Communications in Computer and Information Science 756

Commenced Publication in 2007
Founding and Former Series Editors:
Alfredo Cuzzocrea, Xiaoyong Du, Orhun Kara, Ting Liu, Dominik Ślęzak,
and Xiaokang Yang

Editorial Board

Simone Diniz Junqueira Barbosa
*Pontifical Catholic University of Rio de Janeiro (PUC-Rio),
Rio de Janeiro, Brazil*
Phoebe Chen
La Trobe University, Melbourne, Australia
Joaquim Filipe
Polytechnic Institute of Setúbal, Setúbal, Portugal
Igor Kotenko
*St. Petersburg Institute for Informatics and Automation of the Russian
Academy of Sciences, St. Petersburg, Russia*
Krishna M. Sivalingam
Indian Institute of Technology Madras, Chennai, India
Takashi Washio
Osaka University, Osaka, Japan
Junsong Yuan
Nanyang Technological University, Singapore
Lizhu Zhou
Tsinghua University, Beijing, China

More information about this series at http://www.springer.com/series/7899

Robertas Damaševičius · Vilma Mikašytė (Eds.)

Information and Software Technologies

23rd International Conference, ICIST 2017
Druskininkai, Lithuania, October 12–14, 2017
Proceedings

 Springer

Editors
Robertas Damaševičius
Kaunas University of Technology
Kaunas
Lithuania

Vilma Mikašytė
Kaunas University of Technology
Kaunas
Lithuania

ISSN 1865-0929 ISSN 1865-0937 (electronic)
Communications in Computer and Information Science
ISBN 978-3-319-67641-8 ISBN 978-3-319-67642-5 (eBook)
DOI 10.1007/978-3-319-67642-5

Library of Congress Control Number: 2017953453

Printed on acid-free paper

This Springer imprint is published by Springer Nature
The registered company is Springer International Publishing AG
The registered company address is: Gewerbestrasse 11, 6330 Cham, Switzerland

Preface

We are happy to present you this book, *Information and Software Technologies*, which is a collection of papers that were presented at the 23rd International Conference on Information and Software Technologies, ICIST 2017. The annual conference took place during October 12–14, 2017, in Druskininkai, Lithuania.

The book consists of four chapters, which correspond to the four major areas that are covered during the conference, namely, Information Systems, Business Intelligence for Information and Software Systems, Software Engineering, and Information Technology Applications. These chapters are further subdivided according to the eight special sessions that were held at the conference. They are the following: (a) Innovative Applications for Knowledge Transfer Support, (b) e-Health Information Systems, (c) Information and Software Technologies for Intelligent Power Systems, (d) Intelligent Methods for Data Analysis and Computer Aided Software Engineering, (e) Intelligent Systems and Software Engineering Advances, (f) Smart e-Learning Technologies and Applications, (g) Language Technologies, and (h) Internet of Things in Mobility Applications.

Every year ICIST attracts researchers from all over the world, and this year was not an exception – we received 135 submissions from 35 countries. More importantly, there were participants from many more countries, which indicates that the conference is truly gaining more and more international recognition as it brings together a vast number of brilliant specialists who represent the aforementioned fields and share information about their newest projects. Since we always strive to make the conference presentations and proceedings of the highest quality possible, we only accept papers that present the results of various investigations directed to the discovery of new scientific knowledge in the area of information and software technologies. Hence, only 51 papers were accepted for publishing (i.e., 38% acceptance rate). All the papers were reviewed and selected by the Program Committee, which comprised 106 reviewers (together with 69 additional reviewers) from over 90 academic institutions. As usual, each submission was reviewed following a double-blind process by at least two reviewers. When necessary, some of the papers were reviewed by three or four reviewers. Our deepest thanks and appreciation go to all the reviewers for devoting their precious time to produce truly thorough reviews and feedback to the authors.

We would also like to express our gratitude to the general chair, Prof. Eduardas Bareiša (Kaunas University of Technology), as well as to the session chairs and co-chairs Prof. Irene Krebs (Brandenburg University of Technology Cottbus-Senftenberg), Prof. Justyna Patalas-Maliszewska (University of Zielona Góra), Prof. Rolf Engelbrecht (Pro-Rec), Assoc. Prof. Vytenis Punys (Kaunas University of Technology), Prof. Giedrius Vanagas (Lithuanian University of Health Sciences), Prof. Algirdas Pakštas (Vilnius University), Assoc. Prof. Vira Shendryk (Sumy State University), Dr. Marcin Woźniak (Silesian University of Technology), Prof. Emiliano Tramontana and Prof. Christian Napoli (University of Catania), Assoc. Prof. Danguolė Rutkauskienė

(Kaunas University of Technology), Prof. Radu Adrian Vasiu (Politehnica University of Timisoara), Prof. Audrius Lopata (Vilnius University), Assoc. Prof. Jurgita Kapočiūtė-Dzikienė (Vytautas Magnus University), Peter Dirix (University of Leuven), Prof. Carsten Wolff, and Prof. Christian Reimann (Dortmund University of Applied Sciences and Arts), and Adj. Prof. Pasi Kuvaja (University of Oulu) for their expertise, assistance, and invaluable contribution in making the conference a top-quality scientific event.

In addition, we would like to thank the local Organizing Committee, the Faculty of Informatics, Kaunas University of Technology, for the conference would not have been a great success without their tremendous support. We are also thankful to the Research Council of Lithuania for financial support.

The proceedings of the ICIST 2017 conference are published as an issue in the *Communications in Computer and Information Science* series for the fifth time. This would not be possible without the kind assistance that is provided by Leonie Kunz, Aliaksandr Birukou, and Ingrid Beyer, all from Springer, for which we are utmost grateful. We are very proud of this collaboration and believe that this fruitful partnership will continue for many more years to come.

July 2017   Vilma Mikašytė
                                                              Robertas Damaševičius

Organization

The 23rd International Conference on Information and Software Technologies (ICIST 2017) was organized by Kaunas University of Technology and was held in Druskininkai, Lithuania (October 12–14, 2017).

General Chair

Eduardas Bareiša   Kaunas University of Technology, Lithuania

Local Organizing Committee

Vilma Mikašytė (Chair)	Kaunas University of Technology, Lithuania
Romas Šleževičius	Kaunas University of Technology, Lithuania
Lina Repšienė	Kaunas University of Technology, Lithuania
Gintarė Dzindzelėtaitė	Kaunas University of Technology, Lithuania
Gintarė Lukoševičiūtė	Kaunas University of Technology, Lithuania

Special Section Chairs

Irene Krebs	University of Technology Cottbus, Germany
Marcin Woźniak	Silesian University of Technology, Poland
Danguolė Rutkauskienė	Kaunas University of Technology, Lithuania
Audrius Lopata	Vilnius University, Lithuania
Maria Dolores Afonso Suárez	SIANI University Institute, Spain
Rolf Engelbrecht	ProRec Germany, Germany
Justyna Patalas-Maliszewska	University of Zielona Gora, Poland
Emiliano Tramontana	University of Catania, Italy
Christian Napoli	University of Catania, Italy
Carsten Wolff	Dortmund University of Applied Sciences and Arts, Germany
Christian Reimann	Dortmund University of Applied Sciences and Arts, Germany
Pasi Kuvaja	University of Oulu, Finland
Jurgita Kapočiūtė-Dzikienė	Vytautas Magnus University, Lithuania
Peter Dirix	University of Leuven, Belgium
Algirdas Pakštas	London Metropolitan University, UK
Vira Shendryk	Sumy State University, Ukraine
Radu Adrian Vasiu	Politehnica University of Timisoara, Romania

Vytenis Punys   Kaunas University of Technology, Lithuania
Giedrius Vanagas   Lithuanian University of Health Sciences, Lithuania

Program Committee

Irene Krebs   University of Technology Cottbus, Germany
Marcin Woźniak   Silesian University of Technology, Poland
Danguolė Rutkauskienė   Kaunas University of Technology, Lithuania
Ondrej Krejcar   University of Hradec Kralove, Czech Republic
Marek Krasinski   Wroclaw University of Economics, Poland
Rolf Engelbrecht   ProRec Germany, Germany
Emiliano Tramontana   University of Catania, Italy
Radu Adrian Vasiu   Politehnica University of Timisoara, Romania
Vytenis Punys   Kaunas University of Technology, Lithuania
Giedrius Vanagas   Lithuanian University of Health Sciences, Lithuania
Olga Kurasova   Vilnius University, Lithuania
Jurgita Kapočiūtė-Dzikienė   Vytautas Magnus University, Lithuania
Yuh-Min Tseng   National Changhua University of Education, Taiwan
Constantine Filote   Stefan cel Mare University of Suceava, Romania
Jose Luis Herrero Agustin   University of Extremadura, Spain
Sevinc Gulsecen   Istanbul University, Turkey
Marisa Gil   Polytechnic University of Catalonia, Spain
Achim Schmidtmann   Dortmund University of Applied Sciences and Arts,
                                 Germany
Mehmet Aksit   University of Twente, Netherlands
Saulius Gudas   Vilnius University, Lithuania
Sanda Martinčić-Ipšić   University of Rijeka, Croatia
José Raúl Romero   University of Córdoba, Spain
Marite Kirikova   Riga Technical University, Latvia
Alvydas Jaliniauskas   Harland Clarke Company, USA
Raimundas Jasinevičius   Kaunas University of Technology, Lithuania
Damjan Vavpotič   University of Ljubljana, Slovenia
Sandro Leuchter   Hochschule Mannheim University of Applied Sciences,
                                 Germany
John Gammack   College of Technological Innovation,
                                 United Arab Emirates
Paulo Rupino Cunha   University of Coimbra, Portugal
Jyrki Nummenmaa   University of Tampere, Finland
Algirdas Pakštas   London Metropolitan University, UK
Marcin Paprzycki   Systems Research Institute, Polish Academy
                                 of Science, Poland
Stefano Squartini   Polytechnic University of Marche, Italy
Ana Paula Neves Ferreira da   University of Coimbra, Portugal
  Silva
Tor-Morten Grønli   Oslo School of Arts, Communication and Technology,
                                 Norway

Christophoros Nikou	University of Ioannina, Greece
Elena Sánchez Nielsen	University of San Fernando de la Laguna, Spain
Vira Shendryk	Sumy State University, Ukraine
André Schekelmann	Niederrhein University of Applied Science, Germany
Virgilijus Sakalauskas	Vilnius University, Lithuania
Dalia Krikščiūnienė	Vilnius University, Lithuania
Audrius Lopata	Vilnius University, Lithuania
Aleksandras Targamadzė	Kaunas University of Technology, Lithuania
Peter Thanisch	University of Tampere, Finland
Lovro Šubelj	University of Ljubljana, Slovenia
Karin Harbusch	University of Koblenz-Landau, Germany
Joao Manuel R.S. Tavares	University of Porto, Portugal
Zakaria Maamar	Zayed University, United Arab Emirates
Juan Manuel Vara Mesa	University of Rey Juan Carlos, Spain
Alexander Maedche	University of Mannheim, Germany
Pavel Kordík	Czech Technical University, Czech Republic
Olegas Vasilecas	Vilnius Gediminas Technical University, Lithuania
Rimantas Butleris	Kaunas University of Technology, Lithuania
Tomas Krilavičius	Vytautas Magnus University, Lithuania
Eduard Babkin	National Research University, Russia
Jorg Becker	University of Munster, Germany
Albertas Čaplinskas	Vilnius University, Lithuania
Linas Laibinis	Abo Akademi University, Finland
Benkt Wangler	Stockholm University, Sweden
Valentina Dagienė	Vilnius University, Lithuania
Justyna Patalas-Maliszewska	University of Zelona Gora, Poland
Miloslava Cerna	University of Hradec Králové, Czech Republic
Tomas Blažauskas	Kaunas University of Technology, Lithuania
Prima Gustienė	Karlstad University, Sweden
Vita Spečkauskienė	Lithuanian University of Health Sciences, Lithuania
Petra Poulova	University of Hradec Králové, Czech Republic
Irina Klizienė	Kaunas University of Technology, Lithuania
Renata Burbaitė	Kaunas University of Technology, Lithuania
Kristina Bespalova	Kaunas University of Technology, Lithuania
Jorge Garcia	University of Porto, Portugal
Kęstutis Kapočius	Kaunas University of Technology, Lithuania
Martynas Patašius	Kaunas University of Technology, Lithuania
Rytis Maskeliūnas	Kaunas University of Technology, Lithuania
Jonas Valantinas	Kaunas University of Technology, Lithuania
Lina Čeponienė	Kaunas University of Technology, Lithuania
Raimundas Matulevičius	University of Tartu, Estonia
Rimantas Barauskas	Kaunas University of Technology, Lithuania
Rita Butkienė	Kaunas University of Technology, Lithuania
Maciej Laskowski	Lublin University of Technology, Poland
Agnius Liutkevičius	Kaunas University of Technology, Lithuania

Ana Meštrović	University of Rijeka, Croatia
Andrzej Jardzioch	West Pomeranian University of Technology Szczecin, Poland
Tomas Danikauskas	Kaunas University of Technology, Lithuania
Beata Gavurova	Technical University of Košice, Slovakia
Armantas Ostreika	Kaunas University of Technology, Lithuania
Dominykas Barisas	Kaunas University of Technology, Lithuania
Pavel Jirava	University of Pardubice, Czech Republic
Alius Noreika	Kaunas University of Technology, Lithuania
Eva Rakovska	University of Economics Bratislava, Slovakia
Natalia Loukachevitch	Moscow State University, Russia
Gintaras Palubeckis	Kaunas University of Technology, Lithuania
Reima Suomi	University of Liechtenstein, Liechtenstein
Seweryn Spalek	Silesian University of Technology, Poland
Vytautas Štuikys	Kaunas University of Technology, Lithuania
Maria Dolores Afonso Suárez	SIANI University Institute, Spain
Christian Napoli	University of Catania, Italy
Carsten Wolff	Dortmund University of Applied Sciences and Arts, Germany
Christian Reimann	Dortmund University of Applied Sciences and Arts, Germany
Alfonsas Misevičius	Kaunas University of Technology, Lithuania
Pasi Kuvaja	University of Oulu, Finland
Rimvydas Simutis	Kaunas University of Technology, Lithuania
Peter Dirix	University of Leuven, Belgium

Additional Reviewers

Wojciech Kempa	Silesian University of Technology, Poland
Vytautas Rudžionis	Kaunas University of Technology, Lithuania
Kastytis Ratkevičius	Kaunas University of Technology, Lithuania
Slobodan Beliga	University of Rijeka, Croatia
Zenonas Navickas	Kaunas University of Technology, Lithuania
Ilhan Tarimer	Muğla Sıtkı Koçman University, Turkey
Juha Roning	University of Oulu, Finland
Iwona Paprocka	Silesian University of Technology, Poland
Virginija Limanauskienė	Kaunas University of Technology, Lithuania
Daina Gudonienė	Kaunas University of Technology, Lithuania
Vitaliy Mosiychuk	National Technical University of Ukraine, Ukraine
Jurij Novickij	Vilnius Gediminas Technical University, Lithuania
Robert Nowicki	Częstochowa University of Technology, Poland
Vacius Jusas	Kaunas University of Technology, Lithuania
Grzegorz Chmaj	University of Nevada, USA
Zbigniew Marszałek	Silesian University of Technology, Poland
Antanas Lenkevičius	Kaunas University of Technology, Lithuania

Germanas Budnikas	Kaunas University of Technology, Lithuania
Miloslav Hub	University of Pardubice, Czech Republic
Marcin Gabryel	Częstochowa University of Technology, Poland
Ka Lok Man	Xi'an Jiaotong-Liverpool University, China
Grazia Lo Sciuto	University of Catania, Italy
Lina Narbutaitė	Kaunas University of Technology, Lithuania
Solvita Bērziša	Riga Technical University, Latvia
Ali Isik	Mehmet Akif Ersoy University, Turkey
Vilma Deltuvaitė	Kaunas University of Technology, Lithuania
Wojciech Mitkowski	AGH University of Science and Technology, Poland
Borislav Djordjevic	Institute Mihailo Pupin, Serbia
Valentina Timcenko	Institute Mihailo Pupin, Serbia
Jordan Hristov	University of Chemical Technology and Metallurgy, Bulgaria
Ranka Stanković	University of Belgrade, Serbia
Volkan Tunali	Celal Bayar University, Turkey
Ramūnas Kubiliūnas	Kaunas University of Technology, Lithuania
Aleksandra KawalaJanik	Opole University of Technology, Poland
Dimiter Dimitrov	Technical University of Sofia, Bulgaria
Taflan Gundem	Bogaziçi University, Turkey
Krzysztof Okarma	West Pomeranian University of Technology, Poland
Dawid Polap	Silesian University of Technology, Poland
Alberto Rodriguez	Universidad Miguel Hernandez de Elche, Spain
Damian Slota	Silesian University of Technology, Poland
Marcin Komanda	University of Economics in Katowice, Poland
Slawomir Klos	University of Zielona Góra, Poland
Judita Kasperiūnienė	Vytautas Magnus University, Lithuania
Vytautas Pilkauskas	Kaunas University of Technology, Lithuania
Mariya Eremieva	Naval Academy, Bulgaria
Aparna Vijaya	Vellore Institute of Technology, India
Gytis Vilutis	Kaunas University of Technology, Lithuania
Milan Edl	University of West Bohemia, Czech Republic
Nuno Pombo	University of Beira Interior, Portugal
Marta Wlodarczyk-Sielicka	Maritime University of Szczecin, Poland
Piotr Artiemjew	University of Warmia and Mazury in Olsztyn, Poland
Onder Demir	Marmara University, Turkey
Aleksander Gwiazda	Silesian University of Technology, Poland
Ilmars Slaidins	Riga Technical University, Latvia
Elena Pavlova	Lomonosov Moscow State University, Russia
Simon Dobrisek	University of Ljubljana, Slovenia
Branislav Popović	University of Novi Sad, Serbia
Tuncay Yigit	Suleyman Demirel University, Turkey
Elena Gorbacheva	Universität Münster, Germany
Necmettin Ozkan	Turkiye Finans Participation Bank, Turkey
Vladimir Mityushev	Pedagogical University of Cracow, Poland
Peter Jelinek	Hogeschool van Amsterdam, The Netherlands

Krzysztof Pancerz   University of Rzeszów, Poland
Damian Mazur   Rzeszów University of Technology, Poland
Tomas Rasymas   Vilnius University, Lithuania
Gabriel Svejda   University of West Bohemia, Czech Republic
Josef Basl   University of West Bohemia, Czech Republic
Mokhtar Beldjehem   University of Ottawa, Canada
Krzysztof Cpalka   Częstochowa University of Technology
Darius Birvinskas   Kaunas University of Technology, Lithuania

Co-editors

Robertas Damaševičius   Kaunas University of Technology, Lithuania
Vilma Mikašytė   Kaunas University of Technology, Lithuania

Contents

**Information Systems: Special Session on Information and Software
Technologies for Intelligent Power Systems**

Business Intelligence for Information and Software Systems:
Special Session on Intelligent Methods for Data Analysis
and Computer Aided Software Engineering

Software Engineering: Special Session on Intelligent Systems
and Software Engineering Advances

**Information Technology Applications: Special Session on Smart
e-Learning Technologies and Applications**

Information Technology Applications: Special Session on Language Technologies

Information Technology Applications: Special Session on Internet-of-Things in Mobility Applications

Information Systems: Special Session on Innovative Applications for Knowledge Transfer Support

Role of "Bridge Person" in Software Development Projects

Līga Bormane and Solvita Bērziša[⊠]

Information Technology Institute, Riga Technical University,
Kalku 1, Riga, Latvia
Liga.Bormane@edu.rtu.lv, solvita.berzisa@rtu.lv

Abstract. Well-defined requirements articulating user expectations and needs are a key to successful implementation of software development project. However, business process experts often lack experience in requirement definition, are ill-equipped to interact directly with system developers and sometimes are even unable to agree upon common understanding of the expect end-product. To mitigate this issue, projects frequently involve a so called "bridge person" – a team member with an objective to facilitate smooth communication among technical and non-technical individuals. The objective of this paper is to evaluate "bridge person" importance and summarize aspects that impact selection of a right "bridge person" type in particular software development project. The paper summarizes information about the role of "bridge person" and presents the survey of industry's perception of this role.

Keywords: "Bridge person" · Software development project · Business requirements · Stakeholders · Requirements analysis

1 Introduction

Information system (IS) or software is developed in projects with an objective to satisfy customer requirements within planned time and resources. However, data by to one of the leading research organizations the Standish Group [1] show that it is difficult to complete software development (SD) projects successfully. Every year approximately 20% of the projects fail, about 50% of the projects are delayed, exceed budget or do not deliver all planned functionality, and only 30% of the projects are successful [1].

Another important factor is that since the 1990s one of the TOP 3 reasons of SD project failures has been related to the requirements analysis [1, 2, 3]. Project requirements analysis (PRA) stage problems are divided into three main categories: problems of scope, problems of volatility and problems of understanding [4]. However, all these problems have common reasons related to poor understanding of requirements, lack of communication and conflicting views of users on requirements [4]. These facts suggest that requirements are clearly articulating business needs and user expectations are a key to successful implementation of SD projects [5, 6]. Therefore, the PRA stage has a profound impact on the project success. This stage is one of the most challenging stages of projects because it involves identification of all stakeholders, understanding of their language, understanding, and management of their

R. Damaševičius and V. Mikašytė (Eds.): ICIST 2017, CCIS 756, pp. 3–14, 2017.
DOI: 10.1007/978-3-319-67642-5_1

issues and expectations, as well as expression of the requirements in a form comprehensible to system developers [7].

As customer stakeholders often lack experience in requirement definition, they are
ill-prepared to interact with system developers and sometimes are even unable to agree
upon common understanding of what they would like to have built. "Bridge person" is
involved in projects as a mediator among technical and non-technical individuals [8].
This person sufficiently understands business processes, is able to listen to stakeholders
and at the same time has an understanding of the IS development area, thus being able
to provide the necessary link between two parties in the development project [8].
However, each project has unique requirements and selecting right specialist is a
challenging task, and there is a different type of "bridge person". Therefore, some
guidance for selecting the right "bridge person" is desirable.

The objective of this paper is to evaluate "bridge person" importance and summarize aspects that impact selection a right type of "bridge person" for a particular SD
project. Also, the authors also draw attention to the importance of requirements analysis stage, the significance of "bridge person", represent results of the survey on
industry's perception of this role in SD projects and propose solution how selection a
right type of "bridge person" can be formalized.

The rest of the paper is structured as follows: Sect. 2 describes theoretical background and related studies; Sect. 3 presents the survey results; and the aspects for
"bridge person" type selection and process formalization solution is presented in
Sect. 4. Conclusion and future research are presented at the end of the paper.

2 Literature Review

This section summarizes theoretical background and related studies about the project
requirements analysis stage, the role of "bridge person" and performers of this role in
SD project and different SD models.

2.1 Requirements Analysis Stage

The project requirements analysis (PRA) stage is a first part of the software development process and plays an important role in quality assurance of developed system [9,
10]. The goal of PRA stage is to understand the users' needs, collect and analyze them,
and then document into correct, consistent, verifiable and feasible system requirements
[10, 11]. Incoming and outgoing information and activities of this stage are shown in
Fig. 1. This flow of information is similar for all organizations in all of the types of SD
projects [7]. The activities of PRA stage are divided into two groups – requirement
development and requirement management activities [11].

Requirement development activities must answer to question "WHAT is needed to
be created?". Sequential execution of this group activities provides a road from
incoming information to outgoing [10, 11]. The following activities are performed:
(1) requirements elicitation that records and summarizes available information from all
possible sources of information; (2) requirements analysis that discussed, detailed and
prioritized the elicited requirements with the stakeholders; (3) requirements

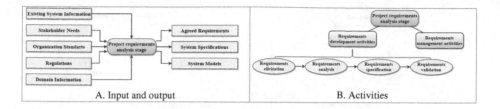

Fig. 1. Overview of PRA stage adopted from [7, 11]

specification that produces requirement document which become a foundation for further software design and development process and (4) requirements validation that makes sure that all previous activities acquired and documented requirements are clear and feasible, and that all the requirements in the document are aligned with the organization standards and industry best practices.

Requirements management activities control accepted requirements, specifications, and models of consistency and constancy of the SD process [10, 11].

2.2 Role of "Bridge Person"

"Bridge person" is an individual who serves as the principal mediator or communication channel between customer stakeholders and system developers. His main task is to provide a link through which the customer stakeholders in non-technical language expresses requirements flow to system developers in a way understandable to them [8, 11, 12].

"Bridge person" is a project role but not necessarily a job title. This person can have different job title – business analyst, requirements analyst, systems analyst, product owner, requirements engineer, project manager, or any other specialist from customer, developer or independent organization, who perform responsibilities of this role. These job titles are used inconsistently from organization to organization. Regardless of the job title, the person performing a moderator role must have right skills, knowledge, and personality to perform this role well [11, 12].

"Bridge person" facilitates SD project incoming and outgoing information flows (Fig. 2), through incoming information transformation, structuring and transfer to system developers [11]. This person helps stakeholders to harmonize expressed and actual needs [11, 13].

According to [11, 13, 14], the main responsibilities of "bridge person" are: (1) define business needs; (2) plan the requirements approach; (3) elicit requirements; (4) analyze requirements; (5) facilitate prioritization; (6) write specifications (7) communicate requirements; (8) lead validation and (9) manage requirements.

Since "bridge person" is more than a person who only records requirements, this role includes many "soft skills" that are more people-oriented than technical [15]. "Bridge person" needs to know how to use many different methods (elicitation, analysis, modeling, etc.) and how to represent information in forms other than natural-language text. An effective "bridge person" combines strong communication, facilitation, and

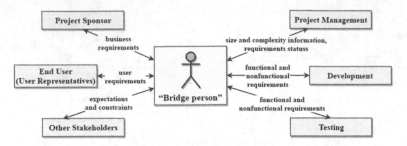

Fig. 2. "Bridge person" as communication channel, adopted from [11]

interpersonal skills with technical and business domain knowledge. Patience and a genuine desire to work with people are this role's executor key success factors [11].

In practice, three types of "bridge person" can be identified. They mainly differ by their affiliation, primary responsibilities and core competencies [16]: (1) "bridge person" on customer side; (2) "bridge person" on developer side and (3) "bridge person" as an independent consultant. All three types are characterized in Table 1. While the main responsibilities and competencies are similar regardless of affiliation, there are some changes in emphasis.

Table 1. "Bridge person" types and their characteristics

Type / Criteria	"Bridge person" on customer side	"Bridge person" on developer side	"Bridge person" as an independent consultant
Affiliation	In-house, align to business	Outsource, embedded in IT	Independent
Primary responsibilities	Define business requirements; Define user requirements; Communicate with business experts, etc. stakeholders; Communicate with the developer; Check proposed/delivered system.	Define user requirements; Define system requirements; Communicate with customer; Communicate with development team; Check system compliance with requirements	Analyze the current situation; Analyze the desired future situation; Define a solution concept; Define business requirements; Evaluate solution proposals.
Advantages , core competencies	Know organization, its goals and challenges; Identifies the "big picture" and detailing; Know organization IS and IT infrastructure – see changes and system that does not fit.	Know the system and its structure; Know different complexity technologies; Identifies detailing.	Know business area related laws and regulations; Know the best practices; Know the various existing solutions.

2.3   "Bridge Person" in Software Development Projects

Software development life cycle (SDLC) covers all software development activities from inception till software deployment and exploitation [17, 18]. To manage SDLC activities, a number of SDLC models have been created, such as traditional or predictive, iterative and incremental and adaptive life cycle model [19]. PRA activities and involvement of "bridge person" varies according to SDLC model used. In addition,

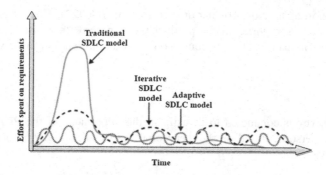

Fig. 3. PRA stage activities on project timeline [11]

depending on SDLC, PRA stage activities can be carried out at one or more times during the project (Fig. 3).

Traditional SDLC models (such as waterfall and V model) are based on a sequence of activities, where each subsequent execution needs previous results. PRA stage activities occur only once at the beginning of SD project. The requirements are only revisited in a testing phase to evaluate the system against the requirements. The largest workload of "bridge person" in these projects is in the first quarter of the total project timeline. In this type of projects, "bridge person" involvement is short but very intense. In addition, all requirements are collected at one point, and their reformulation is not intended. Thus, "bridge person" impact on project results is very high [11, 19, 20].

Iterative and incremental SD (often for simplicity referred to "iterative SD" [21]) is based on the idea of a progressive development process in which the whole system is divided into smaller parts – "steps" or "iterations". At the beginning of the project, only common top-level system requirements are defined, and detailed requirements analysis is repeated at the beginning of each iteration. Duration of one iteration is up to three months. A PRA stage activities workload curve varies. Initially "bridge person" workload is slightly higher than during the next iterations, since of the project beginning in addition to the iterations requirements defines the common top-level system requirements. In general, it may be determined that the "bridge person" participation in these projects is continuous. The amount of work aggregated for all iterations could be almost equivalent to traditional SD projects, but less intensive at times leaving space for correcting errors [11, 21].

Adaptive SD (also known as agile SD) focus on lightweight processes, which allow for rapid changes and continuous involvement of stakeholders. In this methodology, detailed analysis and documentation are not performed in their standard meaning but are tightly coupled with other concurrent activities. When the project is starting, project's top-level system requirements in a form of user story are summarized in the product backlog, and at the beginning of each iteration highest priority user stories are selected, detailed, developed, and tested together with stakeholders. The iterations are shorter than in iterative SD [11, 19–22].

In agile projects, requirements are managed differently than in two earlier SDLC, and "bridge person" has a slightly different role [22]. Often "bridge person" are constantly supporting a product owner or performs this role [23]. The product owner is responsible for all user stories in the product backlog correctness, detailing and prioritization [23]. His participation is continuous, but its intensity strongly varies.

3 Survey

An industry survey is conducted to investigate the importance of the PRA stage and role of "bridge person". Based on the theoretical analysis the following objectives are set for the survey:

- to evaluation a level of recognition of the role of "bridge person";
- to identify a level of involvement of "bridge person" in SD projects;
- to gather information on job titles including "bridge person" responsibilities;
- to summarize most important competencies of "bridge person".

The online survey was selected as a data collection method and sent to a number of organizations in Latvia, as well as it was placed in several social networks with different SD projects related groups. The survey was completely anonymous.

64 respondents participated in the survey and mostly with at least more than five years of experience in software development projects. Distribution of SD project parties and their sphere of activity are shown in Fig. 4. The respondents' breakdown by the sphere of activity shows that the survey respondents have represented a wide number of sectors.

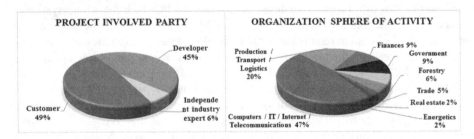

Fig. 4. Respondents breakdown by involved party and organization sphere of activity

To evaluate recognition of the "bridge person" role, the respondents were asked to recognize this role without any additional explanation. That resulted in 33% of the respondents recognizing the role (Fig. 5). After the additional explanation, this role also recognizes by the remaining respondents.

In addition, the majority of respondents (97%) says that they have been in contacts with this role performer on a daily basis in their own or other organization. Figure 6 shows job positions of this role at customer and developer side.

Based on the answers (Fig. 7), it can be concluded that the respondents are not only in contact with the "bridge person", but "bridge person" is also actively involved in almost all organization's projects. According to respondents rating, two most popular

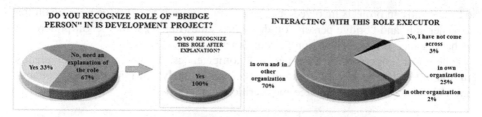

Fig. 5. Respondents' assessment of "bridge person" recognition and contact on a daily basis

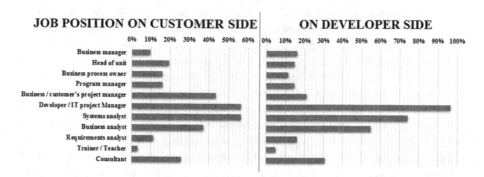

Fig. 6. Respondents marked job positions

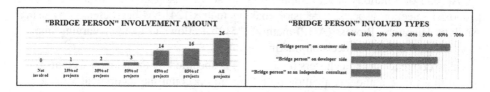

Fig. 7. Respondents' assessment of "bridge person" involvement in projects and it types

Fig. 8. Respondents' assessment of "bridge person" competencies

and frequently in projects involved "bridge person" types is the "bridge person" on the customer side and "bridge person" on developer side (Fig. 7) with a slight preference for having the "bridge person" on the customer side.

The most important "bridge person" competences following the respondent's opinion are shown in Fig. 8. Communication skills, analytical thinking, and collaboration skills are evaluated as three most critical competencies.

4   Selection of "Bridge Person" Type

The aspects that impacts selection of an appropriate "bridge person" type for a given SD project we define as multi-criteria decision-making problem. Hierarchical decomposition of the aspects or criteria for selection of "bridge person" type is given in Fig. 9. The description of SD project situation is based on four groups of criteria including sub-criteria that are defined according to the theoretical analysis of "bridge person" role tasks and required competencies for the particular SD project based on the product that is developed and development process. These four criteria groups or clusters are: (1) criteria related to the customer – "C1: Customer" –; (2) criteria related to the developer – "C2: Developer"; (3) criteria related to the system – "C3: IS development product" and (4) criteria related to the development process – "C4: IS development project". A large impact to selection of "bridge person" type are customers as it existing competencies and need for addition competencies mainly impact decision about "bridge person" type.

As one of solutions and examples how to solve this selection problem and test proposed selection aspects, a decision-making matrix [24] has been created by using Analytic Hierarchy Process (AHP) method [25] that allows to identify varying impact of evaluation aspects to decision-making.

Impact of each criteria clusters (c_i, $i = 1..4$) is specified by the relative weights (w_i'). According to the authors evaluation by taking into account the theoretical knowledge gained in Sect. 2 and the survey data in Sect. 2 the current values of weights are 0.51, 0.32, 0.10 and 0.07. Weight values approve previous assumption that the customer related criteria's have the largest impact on results. Each sub-criterion (c_{ij}, $i = 1..4$, $j = 1.. k$, k – count of sub-criteria in i cluster) also have their own AHP relative weights (w_{ij}''). The summary sub-relative weights of criteria are calculated by multiplying two previously obtained weights ($w_{ij} = w_i' * w_{ij}''$).

For decision-making matrix creation, the mapping between the project situation and the "bridge person" type is established. For every criterion c_{ij}, there are m potential answers characterizing the project situation. Their value is denoted by v_{ijs}, $s = 1.. m$, where s is the answer. The most suitable type of "bridge person" is identified for every answer by assigning a rank using the eleven points rating scale (r_{ijst}, $t = 1..3$, where t – "bridge person" type). These ranking is performed by the authors and these values are also possible to calibrate.

The weights and rankings constitute the setup of the proposed solution. Also, interactive interface based on Excel has been created that helps to guide through number of evaluation criteria and automate calculation of results. To apply the

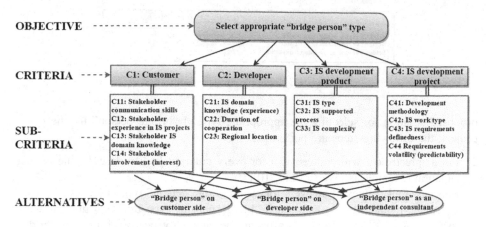

OBJECTIVE ----------→ Select appropriate "bridge person" type

CRITERIA ----→ | C1: Customer | C2: Developer | C3: IS development product | C4: IS development project |

SUB-CRITERIA ----→

C11: Stakeholder communication skills
C12: Stakeholder experience in IS projects
C13: Stakeholder IS domain knowledge
C14: Stakeholder involvement (interest)

C21: IS domain knowledge (experience)
C22: Duration of cooperation
C23: Regional location

C31: IS type
C32: IS supported process
C33: IS complexity

C41: Development methodology
C42: IS work type
C43: IS requirements definedness
C44 Requirements volatility (predictability)

ALTERNATIVES ---→ "Bridge person" on customer side   "Bridge person" on developer side   "Bridge person" as an independent consultant

Fig. 9. Description of "Bridge person" type selection problem

Method for "bridge person" type selection

C1: Customer

	No	Low	Medium	High
C11: Stakeholder communication skills	○	○	○	◉
C12: Stakeholder experience in IS projects	○	○	◉	○
C13: Stakeholder IS domain knowledge	○	○	◉	○
C14: Stakeholder involvement (interest)	○	○	◉	○

C2: Developer

	No	Low	Medium	High
C21: IS domain knowledge (experience)	○	○	○	◉
C22: Duration of cooperation	No	Short	Medium	Long
	○	○	○	◉
C23: Regional location	Close - in one city		Far - in different cities	
	◉		○	

C3: IS development product

	COTS	Adapted COTS	Custom system
C31: IS type	○	○	○
C32: IS supported process	Core business	Support process	Methodical process
	○	◉	○
C33: IS complexity	Low	Medium	High
	○	○	◉

C4: IS development project

	Traditional	Iterative	AGILE
C41: Development methodology	○	◉	○
C42: IS work type	New IS	Adding features	IS replacement
	○	◉	○
C43: IS requirements definedness	Low	Medium	High
	○	◉	○
C44: Requirements volatility (predictability)	Low	Medium	High
	○	◉	○

Fig. 10. Example project criteria values

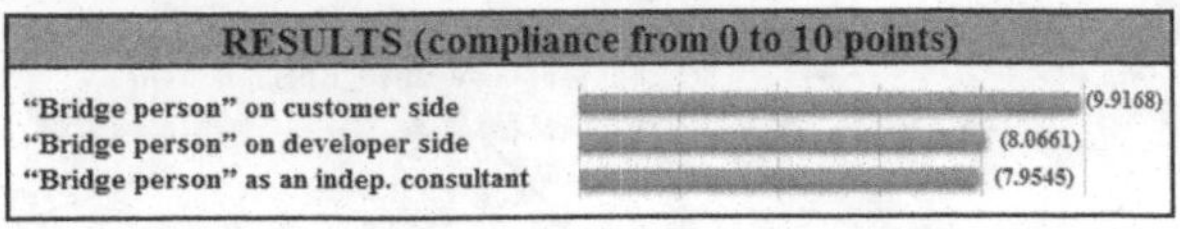

Fig. 11. Example project results

proposed solution for selecting the appropriate type of "bridge person" for the given project, the following steps are performed:

1. Fill a spreadsheet with values (v_{ijs}) for every criterion (c_{ij}) to describe the project situation (example is given in Fig. 10);
2. Read the rank values of answers for each "bridge person" type (r_{ijst});
3. Calculate a suitability rank for each "bridge person" type by using the following formula: $R_t = \sum_{ij} w_{ij} \times r_{ijst}$. As a result, the suitability rank each type of "bridge person" is shown (Fig. 11).

In the example, the highest rank is for the "bridge person" on customer sides. In this case, that is strongly influenced by relatively high internal development competencies at the customer side and the long project duration. The projects situation described is drawn from observations in practice, and a posterior evaluation of this selection corresponds to what was used in the project.

5 Summary and Conclusion

During this research the requirements analysis stage has been analyzed as it has the profound impact on IS development. If requirements analysis is carried out properly, then it can be argued that the SD project will be successful and the system will satisfy customer needs. Even though there is a rich literature on requirements management, not a single method can resolve all the challenges, especially, those associated with the human factors.

The "bridge person" role is one of the solutions to deal with the human factors. Responsibilities of this role are to ensure the proper information flow between the representatives involved in the project. The authors draw a conclusion that involving "bridge person" in SD projects and the PRA stage in particular serves as an enabler of successful project completion.

Selection of the "bridge person" type is influenced by four important factors – customer, developer, system and SD project characteristics. The most significant of them is customer because only they know what is needed. That is why "bridge person" on customer side has significant advantages compared to the other two types.

Based on the analyzed literature and the results of this paper, potential future research directions are:

- consideration of additional factors in the selection problem sphere, for example, costs and more detailed characteristics of systems by area of application and technology used;

- distinguishing between different levels of qualification (e.g., beginner, intermediate and expert) of "bridge person";
- the combination of the "bridge person" role with related roles;
- further evaluation of the solution for selection of the "bridge person" type.

References

1. Standish Group: Standish Group 2015 Chaos Report. https://www.infoq.com/articles/standish-chaos-2015
2. Attarzadeh, I., Siew, H.: Project management practices: success versus failure. In: Proceedings of the 2008 International Symposium on Information Technology (2008)
3. Stepanek, G.: Software Project Secrets: Why Software Projects Fail. Apress, New Zealand (2005)
4. Kumari, S., Pillai, A.: Requirements elicitation issues and project performance: a test of a contingency model. In: Proceedings of the 2015 Science and Information Conference (2015)
5. Liao, H.: Requirement elicitation of enterprise informationization from view of VCA. In: Proceeding of the 2010 International Conference on Networked Computing (2010)
6. Noraini, C., Abdullah, M.: Requirement elicitation: identifying the communication challenges between developer and customer. Int. J. New Comput. Architectures Their Appl., 371–383 (2011)
7. Arif, S., Khan, Q., Gahyyur, S.: Requirements engineering processes, tools/technologies, & methodologies. Int. J. Rev. Comput., 41–56 (2009–2010)
8. More, J., Stieber, A.J., Liu, C.: Breaking Into Information Security. Syngress, USA (2016)
9. Haron, A., Sahibuddin, S.: The strength and weakness of requirement engineering (RE) process. In: 2nd International Conference on Computer Technology and Development (2010)
10. Eleiche, A.M., Ahmad, I., Elish, M.O.: Design requirements in software and engineering systems. Ind. Eng. Manage. Syst., 70–81 (2012)
11. Wiegers, K., Beatty, J.: Software Requirements. Microsoft Press (2013)
12. Hickey, A., Davis, A.: A tale of two ontologies: the basis for systems analysis technique selection. In: 9th Americas Conference on Information Systems (2003)
13. International Institute of Business Analysis: A guide to the business analysis body of knowledge (BABOK). International Institute of Business Analysis (2015)
14. Young, R.R.: The Requirements Engineering Handbook. Artech House Print on Demand (2003)
15. Darvill, L.: The importance of personal skills for the expert business analyst. Analysts Anonymous 11 (2012)
16. Lazdāne, G.: Projekta vadība un Biznesa analīze – duets vai solo? http://www.slideshare.net/IIBA_Latvia_Chapter/ba-pv-21112013lnpva
17. IEEE Computer Society: Guide to the Software Engineering Body of Knowledge (SWEBOK). IEEE Computer Society Press (2014)
18. ISO/IEC 12207:2008 Systems and software engineering – Software life cycle processes (2008)
19. Project Management Institute: A Guide to the Project Management Body of Knowledge (PMBOK). Project Management Institute, Inc. (2013)

20. Yu Beng, L., Wooi Khong, L., Wai Yip, T., Soo Fun, T.: Software development life cycle agile vs traditional approaches. In: 2012 International Conference on Information and Network Technology (2012)
21. Larman, C.: Agile and Iterative Development: A Manager's Guide. Addison-Wesley Professional (2004)
22. Paetsch, F., Eberlein, A., Maurer, F.: Requirements engineering and agile software development. In: 12th IEEE International Workshops on Enabling Technologies: Infrastructure for Collaborative Enterprises (2003)
23. Gregorio, D.D.: How the Business Analyst Supports and Encourages Collaboration on Agile Projects. IEEE (2012)
24. Technology evaluation centers: what is decision matrix? http://www.rfp-templates.com/What-is/Decision-Matrix
25. Triantaphyllou, E., Mann, S.H.: Using the analytic hierarchy process for decision making in engineering applications: some challenges. Int. J. Ind. Eng. Appl. Pract., 35–44 (1995)

A Knowledge-Management System for the Innovation-Strategy Development of SME Enterprises

Sławomir Kłos[✉], Katarzyna Skrzypek, and Karol Dabrowski

Department of Computer Science and Production Management,
University of Zielona Góra, Zielona Góra, Poland
s.klos@iizp.uz.zgora.pl

Abstract. Product and process innovations determine the competitiveness of manufacturing enterprises. The evaluation of a prototype of a new product or technology is a very-important process which sets the strategy of manufacturing or service enterprise development. Research-and-development-processes are expensive and time-consuming. But the most important for a manufacturing or service enterprise is the effectiveness of these processes (as measured by the market success of a product or innovative technology). In this paper is proposed a model for a knowledge-management system for innovation-processes improvement and enterprise-strategy development. The system is aimed at small and medium-sized manufacturing or service companies. The model of the system was created on the base of the results of survey research made in 112 Polish small and medium-sized enterprises. Illustrative examples are given.

Keywords: Knowledge management · Innovation strategy · Survey research · Small and medium-sized enterprises (SME's)

1 Introduction

Effective knowledge-management systems in high technology small and medium-sized enterprises should support research-and-development projects and innovation processes. The improvement of R&D processes is critical for the business strategy of manufacturing enterprises and wrong decisions can even result in the bankruptcy of the company. The most-important problem of small and medium-sized enterprises for new product or technology development is limited resources. Innovation projects are expensive and time-consuming and the results are not guaranteed (a relatively high probability of failure). Therefore, developing and implementing methods and tools for knowledge management to support the R&D strategy of SME's is very important in, inter alia, facilitating the reduction of resource requirements.

There are many research publications in the field of knowledge and innovation management. Dickel and Moura developed a model to measure organisational performance with a focus on knowledge management and innovation management [Dickel]. They used a quantitative research study, in the form of a multi-case study applied to three companies in the metal-mechanic sector in Brazil. The proposed model could be an effective tool for assessing organisational performance in that, in its application, the

© Springer International Publishing AG 2017
R. Damaševičius and V. Mikašyté (Eds.): ICIST 2017, CCIS 756, pp. 15–24, 2017.
DOI: 10.1007/978-3-319-67642-5_2

surveyed organisations have already been able to identify their main weaknesses and to use the reported results to improve their management. Forsman has studied what kinds of innovations have been developed in small manufacturing and service enterprises and what has been the degree of innovation capacity which small enter-prises possess. Roper and Dudas analysed the determinants of companies' innovation outputs and provided new information on the relationship between knowledge stocks, as measured by patents, and innovation-output indicators [3]. They found that existing knowledge resources have moderately negative rather than positive impacts on companies' innovation outputs and knowledge flows derived from internal investment, and external search dominate the effect of existing knowledge resources on innovation performance. Nowacki and Bachnik used a concept of eight processes of knowledge management and identified three broad categories of knowledge management innovations in an organisational context [4]. From the analysis of small, medium-sized, and large companies in Poland it turned out that the investigated enterprises were not very innovative in the area of knowledge management. Donate and Guadamillas suggest that managers should focus their attention on knowledge exploration and utilisation practices, along with a raft of "organisational enablers", in order to achieve high levels of innovation results for the company [5]. They provide new empirical evidence on the relationships between knowledge management, organisational elements such as culture, leadership, HR practices, and innovation, in a large sample of companies. Open innovation establishes the flow of the internal and external information of organisations [6]. Talke, Salomo and Kock point out that the influence of top management teams (TMT) should be crucial, since innovation strategies are shaped at the top-management level [7]. Their study investigated how TMT characteristics affect a company's strategic innovation orientation, and how this related to innovation outcomes and company performance. The results indicate that TMT diversity, measured as heterogeneity in the educational, functional, industry, and organisational backgrounds, has a strong positive effect on a company's innovation orientation.

In this paper a model is proposed for a system for effective knowledge management and strategic-decisions support in the field of innovations. The model was prepared on the basis of the results of a pilot survey conducted in 112 small and medium-sized Polish manufacturing and service enterprises. The main research problem in the paper is formulated as In a small or medium-sized manufacturing or service enterprise, what functions of the knowledge-management system can effectively support innovation management in terms of the strategic development of the enterprise? The model of the knowledge-management system includes its functionality prepared on the basis of the expectations of the investigated manufacturing and service companies. In the next chapter the results of the survey research are presented.

2 The Results of the Pilot Survey Research

The pilot survey research was conducted in 112 manufacturing and service companies and included questions concerning of companies' strategy, innovations and knowledge. The first question was formulated as *Which element of the enterprise's strategy is the most important for its development (in terms of revenue growth)?* The answers were rated on a scale from 1 to 5. The summary results of answers are presented in Fig. 1.

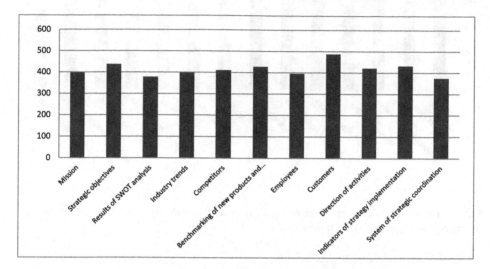

Fig. 1. The results of the survey research – the impact of strategy on the enterprise's development

For the respondents the most-important components of strategy for the business development are the results of customer-satisfaction analysis and properly formulated strategic objectives (and indicators of the strategic implementation). Another important aspect of the research is the analysis of new products and technologies. The results of the research confirm that the development of innovative products and technologies should be stimulated and verified by the customers' evaluation process. It means that for new-project development knowledge about new products, technologies and customer satisfaction (preferences) is crucial for the strategy of innovations.

The next question directed to the respondents was *What knowledge is the most important for strategic development preparation and implementation?* The results of the survey research are presented in Fig. 2. All the answers are concerned with knowledge about business partners. For example, *the IT system* is concerned with knowledge about the IT systems of business partners. The analysis of the presented results shows that the most important for strategic development is knowledge about business partners' products, services and technologies. For effective implementation of new products and services knowledge about the core competences of business partners is also very important. Knowledge about business partners' organisation models and IT systems has relatively little impact on product development. It is interesting to note that knowledge about business partners know-how (patents and licences) is also not crucial for new-product development.

The last question analysed in the paper was *What methods and technologies determine the strategic competitive advantage of the company?* The results of the research are presented in Fig. 3.

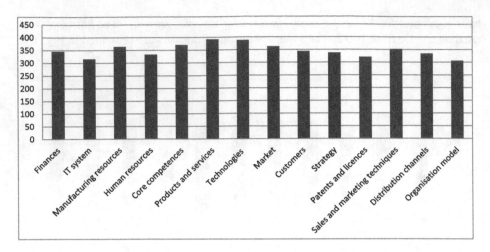

Fig. 2. The results of the survey research – the impact of knowledge about business partners on the enterprise's strategic development

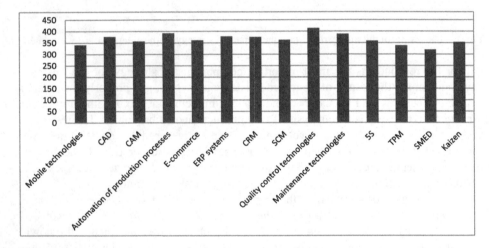

Fig. 3. The results of the survey research – the impact of methods and technologies implementation on the enterprise's strategic development

For the studied enterprises, the most-important methods or technologies which determine the strategy of company development are technologies supporting quality control and the automation of production processes [8]. Kaisen methods and mobile technologies have a relatively small impact on enterprises' strategic development. The survey research enables us to define assumptions and limitations for knowledge-management systems focused on new-product and technological development. In Fig. 4 a model for knowledge-management-system implementation is proposed.

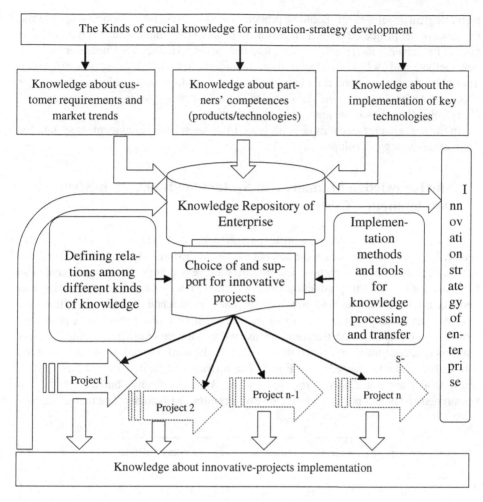

Fig. 4. A model for knowledge-management-system implementation for innovation-strategy development

On the basis of the conducted research the most-important kinds of knowledge for project development in a company could be defined. On the basis of the survey research three general kinds of knowledge resources for innovations development are identified:

- knowledge about customers and market trends,
- knowledge about business partners,
- knowledge about key technologies.

For the support of innovation projects implemented in a company a database and the correlation between different kinds of knowledge should be established. The knowledge-management system should support decisions about innovative project selection and implementation. IA very important function of a knowledge-management system is proper knowledge processing and transfer. The structure of projects for new-product or technological development should be properly defined. Especially important is to define the level of the projected costs and assumed profits of the innovation. Each innovative project implementation results in a new knowledge (experiences, the implementation of new methods and tools, etc.) which is important for the knowledge-management system. Therefore, the system should include tools which facilitate the securing of knowledge about project implementation. The knowledge-management system is an important tool for defining the innovation strategy of an enterprise.

In the next chapter an example is presented a of knowledge-management system for innovation-strategy development.

3   The Knowledge Management System for Innovation-Strategy Development – Case Study

Let us consider the small manufacturing enterprise *Alpha* in the mechanical engineering sector. The core competences of the company lie in the design and production of furnaces for the heat treatments of metals. The products are very complex and innovative. The furnaces are included in production lines dedicated, inter alia, to the automotive and aerospace industries. The company has 15 years' experience in design products and technologies for the heat treatments of metals. Each new order involves a prototype which must be created with the comprehensive commitment of customers and business partners (material suppliers, subcontractors, etc.). The work-breakdown structure of the innovative product is presented in Fig. 5. The furnace system includes 14 key subsystems, which are not always produced by the *Alpha* company, but are very often researched and developed by external research centres or institutes. The manufacturing

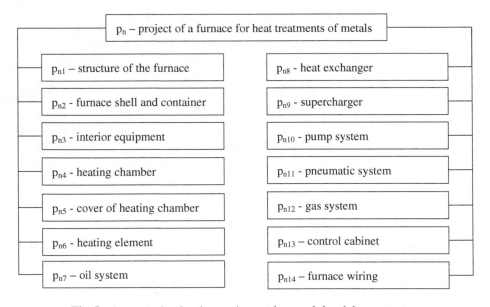

Fig. 5. An example of an innovative-product work-breakdown structure

of the system is often commissioned to external business partners who make the elements of the subsystems on the basis of assigned construction documentation. That means that the product is prepared and allocated into the ambient industry. The knowledge related to the project is also shared around, and without an effective knowledge-resource-planning system it can be lost. On the other hand this knowledge should be accessible to the cooperating companies in limited portions to avoid the possibility of the loss of core competences. Therefore, to support the overall projects implementation a knowledge broker should be engaged who will be responsible for the knowledge transfer to external organisations.

The following examples of the kinds of knowledge should be entered in the knowledge database of the *Alpha* company:

- k_1 - patents and utility models,
- k_2 - results of scientific research,
- k_3 - material properties (strength tests, temperature effects, etc.),
- k_4 - technical approvals,
- k_5 - technological-customer requirements,
- k_6 - exploitation-customer requirements,
- k_7 - market trends,
- k_8 - business partners' products,
- k_9 - business partners' technologies,
- k_{10} - experience in other projects, etc.

For each subsystem of the innovative project, the knowledge-demand rate p_{ij} can be calculated as follows:

$$p_{ij} = \sum_{j=1}^{m} \omega_{ij} \cdot \varphi_{ij} \tag{1}$$

where

ω_{ij}	- the weight of kinds of knowledge $\omega_{ij} = 0, 1, 2, 3, 4, 5$
φ_{ij}	- the demand for knowledge for each subsystem, $\varphi_{ij} \in\ <0;1>$
$i = 1, 2, \ldots, n$	- number of projects,
$j = 1, 2, \ldots, m$	- number of project subsystems

The innovation strategy governs long-term decisions concerning investments in new products and technologies or R&D activities support. Using index (1) the knowledge requirements for the subsystems of innovative products can be determined. In Table 1 a matrix of knowledge demand for the innovative project is proposed. The knowledge-demand index is calculated on the basis of the number of inquiries (percentage) for each knowledge category. For example the highest number of enquiries for knowledge category k_1 was for subsystem p_{n8} - heat exchange, which is relatively high (15% of all enquiries in category k_1). In Table 1 the fields in which the knowledge-demand index is greater than 0.09 are denoted.

Table 1. The matrix of knowledge demand for the innovative project

φ_{ij}	k_1	k_2	k_3	k_4	k_5	k_6	k_7	k_8	k_9	k_{10}
p_{n1}	0.01	0.18	0.08	0.08	0.09	0.06	0.17	0.05	0.11	0.01
p_{n2}	0.04	0.03	0.08	0.02	0.13	0.11	0.01	0.00	0.15	0.08
p_{n3}	0.10	0.03	0.04	0.10	0.03	0.14	0.01	0.06	0.07	0.07
p_{n4}	0.06	0.04	0.08	0.10	0.03	0.00	0.13	0.04	0.02	0.06
p_{n5}	0.06	0.10	0.08	0.01	0.05	0.05	0.03	0.08	0.05	0.14
p_{n6}	0.04	0.16	0.11	0.14	0.10	0.01	0.00	0.08	0.00	0.00
p_{n7}	0.11	0.08	0.06	0.00	0.10	0.02	0.18	0.07	0.06	0.01
p_{n8}	0.15	0.13	0.10	0.07	0.11	0.13	0.00	0.12	0.14	0.01
p_{n9}	0.05	0.11	0.01	0.02	0.11	0.10	0.13	0.07	0.07	0.07
p_{n10}	0.05	0.01	0.11	0.08	0.02	0.07	0.11	0.06	0.13	0.09
p_{n11}	0.10	0.01	0.02	0.12	0.01	0.06	0.01	0.05	0.08	0.15
p_{n12}	0.07	0.05	0.10	0.10	0.02	0.11	0.01	0.11	0.03	0.15
p_{n13}	0.09	0.01	0.05	0.06	0.15	0.06	0.11	0.13	0.08	0.15
p_{n14}	0.08	0.06	0.08	0.10	0.06	0.07	0.09	0.09	0.01	0.02

The matrix presented in Table 1 shows what kinds of knowledge, and for which subsystems, are important. For example, according to the data the greatest demand on knowledge comes from k_4, k_5, and k_7. For the furnace-wiring subsystem only one kind of knowledge is important - k_4 technical approvals. The results of the analysis of knowledge-demand matrix enable us to determine the required kinds of knowledge and areas (technologies or products/subsystems) which should be supported. For the innovation strategy it means what competences (human resources, training, subcontractors, research institutes, etc.) we should develop to guarantee a high level of innovation. The proposed knowledge management for innovation-strategy development should include the learning tools based on artificial neural networks for the adaptation of the knowledge-demand matrices for customer requirements [9]. Of course, the system should include all the innovative projects being undertaken by the whole of the enterprise (including internal projects).

The methodology for implementing the knowledge-management system for innovation-project development is presented in Fig. 6. In the first step of the methodology, the research tools for the identification of vital knowledge in the company should be developed. It means that surveys addressed to customers, employees and business partners should be prepared. On the basis of the results of the research the most-important kinds of knowledge for the enterprise can be defined. In this stage of the methodology the tools for knowledge recording and transfer should be proposed. Next, the work-breakdown structure of the project should be devised and on the basis of the kinds of knowledge and the scope of the projects the knowledge-demand matrix can be developed.

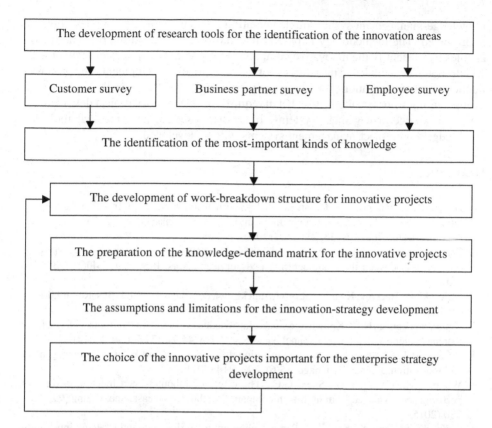

Fig. 6. The methodology of knowledge management system implementation for innovation-strategy development

On the basis of the analysis of the knowledge-demand matrix, the assumptions and limitations of the innovation strategy can be formulated. The assumptions and limitations enable us to support the decision as to which innovative projects should be developed. The innovation strategy can be enhanced by drawing on the feedback as the last stage, and the developing of the work-breakdown structure of new innovative projects.

4 Conclusions

Many SME's do not have a development strategy, and especially an innovation strategy. But for high-tech engineering innovation enterprises this kind of strategy is crucial and in the long-term perspective determines market success or failure. The most-important resources for each innovative company are knowledge and experience, which decide about the implementation of projects (innovative products, technologies or services). In this paper a model of knowledge-management-system implementation for innovation-strategy development is proposed. The model is prepared on the basis of survey research of 121 Polish manufacturing or services SME's. In addition, the methodology of knowledge-management-system implementation for innovation-strategy development is presented. The methodology is based on a knowledge demand matrix. The matrix enables us to identify the innovative components of products, services or technologies which should be included in the strategy for the enterprise's development. The proposed methodology of innovation-strategy development can be relatively easily implemented in engineering-to-order enterprises [10]. It requires simple tools for project development for a knowledge-management systems. In further research, an integrated tools for knowledge- and project-management systems will be developed.

References

1. Dickel, D.G., Moura, G.L.: Organizational performance evaluation in intangible criteria: a model based on knowledge management and innovation management. RAI Revista de Administração e Inovação **13**, 211–220 (2016)
2. Forsman, H.: Innovation capacity and innovation development in small enterprises. A comparison between the manufacturing and service sectors. Res. Policy **40**(5), 739–750 (2011)
3. Nowacki, R., Bachnik, K.: Innovations within knowledge management. J. Bus. Res. **69**, 1577–1581 (2016)
4. Roper, S., Dundas, N.H.: Knowledge stocks, knowledge flows and innovation: Evidence from matched patents and innovation panel data. Res. Policy **44**(7), 1327–1340 (2015)
5. Donate, M.J., Guadamillas, M.J.: Organizational factors to support knowledge management and innovation. J. Knowl. Manage. **15**(6), 890–914 (2011)
6. Wang, C.H., Chang, C.H., Shen, G.C.: The effect of inbound open innovation on firm performance: evidence from high-tech company. Technol. Forecast. Soc. Chang. **99**, 222–230 (2015)
7. Talke, K., Salomo, S., Kock, A.: Top management team diversity and strategic innovation orientation: the relationship and consequences for innovativeness and performance. J. Prod. Innov. Manag. **28**(6), 819–832 (2011)
8. Jasarevic, S., Diering, M., Brdarevic, S.: Opinions of the consultants and certification houses regarding the quality factors and achieved effects of the introduced quality system. Tehnicki Vjesnik-Technical Gazette **19**(2), 211–220 (2012)
9. Burduk, A.: Artificial neural networks as tools for controlling production systems and ensuring their stability. In: Saeed, K., Chaki, R., Cortesi, A., Wierzchoń, S. (eds.) CISIM 2013. LNCS, vol. 8104, pp. 487–498. Springer, Heidelberg (2013). doi:10.1007/978-3-642-40925-7_45
10. Kłos, S.: A model of an ERP-based knowledge management system for engineer-to-order enterprises. In: Dregvaite, G., Damasevicius, R. (eds.) ICIST 2016. CCIS, vol. 639, pp. 42–52. Springer, Cham (2016). doi:10.1007/978-3-319-46254-7_4

Exemplar Functionalities of the Intelligent System for Tacit-Knowledge-Transfer Support for an IT Company

Justyna Patalas-Maliszewska[1(✉)] and Irene Krebs[2]

[1] University of Zielona Góra, Zielona Góra, Poland
J.Patalas@iizp.uz.zgora.pl
[2] Brandenburg University of Technology Cottbus-Senftenberg, Cottbus, Germany
krebs@b-tu.de

Abstract. This article aims to present the usage flow of the intelligent system for Tacit Knowledge-Transfer-Support for an IT company. The following exemplar functionalities of this system are described: C1-F1: Selecting the processes that are carried out by an employee, C1-F2: Determining the employees' knowledge and C2-F2: Determining the weighting of each component of the personnel-usefulness function using the FAHP method. The presented functionalities enable the selection of the employees with the appropriate skills as the main tacit-knowledge source within a company and acquiring the knowledge from them.

Keywords: Tacit knowledge · An intelligent system · Tacit knowledge transfer support

1 Introduction

Companies functioning in a highly competitive environment should appreciate the importance of tacit-knowledge management for securing their competitive advantage. Tacit knowledge in a company is gained from employees who participate in this process, but, however, their knowledge is very difficult to absorb [2, 6, 13, 15]. Nonaka and Takeuchi [10] stated that tacit knowledge can be transferred only through demonstration and the sharing of experience by the employee. However, the problem of tacit-knowledge transfer involves the management of employees, processes, implemented by staff within the company, and the determination of the importance of the knowledge.

According to Wang et al. [16] tacit knowledge can be defined as both employees' professional knowledge (skills, abilities, patents) and experience knowledge. Dhuieba et al. [3] stated that tacit knowledge should be transferred in a company to enable employees understand their activities. We maintain that the most-vital tacit knowledge is associated with employees' knowledge within a company. Our research on employees' knowledge presented a possible method for defining and classifying such employees in a company [13, 14]. We are continuing our research, and we are proposing an intelligent system for Tacit-Knowledge-Transfer Support for an IT company, based on Know-How. When knowledge staff leave a company, their knowledge leaves with them [9]. Our motivation to build this system came from studies of the literature, and also from research results obtained from 62 Polish manufacturing companies in the

© Springer International Publishing AG 2017
R. Damaševičius and V. Mikašytė (Eds.): ICIST 2017, CCIS 756, pp. 25–34, 2017.
DOI: 10.1007/978-3-319-67642-5_3

Lubuskie region, and from 23 German manufacturing companies in the Brandenburg region (in the cross-border cooperative region of Lubuskie/Poland-Brandenburg/Germany) in the automotive and construction sectors (they constitute 20% of such enterprises in the cross-border cooperative region).

In this paper, special attention is paid to present the first part of our intelligent system for Tacit-Knowledge-Transfer Support for the IT company, being the implementation of our concept for the Tacit-Knowledge-Transfer Support Tool: the Know-Board, presented in our previous work [12]. Section 2 shows the literature research related to an approach to Tacit-Knowledge-Transfer Support, and presents the stages which are involved in an intelligent system for Tacit-Knowledge-Transfer Support. Section 3 presents exemplar functionalities of an intelligent system, and Sect. 4 summarises the research results.

2   Related Works and the Approach to the Tacit-Knowledge-Transfer-Support Tool

Tacit knowledge is more difficult than explicit knowledge to transfer among employees [5], but on the other hand managers now pay more attention to the sharing of some important knowledge [7]. Moreover, tacit knowledge is the currency of the informal economy of the workplace [8]. Therefore, any approach to Tacit-Knowledge-Transfer Support should attempt to make tacit knowledge explicit. Our research is focused on the Tacit-Knowledge-Transfer-Support model according to the following stages of the tacit-knowledge-management process. (1) Identifying tacit-knowledge sources (employees' knowledge is the main tacit-knowledge source), (2) Defining the rules for knowledge acquisition, (3) Acquiring knowledge, (4) Classifying knowledge, (5) Understanding knowledge, (6) Using knowledge, (7) Saving knowledge, (8) Building the organisational-knowledge culture.

In this paper we attempt to acquire, codify and convert knowledge within an IT company. So, the proposed approach to an intelligent system for Tacit-Knowledge-Transfer Support for the IT company provides an opportunity to acquire and convert tacit knowledge within the IT company, and, in line with our previous work [12], consists of five components.

- C1: Tacit-Knowledge-Source Identification.
- C2: Tacit-Knowledge-Source Determination using FAHP (The Fuzzy Analytic Hierarchy Process).
- C3: Tacit-Knowledge Acquisition.
- C4: Tacit-Knowledge Transformation.
- C5: Explicit Knowledge Visualisation: A Knowledge-Transfer Board.

Therefore, the following stages are involved in the intelligent system for Tacit-Knowledge-Transfer Support.

Within component C1

Stage C1-1. Defining the processes typically implemented by the staff member

Each employee should identify the processes that are to be carried out by her/him and should allocate in a given month the time spent on each element, within a defined range of 1 h–160 h.

Stage C1-2. Devising a knowledge questionnaire for employees, facilitating the determining of knowledge sources in the company and obtaining the values of each component - GK, PK, A, E, CI - of the personnel-usefulness function [14]:

$$F_n = GK + PK + A + E + CI, \tag{1}$$

where

GK = the general knowledge of the nth worker in the company.
PK = the professional knowledge of the nth worker in the company.
A   = the professional abilities of the nth worker in the company.
E   = the experience of the nth employee in the company.
CI = the capacity for innovation of the nth employee in the company

Stage C1-3. Defining algorithmic solutions for each component GK, PK, A, E, CI of the personnel-usefulness function.

The results: $1 \leq GK \leq 5$; $1 \leq PK \leq 5$, $1 \leq A \leq 5$, $1 \leq E \leq 5$, $1 \leq I \leq 5$.

Stage C1-4. Determining the values of the personnel-usefulness function for each employee.

The result: $1 \leq F_n \leq 25$

Stage C1-5. Devising a knowledge questionnaire for managers in order to evaluate each employee.

The result: $1 \leq ACT \leq 5$; ACT– the acceptance of F_n by the managers in the company.

Within component C2

Stage C2-1. The weighting of each component GK, PK, A, E, CI of the personnel-usefulness function using the FAHP method.

Managers should determine the relative primacy of each factor in the function F_n for each employee, depending on the validity of the given component for the implementation of the new IT project.

Stage C2-2. Determining the main tacit-knowledge sources (MTKS) for new IT projects.

The result: the set of MTKS: MTKS $= <$ MTKS$_1$(F'$_1 \geq 3$ and ACT$_1 \geq 3$), ..., KWj(F$_j \geq 3$ and ACT$_j \geq 3$), j$\in$N

Within component C3

Stage C3-1. Devising a questionnaire for knowledge acquisition for each IT project for each main tacit-knowledge source in the IT company

According to the work of Patalas-Maliszewska and Dudek [11], and the work of Belussi et al. [1], Falkenberg et al. [4], we can acquire useful tacit knowledge in companies by the use the following methods: feedback from customers and suppliers, consultation, analysis-simulation results, observations conducted in real time, using records analysis, demonstrations and training, knowledge audits, and audio and video recordings of activities by experienced employees. In this system, a web questionnaire for knowledge acquisition on each IT project is created and implemented.

Stage C3-2. Creating a knowledge base on IT projects based on results, and on Key-Word Taxonomy.

The result: a complete table on each IT project.

Within component C4

Stage C4-1. The verification of the knowledge base on IT projects by the manager.

The managers should verify the acquired knowledge.

Within component C5

Stage C5-1. The selection of a satisfactory main tacit-knowledge source (employee(s)) for new IT-project-implementation.

The managers can select the most-suitable employee(s) for the new IT-project implementation based on the set of the MTKS.

Stage C5-2. Giving the rights to the use of the knowledge base to new employees in the company.

The managers may give the rights to the use of the knowledge base to new employees for new IT-project implementation.

The issue in this paper is how to select the employees with the appropriate skills as the main tacit-knowledge source, how to acquire knowledge from them, and finally how to codify and convert this knowledge within the IT company. Moreover, how can acquiring tacit knowledge be useful for undertaking new IT projects in companies? The proposed intelligent system for Tacit-Knowledge-Transfer Support provides an opportunity to acquire and convert useful tacit knowledge in the IT company. The next section describes exemplar functionalities of the tacit-knowledge transfer-support system which implements the above stages according to the components C1–C5.

3   An Intelligent System for Tacit-Knowledge-Transfer Support for the IT Company - an Application - Part I Tacit-Knowledge

In Fig. 1 the usage flow of our intelligent system for Tacit-Knowledge-Transfer Support for the IT company is presented. The server administrators perform the server-administration tasks.

Below we describe some sample functions of our system. Within component C1 Tacit-Knowledge Source Identification we have, e.g., the following function:

- C1-F1: Selecting the processes that are carried out by an employee.

A Web-based questionnaire on the typically implemented processes $Pn \in \leq 1$; $69 \geq$ for each employee in the IT company $W = \{W1,\ldots, Wm\}$, $m \in N$ was created (see Fig. 2).

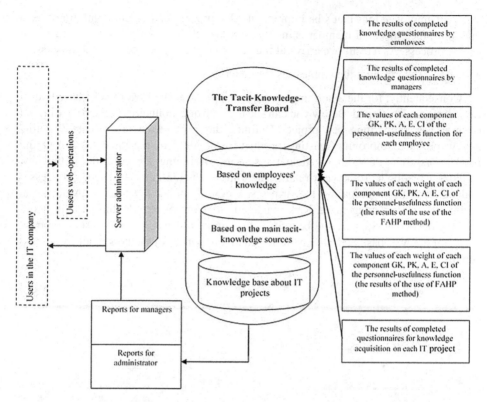

Fig. 1. Usage flow of the intelligent system for Tacit-Knowledge-Transfer Support for the IT company, own work

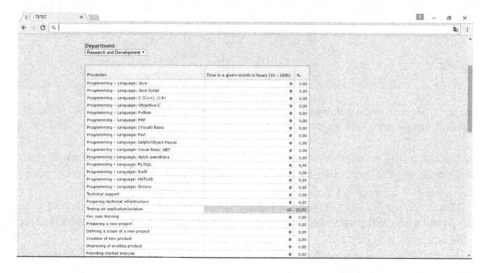

Fig. 2. Web-based questionnaire on typically implemented processes in the IT company, own work

If an employee logs that s/he implements this process in a given month for at least one hour, then this staff member is included in the set of employees who are involved in this process. As a result we arrive at the set of employees assigned to the process.

- C1-F2: Determining the employees' knowledge

Consequently, for the determined groups of processes the various web-based questionnaires are developed. Below you can see the web questionnaire for the following set of processes. Preparing a new project. Defining the scope of the new project. Creating a new product. Improving existing products. Providing market analysis. Providing market research. Providing technical research. Designing the concept of the new product. Creating a prototype. Creating the final product. Sharing marketing processes and best practices. Preparing the firm's strategy. Planning the firm's development. Human-resource management. Risk management. Controlling. Finding new projects. Making decisions. Support and benefits formulation. Figures 3 and 4 present the fragments of the web-based questionnaire for each component of the personnel-usefulness function.

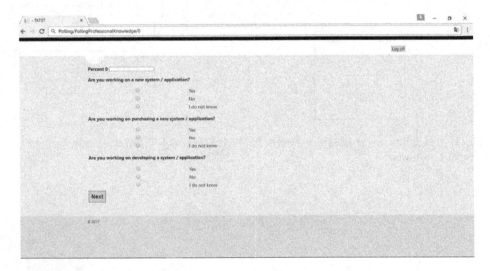

Fig. 3. A fragment of the web-based questionnaire: the professional knowledge (PK) of the nth worker in the company, own work

Thanks to the solution algorithms for these tests, we derive the values of each component of the personnel-usefulness function F_n for each employee, where $1 \leq GK \leq 5$; $1 \leq PK \leq 5$, $1 \leq A \leq 5$, $1 \leq E \leq 5$, $1 \leq CI \leq 5$.

Moreover, the manager in the IT company should also evaluate the employee; so in our system we have the web-based questionnaire Acceptance (ACT) for the nth manager in the company (see Fig. 5).

Accepting the following rules: if $Fn \geq 17$ and $ACT \geq 3$ for each employee then we generate the set of the employees' knowledge.

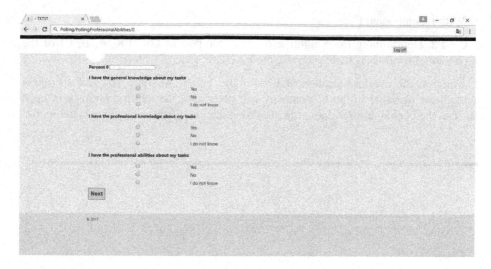

Fig. 4. A fragment of the web-based questionnaire: the professional knowledge (PK) of the nth worker in the company, own work

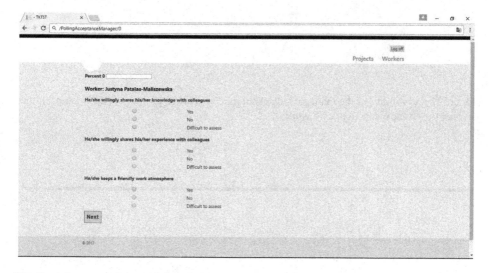

Fig. 5. A fragment of the web-based questionnaire Acceptance (ACT) for the nth manager in the company, own work

The difficulty of the presented approach in our system is that different questionnaires should be defined for each process group. In our system we formulated and implemented different web-questionnaires for four different sets of processes, which means four GK web questionnaires, four PK web-questionnaires, four A web-questionnaires, four E web-questionnaires, and four CI web-questionnaires.

Within component C2:

- C2–F2. Determining the weighting of each component GK, PK, A, E, CI of the personnel-usefulness function using the FAHP method

Through the use and implementation of the Fuzzy Analytic Hierarchy Process method, the manager in the IT company can determine the relative primacy of each factor in the personnel-usefulness function for each knowledge employee (see Fig. 6).

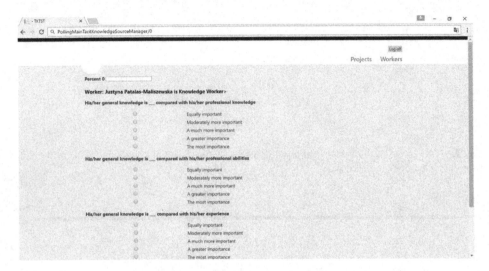

Fig. 6. The possibility of the manager's determining the relative primacy of each factor in the personnel-usefulness function, own work

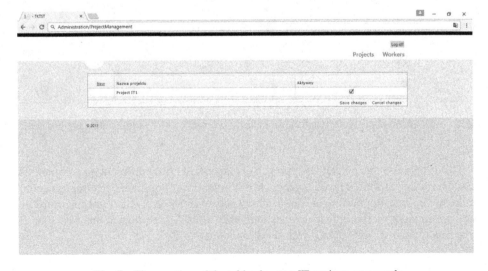

Fig. 7. The creation of the table about an IT project, own work

The FAHP algorithm is also implemented in our system, and we have also defined the rules by which an employee can be assigned to the MTKS. As an example of the implementation of further components we present below a fragment of the report: the table on the IT project (Fig. 7):

This study presents exemplar functionalities of the knowledge-transfer-support system for identifying the main tacit-knowledge sources (MTKS) in the IT company, and for acquiring and converting the tacit knowledge from the MTKS. Further, we plan to conduct experiments to evaluate the usefulness of this system.

4 Conclusions

This paper addresses the challenges and needs of tacit-knowledge transfer as defined by managers in IT companies. Tacit-knowledge acquisition, converting and transferring is becoming crucial for effective software development. In this paper, we have asserted that tacit knowledge cannot be separated from knowledge sources. Our case study presents an intelligent system for Tacit-Knowledge-Transfer Support for an IT company. The use of the system can serve to manage critical tacit knowledge gathered from any identified Main Tacit-Knowledge Source (MTKS) in the IT company.

Several limitations of the proposed system need to be kept in mind; in fact, these limitations might serve as starting points for further research. Firstly, this system should be modified and made relevant to the profile of the company. Future research should extend our theoretical model to other business and company model concepts. Secondly, the present tool focusses on a defined set of business processes in an IT company. Future research should extend this analysis to other relevant processes in an IT company. Finally, due to our personnel usefulness function concept, it will be necessary to formulate a different, web questionnaire for employee knowledge, according to the business processes in each company.

In our further work we will demonstrate the utility of this system through examples of its implementation in IT companies.

References

1. Belussi, F., McDonald, F., Borrás, S.: Industrial districts: state of the art review. Research report, Project West–East id: Industrial districts re-location processes. Identifying policies in the perspective of the European Union enlargement. Report (2005). http://cordis.europa.eu/docs/publications/1001/100123911-6_en.pdf. Last accessed 3 Nov 2016
2. Bennet, R.: Employers' demands for personal transferable skills in graduates: a content analysis of 1000 job advertisements and an associated empirical study. J. Vocat. Educ. Training **54**(4), 457–476 (2002)
3. Dhuieba, M.A., Larochea, F., Bernarda, A.: Context-awareness: a key enabler for ubiquitous access to manufacturing knowledge. Procedia CIRP **41**, 484–489 (2016)
4. Falkenberg, L., Woiceshyn, J., Karagianis, J.: Knowledge sourcing: internal or external? In: Competitiveness and Learning 5th International Conference (2003) http://www2.warwick.ac.uk/fac/soc/wbs/conf/olkc/archive/olk5/papers/paper16.pdf. Last accessed 15 Nov 2016

5. Fernie, S., Green, S.D., Weller, S.J.R.: Newcombe, knowledge sharing: context, confusion and controversy. Int. J. Project Manage. **21**(3), 177–187 (2003)

6. George, E., Chattopadhyay, P.: One foot in each camp: the dual identification of contract workers. Adm. Sci. Q. **50**, 68–99 (2005)

7. Heidemann, J., Klier, M., Probst, F.: Online social networks: a survey of a global phenomenon. Comput. Netw. **56**(18), 3866–3878 (2012)

8. McKinlay, A.: The bearable lightness of control: organizational reflexivity and the politics of knowledge management. In: Pritchard, C., Hull, R., Chumer, M., Willmott, H. (eds.) Managing Knowledge: Critical Investigations of Work and Learning. MacMillan Press, London (2000)

9. Mládková, L.: Management of Knowledge Workers. Wolters Kluwer Business, Bratislava (2012)

10. Nonaka, I., Takeuchi, H.: The Knowledge-Creating Company: How Japanese Companies Create the Dynamics of Innovation. Oxford University Press (1995)

11. Patalas-Maliszewska, J., Dudek, A.: A model of a tacit knowledge transformation for the service department in a manufacturing company: a case study. Found. Manage. Int. J. **8**(1), 75–188 (2016)

12. Patalas-Maliszewska, J., Krebs, I.: A model of the tacit knowledge transfer support tool: cknow-board. In: Dregvaite, G., Damasevicius, R. (eds.) ICIST 2016. CCIS, vol. 639, pp. 30–41. Springer, Cham (2016). doi:10.1007/978-3-319-46254-7_3

13. Patalas-Maliszewska, J., Krebs, I.: Decision model for the use of the application for knowledge transfer support in manufacturing enterprises. In: Abramowicz, W. (ed.) BIS 2015. LNBIP, vol. 228, pp. 48–55. Springer, Cham (2015). doi:10.1007/978-3-319-26762-3_5

14. Patalas-Maliszewska, J.: Knowledge Worker Management: Value Assessment, Methods, and Application Tools. Springer, Heidelberg (2013)

15. Sharma, P., Tam, J.L.M., Namwoon, K.: Demystifying intercultural service encounters. toward a comprehensive conceptual model. J. Serv. Res. **12**, 227–242 (2009)

16. Wang, J.-F., Chen, M.-Y., Feng, L.-J., Yue, J.: The construction of enterprise tacit knowledge sharing stimulation system oriented to employee individual. Procedia Eng. **174**, 289–300 (2017)

A Model of the Knowledge Assessment Using Bayes' Network

Małgorzata Śliwa and Justyna Patalas-Maliszewska[(✉)]

University of Zielona Góra, Zielona Góra, Poland
{M.Sliwa, J.Patalas}@iizp.uz.zgora.pl

Abstract. Modelling of knowledge in production enterprises makes it possible to optimise the processes related to knowledge management. Based on the literature review presented the models using to modeling of knowledge. Following this, the process of acquiring tacit knowledge by the R&D department employees is presented. This article formulates the model of knowledge assessment by means of the Bayesian networks, using the example of a Polish medium manufacturing company from the automotive sector with its own research and development (R&D) department. The authors present the problem of assessing the knowledge acquired from a knowledge form dedicated to this company. The knowledge base has been formulated for which the Bayesian network has been used - the learning algorithm which supports quick identification of the required knowledge and its assessment. Thanks to the implementation of the Bayesian network, it was possible to acquire information on the level of knowledge in a department subject to study; thus it was possible to reduce the time needed for the acquisition of the already gathered resource and its correct identification.

Keywords: Byesian network · Tacit knowledge · Sharing knowledge · Research and development · Production enterprise

1 Introduction

The development of information technology creates the necessity for enterprise managers to make decisions regarding the implementation of the tools assisting in business processes. Knowledge management is classified as one of those processes which not only require support by means of implementing IT tools, but also adequate modelling of the activities conducted by employees as part of this process.

IT systems that support decision-making based on expert knowledge. It encompasses mainly the so-called tacit knowledge which is connected with experience. It comes from the employees and it is acquired by one's own actions. Tacit knowledge is created in the surroundings of generally available and easy to articulate explicit knowledge [1], formalised and concentrated in procedures, regulations, instructions, knowledge bases, etc. [2]. While it is possible to measure the formalised resource, it is hard to acquire and assess the experts' level of knowledge.

Modelling of knowledge and artificial intelligence, even in the case of a simple task, requires the involvement of large resources, while this knowledge is in the state of

© Springer International Publishing AG 2017
R. Damaševičius and V. Mikašytė (Eds.): ICIST 2017, CCIS 756, pp. 35–47, 2017.
DOI: 10.1007/978-3-319-67642-5_4

a constant change [3]. Knowledge representation methods used are based mainly on: predicate logic, production rule and semantic network, and framework. Thanks to ontology it is possible to connect the basic knowledge with the knowledge representation [4].

This article formulates the model of knowledge assessment by means of the Bayesian networks, using the example of a Polish medium manufacturing company from the automotive sector with its own research and development (R&D) department. The authors present the problem of assessing the knowledge acquired from a knowledge form dedicated to this company. The knowledge base has been formulated for which the Bayesian network has been used - the learning algorithm which supports quick identification of the required knowledge and its assessment. Thanks to the implementation of the Bayesian network, it was possible to acquire information on the level of knowledge in a department subject to study; thus it was possible to reduce the time needed for the acquisition of the already gathered resource and its correct identification.

Chapter two presents, based on the literature review, the models of knowledge assessment in enterprises. Following this, the process of acquiring tacit knowledge by the R&D department employees is presented. As a consequence, the Bayesian network has been designed to formulate the model of knowledge assessment and the model has been verified on a real example.

2 Knowledge Modelling

Systems which represent knowledge are generally called knowledge based systems [3]. Based on the review of literature (from the year 2000 to 2015), the researchers explain the models of knowledge used in representing and manipulating knowledge. Four main categories of the models and their representatives have been distinguished [5]:

- the linguistic knowledge bases – FrameNet, WordNet, ConceptNet,
- the expert knowledge bases – Fuzzy Rule based System, Logical Rule based System,
- the ontology – Application Ontology, Domain O., Generic O., Representation O.,
- the cognitive knowledge base.

In manufacturing companies, knowledge modelling tools use algorithms which support the identification of key notions contained in dispersed external and internal sources. The selection of key words, taking into account their frequency or the sequence of their occurrence are made possible by data mining techniques [6] or semantic methods [7].

When assessing risk, making decisions or specifying the probability of a situation that has occurred, the following methods are used: Fuzzy Petri Nets – a method of modelling with a visual representation of knowledge and inferencing in expert systems [8], Bayesian networks [9] or genetic algorithms [10]. The Bayesian networks are used for object classifications, presenting process dependencies, as well as when making decisions in uncertainty conditions [9]. As authors of Agena Risk said Bayesian network "is enabled us to incorporate expert judgement (for example, about the software development process) with limited data from individual component testing and even more limited data from system testing" [11].

Genetic algorithms, as a more complex tool, as a rule, are used for studying the (occurrence) of the final effect through the analysis of multiple factors and their weights. They are useful, for example, in evaluating customers' preferences [12], or in analysing manufacturing processes, accompanied by the index rankings [13].

The presented solutions are used in large manufacturing companies. On the other hand, in the small-medium-enterprises (SME) sector, one should look for techniques which make it possible to design knowledge and assess it adequately to the needs of the company. According to the basic rules presented by Bubenko [14], modelled knowledge in a company refers to conceptual techniques which take into account the information system or the group of elements of the company (business processes, actors, roles, flow of information, etc.) and teleological group, which includes reasons.

Knowledge modelling can be objective, i.e. the definition of knowledge representation in the form of an object, or in the form of a process, i.e. the representation of knowledge encompasses cause-effect dependencies, which, in turn, is reflected in the networks and trees, and directed graphs.

For the needs of formulating the model of knowledge assessment in a manufacturing company, the following knowledge categories have been adopted:

- group of knowledge, group of products, group of models, etc.,
- main fields of knowledge occurring in the R&D department regarding the specified issues related to the project, e.g. technology, material resistance, etc.
- sources of knowledge, i.e. the list of employees who are actively involved in a given project,
- the how? knowledge, i.e. the list of problems during the realisation of the project.

The dispersed knowledge can be acquired and organised using tools such as [15]: questionnaires, forms, thematic panels or message boards of knowledge exchange which should ultimately be connected to internal knowledge bases.

For the manufacturing company under consideration, a knowledge base has been prepared, based on the dedicated knowledge acquisition questionnaire. The base includes specialist knowledge on the executed projects which required the use of an employee's experience. The check boxes have been narrowed down to specifying the item compliant with the closed list. The content of the form and the example answers are presented below:

1. Specify the ID of the project to which the issue belongs. *SF_1369*
2. Specify the group of products. *valves*
3. Select the field of knowledge of the issue. *technology*
4. Select the key word for the issue. *main gasket, gasket*
5. To whom do you make the knowledge available? *R&D department*
6. Specify the activities performed while solving the issue. *Additional laboratory tests, Jan Kowalski, Pressure Value_1369*
7. Which key materials were used while solving the issue (source of knowledge)? *Technical documentation, SafetyValve_1365*

8. Which materials were created while solving the issue (source of knowledge)? Should the acquired knowledge be made available to a new employee? *Technical documentation, SafetyValve_1369*
9. Comments on the acquired knowledge.
10. Person responsible for solving a given issue. *Andrzej Nowak*

The information downloaded automatically while filling in the knowledge questionnaire (the employee is logged in on his/her computer, the employee logs in to the system, etc.)

The knowledge acquired this way is entered to the knowledge base for which the Bayesian network has been implemented.

3 Modelling of Knowledge Using the Bayesian Network

The operating principle of the Bayesian network is based on the Bayesian classification rule. Its graphical interpretation presents the finite, acyclic directed graph which indicates the cause-effect dependency between the apexes (variables) [16]. The Bayesian networks create an effective expert system which is based on statistics. The Bayes theorem (Eq. 1) is the so-called conditional probability (a posteriori) of the event A (belonging to a specified class A) on condition of the occurrence of event B (possessing the properties specified as B).

$$P(A_i \setminus B) = \frac{P(B \setminus Ai)P(Ai)}{P(B)} \tag{1}$$

Assuming the update of the simple probability a priori to a posteriori in the light of new information (e.g. known properties of the project under examination), it should be borne in mind that event B can occur in several mutually exclusive ways A_k (several various routes), where the probabilities of occurrence A_k are significant. Thus, total probability P(B) can be expressed by the equation:

$$P(B) = \sum_k P(A_k)P(B \setminus A_k) \tag{2}$$

The acquired knowledge has made it possible to calculate again the probability of the occurrence of each event A_i, therefore from the first value A_i we arrive at a new value $P(A_i \setminus B)$, using the Eq. 1 [16].

Modelling of the Bayesian networks with the graphical interpretation of the networks with the calculating engine can be made using the following software: AgenaRisk [17], GeNie [18], Belief and Decision Network Tool [19], dedicated computer platform, with traditional interface easy to use by an average user.

Knowledge base build on the basis of a knowledge acquisition form (see Chap. 2) constitutes the so-called training set i.e. the reference point for the Bayesian network. Methodology of implementation and functioning of a network in the company subject to study is described in three basic steps. While step 1 relates to the preparation of a

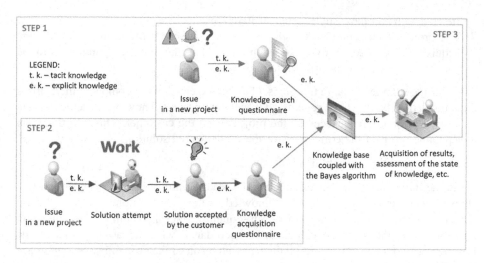

Fig. 1. The methodology of implementing the presented knowledge management supporting algorithm in the R&D department in a manufacturing company

general concept and purposefulness of modelling of knowledge available in the company, steps 2 and 3 present specific actions - they are visually represented by Fig. 1.

STEP 1 Construction of the Bayesian network scheme

The first step involves the definition of the purpose of the network – what question it should answer or what classes should the described object belong to. Based on the analysis of key elements in the company which affect the achievement of the objective, one should define the dependencies between the elements (levels of the net).

STEP 2 Creating the training set

The second step involves the acquisition of knowledge for the bases on which the calculating algorithm shall base its operation. Using the proposed tool (e.g. a questionnaire) one acquires knowledge on a set quantity in a specified period of time. Completing the bases (training set) should be performed in cyclic time intervals. That updates are made realistic results of probability are received. The subsequent steps presented below.

1. A R&D employee receives a new project which includes a problematic issue.
2. The project leader undertakes to search for solutions. First, by their own, and then using the sources of knowledge acquired from outside or from inside of the company.
3. Concepts, visualisations, solutions, and prototypes are devised. Thus, documents of various kind, origin, and format are acquired.
4. The choice of an optimal solution is made.
5. The prototype is put to internal tests and studies carried out by a team composed of the project leader, quality engineer, etc.
6. The project is approved by the authorised entities, i.e. the project leader, CEO...

Items 4 to 6 can have any number of iterations.

7. The project leader completes his/her knowledge bases by filling in the knowledge acquisition (issue solution) questionnaire, assigning the indicated parameters to the specific issue from a specific field.

After the sufficiently large training set has been created in the company, there arises the knowledge base which regards the specified issues. They are entered by the authorised person, having received the project from the customer. This constitutes an indisputable proof of the correctness of the implemented solution.

STEP 3 Algorithm operation

In the initial stage, the Bayesian networks read the probability of occurrence of an element at the input, e.g. the field of knowledge, key word, among previously completed elements in the training base. Subsequently, the algorithm defines the joint probability for the searched elements, in accordance with the assumptions of the Bayesian network (Eq. 1). Based on the received result of the probability, the inference takes place, i.e. the reference thereof to the interpretation of a given probability range and the corresponding inferences (optionally: benefits). For example: if $P(z) > 0.7$, it is assumed that the level of the available knowledge is high. Therefore, one estimates the reception of the assumed benefits at a value suggested by the management board of the company, e.g. completion of the project within the period of time 5% shorter than the standard time.

The knowledge entered to the R&D bases is also coupled with a simple knowledge search engine: key word, field of knowledge, employees, department, source of knowledge, or action. It is assumed that the standard sorting of materials according to the type of knowledge, i.e. the belonging to the base, time of editing, time of addition, alphabetically.

4 Implementation of the Model

The model and its structure has been designed based on the research conducted in previous studies on the distribution of technical knowledge in a manufacturing company [15, 20, 21]. The characteristic of such a department is presented below:

D1: company type: production, automotive sector,

D2: company size: SME, current employment: about 70 workers,

D3: project assumptions: pneumatic valves, assistive devices for assembly and production,

D4: R&D personnel involved in the task: 3 to 4 people,

D5: project budget: from 150 000 PLN to 500 000 PLN,

D6: project representative > age 29 years,

D7: R&D manager: 15 years in the team, 17 years of experience in a similar position,

D8: number of projects carried out: 4–5 per year.

4.1   Assumptions of the Proposed Bayesian Network

Independent variables included in the Bayesian network have been chosen from all the elements contained in the knowledge acquisition form in the R&D department.

Step 1

At first, one should specify the independent variables, i.e. the first layer which has no "predecessors", which have been chosen from all acquired data in the form. Where A, B, C…are symbolic designations of the node, p(a) – means the probability occurring in the node A for the nth an choice.

A {a1, a2, a3}	A–group of products
p(a1), p(a2), p(a3)	probability of the occurrence of a given group of products
Set of values:	valves, blocks, connectors
B {b1…b5}	B–areas of knowledge
p(b1)… p(b5)	probability of the occurrence of a given field of knowledge
Set of values:	structure, material, functionality, technology, research
C {c1…c40}	C– group of key words
p(c1)…p(c40)	probability of occurrence of a given key word
Set of values:	An example set contains 40 defined groups of key words, where some of them are identical and describe one element
D {d1…d5}	D–departments in the company to which the knowledge has been made available
p(d1)…p(d5)	probability of occurrence of a given department
Set of values:	R&D Department (default), Technological Dep., Commercial Dep., Maintenance Dep., Purchasing Dep.
E {e1..e5}	E– activities performed after the issues have been resolved
p(e1)…p(e5)	probability of occurrence of a given activity
Set of values:	feedback from the customer, additional research, external expert consultation, internal expert consultation, other
F {f1..f8}	F– key materials used for solving the issues
p(f1)…p(f8)	probability of occurrence of given materials
Set of values:	technical documentation, literature, customer feedback, knowledge base, website, application/programme, materials catalogue, internal knowledge exchange points
G {g1..g13}	G– materials produced after the task has been resolved
p(g1)…p(g13)	probability of occurrence of given materials
Set of values:	technical documentation, procedure of action, instruction, CAD/CRM simulation, video recordings, audio recordings, visualisation, log analysis, reports, research reports, "brainstorm" panel, graphics, utility model or patent.
H {h1, h2}	H–decision on making the acquired knowledge available to new employees
p(h1), p(h2)	Probability of occurrence of a given decision
Set of values:	Yes, Not
I {i1, i2, i3}	I– employee who deals with the subject-matter

p(i1), p(i2), p(i3)   probability of occurrence of a given employee
Set of values: employee 1, employee 2, employee 3...

Step 2

In the second step, the dependent variables have been defined, that is the subsequent layers of the network which will constitute elements subject to learning. The inference of those levels takes place as a result of the work on the training set.

M {m1, m2}   M– (knowledge base) guidelines
p(m1), p(m2)   Probability of occurrence of knowledge indications (the higher the probability, the more indications)
Set of values: True/False
N {n1, n2}   N– competent team
p(n1), p(n2)   Probability of occurrence of a competent team (the higher the probability, the more competent the team)
Set of values: True/False
O {o1, o2}   O– ready templates
p(o1), p(o2)   Probability of occurrence of a given employee
Set of values: True/False

Description of the dependencies:

M on A, B, C – the level of indications (the so-called knowledge bases) is dependent on the number of the occurrences of the groups of products, fields of knowledge, key words for the issue. The more numerous they are, the better for the company (larger deposits of knowledge).

N on D, E, I – competent team is a result of the components: departments to which the knowledge has been available, actions undertaken to solve the task, and the employee. The more numerous the indications and presence of a given component in the training set, the higher the index of the knowledge in the company.

O on F and G – ready templates are dependent on the number of key materials used while solving a given issue in the project, and on the quantity of materials created after the issue has been solved. The more numerous they are, the better for the company, the higher the index of knowledge in the company.

Step 3

The search for the probability of the occurrence of knowledge which has declared parameters in the company (dependent variable), calculated according to the rule of chain of nodes.

Z {z1, z2}   Z – level of knowledge
p(z1), p(z2)   probability of occurrence of a given knowledge (issue resolution), which can be broken down into three range groups: low, average, high
Set of values: True/False

Description of the dependencies:

Z on M, N, O – level of knowledge of a given project is a result of a joint occurrence of indications (knowledge bases), competent team, and ready templates. The higher the occurrence of the components, the more knowledge the company has.

4.2   Defined Bayesian Network

Presented in the article, the network modelled in the Belief and Decision Network Tool Version 5.1.10. The network has an example probability values for each node (a priory) (Fig. 2), which should be connected with reality values – declared in the training set a fixed number of verified projects, by R&D workers.

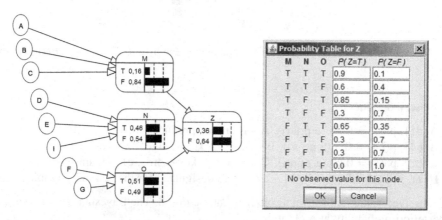

Fig. 2. Bayesian network after fill up of the probability at each node, with the example of probability table for "Z" node. Belief and decision network tool version 5.1.10.

The project of the network does not include the cases of simultaneous observation of several values in a given node.

The inference based on the presented Bayesian network, takes place after the initial analysis of the issue addressed by the network. As first values should be defined from the perspective of which the probability analysis is conducted. Receiving the a prestori probability result, at the outputs one should specify the observation, choosing each time a specific input component. The more specified input components, the more reliable the final probability. For the purpose of the presentation of the operation of the network, it has been assumed that the company subject to the study receives a new project in which main sealing is problematic in the context of the manufacturing technology in products such as valves. Employee 2 is put forward as the project leader; the rest of the team is sufficiently burdened with tasks.

While analysing the decision about taking the project, the management's question is: what is the level of knowledge in the R&D department regarding the given subject-matter, with the availability of employee 2?

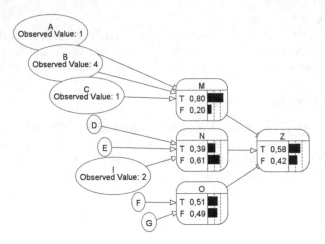

Fig. 3. Example of working network after filling in the form by a R&D manager. B&DNT ver. 5.1.10.

Observed values:

A{a1}, p(a1) = 0.25 (a priori), A - group of products, a1 – connectors,
B{b4}, p(b4) = 0.5 (a priori), B - fields of knowledge, b4 – technology,
C{c1}, p(c1) = 0.20 (a priori), C - group of key-words, c1 – main gasket,
I{i2}, p(i2) = 0.5 (a priori), I – employee designated for the task, i2 – employee 2.

Observed values are shown as observed at the Fig. 3. The Bayesian network shows a posteriori probability at each node.

It represents that the level of knowledge is nearly 58% in department. The output result should be verified with the interpretation of the indicators of benefits (accepted by the management of the company) assigned to the set ranges. Three probability ranges is proposed: low: $0.00 \leq P(x) < 0.30$, average: $0.30 \leq P(x) < 0.70$ and high: $1,00 > P(x) \geq 0,70$.

Managers and the R&D representatives assign attributes to each group. The result of the level of knowledge which takes into consideration the observed values $P(z) = 0.58$ is within the average range; one can assume a moderate probability of the creation of the innovation while preparing the project, occurrence of the reduction by up to 5% of the duration of the project, reduction of complaints, financial efforts up to circa 5% or the reduction of time assigned to introducing and training the employee by circa 5%.

Assuming the expansion of the network by the alternatives of multi-choice observations and creating a hybrid networks (Fig. 4), one can assume the interpretation of the results of the probability of the nodes with the predecessors. Authors understanding "hybrid networks" as a combination of multiple alternatives (multi-choice) in one network, for example: wide-developed C-class nodes. All (C1 through C96) involve a keyword, although the user can observe multiple key words at once.

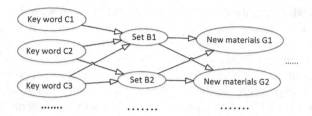

Fig. 4. Example of part of multi-choice Bayesian network, which showed relationship among: Key words → Set of knowledge → New materials → Others nodes

Table 1. The set of indications related to the probability occurring at the dependent nodes.

Example components of probabilities	Example probability of the node	Examples of indications
—Main sealing P(c1), —Chemical resistance P(c2), —o-ring P(c3).	Functionality P(b1) low: $0.00 \leq P$ (b1) < 0.30	Inadequate level of knowledge. Fill in the knowledge bases regarding the issue c1, c2, c3.
—Chemical resistance P(c2), —o-ring gasket P(c3).	Material P(b2) high $1.00 > P(b2) \geq 0.70$	High level of knowledge. It is recommended that the knowledge from the ranges c1, c2, c3 be made available to new employees.

Indications related to the partial probability range would concern the proposed actions to enhance the level of knowledge. Set of interpretations (Table 1) should be proposed by the project leaders on a one-off basis.

It is assumed to test the model in the researched manufacturing company for a period of approximately 6 to 9 months at the turn of 2017 and 2018. At that time, the R&D workers will insert the knowledge into the base. Then, in 3-month intervals, experiments - measuring the level of knowledge will be conducted. At the same time, statistics will be tracked on 4 elements: the number of projects considered as innovative, the duration of the projects, the budget assumed and the budget used, the number of trainings for R&D workers and their activity. Observations will be generated in the user-defined period where goal is to monitor the real benefits of using a designed system (or not) in the enterprise. If it will be required, managements should adjust the conclusions (or hint) attributed to the probability ranges, at their discretion.

5   Conclusions

Modelling of the knowledge assessment may contribute to maintaining market competitiveness by a company. Knowledge management supporting technology with the assessment of knowledge level is significant from the perspective of the employees of the department as well as the management. The R&D department, working with its own base of knowledge, gathers and uses the required know-how, which contributes to a quick access to necessary information. The managing units, in turn, are able to monitor the work of the R&D department. Knowledge modeling (and generally knowledge management) allows for better performance of the processes in the enterprise, mainly because of the time saving access to knowledge [22] and its analysis.

Selecting the appropriate method of knowledge representation adequate to the needs and coupling it with an intelligent system will lead to the interpretation of a set objective which is as precise as possible. The proposed knowledge management supporting model based on the Bayesian networks indicates the dependencies between the objects, constituting a clear graphical representation. This allows for an automatic support of the decision making [16], being based on expert knowledge. The tool for supporting the level of knowledge based on statistics and total probability offers the possibility of optimal quotation of the project, estimating the lead time or selecting a competent team. Subsequent studies will involve conducting research experiments regarding the implementation of the proposed model in a manufacturing company.

References

1. Nonaka, I., Toyama, R., Konno, T.: SECI, Ba and Leadership: a Unified Model of Dynamic Knowledge Creation. Long Range Planning, No. 33 (2000)
2. Jashapara, A.: Zarządzanie wiedzą. Polskie Wydawnictwo Ekonomiczne, Warszawa (2006)
3. Akerkar, R., Sajja, P.: Knowledge-based systems. Jones and Bartlett Publishers, Sudbury (2010)
4. Qiang, Z., Ping, Y., Yang, X.: Research on a knowledge modelling methodology for fault diagnosis of machine tools based on formal semantics. Adv. Eng. Inform. **32**, 92–112 (2017)
5. Bimbaa, A.T., Idris, N., Al-Hunaiyyanb, A., Mahmuda, R.B., Abdelaziz, A., Khana, S., Chang, V.: Towards knowledge modeling and manipulation technologies: a survey. Int. J. Inf. Manage. **36**, 857–871 (2016)
6. Han, J., Kamber, M., Pei, J.: Data Mining: Concepts and Techniques. Elsevier Inc, Waltham (2012)
7. Bergamaschi, S., Martoglia, R., Sorrentino, S.: A semantic method for searching knowledge in a software development context. In: Proceedings of the 20th Italian Symposium on Advanced Database Systems, SEBD (2012)
8. Liua, H.-C., Youb, J.-X., Lic, Z., Tian, G.: Fuzzy petri nets for knowledge representation and reasoning: a literature review. Eng. Appl. Artif. Intell. **60**, 45–56 (2017)
9. Olbryś, J.: Sieć bayesowska jako narzędzie pozyskiwania wiedzy z ekonomicznej bazy danych. Zeszyty Naukowe Politechniki Białostockiej. Informatyka, Zeszyt 93/2, pp. 93–107 (2007)
10. Yanrong, H., Yang, S.X.: A knowledge based genetic algorithm for path planning of a mobile robot, robotics and automation. In: 2004 IEEE International Conference Proceedings ICRA (2004)
11. Fenton, N.E., Neil, M.: Decision support software for probabilistic risk assessment using bayesian networks. IEEE Softw. **31**(2), 21–26 (2014)
12. Haoa, J.-X., Yuc, Y., Lawb, R., Fongd, D.: A genetic algorithm-based learning approach to understand customer satisfaction with OTA websites. Tour. Manag. **48**, 231–241 (2015)

13. Nestic, S., Stefanovic, M., Djordjevic, A., Arsovski, S., Tadic, D.: A model of the assessment and optimisation of production process quality using the fuzzy sets and genetic algorithm approach. Eur. J. Ind. Eng. **9**(1), 15–27 (2015)
14. Bubenko, J.: Enterprise Modelling. Ingénierie des Systems d' Information, vol. 2/6 (1994)
15. Śliwa, M., Patalas-Maliszewska, J.: Model of converting tacit knowledge into explicit knowledge on the example of R&D department of the manufacturing company, including assessment of knowledge workers' usefulness. J. Theor. Appl. Comput. Sci. **9**(3), 25–34 (2015)
16. Król, A.: Sieci bayesowskie jako narzędzie wspomagające proces podejmowania decyzji. Zeszyty Naukowe Politechniki Śląskiej. Organizacja i Zarządzanie, 71/ 1917, pp. 209–218 (2014)
17. http://www.agenarisk.com/
18. https://www.bayesfusion.com/
19. http://www.aispace.org/index.shtml
20. Śliwa, M.: Uwarunkowania procesu modelowania i oceny efektywności systemu wspomagającego zarządzanie wiedzą ukrytą w przedsiębiorstwach produkcyjnych. Przedsiębiorczość i Zarządzanie, Tom XVII, Zeszyt **7**(2), 263–278 (2016)
21. Śliwa, M., Patalas-Maliszewska, J.: A strategic knowledge map for the research and development department in a manufacturing company. Found. Manage. **8**(1), 151–166 (2016). International Journal
22. Tabaszewska, E.: Wprowadzanie i funkcjonowanie systemów zarządzania wiedzą w przedsiębiorstwach. Wydawnictwo Uniwersytetu Ekonomicznego we Wrocławiu, Wrocław (2012)

Object-Oriented Knowledge Representation and Data Storage Using Inhomogeneous Classes

Dmytro Terletskyi[(✉)]

Taras Shevchenko National University of Kyiv, Kyiv 03680, Ukraine
dmytro.terletskyi@gmail.com

Abstract. This paper contains analysis of concept of a class within different object-oriented knowledge representation models. The main attention is paid to structure of the class and its efficiency in the context of data storage, using object-relational mapping. The main achievement of the paper is extension of concept of homogeneous class of objects by introducing concepts of single-core and multi-core inhomogeneous classes of objects, which allow simultaneous defining of a few different types within one class of objects, avoiding duplication of properties and methods in representation of types, decreasing sizes of program codes and providing more efficient information storage in the databases. In addition, the paper contains results of experiment, which show that data storage in relational database, using proposed extensions of the class, in some cases is more efficient in contrast to usage of homogeneous classes of objects.

Keywords: Class · Homogeneous class · Single-core inhomogeneous class · Core of level m · Multi-core inhomogeneous class

1 Introduction

During recent years amount of information, which is used by information systems, has extremely increased, therefore invention of efficient approaches to knowledge representation, storing and extraction of data become more crucial. Nowadays the majority of modern information systems is developed using object-oriented programming (OOP) languages. The main advantage of OOP-languages is simultaneous combining of the programming paradigm implementation and object-oriented knowledge representation model within the language. Moreover, almost all modern languages support such technology as object-relational mapping (ORM), which allows data storing within relational database in terms of classes and objects.

However, one of the important tasks of object-oriented information systems development, is design of classes and their hierarchy, which describes particular domain. Complexity of the whole system mostly depends on the structure of the classes and the structure of their hierarchy. In addition, efficiency of data storage within relational database also depends on the structure of particular classes.

© Springer International Publishing AG 2017
R. Damaševičius and V. Mikašytė (Eds.): ICIST 2017, CCIS 756, pp. 48–61, 2017.
DOI: 10.1007/978-3-319-67642-5_5

Nowadays concept of a *class* is widely used in almost all approaches to knowledge representation. However, its definition and interpretations within various knowledge representation formalisms have some differences. Let us consider the notion of the class within such object-oriented knowledge representation models (KRMs) as *frames* and *object-oriented programming* (OOP).

2   Concept of a Class

In the theory of frames *class* is usually called *class-frame* or *generic frame* [4,9,10]. *Class-frame* is defined as a data structure, which describes a group of objects with common attributes [10]. It defines attributes (properties), relationships with other frames and procedural attachments (methods) for class-instances or other class-frames. In other words, a class-frame defines a stereotypical object, which can be considered as a template for creation of more specific stereotypical or particular objects. Therefore, all frames, which are instances of a class-frame, have the same structure and behavior.

Within the OOP concept of the *class* is associated with a number of different, but not always competing, interpretations [3,5,6,8,19]. It can variously be interpreted as: a set of objects; a program structure or module; a factory-like entity which creates objects; a data type. However, despite all differences, a class defines some set of properties (specification) and (or) set of methods (signature), which are common for all objects of the class, in all of these interpretations. In other words, specification defines the structure of objects, while signature defines their behavior.

Analyzing and comparing notions of a class within the theory of frames and OOP, it is possible to conclude that in both cases a class defines objects with same structure and behavior, i.e. objects of the same type. Therefore, such classes can be called *homogeneous* ones. This feature of classes introduces some limitation, in particular it makes impossible simultaneous definition of a few types of objects within one class. Consequently, description of each new type of objects requires definition of new class. When a few types of objects are similar but not equivalent ones, it can cause duplication of properties and methods in classes, which describe these types. To prevent such situations, frames, as OOP, support the inheritance mechanism, that helps to build class hierarchies in more flexible and efficient way. However, as it was shown in [1,12,18], using of inheritance can cause problems of exceptions, redundancy and ambiguity, which usually arise while constructing of hierarchies and reasoning over them.

3   Homogeneous Classes of Objects

Besides frames and OOP, there is such object-oriented knowledge representation model as *object-oriented dynamic networks* (OODN), which was proposed in [13–15]. All these KRMs have some similarity, however OODN use more extended notion of the class, than frames and OOP, which allows avoiding duplication of properties and methods in representation of types, decreasing sizes of program codes and providing more efficient information storage in the databases. Let us consider concept of class within OODN in more details.

Similarly to frames and OOP, OODN exploit concept of *homogeneous class* (HC) of objects.

Definition 1. *Homogeneous class of objects T is a tuple $T = (P(T), F(T))$, where $P(T) = (p_1(T), \ldots, p_n(T))$ is a specification, which defines some quantity of objects, and $F(T) = (f_1(T), \ldots, f_m(T))$ is a signature, which can be applied to them.*

As it was mentioned early, such concept of the class has widespread practical usage in frames systems and OOP, however there are some objects that simultaneously belong to many different classes, which cannot be described using concept of homogeneous classes. One of the approaches for solving this problem is introduction of concept of *inhomogeneous class* of objects, which extends notion of *homogeneous class* [13, 16]. However, concept of inhomogeneous classes, which is proposed in [13], can be extended by the dividing of inhomogeneous classes of objects on *single-core inhomogeneous classes* (SCIC) and *multi-core inhomogeneous classes* (MCIC) of objects. Let us define these kinds of inhomogeneous classes of objects.

4   Single-core Inhomogeneous Classes of Objects

Concept of single-core inhomogeneous class of objects means the same as concept of homogeneous class of objects, which was defined in [13], i.e.

Definition 2. *Single-core inhomogeneous class of objects T is a tuple*

$$T = (Core(T), pr_1(A_1), \ldots, pr_n(A_n)),$$

where $Core(T) = (P(T), F(T))$ is a core of the class T, which contains properties and methods that are common for objects $A_1, \ldots, A_n$, and $pr_i(A_i) = (P(A_i), F(A_i))$, where $i = \overline{1, n}$, is an i-th projection of the class T, which contains properties and methods that are typical only for the object A_i, $i = \overline{1, n}$.

As we can see, concept of SCIC allows describing two or more different types within one class, using OOP-like style, while describing each new type within OOP requires definition of new class or using mechanism of inheritance if types have common properties and (or) methods.

Analyzing Definitions 1 and 2, we can conclude that any HC defines only one type of objects, while any SCIC defines at least two different types of objects. Therefore, in the first case notions of *class* and *type* mean the same, while in second case they have different meaning. Taking into account that SCIC simultaneously defines a few types of objects, let us introduce the concept of a *type* of objects.

Definition 3. *Type t_i, $i = \overline{1, n}$ of inhomogeneous class of objects $T_{t_1, \ldots, t_n}$ is a homogeneous class of objects $t_i = (Core(T_{t_1, \ldots, t_n}), pr_i(A_i))$, where $Core(T_{t_1, \ldots, t_n})$ is a core of the class $T_{t_1, \ldots, t_n}$, and $pr_i(A_i)$ is its i-th projection.*

Let us consider an example of SCIC of objects.

Example 1. Clearly that such geometric figures as square, rectangle and rhombus belong to the class of convex quadrangles. Let us define SCIC of objects T_{SRRb}, which defines these types of convex quadrangles in the following way

$$T_{SRRb} = (p_1(T_{SRRb}) = (4, \text{sides}),$$
$$p_2(T_{SRRb}) = (4, \text{angles}),$$
$$p_3(T_{SRRb}) = vf_3(T_{SRRb}) = (1),$$
$$f_1(T_{SRRb}) = (v_1(p_2(t_i)) + v_2(p_2(t_i)) + v_3(p_2(t_i)) + v_4(p_2(t_i)), \text{cm}),$$
$$i \in \{S, R, Rb\}$$
$$p_1(t_S) = ((2, \text{cm}), (2, \text{cm}), (2, \text{cm}), (2, \text{cm})),$$
$$p_2(t_S) = ((90°), (90°), (90°), (90°)),$$
$$p_3(t_S) = vf_3(t_S) = (1),$$
$$p_4(t_S) = vf_4(t_S) = (1),$$
$$f_1(t_S) = ((v_1(p_1(t_S)))^2, \text{cm}^2),$$
$$p_1(t_R) = ((2, \text{cm}), (3, \text{cm}), (2, \text{cm}), (3, \text{cm})),$$
$$p_2(t_R) = ((90°), (90°), (90°), (90°)),$$
$$p_3(t_R) = vf_3(t_R) = (1),$$
$$p_4(t_R) = vf_4(t_R) = (1),$$
$$f_1(t_R) = (v_1(p_1(t_R)) \cdot v_2(p_1(t_R)), \text{cm}^2),$$
$$p_1(t_{Rb}) = ((3, \text{cm}), (3, \text{cm}), (3, \text{cm}), (3, \text{cm})),$$
$$p_2(t_{Rb}) = ((80°), (100°), (80°), (100°)),$$
$$p_3(t_{Rb}) = vf_3(t_{Rb}) = (1),$$
$$p_4(t_{Rb}) = vf_4(t_{Rb}) = (1),$$
$$f_1(t_{Rb}) = ((v_1(p_1(t_{Rb})))^2 \cdot \sin(v_1(p_4(t_{Rb}))), \text{cm}^2),$$

where $p_1(T_{SRRb})$ is a quantity of sides, $p_2(T_{SRRb})$ is a quantity of internal angles, $vf_3(T_{SRRb})$ is a verification function, which defines a property "sum of all internal angles is equal to 360°", i.e. $vf_3(T_{SRRb}) : p_3(T_{SRRb}) \to \{0, 1\}$, where

$$p_3(T_{SRRb}) = (v_1(p_4(t_i)) + v_2(p_4(t_i)) + v_3(p_4(t_i)) + v_4(p_4(t_i)) = 360),$$

where $i \in \{S, R, Rb\}$, $f_1(T_{SRRb})$ is a method of perimeter calculation, $p_1(t_S)$, $p_1(t_R)$, $p_1(t_{Rb})$ are sizes of sides, $p_2(t_S)$, $p_2(t_R)$, $p_2(t_{Rb})$ are degree measures of internal angles, $vf_3(t_S)$ is a verification function, which defines a property "all sides of figure have the same length", i.e. $vf_3(t_S) : p_3(t_S) \to \{0, 1\}$, where

$$p_3(t_S) = (v_1(p_1(t_S)) = v_2(p_1(t_S)) = v_3(p_1(t_S)) = v_4(p_1(t_S))),$$

$vf_4(t_S)$ is a verification function, which defines a property "all internal angles are equal to 90°", i.e. $vf_4(t_S) : p_4(t_S) \to \{0, 1\}$, where

$$p_4(t_S) = (v_1(p_2(t_S)) = v_2(p_2(t_S)) = v_3(p_2(t_S)) = v_4(p_2(t_S)) = 90),$$

$f_1(t_S)$ is a method of square calculation, $vf_3(t_R)$ is a verification function, which defines a property "opposite sides of the figure have the same length", i.e. $vf_3(t_R) : p_3(t_R) \rightarrow \{0, 1\}$, where

$$p_3(t_R) = ((v_1(p_1(t_R)) = v_3(p_1(t_R))) \wedge (v_2(p_1(t_R)) = v_4(p_1(t_R)))),$$

$vf_4(t_R)$ is a verification function, which defines a property "all internal angles are equal to 90°", i.e. $vf_4(t_R) : p_4(t_R) \rightarrow \{0, 1\}$, where

$$p_4(t_R) = (v_1(p_2(t_R)) = v_2(p_2(t_R)) = v_3(p_2(t_R)) = v_4(p_2(t_R)) = 90),$$

$f_1(t_R)$ is a method of square calculation, $vf_3(t_{Rb})$ is a verification function, which defines a property "all sides of figure have the same length", i.e. $vf_3(t_{Rb}) : p_3(t_{Rb}) \rightarrow \{0, 1\}$, where

$$p_3(t_{Rb}) = (v_1(p_1(t_{Rb})) = v_2(p_1(t_{Rb})) = v_3(p_1(t_{Rb})) = v_4(p_1(t_{Rb}))),$$

$vf_4(t_{Rb})$ is a verification function, which defines a property of equality of opposite internal angles of the figure, i.e. $vf_4(t_{Rb}) : p_4(t_{Rb}) \rightarrow \{0, 1\}$, where

$$p_4(t_{Rb}) = ((v_1(p_2(t_{Rb})) = v_3(p_2(t_{Rb}))) \wedge (v_2(p_2(t_{Rb})) = v_4(p_2(t_{Rb})))),$$

$f_1(t_{Rb})$ is a method of square calculation.

As we can see, SCIC of objects T_{SRRb} simultaneously describes three types of convex quadrangles t_S, t_R and t_{Rb}. Therefore, concept of SCIC of objects allows describing of classes, which define two and more types of objects. Such approach gives us an opportunity of efficient knowledge representation due construction of core of inhomogeneous class of objects.

Indeed, from the described example, we can see that for representation of types, which define squares, rectangles and rhombuses, it is necessary to describe 7 properties and 2 methods for each type, i.e. 21 properties and 6 methods. Usage of the SCIC provides representation of these types via representation of only 3 properties and 1 method for the class core, and 4 properties and 1 method for each of projections of the class, i.e. 15 properties and 4 methods. In such a way, proposed approach allows avoiding duplication of properties and methods in representation of types, decreasing sizes of program codes and providing more efficient information storage in the databases.

5   Multi-core Inhomogeneous Classes of Objects

According to Definition 2, core of the class contains only properties and methods, which are common for all types of the class and projections of the class contain properties and methods, which are typical only for the particular types. However, sometimes a few projections can contain equivalent properties and (or) methods, which are typical not for all types of the class, therefore they are not parts of the class core. In these cases duplication of such properties and (or) methods will occur. In order to prevent it and to make the class structure more optimal, let us define the concept of *core of level m*.

Definition 4. *Core of level m of inhomogeneous class $T_{t_1,\ldots,t_n}$ is a tuple*

$$Core^m\left(T_{t_1,\ldots,t_n}\right) = \left(P\left(T_{t_{i_1},\ldots,t_{i_m}}\right), F\left(T_{t_{i_1},\ldots,t_{i_m}}\right)\right),$$

where $t_{i_1},\ldots,t_{i_m}$ are arbitrary m types from the set of types $\{t_1,\ldots,t_n\}$, where $1 \le m \le n$, $1 \le i_1 \le \cdots \le i_m \le n$, and $P\left(T_{t_{i_1},\ldots,t_{i_m}}\right)$, $F\left(T_{t_{i_1},\ldots,t_{i_m}}\right)$ are specification and signature of the core of inhomogeneous class $T_{t_{i_1},\ldots,t_{i_m}}$, which contain properties and methods, which are common for all objects of types $t_{i_1},\ldots,t_{i_m}$.

Since, not all types of the class can have common properties and (or) methods, the inhomogeneous class of objects, which defines n types, can contain k cores of level m, where $0 \le k \le C_n^m$. That is why, let us generalize the Definition 2, taking into account Definitions 3 and 4.

Definition 5. *Multi-core inhomogeneous class of objects $T_{t_1,\ldots,t_n}$ is a tuple*

$$T_{t_1,\ldots,t_n} = \Big(Core_1^n(T_{t_1,\ldots,t_n}), Core_1^{n-1}(T_{t_1,\ldots,t_n}),\ldots,Core_{k_{n-1}}^{n-1}(T_{t_1,\ldots,t_n}),\ldots,$$
$$Core_1^1(T_{t_1,\ldots,t_n}),\ldots,Core_{k_1}^1(T_{t_1,\ldots,t_n}), pr_1(t_1),\ldots,pr_n(t_n)\Big),$$

where $Core_1^n(T_{t_1,\ldots,t_n})$ is a core of level n of the class $T_{t_1,\ldots,t_n}$, $Core_{i_{n-1}}^{n-1}(T_{t_1,\ldots,t_n})$ is an i_{n-1}-th core of level $n-1$ of the class $T_{t_1,\ldots,t_n}$, where $i_{n-1} = \overline{1,k_{n-1}}$ and $k_{n-1} \le C_n^{n-1}$, $Core_{i_1}^1(T_{t_1,\ldots,t_n})$ is an i_1-th core of level 1 of the class $T_{t_1,\ldots,t_n}$, where $i_1 = \overline{1,k_1}$ and $k_1 \le C_n^1$, $pr_i(t_i)$ is an i-th projection of the class $T_{t_1,\ldots,t_n}$, which contains properties and methods, which are typical only for the type t_i, where $i = \overline{1,n}$.

Let us consider an example of MCIC of objects.

Example 2. Let us consider all types of convex quadrangles from the previous example and define MCIC of objects T_{SRRb}, which defines all these types in the following way

$$T_{SRRb} = (p_1(T_{SRRb}) = (4, \text{sides}),$$
$$p_2(T_{SRRb}) = (4, \text{angles}),$$
$$p_3(T_{SRRb}) = vf_3(T_{SRRb}) = (1),$$
$$f_1(T_{SRRb}) = (v_1(p_2(t_i)) + v_2(p_2(t_i)) + v_3(p_2(t_i)) + v_4(p_2(t_i)), \text{cm}),$$
$$i \in \{S, R, Rb\}$$
$$p_1(T_{SR}) = ((90°),(90°),(90°),(90°)),$$
$$p_2(T_{SR}) = vf_2(t_i) = (1), \; i \in \{S, R\}$$
$$p_1(T_{SRb}) = vf_1(t_i) = (1), \; i \in \{S, Rb\}$$
$$f_1(T_S) = ((v_1(p_1(t_S)))^2, cm^2),$$
$$p_1(T_R) = vf_1(t_R) = (1),$$
$$f_1(T_R) = (v_1(p_1(t_R)) \cdot v_2(p_1(t_R)), \text{cm}^2),$$
$$p_1(T_{Rb}) = vf_1(t_{Rb}) = (1),$$
$$f_1(T_{Rb}) = ((v_1(p_1(t_{Rb})))^2 \cdot \sin(v_1(p_4(t_{Rb}))), \text{cm}^2),$$

$$p_1(t_S) = ((2, \text{cm}), (2, \text{cm}), (2, \text{cm}), (2, \text{cm})),$$
$$p_1(t_R) = ((2, \text{cm}), (3, \text{cm}), (2, \text{cm}), (3, \text{cm})),$$
$$p_1(t_{Rb}) = ((3, \text{cm}), (3, \text{cm}), (3, \text{cm}), (3, \text{cm})),$$
$$p_2(t_{Rb}) = ((80°), (100°), (80°), (100°))),$$

where $p_1(T_{SRRb})$ is a quantity of sides, $p_2(T_{SRRb})$ is a quantity of internal angles, $vf_3(T_{SRRb})$ is a verification function, which defines a property "sum of all internal angles is equal to 360°", i.e. $vf_3(T_{SRRb}) : p_3(T_{SRRb}) \to \{0, 1\}$, where

$$p_3(T_{SRRb}) = (v_1(p_4(t_i)) + v_2(p_4(t_i)) + v_3(p_4(t_i)) + v_4(p_4(t_i)) = 360),$$

where $i \in \{S, R, Rb\}$, $f_1(T_{SRRb})$ is a method of perimeter calculation, $p_1(T_{SR})$ is degree measures of internal angles, $vf_2(T_{SR})$ is a verification function, which defines a property "all internal angles are equal to 90°", i.e. $vf_2(T_{SR})$: $p_2(T_{SR}) \to \{0, 1\}$, where

$$p_2(T_{SR}) = (v_1(p_1(T_{SR})) = v_2(p_1(T_{SR})) = v_3(p_1(T_{SR})) = v_4(p_1(T_{SR})) = 90),$$

where $i \in \{S, R\}$, $vf_1(T_{SRb})$ is a verification function, which defines a property "all sides of figure have the same length", i.e. $vf_1(T_{SRb}) : p_1(T_{SRb}) \to \{0, 1\}$, where

$$p_1(T_{SRb}) = (v_1(p_1(t_i)) = v_2(p_1(t_i)) = v_3(p_1(t_i)) = v_4(p_1(t_i))), \; i \in \{S, Rb\},$$

$f_1(T_S)$ is a method of square calculation, $vf_1(t_R)$ is a verification function, which defines a property "opposite sides of the figure have the same length", i.e. $vf_1(t_R) : p_1(T_R) \to \{0, 1\}$, where

$$p_1(t_R) = ((v_1(p_1(t_R)) = v_3(p_1(t_R))) \wedge (v_2(p_1(t_R)) = v_4(p_1(t_R)))),$$

$f_1(T_R)$ is a method of square calculation, $vf_1(t_{Rb})$ is a verification function, which defines a property of equality of opposite internal angles of the figure, i.e. $vf_1(t_{Rb}) : p_1(T_{Rb}) \to \{0, 1\}$, where

$$p_1(t_{Rb}) = ((v_1(p_2(t_{Rb})) = v_3(p_2(t_{Rb}))) \wedge (v_2(p_2(t_{Rb})) = v_4(p_2(t_{Rb})))),$$

$f_1(T_{Rb})$ is a method of square calculation, $p_1(t_S)$, $p_1(t_R)$, $p_1(t_{Rb})$ are sizes of sides, $p_2(t_{Rb})$ are degree measures of internal angles.

Analyzing the structure of the class T_{SRRb}, we can see that it is really multi-core, because it has 1 core of level 3, 2 cores of level 2 and 3 cores of level 1. The structures of all cores of the class T_{SRRb} are shown in the Table 1.

As we can see, MCIC of objects T_{SRRb} simultaneously describes three types of convex quadrangles t_S, t_R and t_{Rb} too. Therefore, concept of MCIC of objects also allows describing of classes, which define two and more types of objects. Such approach gives us an opportunity of efficient knowledge representation due construction of cores of level m of inhomogeneous class of objects.

From the previous example, it is known that for representation of types, which define squares, rectangles and rhombuses, it is necessary to describe 7 properties

Table 1. Structures of cores of the class T_{SRRb}

Core	Properties/Methods	Common for types
$Core_1^3(T_{SRRb})$	$p_1(T_{SRRb})$, $p_2(T_{SRRb})$, $p_3(T_{SRRb})$, $f_1(T_{SRRb})$	t_S, t_R, t_{Rb}
$Core_1^2(T_{SRRb})$	$p_1(T_{SR})$, $p_2(T_{SR})$	t_S, t_R
$Core_2^2(T_{SRRb})$	$p_1(T_{SRb})$	t_S, t_{Rb}
$Core_1^1(T_{SRRb})$	$f_1(T_S)$	t_S
$Core_2^1(T_{SRRb})$	$p_1(T_R)$, $f_1(T_R)$	t_R
$Core_3^1(T_{SRRb})$	$p_1(T_{Rb})$, $f_1(T_{Rb})$	t_{Rb}

and 2 methods for each type, i.e. 21 properties and 6 methods. Usage of the MCIC provides representation of these types via representation of only 3 properties and 1 method for the $Core_1^3(T_{SRRb})$, 2 properties for the $Core_1^2(T_{SRRb})$, 1 property for the $Core_2^2(T_{SRRb})$, 1 method for the $Core_1^1(T_{SRRb})$, 1 property and 1 method for the $Core_2^1(T_{SRRb})$, 1 property and 1 method for the $Core_3^1(T_{SRRb})$, 1 property for the $pr_1(t_S)$, 1 property for the $pr_1(t_R)$ and 2 properties for the $pr_1(t_{Rb})$, i.e. 12 properties and 4 methods. In such a way, usage of MCIC similarly to SCIC allows avoiding duplication of properties and methods in representation of types, decreasing sizes of program codes and provides more efficient information storage in the databases.

6   Object-Oriented Data Storage

Nowadays almost all object-oriented information systems use the databases for data storage, therefore efficient representation of classes and objects within the databases (in particular within relational databases) and their further extraction are topical issues. Modern stack of object-oriented technologies contains such tool as object-relational mapping (ORM), which allows mapping of classes and their objects into tables and their records within relation databases [2, 11, 17]. Despite all advantages of ORM, it has some limitations, in particular it still does not provide an ability to map methods of classes into the database that makes impossible precise and complete exchange of classes among different object-oriented software. Moreover, as it was emphasized in [7], inheritance is not a feature that relational databases naturally have, and therefore the mapping is not as obvious.

It is known that during the ORM structures of classes define the structures of future tables in the database. Therefore efficiency of data storage in the database strictly depends on structures of classes. That is why we performed an experiment for checking, how the usage of SCICs and MCICs influences representation of objects and their types in relational databases in contrast to usage of HCs.

As a part of the experiment, we have created three relational databases using HCs, SCICs and MCICs. We used types t_S, t_R and t_{Rb} form the Examples 1 and 2 as a test data.

The database based on HCs has 3 tables, where each of them has 31 columns for every type of objects, i.e. t_S, t_R and t_{Rb}. The database based on SCICs has

4 tables: 1 table with the 9 columns for the $Core(T_{SRRb})$ and 3 tables with the 23 columns for $pr_1(S)$, $pr_2(R)$, $pr_3(Rb)$. The database based on MCICs has 9 tables: 1 table with 9 columns for the $Core_1^3(T_{SRRb})$, 1 table with 11 columns for the $Core_1^2(T_{SRRb})$, 1 table with 3 columns for the $Core_2^2(T_{SRRb})$, 1 table with 3 columns for the $Core_2^1(T_{SRRb})$, 1 table with 5 columns for the $Core_2^1(T_{SRRb})$, 1 table with 5 columns for the $Core_3^1(T_{SRRb})$ and three tables which have 9, 11 and 19 columns respectively, for $pr_1(S)$, $pr_2(R)$ and $pr_3(Rb)$.

The experiment was performed in the environment of operating system Linux Debian Stretch. MariaDB 10.1.23 was chosen as a DB server. The aim of the experiment was to compare sizes of DBs, which are deployed on the server, and sizes of their exported *.sql files. Corresponding measurements were performed for 21 cases. First measurement was done when DBs contained 0 objects, after this we added 4000 objects of each types (i.e. 12000 objects during one insertion session) to every DB and repeated the measurements. Then the procedure was repeated 19 times. At the end of the experiment each DB contained 80000 objects

Table 2. Sizes of DBs based on HCs, SCICs, MCICs and their exported *.sql files

Quantity of objects	Sizes of DB (Mb)			Sizes of DB *.sql file (Mb)		
	HC	SCIC	MCIC	HC	SCIC	MCIC
0	0.046875	0.0625	0.125000	0.006396	0.006080	0.007398
12000	4.546875	4.5625	1.031250	4.730189	2.954480	0.872142
24000	10.546875	7.5625	2.593750	9.456926	5.905566	1.738131
36000	13.546875	8.5625	4.640625	13.747144	8.861661	2.610227
48000	17.546875	11.5625	4.640625	18.928142	11.825956	3.488397
60000	21.546875	14.5625	5.640625	23.666618	14.789045	4.366487
72000	26.546875	17.5625	5.640625	28.405355	17.751929	5.244479
84000	30.546875	20.5625	8.640625	33.143831	20.715019	6.122471
96000	33.546875	21.5625	8.640625	37.882568	23.678108	7.000561
108000	40.546875	23.5625	8.640625	42.621044	26.641197	7.878553
120000	45.546875	26.5625	8.640625	47.359781	29.604286	8.756643
132000	45.546875	29.5625	9.640625	52.098518	32.567581	9.634635
144000	47.546875	29.5625	9.640625	56.837220	35.530940	10.512725
156000	47.546875	29.5625	9.640625	61.575731	38.493554	11.390717
168000	47.546875	29.5625	9.640625	66.314207	41.456849	12.268807
180000	47.546875	29.5625	13.640625	71.053206	44.419733	13.146799
192000	68.640625	43.5625	15.640625	75.791682	47.382822	14.024791
204000	75.640625	47.5625	15.640625	80.530419	50.346117	14.902881
216000	75.640625	47.5625	16.640625	85.268895	53.309206	15.780873
228000	84.656250	52.5625	16.640625	90.007632	56.272295	16.659141
240000	84.656250	52.5625	16.640625	94.746369	59.235385	17.537246

of each types (i.e. 240000 objects in each DB). For simplification of automated database generation, all objects of the same type were initialized in the same way. Results of all measurements are shown in the Table 2.

Using obtained results, we built following dependencies between sizes of DBs and quantities of objects, which they contain

$$S(DB_{HC}) = 0.0003 * Q + 0.793, \tag{1}$$
$$S(DB_{SCIC}) = 0.0002 * Q + 1.253, \tag{2}$$
$$S(DB_{MCIC}) = 0.00007 * Q + 1.0651, \tag{3}$$

where $S(DB_i)$ is a size of DB of i-th type, where $i \in \{HC, SCIC, MCIC\}$, and Q is a quantity of objects within the DB. Corresponding graphs and their linear approximations are shown on Fig. 1.

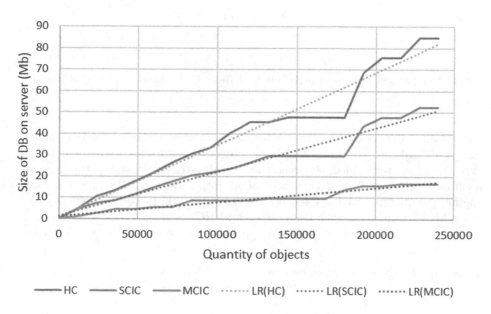

Fig. 1. Comparison of sizes of DBs based on HCs, SCICs and MCICs of objects

In addition, we built following dependencies between sizes of exported *.sql files of DBs and quantities of objects within DBs:

$$S(FDB_{HC}) = 0.0004 * Q - 0.0781, \tag{4}$$
$$S(FDB_{SCIC}) = 0.0002 * Q - 0.0.171, \tag{5}$$
$$S(FDB_{MCIC}) = 0.00007 * Q - 0.0145, \tag{6}$$

where $S(FDB_i)$ is a size of exported *.sql DB file of i-th type, where $i \in \{HC, SCIC, MCIC\}$, and Q is a quantity of objects within the DB. Corresponding graphs and their linear approximations are shown on Fig. 2.

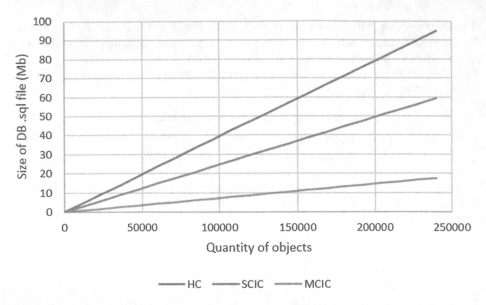

Fig. 2. Comparison of sizes of exported *.sql files of DBs based on HCs, SCICs and MCICs of objects

Obtained dependencies allow us to predict approximate size of DB and its exported *.sql file, based on quantity of objects within the environment where experiment was performed. However, these results strictly depend on the environment of experiment, in particular type of operating system, DB server, database engine, parameters of DB tables, etc. Nevertheless, they show the efficiency of using MCIC comparing with using SCIC and HC.

For convenient usage of proposed approach, we can formulate the following theorem.

Theorem 1. *Efficiency of storage $m_1, \ldots, m_n$ objects of types $t_1, \ldots, t_n$ in relation database, using concept of MCIC in contrast to usage of HC can be calculated in the following way*

$$E = 100 - \frac{M_{MCIC}}{M_{HC}} \cdot 100,$$

where

$$M_{MCIC} = \left(\sum_{i_n=1}^{1} C_1^n + \sum_{i_{n-1}=1}^{k_{n-1}} C_{i_{n-1}}^{n-1} + \cdots + \sum_{i_1=1}^{k_1} C_{i_1}^1 + \sum_{i=1}^{n} Pr_i \cdot m_i \right),$$

and $C_{i_n}^n, \ldots, C_{i_1}^1$ – are memory sizes, which allow storing of $i_n, \ldots, i_1$ cores of level $n, \ldots, 1$ of class $T_{t_1,\ldots,t_n}$ respectively, Pr_i – is memory size, which allows storing of i-th projection of the class, and $M_{HC} = T_1 \cdot m_1 + \cdots + T_n \cdot m_n$, where T_i – is memory size, which allows storing of i-th type of the class.

Analyzing the theorem, let us formulate a few important remarks.

Remark 1. Precise calculation of efficiency of data storage in relation database, using concept of MCIC, before creation of the database itself and its information filling, is impossible, because the storing of equivalent properties for objects of the same type can require different memory sizes.

Remark 2. Theorem 1 allows calculating approximate efficiency coefficient of data storage in relation database, using concept of MCIC, before (without) the database creation. It can be done, if maximum possible memory sizes, which allow storing properties and methods of each type, are used for calculation.

Remark 3. Theorem 1 can be easily reformulated for calculation of efficiency coefficient of using MCIC comparing with using SCIC by applying memory sizes, which allow storing SCICs instead $T_1, \ldots, T_n$.

Summarizing results of performed experiment, it is possible to conclude that in the case of using MCICs:

1. storage of n objects, where $n \in \{0, 12000, 24000, \ldots, 240000\}$, in the DB is more efficient in average by 64.93% in contrast to using of SCICs and 77.89% in contrast to using of HCs;
2. size of exported *.sql file of such DB decreased in average by 70.41% in contrast to using of SCICs and 81.5% in contrast to using of HCs;
3. SQL queries to tables of such DB are performed faster in the contrast to cases of using SCICs and HCs.

Analyzing Definitions 2 and 5, it is possible to conclude, that usage of MCIC or SCIC is efficient, when types of objects has common properties and (or) methods. In such cases structure of the MCICs will be similar to classes hierarchies built using rational single inheritance, which allow avoiding of the redundancy problem. However, MCICs can be used even in situations when types of objects do not have common properties and (or) methods, in these cases classes will have only projections, which are equivalent to HCs.

7   Conclusions and Outlook

In this paper we analized concept of a class within such object-oriented KRMs as frames, OOP and OODN. The main attention was paid to structure of the class and its efficiency in the context of data storage, using object-relational mapping.

The main achievement of the paper is introduction of concepts of single-core and multi-core inhomogeneous classes of objects, which extend notion of homogeneous class of objects. The main idea of SCIC is defining single core of level n, while the main idea of MCIC is defining set of cores of level m. Proposed concepts allow simultaneous defining of a few different types within one class of objects, avoiding duplication of properties and methods in representation of types (especially if they have common properties and (or) methods), decreasing sizes of program codes and providing more efficient information storage in the databases.

The efficiency of proposed concept was proven by the experiment, which showed that data storage in relational database using concept of MCIC is more efficient in contrast to usage of SCIC and HC. Using obtained results of measurements (see Table 2), dependencies between sizes of DBs and quantities of objects, which they contain (see Fig. 1) and dependencies between sizes of exported *.sql files of DBs and quantities of objects within DBs (see Fig. 2), were built. In addition, the method for calculation of approximate efficiency coefficient of data storage in relational database, using concept of MCIC, was proposed in Theorem 1.

However, despite all noted advantages of proposed extension of class notion, it requires further research, at least in the following directions:

- comparison structure of MCICs with HCs hierarchies obtained using single and multiple inheritance;
- adoption of inheritance mechanisms for MCICs;
- building of inhomogeneous poly-hierarchies of MCICs;
- generalization of concept of MCICs to fuzzy case;
- adoption of inheritance mechanisms for fuzzy MCICs;
- building of inhomogeneous poly-hierarchies of fuzzy MCICs;
- studying of object-relation mapping of MCICs into:
  - object-oriented databases;
  - fuzzy object-oriented databases;
  - graph databases;
- adoption and usage of MCICs in object-oriented programming paradigm.

References

1. Al-Asady, R.: Inheritance Theory: An Artificial Intelligence Approach. Ablex Publishing Corporation, Norwood (1995)
2. Ambler, S.W.: Agile Database Techniques: Effective Strategies for the Agile Software Developer. Wiley, New York (2003)
3. Booch, G., Maksimchuk, R.A., Engle, M.W., et al.: Object-Oriented Analysis and Design with Applications, 3rd edn. Addison-Wesley Professional, Boston (2007)
4. Brachman, R.J., Levesque, H.J.: Knowledge Representation and Reasoning. Morgan Kaufmann Publishers, San Francisco (2004)
5. Craig, I.D.: Object-Oriented Programming Languages: Interpretation. UTCS. Springer, London (2007)
6. Dathan, B., Ramnath, S.: Object-Oriented Analysis, Design and Implementation: An Integrated Approach. UTCS, 2nd edn. Springer, London (2015)
7. Goncalves, A.: Beginning Java EE 7. Apress, Berkely (2013)
8. Meyer, B.: Object-Oriented Software Construction, 2nd edn. Prentice Hall, Upper Saddle River (1997)
9. Minsky, M.: A Framework for Representing Knowledge. Technical report No. 306, AI Laboratory, Massachusetts Institute of Technology (1974)
10. Negnevitsky, M.: Artificial Intelligence: A Guide to Intelligent Systems, 2nd edn. Addison-Wesley, Herlow (2004)
11. Philippi, S.: Model driven generation and testing of object-relational mappings. J. Syst. Softw. **77**, 193–207 (2005). doi:10.1016/j.jss.2004.07.252

12. Terletskyi, D.: Inheritance in object-oriented knowledge representation. In: Dregvaite, G., Damasevicius, R. (eds.) ICIST 2015. CCIS, vol. 538, pp. 293–305. Springer, Cham (2015). doi:10.1007/978-3-319-24770-0_26

13. Terletskyi, D.O., Provotar, O.I.: Object-oriented dynamic networks. In: Setlak, G., Markov, K. (eds.) Computational Models for Business and Engineering Domains, vol. 30, pp. 123–136. ITHEA IBS ISC (2014)

14. Terletskyi, D.A., Provotar, A.I.: Fuzzy object-oriented dynamic networks. I. Int. Sci. J. Cybern. Syst. Anal. **51**, 34–40 (2015). doi:10.1007/s10559-015-9694-0

15. Terletskyi, D.A., Provotar, A.I.: Fuzzy object-oriented dynamic networks. II. Int. Sci. J. Cybern. Syst. Anal. **52**, 38–45 (2016). doi:10.1007/s10559-016-9797-2

16. Terletskyi, D.A., Provotar, O.I.: Mathematical foundations for designing and development of intelligent systems of information analysis. Sci. J. Probl. in Program. **15**, 233–241 (2014)

17. Torres, A., Galante, R., Pimenta, M.S., Martins, A.J.B.: Twenty years of object-relational mapping: a survey on patterns, solutions, and their implications on application design. Inf. Softw. Technol. **82**, 1–18 (2017). doi:10.1016/j.infsof.2016.09.009

18. Touretzky, D.S.: The Mathematics of Inheritance Systems. Morgan Kaufmann Publishers, Los Altos (1986)

19. Weisfeld, M.: The Object-Oriented Thought Process, 3rd edn. Addison-Wesley Professional, London (2009)

Information Systems: Special Session on e-Health Information Systems

Beyond Health Apps, Utilize Patient-Generated Data

Asif Akram[1,2(✉)], Gerard Dunleavy[1], Michael Soljak[1], and Josip Car[1,2]

[1] Centre for Population Health Sciences (CePHaS), LKC Medicine,
Nanyang Technological University, Singapore, Singapore
{asifakram,gerard.dunleavy,michael.soljak,josip.car}@ntu.edu.sg
[2] Global eHealth Unit, Department of Primary Care and Public Health, School of Public Health,
Imperial College, London, UK

Abstract. This paper presents the rational for a novel bespoke data-centric digital health platform i.e. Platform for Health Apps, Surveys and Education (PhASE). The conceptual design and prototype development of PhASE is discussed in detail. The aim of the research-centered and patient-centric digital health platform is to enable rapid research-study design; real-time data collection hub; and enable mobile education and training. The mobile collection and curation of health data is on the rise, but without any suitable data collection hub; aggregation and analysis of these isolated data streams is expensive. Digital health is focused on health applications (healthApps) and in last few years there is a growth of disconnected diverse healthApps; which are lacking a sustainable eco-system; compliance to the medical protocols; reliability and any long-term vision. There is also a serious concern as to the clinical effectiveness of the abundantly available healthApps, which exist without any regulatory control.

Keywords: Health application · Mobile data collection · Platform · Digital health · mHealth · eHealth

1 Introduction

The recent advancement in information technology has greatly improved the existing healthcare industry. The latest developments hold a tremendous potential to further enhance disease prevention and management; empowering healthcare workers; and extending core health interventions beyond the reach of traditional care [4]. The combination of smartphones and mobile communication in conjunction with Internet for digital health solutions is generally referred as mobile health (mHealth) [20]. mHealth hasn't yet made a significant impact in our daily life, emerging as a patchwork of incompatible health applications (healthApp). Normally, healthApps are designed with static focus, serving narrow demands, targeting limited audiences and lacking a sustainable eco-system. The impact of healthApps within the health system can be improved by more coordinated development.

The spike in smartphone-use and the rapid proliferation of self-monitoring (or self-tracking) healthApps; well-being assistants; and digital health projects has generated considerable enthusiasm. There are an estimated 165,000 health-and-fitness apps between the Apple store and Android's Google Play store [3]. The existing healthApps

R. Damaševičius and V. Mikašytė (Eds.): ICIST 2017, CCIS 756, pp. 65–76, 2017.
DOI: 10.1007/978-3-319-67642-5_6

cover a broad spectrum of uses from apps with basic functions (step counter, miles cycled, calories consumed, sleep pattern) to apps with sophisticated features for specific specialties (measuring blood pressure, blood sugar, heart rate). Unfortunately, these healthApps have had limited success in revolutionizing patient care, medical research, and digital health. The effectiveness of healthApps (irrespective of their uniqueness) can only be improved when embedded in a larger system that links silos of data, information, knowledge and the digital world with physical entities. These physical entities include healthcare workers, researchers, hospitals, laboratories, pharmacies and above all the patient themselves. The personal data generated by self-monitoring healthApps can be extremely helpful to healthcare providers, agencies and related organizations. The potential richness of isolated data that could be gathered from patient databases/registries, geo-location, movement patterns, chronic conditions, fitness level and lifestyle is mind blowing but underused. The information gained from this potentially mammoth data pool along with the engagement of healthcare professionals, organizations and patients could drive innovation, policy development and recommendations for clinical practices. Current healthcare challenges need the integrated information to support best evidence-based care and policies. The integration will ultimately empower respective organizations to seek change; how population health is managed, how to initiate early detection, diagnosis and implement the most effective treatment.

The large amount of patient-generated data has a huge potential value to improve the level of healthcare provided to patients. Unfortunately, the rich patient-generated data via self-monitoring healthApps is largely not accessible to healthcare providers nor is it available in any useful format. The key to effective use of big data is in the processing of the data to extract useful information. The extracted information should be presented in an easy-to-understand and informative format. The same extracted information should be presented in multiple formats tailored to different audiences i.e. patients, healthcare workers, and policy makers. To illustrate the concept, a heartbeat monitoring sensor capturing every heartbeat for a week will generate a great deal of data, which may not be easy for any healthcare provider to consume. This data then needs to be formulated in to an easy to utilize format such as a single table or graph that summarizes hourly average heartbeat for that week.

There have been various attempts to develop frameworks, platforms and even infrastructure for the rapid development of healthApps, all of which are quite technology focused. The main aim of such initiatives is to lower the technical barriers for the development and roll out effort for healthApps. Generally, healthcare systems help developers to concentrate on the chosen domain for the healthApp rather than boilerplate essentials for the healthApp development. The existing healthcare systems are not designed to focus on the patient's care, primary care services or more broadly population health. Redesign and integration of existing health care systems with other aspects of patient care has become a complex task. There are low expectations from existing systems due to diverse stakeholders with self-focused agendas, unique organizational processes, varying delivery channels and diverse approaches to control the information flow and access.

Already, healthcare professionals and consumers have expressed concerns about the quality of many healthApps. There is an ever-increasing call to establish a formal healthApps regulatory agency or some form of certification to be put in place for vetted medical healthApps. Numerous surveys have highlighted risks, negative issues and worrying deficiencies in existing healthApps. The National Health Service in England ran Health Apps Library [1] for vetted, tested and approved healthApps. The Health Apps Library had issues and was closed down in October 2015. The upgraded and updated version of the Health Apps Library was recently launched again in April 2017. The Health Apps Library will be discussed later in the paper. Similarly, the University of British Columbia eHealth Strategy Office developed the Health-e-Apps [2] resource to encourage health professionals to share useful healthApps.

There is a requirement for patient-centered digital health platforms to ease healthApp development; enable rapid research-study design; real-time data collection hub; and enable mobile education and training. The "Platform for HealthApps, Surveys and Education (PhASE)" is under development in the Centre of Population Health Sciences, LKC School of Medicine to address the concerns and issues outlined above. The PhASE will not only assist in the development of quality healthApps and in conducting secure health surveys but also in aggregating data from multiple healthApps, linking patient-data generated by different healthApps, analyzing patient-data and integrating it in to an easy to utilize format. Finally, the effectiveness of healthApps is coupled with the alignment of general and health literacy levels of consumers [12]. Health literacy is defined as "the degree to which individuals can obtain, process, and understand basic health information and services needed to make appropriate health decisions" [11]. healthApps should also have an educational component to improve the knowledge of patients. Though, a substantial amount of health-related information is available on the Internet, it varies in its accessibility, quality, reading grade level and accuracy [9]. In addition to patient education, PhASE will also include a training component to equip healthcare workers for improved patient-centric services.

The PhASE aims to be a medium for interaction between various parties i.e. developers, patients, healthcare providers, governmental agencies and general users. The PhASE will support the secure communication between different entities, the communication logging facility and the availability of logs to involved parties for quality assurance and control.

2   Platform for Health Apps, Surveys and Education

A "platform" is a system that can be programmed and therefore customized by outside developers i.e. users, managers and administrators. The customization and flexibility of the platform can be adapted to countless needs and niches that may not have been possibly contemplated during the design and development stage [10]. The "Platform for Health-Apps, Surveys and Education (PhASE)" is a patient data driven healthcare interoperable and extendable solution, which allows third parties to integrate their application and tools with it. The proposed PhASE covers all aspects of modern and digital healthcare:

- Application (desktop and mobile) development, capable of generating data
- Data collected from mobile or traditional applications, sensors, wearables and surveys

- Integration of data collected from various streams
- Expert System for decision making on the collected data
- Information extraction in the form of data analysis and data mining
- Reports for easy-to-utilize data by various stakeholders
- Knowledge transfer to improve the health literacy level of users

The reality of life is technology changes within a short time span. All the time new tools and trends are emerging; technical support teams in organizations will never be able to stay completely up-to-date on all of the latest technology that could impact patient care. A platform like PhASE gives health providers the access to a new technology, when required and delivers the content to new media. The ideal solution, will give flexibility to the healthcare industry to adopt new trends at their desired pace and integrate their existing solutions with new technologies.

The PhASE will be built upon four key features. The support for the secure and reliable communication between different physical entities i.e. patient-doctor, nurse-doctor, field health worker-domain expert, researcher-participant etc. The communication from the comfort of users selected medium (mobile or desktop) and at any time of the day will improve the efficiency of the system, minimizing unnecessary delays. The second feature is the extendibility and flexibility. The extendibility allows the integration of heterogeneous devices with minimum efforts; rolling out new features and services to the platform users. The ability to create new services as a mashup is a meta-component or service that utilizes content, information or data from more than one source or existing services and tools [14]. The third important aspect of the platform is to aggregate data collected from different streams in the form of forms/surveys, patient records, health-Apps, wearable censors etc. Finally, utilizing the aggregated data in an easy-to-use format for the various stakeholders for better patient care.

PhASE provides the RESTful [21] based connectivity to integrate third parties' tools in the form of web services Application Programming Interface (API). The PhASE architecture is designed on the well-known principle of "Micro Services" [22] to implement standalone features. The architecture of the PhASE has been designed with extreme care, where each feature and component can be consumed independently. This isolation of individual components enables users to integrate different components to create innovative healthcare mashups.

The PhASE will allow researchers to design and create simple surveys and complex data collection multi-step forms with ease. The complex data collection forms are smart forms. The smart form is a dynamic and flexible form, which shows or hides fields on the fly based on the user input; update field values based on a selected item and perform calculations. The PhASE will also add educational component to surveys by adding the feedback or link to external resources based upon a single or set of options selected. Ultimately, the PhASE is a hub that receives information from all streams and organizes it in one place for the stakeholders to view, analyze, filter and consume.

3   Platform Architecture

The short-sighted vision for any new healthcare platform is to create yet-another app store or app development tool for the healthcare with limited scope. The long term objective of PhASE is to accelerate application development through open standards; interface based third party integration; flexible data model; data analysis algorithms, data mining routines and educational resources for interoperable healthcare applications.

The architecture of PhASE attempts to consolidate fully decentralized information streams to a centralized model. The current decentralized model of the healthcare industry is due to the general practice that each data-generation tool controls its data and stores independently. A sharing of the data, if possible, is upon request only. The data request to every data source brings another level of complication resulting in unwanted delays and incomplete information for analysis. The fully centralized model collects and stores data in a central repository from various streams where stakeholders agree and consented to share data. The centralized data can be accessed and used by participants in accordance with well-defined policies and procedures. A centralized model may offer best technical performance regarding data availability and response time [13]. Unfortunately, due to lack of trust and cutting throat competition among stakeholders, a fully centralized model is not possible and bringing all stakeholders to the same level is a daunting task. A feasible approach is to design some sort of hybrid method. The hybrid sharing model doesn't store all data in a centralized repository but retrieves data when required on behalf of the requester. The data normally stays with the owner of the data, who agreed to share the data with other stakeholders in accordance with agreed policies. The hybrid approach solves a few major issues of the decentralized model, the bottle-necking i.e. information stored in a single repository; stakeholders agreeing separate sharing agreement and policies; and a high number of data requests from interested entities to the data owner.

The main communication architecture of the PhASE is aligned with the hybrid model. The PhASE is a one-stop shop for all data queries and for data collection in accordance with patient consent and agreed terms and conditions for data sharing. The healthApp can retrieve information from trusted resources or 3rd party service providers to produce quality patient-centric data. The possible example is any external server hosting the domain specific survey and the PhASE hosting the domain specific rules to compliment the survey resulting in the flexible expert system.

The information is collected in a self-organized and automated manner over wireless networks (IEEE 802.11, IEEE 802.15.4/ZigBee, and Bluetooth) and is periodically uploaded to the PhASE. The PhASE is a client-server architecture utilizing current cloud computing paradigms. The cloud-based healthcare platform with Software-as-a-Service (SaaS) enables PhASE in delivering healthcare information services with high clinical value, low cost, and high usability. The technical management of the PhASE relies on best practices of cloud services, which itself adopt the design principles of OpenStack cloud architecture [5] and the Open Cloud Computing Interface (OCCI) [5].

The heterogeneous (varying data structure and format) nature of the data generated by various healthApps and wearables can't be stored in traditional databases. The conventional databases are optimized for the storage and querying of structured data.

The unstructured data collected by the PhASE requires innovative data solution. The PhASE, internally deploys NoSQL [23] storage model for initial data storage capable of handling arbitrarily flexible data structure. The collected data will be harmonized, converted to JSON format (agnostic of healthApps, sensors, wearables and programming languages) and data from various data streams will be potentially linked. The flexibility of data structure allows third parties to integrate their tools with PhASE without any complicated restructuring or formatting. The current data trend in the health care industry moving from structured data to semi-structured data (self-monitoring, mHealth, wearable devices, and sensors) and even to unstructured data (transcribed notes, images, and videos). The PhASE data-storage architecture is horizontally and vertically scalable. The horizontal scalability is crucial for the storage of big data generated by healthApps and sensors. This big data will continue to grow significantly not only in the storage size but in the frequency too.

4   Components of the Platform

The "Platform for HealthApps, Surveys and Education (PhASE)" is a challenging project with various facets. The objective of the PhASE is not to re-design existing health systems but to implement a new patient-centric platform with a different strategy and vision. The PhASE addresses limitations of existing health systems by providing an integration hub in the form of generic but extendable Application Programming Interface (API).

4.1   Health Information Exchange

The lack of data sharing and ineffective utilization of patient data is a hindrance to the healthcare industry. Patient clinical data linked with patient-generated data can reduce the burden of care delivery and over treatment by early detection and effective prevention. A properly designed, developed and deployed Health Information Exchange (HIE) and Health Information Exchange Interoperability (HIEI) will result in enormous savings. According to one study, the properly standardized and implemented HIE could yield a net value of $77.8 billion per year [7]. The clinical impact of HIEI for which quantitative estimates cannot yet be made would likely add further value.

The standardization of HIE will result in effective collaboration and partnership among various stakeholders. The long-term collaboration will result in reliable and accurate information. The concept of HIE is relatively recent and is quickly evolving. The first iteration of HIE involved the basic clinical data exchange e.g. laboratory results, hospitals discharge, referrals etc. The current stage of HIE needs to handle more heterogeneous data from a broader spectrum. The nature of data is extended to analytical capabilities, quality improvement, population health management, research and evaluation [8].

The technical architecture of HIE is designed with advanced features to incorporate various data streams, existing registries and databases, patient-reported outcomes and most importantly data from home tele-monitoring devices. The current trend for HIE is moving from fully decentralized architecture to the fully centralized infrastructure. The support for the HIE is with a RESTful API based component creating a secure network for collaborators for bi-directional health data sharing. The HIE will be gateway to the Data Collection Hub (discussed in next section) creating a comprehensive health data from multiple data streams.

4.2 Data Collection Hub

One of the most important components of the PhASE is the Data Collection Hub that will collate and retrieve information related to all aspects of health care research. The end-result will be organized information in one place for the mobile end user. The information will be collected from various streams i.e. health questionnaires and surveys, consented patient visit data, patient-generated data e.g. wearable devices, self-monitoring healthApps or self-reported data. The hub will be extendable to collate secure communication between physician, nurse or patient; notification sent to patients or participants; and exchanges between mobile health workers and remote experts. The aggregated data confined in huge databases or data warehouses will give access to sortable, useable, searchable and actionable data. The outcome will be quick access to real-time health information, improved health care services, lower costs and effective solutions.

4.3 Survey Designer with Roll-Out Feature

One of the main components of the PhASE is to allow researchers to design and create smart, interactive and complicated data collection forms and surveys. The interactivity of forms means dynamically reacting to user actions. The smart data collection forms show or hide fields, update field values and perform calculations according to the user interactions and choices. Large forms can be arranged as multi-page forms, for logical and smooth navigations. Researchers will be able to design and create complicated data collection forms without dependency on developers. The form created will be deployed to the server and collected data will be automatically persisted to the backend database.

4.4 Data Mining and Analysis

Patient-generated data is growing exponentially, but the potential value of this data is not yet being realized. The limited utilization of the data is due to lack of adequately developed predictive modeling and simulation techniques for analyzing healthcare data. This shortcoming is not due to a lack of innovative hardware, software or technological development, as they are readily available to improve the patient care. The major bottleneck is the aggregating, processing and displaying of the data.

In the later stages of the PhASE design and development, the generic data mining and analysis component will be created from open source projects RapidMiner [24] and WEKA [25]. The generic component will allow researchers and users to create their own data mining and analysis tools. The data mining and analysis tool will be capable of consuming local data or data from third parties to create a mashup for analytical service.

4.5 Clinical Decision Support

The clinical decision support CDS system is an application that analyzes patient data to help healthcare providers make clinical decisions. It is an adoption of the expert system used in various other domains. There is an improvement in patient care by the early detection and intervention with the CDS [18]. The currently available CDS systems are static and tightly integrated with the data collection tools; any update or changes require another iteration of development. PhASE will deploy more dynamic and sustainable approach; the data collection is independent in the form of questionnaires and surveys and can be separately linked with rules for decision making (if required). The long term plan for PhASE is to host multiple CDS for various symptoms which can be designed and modified by clinicians via a web interface. The dynamic approach will allow the reuse of the same CDS for multiple data collection questionnaires. Similarly, the same data collection questionnaires can be linked to various CDSs according to the local practice and jurisdiction.

4.6 Education and Training

The general workforce including healthcare staff is looking for ways to increase efficiency, reduce errors, improve knowledge, and compliance with regulations, while increasing competitive advantages wherever possible. Smartphone/tablet based education and training is an innovative means, for a new technologically savvy group of young people, entering the workforce and many people work from nontraditional workspaces. learning has been assessed in the clinical setting, resulting in learners increasing their knowledge of clinical skills by a means that was interesting while being time- and place flexible [19]. PhASE aims to host educational resources of interest for healthcare providers and patients allowing portable, personal, interactive and exciting learning. PhASE will support healthApps providing visual simulation, review, self-knowledge testing, direct communication and feedback. This will allow healthcare providers to stay connected with their patients; post new information and continue to answer questions regarding the technical and clinical aspect of a medical treatment.

5   Relevant Projects

There are various initiatives in recent years to aggregate the patient information or to support patient centric data to varying levels. Neither all of these projects are success story nor are they regularly maintained. This section discusses a few of the relevant and appropriate projects in no particular order.

5.1 Health Hub Singapore

Health Hub Singapore [15] launched in 2015, is one of the most comprehensive initiatives allowing Singaporeans and permanent residents (PRs) to access their public health records online. The Health Hub Singapore is designed on the hybrid model to draw data from public healthcare databases (the National Electronic Healthcare Records and School Health System). The platform allows users to access their health records, track appointments, life style and directory of healthcare providers.

5.2 Microsoft HealthVault

Microsoft HealthVault [26] is a secure web-based health solution platform enables individuals to store, manage, and share their health and fitness information available since 2007. The Microsoft HealthVault is intended for both patients and healthcare professionals. The main selling point of Microsoft HealthVault is its 3rd party integrations based on industry standards exchange formats. It supports seamless updates of data from major sensors wearable devices i.e. FitBit, Garmin etc.

5.3 Google Health

Google Health [27] was a personal health record service that allowed users to centrally store and manage their health information. The service stored user's personal information, health conditions, medications and lab results with options to share with others. The service was introduced in 2008 and discontinued in 2011. The volunteer and manually logging of the data was not popular among users.

5.4 HealthKit by Apple

HealthKit by Apple [17] is a tool for developers to design health applications. The application is intended to be personal and a central data collection point from electronic accessories and wearables. The HealthKit allows users to discover other compatible healthApps in the Apple Store but the data generated by healthApps is not integrated.

5.5 HealthKit (The Global Health Community)

HealthKit [16] is a global platform for patients and practitioners around the world that is making healthcare efficient and effective. HealthKit allows users to manage their health, share records with doctors and locate a practitioner with one of the most extensive directories.

5.6 myChart

myChart [28] is a platform for patients to access their medical information online e.g. lab results, past and upcoming appointments and referrals. The key feature of myChart is support for messaging health providers and refilling medications. Users of myChart can also access medical records of dependent children.

5.7 CONNECT Community Portal

CONNECT [29] is an open source project promoting interoperability for exchange of information. CONNECT enables secure, health data exchange among various stake-holders and implements the Nationwide Health Information Network (NwHIN) [32] standards and specifications.

5.8 PhiCollect

PhiCollect [30] is a cloud-based open source data collection platform. PhiCollect allows users to collect data from and publish to a variety of platforms. PhiCollect is based on Open Data Kit [31], which itself is not actively maintained. PhiCollect has also appli-cation outside healthcare sectors i.e. emergency response, food security and facilities management.

5.9 Health Apps Library

The National Health Service (NHS) of United Kingdom launched the Health Apps Library [2] in 2013 to promote safe, effective health apps. The NHS was one of the early pioneers among healthcare providers in the curation of health apps for patients. Health Apps Library was closed in 2015 after a number of issues, including security concerns, dummy data, lack of encrypted data on the device and during data transfer, were high-lighted in a study by Imperial College [19]. Health Apps Library was relaunched this year along with – the Digital Apps Library. Health Apps Library lists apps as either "being tested" or "NHS Approved".

5.10 Health-e-Apps

Health-e-Apps [1] was developed with funding from the Ministry of Health, British Columbia to promote the use of health apps by health professionals and the public. Health-e-Apps encourages health professionals to share useful health apps with the public and among themselves, while also encouraging the general public to access health apps recommended by health professionals.

6 Conclusion

The paper outlines the rational for the digital platform to integrate various components of the healthcare sector. The rapid growth of self-monitoring apps, sensors and wearable gadgets generate enormous amount of patient-centric data which can improve popula-tion health and primary care. The patient-centric data needs to be aggregated, linked and made available to various stakeholders in easy-to-utilize format. The richness of collected data can be further exploited with the use of technical development of data analysis and data mining. Finally, the platform should validate healthApps against set policies for compliance with standards and medical evidence. The educational aspect, integrated within healthApps will improve health literacy level of end-users.

Acknowledgments. We acknowledge the funding from the Nanyang Technological University to the Lee Kong Chian School of Medicine/Centre for Population Health Sciences (CePHaS).

References

1. National Health Service. NHS: Health Apps Library. http://bit.ly/15rxYyB. Accessed 20 May 2017
2. Shaw, G.: UBC's Health-e-Apps project helps patient help themselves. http://apps.nhs.uk/. Accessed 20 May 2017
3. IMS Institute for Healthcare Informatics: IMSHelath. Patient Adoption of mHealth (2015). http://www.imshealth.com/files/web/IMSH%20Institute/Reports/Patient%20Adoption%20of%20mHealth/IIHI_Patient_Adoption_of_mHealth.pdf. Accessed 20 May 2017
4. Estrin, D., Sim, I.: Open mHealth architecture: an engine for health care innovation. Science **330**(6005), 759–760 (2010)
5. Open Source Cloud Computing Software. https://www.openstack.org. Accessed 20 May 2017
6. Open Cloud Interface. http://occi-wg.org. Accessed 20 May 2017
7. Walker, J., Pan, E., Johnston, J., Adler-Milstein, J.: The value of health care information exchange and interoperability. Health Aff. **24**, 10–18 (2005)
8. McCarthy, D.B., Propp, K., Cohen, A., Sabharwal, R., Schachter, A.A., Rein, A.L.: Learning from health information exchange technical architecture and implementation in seven beacon communities. EGEMS **2**(1), 1060 (2014). doi:10.13063/2327-9214.1060
9. Berland, G.K., Elliott, M.N., Morales, L.S., Algazy, J.I., Kravitz, R.L., Broder, M.S., Kanouse, D.E., Muñoz, J.A., Puyol, J., Lara, M., Watkins, K.E., Yang, H., McGlynn, E.A.: Health information on the internet accessibility, quality, and readability in English and Spanish. JAMA **285**(20), 2612–2621 (2001). doi:10.1001/jama.285.20.2612
10. Anderson, M.: The three kinds of platforms you meet on the internet. http://pmarchive.com/three_kinds_of_platforms_you_meet_on_the_internet.html. Accessed 20 May 2017
11. Ratzan, S.C., Parker, R.M.: Introduction. In: National Library of Medicine Current Bibliographies in Medicine: Health Literacy. National Institutes of Health, U.S. Department of Health and Human Services (2000)
12. Kim, H., Xie, B.: Health literacy and internet- and mobile app-based health services: a systematic review of the literature. Proc. Assoc. Info. Sci. Tech. **52**, 1–4 (2005). doi:10.1002/pra2.2015.145052010075
13. Lapsia, V., Lamb, K., Yasnoff, W.A.: Where should electronic records for patients be stored? Int. J. Med. Inform. **81**(12), 821–827 (2012)
14. Grannis, S.J., Biondich, P.G., Mamlin, B.W., Wilson, G., Jones, L., Overhage, J.M.: How disease surveillance systems can serve as practical building blocks for a health information infrastructure: the Indiana experience. AMIA Annu. Symp. Proc., 286–290 (2005)
15. Health Hub Singapore. https://www.healthhub.sg/
16. HealthKit (global health community). https://www.healthkit.com/
17. HealthKit by Apple. https://developer.apple.com/healthkit/

18. Kensaku, K., Houlihan, C.A., Balas, E.A., Lobach, D.F.: Improving clinical practice using clinical decision support systems: a systematic review of trials to identify features critical to success. BMJ **330**, 765 (2005)
19. Clay, C.A.: Exploring the use of mobile technologies for the acquisition of clinical skills. Nurse Educ. Today **31**, 582–586 (2011)
20. Huckvale, K., Prieto, J.T., Tilney, M., Benghozi, P.J., Car, J.: Unaddressed privacy risks in accredited health and wellness apps: a cross-sectional systematic assessment. BMC Med. **13**, 214 (2015). doi:10.1186/s12916-015-0444-y
21. Free, C., Phillips, G., Watson, L., Galli, L., Felix, L., Edwards, P., Patel, V., Haines, A.: The effectiveness of mobile-health technologies to improve health care service delivery processes: a systematic review and meta-analysis, 15 January 2013. https://doi.org/10.1371/journal.pmed.1001363
22. Christensen, J.H.: Using RESTful web-services and cloud computing to create next generation mobile applications. In: Proceedings of the 24th ACM SIGPLAN Conference Companion on Object Oriented Programming Systems Languages and Applications, pp. 627–634. ACM
23. Newman, S.: Building Microservices. O'Reilly Media Inc., Sebastopol (2015)
24. Leavitt, N.: Will NoSQL databases live up to their promise? Computer **43**(2), 12–14 (2010)
25. Klinkenberg, R. (ed.): RapidMiner: Data Mining Use Cases and Business Analytics Applications. Chapman and Hall/CRC, Boca Raton (2013)
26. Hall, M.: The WEKA data mining software: an update. ACM SIGKDD Explor. Newsl. **11**(1), 10–18 (2009)
27. Microsoft HealthVault. https://www.healthvault.com/sg/en
28. Google Health. https://en.wikipedia.org/wiki/Google_Health
29. myChart. https://www.ucsfhealth.org/ucsfmychart/
30. CONNECT Community Portal. http://www.connectopensource.org/
31. PhiCollect. https://www.webfirst.com/phicollect
32. Open Data Kit. https://opendatakit.org/
33. Nationwide Health Information Network (NHIN). https://www.healthit.gov/sites/default/files/what-Is-the-nhin–2.pdf

Privacy Matters: Detecting Nocuous Patient Data Exposure in Online Physician Reviews

Frederik S. Bäumer[(✉)], Nicolai Grote, Joschka Kersting, and Michaela Geierhos

Heinz Nixdorf Institute, University of Paderborn, Paderborn, Germany
{fbaeumer,ngrote,jkers,geierhos}@hni.upb.de

Abstract. Consulting a physician was long regarded as an intimate and private matter. The physician-patient relationship was perceived as sensitive and trustful. Nowadays, there is a change, as medical procedures and physicians consultations are reviewed like other services on the Internet. To allay user's privacy doubts, physician review websites assure anonymity and the protection of private data. However, there are hundreds of reviews that reveal private information and hence enable physicians or the public to identify patients. Thus, we draw attention to the cases when de-anonymization is possible. We therefore introduce an approach that highlights private information in physician reviews for users to avoid an accidental disclosure. For this reason, we combine established natural-language-processing techniques such as named entity recognition as well as handcrafted patterns to achieve a high detection accuracy. That way, we can help websites to increase privacy protection by recognizing and uncovering apparently uncritical information in user-generated texts.

Keywords: Physician reviews · User privacy · Nocuous data exposure

1 Introduction

Physician Review Websites (PRWs) receive an increasing amount of attention from the media as well as from physicians and patients. They enable users to rate medical services anonymously and freely access this content on the Web. We define anonymity as being not known, named or being regarded as nameless [4]. These reviews help other patients to look about for an adequate service. Reviews, as shown in Fig. 1 can be divided into a qualitative (i.e. review text) and a quantitative (i.e. numerical ratings) part. Moreover, Health Care Providers (HCPs) comment on the reviews and reviewers can even provide meta data (e.g. age, insurance). The anonymity the Web conveys to its users enables a truthful way of communicating one's ratings. Though, to be able to provide an authentic rating, patients add information about their person, treated disease and the visit at the physician in general. Hence, they may risk damaging the sensible physician-patient relationship or to be identifiable for other people because a limited amount of information like age and number of children can already threaten anonymity. Additional to such consciously published information, users tend to reveal further information unintended [24]. This kind of information, especially in combination with other and meta data like the physician's name or location, endangers anonymity although only a very limited

© Springer International Publishing AG 2017
R. Damaševičius and V. Mikašytė (Eds.): ICIST 2017, CCIS 756, pp. 77–89, 2017.
DOI: 10.1007/978-3-319-67642-5_7

amount of information is provided [35]. Leading PRWs are aware of this risk and are encouraged by law to introduce control mechanisms, which automatically test and identify user statements that harm anonymity and privacy. However, our analysis of published reviews uncovers that still a lot of ratings with privacy violations exist, which at worst enable readers to de-anonymize a reviewer.

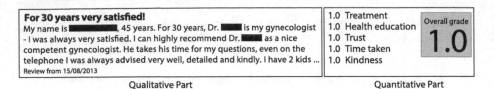

| Qualitative Part | Quantitative Part |

Fig. 1. Sample physician review on jameda.de (translated from German)

In the context of patient reviews, it is important to distinguish between reviewers and patients because these roles do not necessarily appear *in persona* [17]. Patients can report their own experiences. But a reviewer can also write about the medical treatment of a third person (e.g. a child). Therefore, we need to distinguish between revealing information about oneself or a third person. Such specific and general difficulties to the PRW domain lead to the necessity of protecting patients' privacy. This is especially important when the privacy of a third person is risked. Privacy protection and threats to privacy receive an increasing amount of attention in the public. Even the New York Times wrote years ago about this topic, a long time before greater revelations were made [25]. For this reason, we developed an approach for recognizing potentially nocuous patient data exposure in patients' reviews (shown in the left part of Fig. 1). In particular, our algorithm analyzes the semantic information of the qualitative part of reviews as well as their meta data. Therefore, information that would cause a break of privacy is detected. By highlighting potentially private information and providing an explanation about the privacy risk, patients are warned and maybe discouraged from publishing. Apart from that, we discuss limitations and constraints that our actual approach faces. We encourage the community or PRWs themselves to apply our method. Up to now, e.g. the German PRW jameda.de already identifies 'irregularities' containing spam and fake review in order to reduce data noises. Such cases are then manually treated and people decide whether to delete the reviews [23]. However, as we will later show, we believe that jameda's system can be improved to detect even more issues.

The structure of the paper is as follows: In Sect. 2, we provide an overview of the related work. Then, we give an insight into our categorization of potential privacy threats (Sect. 3). We present our approach for uncovering potential privacy threats in patient's online reviews in Sect. 4, before we discuss the strengths and weaknesses of our approach (Sect. 5). Finally, we summarize our results in Sect. 6.

2 Current State of Research

As a great and increasing number of people is using social networks, many studies are focused on their usage. An important phenomenon is that people are revealing too many information about themselves [13, 20]. In many cases, it happens unwittingly and unintentionally [1, 24], but creates physical and cyber risks [18]. Since PRWs are widely used [11] and investigated [9], most researchers focused on aspects like quality [7, 10, 11, 31, 32, 34] or their awareness in public and in scientific controversies [6, 12]. Ethical issues and data protection are studied as well [12, 21, 33]. The last-mentioned point is fundamental for our work, since we focus on de-anonymization issues. During the last years, there have been discussions how PRWs have impact on relationships between physicians and their patients, about the quality of physician's work, and on how evaluated physicians should behave according to their ratings [11, 19, 39]. Moreover, the reviewer behavior is studied. Why physicians are rated online is one of the crucial research questions [6, 22]. Other features like psycho-graphic [37] and socio-graphic are considered, too [3, 9, 37]. Additionally, aspects like the medical condition of reviewers were investigated [9, 37] as well as the importance of specific criteria for users of PRWs [8]. Further studies focused on the review's sentiment [6, 11, 16, 26] and quantified parts [11] as well as on the number of ratings per physician [6, 16]. Since different works on privacy issues in other established social networks have been conducted [28], there is little to find about the medical context, which can be considered as privacy sensitive. Especially, de-anonymization is a considerable threat to people's privacy. For example, Acquisti and Gross [18] showed in their study 2005 that it is possible to identify one's social security number by using information from profile sites. Organizations could use such information for sending spam or starting phishing attacks [18]. Sweeney [35] figured out that it is possible to identify 87% of the U.S. population only by combining ZIP code, gender and date of birth information: "In general, few characteristics are needed to uniquely identify a person". Therefore, it is not sufficient to remove person names and addresses to anonymize a set of data [36].

Hence, there exist different attack scenarios. Renoth [30] provides an overview on different methods of de-anonymization. Wondracek et al. [40] introduce a de-anonymization approach, which is based on group memberships that are available on social network sites. Thus, they can identify a user with his or her belonging. Another attack method was developed by Korayem and Crandall [24], who use temporal, social, textual and geographic user properties from two different social networks for machine learning purposes. That way, two corresponding accounts help to identify a user.

Within the context of PRWs, we can assume that the same problems and potential attacks on users' privacy that account for social networks are relevant for PRWs as well. PRWs share the same characteristics as social networks, which are defined as "a dedicated website or other application which enables users to communicate with each other by posting information, comments, messages, images, etc." [29]. Therefore, it is important to protect the information that users are revealing in social networks, especially if this information has a medical background. Some research is done in the field of protecting medical data of patients. One protection model is K-anonymity. These models consider the issue that many information in patient data can lead to the recognition of individuals. In one example, Ganta showed that it is possible to identify a single person, including his or her medical condition and treatments, simply by comparing patient-discharge information, which was supposed to be anonymized [15]. K-anonymity provides protection against linking attacks, which means the interlinking of private information such as gender, ZIP code and other publicly available data [14]. This problem is extended by legal regulations which oblige holders of patient data to protect people's privacy [38]. Due to the fact that information about diseases is considered as highly confidential, even though it is often included in reviews, privacy protection has to be strict. Publishing ratings without names is not sufficient for privacy protection because reviewers should not fear to be recognized by their physicians or anyone else. For example, the German PRW jameda.de takes this into account and developed guidelines as well as testing mechanisms together with patients and physicians in order to protect privacy and prevent deceptive ratings [23]. Therefore, popular German PRWs such as jameda.de and docinsider.de seem to protect their user's privacy inconsistently because there is no information available how names provided by users in their ratings (e.g. names are crossed out using curved or squared brackets) are deleted. Consequently, since everyone can publish a rating, there comes up the question of roles. The person treated by a physician does not have to be the reviewer. As Geierhos and Bäumer [17] showed in previous work, different roles like parents providing a rating for their underage children or children for their aging parents can be widely found.

3   Data Exposure Classification

In the following, the data exposure regarding affected persons is categorized and the risk of de-anonymization is carried out. For this purpose, we first present the underlying data set in Sect. 3.1 before we present our data exposure classification (cf. Sect. 3.2).

3.1   Data Acquisition and Preprocessing

Our text collection was created by crawling data from the most popular German PRW jameda.de between October 2013 and January 2015. More than 213,000 HCP records and 860,000 individual reviews cover the time period from January 2009 to January 2015. The HCP repository contains personal information such as name, address and specialty. It consists of various types of HCPs, especially physicians (67.6%), health practitioners (7.9%), psychotherapists (6.8%), pharmacists (5.5%) and physical therapists (5.3%). The review collection contains the title and text of each review and consists of 327,625 types and 45,023,119 tokens.

In order to achieve a higher data quality, we applied preprocessing. Thus, we preselected reviews including possible data exposure for further analysis. This includes, on the one hand, the removal of non-textual evaluations and, on the other hand, the recognition and annotation of person and location entities. Named entity recognition (NER) is a sub-task of information extraction (IE) with the goal to automatically detect and classify named entities. While many NER algorithms work on the English language, various other languages have also been studied. The challenge for NER tasks heavily depends on several factors, e.g. the domain or the language. Often NER systems are optimized for a specific domain and cannot easily be adapted [27]. We used the well-known GATE Toolkit for the NER part with self-developed gazetteers for the German language. The gazetteers for drugs (e.g. "paracetamol"), diseases (e.g. "kidney failure") and medical jargon (e.g. "I was on sick leave") are to be emphasized here. Next, we applied a rule-based preselection that highlights entries containing an increased number of person or location entities. Furthermore, those entries which contain personal details etc. were highlighted, e.g. drug indications. In addition, a phrase search is applied to reveal patterns such as *"meine Tocher"* ("my daughter"), *"in Behandlung seit"* ("in treatment since"), *"Ich wohne in"* ("I am living in") or *"Jahre alt"* ("years old"). Based on the results of the preselection, we identified even more patterns that allow us to find more reviews suspected of nocuous data disclosure (so-called bootstrapping). Table 1 shows examples for sentences containing possible data exposures.

Table 1. Selected results of the pattern-based pre-selection process

#	Examples of exposed sentences	Feature
1	My name is <**Name**>. Mrs. <**Name**> and Mr. <**Name**> recommended me that I can visit you	Name
2	My name is <**Name**> und I am the singer at the <**Job**>	Name, Job
3	My name is <**Name**> and I live in <**Location**>	Name, Location
4	Hello, my name is <**Name**>, at <**Age**> Years the first time an <**Disease**>	Name, Age, Disease
5	[...] suffered from a <**Disease**> and I wasn't able to make it to my family physician in <**Location**> (I live in <**Location**> and work at <**Location**>). I have never (I'm now <**Age**> years old) [...]	Disease, Location, Age
6	[...] get sick (I work as a <**Job**>), I was told that I am healthy and able to work	Job

In order to get an insight into how often information is published in reviews, we have examined a random sample of 5,000 reviews. We have investigated whether information about the person (e.g. name), the place of residence (e.g. city), the family (e.g. number of children), the place of work (e.g. company name) or diseases (e.g. cancer) is provided. We have not yet considered the additional meta data at this point. In 1,102 reviews, at least one information bit was given, which mostly concerns the family situation (e.g. "as a mother of three children"). In 142 reviews, we found two information bits (e.g. place of residence and number of children). It is surprising, how often the roles (reviewer, patient) are explicitly mentioned in the reviews. For example, mothers and fathers often mention that they were at the doctor with their children and provide further information about their age and their illness (e.g. "Our 5-year-old daughter has been suffering from chronic abdominal pain for several weeks"). There are 24 reviews that contain at least three items that we classify as possibly harmful for patient's privacy.

3.2   Classification

As shown in Table 1, the extent to which data is revealed as well as the type of information varies heavily. Partwise, the full name as well as location of residence and age
are given. Oftentimes, there are indications of the disease, treatment and treatment duration, too. While personal data like full names and locations enable third parties to identify
a person, indications about diseases and treatment allow the de-anonymization by a
physician. Even information about the number of children and their age at a given point
in time (timestamp) can lead in combination with a disease or employer to a de-anonymization in small towns. This is especially possible when further meta data is provided
(e.g. the location of the physician's office). Within our data set, we discovered examples
in which reviewers were identifiable because of uniquely matching information
regarding the job, name and additional meta information. For example, it was possible
to find the website of the reviewer's employer and therefore identify the reviewer
because of the given information.

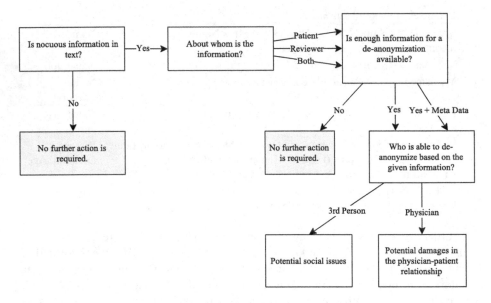

Fig. 2. Classification of qualitative reviews

In the following, we want to show some examples in which revelations appeared.
We exemplify how the information can be used alone or in combination for de-anonymization. In the first classification step, we distinguish between reviews that contain or do
not contain private information. If there is private information (like name, age, location,
drugs, date of visit), we distinguish whether it has to be assigned to the reviewer or
patient, as long as these roles are not *in persona*. Applied to the sample review (Fig. 1),
we can yet identify the following features: Name[1], age (45 years), number of children

---
[1] Some data is not given here for privacy reasons, even if it is freely accessible.

(2), medical specialist, location of the physician's office, period of treatment (August 2013), length of the physician-patient relationship (30 years). Obviously, all information details concern the patient and reviewer *in persona*. But other reviews abound, especially by parents writing about the experiences of her children: *"My daughter has been with <physician> since her birth. Meanwhile she is <age>"*. Furthermore, we discovered examples in which a reviewer describes the visit of a third person, without being present in the certain situation. This could damage the physician-patient relationship because of hearsay.

Table 2. Various personal information available on PRWs (shortened list)

Role	Feature	Source	Feature
Patient	Age	Text, Meta data	* years old
	City	Text	I live in *
	Date of visit	Meta data	–
	Disease(s)	Text	I am diabetic patient
	Duration of PP-relation	Text	for * **weeks** in treatment
	Duration of disease/treatment	Text	in treatment since *
	Drugs	Text	cortisone
	Gender	Text	I'm **mother** of
	Insurance	Meta data	–
	Job	Text	and work at
	Marriage status	Text	**my wife** has
	No. of children	Text	With * children
	Place of birth	Text	from *, my hometown
	Treatment	Text	was prescribed a *
	Waiting time (date)	Text	waited for * months
Reviewer	Date of review	Meta data	–
	Relation (to patient)	Text	Accompanied my *
	Patient *in persona*	Text	–
	Stylometry data	Text	–
Physician	City	Meta data	–
	Federal state	Meta data	–
	Full name	Meta data	–
	Response on a review	Meta data	–
	Speciality	Meta data	–
	Street	Meta data	–
	ZIP	Meta data	–

In the following, the decision takes place whether a single information allows the de-anonymization (e.g. full name) or whether further information (e.g. meta data like the location of the physician's office) is required. In this step, it is particularly important whether a patient can be identified by the physician and his/her team or by anyone else. While the former can damage the sensible physician-patient relationship, the latter may cause problems at the workplace or in the social environment [15]. Example no. 2 in

Table 1 shows when a de-anonymization in public is possible. Here, a short web search is sufficient to identify the concrete person. By contrast, example no. 4 allows the de-anonymization by physicians, because name, age, illness and meta data such as review date and health insurance are given. Our current decision tree is depicted in Fig. 2.

The remaining question is at the moment, how much information is necessary to de-anonymize a person. Fact is, that, due to the already available information and a well-known patient group, a physician needs less information to de-anonymize his or her patient in comparison to the general public. However, Sweeney [35] showed that it is possible to de-anonymize 87% of the US population with only three information bits (ZIP, gender, date of birth). At this point, it is recommended to take a closer look at the demographic details in reviews, either available as plain text or meta data (cf. Table 2). Table 2 shows more risky data apart from age, location and name. The forenamed details provide an overview on their harmfulness to privacy. Other features are gender, marriage status or date, which are not always mentioned in texts, but can help others to identify a person. That is, when the reviewer is, for example, "A mother of three children [...]", the number of children (3) and the gender (female) are provided. A similar case applies when stated "My husband went with my son [...]" (marriage status, gender of the child is mentioned). Apart from this kind of information patients reveal in form of texts or meta data, further details are available. For example, it is known that patients prefer physicians close to their place of residence, which can serve as an additional location information [2].

4   Approach

In the following, we present our approach which enables PRWs to automatically screen incoming reviews for potential privacy threats and to make them visible to users. Therefore, we explain the underlying data processing pipeline (Sect. 4.1) before we present our applied natural language (NL) patterns (Sect. 4.2) and quality constraints (Sect. 4.3).

4.1   Data Processing Pipeline

Our data processing pipeline (cf. Figure 3) is built upon the preprocessing step described in Sect. 3.1 and is applied on the presented data set. Based on annotations that were done by the NER that are especially related to person and location entities as well as organizations, drugs, data, etc., we apply our detection rules (cf. Sect. 4.2) (currently 30 predefined rules in the so-called rule repository), which are able to detect correlating information or including and annotate contextual information such as family relations or dosages of drugs.

After the NER, additional quality constraints (cf. Sect. 4.3) reduce the number of annotations to present only essential information. The remaining annotations are enriched with explanations for the users, which provide further details why users' privacy might be violated.

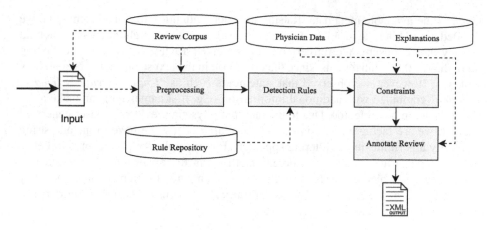

Fig. 3. Data processing pipeline

4.2 NL Pattern-Based Detection of Patient Data Exposure

The information, which has been found up to now by the NER approach and the defined NL patterns, provide a first hint for data revelation (e.g. location, name). They alone are not sufficient. The phrase "My daughter Leonie" indicates that a parent writes about a female child called "Leonie". A connection between Leonie and the role as daughter is, up to now, not made. For this reason, we apply NL patterns, which consist of strings and the NER results. A pattern is for example (*daughter\son\child\children*) + NER(*Name*). This pattern enables us to combine results that have not been connected before. The allegation "I am 25 years old" corresponds to the reviewer. If there exists more information about a third person, e.g. a child, we have to assign it to the child. But if there is just one role mentioned in the whole text, all textual and meta information is related to the same role. When detecting privacy issues, our method displays a warning with information about the threat and an explanation is attached to the text passage.

4.3 Quality Constraints

To enhance the quality of the results and to reduce the number of incorrect or irrelevant information for the user, we perform a constraint-based filtering after the NL pattern-based detection. This includes, on the one hand, detecting incorrect annotations due to NER errors such as invalid names (e.g. annotated names including numbers) or single titles ("Mr.") and, on the other hand, ignoring of annotations, which are evidently not related to the patient or reviewer. Especially, the corresponding physician's name that is above average represented in reviews, is an example for such a constraint-based filtering. Furthermore, this technique also operates on very general location descriptions like "Germany", "Republic", "Medical Office" or "Hospital" because they can be classified as innocuous and might distract the user from nocuous annotations. At this point, the question comes up whether it is necessary to filter the location of the medical office given in the available meta data. Raising the user's attention for this information, we decided not to filter the location of the medical office and thus highlight it as a potential privacy data exposure. We furthermore implemented a white list of cities containing more than 100,000 inhabitants, since their mention in the text seems not to be a privacy violation. However, we observed that statements such as "*I have previously lived in Cologne*" combined with additional information (e.g. first name, age) can make a de-anonymization possible, too. Due to the fact that physician reviews are user-generated content, we are facing high variance in text quality. Thus, we have to include string similarity algorithms in our filtering approach. For example, the physician "Dr. Peter-meyer" appears in at least five different spellings in the reviews (i.e. "Petremayer", "Petermayer"), which all needs to be filtered and compared to the meta data since they are not names of the reviewer. This is currently done by using Jaro-Winkler distance which currently produces good results [5].

5   Discussion

First and foremost, there are possibilities of de-anonymization based on public available physician reviews. As one first counter step, our approach detects serious privacy threats that may lead to de-anonymization and therefore may damage personal relationships or one's general personal well-being. On the one hand, there is a relatively decent number of reviews that forms a threat. But even a small number, in our case several thousand reviews, of de-anonymization threats can cause damages that may be disastrous to individuals.

Additionally, it should be mentioned that reviews to this day have already been quality-checked by most PRWs before publication. Having that in mind, we defined different categories based on the issues we have manually identified. However, our approach shows ambiguous results: We have solved different threats, whereas we may have not found some issues due to missing or too strict NL patterns. Our idea is to scan through existing reviews and identify threats in. Therefore, we may have not come up with issues we did not have in mind, what is a limitation. Misspellings or reviews using dialects, bad language and suchlike will not be covered in the current version of our approach. Another constraint is the degree of harmfulness. A location may be more harmful when it is more unique (very small town) and furthermore not identical with the physician's location. Combinations of potential harmful information are regarded as an even bigger threat. Another constraint is that a patient's name cannot be part of a physician's name, but it actually can be. The very common German name "Meyer" may fit to the patient as well as to the physician. Anyhow, we solved a broad number of privacy threats whereas our approach is easy to adapt. We have shown a working solution that may be used by PRWs *ad hoc*.

6   Conclusion

As we have shown, the current efforts of German PRWs are too weak when it comes to protect the anonymity of reviewers or patients. Indeed, there exist PRWs like the German portal jameda, which has already introduced a very fine-meshed protection system, filtering fake reviews and private data such as names. At the same time, dozens of evaluations show that de-anonymization is enabled by providing several pieces of private information in combination with meta data. Therefore, we would like to draw attention to the necessity of encountering the extensive issue. By using our approach that combines existing NLP techniques (e.g. NER, string similarity algorithms), PRWs can support users with context-sensitive warnings, which show possible data exposure and explain its danger to reviewer's anonymity.

References

1. Almishari, M., Gasti, P., Tsudik, G., Oguz, E.: Privacy-preserving matching of community-contributed content. In: Crampton, J., Jajodia, S., Mayes, K. (eds.) ESORICS 2013. LNCS, vol. 8134, pp. 443–462. Springer, Heidelberg (2013). doi:10.1007/978-3-642-40203-6_25
2. Bäumer, F.S., Geierhos, M., Schulze, S.: A system for uncovering latent connectivity of health care providers in online reviews. In: Dregvaite, G., Damasevicius, R. (eds.) ICIST 2015. CCIS, vol. 538, pp. 3–15. Springer, Cham (2015). doi:10.1007/978-3-319-24770-0_1
3. Beck, A.J.: Nutzung und bewertung deutscher arztbewertungsportale durch patienten in deutschen hausarztpraxen. Ph.D. thesis, Ulm University (2014)
4. Bibliographisches Institut. Duden – Anonymität. http://www.duden.de/suchen/dudenonline/anonymit%C3%A4t (2017). Accessed 20 Mar 2017
5. Cohen, W.W., Ravikumar, P., Fienberg, S.E.: A comparison of string distance metrics for name-matching tasks. In: Proceedings of IJCAI-03 Workshop on Information Integration on the Web (IIWeb-03), 9–10 August 2003, Acapulco, Mexico, pp. 73–78 (2003)
6. Emmert, M., Gerstner, B., Sander, U., Wambach, V.: Eine bestandsaufnahme von bewertungen auf arztbewertungsportalen am beispiel des nürnberger gesundheitsnetzes qualität und effizienz (QuE). Gesundheitsökonomie & Qualitätsmanagement 19(04), 161–167 (2014)
7. Emmert, M., Maryschok, M., Eisenreich, S., Schöffski, O.: Arzt-bewertungsportale im internet – geeignet zur identifikation guter arztpraxen? Das Gesundheitswesen 71(04), e18–e27 (2009)
8. Emmert, M., Meier, F., Heider, A.-K., Dürr, C., Sander, U.: What do patients say about their physicians? An analysis of 3000 narrative comments posted on a German physician rating website. Health Policy 118(1), 66–73 (2014)
9. Emmert, M., Meier, F., Pisch, F., Sander, U.: Physician choice making and characteristics associated with using physician-rating websites: cross-sectional study. J. Med. Internet Res. 15(8), e187 (2013)
10. Emmert, M., Sander, U., Esslinger, A.S., Maryschok, M., Schöffski, O.: Public reporting in germany: the content of physician rating websites. Methods Inf. Med. 51(2), 112–120 (2012)
11. Emmert, M., Sander, U., Pisch, F.: Eight questions about physician-rating websites: a systematic review. J. Med. Internet Res. 15(2), e24 (2013)

12. Fischer, S., Emmert, M.: A review of scientific evidence for public perspectives on online rating websites of healthcare providers. In: Gurtner, S., Soyez, K. (eds.) Challenges and Opportunities in Health Care Management, pp. 279–290. Springer, Cham (2015). doi: 10.1007/978-3-319-12178-9_22

13. Forkefeld, N.: The invisible hand of social network: Wie viel Transparenz in Sozialen Netzwerken ist ökonomisch? Discussion Papers 24/2012, Witten/Herdecke University, Faculty of Management and Economics (2012)

14. Gal, T.S., Chen, Z., Gangopadhyay, A.: A privacy protection model for patient data with multiple sensitive attributes. Int. J. Inf. Secur. Priv. 2(3), 28–44 (2008)

15. Ganta, S.R., Kasiviswanathan, S.P., Smith, A.: Composition attacks and auxiliary information in data privacy. In: Proceedings of the 14th ACM SIGKDD International Conference on Knowledge Discovery and Data Mining, pp. 265–273. ACM, New York (2008)

16. Gao, G.G., McCullough, J.S., Agarwal, R., Jha, A.K.: A changing landscape of physician quality reporting: analysis of patients' online ratings of their physicians over a 5-year period. J. Med. Internet Res. 14(1), e38 (2012)

17. Geierhos, M., Bäumer, F.S.: Erfahrungsberichte aus zweiter Hand: Erkenntnisse über die Autorschaft von Arztbewertungen in Online-Portalen. In: Book of Abstracts der DHd-Tagung 2015, pp. 69–72, Graz (2015)

18. Gross, R., Acquisti, A.: Information revelation and privacy in online social networks (The Facebook case). In: Proceedings of the 2005 ACM Workshop on Privacy in the Electronic Society, pp. 71–80. ACM, Alexandria (2005)

19. Hanauer, D.A., Zheng, K., Singer, D.C., Gebremariam, A., Davis, M.M.: Public awareness, perception, and use of online physician rating sites. J. Am. Med. Assoc. 311(7), 734 (2014)

20. Heidemann, J.: Online Social Networks – Ein sozialer und technischer Überblick. Informatik-Spektrum 33(3), 262–271 (2010)

21. Hennig, S., Etgeton, S.: Arztbewertungen im Internet. Datenschutz und Datensicherheit 35(12), 841–845 (2011)

22. Hinz, V., Drevs, F., Wehner, J.: Electronic word of mouth about medical services. Technical report, HCHE Research Paper (2012)

23. Jameda. Frequently Asked Questions (FAQ) für Nutzer (2016). https://www.jameda.de/hilfe/?show=user. Accessed 14 Mar 2017

24. Korayem, M., Crandall, D.J.: De-anonymizing users across heterogeneous social computing platforms. In: Proceedings of the 7th International Conference on Weblogs and Social Media, Cambridge, MA, USA, pp. 689–692 (2013)

25. Lohr, S.: How privacy vanishes online (2010). http://www.nytimes.com/2010/03/17/technology/17privacy.html?scp=1&sq=how%20privacy%20can%20vanish%20steve%20lohr&st=cse. Accessed 20 Mar 2017

26. López, A., Detz, A., Ratanawongsa, N., Sarkar, U.: What patients say about their doctors online: a qualitative content analysis. J. Gen. Intern. Med. 27(6), 685–692 (2012)

27. Nadeau, D., Sekine, S.: A survey of named entity recognition and classification. Linguisticae Investigationes 30(1), 3–26 (2007)

28. Narayanan, A., Shmatikov, V.: De-anonymizing social networks. In: Proceedings of the 30th IEEE Symposium on Security and Privacy, pp. 173–187. IEEE, Oakland (2009)

29. Oxford University Press. social network - definition of social network in english – oxford dictionaries. https://en.oxforddictionaries.com/definition/social_network. Accessed 15 Mar 2017

30. Renoth, J.: Data mining and data analysis in online social networks (2011)

31. Sander, U., Emmert, M., Grobe, T.: Effektivität und Effizienz der Arztsuche mit Arztsuch- und Bewertungsportalen und Google. Das Gesundheitswesen 75(06), 397–399 (2012)

32. Schaefer, C., Schwarz, S.: Wer findet die besten Ärzte Deutschlands?: Arztbewertungsportale im Internet. Zeitschrift für Evidenz, Fortbildung und Qualität im Gesundheitswesen **104**(7), 572–577 (2010). 15 Jahre ÄZQ
33. Strech, D.: Arztbewertungsportale aus ethischer Perspektive. Eine orientierende Analyse. Zeitschrift für Evidenz, Fortbildung und Qualität im Gesundheitswesen **104**(8–9), 674–681 (2010)
34. Strech, D., Reimann, S.: Deutschsprachige Arztbewertungsportale. Das Gesundheitswesen **74**(08/09), e61–e67 (2012)
35. Sweeney, L.: Simple demographics often identify people uniquely. Health (San Francisco) **671**, 1–34 (2000)
36. Sweeney, L.: Achieving k-anonymity privacy protection using generalization and supression. Int. J. Uncertainty, Fuzziness Knowl.-Based Syst. **10**(05), 571–588 (2002)
37. Terlutter, R., Bidmon, S., Röttl, J.: Who uses physician-rating websites? differences in sociodemographic variables, psychographic variables, and health status of users and nonusers of physician-rating websites. J. Med. Internet Res. **16**(3), e97 (2014)
38. van der Haak, M., Wolff, A., Brandner, R., Drings, P., Wannenmacher, M., Wetter, T.: Data security and protection in cross-institutional electronic patient records. Int. J. Med. Inf. **70**(2–3), 117–130 (2003)
39. Verhoef, L.M., de Belt, T.H.V., Engelen, L.J., Schoonhoven, L., Kool, R.B.: Social media and rating sites as tools to understanding quality of care: a scoping review. J. Med. Internet Res. **16**(2), e56 (2014)
40. Wondracek, G., Holz, T., Kirda, E., Kruegel, C.: A practical attack to de-anonymize social network users. In: Proceedings of the IEEE Symposium on Security and Privacy, pp. 223–238. IEEE, Berkeley/Oakland (2010)

Classifying Cognitive Workload
Using Eye Activity and EEG Features
in Arithmetic Tasks

Magdalena Borys[(✉)], Małgorzata Plechawska-Wójcik,
Martyna Wawrzyk, and Kinga Wesołowska

Lublin University of Technology, Lublin, Poland
{m.borys, m.plechawska}@pollub.pl,
{martyna.wawrzyk, kinga.wesolowska}@pollub.edu.pl

Abstract. The paper presents the results of classification of mental states in
a study of the cognitive workload based on arithmetic tasks. Different classification methods were applied using features extracted from eye activity and EEG
signal. The paper discusses results of two datasets. The first one covers binary
classification discriminating between the cognitive workload condition and the
no-task control condition. The second one discriminates between three mental
states: the high cognitive workload condition, the low cognitive workload
condition and the no-task control condition. The results obtained for the first
dataset reached the accuracy of 90% with 6 eye-tracking features as input and an
SVMs classifier. The second dataset was classified with the maximum accuracy
of 73% due to its complexity.

Keywords: Cognitive workload · Classification · Eye-tracking ·
Electroencephalography

1 Introduction

Cognitive workload is a term defined as a quantitative usage measure of the limited
amount of working memory [1]. Measuring cognitive load changes can contribute to
better diagnosis and treatment of patients, help design effective strategies to reduce
medical errors among clinicians and facilitate user evaluation of any information
systems. It is worth indicating that the highest productivity of human cognitive processing is reached if a mental task is within an optimal range.

Estimation of cognitive workload, although profitable, is still considered as a difficult task. There are two major kinds of cognitive load evaluation: subjective
(non-direct, based on questionnaires) and objective (based on biomedical signal measuring) [2]. Nowadays, however, researchers focus evaluation of mental effort mainly
on such techniques as electroencephalography (EEG), eye-tracking (ET) or electro-
cardiogram (ECG). Among human physiological indices one can find pupil diameter
change, duration of fixation and amplitude of saccades, ratio, amplitude and power of
specific brain wave components, as well as many others. Composing different features

© Springer International Publishing AG 2017
R. Damaševičius and V. Mikašytė (Eds.): ICIST 2017, CCIS 756, pp. 90–105, 2017.
DOI: 10.1007/978-3-319-67642-5_8

gives a possibility to receive better results in distinguishing cognitive workload in different type of workload tasks as well as between cognitive workload and relaxation.

The aim of the paper is to perform classification of the mental states of the participants of the study. The features applied in the classification were extracted from eye activity and EEG signals.

The paper is structured as follows. The second section covers a literature review of research conducted in the cognitive load area. The third one presents the particulars of the experiment, whereas the fourth discusses details of the data analysis process. The measurement of cognitive load is presented in the fifth section and the classification details – in the sixth. The last section discusses the results obtained.

2   Related Work

In the literature there are more and more works devoted to assessing cognitive load with objective measures. Once popular, subjective reports and psychophysiological measurements [3, 4] are rarely applied and are useful rather in combination with others, more objective indicators such as EEG, ECG or eye-activity (including eye-movements as well as pupillometry) [5].

2.1   Statistical Analysis and Relationships

The most popular is statistical and correlation analysis of such features as pupil dilation [6], blink number [7, 8], eye-movement measures (fixation duration and rate, saccade amplitude) or EEG band spectra and pupil diameter size [9, 10]. Some results show that eye-tracking features complement EEG data and ensure comprehensive cognitive load analysis [2, 5]. Also pupillometry measures gain more and more recognition in the context of mental activity [11].

2.2   Regression Analysis and Supervised Classification

Other papers describe regression analysis [12] and supervised classification. Classifiers such as Gaussian mixture models to determine a level of cognitive load based on blink number, saccade amplitude and pupil dilation [13] or MLP to recognize affective states (stress and relaxation) using pupil diameter [14] were used in former research. Eye-based measures are often combined with other signals. An example of such study can be find in [15], where the GSR signal with blink measures was applied in cognitive load classification using methods like SVMs or Naïve Bayes. Eye activity features are also often linked with EEG data. Classification based on joined features appears to gain better results than classical EEG-based analysis. Example studies cover pupil diameter features and band power EEG analyzed with Naïve Bayes classifier [16]; pupil diameter, blink and fixation duration with the SVM classifier [17]. The literature shows that the most popular classifiers applied in cognitive workload detection are the LDA and SVM methods. They are willingly used in the classification of joined features of pupil dilation and EEG frequency bands (theta, alpha, and beta) [18] as well as in the study of eye-tracking features, pupil dilation and EEG frequency [19]. An often applied classifier in the study of EEG data (such as spectral edge frequency, entropy or wavelet coefficients) complemented with other features (response time) is neural networks, typically the MLP method [20].

3 The Experiment

3.1 Participants

The study was approved by the Research Ethics Committee of Lublin University of Technology (Approval ID 3/2015 from 12 November 2015r) and all participants received verbal and written information about the study. All participants signed an informed consent.

Twenty healthy male graduate students (age: 22,8 years with standard deviation of 10 months; education: 1st year of Computer Science Master degree) participated in the study. All were right handed with normal or corrected-to-normal vision, they were not under pharmacological treatment. Participation was voluntary and no compensation was offered. Due to the quality of the EEG recording only 13 participants were selected for further analysis to obtained reliable results.

3.2 Experimental Task

The experiment was composed of eleven intervals, six task intervals (Interval 1: Interval 6) and five break intervals (Break 1:Break 5), run alternately. Each task interval consisted of a series of 17 arithmetic tasks (adding and subtracting integers) of different level of difficulty. This difficulty level rose in each consecutive interval. Interval 1 contained the easiest tasks (adding numbers in the range 1 to 10), whereas Interval 6 covered the hardest ones (adding and subtracting numbers ranging from 20 to 100). Each single arithmetical task was composed of two elements: an arithmetical operation (e.g. 10 + 5) and its result (e.g. 15). The result could be correct or incorrect. A participant was asked to click the left mouse button in case the answer was correct and do nothing in case of incorrect answer.

Each arithmetic task was displayed totally for 5500 ms including 1000 ms of delay at the beginning. An arithmetic operation was displayed for 400 ms with a 300 ms delay time before it. The result was displayed for 200 ms after 700 ms delay time before it. The rest of the time was dedicated to the participant's reaction. In a single task interval there were 6–7 correct answers.

All break intervals were the same, displaying an empty white screen with the word "Break" and calming music being played. The purpose of the break was to bring the participants' mental activities to a normal level and remove any mental effect of the previous set of tasks.

3.3 Procedure

Participants took part in the experiment in quiet conditions in the testing room in Laboratory of Motion Capture and Interface Ergonomics at Lublin University of

Technology [21]. The room was illuminated with standard fluorescent light and outside light was blocked to ensure stable conditions for the duration of the experiments. The mean light intensity in the room was 487,4 lx with a standard deviation of 15 lx. The light intensity was measured using digital luxmeter HT309 with accuracy 3% and resolution 0.1. The change of light intensity influenced by stimuli brightness at the level of the participants' eyes was minimized.

The experiment was designed and carried out using the tool dedicated to psychophysics and psychophysiology experiments (PsyTask). The prepared experiment was run directly the EEG recording and analyzing software (EEGStudio). It enabled to synchronize EEG data with stimulus displayed to a participant.

The experimenter explained the procedure and left the participant alone to give him a chance to focus on the tasks. The participants were instructed to minimise body movement to reduce potential artefact influence on their EEG signals and to fix (ate) their gaze on the centre of the monitor. The only movement to be performed was mouse clicking.

3.4 ET Data Acquisition

The eye-tracking data were captured simultaneously, but independently of the EEG signal. Eye events as well as pupil diameter size were tracked with binocular eye-tracking glasses (ETG2.0 manufactured by SensoMotoric Instruments) with a sampling rate of 30 Hz each eye and a resolution of 0.01 mm. The ETG2.0 uses video based oculography technique with a dark pupil with corneal reflections method. Each recording was preceded by a 3-point calibration procedure within build-in by manufacturer software.

3.5 EEG Data Acquisition

EEG equipment used in the study consisted of a 21 channel amplifier (Mitsar EEG 201), an electrode cap and dedicated EEG cup gel electrodes. Monopolar average mounting based on ear electrodes was applied. The sampling frequency was 500 Hz. All 21 electrodes were located according to the 10–20 system.

The recording procedure covered such initial steps as equipment setting, electrode mounting and impedance testing. Signal recording for each participant was performed as follows. In the first part of the recording the participant was in the resting state – he was asked to sit motionless for a minute with his eyes respectively opened and closed. The second part was dedicated to the main study described in the Experimental task section. The last part of the recording was a repetition of the resting state EEG recording. The resting state recordings are necessary to obtain material for the baseline estimation to determine real differences between participant activity and calm.

4 Data Processing

ET and EEG signal processing was composed of several steps presented in Fig. 1 and described in details in the following sections.

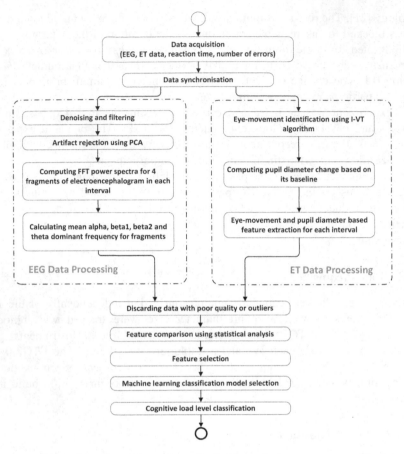

Fig. 1. Diagram of data processing in the study (source: own work)

4.1 ET Data Processing

Since the eye-tracking data were not synchronised with the stimuli of the experiment, they were synchronised manually based on a video recorded by the ETG2.0 scene camera with a frame rate 30 Hz.

All eye-tracking features were calculated as the average over both eyes. Eye related events such as fixations, saccades and blinks as well as pupil diameter were exported from ETG2.0 data recording using the dedicated BeGaze3.6 software. Fixations and saccades were detected using a dispersion-based identification (I-DT) algorithm. The minimum duration window threshold was set to 80 ms and maximum dispersion was set to 100 px). Adjacent fixations were merged and fixations smaller than 80 ms were discarded. Blinks were filtered out of the raw data using the build-in blink identification algorithm. Blinks shorter than 70 ms were discarded. Pupil diameter data were associated with fixation events. Pupil responses (diameter change) were calculated individually for each participant in each interval based on the average pupil diameter size during the first fixation.

4.2   EEG Data Processing

Firstly, the Notch filter was applied to remove electrical power artifact from the signal. Then, the signal was filtered to the range of 3–50 Hz. This filtration removed delta and high gamma waves, which were not intended to be included in the analysis. Initially filtered signal was corrected in order to remove unwanted artifacts, such as muscle noise (for example eye blinks or tongue moves), the imperfection of the electrode-skin contact (caused for example by sweating or gel drying) or other problems. In order to eliminate unwanted artifacts, Principal Component Analysis (PCA) method was applied [22]. Two primary PCA components were selected to perform the artifacts correction. Visual inspection of the data was also applied.

Next step was dedicated to the selection of the signal fragments with the highest signal-to-noise ratio values. Four fragments of approximately 5 s were selected from each interval. These selected fragments were processed with WinEEG software for further analysis. EEG spectra were generated using FFT for each selected fragment. For the statistical analysis, the values of wave frequency (beta1, beta2, theta and alpha) for electrodes Cz, F3, F4, P3 and P4 were used. Four values from the chosen fragments for each interval were averaged in order to compare the task and break activities.

4.3   Collected Data

As was mentioned, for the purpose of the study the ET and EEG features were calculated individually for the participants at each interval. Each calculated set of values in an interval is considered as a single observation in further analysis. In particular, each observation contains the following ET and EEG features:

- Cz_Alpha, ... P4_Alpha – alpha dominant frequency from channel Cz, F3, F4, P3 and P4 of the EEG device (in Hz);
- Cz_Beta_1, ... P4_Beta1 – beta1 dominant frequency from channel Cz, F3, F4, P3 and P4 of the EEG device (in Hz);
- Cz_Beta_2, ... P4_Beta2 – beta2 dominant frequency from channel Cz, F3, F4, P3 and P4 of the EEG device (in Hz);
- Cz_Theta, ... P4_Theta – theta dominant frequency from channel Cz, F3, F4, P3 and P4 of the EEG device (in Hz);
- Fix_N – fixations number (number of fixation in the interval);
- FixDur_Mean, FixDur_Median FixDur_Std, FixDur_Max – mean, median, standard deviation and maximum of fixation duration in the interval (in seconds);
- Sacc_N – fixation number (number of fixation in the interval);
- SaccDur_Mean, SaccDur_Median, SaccDur_Std, SaccDur_Max – mean, median, standard deviation and maximum of saccade duration in the interval (in seconds);
- SaccAmp_Mean, SaccAmp_Median, SaccAmp_Max – mean, median and maximum of saccade amplitude in the interval (in degrees);
- SaccAccel_Mean, SaccAccel_Median, SaccAccel_Max – mean, median and maximum of saccade acceleration in the interval (in degrees/s^2);
- PD_Mean, PD_Median, PD_Std, PD_Max, PD_Skewness, PD_Kurtosis – mean, median, standard deviation, maximum, skewness and kurtosis of normalised pupil diameter in the interval (in mm);

- Blinks_N – blink number (number of blinks in the interval);
- BlinksDur_Mean, BlinksDur_Median, BlinksDur_Std, BlinksDur_Max – mean, median, standard deviation and maximum of blink duration in the interval (in seconds);
- BlinksDur_Total – total time of eye closure during blinks in the interval (in seconds).

Since some participants closed their eyes to relax during the break intervals (despite the instructions), the eye-tracking data for those observations can distorts the results of analysis and should be treated as outliers. That is why the observations where for more than 20% of interval duration a participant has his eyes closed (the value of Blinks-Dur_Total feature), as well other outliers, were excluded from further analysis. A total of 115 observations with 48 presented features constructed Dataset 1 and Dataset 2 (described in next section) and were applied in the analysis.

5 Cognitive Load Measurement

The statistical test was applied to assess discrimination ability of each feature as well as the relationships between features to reduce the dimension of the applied classification model.

The statistical analysis was performed for two sets of data. The purpose of the first dataset (Dataset 1) was to discriminate between two mental states: the cognitive workload condition and the no-task control condition. Therefore each observation data representing the task interval was labelled as "1" (cognitive workload condition) and representing the break interval as "0" (no-task control condition, in which participants were asked to remain relaxed).

The purpose of the second dataset (Dataset 2) was to discriminate between three mental states: a high cognitive workload condition, a low cognitive workload condition and a no-task control condition. The data assignment to label "0" (no-task control condition) remained the same as in Dataset 1, but all data observations representing task intervals were classed based on its cognitive workload level (assessed by participants' mean response time).

In contrast to other studies, in which the task difficulty level (and therefore the cognitive workload level) were assigned based on the subjective ratings [13, 15, 16] or arbitrary classification [23], to class each interval (but not observation) the mean response time to stimuli was used. The analysis of variance (ANOVA) with the significance level of 5% showed that in triples of task intervals (1–3–5 and 7–9–11) there are no significant differences in the mean values of the mean response time variable (mean response time did follow the normal distribution). The pairs of intervals 1–9, 1–11, 3–11, 5–7, 5–9, 5–11 were found significantly different using Fisher's Least Significant Differences method with the significance level of 5%.

Both datasets are imbalanced. In Dataset 1 there are approximately 37% of "0" samples and 63% of "1" samples, while in Dataset 2 there are approximately 32% of "1" samples, 31% of "2" samples and 37% of "0" samples.

5.1   Dataset 1

The major features for both classes ("0" and "1") do not follow the normal distribution (tested using Shapiro-Wilk normality test with significance level of 5%), so the non-parametric statistical methods were applied.

The correlation between 48 calculated features and the class variable were measured using Spearman's rank correlation coefficient. As many as 19 features turned out to be correlated with the class variable with the significance level of 5%, where the strongest correlation coefficient was detected for features based on blinks duration.

The analysis of Spearman's rank correlation coefficient between all features revealed also several almost perfect correlations (rho > 0.9) in pairs such as: Fix_N–FixDur_Mean (rho = −0,99), Fix_N–FixDur_Std, FixDur_Mean–FixDur_Std, Fix-Dur_Max–FixDur_Std, PD_Mean–PD_Median (rho = 0,98), BlinksDur_Max–BlinksDur_Std; as well as many other strong correlations between ET features. The correlation between the features does not surprise, since the eye-movements are connected (e.g. the number of fixations can suggests the number of saccades) as well as eye-movement features (e.g. the longer the duration of a saccade, the higher its amplitude and the greater its acceleration).

Moreover, to investigate the differences between independent groups (two mental state classes) the Mann-Whitney U test and the Kolmogorov-Smirnov test were used. The Mann-Whitney U test found statistical differences in medians of 22 features (4 EEG and 18 ET) while the Kolmogorov-Smirnov found statistical differences in empirical distribution functions of 17 (1 EEG and 16 ET) features between classes with the significance level of 5%. Among those features in which statistical difference between classes was found, 15 features were the same. All features identified as significantly different between classes in the Mann-Whitney U test were consistent with the Spearman correlation results. The statistical significance proved that a relationship observed in the data occurred not by chance, therefore the data can be used to build a classifier for automated cognitive workload level identification.

5.2   Dataset 2

As in the previous dataset, the major features for the three groups do not follow the normal distribution (again tested using Shapiro-Wilk normality test with significance level of 5%), thus the non-parametric statistical methods were applied.

The correlation between 48 calculated features and the class variable were measured using Spearman's rank correlation coefficient. While 14 features were correlated with the class variable with the significance level of 5%, the moderated correlation (with rho > 0.4) was detected for 2 features based on fixation duration (the highest relationship was for FixDur_Max, where rho = −0.49) and 2 features based on blink duration. Only one correlation with an EEG feature (Cz_Alpha) was found as significant, but the relationship is rather weak. The analysis of Spearman's rank correlation coefficient between all features is presented in Sect. 5.2.

To examine the differences between multi groups, the nonparametric equivalents to analysis of variance were used. The Kruskal-Wallis analysis of ranks indicated the statistically significant difference in at least one group distribution for 24 features (including all those correlated with a class variable except Cz_Alpha) with the significance level of 5%. The Median test showed that 17 features had statistically significant differences in medians of class populations with the significance level of 5%. Among those features are all those correlated with a class variable (except Cz_Alpha, Fix_N and FixDur_Mean). Analogically, the statistical significance gave proof that a relationship observed in the data occurred not by chance.

6   Cognitive Load Classification

Data from Dataset 1 and Dataset 2 was used to train and evaluate a set of classifiers. The different classifiers were selected in order to compare different approaches presented in other scientific works. The implementation of the following classifiers in MATLAB R2016a Statistics and Machine Learning Toolbox were used:

- Decision Trees (with maximum number of splits: 4, 20 and 100) [24].
- Discriminant Analysis (linear and quadratic) [25, 26].
- Logistic Regression [27].
- Support Vector Machines, SVMs (with kernels: linear, quadratic, cubic or Gaussian, multiclass method: one-vs-one and box constraint level: 1) [28].
- k-Nearest Neighbour Classifiers, k-NN (with Euclidean distance metric and number of neighbours is set to 1, 10 and 100; with Euclidean distance metric using a distance weight and the number of neighbours is set to 10; with Cosine distance number of neighbours is set to 10 and with cubic distance number of neighbours set to 10) [29].
- Ensemble Classifiers (Boosted Trees, Bagged Trees, Subspace Discriminant, Subspace k-NN, RUSBoost Trees; accordingly with maximum number of splits: 20, number of learners: 30 and learning rate: 0.1) [30–32].

For all k-NN and SVMs classifiers the data were standardised. Taking into account the small size of the datasets, to evaluate and compare the accuracy of the predictive model 5-fold cross-validation was used in the study.

As mentioned in Sects. 5.1 and 5.2, the major features do not follow the normal distribution, therefore the linear discriminant analysis (LDA) could not be applied to find the combination of features that separates two classes and then reduce the dimension of the classification model. Moreover, the response (class feature) has a categorical type in both datasets, therefore the Chi-squared test was used to select a subset of features with reasonable predictive power.

6.1   Dataset 1 – Binary Classification

The 12 features were indicated as the key features for binary classification in the feature selection process using the Chi-squared test with the significance level of 1%. All were eye-tracking based features, among which most were related to blinks (4 features), the number of fixations and fixation duration (3), saccade duration and amplitude (2) as well as pupil diameter (2). In addition, the feature selection performed using same test with the significance level of 5% indicated 20 features (among them 3 EEG features:

P3_Theta, Cz_Beta2 and P4_Theta) as the best predictors (key variables for classification).

Taking into consideration the results of the feature selection process, several classification models were built and compared. Table 1 shows the results of classification using different sets of features with the classifiers that performed with the highest accuracy for those sets. To compare the classification models the accuracy, area under curve (AUC) as well as positive predictive values (PPV) for classes "0" and "1" were calculated. The Bagged Trees classifier performed the best among other classifiers with all dataset features, all the key features identified with the Chi-squared test with the significance level of 5% as well as only with the eye-tracking based best predictors. While the accuracy of all sets of features was almost the same, the reduction of a set's dimensions in the models increased the precision to identify class "1". The classification model with only EEG features identified as the best predictors allowed to achieve 74% of accuracy, which is less than in the model with only the BlinksDur_Max feature included.

The best predictors identified with the Chi-squared test with the significance level of 1% allow to achieve the accuracy at 90% (with *precision* = 93.1%, *sensitivity* = 91.8% and *specificity* = 88% in the classifying of cognitive workload condition) with the nearest neighbours algorithm with the most commonly used Euclidean distance and a single nearest neighbour (k = 1). The same accuracy (but with *precision* = 90.8%, *sensitivity* = 94.5% and *specificity* = 83.35% in the classifying of cognitive workload condition) was achieved for the set with the number of features reduced to 6 (by discarding the features with a high correlation with the already included ones). However, in this case, the SVMs with Quadratic kernel were used as classifier and achieved a higher value of AUC.

Additionally, to ensure that the high accuracy of classification models does not dependent only on blink duration based features and specific participants behaviour during break intervals, a classification founded only on fixation, saccade and pupil diameter based features was performed. The model with 7 features reached almost 90% of accuracy (*precision* = 90.5%, *sensitivity* = 91.8% and *specificity* = 84.1% in the classifying of cognitive workload condition), but it had a slightly lower precision in predicting class "0".

6.2   Dataset 2 – Multiclass Classification

In the feature selection process, the 13 features were indicated as the best predictors for multiclass classification using the Chi-squared test with the significance level of 1%. All predictors are very similar to those in binary classification, but additionally the saccade acceleration median was revealed as significant. In addition, the Chi-squared test performed with the significance level of 5% indicated 21 features (among them 4 EEG features: Cz_Beta2, Cz_Beta1, P3_Theta, and Cz_Alpha) as key for the classification.

Table 2 shows the results of classification using different sets of features with the classifiers that performs with the highest accuracy for those sets. Similarly, to compare the classifiers and sets of features, the accuracy as well as positive predictive values for classes "0", "1" and "2" are reported. The highest accuracy was reached for the k-NN

Table 1. The results of classification on different sets of features

Features used in a model	Classifier	Accuracy	AUC	PPV for "0"	PPV for "1"
All 48 features	Bagged Trees	85.2%	0.93	88%	84%
The best predictors with p-value < 0.05 (20 features)	Bagged Trees	87%	0.93	85%	88%
Only ET based the best predictors with p-value < 0.05 (17 features)	Bagged Trees	86.1%	0.93	84%	87%
Only ET based the best predictors with p-value < 0.05 (17 features)	RUSBoosted	88.7%	0.91	81%	94%
Only EEG based the best predictors with p-value < 0.05 (3 features)	Quadratic Discriminant with diagonal covariance regularisation	73.9%	0.66	73%	74%
The best predictors with p-value < 0.01 (12 features)	KNN with the Euclidean distance, k = 1	90.4%	0.90	86%	93%
BlinksDur_Max	KNN with cosine distance, k = 10	78.3%	0.71	79%	78%
BlinksDur_Max, SaccAmp_Mean	SVMs with Gaussian kernel	82.6%	0.8	81%	84%
BlinksDur_Max, SaccAmp_Mean, FixDur_Max	Bagged Trees	88.7%	0.90	85%	91%
BlinksDur_Max, SaccAmp_Mean, FixDur_Max, PD_Std	SVMs with Quadratic kernel	88.7%	0.93	91%	88%
PD_Std, BlinkDur_Max, SaccAmp_Mean, FixDur_Max, SaccDur_Std, SaccAmp_Median	SVMs with Quadratic kernel	90.4%	0.93	90%	91%
SaccAmp_Mean	Linear Discriminant	73,9%	0.63	80%	73%
SaccAmp_Mean, FixDur_Max	Logistic Regression	80.9%	0.79	86%	79%
SaccAmp_Mean, FixDur_Max, PD_Std	Quadratic Discriminant	82.6%	0.83	89%	80%
Fix_N, FixDur_Max, FixDur_Std, SaccDur_Std, SaccAmp_Mean, PD_Std, PD_Max	k-NN with the Euclidean distance, k = 1	88.7%	0.88	85%	91%

Table 2. The results of classification on different sets of features

Features used in a model	Classifier	Accuracy	PPV for "0"	PPV for "1"	PPV for "2"
All 48 features	Bagged Trees	63.5%	71%	63%	52%
The best predictors with p-value < 0.05 (21 features)	Bagged Trees	71.3%	77%	67%	70%
Only ET based the best predictors with p-value < 0.05 (17 features)	k-NN with the Euclidean distance, distance weight: squared inverse, k = 10	73%	97%	64%	66%
Only EEG based the best predictors with p-value < 0.05 (4 features)	k-NN with the Euclidean distance, k = 1	50.4%	53%	43%	55%
The best predictors with p-value < 0.01 (13 features)	Bagged Trees	71.3%	79%	65%	69%
SaccAmp_Mean	Quadratic Discriminant	55.7%	73%	48%	55%
SaccAmp_Mean, BlinksDur_Max, PD_Std, PD_Max, FixDur_Max, SaccAccel_Median, SaccDur_Mean, SaccAmp_Max, Fix_N, SaccDur_Median, SacccDur_Max, FixDur_Mean	k-NN with the Euclidean distance, distance weight: squared inverse, k = 10	69.6%	97%	60%	60%

classifier and the set of 17 best predictors based on eye-tracking features. The accuracy in the model is the highest thanks to perfect discrimination of class "0" (as positive predictive values show). A slightly lower accuracy, but better prediction precision (PPV) for all the classes is obtained by the models with the Bagged Trees method and the set of 13 best predictors (or 21).

As presented in Table 3, the false discoveries occur mainly between observations from class "1" and "2", but as the false discovery rate (FDR) shows the rate of type I errors is the highest for class "1". Furthermore, in all models the observations from class "2" are more often falsely classified as "0" than observations from class. Additionally, the classification of class "0" has still the best precision.

Table 3. PPV and FDR for Bagged Trees classifier and the set of 13 best predictors/features

		Predicted class		
		0	1	2
True class	0	79%	13%	9%
	1	9%	65%	22%
	2	12%	23%	69%
	PPV	79%	65%	69%
	FDR	21%	35%	31%

7 Discussion and Conclusions

The results of classification for both datasets show that it is possible to discriminate between mental states. The binary classification of Dataset 1, discriminating between the cognitive workload condition and the no-task control condition, achieved the accuracy of 90% with 6 eye-tracking features as input and the SVMs classifier. A similar accuracy was also obtained by the classification model with a simpler k-NN classifier and 12 eye-tracking features as input, but in this model the positive prediction rate for the cognitive workload condition was slightly higher than the positive prediction rate for the no-task control condition. In this case, the achieved accuracy was satisfactory. Moreover, the relationships between features allowed to reduce the dimension of the classification model.

On the other hand, the multiclass classification of Dataset 2, discriminating between three mental states: a high cognitive workload condition, a low cognitive workload condition and a no-task control condition, achieved much lower accuracy due to its complexity. The maximum accuracy was 73% and was obtained for a model with the k-NN classifier and 17 eye-tracking features as input. Although the model has very high positive prediction rate for a no-task control condition, it works poorly in distinguishing between two cognitive workload conditions. For this reason, the classification model based on the Bagged Trees algorithm and a set of 13 features, identified as the key predictors with p-value < 0.01, is better for classing all states. For Dataset 2 the process of dimension reduction did not provide expected results. Moreover, the results of classification show the selection of the classification model depends on classification purpose. The best accuracy of the model does not always provide expected precision to classify the selected class or classes.

It is difficult to directly compare obtained results with other works since they compared different cognitive load levels (e.g. low-high, low-medium-high) without resting (no cognitive workload condition). The binary classification between affective states such as relaxation and stress presented in the work of Ren et al. [14] achieved the highest accuracy of 84%.

Furthermore, in multiclass classification all models more often falsely classified the observations with a high cognitive workload condition as a no-task control condition, than observations with a low cognitive workload condition as a no-task control condition, which shows more similarity between a high cognitive workload condition and a no-task control condition. It could be explained by the fact that some participants, especially in the last task interval, were fatigued and stopped to perform the arithmetic tasks. The same problem occurred during the previous designed case study and was addressed by simplifying the tasks, but apparently insufficiently for all participants. Some insights may be provided by analysis of not only the participants' reaction time, but also their number of errors in the interval. Therefore, the high and low cognitive workload condition should be assigned to an interval based on more complex analysis than only on reaction time.

Another issue was participants' eye closure during break intervals. The participants were asked to look at the centre of the computer screen with the word "Break" on it, however some of them closed their eyes to relax. Therefore, some observations had to be excluded from the analysis. To address that problem an additional warning sound could be provided when a participant looks away, as mention in another work [12]. However, with the presented hardware setup (mobile eye-tracking glasses) it was not possible. Nevertheless, to ensure that classification as a no-task control condition (and thus break intervals) does not depend on features related to blinks, additional classification was provided without those features as a input.

All participants performed the experimentation under similar stable lighting condition (fluorescent light) and during the whole experiment the light intensity of the computer screen was the same, but the participants could freely move their heads. That could affect their visual angle and change the intensity (luminance) of the light that fell on the eye. For that reason, the pupil diameter, otherwise recognised as a good indicator of cognitive workload, in the present study proved to be a weaker predictor than eye event related features.

Finally, none of the included EEG features was included as an input in the classification models with the best accuracy. The explanation may be the fact that EEG features were calculated as a dominant frequency for each waveform, and maybe another EEG measure could provide more distinction between mental states. Other issues may be the signal artifacts caused by the participants' movements since as many as 7 participants' data were excluded from analysis due to the noisy EEG signal. Increasing the number of participants in the study would allow to obtained more observations without noisy EEG signal and thus overcome those limitations.

The obtained results might be considered as exploratory work and cannot be treated as final. Additional investigation about classifier parameter's selection with the extended dataset is needed. What is more, more extended studies are necessary to provide proper validation of model accuracy and flexibility.

References

1. Gevins, A., Smith, M.E., McEvoy, L., Yu, D.: High-resolution EEG mapping of cortical activation related to working memory: effects of task difficulty, type of processing, and practice. Cereb. Cortex **7**, 374–385 (1997). doi:10.1093/cercor/7.4.374
2. Kruger, J., Doherty, S.: Measuring cognitive load in the presence of educational video: towards a multimodal methodology. Australas. J. Educ. Technol. **32**, 19–31 (2016). doi:10.14742/ajet.3084

3. O'Donnell, R.D., Eggemeier, F.T.: Workload assessment methodology. In: Handbook of Perception and Human Performance. Cognitive Processes and Performance, vol. 2. Wiley (1986)

4. Tsang, P.S., Vidulich, M.A.: Mental workload and situation awareness. In: Handbook of Human Factors and Ergonomics, 3rd edn., pp. 243–268. Wiley Online Library (2006)

5. Matthews, G., Reinerman-Jones, L.E., Barber, D.J., Abich IV, J.: The psychometrics of mental workload: multiple measures are sensitive but divergent. Hum. Factors **57**, 125–143 (2015)

6. Marshall, S.P.: The index of cognitive activity: measuring cognitive workload. In: Proceedings of IEEE 7th Conference on Human Factors and Power Plants, pp. 5–9 (2002). doi:10.1109/HFPP.2002.1042860

7. Chen, S., Epps, J., Ruiz, N., Chen, F.: Eye activity as a measure of human mental effort in HCI. In: Proceedings of the 16th International Conference on Intelligent User Interfaces, pp. 315–318. ACM, New York (2011)

8. Kiefer, P., Giannopoulos, I., Duchowski, A., Raubal, M.: Measuring cognitive load for map tasks through pupil diameter. In: Miller, J.A., O'Sullivan, D., Wiegand, N. (eds.) GIScience 2016. LNCS, vol. 9927, pp. 323–337. Springer, Cham (2016). doi:10.1007/978-3-319-45738-3_21

9. Savage, S.W., Potter, D.D., Tatler, B.W.: Does preoccupation impair hazard perception? A simultaneous EEG and eye tracking study. Transp. Res. Part F Traffic Psychol. Behav. **17**, 52–62 (2013)

10. Kruger, J.-L., Hefer, E., Matthew, G.: Measuring the impact of subtitles on cognitive load: eye tracking and dynamic audiovisual texts. In: Proceedings of Eye Tracking South Africa, pp. 6–11 (2013)

11. Ren, P., Barreto, A., Huang, J., Gao, Y., Ortega, F.R., Adjouadi, M.: Off-line and on-line stress detection through processing of the pupil diameter signal. Ann. Biomed. Eng. **42**, 162–176 (2014). doi:10.1007/s10439-013-0880-9

12. Ryu, K., Myung, R.: Evaluation of mental workload with a combined measure based on physiological indices during a dual task of tracking and mental arithmetic. Int. J. Ind. Ergon. **35**, 991–1009 (2005). doi:10.1016/j.ergon.2005.04.005

13. Chen, S., Epps, J.: Automatic classification of eye activity for cognitive load measurement with emotion interference. Comput. Methods Programs Biomed. **110**, 111–124 (2013). doi:10.1016/j.cmpb.2012.10.021

14. Ren, P., Barreto, A., Gao, Y., Adjouadi, M., Member, S.S., Barreto, A., Member, S.S.: Affective assessment by digital processing of the pupil diameter. IEEE Trans. Affect. Comput. **4**, 2–14 (2013). doi:10.1109/T-AFFC.2012.25

15. Nourbakhsh, N., Wang, Y., Chen, F.: GSR and blink features for cognitive load classification. In: Kotzé, P., Marsden, G., Lindgaard, G., Wesson, J., Winckler, M. (eds.) INTERACT 2013. LNCS, vol. 8117, pp. 159–166. Springer, Heidelberg (2013). doi:10.1007/978-3-642-40483-2_11

16. Haapalainen, E., Kim, S., Forlizzi, J.F., Dey, A.K.: Psycho-physiological measures for assessing cognitive load. In: Proceedings of the 12th ACM International Conference on Ubiquitous Computing, pp. 301–310. ACM, New York (2010)

17. Halverson, T., Estepp, J., Christensen, J., Monnin, J.: Classifying workload with eye movements in a complex task. Proc. Hum. Factors Ergon. Soc. Annu. Meet. **56**, 168–172 (2012)

18. Rozado, D., Duenser, A.: Combining EEG with pupillometry to improve cognitive workload detection. Computer (Long. Beach. Calif) **48**, 18–25 (2016). doi:10.1109/MC.2015.314

19. Lobo, J.L., Del Ser, J., Moravek, Z., De Simone, F., Presta, R., Collina, S.: Cognitive workload classification using eye-tracking and EEG data. In: Proceedings of the International Conference on Human-Computer Interaction in Aerospace, pp. 16:1–16:8. ACM, New York (2016)
20. Zarjam, P., Epps, J., Lovell, N.H.: Beyond subjective self-rating: EEG signal classification of cognitive workload (2015)
21. Skublewska-Paszkowska, M., Łukasik, E., Smołka, J., Miłosz, M., Plechawska-Wójcik, M., Borys, M., Dzieńkowski, M.: Comprehensive measurements of human motion parameters in research projects. In: Candel Torres, I., Gomez Chova, L., Lopez Martinez, A. (eds.) INTED2016 Proceedings, pp. 8597–8605. IATED Academy (2016)
22. Jolliffe, I.: Principal component analysis. Wiley Online Library (2002)
23. Kumar, N., Kumar, J.: Measurement of cognitive load in HCI systems using EEG power spectrum: an experimental study. Procedia - Procedia Comput. Sci. **84**, 70–78 (2016). doi:10.1016/j.procs.2016.04.068
24. Breiman, L., Friedman, J., Stone, C.J., Olshen, R.A.: Classification and Regression Trees. CRC Press, New York (1984)
25. Fisher, R.A.: The use of multiple measurements in taxonomic problems. Ann. Eugen. **7**, 179–188 (1936)
26. Krzanowski, W.J.: Principles of Multivariate Analysis: A User's Perspective. Clarendon, Oxford (1988)
27. Friedman, J., Hastie, T., Tibshirani, R., et al.: Additive logistic regression: a statistical view of boosting (with discussion and a rejoinder by the authors). Ann. Stat. **28**, 337–407 (2000)
28. Christianini, N., Shawe-Taylor, J.: An Introduction to Support Vector Machines and Other Kernel-Based Learning Methods. Cambridge University Press, Cambridge (2000)
29. Mitchell, T.M., et al.: Machine learning (1997)
30. Mason, L., Baxter, J., Bartlett, P.L., Frean, M.R.: Boosting algorithms as gradient descent. In: NIPS, pp. 512–518 (1999)
31. Breiman, L.: Bagging predictors. Mach. Learn. **24**, 123–140 (1996)
32. Ho, T.K.: The random subspace method for constructing decision forests. IEEE Trans. Pattern Anal. Mach. Intell. **20**, 832–844 (1998)

Evaluating Electronic Health Records Interoperability

Fadoua Khennou[1(✉)], Youness Idrissi Khamlichi[2],
and Nour El Houda Chaoui[1]

[1] TTI Laboratory, Higher School of Technology,
Sidi Mohamed Ben Abdellah University, Fes, Morocco
{fadoua.khennou,houda.chaoui}@usmba.ac.ma
[2] REIS Laboratory, Faculty of Science and Technology,
Sidi Mohamed Ben Abdellah University, Fes, Morocco
youness.khamlichi@usmba.ac.ma

Abstract. Nowadays, ensuring clinical interoperability is considered a challenging situation for health practitioners. This is due to the development of an excessive amount of electronic health record (Ehr) softwares, which do not consider the integration of the interoperability modules at an early stage. Actually, many isolated solutions are present and are unable to exchange data with other systems.

Instead of presenting new distinct solutions in terms of modeling, storage and processing techniques, we need to shed light and upgrade their current capabilities in order to end up with compatible platforms.

In this paper, we formalize and assess the interoperability concept in regards to the health sector. Our approach is an extended version of the legacy Levels of Information Systems Interoperability Model (LISI), which was originally designed in the context of The Joint Task Force (JTF) system. Through this, we define representative metrics that have to be achieved within an Ehr, and classify them according to semantical, syntactic and technological attributes. The model revealed meaningful results in firstly measuring the level of the interoperability then generating a matrix profile able to display the main gaps and shortfalls need to be enhanced so as to attain a mature stage.

Keywords: Clinical interoperability · Electronic health record · Levels of Information Systems Interoperability Model (LISI) · Semantical · Syntactic · Technical

1 Introduction

Electronic health record systems are designed to contain and share information from all providers. Their main purpose is to enable, for physicians and health care professionals, access unstructured data, perform rapid interventions and quality follow-up with their patients.

In addition to that, their integration allows patients and health care providers to securely access and share medical information from their medical records electronically. While an electronic medical record is represented just as a digital version of

© Springer International Publishing AG 2017
R. Damaševičius and V. Mikašytė (Eds.): ICIST 2017, CCIS 756, pp. 106–118, 2017.
DOI: 10.1007/978-3-319-67642-5_9

paper, an electronic health record is much more developed and can provide diversified features. From preliminary interviews, diagnostics, follow-up examinations to treatments, the information flow is always present between different Ehrs. The primary goal behind the implementation of these systems is to improve the patients' care, accelerate clinical and diagnostic analysis, manage patient history reports, avoid repetitive laboratory tests and overall boost the quality of care within health organisms.

However, if this implementation is not followed by interoperability solutions [5] to connect hospitals, community laboratories, clinics and other health institutes, so as to facilitate a secure electronic exchange of applications and clinical data, it will be arduous to take advantage from these systems' features and their added value.

That's to say, we must define, study and analyze health interoperability metrics, that will help us examine whether two health systems are interoperable or not. For that, the LISI assessment model [4] has been presented and applied for the health sector in order to measure potential interoperability between systems.

This prototype approach is beneficial for both researchers and health practitioners. Once applied, it will assist them in suggesting improvement and integrate new semantic, syntactic and technological solutions for their Ehrs.

2 Related Work

Peter Drucker said: 'if you can't measure it, you can't improve it'. Actually, the interoperability concept is represented as an abstract term, and because of that many health organisms find difficulties in enhancing it within their Ehr [7]. This has pushed us to think wisely on how to quantify this concept.

Unfortunately, there is a very minimal focus on the implementation of a conceptual model that can formalize and measure the interoperability of some given systems. Those that do exist are based only on implementing very specific technical health standard infrastructures, and do not introduce a comprehensive model that can be applied as a general case study.

Authors in [8], have presented a comparative study of some legacy interoperability models, which are based on the leveling approach. This was mainly introduced by Levels of Information Systems Interoperability (LISI) and Level on conceptual Interoperability Model (LCIM) [12], both of them can be applied for the classification of interoperability in the fields of applications and systems. While the first approach is based on the study of the technological interconnection of interoperating applications, the second focuses only on the conceptual aspect through the definition of data exchange interfaces between the communicating systems. Another leveling based approach that was proposed by ATHENA [9] (Advanced Technologies for Interoperability of Heterogeneous Enterprise Networks and their Applications) is a maturity model that covers business aspects and services within an independent enterprise.

A common drawback that can be noted toward these models, is that they are very limited and did not cover specific modules of interoperability of some actual field of studies such us the healthcare [2]. Yet, even though LISI was conceived in 1990 it has proven to be of considerable value. Introduced by the Department of Defense in the United States of America (DoD), the model proposes not only an interoperability profile but also a platform for measuring and assessing the degree of potential inter-operability between systems.

Our main goal throughout this paper is to analyze the methodological process of the LISI model and propose an extended prototype for application to healthcare. To do so, we firstly formalize the concept of interoperability based on semantical, syntactic and technological attributes, evaluate these parameters in regards to the existing systems and generate a system profile matrix. Through this process, we measure the degree of potential data exchange between two given electronic health records and define the major gaps and shortfalls.

The reminder of this paper is presented as follows. Section 3 presents a description of the LISI model and its methodological process. Section 4 describes our proposed extended model for application to healthcare. Section 5 sheds light on the implementation of a case study, for the evaluation of some existing electronic medical records. Finally, Section 6 features a conclusion of the study.

3   LISI Interoperability Model

The Levels of Information Systems Interoperability (LISI) aims at developing an interoperability profile between independent systems, the correlation of these profiles makes it possible to study the degree of potential interoperability between parties. LISI presents a reference model that defines, measures and estimates the level of interoperability that can be achieved between systems.

3.1   The Reference Model

The reference model (Fig. 1) includes five levels of maturity for interoperability, as well as a set of characteristics described below:

- **Isolated Systems:** There is no communication between applications.
- **Connected systems:** Applications are connected electronically in a local network.
- **Distributed Systems:** Heterogeneous applications can exchange data.
- **Integrated systems:** Applications can collaborate in a sophisticated way.
- **Universal systems:** The applications and their data are shared within the same organism or between distributed ones in a developed mechanism.

A classification of the interoperability through the LISI approach, is defined under the PAID abbreviation:

- **P** for procedures, reflects the procedures, approaches and standards used to establish information exchange between systems.
- **A** for applications, describes the applications that permit data exchange.
- **I** for infrastructures, outlines the hardware and network platform that insure the interaction between systems.
- **D** for data, describes the formats, protocols and semantic exchange of data.

The intersection of the presented interoperability attributes and the five levels of maturity, led to the definition of the reference model presented in Table 1.

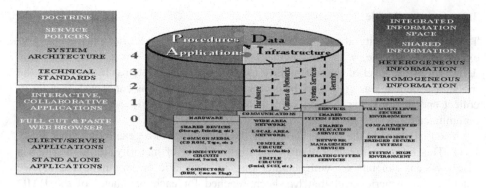

Fig. 1. LISI reference model and its related PAID modules [12]

Table 1. The current LISI reference model (LISI 1998)

Level of interoperability		Interoperability attributes			
		P	A	I	D
4-Enterprise	c	Multi-national enterprise	Interactive (cross application)	Multiple topologies	Cross enterprise
	b	Cross government			
	a	Govt enterprise			Enterprise model
3-Domain	c	Domain level	Groupware	World wide networks	Domain models
	b				
	a				
2-Functional	c	Common operating environment	Desktop automation	Local networks	Program model and advanced data formats
	b				
	a	Program			
1-Connected	d	Standards compliant	Basic messaging	Single connection	Basic data formats
	c				
	b	Site level	System drivers		
	a				
0-Isolated	d	Access	N/A	Removable media	Media
	c				
	b	Control		Manual entry	Private
	a				
	0	No known interoperability			

The background of the PAID concept, was originally conceived in the context of the US task force missions. Each part of the described modules was particularly perceived to enhance system to system interactions. These attributes define a set of components for the commutation of services at each level of sophistication. It helps in specifying the point of weaknesses and gaps within a given architectural system.

3.2   System Profile

The main particularity about the implementation of LISI model lies on its ability to express the outcome, with the calculation of three metrics. These latter allow the definition of the level of interoperability for two operating systems. In this sense, the model assessment was guided by Inspector, a software that was conceived in order to collect and illustrate the features on which two systems could be based on so as to communicate.

The first phase of the process concerns the calculation of a generic interoperability level. This refers to the definition of the highest level of maturity, through which a given system can interact with another one in a specific environment. Hence, we calculate the generic level that has been reached for each parameter of the PAID modules. The second stage reflects the measurement of an expected interoperability level, which is accomplished by comparing two systems' generic level and designating the lowest one. This metric is generally calculated in order to demonstrate the expected level where two systems can operate. At last, a specific interoperability level is needed so as to compare two systems' detailed implementations and features that are checked in regards to the PAID modules.

3.3   System Interoperability Matrix

The final stage of the implementation of the model depicts a matrix, which takes the generic level as a parameter. The intersection of the values for each couple of systems gives rise to the specific interoperability level.

Let's consider an example of an assessment matrix represented in Table 2. The intersection of the generic levels for system D and system C is represented by the specific level 1c. Furthermore, the expected level is calculated by defining the lowest value for both systems, which is also 1c. Here the LISI model indicates that, if the specific level is equal to the expected one, both systems are able to communicate and operate appropriately. However, if the specific level is less than the expected one, then the communication process is limited and there are some actual differences in the features of the examined systems. At last, if the specific level is higher than the

Table 2. Interoperability LISI matrix

Generic Level		A	B	C	D	E	F	G
		2a	1a	1c	2b	3c	2b	1a
A	2a	2a						
B	1a	1a	2a					
C	1c	1a	1a	1b				
D	2b	2a	1a	1c	2b			
E	3c	2a	1a	2c	2b	3c		
F	2b	2a	1a	2b	2b	1c	2b	
G	1a	1a	2a	1a	2a	1a	1a	1a

expected one, we can say that the communication process is very mature and major capabilities of the PAID modules give the qualification to communicate in a high sophisticated level.

4 Proposed Extended Model

In this section, we introduce and analyze the main attributes that define health inter-operability, then we describe the process of their integration to the extended prototype based LISI model.

4.1 Health Interoperability Metrics

We can consider an Ehr as interoperable, if it has the ability to operate with other existing or future systems without any barriers. In other words, the interoperability concept is based on a common and explicit understanding of the information exchanged between different partners, and carried out to enable applications exchanging and interpreting information in a homogeneous way. Besides, the workflow has to guarantee an exchange based on three major attributes: semantics, syntax and technology.

Semantic
The aim is to define a common vocabulary that will be used in electronic health records to name a particular medical concept. Semantic interoperability needs to ensure that the exact meaning of the information exchanged is understandable by any other application.

For an electronic healthcare system, this interoperability aspect has to guarantee the development of health reference models, templates and terminologies, allowing formal representation of health data according to international standards.

Reference Model
A reference model combines various assets and health standards, allowing the defini-tion of a common format between several medical organizations. The benefit, is to improve communication, define the scope, the context of health services and enable the re-use for health programs. In this context, several health standards [3] are adopted e.g. HL7, OpenEHR, EN 13606, EN/ISO 12967, HPRIM. Through these, the modeling of clinical data structures such as medical prescriptions, structured documents, blood pressure results and others can be attained with the use of archetypes or special entities, which are designed specifically to accommodate the concepts of health services.

Terminologies and Bindings
This concerns a common modeling of health data types by defining terminology sys-tems for an electronic health record. Coding health data entries is a way of using different terminologies and clinical code domains systems [1] e.g. LOINC, SNOMED CT. As for terminology bindings, it refers to the association of terminology components and an information model of a given health standard. Through this, each terminology set or coded value, which corresponds to specific clinical domains, are

mapped to the information model classes and attributes used to describe a medical concept. In this level, semantic interoperability can evolve by incorporating data from varied systems in one place and interpret exchanged data by its relevant meaning.

Syntactic

This expresses the definition of a common computer formats in order to interconnect various softwares and exchange data. In other words, this requires the definition of a common structure and context between varied medical parties. The syntactic interoperability concerns the way in which data is encoded and formatted. Different formats can be included for sound, photo, image, character encoding, aggregates of several objects and documents formats. In this context, messaging standards are adopted such as Health Level 7, which describes the format for a computerized exchange of clinical data. This leads to the implementation of an open system allowing to assume the heterogeneity of its components.

Technical

Technical interoperability delineates the integration of communication, network protocols and infrastructural technologies. Here, we can define the characteristics of physical medias allowing the storage of the data, its management, security and migration to other supports. It also maintains the replication of records and documents on distant sites.

4.2   Extended Model

As the LISI model demonstrated a broad use of the profiling concept in order to calculate the level of interoperability between systems, the health sector is among the leading industries that requires an interoperable platform [6, 10], which not only supports an information health system, but also a technological platform able to exchange medical data at different levels. In this vein, it is necessary to classify the general attributes defining the interoperability within an electronic health system.

We integrated the interoperability components need to be achieved within an electronic health record system, into the formal model of interoperability LISI. The level of maturity increases according to the attributes related to the semantics, the syntax and the technologies SST used within a health organization. In Table 3, we present our extended LISI model for application to the health sector.

1. **Isolated:** This level describes an initial primitive layer, though which no interoperability can be distinguished. The latter does not define any communication channel and known to be as "not connected".
2. **Connected:** We considered splitting this layer into two parts. The first concerns an elemental communication process of unstructured medical data records such as: clinical notes, prescription paper charts and discharge summaries. The delivery of these documents is based on a basic platform, which does not support any technological structure. The second one defines a first semantical contextualization of data exchanged between small services of a given health institute.
3. **Functional:** In the third layer, a gradual progression has been demonstrated by an internal local network, allowing a continuous flow of medical data to be stored,

Table 3. The extended prototype of LISI for e-health systems

Level of interoperability			Health interoperability attributes		
			Semantic	Syntactic	Technology
Enterprise	4	b	Multi-national agreement	Cross enterprise model	Multiple topologies
		a	National agreement	Enterprise model	Centralized topology
Domain	3	c	Reference model	Advanced Electronic health records	Security compliance
		b	Terminology bindings	Electronic health records (Ehr)	Metropolitan network (MAN)
		a	Terminologies, ontologies	Domain based data models	Subdomains network
Functional	2	b	Standards compliance	Program model (Emr)	Web based access
		a	Health information system	Advanced data formats	Local network (LAN)
Connected	1	b	Contextualization	Administration data entry support	Single connection
		a	N/A	Clinical notes, prescription paper charts, discharge records, nurse/doctor notes...	Basic messaging
Isolated	0	0	N/A	N/A	N/A

queried and manipulated. This consists of using web services, databases, Electronic Medical Records to store, process and model a Health Information System (HIS).

4. **Domain:** Here we attain a high level of maturity, since we recognize a partial or complete integration of health standards for instance: OpenEHR, HL7, HPRIM and others. The domain level can be earned by implementing an Electronic Health Record using common clinical code domains, health terminologies and ontologies. As for ensuring an integral exchange between different medical domains, we note the integration of security and privacy modules in the Ehr system.

5. **Enterprise:** The last layer allows to define a communication process at a high level. It consists of ensuring a centralized or distributed architecture of several connected Ehr coming from myriad health organizations. Semantically, this can be carried out through a formalization of a national or international standard allowing to regroup major health procedures.

Through the presented prototype (see Fig. 2), we apprehend that in order to communicate at a mature level, it is necessary to acquire procedures, health standards, technologies and primordial methods to meet the three major criterion of health interpretability.

Therefore, this makes it easy to define the current state of a given medical organization and improve it by acknowledging the SST modules.

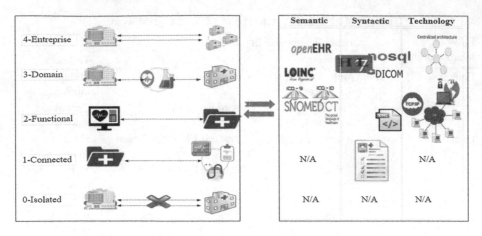

Fig. 2. Extended (SST) metrics for application to healthcare

5 Evaluation

In this part of our paper, we emphasize on the implementation of the described approach, using a case study, in order to measure and evaluate health interoperability of some existing Ehrs.

5.1 A Case Study

The first step is the generation of a generic interoperability profile for each presented system. Table 4 summarizes an interoperability profile generated for the OpenEmr project [11]. This is based on the assessment of the main capabilities (SST) that we previously described for the extended prototype.

Through an in-depth research analysis, we summarized the key features and usage components of OpenEmr and applied them to the extended prototype. As for its generic interoperability metric, it can be calculated by specifying the highest level of sophistication that can be achieved, using the described system's components. In this case, the metric is 3a which is a result of the lowest value of the defined SST (S:3a, S:3a, T:3c).

We applied the same process for a sample of some existing Emrs and Ehrs [13]. Table 5, outlines the results of their reported generic level.

While the generic level measures only the value that corresponds to each particular system, the expected and specific levels calculate the degree by assembling two distinct electronic health records. Meaning, we compare the ability of two systems to operate and exchange data in a specific level of sophistication. Figure 3, displays the generated assessment matrix of the presented Ehrs.

Here, the matrix indicates the specific level of interoperability resulting from the comparison of distinct electronic health records. By doing so, we can summarize the gaps and shortfalls need to be enhanced for each Ehr.

Table 4. The generic interoperability profile (OpenEmr)

Level of interoperability			Health Interoperability Attributes		
			Semantic	Syntactic	Technology
Enterprise	4	b	Multi-national agreement	Cross enterprise model	Multiple topologies
		a	National agreement	Enterprise model	Centralized topology
Domain	3	c	Reference model	Advanced Electronic health records	HIPAA
		b	Terminology bindings	Electronic health records	Metropolitan network (MAN)
		a	ICD-9 ICD-10 SNOMED RxNorm SNOMED	Domain based data models	Subdomains network
Functional	2	b	Standards compliance	Medical practice management software	HTTP
		a	Health information system	Advanced data formats	Local network (LAN)
Connected	1	b	Contextualization	Administration data entry support	Single connection
		a	N/A	Clinical notes, prescription paper charts, discharge records, nurse/doctor notes…	Basic messaging
Isolated	0	0	N/A	N/A	N/A

Table 5. Generic interoperability level of a sample of Ehr systems

Electronic health records		Reported level
A	OpenEmr	3a
B	Cottage Med	2a
C	Gnuhealth	3c
D	HospitalOS	2b
E	OpenEhr	4a

Generic		A	B	C	D	E
Level		3a	2a	3c	2b	4a
A	3a	3a				
B	2a	2a	2a			
C	3c	3a	1a	3c		
D	2b	2b	2b	3a	2b	
E	4a	3a	2a	3c	1b	4a

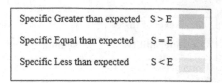

Specific Greater than expected   S > E

Specific Equal than expected   S = E

Specific Less than expected   S < E

Fig. 3. Specific versus expected level assessment matrix

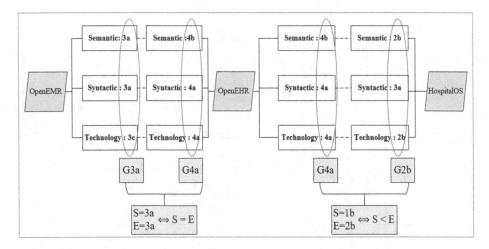

Fig. 4. Evaluation of interoperability level based on (SST)

The results revealed form the evaluation matrix that, while some Ehrs can communicate in synchronization without barriers (OpenEmr to OpenEhr), others have limited capacities with respect to the SST modules.

In fact, if we take for instance OpenEHR and HospitalOS, we note the existence of major gaps (see Fig. 4). This is mainly due to the HospitalOS profiling system, which has lower capabilities in regards to the SST metrics. Hence, in order to improve their exchange, it is necessary to integrate the needed health modules starting from the connected level, as it is the high level of sophistication that HospitalOS has achieved.

On the contrary, OpenEHR to OpenEmr link indicates that an exchange of data can be performed without problems, since the specific and the expected level are equivalent. In fact, OpenEHR has a widely developed platform and represents a reference model that allows an easy integration of different health terminologies and ontologies. In this sense, the two Ehrs will operate and share data according to the lowest level which corresponds to the OpenEmr system profile.

As a summary, the Ehr systems can exchange data at the basis of their system profile, which may either meet the requirements of the SST attributes or need to upgrade their capabilities starting from their achieved level.

6 Conclusion

In this paper, we presented an evaluation methodology based on LISI interoperability model, through which we proposed a novel prototype for application to the health sector. This was assessed by the integration of the semantic, syntactic and technology (SST) modules. The implementation process allowed the evaluation of some existing electronic health records along with a successful measurement of the interoperability level. At last, an assessment matrix was generated to illustrate the ability of two systems to exchange health data.

This study will push researchers to focus more on improving interoperability solutions, rather than conceiving new Ehr softwares with novel distinct technologies. A major perspective of this prototype is the conception of a linear regression model based on the correlation between the (SST) modules, in order to measure precisely the metrics of each defined parameter.

References

1. Aso, S., et al.: Analyzing SNOMED CT and HL7 terminology binding for semantic interoperability on post-genomic clinical trials. Stud. Health Technol. Inform. **192**, 980 (2013)
2. Bhartiya, S., Mehrotra, D., Girdhar, A.: Issues in achieving complete interoperability while sharing electronic health records. Procedia Comput. Sci. **78**, 192–198 (2016)
3. Ed Hammond, W.: Standards for global health information systems. In: Global Health Informatics, pp. 94–108. Elsevier (2017)
4. C4ISR Architecture Working Group: Levels of Information Systems Interoperability (LISI) (1998)
5. Iroju, O., et al.: Interoperability in healthcare: benefits, challenges and resolutions. Int. J. Innov. Appl. Stud. **3**(1), 262–270 (2013)
6. Jaulent, M.-C., et al.: Semantic interoperability challenges to process large amount of data perspectives in forensic and legal medicine. J. Forensic Leg. Med. (2016)
7. Noumeir, R.: Requirements for interoperability in healthcare information systems. J. Healthc. Eng. **3**(2), 323–346 (2012)
8. Rezaei, R., Chiew, T.-k., Lee, S.-p.: A review of interoperability assessment models. J. Zhejiang Univ. Sci. C **14**(9), 663–681 (2013)
9. Ruggaber, R.: ATHENA - Advanced technologies for interoperability of heterogeneous enterprise networks and their applications. In: Konstantas, D., et al. (eds.) Interoperability of Enterprise Software and Applications, vol. 1, pp. 459–460. Springer, London (2006)
10. Sachdeva, S., Bhalla, S.: Semantic interoperability in standardized electronic health record databases. J. Data Inf. Qual. **3**(1), 1–37 (2012)

11. Synitech. openemr/openemr. GitHub. https://github.com/openemr/openemr. Accessed 28 Mar 2017
12. Wang, W., Tolk, A., Wang, W.: The levels of conceptual interoperability model: applying systems engineering principles to M&S. arXiv:0908.0191 [cs] (2009)
13. Zaidan, A.A., et al.: Multi-criteria analysis for OS-EMR software selection problem: a comparative study. Decis. Support Syst. **78**, 15–27 (2015)

Implementation and Evaluation of a Decision Support Systems for the Patients of a Laboratory Service

Georgy Kopanitsa[1,2(✉)] ⓘ and Zhanna Kopanitsa[1]

[1] Institute Cybernetic Center, Tomsk Polytechnic University, Tomsk, Russia
georgy.kopanitsa@gmail.com
[2] Tomsk State University for Architecture and Building, Tomsk, Russia

Abstract. The problem of a decision support of a laboratory service patients originates from the fact that in Russia most patients address laboratory services directly without being referred by a doctor. This leads to the problem of interpretation of test results by the patients without sufficient medical background. So, we have a situation when there is no doctor who can professionally interpret the results. This problem can be solved by a laboratory service if it can provide not only the results of the tests but also their interpretations. This task can be delegated to a decision support system, which can automatically generate interpretation reports and send them to the patients. We have implemented and evaluated such a system in the Helix laboratory service in Saint-Petersburg, Russia. Now, it generates about 3500 reports a day. The implementation of the system allowed increasing the number of patients who refer to a doctor after laboratory tests by 14%. A qualitative study with 100 patients demonstrated a high acceptance of the system. The majority (82%) of the patients reported that they trust the system and follow its advice to visit a doctor if necessary.

Keywords: Decision support · Laboratory information system · Telemedicine · First order predicates

1 Introduction

Automated decision support systems that have proved their efficiency for doctors can be a good solution for the problem of diagnostics decision support [1]. The experience of development and implementation of decision support systems for doctors shows the efficiency of such solutions for the doctors, however, developers face problems when it comes to the decision support for patients. They require different approach in data presentation and interpretation [8, 9, 14, 15].

Studies [19, 20] have demonstrated that many providers do not have systems, which can ensure that the results of the tests completed reliably communicated to patients. As shown in [5, 26] normal and abnormal test results are commonly missed, even in when a health care system has a wide use of electronic health records (EHRs), and that providers miss 1–10% of abnormal test results. A systematic review made by Callen et al. found that, across 19 published studies, 6.8–62% of lab tests were not followed up on [4].

R. Damaševičius and V. Mikašytė (Eds.): ICIST 2017, CCIS 756, pp. 119–128, 2017.
DOI: 10.1007/978-3-319-67642-5_10

In a specific situation when a patient directly refers to a laboratory service, one shall be very careful when sending results by mail or providing them on a web portal [11, 13, 17]. It should be presumed that the recipient of the reports will not correctly understand the meaning of the results [10, 12, 16, 21]. So, the ability of the system to deliver information in a way it will be understood by a non-health care professional is crucial to inform motivate a patient refer to a doctor especially in case of abnormal results [4].

Interpretation of test results is a resource consuming task that can delay the results and increase costs of each test [22, 23, 27]. However, this can be done by computer decision support systems that proved to solve such tasks efficiently [24, 25]. So the design and implementation of a decision support system that would generate reports for the patients who referred to a laboratory service without a doctor's referral can increase motivation and support patients to make better informed decisions to follow up on the results of the tests.

The goals of the design and implementation of the decision support system for the patients were to:

1. deliver a personalized tool to inform patients on the results of laboratory tests.
2. empower patients to make informed decision on the tactics of their treatment.
3. help patients understand the doctor and be prepared for a visit.

To achieve these goals, we have developed a decision support system that solves a classification problem and defines the following parameters based on the results of laboratory tests:

1. diagnosis (group of diagnoses).
2. recommendations to run other laboratory tests.
3. recommendation to refer to a specialist doctor.

This paper presents the development, implementation and evaluation of a decision support system for the patients of a test center.

2   Methods

2.1   Implementation

To achieve the described above goal a decision support system must solve a classification problem by associating a vector of test results to a set of diagnoses and find a set of recommendations associated with every diagnosis from this set.

On the next step, we have developed a classification algorithm that has the following possible outcomes:

Found a set of diagnoses that can be associated to the results of the laboratory test. No diagnosis found.

Found a set of diagnoses, but the system requires extra test or vital signs to choose the proper diagnosis form this set.

To organize a communication between the system and an expert we have implemented a knowledge representation language (KRL) that is based on the first order predicate logic [18].

After the knowledge representation language was implemented we have developed a graphical user interface to allow experts filling in the knowledge base. For the pilot project, we have chosen a limited set of laboratory tests that could be interpreted by the system to test the feasibility of the approach. We have invited 3 laboratory doctors and 3 specialist doctors (gynecologist, urologist and general practitioner) to fill in the system's knowledge base.

The inference engine if the system generated and sent a patients' report when all the tests of an order were completed.

We did not intend to make the system prescriptive and make the patient come to a specific treatment decision. So we made the generated patients' reports as descriptive as possible to be rather informative than indicatory. The reports intended to motivate patients refer to a doctor for a consultation.

The knowledge representation language, knowledge base and the classification algorithm were developed as a Doctor Ease decision support system, which was implemented in the Helix laboratory service in Saint-Petersburg, Russia.

2.2   Evaluation

Correctness of the decision support

To evaluate the correctness of the generated reports a validation of a sample of 256 reports was sent to two independent laboratory service physicians for independent expert review. The results of the review was used to calculate precision ((All terms − Mistakes)/All terms), recall (ratio of true positives to (true positives + false negatives)), and F-measure $\left(2 \cdot \frac{recall \cdot precision}{recall + precision}\right)$ [7]. All the disagreements between reviewers were settled by consensus. Cohen's kappa has been calculated to rate the disagreement between experts [2].

User acceptance

To evaluate the user acceptance of the decision support system we have applied a Wilson and Lankton's model of patients' acceptance of e-health solutions [23]. The model was applied to measure behavioral intention to use (BI), intrinsic motivation (IM), perceived ease-of-use (PEOU), and perceived usefulness (PU) of the system.

BI denotes the intention to use and rely on the decision support system, IM denotes the readiness to use the decision support system without any compensation, PEOU denotes the extent to which the generated reports are clear and understood by the patients, and PU refers to the degree to which the user believes that the use of the system would enhance their experience with laboratory tests.

We have applied the method proposed by Davis et al. [6] in the revision of Wilson and Lankton [28] to measure BI, PEOU, and PU. IM was measured using the method provided by Davis et al. [25].

BI measure contained of 2 items whereas IM, PEOU, and PU contained 3 items each. We used Russian translations of the measurement tools made by the research team. To rate each item a Likert scale from 1 (not at all) to 7 (very much). was applied.

Table 1. Demographic details of the patients

Gender	Average age	Age >60	Education			IT habits		
			Higher	Secondary	Below secondary	Beginners	Intermediate	Advanced
28 Males	41.3	8	9	14	5	3	17	8
32 Females	42.3	6	11	18	3	8	4	0
Total 60								

Recruitment

Participants were recruited in Saint-Petersburg, Russia. The inclusion criteria were: having experience with the decision support system with at least 5 reports on the test results.

Demographic details of the patients are presented in the Table 1. IT literacy of the patients was evaluated based on how often they use PC or Smartphones. The IT literacy was graded from beginners – users that have started using PC within 6 months; intermediate – users of PC at least twice a week; and advanced – for those using PC on the daily basis.

Data collection and analysis

The participants were asked to complete an online questionnaire. Each participant got an individual link and could work only with one questionnaire. A detailed instruction on how to work with a questionnaire and the meaning of the scale was provided to each participant.

GNU Octave was used to calculate statistics of the participants' general characteristics and user acceptance measurements.

The study got the approval by the regional ethics committee. All the participants invited to the study were notified of the objectives of the study and of the purpose of the questionnaires. Each participant was assured, in writing, of their entitlement to anonymity and confidentiality. Written consent was acquired from each participant and each participant was reminded of their entitlement to withdraw data from the study database for up to three months after their approval.

3   Results

The developed decision support system has a traditional structure and consists of the following modules:

- Data base;
- Data extraction system;
- Knowledge base;
- Inference engine;
- Knowledge base editor;
- Explanation system;
- Results generator;

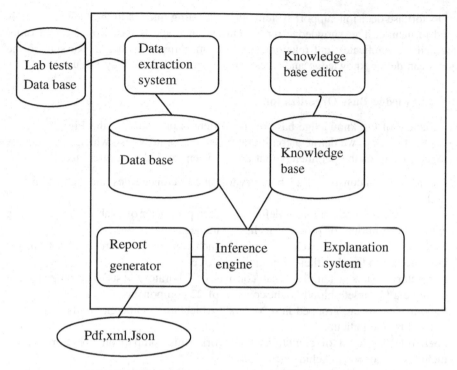

Fig. 1. Structural scheme of the decision support system

A structural scheme of the system is presented in the Fig. 1.

- Each module provides the following functionality to the expert system.
- Data base with a dynamical structure stores facts (test results) and intermediate results of the logical inference. The facts are taken from a laboratory information system (LIS).
- Knowledge base of the DoctorEase stores expert knowledge and inference rules.
- Inference engine applies knowledge and rules form the knowledge base to the facts form the data base to solve the classification task.
- Knowledge base editor provides a user interface to define new knowledge and rules.
- Explanation system analyses the sequence of the rules to explain how the system achieved the result.

The developed decision support system has two main use cases: knowledge acquisition and decision support. Knowledge acquisition mode allows defining inference rules, which are complex objects and each of them adds its element to the resulting inference. The knowledge is defined by associating test results and its reference value to a set of diagnoses. In the decision support mode, the system generates recommendations applying a set of knowledge and rules to the facts that are derived form a LIS data base.

DoctorEase decision support system allows creating queries in the language that is closed to natural. The knowledge representation language is based on the first order logic and the predicates and relationships have meaningful names in Russian so the experts can define knowledge and rules using the terminology they are used to.

3.1 Knowledge Base Organization

The structure of the knowledge base of the system is presented in the Fig. 2.

On the first step, we define a configuration of a laboratory test, which is a complex object consisting of the parameters that are sufficient to make an inference.

- A configuration consists of a laboratory test and inference rules, that can be applied to the test.
- A direct rule is an object that is defined for each parameter of a laboratory test along with the conditions for processing these parameters.
- Each rule has a list of exclusion rules, which can exclude direct rules from the inference provided that their conditions are true.
- Laboratory test is a template that consists of laboratory tests' components. For example a Complete blood count consists of 22 components.
- Laboratory tests are grouped into "orders", which are commercial units that can be ordered by the patients.
- Each rule has a set of conditions that work with comparison operators: =, <>, includes (>= or =<), excludes (>= and =<).
- Conditions are associated with each other by logical operators "and", "or" and "not".

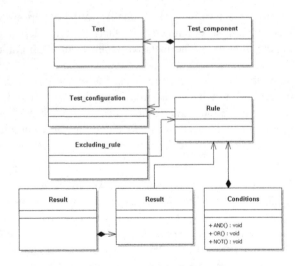

Fig. 2. Object model of DoctorEase

3.2   Inference Process

After the system has received a notification that the laboratory test results are available it starts the inference according to the following algorithm:

1. Patient's order is analyzed to understand if there exist configurations for such orders.
2. Fact (test results) are loaded to the decision support system's data base.
3. The inference engine defines a sequence of rules from the knowledge base to be applied to the facts.
4. Exclusion rules are applied to the facts to exclude non-valid rules from the inference.
5. Result blocks are added to the result file according to the rules' sequence.

3.3   Implementation

The system was implemented in the Helix laboratory service in Saint-Petersburg, Russia. At the moment it generates about 3500 reports a day.

3.4   Evaluation

Correctness

As described in the methods section a sample of 256 reports was independently reviewed by two laboratory physicians of the laboratory service.

The results of evaluation (e.g. precision, recall and F-measure) for each are presented in Table 2. Cohen's kappa was calculated to check the inter-rater agreement between the two laboratory physicians. The physicians showed disagreement in the case of 2 reports.

Table 2. Reports' quality evaluation

Analyzed reports	Mistakes	Precision	Recall	F-measure	Cohen's kappa
256	19 (7%)	0.93	0.93	0.93	0.99

Acceptance

The mean values for BI, IM, PEOU, and PU (5.9, 6.2, 5.7, and 5.9 respectively) showed the high acceptance of the decision support system and the reports, which it generates (Table 3).

Table 3. Acceptance evaluation metrics

Criterion, item	Mean value
Behavioral intention to use	5.9
I intend to use the	5.7
I feel like I will use it in the future	6.1
Intrinsic motivation	6.2
I find the system to be useful for me	6.2
The system helps me to make more informed decisions	5.9
The system is reliable and I trust it	6.4
Perceived ease of use	5.7
The reports are clear and understandable	6.3
It is easy to access the reports	5.7
I like that I can keep all my reports in the electronic format	5.4
Perceived usefulness	5.9
Using the system enhances the effectiveness of managing my health conditions	5.7
It explains me what my health status is	6.1
I can provide all the information about my test results to any doctor I visit	5.9

4 Discussion and Conclusion

The paper presents a process of development and implementation of a decision support system for laboratory service patients. The system allows patients reading and understanding medical records in natural language. For the laboratory service the system allowed increasing the level of satisfaction of the patients and the number of patients who came back to the laboratory service for more detailed testing.

One of our measures of feasibility was the percent of patients who agreed to pilot test the decision tool. We were surprised that 100% agreed, given the fact that this population is older and therefore may be more likely to favor a more traditional, paternalistic approach to decision-making.

Current research is focused on the extension of the knowledge representation language by adding an ability to work with fuzzy sets [3]. This will provide experts with flexibility in definition of knowledge and rules. We also are studying the possibility to validate the reports that are produced by DoctorEase to enable the system acquiring knowledge based on its experience.

We also are working on the mobile application to enhance user experience and make the tool interactive.

References

1. Ahmadian, L., van Engen-Verheul, M., Bakhshi-Raiez, F., Peek, N., Cornet, R., de Keizer, N.F.: The role of standardized data and terminological systems in computerized clinical decision support systems: literature review and survey. Int. J. Med. Inform. **80**, 81–93 (2011)

2. Berry, K.J., Johnston, J.E., Mielke Jr., P.W.: Weighted kappa for multiple raters. Percept. Mot. Skills **107**, 837–848 (2008)

3. Boegl, K., Adlassnig, K.P., Hayashi, Y., Rothenfluh, T.E., Leitich, H.: Knowledge acquisition in the fuzzy knowledge representation framework of a medical consultation system. Artif. Intell. Med. **30**, 1–26 (2004)

4. Callen, J.L., Westbrook, J.I., Georgiou, A., Li, J.: Failure to follow-up test results for ambulatory patients: a systematic review. J. Gen. Intern. Med. **27**, 1334–1348 (2012)

5. Casalino, L.P., Dunham, D., Chin, M.H., Bielang, R., Kistner, E.O., Karrison, T.G., Ong, M. K., Sarkar, U., McLaughlin, M.A., Meltzer, D.O.: Frequency of failure to inform patients of clinically significant outpatient test results. Arch. Intern. Med. **169**, 1123–1129 (2009)

6. Davis, F.D., Bagozzi, R.P., Warshaw, P.R.: User acceptance of computer technology: a comparison of two theoretical models. Manage. Sci. **35**, 982–1003 (1989)

7. Kawada, T.: Sample size in receiver-operating characteristic (ROC) curve analysis. Circ. J. **76**, 768 (2012). Author reply 769

8. Kopanitsa, G.: Standard based multiclient medical data visualization. Stud. Health Technol. Inform. **180**, 199–203 (2012)

9. Kopanitsa, G.: Evaluation study for a multi-user oriented medical data visualization method. Stud. Health Technol. Inform. **200**, 158–160 (2014)

10. Kopanitsa, G.: Evaluation study for an ISO 13606 archetype based medical data visualization method. J. Med. Syst. **39**, 82 (2015)

11. Kopanitsa, G.: Development of a web portal using open source information visualization libraries. Stud. Health Technol. Inform. **221**, 123 (2016)

12. Kopanitsa, G., Hildebrand, C., Stausberg, J., Englmeier, K.H.: Visualization of medical data based on EHR standards. Methods Inf. Med. **52**, 43–50 (2013)

13. Kopanitsa, G., Karpov, A., Lakovenko, G., Laskovenko, A., Yampolsky, V.: Exploring barriers and opportunities for adoption of web portals in Russia. Example of a Tuberculosis portal. Stud. Health Technol. Inform. **224**, 170–174 (2016)

14. Kopanitsa, G., Tsvetkova, Z., Veseli, H.: Analysis of metrics for the usability evaluation of EHR management systems. Stud. Health Technol. Inform. **180**, 358–362 (2012)

15. Kopanitsa, G., Tsvetkova, Z., Veseli, H.: Analysis of metrics for the usability evaluation of electronic health record systems. Stud. Health Technol. Inform. **174**, 129–133 (2012)

16. Kopanitsa, G., Veseli, H., Yampolsky, V.: Development, implementation and evaluation of an information model for archetype based user responsive medical data visualization. J. Biomed. Inform. **55**, 196–205 (2015)

17. Kopanitsa, G., Yampolsky, V.: Exploring barriers and opportunities for adoption of web portals in Russia. Stud. Health Technol. Inform. **221**, 87–91 (2016)

18. Michalski, R.S.: Pattern recognition as rule-guided inductive inference. IEEE Trans. Pattern Anal. Mach. Intell. **2**, 349–361 (1980)

19. Murff, H.J., Gandhi, T.K., Karson, A.K., Mort, E.A., Poon, E.G., Wang, S.J., Fairchild, D. G., Bates, D.W.: Primary care physician attitudes concerning follow-up of abnormal test results and ambulatory decision support systems. Int. J. Med. Inform. **71**, 137–149 (2003)

20. Poon, E.G., Gandhi, T.K., Sequist, T.D., Murff, H.J., Karson, A.S., Bates, D.W.: "I wish I had seen this test result earlier!": Dissatisfaction with test result management systems in primary care. Arch. Intern. Med. **164**, 2223–2228 (2004)

21. Pyshniak, V., Fotina, I., Zverava, A., Siamkouski, S., Zayats, E., Kopanitsa, G., Okuntsau, D.: Efficiency of biological versus physical optimization for single-arc VMAT for prostate and head and neck cases. J. Appl. Clin. Med. Phys. **15**, 4514 (2014)

22. Quanjer, P.H., Stanojevic, S., Thompson, B.R.: Spirometric thresholds and biased interpretation of test results. Thorax **69**, 1146 (2014)

23. Ross, J.S.: Ensuring correct interpretation of diagnostic test results. JAMA Intern. Med. **174**, 993 (2014)
24. Semenov, I., Kopanitsa, G.: Implementation of a decision support system for interpretation of laboratory tests for patients. Stud. Health Technol. Inform. **221**, 79–83 (2016)
25. Semenov, I., Kopanitsa, G., Karpov, A., Lakovenko, G., Laskovenko, A.: Implementation of a clinical decision support system for interpretation of laboratory tests for patients. Stud. Health Technol. Inform. **224**, 184–188 (2016)
26. Sung, S., Forman-Hoffman, V., Wilson, M.C., Cram, P.: Direct reporting of laboratory test results to patients by mail to enhance patient safety. J. Gen. Intern. Med. **21**, 1075–1078 (2006)
27. Trotz-Williams, L.A., Mercer, N.J., Paphitis, K., Walters, J.M., Wallace, D., Kristjanson, E., Gubbay, J., Mazzulli, T.: Challenges in interpretation of diagnostic test results in a mumps outbreak in a highly vaccinated population. Clin. Vaccine Immunol. **24** (2017)
28. Wilson, E.V., Lankton, N.K.: Modeling patients' acceptance of provider-delivered e-health. J. Am. Med. Inform. Assoc. **11**, 241–248 (2004)

AHP Model for Quality Evaluation
of Healthcare System

Dalia Kriksciuniene and Virgilijus Sakalauskas[✉]

Department of Informatics, Vilnius University,
Universiteto str. 3, Vilnius, Lithuania
{dalia.kriksciuniene,
virgilijus.sakalauskas}@khf.vu.lt

Abstract. The issue of healthcare quality is continuously analysed worldwide, as it is a costly investment which takes significant part of country budgets. The EU wide healthcare costs have already overcome €1,400 billion/year, and have a faster raising trend comparing to the GDP levels of member countries. The variety of models, abundance of indicators and inconsistency of statistical information used for quality evaluation in healthcare leads to numerous attempts of solving this task in the scientific literature. The article aims to evaluate healthcare quality by taking into account the importance of indicators by applying expert based AHP (Analytic Hierarchy Process) method and the regression analysis of health statistics. The rankings of EU countries according to their healthcare investment types and costs were developed and evaluated.

Keywords: Quality evaluation · Healthcare system · Analytic Hierarchy Process (AHP) · EU countries healthcare statistics

1 Introduction

The main concepts of discussion in the contemporary healthcare are related to defining the standards of quality of care, increasing efficiency of investments and exploring of cost containment problem, which could reduce healthcare costs without losing its quality.

Following the Institute of Medicine, quality of care is defined as "the degree to which health services for individuals and populations increase the likelihood of desired health outcomes and are consistent with current professional knowledge" (Institute of Medicine 2001). Quality of healthcare includes the aspect of decision making, as it should allow individuals have their preferences met in terms of treatment options.

Quality of healthcare is evaluated according to six main dimensions (Institute of Medicine 2001):

- Effective, and improve health outcomes;
- Safe, and prevent avoidable harm related with care;
- Appropriate, and comply with current professional knowledge as well as meeting agreed standards;

© Springer International Publishing AG 2017
R. Damaševičius and V. Mikašytė (Eds.): ICIST 2017, CCIS 756, pp. 129–141, 2017.
DOI: 10.1007/978-3-319-67642-5_11

- Involve persons/patients as key partners in the process of care;
- Efficient and leading to the best value for money invested and to equal access to available care of the same level of quality for all.

The task is to investigate how quality of care can be assessed in order to validate processes, tools, treatments in healthcare systems without undermining accessibility and affordability. However, the dimensions and determinants that define quality of care have no standard format yet. Numerous indicators are evaluated by the medical organizations for characterizing the situation and dynamics of healthcare issues.

The model proposed by Donabedian (1988) is a common framework for assessing health care quality and identifies three domains in which health care quality can be assessed: structure, process, and outcomes (Shi and Singh 2015).

The research presented in this article analyses the problem of EU healthcare system performance measurement by suggesting quality/efficiency measurement framework using AHP method. The research takes into account complex interrelations of the performance criteria, which are arranged to hierarchical structure, and possibility to introduce expert judgment. The following sections discuss the importance of weighting of healthcare quality evaluation criteria and their arrangement in hierarchical structure as proposed by group of experts. The Sect. 3 analyses principles of the selected research method AHP. The last section of the paper illustrates the feasibility of the proposed methods in the area of healthcare quality/efficiency evaluation and discusses the allocation of EU countries to the most adequate segments of healthcare level.

2   Healthcare Quality Evaluation Frameworks

The concept of quality in the healthcare is developed in the comparative basis. Performers of quality evaluation create vast variety of models used for country rankings, where different input and output variables are included. This leads to even contradictory results where the same country can be is opposite ranking positions due to differences of the ranking models. Some of the ranking examples include models by Bloomberg, EU reports, USA efficiency reports and others.

The country ranking worldwide by their quality and efficiency in healthcare as proposed by Bloomberg is based on three criteria: life expectancy; relative per capita cost of health care (percentage of GDP per capita); and the absolute per capita cost of health care (expenditures covering preventive and curative services, family planning, nutrition and emergency aid). The ranking included countries with populations of at least five million, life expectancy of at least 70 years and GDP per capita of at least $5,000 (Lu and Du 2016).

The variables which indicate quality of healthcare are not standardized. Various statistical data as well as survey data are used for measuring quality of healthcare. World Health organization classifies the indicators into main groups of Health status, Risk factors, Service coverage, Health systems. The report presents 100 indicators for monitoring health status (World Health Statistics 2016). The prevailing indicators in the research works are: expected life duration at birth, expected life duration after 65 or expected duration of healthy life after 65. However these indicators reveal significant differences of population health indicators in various countries. The EU country statistics indicate differences of life expectancy at birth from 73.7 (LT) to 82.6 (ES) (Medeiros and Schwierz 2015). The survey published in Patient safety and quality of care (2013) also reveals differences in perceived quality of healthcare by population: most all respondents in Belgium (97%), Austria (96%), and Malta and Finland (both 94%) evaluate the overall healthcare quality in their countries as good, yet only around a quarter of respondents in Romania (25%) and Greece (26%) say the same. Despite of efforts for collecting statistical data on various indicators, it is not clear which of them are responsible for healthcare status and could provide guidance where and how much has to be invested for achieving desired level of healthcare.

In our research we prefer the factors consistently measured by all EU countries, which include various statistical data or survey information of healthcare.

The first stage of the research aimed to explore interrelationship and importance of groups of indicators of different origin. We have divided the healthcare factors into 5 big groups (Fig. 1): Infrastructure, Life style, Country general statistics, Service consumption and Subjective healthcare measures.

Each group of factors which can potentially affect quality and efficiency of healthcare, and imply significant costs consist of subgroups (as in Fig. 1). There can be used many indicators for characteristics, but for each group we have limited splitting

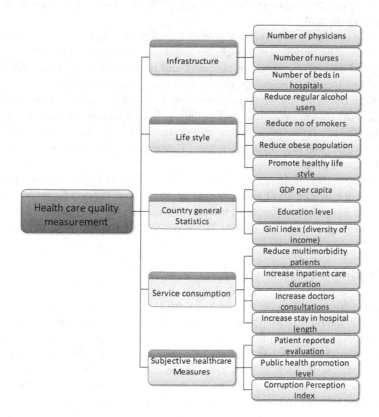

Fig. 1. Factors describing the healthcare quality

only to 3 or 4 subindicators (factors), as the further applied research method is very sensitive to big number of input variables.

The indicators falling in to the *Infrastructure* group characterize the investment of the country to main infrastructural compounds of healthcare provision, such as hiring professional physicians and nurses, general equipment of hospitals, also including number of beds for patients. EU countries have different strategies and initiatives related to these indicators which have taken place in many EU countries (Denmark, Sweden, Latvia and others), such as centralizing professional treatment to big hospitals, and reducing number of small regional healthcare institutions, reducing number of beds in hospitals, creating compensation systems for motivating nurses and doctors, increasing role of family doctors versus direct access to the specialists, etc.

The *Life style* group contains indicators which characterize general attitude to the health issues by people, also includes preventive measures and treatment priorities to risk groups. The group describes country investments to promoting healthy life style, access to healthy environment, food, and preventive activities to alcohol consumption, also concern about people which sometimes are not treated as patients who deserved medical care (e.g. obese population, smokers).

The group of *Country general statistics* provides objective economical characteristic of countries which could make impact to healthcare. As the general spending of countries to healthcare purposes make about 8–10% of GDP, the budgets in financial terms differ significantly.

The group of *Service consumption* provides indicators which show how the medical services are used by population. It includes number of direct contacts with doctors for consulting and treatment examining purposes and preventive exploration and depends of efficiency of treatment planning, assignment of treatment procedures.

The group of *Subjective healthcare measures* provides characteristics of countries as differences of patient behaviour and attitudes. It also includes indicators of patient reported healthcare, however only few EU countries collect this type of data (some these data are available in Denmark, Sweden, Estonia, however different questionnaires are used for these purposes).

For all the factors of the second level, we have applied statistical data except for *Public health promotion level* and *Corruption Perception index* which are calculated only for some countries, so we don't include this data to our calculations. The data set of all used healthcare quality variables is presented in Appendix A.

3   Principles of AHP Method

In this research we deal with the problem of evaluation healthcare quality in EU countries. We intend to rate the level of quality in different countries and try to envisage the relation between the quality and healthcare outcome variables – long and healthy life expectancy. The indicators influencing the level of healthcare were discussed and selected in Sect. 2. Now we will describe AHP (Analytic Hierarchy Process), the method suitable for quality evaluation. It enables to use both expert knowledge and the available statistical data for defining weights of the indicators.

The AHP method enables decision makers to convert complex problems into simplified hierarchical structures to find the optimal decision alternative. The method was implemented in practice for solving tasks in economic, financial, social, managerial and technical domain areas (Saaty 1980, Saaty and Kearns 1985, Crowe et al. 1998, Drake 1998, Chuang 2001, Kumar Dey 2001, Korpela et al. 2001, Banuelas and Antony 2003, Kriksciuniene et al. 2015).

The application procedure of AHP method is divided into four major steps:

1. Problem modeling and representation of indicators in the hierarchical form,
2. Valuation of weights by pairwise comparisons,
3. Weight aggregation into priority vector by using the eigenvalue method, and
4. Sensitivity analysis.

Further we will shortly describe these steps.

Problem modelling step means decomposition of complex problem into a set of indicators arranged as hierarchy structure.

The step of *valuation of weights* is performed by collecting opinions of experts. The main feature of the method is that the expert valuation of importance of all indicators (factors or criteria) is made by pairwise comparison by defining which element of the pair is more important and in which extent. The logical consistency of opinions regarding to all pairs is checked and evaluated. The results of pairwise valuation step of all factors are arranged into matrix. Let us have n criterion of one level, then the criteria ranking matrix has $n \times n$ rank, has a following representation:

$$A = \begin{pmatrix} 1 & a_{12} & \dots & a_{1n} \\ a_{21} = 1/a_{12} & 1 & \dots & a_{2n} \\ \dots & \dots & 1 & \dots \\ a_{n1} = 1/a_{1n} & a_{n2} = 1/a_{2n} & \dots & 1 \end{pmatrix}$$

Each a_{ij} is a natural number between 1 to 9 or it's reciprocal, and express the comparison level between element i and j – the larger number means more important criteria. This matrix is called the priority or comparison matrix.

The step of *weight aggregation into priority vector* can be fulfilled by applying methods described by Saaty (1980). At first each element of matrix A is normalized by the column total sum $\overline{a_{ij}} = a_{ij} / \sum_{i=1}^{n} a_{ij}$. The priority vector elements are equal to average value of each row $p_i = \frac{1}{n} \cdot \sum_{j=1}^{n} \overline{a_{ij}}$.

The sum of priority criteria vector (vector of weights W) elements is equal to one. The large value in the priority weight indicates the most important criterion.

The calculation of priority vector makes sense only if derived from consistent comparison matrixes. Comparison matrix is called perfectly consistent, if the parity $a_{ij} = a_{ik} \cdot a_{kj}$ is valid for all comparisons. In practice this condition can be met extremely rarely, therefore the allowed deviation for consistency is set. There are several methods for consistency evaluation. As it is shown in Saaty (1980) the *consistency index* (*CI*) can be calculated by using the eigenvalue method:

$CI = \frac{\lambda_{max} - n}{n - 1}$, where n is the dimension of the comparison matrix, λ_{max} - maximal eigenvalue. The *consistency ratio*, is defined by the equation $CR = \frac{CI}{RI}$, where RI is the random index, computed as the average *CI* of 500 randomly filled matrices. If *CR* is less than 0.1 or 10%, then the matrix can be considered as having an acceptable consistency rate.

After calculating the vector of weights *W* for criteria and subcriteria, we need to rank alternatives. This step is performed by calculating priority vector for each decision alternative. If we have m alternatives and n different criterion, we have to calculate n priority vectors with $(m \times 1)$ dimensions each. All these vectors are combined into one *alternatives priority matrix* (ALM) with dimensions $(m \times n)$. In order to rank the alternatives across all criteria and get *alternatives global priorities vector* (*AGPV*) we should use the additive aggregation procedure, which essentially means product of the matrixes *ALM* and *W*.

The weight valuation stage of AHP method by pairwise comparisons of criterion carries the biggest subjectivity and concern. The general approach for fulfilment of this stage is employing the number of domain experts and aggregation of all opinions. In our case for evaluating the healthcare level of EU countries we have invite as experts' health specialist. We distribute the pairwise comparison sheet using BPMSG AHP Online System (http://bpmsg.com/academic/ahp.php).

4 Research Results

The research attempted to look at assessment of healthcare quality problem appealing on subjective decision of healthcare experts using AHP method. As it was described in Sect. 3, AHP application should start with the problem modelling and representation of all influencing indicators in the hierarchical form. In Sect. 2 we have discussed the selection of factors stimulating the growth of healthcare quality. The hierarchical structure of these indicators was presented in Fig. 1.

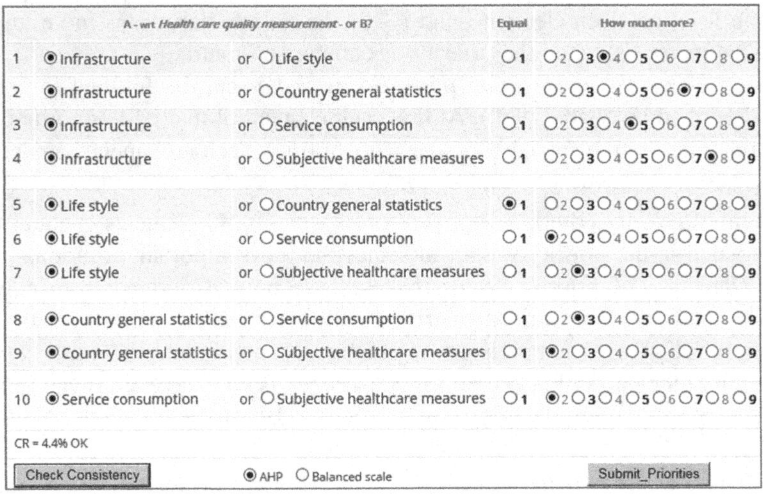

Fig. 2. Example of pairwise comparison set

We have selected the indicators from the set of attributes for which we have EU statistics, as only in this situation we can apply AHP method and calculate alternatives global priorities. The dataset of selected quantitative indicators, used in the calculations is presented in Appendix A.

To establish the weights of these factors, we distribute the pairwise comparison sheet (see example in Fig. 2) to experts' using BPMSG AHP Online System. This system allows in simple way decide the importance of each pair of factors, and let to justify the consistency of answer set.

The Fig. 2 show that the example answer set is consistent with CR = 4.4%. We got 10 consistent answers sets from experts about their opinion on importance the factors

Table 1. Global priorities of healthcare factors

Level 0	Level 1	Level 2	Global priorities
Health care quality measurement	Infrastructure **30.0%**	Number of physicians	10.7%
		Number of nurses	10.0%
		Number of beds in hospitals	9.3%
	Life style **25.8%**	Reduce regular alcohol users	8.2%
		Reduce no of smokers	4.6%
		Reduce obese population	6.4%
		Promote healthy life style	6.6%
	Country general statistics **18.1%**	GDP per capita	12.0%
		Education level	2.9%
		Gini index (diversity of income)	3.2%
	Service consumption **14.0%**	Reduce multimorbidity patients	5.1%
		Increase inpatient care duration	1.8%
		Increase doctors consultations	5.5%
		Increase stay in hospital length	1.7%
	Subjective healthcare measures **12.1%**	Patient reported evaluation	4.5%
		Public health promotion level	3.8%
		Corruption Perception Index	3.8%

affecting healthcare system quality. It can be noticed that the vision on most important factors vary in rather big interval. We can assume that in different EU countries there are different insights on importance of health care factors. In Table 1, we present the aggregated results about the constructive weights of influencing factors. The weights are expressed in percent's, and called as Global Priorities values.

As we see in Table 1 the most important factor is *Infrastructure* which is expressed by number of physicians, nurses and beds in hospitals. Its influence makes 30%. The 25.8% goes to *Life Style*, as most of experts conclude importance of the individual efforts to care about own healthy living style. The high impact (18.1%) on healthcare quality has overall country development status characterized by GDP per capita, Education level, Gini index (reflecting diversity of income). The *Service consumption* factor has not so high score of 14%. Maybe this is resulting of disparity the factors

Table 2. Quality rating and ranking of EU countries

	AHP method		Regression method		
	Quality rating	Rank	Quality rating	Rank	
AT	4.68	2	5.44	2	AT
BE	4.54	4	4.59	6	BE
BG	2.80	26	1.97	28	BG
CY	2.77	27	2.30	24	CY
CZ	3.99	8	4.35	7	CZ
DE	5.03	1	5.55	1	DE
DK	4.29	7	4.07	10	DK
EE	3.27	16	3.67	13	EE
EL	3.23	18	2.50	22	EL
ES	2.84	24	2.14	25	ES
FI	4.42	6	5.17	3	FI
FR	3.56	12	3.70	12	FR
HR	2.95	23	3.11	19	HR
HU	3.25	17	4.01	11	HU
IE	3.35	15	3.12	18	IE
IT	3.44	13	2.32	23	IT
LT	3.78	10	3.48	15	LT
LU	4.44	5	5.08	4	LU
LV	2.83	25	2.96	20	LV
MT	3.22	19	2.67	21	MT
NL	3.97	9	4.75	5	NL
PL	3.13	21	3.44	16	PL
PT	2.42	28	2.07	27	PT
RO	2.95	22	2.14	26	RO
SE	4.55	3	4.28	8	SE
SI	3.37	14	3.58	14	SI
SK	3.71	11	4.09	9	SK
UK	3.22	20	3.43	17	UK

rating by experts. Very similar situation is with the *Subjective healthcare measures*. The aggregated influence of this factor is set to 12.1%. In some EU countries the patient reported healthcare quality evaluation is in high importance whereas in other it's very difficult to find such valuation. Some countries has high Corruption Perception Index, others don't have any corruption in health care and don't calculate corruption index. We couldn't find any appropriate statistical data for these variables, so, in further calculations we assume that these two variables are equally distributed for all EU countries.

Using the global priority values from Table 1, and quantitative date set (Appendix A), we apply the AHP method described in Sect. 3, and calculate the healthcare quality rating (in %) from the set of picked indicators of all 28 EU countries. The results are presented in left part of Table 2. Here we can also see the overall ranking of countries.

One of the biggest challenges using AHP is to get the weights evaluation from area experts. This task takes a lot of time and expected a deep knowledge's in the subject. So we decided to try get the factor weights using multiply regression analysis and compare the obtained results. As dependent variable we select the *Total health expenditure per capita in PPP* (see in Appendix A). All other variables from this table we analyse as independent and attempted to find reliable number of significant input variables. For this task we use STATISTICA software and get the following multiple regression results (Table 3):

Table 3. Regression summary with selected relevant factors

N = 28	Regression summary for dependent variable: Total health expenditure per capita, in PPP R = ,95056350 R* = ,90357097 Adjusted R^2 = ,86296927 $F_{(B,19)}$ = 22,255 p < ,00000 Std. error of estimate: 256,26					
	Beta	Std. err. of Beta	B	Std. err. of B	t(19)	p-level
Intercept			1551,763	847,2315	1,83157	0,082742
Physicians per 100000 population	0,227461	0,075007	196,097	64,6644	3,03254	0,006849
Beds per 1000 population	0,324010	0,112032	140,139	48,4555	2,89212	0,009339
GDP per capita, in PPP	0,341560	0,100917	0,023	0,0069	3,38457	0,003111
Education	−0,273435	0,090725	−15,316	5,0817	−3,01388	0,007139
Gini	−0,344302	0,086249	−56,074	14,0467	−3,99195	0,000780
Doctors consultations (in all settings)	0,223073	0,092756	83,502	34,7208	2,40496	0,026530
Average length of stay in hospitals	−0,230098	0,089081	−107,696	41,6939	−2,58301	0,018234
Corruption Perception Index	0,575371	0.113963	26.674	5.2832	5,04877	0,000071

We can notice that regression coefficient of determination is rather high and equal 0.90. All selected variables are significant and its influence is shown in column *Beta*. It's very interesting that most important is *Corruption Perception Index*. *GDP per capita in PPP* and *Gini index* are of second importance row. The weights of selected variables we adjust from column *Beta* values. The weight for rest of variables we set to 0. Using elementary mathematical operations, we have calculated the quality rating and rank of all EU countries. See the results in the right part of Table 3.

If we parallel the results of healthcare quality ratings using AHP and Regression methods, we can notice very slight differences in quality values and obtained rank of countries. We have calculated that average difference of ranks is equal to 3. This let us assume that usage the multiple regression method in factors weight evaluation is reasonable and can replace the poll of experts.

It is very interesting to estimate the relationship of healthcare quality and *Total health expenditure*. This relationship we have visualized be scatterplot graph (Fig. 3).

The results we got are very predictable – the bigger is expenditure per capita in PPP, the higher is healthcare quality of the country. The EU countries can be divided in two sets: high quality and expenditure (upper right square on Fig. 3), low quality and expenditure (lower left circle on Fig. 3). The countries like Germany, Finland, Austria, Luxembourg, Sweden have very high healthcare quality and at the same time high percent of expenditure per capita. Nevertheless the Lithuania, Czech Republic and Slovakia belongs to second group of countries with the low expenditure level, they have healthcare quality comparable with the countries enjoying higher healthcare budget.

The research show that quality of healthcare system of EU countries is in very distinct position. The 'old' EU countries allocate the considerable amount of GDP for this sector and this secure the high level of healthcare.

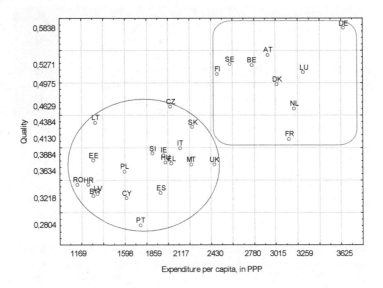

Fig. 3. Scatterplots of healthcare quality vs. expenditure

5   Conclusions and Main Results

The article is based on AHP method for evaluating quality of healthcare systems in EU countries. We have collected opinion of experts for deriving consensus value of weights for the factors included into evaluation healthcare quality model. The weights of selected factors were evaluated also by using multiply regression framework. We have selected the set of variables mostly influencing the healthcare expenditure in EU countries. Though the evaluation of factors weights by experts and by multiply regression analysis don't coincide in some details, we found the healthcare quality ratings and EU countries ranking very similar. This fact let us in some situations replace the long-time consuming poll of experts process using AHP by application of simple multiply regression for factors weight estimation.

The research show that quality of healthcare system of EU countries is in very distinct position. The 'old' EU countries allocate the considerable amount of GDP for this sector and this secure the high level of healthcare.

We also noticed that some countries with the low healthcare budget can boast the long *Healthy life expectancy,* but this mostly happens not through good level of healthcare, but due to other country peculiarity – good climate, healthy food, no stress living conditions and so on.

The results obtained by our research will help the healthcare authorities to identify the shortage in country healthcare system and provide for action improving healthy life expectancy for all EU population.

Acknowledgement. This work was performed within the framework of the COST action "European Network for cost containment and improved quality of health care" http://www.cost. eu/COST_Actions/ca/CA15222.

Appendix A. Data Set of Healthcare Quality Factors

	Infrastructure				Life style				Country general			Service consumption				Subjective quality measures		
	Total health expenditure per capita, in PPP	Physicians per 100000 population	Nurses per 100000 population	Beds per 1000 population	Alcohol consumption in litres per capita	Regular smokers, % of population aged 15+	Population with Body mass index >=30, in %	People taking care on health-enhancing in %	GDP per capita, in PPP	Education	Gini	Multimorbidity patients, in %	Inpatient care duration	Doctors consultations (in all settings)	Average length of stay in hospitals	Corruption Perception Index	Patient reported evaluation	Public health promotion level
AT	2935	4,8	7,9	7,6	13,8	27,7	8,8	74,9	31588	77,1	27,2	35,8	8,2	8,8	9,8	75		
BE	2780	2,9	15,4	6,3	11	28,1	11,5	51,2	29520	68,1	26,2	24,9	8	6,4	8,4	77		
BG	1319	3,7	4,7	6,4	10	33,7	12,4	17,3	11259	76	37	20,5	8	6,4	5,4	41		
CY	1619	3	4,9	3,5	9,2	30,7	12,3	39,8	23133	71,7	33,6	32	8	6,4	5,8	55		
CZ	2025	3,6	8,5	6,8	11,7	25,4	12,9	52,6	20094	86,1	25	31,5	9,4	6,4	9,4	55		
DE	3625	3,8	11,6	8,2	11,2	24,5	12,2	71,2	30172	81,6	30,1	38,7	9	9,9	9	81		
DK	3015	3,5	15,7	3,5	12,2	35	8,6	81,3	31405	69,3	27,4	28	8	4,5	5,5	90		
EE	1315	3,3	6,5	5,3	7,3	31,6	13,3	47,7	17218	82,3	34,8	45,8	7,6	6,3	9,2	70		
EL	2032	6,1	3,3	4,9	10	38,2	10,7	25,9	20159	62,9	34,2	23,9	8	6,4	6,1	44		
ES	1937	4,1	5,5	3,1	11,9	31,8	11,3	49,0	23793	53	34,6	29,6	8	6,4	5,7	58		
FI	2461	2,7	10,7	5,5	8,8	24,1	10,1	77,0	28560	77,1	25,2	45,9	10,6	4,2	10,5	89		
FR	3127	3,1	9	6,4	14,8	28,1	7,3	51,0	27812	68,9	29,2	37	8	6,3	5,6	69		
HR	1266	2,8	5,7	5,8	12,9	27,4	11	41,4	14703	74,7	30,6	30,6	8	6,5	9,6	49		
HU	1978	3	6,4	7,2	12,8	34,9	18,5	56,6	16433	76,2	28,2	37	9,5	11,8	9,5	48		
IE	1962	2,7	12,6	2,9	12,6	29,3	13	51,2	31933	70,3	32	27,1	6	6,5	6,1	73		
IT	2117	4,1	6,6	3,4	9,5	25,2	8,4	35,0	25380	54,6	32,4	24,7	8	6,5	7,8	47		
LT	1335	3,7	7,2	7,4	7,1	28,6	16	36,3	16413	84,1	37,9	32,3	8	8,7	7,7	59		
LU	3259	2,8	11,6	5,4	14,9	28,3	16,5	63,5	63892	70,9	28,5	22,6	8,8	5,9	8,4	81		
LV	1352	2,9	4,9	5,9	8,7	32,3	15,5	48,6	14439	80,5	35,4	40,6	8,3	5,8	8,5	57		
MT	2218	3,1	6,8	4,5	6,4	25,2	23	52,7	21524	41,1	28,1	28,1	8	6,5	7,9	55		
NL	3172	3	8,6	4,7	9,9	34,1	7,8	51,2	31853	68,3	26,7	34,8	8	8	9	83		
PL	1598	2,2	5,8	6,5	8,4	34,9	11,4	41,2	16092	82,5	30,6	33,9	6,9	7,2	6,9	62		
PT	1748	3	6,3	3,4	13,7	22	12,2	37,2	19500	35,8	34	40,3	8,9	6,5	7,5	62		
RO	1169	2,4	5,4	6,1	10,8	21,7	8,6	15,6	12742	70,6	37,4	18,9	7,4	6,5	7,5	48		
SE	2578	3,9	11,1	2,7	6,3	21,3	8,9	75,4	30807	75,6	25,2	32,5	5,7	2,9	7,1	88		
SI	1859	2,5	8,4	4,6	11,8	25,8	12,3	61,0	20695	80,3	24,5	32,2	6,9	6,6	6,9	61		
SK	2232	3	6,3	6,1	10,5	23,3	16,8	52,3	18777	84,3	23,7	30,3	7,3	11,3	7,3	51		
UK	2430	2,8	10,3	2,9	10	27,4	18,3	58,8	26206	76,2	32,4	34,2	7,1	5,7	6,9	81		

References

Banuelas, R., Antony, J.: Going from six sigma to design for six sigma using AHP. TQM Mag. **15**, 34–44 (2003)

Chuang, P.T.: Combining the analytic hierarchy process and quality function deployment for a location decision from a requirement perspective. Int. J. Adv. Manuf. Technol. **18**, 842–849 (2001)

Crowe, T., Noble, J., Machimada, J.: Multi-attribute analysis of ISO-9000 registration using AHP. Int. J. Qual. Reliab. Manag. **15**, 205–222 (1998)

Donabedian, A.: Quality assessment and assurance: unity of purpose, diversity of means. Inquiry **25**(1), 173–192 (1988). JSTOR 29771941

Drake, P.: Using the analytic hierarchy process in engineering education. Int. J. Eng. Educ. **14**, 191–196 (1998)

Institute of Medicine (IOM): Crossing the Quality Chasm: A New Health System for the 21st Century. National Academy Press, Washington, D.C. (2001)

Korpela, J., Lehmusvaara, A., Tuomine, M.: An analytic approach to supply chain development. Int. J. Prod. Econ. **71**, 145–155 (2001)

Kriksciuniene, D., Sakalauskas, V., Strigunaite, S., Masteika, S.: Project performance evaluation by modified analytic hierarchy process model. Transf. Bus. Econ. **14**(1), 192–211 (2015). Vilnius University, Kaunas. ISSN: 1648-4460

Kumar Dey, P.: Decision support system for risk management: a case study. Manag. Decis. **39**, 634–649 (2001)

Lu, W., Du, L.: U.S. health-care system ranks as one of the least-efficient (2016). https://www.bloomberg.com/news/articles/2016-09-29/u-s-health-care-system-ranks-as-one-of-the-least-efficient

Medeiros, J., Schwierz, C.: Efficiency estimates of health care systems in the EU, European Commission, Directorate-General for Economic and Financial Affairs, Economic Papers 549, June 2015

Saaty, T.L., Kearns, K.P.: Analytic Planning: The Organisation of Systems. Pergamon, Oxford (1985)

Saaty, T.L.: The Analytical Hierarchy Process. McGraw Hill, New York (1980)

Shi, L., Singh, D.A.: Delivering Health Care in America: A Systems Approach, 6th edn. Jones and Bartlett, Sudbury (2015)

World Health Statistics 2016: Monitoring health for the SDGs (2016). http://www.who.int/gho/publications/world_health_statistics/2016/en/

Investigation of Predicting Functional Capacity Level for Huntington Disease Patients

Andrius Lauraitis and Rytis Maskeliūnas[✉]

Kaunas University of Technology, Kaunas, Lithuania
{andrius.lauraitis,rytis.maskeliunas}@ktu.lt

Abstract. This paper introduces a model to forecast functional capacity level for people having disorders such as hand tremors, disturbed balance, involuntary movements, chorea etc. These motor features are very closely related the symptoms occurring for Huntington or Parkinson patients in various stages of the disease. Proposed model is designed by applying one of supervised learning artificial neural network models for data collected with smart phones or tablets. Feed-forward backpropagation (FFBP), feed-forward time delay neural network (FFTDNN), cascade forward backpropagation (CFBP), nonlinear autoregressive exogenous model (NARX), Elman, layer recurrent neural network (RNN) and generalized regression neural network (GRNN) were used in investigation. Moreover, the processes of preparing and labeling data, choosing a learning algorithm, training particular neural network, evaluating and comparing each model performance, making predictions on new data, are described in the paper.

Keywords: Artificial neural network (ANN) · Supervised learning · Smart devices and interfaces · Non-linear predictive systems · Huntington disease

1 Introduction

In computer science, data prediction problematics evolved with the rise of artificial intelligence (AI) and machine learning (ML) field and its algorithms [1]. Machine learning enables the acquisition of structural descriptors from given data examples in many applications. Found descriptors can be used for prediction, explanation and understanding [2]. In addition, ML spread widely in medicine e.g. doctors making diagnosis often need to collaborate with computers or computer scientists, thus leading to impossible adequate health and health care without proper data supervision from modern ML methodologies [3]. Furthermore, ML is intensively used in rapidly progressing multidiscipline of bioinformatics, which refers to the development of computer methods for pattern analysis, interpretation and prediction. In bioinformatics, scientists try to find causes to interpret predictive variables i.e. phenotypic data. Such process is achieved by invoking supervised (Support Vector Machines (SVM), multi-layer perceptron neural networks (MLP), Linear Discriminant Analysis (LDA), Hidden Markov Models (HMM), Random forests, Regression Trees, Radial-basis functions etc.) or unsupervised (Self-organizing Maps (SOM), Cluster Analysis, Principal Component Analysis (PCA), Probability Density Estimation etc.) learning methods [4]. Therefore, AI systems

© Springer International Publishing AG 2017
R. Damaševičius and V. Mikašytė (Eds.): ICIST 2017, CCIS 756, pp. 142–149, 2017.
DOI: 10.1007/978-3-319-67642-5_12

application domain in medicine and similar multi disciplines are growing, thus main goal of this investigation is to create a computerized model, which predicts functional capacity level for disabled people. In addition, created model should draw further guidelines for adapting it for patients suffering from neurodegenerative disorders such as Huntington or Parkinson disease.

Objectives of this work: (1) develop a mobile application, which generates circular visual objects and let locating circular objects in device screen for disabled people using their fingers; (2) create a dataset from people using the mobile app by tracking how accurate and fast displayed object was touched (3) create ANN, which predicts functional capacity level for person. In next section, similar approaches are analyzed focusing on those that are closely related to the problematics presented in this paper.

2   Related Work

Dozens of scientific researches and publications exists investigating various ML algorithms and application areas. However, the emphasis of this section is to analyze intelligent systems which one-way or another use artificial neural networks to carry out prognosis in neurology area for Huntington/Parkinson or similar patients' e.g. diagnosis and measurement of disease etc. Artificial neural network can be used for classification of accelerometer based tremor signals invoked from Parkinson patient's involuntary movements [5], also to predict Parkinson disease onset by adapting radial basis function neural network (RBFNN) for tremor activity data recorded via the stimulation electrodes [6]. Dynamic neural network solutions can be found to detect time-varying occurrences of tremor and dyskinesia from time series data acquired from electromyographic sensors and tri-axial accelerometers worn by Parkinson patients [7]. Another approach of designing a prediction model for Parkinson disease is mentioned in scientific article [8] where data is collected from symptoms e.g. age environmental factor, trembling in the legs, arms, hands, impaired speech articulation and production difficulties. To sum up, described related work is just a very small part of the science articles and books that fall into category of ML and its applications in medicine. Next, materials and methods used to compose model are analyzed.

3   Materials and Methods

First, mobile application for collecting data is described. Then, the dataset itself is introduced, explaining input features used. Afterwards, data labeling, neural network configuration setup is investigated.

3.1 Dataset Formation

Working principle of mobile application: circular shape objects of particular color are randomly generated in device screen. Three different modes are supported i.e. 2, 3 and 5 circles at time. Each circle is located in different position of screen thus no possible collisions (overlapping) between two particular circles are possible. Aim for the mobile app user is to touch every object, starting from first in sequence, by finger as close to center as possible. Moreover, the faster an object is touched, the better. Active circle that needs to be touched is marked by a black contour. When the subject finishes the test, collected data is stored in external mobile device storage and sent to the database. Multiple test attempts for subject are allowed if necessary.

Dataset is formed from data collected via mobile application. Currently, dataset consists of 200 data examples from 10 subjects, half of them had minor hand tremors or body movement distractions due to aging. However, no patients suffering from Huntington/Parkinson neurodegenerative disorders were involved in investigation at this stage. Gathered data (parameters and their explanations), together with random sample are listed below in Table 1:

Table 1. Collected data from mobile application (random sample data of 5 records)

x	y	xt	yt	nC	rad	rT	delta
267	818	284	814	2	100	4,423	17,464
610	392	605	390	3	100	8,451	5,385
524	306	539	319	5	100	1,110	19,849
730	159	727	111	2	100	0,960	48,094
245	135	243	138	5	100	1,113	12,010

x, y – generated x, y coordinates of circular object
xt, yt – user touched screen x, y coordinates
nC – number of circular objects show in device screen
rad – circular object radius in density pixels (dp)
rT – reaction time in seconds user touched particular object
delta – Euclidian distance between two points (x; y) and (xt; yt).

Further stage is to extract data descriptors (features) from collected data. This is achieved by having consultations with expert's neurologists. After few consultations, it was decided that rT and delta are sufficient and the most important features for this kind of investigation. Moreover, data preparation for neural network supervised learning approach was made with the help of neurologists. Labeling was done by adding an output variable Y to the neural network model. Generally, Y was chosen to have deterministic real (floating-point) values in interval [0; 10] for fitting (prediction) problem. Y determines the functional capacity of a person i.e. bigger Y value indicates that a person is more capable to do activities than one with a smaller Y value. Such scenario imitates TFC scale measurement system for Huntington disease patients [9].

3.2   Functional Capacity Level Prediction with ANN

Neural network is composed of single neurons that are treated as a simple unit carrying signals (data) to each other or different layers via transfer functions, which correspond to sum of input signal. Most commonly, transfer functions are Tan-Sigmoid (TANSIG), Log-Sigmoid (LOGSIG), linear (PURELIN), hard-limit (HARDLIM) or radial basis transfer function (RADBASN). Neural network has 2 inputs (rt, delta) and 1 output (Y). Seven different neural network models were used in investigation: (1) Feed-forward backpropagation (FFBP); (2) Feed-forward time delay neural network (FFTDNN); (3) Cascade-forward backpropagation (CFBP); (4) Nonlinear autoregressive exogenous model (NARX); (5) Elman Neural Network; (6) Layer Recurrent Neural Network (RNN); (7) Generalized Regression Neural Network (GRNN). Such models for the investigation were chosen due to several reasons. One, all networks deal with supervised learning regression problems. Second, choosing more models gives higher possibilities to verify proper prediction result. Generally, large variety of others models that are not in scope of this investigation exist, however only seven are analyzed which is supposed to be sufficient.

FFBP adjusts the weights of the connections in the networks to minimize the difference between actual output of the net and the desired one [10]. FFTDNN is used in recognition tasks with 3-layer hierarchical arrangement and time-delay [11]. CFBP enables more connections between layers i.e. is each layer of neurons are related to all previous layer of neurons [12]. NARX applies feedback connections enclosing several layers of the network to model dynamic time series [13]. Elman network has the typical connections from input units to hidden units, from hidden units to output and additionally context units, which are activated on a one-for-one basis by the hidden units, with a fixed weight of 1 [14]. RNN represent connectionist architecture using labeled directed acyclic graphs (DAG) structure [15]. GRNN provides estimates of continuous variables and converges to the underlying (linear or nonlinear) regression surface using parallel structure [16].

Table 2 illustrates configuration setup for models used in investigation. All networks have one output layer with one neuron, so it not displayed in table. Hidden layer column refers to number of layers for the model with number of neurons specified in parentheses. In most networks (except GRNN), a simple case with 1 hidden layer and 10 neurons was used. Training function corresponds the optimization algorithm, which is used in network training process to try finding global minimum of a function. TRAINLM refers to Levenberg-Marquardt optimization method [17] and TRAINGDA to method of gradient descent with adaptive learning rate back propagation [18]. Number of network weight elements (gathered from weight and bias matrices) is included, model time delay support of dynamic systems. What is more, it is noted that shown parameters in table are customizable and can be modelled slightly different, depending on varying prediction result.

Table 2. Summary of different neural network models and their configuration parameters

Network	Hidden layer (neurons)	Transfer function	Training function	No. of weight elements	Time delay
FFBP	1 (10)	LOGSIG, PURELIN	TRAINGDA	41	–
FFTDNN	1 (10)	TANSIG	TRAINLM	101	+
CFBP	1 (10)	TANSIG	TRAINLM	43	–
NARX	1 (10)	TANSIG	TRAINLM	81	+
Elman, RNN	1 (10)	TANSIG	TRAINLM	141	+
GRNN	1 (200)	RADBASN, PURELIN	TRAINLM	800	–

In addition, all seven models were used by automatically diving the dataset into training, validation and testing sets. Training set use 70% of all samples and is presented to network during training. Validation set (15%) is used to measure network generalization stop training when necessary. Testing set (15%) have no effect on training and provides independent performance of the network afterwards. Performance and evaluation of each model is analyzed in the 5-th section of this paper with independent data sample.

4   Proposed Prediction Model

Model is composed of two sub models: (1) Dataset formation; (2) ANN functional capacity level prediction model. Figure 1 illustrates model schema. During dataset formation, N disabled people (Huntington disease patients or test subjects), where N is the number of test subjects, uses smart devices to perform reaction and accuracy test experiments with their fingers. After completing the test, collected data is stored in database. ANN sub model predicts functional capacity level of a person by first gathering data from database. Second, data is prepared and labeled for the neural network. Third, network is trained by observing regression (R) i.e. correlation measurement between outputs and targets and mean squared error (MSE) values. ANN training process is iterative i.e. in pursuance of getting regression values as close to 1 and mean squared error as close to 0 as possible. Once the network is trained, it can make predictions on new sample data.

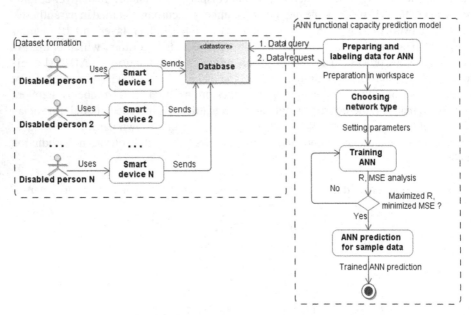

Fig. 1. Model schema to forecast functional capacity level for disabled person

Evaluation results of prototype hybrid model after conducting an investigatory experiment are described in the fifth section of this paper.

5   Experimental Results

Sony Xperia Z3 Compact mobile phone was used to carry out experiment. ANN performance is evaluated with regression (R) and mean squared error (MSE) metrics. Table 3 shows the comparison of ANN regression, performance and value predictions. R metric measure the correlation between output and targets (closer to 1 is preferred) whereas MSE metric is the average squared difference between outputs and targets (closer to 0 is better). "Expected" field indicates the estimations calculated with human intellect i.e. computer scientists and doctors neurologists on a random new data (5 examples). However, expected values are quite rough estimates considering, that dataset

Table 3. Regression, performance and prediction results comparison of different ANN models

Functional capacity level predictions (5 new data samples)						R	MSE
Expected	7,00	1,00	10,00	8,00	1,00	–	–
FFBP	7,06	3,18	9,88	7,90	0,98	0,99526	0,10858
FFDTDNN	6,89	1,03	9,71	7,68	0,76	0,99704	0,04950
CFBP	7,20	0,87	9,81	8,32	0,72	0,99580	0,06714
NARX	6,88	0,97	9,76	7,76	0,56	0,99700	0,05487
Elman	7,16	1,95	9,68	8,20	1,00	0,99533	0,06269
RNN	7,10	0,60	9,79	7,99	0,83	0,99686	0,07392
GRNN	7,00	2,00	10,00	7,19	1,01	0,99985	0,00200

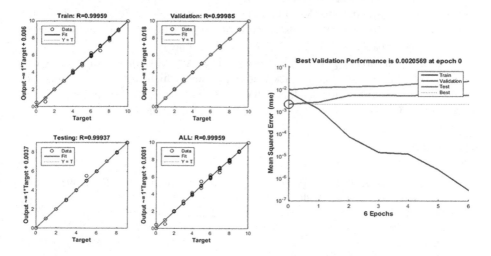

Fig. 2. GRNN performance evaluation using R (left side) & MSE (right ride) metrics

set is rather small (200 examples, 10 test subjects), data labelling process can be improved and further ANN training may be needed etc.

Figure 2 shows an example of GRNN best performance equal to 0.002 on validation set and R 0.99.

6   Conclusions and Further Work

To sum up, FFBP, FFDTDNN, CFBP, NARX, Elman, RNN and GRNN neural networks were used to predict functional capacity level. Dataset was formed using a mobile application developed in Android SDK. Hybrid model was implemented with MATLAB Neural Network Toolbox software. Conclusions:

1. No existing data sets, related to Huntington disease, in ML repository were found. What is more, collected dataset is still in its preliminary stage, meaning more features i.e. typical symptoms of Huntington/Parkinson disease patients should adequately considered. In order to achieve this, a mobile application – suite, which tracks following features, needs to be developed: hand tremors or movement distractions with accelerometer, trajectory following on spiral form object, touch force and brightness level of smart device screen, recording audio to track voice signals, checking typing capabilities of a patient etc.
2. FFBP, FFDTDNN, CFBP, NARX, Elman, RNN, GRNN networks, which were used in investigation, provide high performance results i.e. obtained regression (R) value not less than 0.99 and mean squared values (MSE) not more than 0.11. However, for more reliable network generalization and model verification a larger dataset is required with more test subjects e.g. Huntington/Parkinson disease patients. Moreover, a cross-validation procedure can be applied for performance evaluation.
3. Proposed model is intended to be applied for Huntington/Parkinson early or middle stage patients, so in order to make proper predictions data must be collected accordingly to create a balanced dataset.
4. So far, created model enables functional capacity level predictions on provided dataset. Next step is to adapt a classification algorithm which determines the reaction condition of a patient e.g. Healthy, Early, Middle, Late etc.
5. Model is in its early stages, which indicates that many additional data features will need to be tracked. This concludes that techniques, which were not mentioned in this paper (Support vector machines (SVM), Deep Learning Convolutional Neural Networks (CNN) etc.), could be integrated into a hybrid model.

References

1. Kohavi, R., Provost, F. Glossary of terms. J. Mach. Learn. **30**, 271–274 (1998). http://robotics.stanford.edu/~ronnyk/glossary.html. Accessed 09 May 2017
2. Witten, H.I., Frank, E., Hall, A.M., Pal, J.C.: Data Mining: Practical Machine Learning Tools and Techniques. Morgan Kaufman, Cambridge (2016). ISBN 0128043571, 9780128043578
3. Cleophas, T.J., Zwinderman, A.H.: Machine Learning in Medicine – A Complete Overview, p. 516. Springer, Cham (2015). ISBN 978-3-319-15194-6

4. Yang, R.Z.: Machine learning approaches to bioinformatics. Sci. Eng. Biol. Inf. **4**, 322 (2010). ISBN: 9814287318, 9789814287319, 978-3-319-15194-6

5. Engin, M., Demirag, S., Engin, Z.E., Celebi, G., Ersan, F., Asena, F., Colakoglu, Z.: The classification of human tremor signals using artificial neural network. Expert Syst. Appl. **33**(3), 754–761 (2007)

6. Wu, D., et al.: Prediction of Parkinson's disease tremor onset using a radial basis function neural network based on particle swarm optimization. Int. J. Neur. Syst. **20**(02), 109 (2010)

7. Cole, B.T., Roy, S.H., De Luca, C.J., Nawab, S.H.: Dynamic neural network detection of tremor and dyskinesia from wearable sensor data. In: 2010 Annual International Conference of the IEEE Engineering in Medicine and Biology Society (EMBC) (2010)

8. Chandrashekhar, A., et al.: Design and analysis of data mining based prediction model for Parkinson's disease. Int. J. Comput. Sci. Eng. (IJCSE) **3**(03) (2014). ISSN: 2319-7323

9. Nguyen, H.H.P., Cenci, M.A. (eds.): Behavioral Neurobiology of Huntington's Disease and Parkinson's Disease. Current Topics in Behavioral Neurosciences, vol. 22. Springer, Heidelberg (2015). doi:10.1007/978-3-662-46344-4

10. Rumelhart, D.E., Geoffrey, E., Williams, R.J.: Learning representations by back-propagating errors. Nature **323**(6088), 533–536 (1986)

11. Waibel, A., et al.: Phoneme recognition using time-delay neural networks. IEEE Trans. Acoust. Speech Signal Process. **37**(3), 328–339 (1989)

12. Goyal, S., et al.: Cascade and feedforward backpropagation artificial neural network models for prediction of sensory quality of instant coffee flavored sterilized drink. Can. J. Artif. Intell. Mach. Learn. Pattern Recognit. **2**(6), 78–82 (2011)

13. Billings, S.A.: Nonlinear System Identification: NARMAX Methods in the Time, Frequency, and Spatio-Temporal Domains. Wiley, Hoboken (2013). ISBN 978-1-1199-4359-4

14. Elman, J.L.: Distributed representations, simple recurrent networks, and grammatical structure. Mach. Learn. **7**, 195–224 (1991)

15. Goller, C., Küchler, A.: Learning task-dependent distributed representations by backpropagation through structure. IEEE Neural Netw. (1996). doi:10.1109/ICNN.1996.548916

16. Specht, D.F.: A general regression neural network. IEEE Trans. Neural Netw. **2**(6), 568–576 (1991)

17. Levenberg, K.: A method for the solution of certain non-linear problems in least squares. Q. Appl. Math. **2**, 164–168 (1944)

18. Moreira, M., Fielser, E.: Neural networks with adaptive learning rate and momentum terms. IDIAP Technical report (1995)

Algorithm Defining the Correctness of an Ergometer Rower's Technique Using Three-Dimensional Data

Edyta Lukasik[(✉)], Jakub Smolka, and Jerzy Montusiewicz

Institute of Computer Science, Lublin University of Technology,
Nadbystrzycka St. 38D, 20-618 Lublin, Poland
{e.lukasik, jakub.smolka, j.montusiewicz}@pollub.pl

Abstract. The aim of the article is to present a model of the rower, taking into account the most important angles and the new algorithms for studying the position of the rower's body at different phases of rowing. The positions of the rower's back, elbows and wrists during rowing were analyzed. The paper presents research on the motion capture of rowers practicing on the Concept II Indoor Rower ergometer, using a motion capture system produced by Vicon. The data obtained with the motion capture system and the results generated with the proposed algorithm(s) allow to clearly identify the studied subjects' degree of training and rowing technique on the basis of the analysis of changes in the inclination of the body parts in different phases of rowing.

Keywords: Motion capture · Ergometer rowing · Study of body motion · Algorithms for rowing technique

1 Introduction

Combining multiple disciplines is very common these days. The use of modern 3D technology in various sports disciplines is becoming more and more frequent. The aim of such applications is to conduct quantitative studies of sports performance and use the results to help athletes improve their technique and make progress in a given discipline. Creating an effective tool in support of athletic activities is the subject of the work of many scientists.

One possible technology to use in monitoring sport is a system which records the three-dimensional movement. Registration of movement using a passive optical motion capture system makes it possible to generate reference trajectories of selected elements of the athlete's body during its motion. It allows for precise analysis of the position of individual body parts. Calculated indicators allow for a precise characterization of an athlete's technique and determine its level relative to a standard accepted as correct.

The created algorithms are applicable to quantitative assessment of a rower's technique. In this study of rowers an optical Vicon Motion Capture (MC) system was used to register three-dimensional movement. The study was conducted in the Laboratory of Motion Analysis and Interface Ergonomics of the Institute of Computer Science at the Lublin University of Technology. The analysis of the signal from the

© Springer International Publishing AG 2017
R. Damaševičius and V. Mikašytė (Eds.): ICIST 2017, CCIS 756, pp. 150–163, 2017.
DOI: 10.1007/978-3-319-67642-5_13

MC system allows to search for correlations between the biomechanical properties of specific athletes, their technical skills and individual predispositions. The use of these algorithms allows the assessment of an athlete's performance and progress in the sport.

2 Related Research

Indoor rowing is a sports discipline developed in the academic environment. Water rowers off season use ergometers to maintain the correct body condition. The differences between the kinematics of rowers exercising on a Concept II ergometer and real on-watering were examined in [1]. The results of studies of biomechanical parameters and the movement effectiveness and efficiency of rowers' legs and hands were presented in [2–4]. The biomechanical analysis of rowers carried out using a wireless motion system based on accelerometers is described in [5, 6].

Cerne and others [7] used the Optotrak Certus optical system to research the technique of rowing on a Concept II type ergometer for three groups of rowers: experienced, beginners and amateurs. Fourteen markers were used in the study. They were used for measuring the trajectory of the ergometer rod, the rower's back tilt, speed and accuracy of rowing. The length of the rowing cycle, the strength of strokes and the pressure exerted by the rower on the ergometer footrests were measured. The conclusion was drawn that the movement of the rod and the angle of the trunk at the beginning of the ramp-up phase of experienced and novice rowers are constant and independent of the speed of rowing.

An analysis of a rowing technique and the participant's fatigue based on the handle's trajectory with the use of Vicon motion capture was study in [8]. Seven men were participants in the research and 42 strokes were analysed in three phases of rowing. Such parameters as: the proper handle's position, time of the incorrect rowing technique and the handle's tilt was analysed.

A very important element while rowing is the position of the rower's back. There are authors who say that torso inclination is the most important parameter of body posture during the stroke [9, 10]. Sforza in [11] and Panjkota in [12] studied the kinetics and kinematics of 12 men and 15 women (professional rowers), recorded with an optoelectronic system with 21 markers at the sampling frequency of 120 Hz. The number of strokes per minute was the same for all. The results were as follows: the average slope of the thoracic spine was equal to 52° in the catch position and 120° in the finish position.

Jones et al. [13] compared the work of the lower limbs on two different rowing ergometers: Concept II and RowPerfect. They used the Swedish MC system Qualisys, with the sampling frequency of 60 Hz. The test results indicate that the RowPerfect ergometer is suited for recreational use. Similar studies comparing the Concept II and WaterErgometer machines are described in [14].

Research was conducted using a sophisticated biomechanical model consisting of 41 markers (compared to 14 in [7] and 21 in [12]), covering the movement of the rower [15]. The authors studied the position of the subject's back in 4 different phases of the rowing cycle: the catch, the leg drive, the finish and the body over. The study was conducted after doing the subsequent partial distances: 100 m, 200 m, 300 m, 400 m and 500 m. Comparison of the position of the back, the heart rate, the power and other performance parameters of a professional rower and an amateur made it possible to determine the state of their fatigue during rowing.

In the paper the authors present new algorithms for studying the position of the rower's body at the finish phase of rowing. The positions of forearms, elbows, wrists and back during rowing are analyzed using the proposed algorithms. In order to verify the algorithms and examine their suitability for evaluating the level of the rowers' training, the study was performed on the Concept II Indoor Rower ergometer, using a motion capture system produced by Vicon. The results allow to clearly identify the degree of training of the subjects studied and their rowing technique on the basis of the analysis of changes in the inclination of selected body parts in different positions of the successive phases of rowing. The criteria used for the assessment of the rowing technique correctness were based on the Concept II ergometer user's guide [16].

The proposed geometric model of the upper body of the rower is a new approach to the analysis of athlete's motion in the rowing ergometer discipline. It enables accurate quantitative assessment of the rowing technique. Such an approach and analysis have not been found in the literature by the authors of this study.

3   Research Methodology

Research on ergometer rowing was conducted in the Laboratory of Motion Analysis and Interface Ergonomics (LMAIE) of the Institute of Computer Science at the Lublin University of Technology. The test stand consisted of a three-dimensional motion acquisition system and the Concept II Indoor Rower ergometer.

The optical system from Vicon used in the study consists of eight T40S type cameras operating in the near infrared, two reference Bonita video cameras and a Giganet hub collecting data. The framerate was set to 100 fps. The Nexus 2.0 software from Vicon was used for system calibration, for data recording and post-processing. The system records the movement of the markers placed on the body of a subject, provided that they are seen by at least two infrared cameras.

The study used a procedure developed and presented in [17]. The participant had 41 retroreflective markers attached to the skin with double-sided tape. The location of 39 of them was compatible with the Plug-In Gait Model [18]. Two additional markers, T10.1 and T10.2, were placed on the participant's back, as shown in [17]. The biomechanical Plug-in Gait Model from Vicon can calculate a number of different biomechanical parameters, including angles, moments and forces in the joints of a subject. The names and locations of the markers used are show in Table 1.

Table 1. Marker location on the body [18]

Marker	Location
LWRA/RWRA	Left/right wrist bar thumb side
LWRB/RWRB	Left/right wrist bar pinkie side
LFIN/RFIN	Left/right hand dorsum just below the head of the second metatarsal
LELB/RELB	Lateral epicondyle approximating left/right elbow joint axis

Three retro-reflective markers for tracking the handle trajectory were placed on the handle. They were located in the same position as in the research presented in [15].

The study involved three participants: age 32 ± 4, weight 81.8 ± 4.5 kg, height 1.83 ± 0.2 m. One was a rower of the Academic Sports Association and two were non-rowers. The participants in the experiment were briefed about the study and agreed to take part. They presented different levels of skills and abilities of rowing an ergometer. After a 15-minute warm-up they were to row a distance of 500 m with the maximum possible effort.

4   Model of Rowers

Rowing an ergometer requires a very precise technique. The correct technique is described in the manual [16]. On the basis of this document an oarsman's template was built, taking into account the relevant angles of selected parts of the human body. Four positions during rowing were considered: the catch, the drive, the finish and the recovery. They are presented in Fig. 1. They come from the recording which underwent post-processing in the Vicon Nexus software.

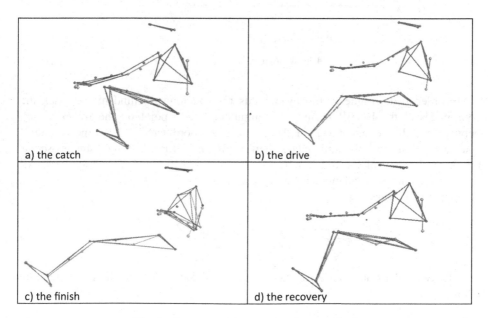

a) the catch   b) the drive   c) the finish   d) the recovery

Fig. 1. Rower positions (Color figure online)

The green color in the Fig. 1 is used for the right side of the human body, and the red color for the left. Yellow-marked elements are also added by the authors of the study: two markers on the back and three on the ergometer handle.

For each of the phases (positions) it is possible to identify the proper (optimum) position of arms and back. A model was created for the most important angles in the position of the rower's hands and back when rowing.

The article focuses on the finish position. In the course of its implementation it is possible to commit numerous technical errors. A template was constructed based on the calculation of the angles. The first important issue is the position of the hands. The elbows should be behind the trunk, as shown in Fig. 2.

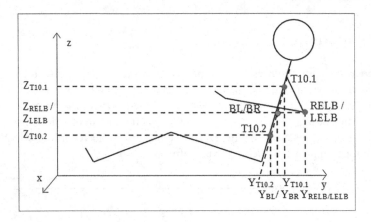

Fig. 2. Elbow position with respect to torso

In order to determine if the rower holds his/her elbows behind his/her back the coordinates of the BL/BR points are computed. It is a point on the rower's back between the T10.1 and T10.2 markers whose Z coordinate is the same as the Z coordinate of the corresponding elbow marker (RELB/LELB). A straight line is used as the approximation of the rower's back between the T10.1 and T10.2 markers. All markers used in the calculations are projected onto the YZ plane. The Y_{BL} and Y_{BR} are computed as follows.

$$Y_{BR/BL} = \frac{(Y_{T10.2} - Y_{T10.1})(Z_{RELB/LELB} - Z_{T10.1})}{Z_{T10.2} - Z_{T10.1}} + Y_{T10.1} \tag{1}$$

The two values are then subtracted from the Y coordinates of the corresponding elbows.

$$\Delta Y_{L/R} = Y_{LELB/RELB} - Y_{BL/BR} \tag{2}$$

For positive $\Delta Y_{L/R}$ values the rowing technique is correct.

Another important element of the technique is to hold the forearms parallel to the floor in the finish position. The wrists should also be held parallel to the floor. The methodology for calculating the angles is shown in Fig. 3.

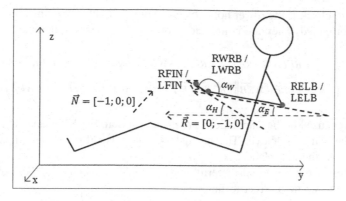

Fig. 3. Forearm and wrist positions with respect to the floor

The angles α_E and α_H are computed using the following formulas:

$$
\begin{aligned}
\alpha_H &= \operatorname{atan} 2\left(\left\|\vec{R} \times \overline{WRB\ FIN}\right\|, \vec{R} \cdot \overline{WRB\ FIN}\right) \cdot \operatorname{sgn}\left(\left(\vec{R} \times \overline{WRB\ FIN}\right) \cdot \vec{N}\right) \\
\alpha_E &= \operatorname{atan} 2\left(\left\|\vec{R} \times \overline{ELB\ WRB}\right\|, \vec{R} \cdot \overline{ELB\ WRB}\right) \cdot \operatorname{sgn}\left(\left(\vec{R} \times \overline{ELB\ WRB}\right) \cdot \vec{N}\right)
\end{aligned}
\tag{3}
$$

The computations are carried out for both sides of the body, substituting WRB FIN and ELB with RWRB, RFIN and RELB or LWRB, LFIN and LELB. The reference R and normal N vectors are the same as above (are presented in Fig. 3). All markers used in the calculations are projected onto the YZ plane. The wrist angle α_W is computed as follows:

$$
\alpha_W = 180^o - \alpha_H + \alpha_E
\tag{4}
$$

Keeping the elbows next to the sides is also an element of the correct rowing technique. The methodology for calculating the angles of forearm position is shown in Fig. 4.

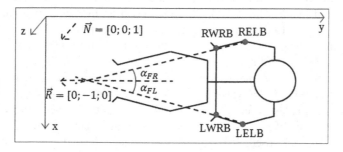

Fig. 4. Forearm position with respect to torso

In order to check if the rower holds his/her arms straight in the finish position, two angles are computed. They are computed using the following equations:

$$\begin{aligned}
\alpha_{FR} &= \text{atan } 2\left(\left\|\vec{R} \times \overrightarrow{RELB\ RWRB}\right\|, \vec{R} \cdot \overrightarrow{RELB\ RWRB}\right) \cdot \text{sgn}\left(\left(\vec{R} \times \overrightarrow{RELB\ RWRB}\right) \cdot \vec{N}\right) \\
\alpha_{FL} &= \text{atan } 2\left(\left\|\vec{R} \times \overrightarrow{LELB\ LWRB}\right\|, \vec{R} \cdot \overrightarrow{LELB\ LWRB}\right) \cdot \text{sgn}\left(\left(\vec{R} \times \overrightarrow{LELB\ LWRB}\right) \cdot \vec{N}\right)
\end{aligned} \tag{5}$$

All markers used in the calculations are projected onto the XY plane. The reference R used is the same as above. The normal N vector is different and in this case is perpendicular to the XY plane.

The values of the wrist and forearm angles should be as close as possible to zero. The values indicate the correct technique.

5   The Proposed Algorithms

Each 3D recording was post-processed using the Vicon Nexus software. The recordings were exported as C3D files. These files were used for further analysis. The files were processed by the authors' own piece of software created in C++ and using the Biomechanical toolkit (b-tk) and Eigen libraries.

5.1   Algorithm for Finding the Finish and the Catch Positions

An algorithm was implemented which cuts out successive strokes out of the entire recording covering the distance 500 m. It produces data crucial to the later analysis of the rower's position. The data contain starting and ending frames of a stroke – the frames in which the rower is in the catch and in the finish positions.

During rowing, the handle moves backwards and forwards, and the movement is repetitive. In our equipment arrangement the most significant movement happens along the Y axis. There are many local minima and maxima in the markers' trajectories. The local minima and maxima of the Y axis are of particular interest. To find consecutive strokes one has to find the locations of the local minimum and maximum values in the Y coordinates of the marker placed in the middle of the handle: HM. The locations of the local extrema correspond to the times of their occurrence. Once the locations of the local minima and maxima are found, the finish position in each stroke can easily be found – it corresponds to the maximum value of the Y coordinate. The localMinMax() function was implemented for this purpose. The algorithm is universal and can be used for any of the X/Y/Z coordinates.

The algorithm consists of the following steps. First the function initializes the variables. It sets the minimum value to $-\infty$, the maximum value to ∞, their locations to -1 and the variable last is set to the NOTHING constant. The last variable allows for tracking what type of a value change was found last (minimum/maximum/increase/decrease). It is used for resetting the values of the local minima/maxima. Once the variables are initialized the function proceeds to finding local minimum/maximum values by examining consecutive values of the chosen marker coordinate (its values in consecutive frames):

a. when the value in the current frame is larger than the values half a window away (a window whose size was set to 0.1 s), it is considered to be a possible local maximum. When the value is larger than the current temporary maximum value, the old maximum value and its location are replaced. The algorithm registers that it found a local maximum;

b. when a new possible minimum is found, the algorithm proceeds analogously to the maximum case;

c. when the value in the current frame is larger than the value half a window before it and smaller than the value half a window after it, then the coordinate value is considered to be increasing. If additionally a local minimum was found previously, the algorithm erases the temporary maximum value and location. This allows for the new local maximum to be found. The algorithm registers that it found an "increase";

d. when the value is decreasing, the algorithm proceeds analogously.

```
function localMinMax(marker,coord,window)
begin
  //find local minima and maxima
  tmpMax ← -MAX_DOUBLE; maxLoc ← -1;
  tmpMin ← MAX_DOUBLE; minLoc ← -1;
  //type of change last detected
  last ← NOTHING;
  for frame ← 0 .. frameCount-1 do
   begin
     prev ← frame - window / 2; next ← frame + window / 2;
     //is possible local maximum found
     if ((prev<0 or marker.coords(coord).value(prev)<
                     marker.coords(coord).value(frame)) and
        (next>=frameCount or marker.coords(coord).value(frame)>
                       marker.coords(coord).value(next))) then
      begin
        //verify maximum's significance
        if (tmpMax < marker.coords(coord).value(frame)) then
        begin
          locations.erase(maxLoc);
          tmpMax ← marker.coords(coord).value(frame);
          maxLoc ← frame;
          //insert new maximum location
          locations.insert(maxLoc);
        end
        last ← MAXIMUM;
      end
     //is possible local minimum found
     else if ((prev < 0 or marker.coords(coord).value(prev) >
                          marker.coords(coord).value(frame)) and
```

```
                    (next>=frameCount or marker.coords(coord).value(frame)<
                              marker.coords(coord).value(next))) then
    begin
      //verify minimum's significance
      if (tmpMin < marker.coords(coord).value(frame)) then
      begin
        //erase previous minimum location
        locations.erase(minLoc);
        tmpMin ← marker.coords(coord).value(frame);
        minLoc ← frame;
        locations.insert(minLoc); //insert new minimum location
      end
      last ← MINIMUM;
    end
    //is increase found
    if ((prev < 0 or marker.coords(coord).value(prev) <=
                      marker.coords(coord).value(frame)) and
       (next >= frameCount or marker.coords(coord).value(frame)
                      <= marker.coords(coord).value(next))) then
    begin
      //in case of increase erase last local maximum
      if (last == MINIMUM) then
      begin tmpMax ← -MAX_DOUBLE; minLoc ← -1; end
      last ← INCREASE;
    end
    //is decrease found
    if ((prev < 0 or marker.coords(coord).value(prev) >=
                      marker.coords(coord).value(frame)) and
       (next >= frameCount or marker.coords(coord).value(frame)
                      >= marker.coords(coord).value(next))) then
    begin
      //in case of decrease erase last local maximum
      if (last == MAXIMUM) then
      begin tmpMin ← MAX_DOUBLE; maxLoc ← -1; end
      last ← DECREASE;
    end
  end
  result ← locations;
end
```

5.2   Computing Angles

The second algorithm was implemented for computing changing angles that characterize a rower's performance. It was implemented as the *angleToVector()* function. It takes, as arguments: two markers, a reference vector, a normal, and coordinates that are taken into account. The two markers constitute a moving vector which may be projected onto a plane if only two coordinates are specified in the cords parameter. The function computes the angle between the moving vector and the reference vector. The angle sign is determined using an arbitrary normal vector (the sign is positive if the dot product of the normal and the cross product of vectors is positive, otherwise it is negative). The function computes angle values in the following steps:

1. Compute the coordinates of the moving vector (using two markers).
2. Optionally project the moving vector onto a selected plane (by zeroing coordinates specified by the *coords* parameter).
3. Compute cross and dot products of the moving vector and the reference vector in all frames of the recording.
4. Compute norms of the cross products.
5. Using the *atan2* function, the norms and the cross products – compute the changing angles.
6. Using the normal vector determine the sign of the angle in consecutive frames.

6 Evaluation of Algorithms and Discussion of Results

6.1 Description of the Experiment

Experimental research will first of all verify the correctness of the algorithms developed, and allow for the assessment of selected elements of the rowing technique. The rowing research concern the following aspects: isolating a single stroke and analysis of the rower's technique in the finish position. In particular the study covers: the position of the elbow relative to the back, forearm distance from the torso, wrist position relative to the floor and back position.

For each rower, individual strokes were extracted: the moment of the stroke, the finish position and the time of the completion of the return. The *localMinMax()* function was used. At the test distance of 500 m the number of full strokes of the individual rowers was 71, 69 and 78, respectively. The first and last stroke were rejected and not included in further calculations.

The study referred to the finish position. The analysis involved an assessment of the correct rowing technique presented by each participant. The end-of-stroke phase, in which the handle is pulled up to the rower's body and the direction of the handle movement changes, was subjected to analysis. For each full stroke the frame number of the end position, i.e. the time of its occurrence, was determined. Finally, the correctness of the rowing movements for the position of the back, elbows, metacarpus and wrist was examined.

6.2 Results of the Experiment

The elbow position with respect to the torso, calculated according to the methodology shown in Fig. 2, is shown in Table 2. The results are shown with an accuracy of 1 mm, although the calculation model is more accurate, but with regard to rowing on the ergometer higher accuracy is not necessary.

Table 2. Elbow position relative to the back in the finish position

Participant	Left elbow		Right elbow	
	mean [m] ± SD	Correct location [%]	mean [m] ± SD	Correct location [%]
Part. 1	0.023 ± 0.006	100	0.027 ± 0.007	100
Part. 2	0.004 ± 0.018	60	−0.005 ± 0.024	39
Part. 3	−0.135 ± 0.040	0	−0.072 ± 0.021	0

Table 3. Forearm position in the finish position

Participant	Left forearm		Right forearm	
	mean [°] ± SD	min [°]÷max [°]	mean [°] ± SD	min [°]÷max [°]
Part. 1	−19.3 ± 0.8	−17.3 ÷ −21.5	−18.7 ± 0.9	−16.2 ÷ −21.3
Part. 2	22.0 ± 2.8	15.8 ÷ 29.5	−27.5 ± 4.7	−15.7 ÷ −36.9
Part. 3	38.7 ± 5.5	29.9 ÷ 50.4	−29.3 ± 4.6	−36.8 ÷ −19.5

The angular position of the forearm, calculated according to Fig. 3, is shown in Table 3, which results in the values of the angles for the right forearm being negative and for the left positive.

The alignment of the wrist with respect to the floor plane, calculated according to Fig. 3, is shown in Table 4. The angle values shown in Tables 3 and 4 are calculated using the *angleToVector()* function with the appropriate parameters for each situation. The back location in the finish position is shown in Table 5.

Based on the implemented algorithms, it is possible to trace the values of each of the time-domain angles including the entire drive stroke, subdivided into the drive and the recovery phases (according to Fig. 1). Figures 5a and b show examples of changes in the forearm angle of the same rower in one stroke.

Table 4. Wrist position in the finish position

Participant	Left forearm		Right forearm	
	mean [°] ± SD	min [°]÷max [°]	mean [°] ± SD	min [°]÷max [°]
Part. 1	7.0 ± 2.1	2.3 ÷ 10.7	7.5 ± 1.8	2.8 ÷ 11.2
Part. 2	−6.4 ± 4.0	−15.5 ÷ 1.7	13.1 ± 8.0	−3.9 ÷ 30.4
Part. 3	48.5 ± 4.0	37.9 ÷ 61.4	24.4 ± 5.1	15.1 ÷ 39.0

Table 5. Parameters of the back position in the finish position

Parameter	mean [°] ± SD	min [°] ÷ max [°]
Part. 1	−29.9 ± 3.1	−35.1 ÷ −22.2
Part. 2	−22.6 ± 5.5	−36.7 ÷ −15.5
Part. 3	−5.6 ± 4.7	−19.0 ÷ 5.3

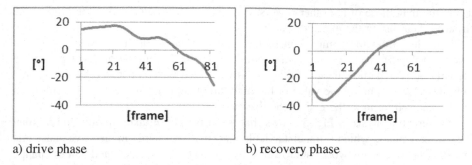

a) drive phase   b) recovery phase

Fig. 5. Change over time in the angle value of the right forearm of the rower 3

Each rower presented a different level of training, which is clearly reflected by the results. They also allow to determine the level of symmetry of individual body parts of each rower.

6.3   Discussion of the Results

The results obtained make it possible to draw many conclusions. The values presented in Tables 2, 3 and 4 allow to determine the level of asymmetry of each competitor's rowing technique. The smallest divergences of values are visible in the 1st player. The algorithms computed calculate the values that are sufficiently selective to allow to accurately determine the level of the rowing technique of individual rowers.

There are negative values in Table 2 with elbows on the back, which means that the elbow in question did not cross the back line. This information indicates that the elbow is in the wrong position, which is a sign of poor training of the rower. The rowers' level of training is indirectly evidenced by the percentage of correct elbow positions. Rower 3 had the weakest rowing technique. It is clear from the analysis of the calculated SD values for individual athletes that for rower 2 these values are the highest. This is due to the fact that only some of the strokes were correct. The values obtained also show that the rowing process is not symmetrical.

The values of the forearm position relative to the floor surface (Table 3) clearly show that for rowers with a better rowing technique the absolute values of these angles are lower. This proves that the forearm in the finishing phase is more parallel to the floor surface. This means that the horizontal component of the force vector generated in the forearm, directed along the axis of the ergometer and determining the efficiency of rowing, is many times greater than the perpendicular component, which does not translate into the desired distance. The vertical component of the force vector in the forearm reflects the energy wasted by the rower. The SD values calculated for rower 1 are indicative of the repetition of the moves in successive runs, which testifies to his good level of training.

Table 4 shows the angular position of the rowers' wrists in relation to the direction of the forearm. The smaller values obtained by athlete 1 indicate that the wrist is arranged more on the extension of the forearm, which demonstrates a better rowing technique than those of the other rowers. Low SD values indicate the repetition of the strokes taken during the entire distance.

It is clear from the comparison of back inclination in the finish position of two rowers (Table 5) that the first has a significantly better technique of rowing than the second one. The particular position is repetitive, which is demonstrated by a relatively low SD value. Changing the value of the inclination angle of the back may result from the fatigue setting in at the end of the distance.

The graph analysis in Fig. 5 shows that the drive phase takes slightly longer than the recovery phase, which is understandable, because it is mainly in the drive phase that the player performs his work as a rower. After some time the calculated values change sign. In the drive phase this happens around frame 60, and in the recovery phase around frame 40. The angle change is generally correct and follows from the fact that the player performing the drive phase reaches the finishing position, where the backward deflection lowers his whole figure. This affects the fundamental change in the value of the angle. The graphs allow the trainer to accurately observe the passage of the zero point, as well as the course of the final drive phase. The smooth change in the angle value in the recovery phase shows that at this time the athlete does not exert a greater physical effort – he is partly resting.

7 Summary

(a) A geometric model of the elbow and the angles defined by the forearms and the wrists of the rower is a translation into the mathematical language of the verbal description of the rowing technique given in the guide to this discipline [16].

(b) The algorithms developed on this model allow for efficient use of data from C3D files that contain a record of three-dimensional rowing movement recorded using Vicon's motion capture system. The results of the experiment conducted show that it is possible to accurately estimate the forearm and wrist angle values present in the rower model. In this article the research was concentrated on the finishing position in each rower stroke.

(c) The obtained values of the elbow position and the forearm and wrist angles provide the basis for trainers to quantify the technique level and capture the technical deficiencies of the rower. The calculated values for individual athletes are significantly different from each other, which makes them applicable in the analysis of the rowing technique on an ergometer.

Acknowledgments. The research program titled "Optimization of training ergometer rowers based on the analysis of 3D motion data, EMG, ergometer and heart rate", carried out in the Laboratory of Motion Analysis and Interface Ergonomics, was approved by the Commission for Research Ethics at the Lublin University of Technology, No. 7/2015 dated 12.11.2015.

References

1. Geng, R., Li, J.S., Gu, Y.: Biomechanical evaluation of two rowing training methods, vibration, structural engineering and measurement. Applied Mechanics and Materials, vol. 105–107, pp. 283–285 (2012)
2. Baker, J., Gal, J., Davies, B., Bailey, D., Morgan, R.: Power output of legs during high intensity cycle ergometry: influence of hand grip. J. Sci. Med. Sport **4**(1), 10–18 (2001)
3. Buckeridge, E., Hinslop, S., Bull, A., McGregor, A.: Kinematic asymmetries of the lower limbs during ergometer rowing. Med. Sci. Sport Exerc. **44**(11), 2147–2153 (2012)
4. Kurihara, K.: Optical motion capture system with pan-tilt camera tracking and real-time data processing. In: ICRA, pp. 1241–1248 (2002)
5. Llosa, I., Vilajosana, X., Vilajosana, J.: Manuel Marques, Design of a motion detector to monitor rowing performance based on wireless sensor networks. In: 2009 International Conference on Intelligent Networking and Collaborative Systems, pp. 397–400 (2009)
6. Ruffaldi, E., Peppoloni, L., Filippeschi, A.: Sensor fusion for complex articulated body tracking applied in rowing. Proc. Inst. Mech. Eng. Part P J. Sports Eng. Technol. **229**(2), 92–102 (2015)
7. Cerne, T., Kamnik, R., Vesnicer, B., Gros, J.Z., Munih, M.: Differences between elite, junior and non-rowers in kinematic and kinetic parameters during ergometer rowing. Hum. Mov. Sci. **32**, 691–707 (2013)
8. Skublewska-Paszkowska, M., Montusiewicz, J., Lukasik, E.: Analysis of rowing based on handle trajectory. In: 9th International Conference on Human System Interaction, pp. 62–68. IEEE, New York (2016)
9. Lamb, D.H.: A kinematic comparison of ergometer and on-water rowing. Am. J. Sports Med. **17**, 367–373 (1989)
10. Nolte, V.: Rowing Faster, pp. 125–140. Human Kinetics Inc., Champaign (2011)
11. Sforza, C., Casiraghi, E., Lovecchio, N., Galante, D., Ferrario, V.F.: A three-dimensional study of body motion during ergometer rowing. Open Sports Med. J. **6**, 22–28 (2012)
12. Panjkota, A., Stancic, I., Supuk, T.: Outline of a qualitative analysis for the human motion in case of ergometer rowing. In: Rudas, I., Demiralp, M., Mastorakis, N. (eds.) WSEAS International Conference, Proceedings. Mathematics and Computers in Science and Engineering, No. 5, WSEAS (2009)
13. Jones, A., Allanson-Bailey, L., Jones, M.D., Holt, C.A.: An ergometer based study of the role of the upper limbs in the female rowing stroke. Procedia Eng. **2**, 2555–2561 (2010)
14. Steer, R.R., McGregor, A.H., Bull, A.M.: A comparison of kinematics and performance measures of two rowing ergometers. J. Sports Sci. Med. **5**(1), 52–59 (2006)
15. Montusiewicz, J., Smolka, J., Skublewska-Paszkowska, M., Lukasik, E., Baran, K.R., Pszczola-Pasierbiewicz, I.: Analysis of selected elements of a rower's posture using motion capture – a case study. In: Dregvaite, G., Damasevicius, R. (eds.) ICIST 2016. CCIS, vol. 639, pp. 107–118. Springer, Cham (2016). doi:10.1007/978-3-319-46254-7_9
16. The Concept II ergometer user guide
17. Skublewska-Paszkowska, M., Montusiewicz, J., Lukasik, E., Pszczoła-Pasierbiewicz, I., Baran, K.R., Smolka, J., Pueo, B.: Motion capture as a modern technology for analysing ergometer rowing. Adv. Sci. Technol. Res. J. **10**(29), 132–140 (2016)
18. Plug-in Gait Model. http://www.irc-web.co.jp/vicon_web/news_bn/PIGManualver1.pdf

Improved Watershed Algorithm for CT Liver Segmentation Using Intraclass Variance Minimization

Alaa Salah El-Din Mohamed[1]([⊠]) [iD], Mohammed A.-M. Salem[1,2] [iD], Doaa Hegazy[1] [iD], and Howida A. Shedeed[1] [iD]

[1] Scientific Computing Department, Faculty of Computer and Information Science, Ain Shams University, Cairo, Egypt
{alaa_salah, salem, doaa.hegazy, dr_howida}@cis.asu.edu.eg
[2] Faculty of Media Engineering and Technology, German University in Cairo, GUC, New Cairo, Egypt
mohammed.salem@guc.edu.eg

Abstract. Liver segmentation in CT images is a complex and challenging process. This is due to wide variability of liver sizes and shapes from one image to another, in addition to the inhomogeneity of the gray-level within the liver region and the low contrast to the background levels. In this paper, a fully automatic approach for liver segmentation is introduced. The approach consists of three main stages; pre-processing, segmentation and post processing. Watershed segmentation algorithm is used in the main processing stage to detect the borders and edges accurately between the liver regions and the background. However, because of the over-segmentation caused by the watershed algorithm, region merging algorithm is applied in the post processing stage. The merging criteria were proposed to maximize the disparity between the liver regions and the background and in the same time to keep the variance of the gray-level in the liver regions under certain threshold. The algorithm achieved 91% overall accuracy when evaluated using CT images from the MICCAI dataset.

Keywords: Liver segmentation · Watershed segmentation algorithm · Region merging · Inter-class distance maximization · Intra-class variance minimization

1 Introduction

According to WHO (World Health Organization) [1] about 1.45 million people die annually from all types of viral hepatitis, mostly from liver disease and liver cancer. Egypt has the highest rates of hepatitis C virus (HCV) in the world. Every year, about 150,000 new infections appear in Egypt. Liver diseases can infect people of all ages. The Egyptian National Committee developed new Treatment for HCV. However, other liver diseases' and liver cancer's treatment is under investigation.

Medical Imaging is a useful tool that can help physician in diagnosis or treatment. It can monitor the disease effectiveness. Medical imaging has several technological types like Computed Tomography (CT), Magnetic Resonance Imaging (MRI), Ultrasound (US), and so on. Nowadays, medical image processing techniques are used widely in

© Springer International Publishing AG 2017
R. Damaševičius and V. Mikašytė (Eds.): ICIST 2017, CCIS 756, pp. 164–176, 2017.
DOI: 10.1007/978-3-319-67642-5_14

medical fields. The time is a crucial factor for early detection and diagnosis of different diseases. Segmentation of regions of interest is the most important technique in medical image processing [2]. However, the process is a complicated and challenging one.

Liver segmentation from abdominal CT images is the process of extracting the liver parenchyma from the liver area [3]. Diagnosticians often preferred CT images because they provide an accurate anatomical information, better spatial resolution and less noise ratio.

Liver segmentation of abdominal CT images is the main step in many clinical applications since it is very useful in many diagnostic and surgical processes. It is also useful in many computers aided diagnosis and surgery systems, and constructing anatomical atlases for the abdominal area.

One of the main challenges for liver segmentation from abdominal CT images is the similarity in the gray-level between the liver and other organs like stomach, heart and spleen, makes it harder to segment the liver.

Another challenge, one liver CT could stretch in 150 slices which makes the accurate segmentation process more complex.

This paper presents some recent techniques based on watershed algorithm. Moreover, it addresses the over-segmentation problem and provides a solution for it. We surveyed similar approaches with different applications. The proposed algorithm labeled an accurate segmentation by minimizing the intra-class variance.

This paper is formed as follows; recent techniques based on watershed algorithm are introduced in Sect. 2. The proposed method is presented in Sect. 3. Results and evaluation are presented and discussed in Sect. 4. Conclusion is drawn in Sect. 5.

2 Recent Techniques Based on Watershed Algorithm for Image Segmentation

This section presents one of the most valuable region based method in medical image segmentation techniques. Watershed segmentation method is applied with different medical application such as segmentation of liver, lung, brain, cervical and cardiac.

The algorithm in [4] consists of three main processing stages for segmenting liver CT images; pre-processing stage, segmentation stage and post-processing stage. Pre-processing stage relies on filtering method for noise removal. The authors use Wiener filter because it deburrs the edges of the objects and due to its high frequency areas. The Wiener filter function needs three input parameters: the input image, point spread function and noise to signal ratio. In the Segmentation stage, the authors apply the marker-control watershed transform method. Watershed transform method produces non-overlapped regions and preserves the edges. As the watershed segmentation algorithm results over-segmentation, the authors use morphological operations, as a post-processing stage, after segmentation to enhance the segmentation. First, they find markers for foreground objects by opening operation and opening by reconstruction operation followed by closing operation and closing by reconstruction operation. Then, they find markers for background by calculating regional maxima of opening-closing reconstruction. Finally, they superimpose the resulted image with the original image and visualize it. The accuracy of this algorithm is 92.1%.

Mathematical method based on Fuzzy C-Mean and watershed is proposed in [5] to segment the brain tumor from MR Brian Images. Benson et al. used 90 glioma MR Brain images. The method is divided into three phases; preprocessing phase, clustering phase and segmentation phase. MR brain images are prone to a lot of noise varieties like salt and paper noise and Gaussian noise. Due to noise removal, the authors used Median filter to improve the MR brain images. Also, they used morphological operations to get rid of irrelevant non-brain tissues and to enhance contrast. The basic idea of Fuzzy C-Mean algorithm is that each data element in the dataset is given a membership value to each cluster. Each cluster has a center; the authors calculate the centroid of each cluster by Histogram calculation. In clustering phase, Fuzzy C-Mean algorithm clusters the brain tumor from MR brain images. In segmentation phase, watershed segmentation algorithm is used to enhance the clustered brain tumor. The authors identify internal and external markers. Internal markers for foreground regions i.e. (tumor region) and external markers for background regions. The result is compared with ground truth images with Dice and Tanimoto coefficients. The Dice coefficient is a similarity coefficient measurement that is commonly used in validating medical images segmentation. It measures the similarity between the resulted image and the ground truth image. The Tanimoto coefficient is a performance coefficient measurement that measures the ratio between the common features of the resulted image and the ground truth image. The method achieved accuracy 93.13% for Dice coefficient and 88.64% for Tanimoto coefficient.

New method is proposed in [6] based on watershed Segmentation Technique for Lung Cancer detection. The method consists of three stages; preprocessing stage, segmentation stage and feature extraction stage. In preprocessing stage, the authors aim to enhance image. They used Gabor filter in enhancement stage. The advantage of the Gabor filter is it gives an optimal localization property in spatial and frequency domain. In segmentation stage, marker-controlled watershed segmentation algorithm is applied. In feature extraction stage, the authors used the segmented lung to extract features from it such as geometric and intensity-based statistical features.

A hybrid segmentation technique is applied in [7] to detect the Cervical Cancer from MR images. The technique is divided into four basic stages; pre-processing stage, edge detection stage, segmentation stage, and morphological operations. The author aims in pre-processing stage to enhance edges in the image. After the Histogram is drawn, they applied Histogram Equalization method to get better enhancement. The image is divided into frames and Histogram Equalization based on intensity calculated for each frame. Then, these frames are combined by Bilinear Interpolation method. The pre-processing stage is followed by Edge detection stage. In segmentation stage, the authors perform hybrid segmentation by using thresholding and watershed Segmentation method. They calculate double threshold to isolate background objects from any cervix area. The watershed segmentation algorithm is applied on the gradient image to segment the tumor. Then, some morphological operations are done to get accurate dimension of tumor.

A fully automatic method for intra-retinal cysts segmentation from Optical Coherence Tomography (OCT) is proposed in [8]. The method depends on marker-controlled watershed Transform method. The authors build the method architecture by four main steps; pre-processing step, retinal layer segmentation step, cyst segmentation step and post-processing step. The authors applied Bayesian Non-Local Means filter for noise removal. In order to segment the retinal cyst, retinal layer must be segmented first. Optical Coherence Tomography Segmentation and Evaluation GUI Tool (OCTSEG) is used for retinal segmentation. In cyst segmentation step, marker-controlled watershed segmentation method is performed. The authors used k-means algorithm to detect the markers of the OCT image and three clusters are used. There exists a fact that the cysts are low intensity regions. So, the authors selected the cluster with the minimum centroid value. In post-processing step, two thresholds are selected to remove additional regions that have same cyst intensity. The authors used OPTIMA Cyst Challenge Dataset with four OCT volumes. The method achieved 96% correlation rate with ground truth.

The authors in [9] focused on non-erosive reflux disease (NERD). They used Cell Microscopic images. They proposed a method that combines four stages. First stage is input image preparation and it consists of three steps. The input image is converted to grayscale image. Then, they used color deconvolution to separate immunohistochemistry (ihc) markers, and they used the averaging filter five times to blur the input image. To avoid over-segmentation caused by watershed segmentation, the authors applied the gradient vector flow (GVF). The authors used GVF to improve the watershed segmentation. The direction of the GVF field forces each water drops to point to one local minimum only. Then, watershed segmentation method is applied. In post processing stage, the authors applied region merging algorithm based on statistical characteristics of each region. The method segments 75% of the cells correctly.

Magnetic resonance imaging (MRI) is used to monitor and diagnose iron overload in Heart Cardiac. The most used method to diagnose iron overloading is calculating cardiac T2* parameter from MRI images. The authors in [10] developed a fully automatic method to segment interventricular septum and measure cardiac T2* parameter by marker-controller watershed segmentation algorithm and some morphological operations. The method consists of five stages; denoising stage, gradient magnitude calculation stage, initial markers detection stage, background markers detection stage and watershed segmentation method stage. In denoising stage, first the image is converted to grayscale image, then the median filter is used to denoise the MRI image. The authors applied edge detection by Sobel operator to calculate gradient magnitude. To detect the initial markers, the authors applied some morphological operations like opening, holes filling and closing. Then, they converted the image to binary image by thresholding algorithm. In background markers detection stage, the distance transform is computed from binary image. Finally, the watershed segmentation algorithm is applied to segment left and right ventricles (LV and RV) from cardiac MRI images. After LV and RV are defined, the interventricular septum is extracted and T2* parameter is easy to calculate.

F. Ouertani et al. in [11] focused on Leishmaniasis disease that infects many countries. They developed an automatic method for Leishmanial Parasite segmentation from fluorescent images. The method divided into three steps; pre-processing step, segmentation step and region merging step. In pre-processing step, the authors used a shading correction method called cubic B-spline method. This method is an iterative method; in each iteration, the background pixels are estimated. In segmentation step, the watershed segmentation algorithm based on gradient magnitude is applied. Because of the noise of the original image, the watershed algorithm caused an over-segmentation.

Therefore, region merging step is required. The region merging algorithm is applied based on two criterions; homogeneity criterion and edge integrity criterion. Two regions are homogeneous, if overlap value is greater than specific threshold. The edge integrity criteria work if the edge height that corresponding to the highest gradient value is greater than specific threshold. The number of corrected parasites segmentation is 1021 form 1438 parasites that tested on 40 images.

Many people are infected by Schistosomiasis. Schistosomiasis is a kind of a parasite worm. It lives in water and infects people during swimming, fishing, agriculture. Hyperspectral Imaging (HSI) is the best way to identify and analysis the infected regions [12]. The authors proposed a method to parasite segmentation from HSI, that make the treatment operation easier and faster. Marker-controlled watershed segmentation method is used. First, the authors applied the low pass filter to remove noise from the input data (gray scale image). Then, they identify the markers and apply watershed segmentation method. Due to overcome the over-segmentation caused by watershed algorithm, statistical region merging is performed.

The authors in [13] used region growing segmentation technique for liver segmentation from abdominal CT images. They combined the region growing method with watershed segmentation method. The proposed method consists of two main phases; pre-processing phase and segmentation phase. The pre-processing phase divided into two steps; noise removal step, applying texture filter and k-means step. First, the median filter is used to clean the input image. Then, texture filter and k-means algorithm are applied to remove other organs that have the same intensities values with the liver. In segmentation phase, region growing method is used to segment the whole liver. The region growing method starts with specific seed point and grows to the liver boundary based on neighbors' pixels' similarity. Then, the authors applied the watershed segmentation method to extract the regions of interest in the liver. Watershed segmentation method starts with several local minima and each pixel could belong to one local minima (region) or more than one local minima; in that case, the pixel classified as boundary or edge. The authors compared the proposed method with region growing method. They used 44 CT images and reached 92.38% accuracy value.

Based on this review, we conducted that the watershed segmentation algorithm is very useful in several medical applications especially in segmentation of liver, lung and brain. It achieved a high rate of success in medical images segmentation. In this paper, we applied the watershed segmentation algorithm on abdominal CT images. The aim of using watershed algorithm is segmenting the liver from abdominal CT images without any user interaction. To overcome the over-segmentation problem caused by watershed algorithm, we used a region merging approach based on two criterions; distance criteria and variance criteria.

3   Methodology

We developed an automatic segmentation algorithm for liver segmentation from abdominal CT images. The algorithm composed of three main stages/blocks as shown in Fig. 1: preprocessing, segmentation and post processing. Algorithm 1 lists the proposed method steps.

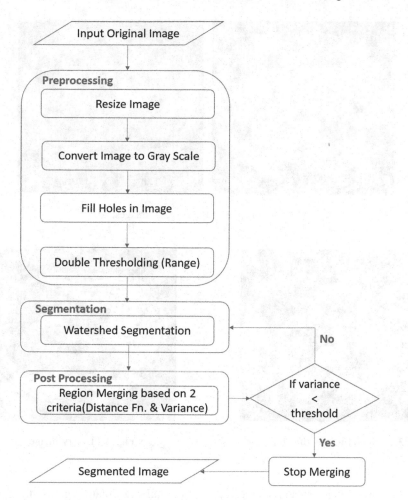

Fig. 1. Block diagram of the proposed algorithm.

3.1 Preprocessing Stage

Preprocessing stage depends on initial segmentation. First, we resize the original image to the half; Fig. 2. The original image is in a DICOM format, therefore, we convert the image to gray scale values. Due to the noise in several medical images, we used holes filling [14] on the original image; Fig. 3. Then, double/range thresholding is used to isolate the foreground form background. Figure 4 shows the resulted binary image.

3.2 Watershed Segmentation Algorithm

The main idea of watershed segmentation algorithm is that it treats the image as a surface with some relief. Each relief has regional minima where water source starts to flood the relief.

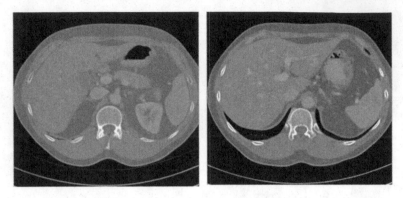

Fig. 2. Sample of the original images.

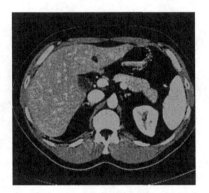

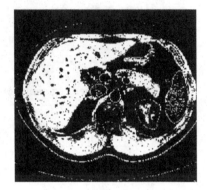

Fig. 3. Original image after filling holes   **Fig. 4.** Binary image

When two different water sources met, a line build to isolate regions. These lines called watershed lines and the new regions called catchment basins. If the pixel has only one water source, then it belongs to single region; and if the pixel has more than one water source, then it could be a boundary/edge between two different regions. Figure 5 shows a gray scale image of two overlapped objects. If a horizontal line is considered as presented in the figure, we see how watershed algorithm is working in Fig. 6. Watershed segmentation algorithm needs binary image to calculate the distance between local maxima pixels to get the catchment basins that segment regions from each other. Watershed algorithm output labeled image from '0' to number of segmented regions. The advantages of the watershed segmentation algorithm are that it detects more accurate object borders than many other algorithms and is useful when objects are overlapped and their borders are hardly detectable. The main disadvantage of watershed segmentation algorithm is over-segmentation. Over-segmentation occurs due to noise or gray-level inhomogeneity that causes several local minima in the image.

In segmentation stage, watershed segmentation algorithm is applied on binary image. First, the distance transform function is calculated between each pixel and

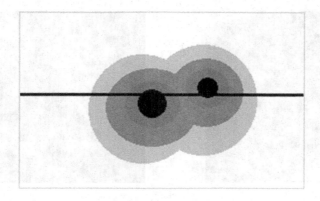

Fig. 5. Sample gray scale image of two overlapped objects

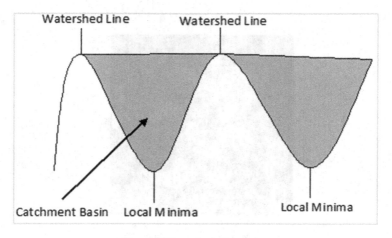

Fig. 6. Watershed Illustration

nearest non-zero pixel. Euclidean distance function is used as a distance transform function. The Euclidean Distance (ED) function formula [15] is formed as

$$ED = \sqrt{(x_1 - x_2)^2 + (y_1 - y_2)^2} \qquad (1)$$

Figure 7(A) shows the distance transform function image after applying on the binary image. The distance transform function is calculated to separate the overlapped and touching objects. To make the centers of the objects white and background black, we calculate the distance transform function of the complement of the binary image. Figure 7(B) shows the distance transform of the complement of the binary image.

Then, the watershed algorithm is performed. The result is shown in Fig. 8.

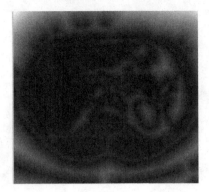 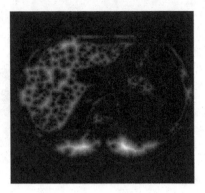

Fig. 7. (A) Distance transform of binary image (B) Complement of the distance transform.

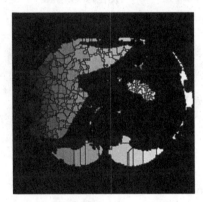

Fig. 8. Watershed gray scale image

3.3   Post Processing Stage

In post processing stage region merging is needed, to get more meaningful objects and to obtain the segmented object. Due to over-segmentation caused by watershed algorithm, region merging is applied to overcome watershed's over-segmentation. Region merging is applied based on two criteria: distance between a center of two regions and variance.

Distance Criteria

The aim of distance criteria is to maximize inter-class distance between classes (regions). For each region in the watershed image, vector feature is calculated from mean (μ), standard deviation (σ), energy (E), homogeneity (H) and correlation (C). Given the adjacency matrix between regions, the Euclidean Distance is computed between the feature vectors of each two regions as shown in Eq. 2. Then, the two regions that have the minimum distance are passed to Variance Criteria.

$$ED = \sqrt{(\mu_1 - \mu_2)^2 + (\sigma_1 - \sigma_2)^2 + (E_1 - E_2)^2 + (H_1 - H_2)^2 + (C_1 - C_2)^2} \quad (2)$$

Variance Criteria

Variance criteria works as a stopping condition for merging. In variance criteria, we want to guarantee to minimize the intra-class variance to specific threshold. The two chosen regions are merged in a temporary image and then, the variance for the temporary image is calculated. If the variance is less than specific threshold, these two regions are merged in the original image. Otherwise, merging process is stopped.

```
Step 1: Read the input image.
Step 2: Resize the image to the half.
Step 3: Convert the DICOM image to gray scale image.
Step 4: Fill holes in the image.
Step 5: Convert the image to binary image by using double
threshold.
Step 6: Apply watershed segmentation algorithm.
Step 7: Calculate the adjacency matrix between regions.
Step 8: While variance > threshold
Step 9: For each two adjacent regions
Step 10: Calculate feature vectors between these two regions.
Step 11: Calculate the Euclidean distance between feature
vectors.
Step 12: Get the two regions with the minimum distance.
Step 13: Merge these two regions.
Step 14: Calculate variance between regions in the image.
Step 15: Stop merging.
```

Algorithm 1. The Proposed Algorithm Pseudocode

4 Results and Evaluation

4.1 Dataset

MICCAI dataset [16] (Medical Image Computing and Computer Assisted Intervention for Liver Segmentation) is used in our experiments. It's a grand challenge competition in segmentation called "SLIVER07" which is used in more than 90 research. MICCAI dataset contained a training data that has 20 volumes and a testing data that has 10 volumes. The size of all slices is 512 × 512. Figure 2 shows sample of the dataset.

4.2 Results

When we apply the algorithm on a sample from the dataset, the resulted image is an over-segmented image. As we illustrate in Sect. 3.2, watershed algorithm always produces an over-segmentation due to noise and surface irregularities. Therefore, we need a post processing operations to overcome the over-segmentation. Region merging is needed.

We compute several statistical factors to obtain the overall accuracy and over-segmentation percentage. True positive factor (TP); that means the number of pixels segmented as liver regarding ground truth image, true negative factor (TN); that means the number of pixels segmented as background regarding ground truth image, false positive factor (FP); that means the number of pixels segmented as liver but in ground truth they are background pixels and false negative factor (FN); that means the number of pixels segmented as background but in ground truth they are liver pixels.

$$Overall\ Accuracy = \frac{TP+TN}{TP+TN+FP+FN} \tag{3}$$

$$Over\ Segmentation = \frac{FP}{TP+FP} \tag{4}$$

Table 1 shows true positive percentage, true negative percentage, over-segmentation and the overall accuracy of the developed algorithm when applying on four subsets extracted from the MICCAI dataset. The average of the overall accuracy is 91%.

Table 1. Results

	Dataset 1	Dataset 2	Dataset 3	Dataset 4
True positive (TP)	96%	97%	97%	98%
True negative (TN)	90%	90%	90%	88%
Over segmentation	35%	40%	37%	43%
Overall accuracy	91%	91%	91%	89%

5   Conclusion

An automatic algorithm has been developed to segment liver from abdominal CT images. The algorithm is divided into three stages; preprocessing, segmentation and post processing. Watershed segmentation algorithm is used for segmentation process. Due to the over-segmentation problem caused by watershed algorithm, region merging algorithm is applied in the post processing stage. The merging criteria were proposed to maximize the disparity between the liver regions and the background and in the same time to keep the variance of the gray-level in the liver regions under certain threshold. The proposed method produced an accurate segmentation by minimizing the intra-class variance and maximizing the inter-class distance between regions. We used MICCAI dataset for abdominal CT images. The algorithm achieved an average of 91% overall accuracy. For the future work, we proposed to use classification algorithm to classify the liver and get better segmentation results.

References

1. World Health Organization. http://www.emro.who.int/media/news/world-hepatitis-day-in-egypt-focuses-on-hepatitis-b-and-c-prevention.html. Accessed 17 Mar 2017
2. Salem, M., Atef, A., Salah, A., Shams, M.: Recent survey on medical image segmentation. In: Hassanien, A., Gaber, T. (eds.) Handbook of Research on Machine Learning Innovations and Trends, pp. 424–464. IGI, USA (2017)
3. Mohamed, A.S.E.D., Salem, M.A.M., Hegazy, D., Shedeed, H.A.: Probablistic-based framework for medical CT images segmentation. In: 2015 IEEE Seventh International Conference on Intelligent Computing and Information Systems (ICICIS), pp. 149–155. IEEE, Cairo (2015)
4. Lawankar, M., Sangewar, S., Gugulothu, S.: Segmentation of liver using marker watershed transform algorithm for CT scan images. In: 2016 International Conference on Communication and Signal Processing (ICCSP), pp. 0553–0556. IEEE, Melmaruvathur (2016)
5. Benson, C.C., Deepa, V., Lajish, V.L., Rajamani, K.: Brain tumor segmentation from MR brain images using improved fuzzy c-means clustering and watershed algorithm. In: 2016 International Conference on Advances in Computing, Communications and Informatics (ICACCI), pp. 187–192. IEEE, Jaipur (2016)
6. Avinash, S., Manjunath, K., Kumar, S.S.: An improved image processing analysis for the detection of lung cancer using Gabor filters and watershed segmentation technique. In: 2016 International Conference on Inventive Computation Technologies (ICICT), pp. 1–6. IEEE, Coimbatore (2016)
7. Garg, S., Urooj, S., Vijay, R.: Detection of cervical cancer by using thresholding & watershed segmentation. In: 2015 2nd International Conference on Computing for Sustainable Global Development (INDIACom), pp. 555–559. IEEE, New Delhi (2015)
8. Girish, G.N., Kothari, A.R., Rajan, J.: Automated segmentation of intra-retinal cysts from optical coherence tomography scans using marker controlled watershed transform. In: 2016 38th Annual International Conference of the IEEE Engineering in Medicine and Biology Society (EMBC), pp. 1292–1295. IEEE, Orlando, FL (2016)
9. Wdowiak, M., Slodkowska, J., Markiewicz, T.: Cell segmentation in desmoglein-3 stained specimen microscopic images using GVF and watershed algorithm. In: 2016 17th International Conference Computational Problems of Electrical Engineering (CPEE), pp. 1–3. IEEE, Sandomierz (2016)
10. Wantanajittikul, K., Saekho, S., Phrommintikul, A.: Fully automatic cardiac T2* relaxation time estimation using marker-controlled watershed. In: 2015 IEEE International Conference on Control System, Computing and Engineering (ICCSCE), pp. 377–382. IEEE, George Town (2015)
11. Ouertani, F., Amiri, H., Bettaib, J., Yazidi, R., Salah, A.B: Hybrid segmentation of fluorescent leschmania-infected images using a watershed and combined region merging based method. In: 2016 38th Annual International Conference of the IEEE Engineering in Medicine and Biology Society (EMBC), pp. 3910–3913. IEEE, Orlando, FL (2016)
12. Devi, T.A.M., Benisha, S., Raja, M.M., Kumar, P., Kumar, E.S.: Meyer controlled watershed segmentation on Schistosomiasis in hyper spectral data analysis. In: 2015 International Conference on Control, Instrumentation, Communication and Computational Technologies (ICCICCT), pp. 829–834. IEEE, Kumaracoil (2015)
13. Mostafa, A., Elfattah, M.A., Fouad, A., Hassanien, A.E., Hefny, H., Kim, T.: Region growing segmentation with iterative K-means for CT liver images. In: 2015 4th International Conference on Advanced Information Technology and Sensor Application (AITS), pp. 88–91. IEEE, Harbin (2015)

176   A.S.E.-D. Mohamed et al.

14. Soille, P.: Morphological Image Analysis: Principles and Applications, 2nd edn. Springer, New York (2003)
15. Deza, E., Deza, M.M.: Encyclopedia of Distances, 1st edn. Springer, Heidelberg (2009)
16. SLIVER07. http://www.sliver07.org. Accessed 26 Mar 2017

Analysis of the Preconditions for Implementation of Nationwide EHR Systems

Irena Skrceska[1](✉), Goran Velinov[2], Margita Kon-Popovska[2],
Marijana Neskovska[3], Miroslav Pevac[4], Leonid Stoimenov[5],
Daniela Ivanova Panova[6], Berislav Vekic[7], and Boro Jakimovski[2]

[1] Faculty of Informatics, European University of Republic of Macedonia,
Skopje, Republic of Macedonia
`irena@eurm.edu.mk`
[2] Faculty of Computer Science and Engineering,
Ss. Cyril and Methodius University in Skopje, Skopje, Republic of Macedonia
[3] Ministry of Health of Macedonia, Skopje, Republic of Macedonia
[4] Ministry of Health of Serbia, Belgrade, Serbia
[5] Faculty of Electronic Engineering, University of Niš, Niš, Serbia
[6] Medical Faculty, Ss. Cyril and Methodius University in Skopje,
Skopje, Macedonia
[7] Faculty of Medicine, University of Belgrade, Belgrade, Serbia

Abstract. The implementation of e-Health or EHR systems at national level is a major challenge for any country in the world. This is due to complexity of the architecture of the technical solution, significant number of involved parties – institutions, professionals, patients, etc., but also because of the great changes that are made with the introduction of the system. In order to have successful implementation, i.e. to reach the planned goals and benefits, certain key conditions need to be met. This paper provides a detailed analysis of health and e-health systems in Macedonia (MK) and Serbia (RS) that was used to meet several key prerequisites before or during the implementation of national e-health systems. The undertaken legislative changes are explained and a description of the selected system on conceptual level that most appropriately fits the required prerequisites for the implementation of e-health system is provided.

Keywords: National e-Health systems · EHR

1 Introduction

Many countries in the world and almost all countries in Europe have perceived the benefits and need for implementation of national electronic health (e-health) system or national Electronic Health Record (EHR) system as its central part. Different countries have chosen different system models and different approaches to their implementation [1–5].

© Springer International Publishing AG 2017
R. Damaševičius and V. Mikašytė (Eds.): ICIST 2017, CCIS 756, pp. 177–189, 2017.
DOI: 10.1007/978-3-319-67642-5_15

Although research from the World Health Organization (WHO) in 2015 [2] shows that a higher percentage of European countries have implemented a national EHR system, however in many cases these systems do not provide a complete EHR. In different countries the national EHR is implemented at certain levels of care includes only part of national health facilities or covering only certain modules and functionalities. In other words, small number of countries have managed to implement complete national EHR system at all three levels of health care and thus cover all health facilities and institutions.

A large number of countries had difficulties in implementation and have encountered a variety of problems that slow down or in the worst case temporarily or permanently stop the implementation process. Although as a barrier to implementation of national e-health or EHR system in up to 50% is considered (1) financing [2] or high planned budgets and most often their surpassing, the problems belong to one of the following categories: (2) problems in defining the objectives and scope of the system (France [4, 7], Britain [3]), (3) problems with the development team (Greece), (4) choice of implementation concept (Italy), (5) timeframe (Britain) - projects lasting a decade or more and (6) laws (Greece).

In MK in 2011 and RS in 2015 were initiated projects for the development and implementation of national e-health systems that incorporated EHR systems within. In MK, the project was organized in three phases: Phase one (2011–2012) - booking and referral system; Phase two (2013–2014) - EHR system nationwide and Phase three (2015–2016) - comprehensive national e-health system. In RS the project was conducted in two phases: Phase one (2015) - development; Phase two (2016) - dissemination. Despite numerous challenges and difficulties, stages completed by the end of 2016 were largely successful or fulfilled the planned targets. Thus the deadlines for development and implementation of this type of systems - national e-health systems, were extremely short. In MK national EHR system was launched in less than two years, and within five years was implemented comprehensive national e-health system. Similarly in RS, the implementation of national e-health system, named Integrated Health Information System (IHIS) [17], at the national level (with EHR) was completed in less than a year. In both countries the implemented systems are based on the same e-health platform. What is more important, the projects were being completed within the planned budgets.

The effects of the introduction of e-health systems are evident and touch almost all segments of the healthcare systems in both countries. MK national e-health system success story was identified and recognized by the wider European professional community. The country scored significantly high in the healthcare ranking made by European Healthcare Consumer Index (EHCI) in their 2014 [8], 2015 [9], 2016 [10] reports. The success that the system achieved in MK is repeating in RS [13]. The positive effects of the national e-health system implementation in MK were also noted in the WHO eHealth report [2].

Aware of the problems (1–6) in a number of countries, prior to the start of the projects an emphasis was given on meeting the preconditions for starting the projects. As a first step detailed analyses were carried out. This paper is an analysis of health systems in the two countries - the method of operation and connectivity of health facilities, as well as interoperability, roles and responsibilities of central government institutions. Analysis is given of the computerization of health facilities of the network of public health facilities. Then a detailed description is provided of the pre-conditions that had to be fulfilled before start of any stage in the implementation of systems. An emphasis is given on changing laws related to e-health and choosing the appropriate model of integrated e-health system nationwide.

In section two there is a description of health and e-health systems in both countries, section three is a comparison of the laws in some EU countries regarding e-health and the specifics of the legislation in MK and RS are presented. In the fourth section a description of the conceptual model of a national e-health system is given and finally number five section provides discussion and some conclusions.

2   Health and e-Health Systems in Macedonia and Serbia

In order to precisely define the (business) processes that would be covered by a national e-health system, such as for instance, the processes of scheduling and booking, referrals or prescriptions, it is necessary to make detailed analysis of health systems in both countries. Moreover, in order to provide functional integration of health systems in central state institutions, and to define the data flow between them, it is necessary to analyze their roles and interconnectedness.

Health systems in RS and MK come from the common system of Yugoslavia [11]. After 25 years, the systems still have many common characteristics but also some significant differences. In Figs. 1 and 2 there is a visual representation of the network of public health facilities in RS and MK. Common features standing out are: the organization of the health system on three levels – primary (I), secondary (II) and tertiary (III) level of health care with institutions at every level having similar responsibilities [12, 13]. The systems are organized to meet the needs of the population throughout the territory and because of that regional approach of organization, some institutions provide services of two levels. For example, GPs/CHC in both countries are set to perform services from primary level, but provide specialist services too, carried out by institutions in the second level (E.g. green color in the GP square). In MK Institutes or Clinical hospitals (CHs) provide specialized consultative care at the secondary level, but educational activities and professional specialization are also carried out which are usually provided in the third level [12] (blue color in the CH squares). Similarly, the five Clinical hospital centers (CHs) in RS provide services defined for secondary and tertiary health care [13].

In Figs. 1 and 2, the numbers represent: doctors, health facilities (in round brackets) and different Hospital Information Systems (HIS) – electronic systems already implemented in the health facilities (in square brackets). The colors of the squares represent that the healthcare facilities use third party IS integrated with the central national e-health system (left side, dark color) or use the central national e-health system through web interface (right side, light color). For example, almost all general practitioners (GPs) in MK and lot of the community health centers (CHCs) in RS use third party IS. Abbreviations Fig. 1: Pharmacies (PH); Gynecologist (GYN); General Practitioners (GP); Laboratories (LAB); Dentistry (DEN); Biomedical Assisted Fertilization, Inpatient Health Care Cardiovascular Surgery, Ophthalmology, Natural

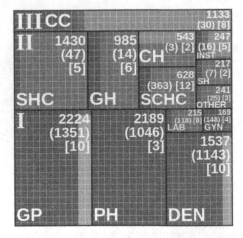   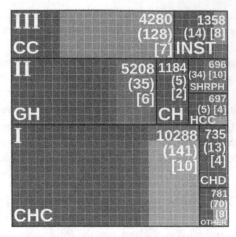

Fig. 1. Net. of public health institutions in MK

Fig. 2. Net. of public health institutions in RS

Healing, Factory Clinics (OTHER); Institutes (INST); Clinical Hospitals (CH); General Hospital (GH); Specialist - Consultative Health Care Public Health Institutions (SHC); Specialist - Consultative Health Care, Dialysis, Public Health Centers, Dentistry (SCHC); Special Hospitals (SH); Clinical Center (CC). Abbreviations Fig. 2: Community Health Centre (CHC); Health Center and Dispensary (CHD); Immediate Care Departments, Public Health Centers, Social Care Institutes, Hospital Institutions for Health Care Workers, Blood Transfusion Institutes (OTHER); Clinical Hospital Centers (CH); General Hospital (GH); Special Hospitals for/without Rehabilitation, Special Psychiatric Hospital (SHRPH); Health Centers (HCC); Institutes (INST); Clinical Centers (CC).

In terms of ownership, in both countries besides the institutions that are state-owned, there is significant number of health facilities in private ownership. In terms of financing, in both countries there is single state (Republic) Health Insurance Fund (RHIF). The institutions that perform public services make agreements with RHIF, which includes them in the network of public health facilities. All state-owned institutions in the two countries are financed by RHIF, based on signed agreements for provision of services of public interest. Private institutions may be included in the network of public health facilities, in such a manner that RHIF contracts out some health services, under the same conditions as with the state institutions. Mostly it is for services not performed in state institutions or in case the state institutions do not have enough capacity (resources) to meet the needs.

General impression is that the health system in MK underwent more changes. In terms of ownership, there is a higher number of private health facilities at all three levels of care, involved in the network of the public health system. For example, primary healthcare is privatized - all doctors working in private clinics which have an agreement with RHIF for funding through capitation mechanism. This applies for children's dentistry, gynecology and pediatrics too. In RS this level of care is still financed within the state public health facilities. Also, in MK there are several private hospitals on the second level of health care and dental clinical center on third level, involved in the network of public health facilities. In MK is introduced a model of registration and financing of health services, called Diagnosis Related Groups (DRG), based on the Australian Refined DRG (AR-DRG) version 5.2 [14]. RS still applies the model of funding through block grants.

In terms of scheduling the examination with GP in MK the scheduling is organized by the clinics in which doctors work. It is interesting to emphasize that these clinics do not have waiting lists of patients. In RS in most health centers there is no system for scheduling the examination by a GP. The exceptions are few major health centers, which provide call centers for phone appointment. For scheduling the examination by a specialist at a medical institution of secondary or tertiary level of health care, in both countries there was no transparent system of appointment. Moreover, for many specialties, types of services in many institutions there were months long waiting lists, even for the time critical diseases. Patients waiting even several hours in the doctor's office was not rare situation.

Regarding the manner of referral, before the start of the implementation of the system in MK a model of reference was defined, reference can be either at the same level of care or at a one-step higher level, i.e. the patient is not returned to a lower level of health care and is not referred directly from first to third level of health care. In RS reference is always made by a GP to higher levels. For certain services of a higher level, a recommendation from a medical specialist is requirement. The territory of RS according RHIF is divided into 31 districts and the patient is always referred to health care within the district to which he belongs. Referral to health facility outside the district requires approval by doctors' committee, which is part of RHIF.

In terms of drugs prescription, prescribing in both countries is performed by GPs, in MK generics of the drug is prescribed, while in RS the specific medication that should be used is prescribed. In both countries it is obligatory to prescribe the drugs from the positive list of RHIF (cost for them being covered). The fulfillment of these prescriptions is made in pharmacies that are contracted with RHIF.

Although the laws on health care in both countries [12, 13] clearly defined responsibilities of the Ministries of Health (MoH) for the organization of health care and healthcare provision, in practice these laws in both countries are not enforced consistently. Above all this refers to the work of RHIF in both countries. Although the RHIFs are financial institutions, in many cases they are largely involved in the competences of the MoH in creating health policies or in the implementation of health activities. E.g., in MK, RHIF defines content of the forms which is in no way related to health insurance of patient or GPs are obliged to send reports to the RHIF for performed preventive examinations of their patients. Similarly, in RS the referrals types and their content are defined by the RHIF and also, its committee determines whether a patient may be referred to a higher level of health care. Another illustrative example is that in both countries prescriptions for medicines that are not on the positive list of RHIF are not recorded.

In both countries apart from MoH and RHIF, other institutions in the system of management are the Institutes for Public Health (IPH) – they have a role in caring for population health prevention through monitoring, research and study of health condition, the causes for occurring and spreading of communicable and non-communicable diseases of social and medical importance, the impact of environmental factors and taking measures to protect and promote health. The Agency for Medicines and Medical Devices (AMMD) that perform registration of drugs and medical devices. In MK in 2015 was formed Directorate for e-health within the MoH [6].

In recent years in both countries there are activities by which the MoH get their legal and expected role - to create health policies for upgrading and improving health systems in both countries. In MK this is also supported by changes in the laws on health care [12] and the law on records in the field of health [6] (see also the next chapter). Similar is expected to happen with the relevant laws in the RS [13, 19].

Introduction and implementation of e-health or HIS in the health facilities in both countries is a continuous process that lasts from late '80. As more important stages of computerization stand out the computerization of primary health care in MK, which took place intensively along with the privatization process - in the period 2001–2006. During that period, all private clinics on primary level acquired appropriate HIS. The Association of Doctors of MK financed the development of a software product that covered the needs of operation of the newly opened clinics of primary health care that have received it for free. In parallel were developed few more products and are used in a number of clinics. The core functionalities of these systems are: booking, medical daybook, the admission of patients, examinations carried out (anamnesis, status by systems, diagnoses, therapies, referrals etc.), creating referrals, drug prescription, dispensing ampullar therapy. The introduction of HIS in hospitals, specialized hospitals and clinics of Clinical Center Skopje (of second and third level of health care) happened independently, where only a small number of hospitals and clinics already implemented information systems (IS).

Computerization of the health system in RS in the period from 2006 to 2013 was performed through projects financed by the World Bank (WB). Within the DILS project [16] were developed and implemented health information systems in most health centers on primary level of health care. Computerization of secondary and tertiary health care is at a very low level - hospitals that have health information system are rare and only one of the four clinical centers has information system.

Numerous are examples in the region, but also in EU and the world, of the implementation of information systems at the national level that did not complete successfully [5]. In the region, the projects are formally closed as successful, but most of them remain on the stage of delivery of technical solution which has little or no use. The WB report concerning the performance of projects financed trough foreign financial support: "Many public sector digital technology projects fail" [18]. In both countries there were attempts to establish integrated health information systems on national level.

In MK was organized a project for development and implementation of a centralized e-health system on national level. The system should have been used in all health facilities in public health in MK and be integrated with systems in other central state institutions. The project had started in 2009. For a period of two years only one module was partly implemented, while the rest did not even start. The project was stopped in 2011 by the MoH. Although there were some technical and organizational problems in the implementation, the main reason for project failure was the selected concept - in one project, in short deadline at national level to develop and implement almost all of the components of a complete e-health system. Taking into account the (little) technical knowledge of health professionals (doctors, nurses, etc.), the resistance to change of almost all of the parties involved, organizational and management capacity of the MoH and of health institutions, such projects could not have been successfully completed.

In RS was also organized project that should develop an integrated health information system. The system should have provided building EHR nationwide [18]. The proposed model of building EHR was decnetralized with planned standards for interopreability and infrastructure for interconnecting the institutions. The project envisaged only a pilot implementation.

3 National Laws on e-Health

One One of the key prerequisites to be fulfilled for successful implementation of national e-health system is adjusting legislation for incorporation of the electronic system in the national health system [5], by defining the model the electronic system - functionality, data sets, the way for its use and others. In Europe, out of 27 countries in which EHR system is implemented nationwide, only in 18 countries there is legislation that regulates the functioning and use of e-health or EHR systems [19].

In the laws to provide a legal framework for the implementation of a nationwide EHR system in European countries as minimal challenges are considered:

- The details and the content of EHR records (specific general health information and exhaustive or detailed elements for certain categories of data).
- Defining the model of interoperability of EHR records – way of data exchange and content of the set of health data.
- Legally establish standardized terminology and the form of coding and categorization of healthcare data.
- In terms of protection of health data at national level, legislation should be established that will introduce special rules for EHRs or accept existing legislation on data protection that is based on general healthcare records.

Comparison of the legislation of the two countries with the EU countries can give a few observations and conclusions. In MK the issues related to e-health are regulated primarily in two laws [6, 15]. It is specific that the laws give very detailed description of the national system for electronic healthcare, which is not typical to most EU countries. Moreover, besides the description of the data set, there is a description of the processes required that should be completed through the system and envisages very strict penalties in case of misuse of the system. This means that changes in the laws that regulate the role and functionality of the national e-health system were adopted and prerequisites were created for providing organizational and personnel resources to manage and support the national system. The most important include the following three changes:

- In the health care bill of RM [15] published in the Official Gazette no. 87 dated 17.06.2013, there is a detailed description of the processes that the national system should cover, as well as the role of all stakeholders in these processes. Eg. For reference: "chosen doctor is obliged to refer patients to secondary and tertiary level of health protection for specialist advisory services through the electronic list of scheduled examinations and interventions." Similarly, the specialists, for additional specialist advisory services, should obligatory referr the patients through the system. Unusually for legislation in MK and well beyond (EU) in law were specified technical conditions for the functioning of the system, the description of the system with many details was given and were envisaged severe penalties for anyone not using the system properly. For example, in the law it is specified that health facilities are obliged to provide two permanent Internet connections (primary and backup) with availability of 99.9%, or that the health facility shall cover the travel costs of the patient, in case "properly scheduled admission can not be used from any reason related to the health facility". These changes enabled successful launch and good functioning of the national system on 01.07.2013.

- With the changes of the law for health records [6] (Official Gazette of RM No. 164 dated 27.11.2013), an accurate definition of the national system of electronic health records has been given: "Electronic system that stores and processes all medical and health information for patients, information for health professionals and associates, data on health institutions, health interventions and services provided in health facilities, data from electronic referrals and electronic prescriptions, data on bookings for specialist examinations and interventions and other data as determined by this and other laws". The same law precisely defines the set and method of collecting and storing all medical data. With these changes is given a legal framework for the development of the system in the coming years (2014–2016).

- With the amendment and extension of the Law for Healthcare (Official Gazette No. 10 dated 22.01.2015) was formed Directorate for Electronic Health as "State administrative body within the Ministry of Health as a legal entity which performs professional activities relevant to the development and promotion of national integrated health information system, and the creation of concepts for the development of health policy on the basis of the analysis of data entered in the national system". Its organizational structure and responsibilities were defined too: "The Department is responsible for upgrading, optimization, execution, regulation, maintenance, control, education of health personnel and analysis of all processes and functionalities associated with the integrated national e-health system with an aim to improve use of the system". With the establishment of a separate institution for e-Health, HR capacities were provided to support the system that is already intensively used but also capacities for its improvement and future development.

In RS the work of e-health systems is regulated by two laws [13, 15]. Using the experiences from MK, one of the basic requirements before starting the project for implementation of an integrated e-health system at the national level, was to analyze the legislation (laws and bylaws) and to propose changes in order to accommodate the system. Unlike in MK, in RS the regulation for the most part was done by preparing appropriate regulations (bylaws). This approach allows greater flexibility and more frequent changes, that do not depend on the Assembly.

Changes in the laws (and bylaws) in both countries have been made to meet the preconditions to start each subsequent stage of implementation of electronic systems. The timeframe of implementation and the success of the implementation of reforms in the health sector in general, is closely linked to the dynamics of change of legislation. The experience of both countries shows that the change in legislation should be made on time, so as not to slow down the implementation of electronic systems, but also well defined to ensure successful change management and proper implementation of new electronic systems.

4   The National e-Health Functional Ecosystems

One One of the most important decisions to be taken before starting the process of development of national e-health system and EHR system is to determine the model of data storage. Generally, this model can be centralized or decentralized. In the centralized model of data storage, as shown in Fig. 3(a), is stored centrally copy of the data that construct EHR. In this model health organizations that are integrated into the system have autonomous and heterogeneous systems where patient health data are stored locally, but one part of the data set in the process of integration of healthcare organization into the EHR system is recorded in a centralized data center. In the decentralized model, shown in Fig. 3(b), there is independent EHR system on health organization level or on regional level. In this model the EHR system it is necessary to ensure interoperability of existing autonomous and heterogeneous systems developed at different times, with different objectives, different data model, platform, technology, and level or type of implemented standards. Achieving semantic interoperability for a large number of distributed systems is complex task.

Both models have their advantages. Keeping health data in the central location allows access to relevant health information about patients in real time; allows patients to receive treatment by doctors from different health organizations which have access to health data of EHR system. Given that health data are available at national level, duplicate tests are avoided and the risk of misdiagnosis is reduced. On the other hand, the decentralized model allows for easier management of risks associated with the security and the privacy of sensitive health data.

Other models are possible, as variation, adaptation or a hybrid of these two that would use the strengths of each of the two models. Based on the analysis of health systems and level of implementation of e-health systems in both countries, but also taking into account the risk factors and the experiences of previous implementations of health systems in the region, it was assessed that adapted centralized model of data storage (Fig. 3(c)) should be implemented, in which some institutions have local copies of the data (they have local systems), while others do not have copies of the data - institutions that do not have local hospital systems and they have to start using the new central system. It was assessed that the proposed model has the "best chance of success."

The functionalities that each institution had to use depended on the services that institution provides. For example, the health centers use the modules for scheduling and referrals, whereas the hospitals use the module for hospital work. Electronic

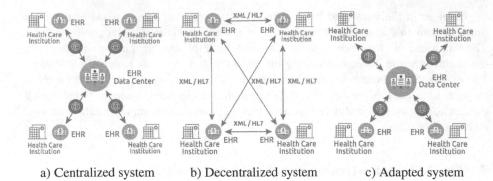

a) Centralized system   b) Decentralized system   c) Adapted system

Fig. 3. (a) Centralized system (b) Decentralized system (c) Adapted system

systems that were used in institutions, had to be integrated with the central system for all modules for which it was necessary. For example, all primary health level clinics, who had their own electronic systems, had to be integrated for functionality: e-booking, e-referral, e-prescription etc. The integration of these systems with the central system enables integrated execution of business processes taking place partly in the local systems, and partly in the central system. In addition, the integration provides bi-directional data exchange - local systems provide the necessary data to the central system and download the necessary data for storage into the local systems. This model of integration of the central system was to allow local systems to continue to operate independently, but also integrated into the national e-health system.

So, concept of e-health system at the national level was elected, which was to build a functional ecosystem involving all health facilities of public healthcare - as providers and users of information in this ecosystem. The aim of the system is not only building functional EHR system, but rather a complete e-health system at the national level, that will play an important role in improving the operational management and the strategic planning of the reforms in public health. For this purpose, the selected model should integrate all systems used in the central state institutions: RHIF, AMMD, IPH and others. E.g. for data retrieved from RHIF - insurance status of patients. For institutions who do not have an electronic system, to provide authorized access to the function-alities of the system via a web interface. For example, it was planned the IPH to have access to all functionalities of the Business Intelligence (BI) module through an interactive web interface. Also, some specific modules or functionalities of the national e-health system are used only through a web user interface. Context level Data Flaw Diagram (DFD) is shown in Fig. 4.

It was also assessed that in order the integration to be successful, on the side of the central system it is necessary to define unambiguous semantics of data exchanged between systems and precisely define and develop Application Programming Interface (API) for integration and interoperability.

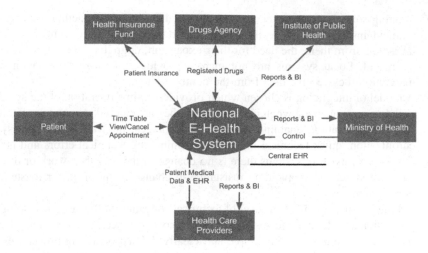

Fig. 4. DFD diagram on conceptual level

5 Discussion and Conclusion

In In designing the multiannual plan for the introduction of e-health system nationwide, which includes nationwide EHR, a comprehensive analysis of the situation of health systems in both countries was made and were achieved all the necessary prerequisites for the start of implementation. This was necessary in order to eliminate most (risk) factors that could adversely affect the implementation of the system and then adversely affect the way the system is used and thereby reduce the positive effects of its use. These factors are: (a) Resistance to change by most stakeholders; (b) Not very large capacities of the participants in the process; (c) The complexity of the system and expectations - very fast results and great expectations.

To successfully overcome the noticed challenges from previous projects for implementation of e-health system in both countries, but also using the experiences from Europe and the world, it was necessary:

1. To provide strong political support. Throughout the period of implementation of the national e-health system strong political support from the MoH should be provided. It should consist of continuous operational support to project teams to easily overcome the resistance to change. Also, it is needed to make changes in the laws governing the role and functionalities of the national e-health system, and to provide organizational and personnel resources to manage and support the system.
2. To find a suitable model to fit the central system and appropriate technical solution. A new concept of architecture was applied – model of adapted centralized system, which involves the integration of a central national e-health system with existing local systems used in healthcare facilities, but also functional user interface for users in institutions that do not have an electronic system. Thus a functional ecosystem is formed where all information systems can function and develop and all members of that ecosystem can have certain benefits. Thereby several advantages are provided:

- Existing software systems continue to be used in the health facilities and government institutions, where they gain importance because the central system takes data from them, the need for their expansion, upgrading and improvement is created. Local systems are not merely providers of information; with the integration they receive data from the central system.
- A model of integration is chosen which provides on-line operation of the system - all data are actualized when in the moment they are entered. Accurately defined API for integration, enabling following advantages: no waiting for data synchronization, quick technical integration, minimizing technical errors and etc.
- For users of existing systems there is no change of the way they work or of the software system, thus avoiding resistance to change or the need for mastering new systems.
- Taking into account the low level of technical education of the new users (health professionals - doctors, nurses, etc.) that did not have electronic health systems, intuitive user interface with simple and clearly defined operating procedures is preferred. Appropriate training models - train the trainers, train the admins, train the end users, should be planned.
- System that is most suitable for users. To avoid the resistance to change of new users - agile (incremental and iterative) approach to the definition, development and implementation of new functionalities should be chosen. In the case of functionality that does not meet the real needs, after feedback form the users, fast repair and improvement should be done.
- Great emphasis on data security, due to privacy and confidentiality.

3. To apply appropriate project methodology for implementation. To find an approach for successful implementation of such a complex system, an analysis of all factors that could affect the process of implementation was performed, and in both countries were applied different approaches, i.e. the projects were organized in different ways and with different duration. In the subsequent research a detailed description of the project methodology will be given and the outcomes and benefits from the use of the systems will be presented.

References

1. Stroetmann, K.A., Artmann, J., Stroetmann, V.N.: European countries on their journey towards national eHealth infrastructures, Final European progress report (2011). http://www.ehealth-strategies.eu/report/eHealth_Strategies_Final_Report_Web.pdf. Accessed 24 Oct 2014
2. WHO Regional Office for Europe. From innovation to implementation. E-Health in the WHO European Region. Copenhagen, Denmark (2016)
3. Bonomi, S., Badr, N.G., Zardini, A., Rossignoli, C.: Improving the introduction of electronic health record: lessons from European and North American Countries. In: Borangiu, T., Drăgoicea, M., Nóvoa, H. (eds.) IESS 2016. LNBIP, vol. 247, pp. 635–648. Springer, Cham (2016). doi:10.1007/978-3-319-32689-4_48

4. Grandy, A.: Electronic health records: how the United States can learn from the french dossier medical personnel. Wis. Int. Law J. **30**(2), 374 (2012)
5. Stone, C.P.: A Glimpse at EHR Implementation Around the World: The Lessons the US Can Learn (2014)
6. Zakon za evidenciite vo oblasta na zdravstvo (Law for health records of Macedonia). http://zdravstvo.gov.mk/wp-content/uploads/2015/05/ZAKON-ZA-EVIDENTSIITE-VO-OBLASTA-NA-ZDRAVSTVOTO-konsolidiran-tekst-2013.164.pdf. Accessed 10 Feb 2017
7. MacDougall, J.: France still seeks an electronic health record (2015). http://www.healthcare-in-europe.com/en/article/14069-france-still-seeks-an-electronic-health-record.html. Accessed 10 Feb 2017
8. European Healthcare Consumer Index Report 2014 (2015). http://www.healthpowerhouse.com/files/EHCI_2014/EHCI_2014_report.pdf. Accessed 15 Mar 2017
9. European Healthcare Consumer Index Report 2015 (2016). http://www.healthpowerhouse.com/files/EHCI_2015/EHCI_2015_report.pdf. Accessed 15 Mar 2017
10. European Healthcare Consumer Index Report 2016 (2017) http://www.healthpowerhouse.com/files/EHCI_2016/EHCI_2016_report.pdf. Accessed 15 Mar 2017
11. Saric, M., Rodwin, V.G.: The once and future health system in the former Yugoslavia: myths and realities. J. Public Health Policy **14**(2), 220–237 (1993)
12. Zakon za zdravstvena zashtita na (Law of Health care of Macedonia). http://zdravstvo.gov.mk/wp-content/uploads/2015/10/0-ZAKON-ZA-ZDRAVSTVENATA-ZASHTITA.pdf. Accessed 15 Mar 2017
13. Zakon o zdravstvenoj zashtiti (Law of Health care of Serbia). http://www.zdravlje.gov.rs/tmpmz-admin/downloads/zakoni1/zakon_zdravstvena_zastit.pdf. Accessed 15 Mar 2017
14. Australian refined diagnosis-related groups (AR-DRG) data cubes. http://www.aihw.gov.au/hospitals-data/ar-drg-data-cubes/. Accessed 15 Mar 2017
15. Zakon o zdravstvenoj dokumnetaciji (Law for health records of Serbia). http://www.rfzo.rs/download/zakoni/Zakon%20o%20zdravstvenoj%20dokumentaciji%20i%20evidencijama%20u%20oblasti%20zdravstva.pdf. Accessed 15 Mar 2017
16. DILS Project Serbia. http://www.worldbank.org/en/news/loans-credits/2008/03/18/serbia-delivery-of-improved-local-services-dils-project. Accessed 15 Mar 2017
17. EU IHIS. http://www.eu-ihis.rs/index_EN.html. Accessed 15 Mar 2017
18. Digital Dividends, World Development Report 2016, p. 165 (2016). http://documents.worldbank.org/curated/en/896971468194972881/pdf/102725-PUB-Replacement-PUBLIC.pdf. Accessed 15 Mar 2017
19. Overview of the national laws on electronic health records in the EU Member States and their interaction with the provision of cross-border eHealth services (2014). http://ec.europa.eu/health//sites/health/files/ehealth/docs/laws_report_recommendations_en.pdf. Accessed 15 Mar 2017

TIROL: The Extensible Interconnectivity Layer for mHealth Applications

Christoph Stach[✉], Frank Steimle, and Ana Cristina Franco da Silva

Institute for Parallel and Distributed Systems, University of Stuttgart,
Universitätstraße 38, 70569 Stuttgart, Germany
{stachch,steimlfk,francoaa}@ipvs.uni-stuttgart.de

Abstract. The prevalence of various chronic conditions is on the rise. Periodic screenings and a persistent therapy are necessary in order to aid the patients. Increasing medical costs and overburdened physicians are the consequences. A telemedical self-management of the illness is considered as the answer to this problem. For this purpose mHealth applications, i.e., the synergy of common smartphones and medical metering devices, are vitally needed. However, poor device interoperability due to heterogeneous connectivity methods hamper the usage of such applications. For this very reason, we introduce the concept for an exTensible InteRcOnnectivity Layer (*TIROL*) to deal with the interconnectivity issues of mHealth applications. Furthermore, we present a prototypical implementation for TIROL to demonstrate the benefits of our approach.

Keywords: mHealth · Medical devices · Harmonization · Interconnectivity layer

1 Introduction

Today, smartphones became constant companions for almost everybody. Due to their consistent connection to the Internet and their ever increasing battery capacity, they serve as a permanent information source as well as communication tool. However, the most outstanding feature of these devices is that any developer can provide new applications for them. Since the number of built-in sensors raises with each smartphone generation, the application possibilities for smartphone are virtually unlimited. Even ordinary smartphones contain hardware required for e.g., basic health and wellness tracking. Moreover, additional sensors tailored to special use-cases can be connect to smartphones, e.g., via Bluetooth.

As a consequence, it is hardly surprising that, especially in the health sector, the use of smartphones can be highly beneficial in terms of saving treatment costs and helping patients who cannot visit their physicians regularly [17]. Patients at any age benefit from health applications for their smartphone—the so-called *mHealth applications* [16]. Particularly advantageous is the telemedical treatment of chronic disease such as diabetes mellitus or the chronic obstructive pulmonary disease (short *COPD*). While hitherto an episodic care in a clinic

© Springer International Publishing AG 2017
R. Damaševičius and V. Mikašytė (Eds.): ICIST 2017, CCIS 756, pp. 190–202, 2017.
DOI: 10.1007/978-3-319-67642-5_16

is required for chronic diseases, mHealth is an enabler for home healthcare. With the help of a smartphone, medical metering devices, and proper mHealth applications, patients are able to diagnose, screen, and therapy their disease by themselves and have to visit their physicians only in case of an emergency, since the required measurements can be carried out very easily with affordable medical measuring devices [24]. That way, not only the physicians' workload gets reduced both also insurance companies safe a lot of money.

However, in order to operate hitch-free, mHealth applications need to be compatible to any available medical metering device, i.e., the application running on a smartphone has to be able to interchange data with the (mostly) external medical hardware. The data interchange constitutes a crucial weak spot for mHealth due to heterogeneous connection types and non-uniform communication protocols [1]. Users are repelled by device incompatibilities, that is, every application supports certain devices only and in some circumstances users have to own several similar medical devices to be able to use all of their mHealth applications. As a consequence, mHealth does not get unreserved approval by the patients despite all of its unquestionable benefits [13].

On that account, this paper provides the following key contributions:

(1) We postulate a requirements specification for an interconnectivity layer which harmonizes the connection techniques.
(2) We introduce the concept for an exTensible InteRcOnnectivity Layer (*TIROL*) to deal with the interconnectivity issues of mHealth applications.
(3) We implement TIROL as an extension for the **P**rivacy **M**anagement **P**latform (*PMP*) [20,21].
(4) We assess the utility of TIROL.

The remainder of this paper is structured as follows: Sect. 2 details on the state of the art concerning connection techniques used by medical metering devices and Sect. 3 looks at related work dealing with the interconnectivity issues of mHealth applications. Based on the shortcomings of these approaches, Sect. 4 postulates a requirements specification for an interconnectivity layer which harmonizes the connection techniques. Following this, the conceptual specification for TIROL is introduced in Sects. 5 and 6 gives some insights on the implementation of TIROL. Section 7 assesses whether TIROL fulfills the requirements specification. Finally, Sect. 8 gives a conclusion and a brief outlook on future work related to mHealth applications.

2   State of the Art

Basically almost every modern medical metering devices in home healthcare is a standalone system. Yet, these devices are designed mainly focusing on their primary task—the metering of health data—and the visual processing of the data is often missed out. Here smartphones come into play. They can be used for both, as a guidance of how to perform a metering as well as a comprehensible presentation of the results [16]. Nowadays the connection is usually realized via

Bluetooth in order to ensure a user-friendly operation. However, concerning the communication protocols such a de facto standard is not in sight. There are several proposals for a uniform connection type, but none of them prevailed yet.

The Bluetooth SIG came up with the *Bluetooth Health Device Profile* (*HDP*) [6] in order to supersede the outdated *Bluetooth Serial Port Profile* (*SPP*) as the SPP causes a poor level of interoperability with different medical devices. The HDP was adopted in 2008 as part of the ISO/IEEE 11073 family of standards. Its main focus is to support a variety of applications for home healthcare. For that purpose, a new communication protocol is introduced, the *Multi-Channel Adaptation Protocol* (*MCAP*). The MCAP is responsible for a reliable connection between a data source (i. e., a medical device) and a data sink (i. e., a smartphone or a PC). Initially, it establishes a control channel between source and sink, e. g., to synchronize the two devices. Then, the devices are able to open multiple channels for payload data. This mode of data transmission is optimized for devices with low resources, as medical devices often have limited computational power. The Bluetooth SIG provides furthermore an optimized exchange protocol to enable interoperability between sensors and data management devices [7]. This includes device data specializations which define how certain families of medical devices (e. g., glucose meters or peak flow monitors) provide their data. I. e., the Bluetooth SIG specifies service IDs and data models for these families. Whereas it is highly recommended that vendors of medical devices should comply with these specifications, it is no necessity for the HDP. As a result, developers of mHealth applications cannot rely on these specializations and they still have to create multiple versions of their applications in order to support medical devices from different vendors (see Fig. 1a). Although each version differentiates only in the connector component, the HDP is still no enabler for mHealth interoperability.

Moreover, HDP belongs to the Classic Bluetooth profiles, i. e., it does not support *Bluetooth Low Energy* (*BLE*). BLE is designed primary for smart devices

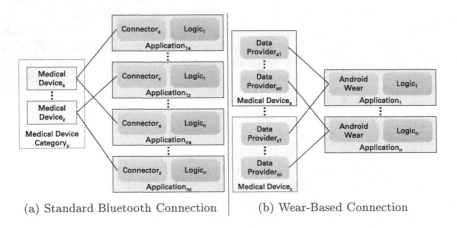

(a) Standard Bluetooth Connection   (b) Wear-Based Connection

Fig. 1. Comparison of standard bluetooth and wear-based connections

where low power consumption is crucial. Due to the new introduced Low Energy protocol stack, BLE is able to reduce power costs considerably. Contrary to Classic Bluetooth, in BLE the devices remain in sleep mode most of the time and initiate a connection only as long as data needs to be transferred. Especially in an mHealth setting where only small amounts of data have to be exchanged and the interval between two measurements (and thus data transfers) is relatively long, BLE is particularly favorable [4]. Thus, a lot of novel medical devices prefer BLE over Classic Bluetooth in order to prolong its battery life. As BLE specifies the communication protocol only but neither standardized device IDs nor message formats for the data exchange, similar medical devices from different vendors establish heterogeneous proprietary communication norms. The Personal Connected Health Alliance consortium promotes various health care profiles in order to counteract this fragmentation [2]. However, the number of proprietary communication protocols such as *Terminal I/O* [23] does not decrease sustainably.

Android Wear is an Android version designed for accessing sensors in wearables. Android Wear facilitates the pairing of wearables with smartphones. For this purpose, it provides a generic API to the sensors of the wearable. This API abstracts from specific communication techniques and protocols. In order to be able to use this API, an mHealth developer has to implement a data provisioning component for each and every of his or her applications. The provisioning component is installed on the wearable. It is needed to establish the connection to the smartphone and it prepares the sensor data for the transmission. This implies that each mHealth application on the smartphone needs a counterpart running on the wearable (see Fig. 1b). Thereby not only the storage consumption but also the power consumption of the wearable increases. Moreover, Android Wear is only compatible to a few certified wearables [12]. Thus, this is also not a comprehensive solution for the interconnectivity issues of mHealth applications.

While most modern medical metering devices in home healthcare have a Bluetooth interface, some vendors still rely on tethered technologies. E.g., the *PO 80* by Beurer Medical[1] has an USB port, only. Other devices such as the *iHealth Vista* by iHealth Labs[2] sends any captured data to an online health service provider. This provider preprocesses the data and makes it available via a web-based interface and/or via APIs for third-party RESTful applications. As a consequence, the already heterogeneous connectivity landscape for medical metering devices gets even more fragmented.

Since it is not conceivable that any of the available connection methods or communication protocols prevail anytime soon, both, developers and users are in great want of a reasonable solution for this fragmentation issue. Currently developers are forced to implement their applications several times in order to support various devices. This leads to long waiting times for patches, since each update has to be applied to every version of the application. Needless to say, that no application is compatible with every device and therefore, users gets furthermore frustrated. That is why also research projects deal with this issue.

---

[1] See www.beurer.com/web/us/products/pulseoximeter/pulse_oximeter/PO-80.

[2] See www.ihealthlabs.com/wireless-scales/wireless-body-analysis-scale.

3   Related Work

The state of the art approaches show, that the solution for the interconnectivity issues of mHealth applications cannot lie in the definition of another standard. Rather promising is the introduction of a unifying interlayer realizing the interconnection between medical devices and mHealth applications [18]. Instead of the huge number of connectors or data providers required per mHealth application (see Fig. 1) a connection interlayer establishes a hub and spoke architecture (see Fig. 2). This reduces the number of required connections sustainably.

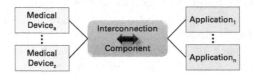

Fig. 2. Hub and spoke architecture realized by a connection interlayer

The *Data Management System* [14] introduces a layer architecture gathering data from input streams (e.g., medical devices) and sending this data to output streams (e.g., smartphones). The focus of this work is on input stream validation and data consistency. For establishing the data streams—and therefore the connection of medical devices—an agent middleware is required which is not included in the approach. Masaud-Wahaishi and Ghenniwa [11] introduce a brokering layer connecting service providers (i.e., data sources) with service requesters (i.e., applications). The brokering layer however does not focus on the connection itself, but on the privacy-aware processing and provisioning of data.

The *Mercury* system [9] deals with this problem by setting up a wireless sensor network for all health sensors. This network provides a single and unified access point for applications. However, specialized microcontrollers are required in the sensors to join the network. Likewise Otto et al. [15] suggest to use wireless body area networks to connect medical devices with smartphones. The smartphone can be used as both, a runtime system for applications as well as a connection to the Internet. Yet, this approach also requires particular hard- and software.

Kouris and Koutsouris [8] recommend to use IoT techniques for the data transfer. Therefore, all sensors are connected to the Internet and send their data to a cloud-based database. mHealth applications can access the sensor data via this database. Even though there are secure transfer protocols for health data such as *Hide-n-Sense* [10], a permanent and unrestricted transmission of sensitive health data to an unknown server is ineligible for most users.

Sorber et al. introduce a vision for a central component called *Amulet* harmonizing the communication with any kind of medical device [19]. Moreover, the Amulet is able to connect to a smartphone, either for providing application with health data or for sending the data to online health services. Amulet should have a small form-factor so that patients are able to carry it always along. This vision is realized as part of the Amulet platform [5]. However, the platform requires a proprietary firmware for the sensors alongside with a distinct runtime-system for the applications. Stock devices are not supported. *BodyScan* [3] has a similar strategy. Their so-called *Wearable Platform*, i.e., the central component of BodyScan, is additionally able to analyze changes on the radio signals of the medical devices. Via these signal changes BodyScan is able to recognize activity pattern in order to enrich the gathered data. Nonetheless, BodyScan has the same disadvantages as Amulet, namely the need for a particular hardware.

As none of these approaches is outright promising, we postulate a requirements specification for an mHealth interlayer in the next section.

4   Requirements Specification

Based on the features as well as shortcomings of the state of the art approaches and related work towards a solution for the interconnectivity issues of mHealth applications, we devise the following requirements which are vital for a unifying interlayer that deals with these problems:

(*A*) **Heterogeneous Connectivity.** As shown above, mHealth applications are executed in a heterogeneous environment. In order to homogenize the environment, the interlayer has to able to support various connection types (such as Classic Bluetooth, BLE, or tethered connections) as well as communication protocols (such as HDP or Terminal I/O).

(*B*) **Flexible Connectivity.** Similar to Android Wear, the interlayer has to abstract from a certain hardware. From an mHealth application's point of view, it is irrelevant which medical device provides a certain kind of health data. Therefore, the devices can be bundled into categories characterized by their features (e.g., respiratory devices or cardiac devices). In this way, an application has to address its data request to a certain category only instead of a certain device and the interlayer forwards it to the right device.

(*C*) **Extensible Interface.** The mHealth landscape is constantly evolving, i.e., new connection types, communication protocols, health devices, and even device categories emerge consistently. Because of that, the interlayer has to be extensible. Otherwise it would be deprecated and thus useless in no time.

(*D*) **Abstract Interface.** The interlayer should provide an abstracted interface to the medical devices. I.e., an application developer has just to define which data s/he wants to access and the interlayer arranges the access.

(*E*) **Resource-Efficient Data Access.** In an mHealth environment, a long battery life is a key issue. Therefore, the data access by the interlayer has to be very resource-efficient. First and foremost, it has to be prevented that every application has to install its own connector on every medical device, as it is needed for Android Wear.

(*F*) **Reliable Data Access.** The interlayer should be able to validate the transmitted values and counteract transmission failures.

(*G*) **No Dependencies.** The interlayer must not require any special hard-
or software. In particular, a manipulation of the health device (e.g., by
installing an additional transmission module) has to be preempted by any
means, due to safety issues. Such an interference could result in corrupted
data.

5   Conceptual Specification

On a conceptual level, our proposed exTensible InteRcOnnectivity Layer
(*TIROL*) is located in between the application layer which executes the applications and the hardware abstraction layer which manages the devices (see Fig. 3).
So, mHealth applications are completely independent from the devices. TIROL
offers them data domain specific interfaces (e.g., respiratory data or cardiac data)
to the devices. The key characteristics of TIROL are detailed in the following:

TIROL is extensible due to a dynamic plugin system towards the hardware
abstraction layer. Each plugin represents a certain data domain. It specifies
which data is available in the respective domain. This specification is completely
device independent—i.e., it uses a uniform data format defined by TIROL—
and it abstracts from a specific access procedure of the devices. Each plugin
offers only data from its domain. If a health device offers data from multiple
domains (e.g., the peak expiratory flow *[respiratory]* heart rate *[cardiac]*), then
two separated plugins are responsible for that device.

The plugins can be added or removed at any time. This is necessary since
some data is only temporarily available. E.g., some medical devices are turned
on only to perform a metering, to broadcast the results, and are shut down
subsequently. A patient is also able to add new device types to TIROL, e.g., when
his or her physician wants to monitor additional health values. Any application
has then automatically access to the newly added data.

Additionally, each plugin is also extensible due to a flexible connection interface. While the plugin itself represents the interface towards the applications,
this connector is the interface towards the devices. The connector manages the
connections to the devices including the individual connection types and communication protocols. Since a patient might have several devices of a certain device
type (e.g., a smart watch and a heart monitor that provide heart rate data), the
connection interface has to be able to exchange the connected device at runtime.
Thereby it is always possible to select the device with the best accuracy which
is currently available. Whenever a new connection type or protocol evolves, it
is only necessary to adapt the connector and afterwards devices uses this new
connection technique are instantly available to any application.

TIROL also reduces the number of required components for the connection
of health devices and applications. While the state of the art approaches require
$a \times d$ connecting components[3] either on the application side (see Fig. 1a) or on the
device side (see Fig. 1b), our approach gets by with h plugins and m extensions

---

[3] Let a be the number of application and d the number of devices.

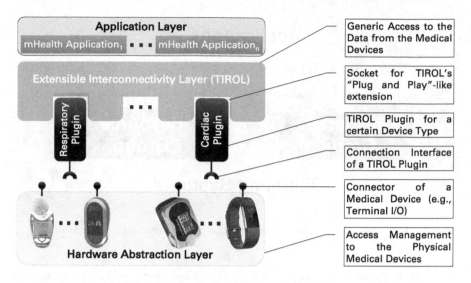

Fig. 3. Conceptual design of the extensible interconnectivity layer (TIROL)

for the connection interface per plugin—i.e., $\sum_h m \in h \approx d^4$. In other words TIROL requires approximately one connecting component per device, no matter how many applications are used. Moreover, since the interlayer harmonizes the heterogeneous connectivity landscape via these connecting components (plugins as well as connection interfaces), no special hardware or software is required. I.e., any standard device and application can be connected to TIROL.

That way, TIROL is very user-friendly: TIROL informs the user which plugins are required by an mHealth application. These requirements are specified by the application developer. Then, the user can obtain the involved plugins from an online repository in case s/he has not installed the plugin already for another application. The plugins contain connectors to all devices from the respective domain and select the best one, regarding a certain quality attribute. I.e., most of the steps are executed automatically by TIROL without any user interference.

6   Implementation Description

The prototypical implementation of TIROL is based on the **P**rivacy **M**anagement **P**latform (*PMP*) for Android-based smartphones. Although the presented prototype is based on Android, the underlying concepts can be applied to any other application platform. The PMP is an interlayer for application platforms separating applications from the operating system (see Fig. 4). Its main purpose is to provide users a fine-grained and context-based mechanism to restrict the applications' access to private data. To that end, it encapsulates all the sensors of the smartphone into so-called *Resource Groups* and applications

---

[4] Let h be the number of health domains and m the number of device models.

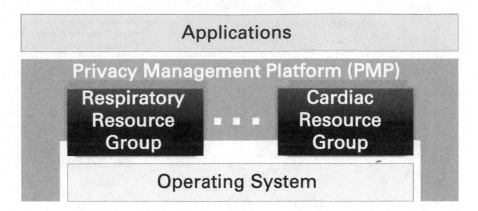

Fig. 4. Simplified layer architecture of the privacy management platform

have to access these groups via predefined interfaces. As the PMP is extendable, i.e., new Resource Groups can added at any time, it is a suitable foundation for TIROL. Thus, TIROL can be realized as an extension for the PMP and each plugin of TIROL can be mapped to a Resource Group of the PMP. In the following, we focus on the PMP's characteristics which are relevant for TIROL, only. For more information about the PMP, please refer to the respective literature [20,21].

Since the PMP enables users to limit or prohibit an application's permissions to access a Resource Group at runtime, it is designed to deal with failed access attempts and missing data due to such restrictions. For that purpose, the PMP segments the program logic of applications into so-called *Service Features*. The data requirements are assigned to these program sections. Each Service Feature can be deactivated individually in case of missing permissions, i.e., missing data. This is highly advantageous for TIROL. In the mHealth context, a patient might have a subset of the medical devices required for a certain applications, only. As a missing medical device is tantamount to a total restraint of the access to this device, a PMP-based implementation of TIROL is able to deactivate the respective Service Features. Thus, the patient can still make use of the remaining features of the application.

From an application's point of view, a Resource Group represents an interface to a certain kind of data (e.g., location data). The interface specifies generic access functions that abstract from the underlying data sources (e.g., `getLatitude`). The Resource Groups are no inherent parts of the PMP but act as independent services. That way, further Resource Groups can be added to the PMP at any time via an external repository. Accordingly, Resource Groups act similar to the plugins of TIROL.

Each Resource Group bundles several *Resources*. A Resource represents an access method to a certain data source (e.g., GPS). As a consequence, a Resource Group can comprise different implementations for the access functions specified therein. The Resource Groups dynamically select the best Resource[5]—and accordingly the best data source—in the current context. Therefore the connection interfaces of the TIROL plugins can be implemented as Resources. Additionally, Resources can implement a buffer, e.g., to cache the latest sensor data. So the Resource is able to provide these data even if the sensor is currently not connected or available. They are also able to perform domain-specific validation procedures to verify the received data and intervene as necessary.

For each Resource Group so-called *Privacy Settings* are defined. A Privacy Setting is an adjustment method for the Resource Group. The PMP uses the Privacy Settings to restrain the access to the data sources which are managed by the Resource Group. E.g., one of the Privacy Setting for the Location Data Resource Group specifies the maximum permissible accuracy of the location data. While the PMP uses the Privacy Settings as a mechanism to assure the user's privacy by defining an upper limit for the quality of the available data, TIROL benefits from these settings in another way. If an application does not require the best data quality, this can be expressed via a Privacy Setting. Then the PMP is able to select another less-accurate but energy-saving Resource within the Resource Group in order to reduce the battery drain.

A *Policy Rule* defines which Service Feature requires access to which type of data, i.e., to which Resource Group, and which Privacy Settings are applied to this access. TIROL is able to create such rules optimizing both, data quality and energy performance for any mHealth application and medical devices in this manner. The Policy Rule can be provided via so-called *Presets*.

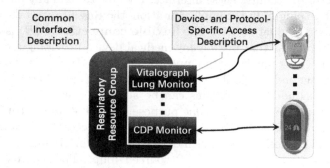

Fig. 5. Model of a health device resource group in the respiratory domain

For the implementation of TIROL, we introduce a model of a generic *Health Device Resource Group* as a blueprint for the plugins of TIROL. Figure 5 depicts the Respiratory Resource Group which is deduced from this generic model. Analogously, there is a Resource Group for each category of medical devices. Within the Resource Groups is one Resource for each medical devices of the respective category. While the Resource Groups define abstract data access functions, the

---

[5] The quality of a Resource is defined respecting a given criterion, e.g., *accuracy*.

Table 1. Realization of the requirements in TIROL's concept and implementation

Requirement	Concept	Implementation
(A)	Connection interfaces	Resources
(B)	TIROL plugins	Resource groups
(C)	"Plug and Play"-like sockets	Resource repository
(D)	Domain-specific plugins	Domain-specific resource groups
(E)	Minimal number connectors	Economic data source selection
(F)	Data preprocessing in plugins	Data preprocessing in resources
(G)	Extensible plugins	Extensible resources

Resources provide the specific implementations of these functions, including the connection establishment and the compliance with the communication protocols.

7 Assessment

In the following, we assess how well TIROL meets the requirements towards a unifying interlayer for mHealth applications (see Sect. 4). Table 1 shows, which component or feature of TIROL fulfills the particular requirement. We consider both, the underlying concept as well as the PMP-based implementation.

The **heterogeneous connectivity** (A) is realized by the connection interfaces of the TIROL plugins. These interfaces are able to bind any medical device to the respective plugin. In the implementation, the Resources establish the connection to the individual devices. The **flexible connectivity** (B) is considered by the TIROL plugins that bundle any medical device providing a certain kind of health data. These plugins are mapped to Resource Groups in the implementation. The "Plug and Play"-like sockets for the plugins provide the **extensible interface** (C) as additional plugins can be added if necessary. The Resource repository of the PMP serve the same purpose. The **abstract interface** (D) is given by the plugins since each plugin provides only access to data of a certain domain without disclosing from which device this data originates. For the implementation the same holds true for the Resource Groups. The **resource-efficient data access** (E) is given by the minimal number of required connectors in the concept. On top of that, the implementation is even able to reduce the power consumption by selecting the most economical data source currently available. Both, the TIROL plugins as well as the Resources are able to preprocess the sensor data. In this way, the data can be validated in order to assure a **reliable data access** (F). TIROL and the PMP are compatible to any given device as both can be extended by plugins or Resources. So there are **no dependencies** (G) whatsoever.

Therefore both, TIROL's concept as well as its implementation meet all of the requirements towards a unifying interlayer for mHealth applications.

8   Conclusion and Outlook

In times of rising medical costs, novel methods of treatment are required. Especially for chronic diseases, the usage of mHealth applications seems to be highly beneficial. However, users are often repelled by device incompatibilities. Therefore, we postulate a requirements specification for an interconnectivity layer to solve these incompatibility issues. Based on this requirements specification, we devise TIROL, an extensible interconnectivity layer for mHealth applications, and a PMP-based implementation of it. Our assessment shows that TIROL constitutes a sound solution for the incompatibility issues of mHealth applications.

Since privacy concerns are another key issue for mHealth applications [1], our PMP-based implementation of TIROL might also be able to solve this problem. As the PMP's main focus is on privacy and data security [20–22], we could piggyback on these strengths by adding such functionalities to our Health Device Resource Group as well. That way TIROL would be able to provide an mHealth infrastructure assuring privacy and data security.

References

1. Chan, M., et al.: Smart wearable systems: current status and future challenges. Artif. Intell. Med. **56**(3), 137–156 (2012)
2. Continua: H.811 Personal Health Devices Interface Design Guidelines. Specification, Personal Connected Health Alliance (2016)
3. Fang, B., et al.: BodyScan: Enabling radio-based sensing on wearable devices for contactless activity and vital sign monitoring. In: MobiSys 2016 (2016)
4. Gupta, N.: Inside Bluetooth Low Energy. Artech House Publishers, Boston (2013)
5. Hester, J., et al.: Amulet: an energy-efficient, multi-application wearable platform. In: SenSys 2016 (2016)
6. Hughes, R.D., et al.: Health Device Profile. Specification, Bluetooth SIG (2012)
7. IEEE: ISO/IEC/IEEE Health informatics-Personal health device communication-Part 20601. IEEE Standard ISO/IEEE 11073–20601:2014 (2014)
8. Kouris, I., Koutsouris, D.: Identifying risky environments for COPD patients using smartphones and internet of things objects. Int. J. Comput. Intell. Stud. **3**(1), 1–17 (2014)
9. Lorincz, K., et al.: Mercury: a wearable sensor network platform for high-fidelity motion analysis. In: SenSys 2009 (2009)
10. Mare, S., et al.: Hide-n-Sense: preserving privacy efficiently in wireless mHealth. Mobile Netw. Appl. **19**(3), 331–344 (2014)
11. Masaud-Wahaishi, A., Ghenniwa, H.: Privacy based information brokering for cooperative distributed e-Health systems. J. Emerg. Technol. Web Intell. **1**(2), 161–171 (2009)
12. Mishra, S.M.: Wearable Android: Android Wear and Google FIT App Development. Wiley Online Library (2015)
13. Murnane, E.L., et al.: Mobile health apps: adoption, adherence, and abandonment. In: UbiComp/ISWC 2015 (2015)
14. O'Donoghue, J., Herbert, J.: Data management within mHealth environments: patient sensors, mobile devices, and databases. J. Data Inf. Qual. **4**(1), 5:1–5:20 (2012)

15. Otto, C., et al.: System architecture of a wireless body area sensor network for ubiquitous health monitoring. J. Mobile Multimed. **1**(4), 307–326 (2005)
16. Siewiorek, D.: Generation smartphone. IEEE Spectr. **49**(9), 54–58 (2012)
17. Silva, B.M., et al.: Mobile-health: a review of current state in 2015. J. Biomed. Inform. **56**, 265–272 (2015)
18. Soceanu, A., et al.: Towards interoperability of eHealth system networked components. In: CSCS 2013 (2013)
19. Sorber, J., et al.: An amulet for trustworthy wearable mHealth. In: HotMobile 2012 (2012)
20. Stach, C., Mitschang, B.: Privacy management for mobile platforms - a review of concepts and approaches. In: MDM 2013 (2013)
21. Stach, C., Mitschang, B.: Design and implementation of the privacy management platform. In: MDM 2014 (2014)
22. Stach, C., Mitschang, B.: The secure data container: an approach to harmonize data sharing with information security. In: MDM 2016 (2016)
23. Stollmann: Terminal I/O Profile. Client implementation guide. Stollmann Entwicklungs- und Vertriebs-GmbH (2015)
24. de Toledo, P., et al.: Telemedicine experience for chronic care in COPD. IEEE Trans. Inf Technol. Biomed. **10**(3), 567–573 (2006)

Decision Support System for Medical Care Quality Assessment Based on Health Records Analysis in Russia

Maksim Taranik[1(✉)] and Georgy Kopanitsa[1,2]

[1] Tomsk Polytechnic University, Tomsk, Russia
taranik@tpu.ru
[2] Tomsk State University for Architecture and Building, Tomsk, Russia

Abstract. The paper presents developed decision system, oriented for healthcare providers. The system allows to healthcare providers to detect and decrease medical nonconformities in health records and forecast the sum of insurance payments taking into account-detected nonconformities. The main components are ISO13606, fuzzy logic and case-based reasoning concept. The result of system implementation allowed to 10% increase insurance payments for healthcare provider.

Keywords: Standards · Case based reasoning · Quality assurance

1 Introduction

Quality of medical care is an important factor that determines the life standard of a country (region) [1, 12]. Unification was one of the steps to increase the quality of medical care in Russia. As a result, treatment standards were developed and implemented in Russia. A standard provides a reference model of a treatment case and describes the necessary medical services and drug prescriptions. Each medical service and drug prescription has a coefficient determining the probability of its application. Therefore, a medical specialist has to make a treatment decision based on these coefficients. This fact identifies medical standards as reference documents with uncertainties and makes fuzzy logic [3] a relevant tool to work with them.

Payment for healthcare can be form insurance company, patient or different funds. In the present work payments from insurance companies are figured. In this case there is medical expert's evaluation of health records and invoices documents. Employees of a medical insurance company perform these procedures. Invoice documents contain the data of insurance payment for a medical service [2]. During the expert evaluation, a medical expert measures a deviation of the medical services presented in the health records from medical standards. Medical experts do not only use standards but also their personal knowledge and experience, which can lead to a subjective conclusion. Therefore, the personal experience of a medical expert is the main element of an expert evaluation. As a result, an expert produces a document, which presents all nonconformities. This document evaluates the quality of medical care provided and specifies the sum of insurance payments for the analyzed treatment case.

© Springer International Publishing AG 2017
R. Damaševičius and V. Mikašytė (Eds.): ICIST 2017, CCIS 756, pp. 203–209, 2017.
DOI: 10.1007/978-3-319-67642-5_17

We can distinguish between two approaches to medical care quality assessment during the health records expert evaluation: based on the medical standards (explicit knowledge) and based on the expert's personal experience (implicit knowledge). In the Russian practice, the use of implicit knowledge is more common. That is why it is necessary to use case-based reasoning (CBR) [4–6, 11] in decision support systems of medical aid quality control and management.

In our work, we propose a concept of a decision support system for medical aid quality management. This system allows healthcare providers to detect and ultimately reduce medical nonconformities in health records. Moreover, it makes use of the detected nonconformities to forecast the sum of insurance payments.

2   Methods

The object of the presented research is the process of planned surgical treatment in the Institute of Microsurgery (Tomsk, Russia). It consists of six steps and each step involves registering a set of medical documents in health records. We acquired a set of health records of the year 2015 inspected by medical experts as well as the results and conclusions of their evaluation. Combinations of treatment cases of 2015 and results of expert evaluation determined a set of treatment cases. Therefore, being the key elements of the CBR concept, the treatment cases represented a training set for the developed system. Linking the medical conclusions to the results of the expert evaluation allowed us to formulate the logical inference rules. To find the treatment cases closest to the one under study, the system primarily selected a set of cases based on the ICD-10 code. Then the obtained set of cases and the investigated case were formalized in vectors, where vector variables conform to the numbers of medical documents at each step of the medical aid process. We used the Euclidean metric to limit the set of cases.

The final set of treatment cases was used to form four reference models. We used fuzzy logic (Mamdani algorithm) to determine the probability coefficients of the entities of each reference model. In accordance with the developed models, we determined how many medical documents are required at each step of the medical aid process based on the logical inference rules. Moreover, Mamdani algorithm was used to evaluate the quality of the whole treatment case and to forecast the amount of the insurance payment based on the detected nonconformities.

The developed algorithm was tested using the health record archive of the Institute of Microsurgery. The evaluation was based on the accuracy of the forecast of insurance payments. The actual amounts of insurance benefits paid to the Institute of Microsurgery were cross-referenced with the estimated values obtained using the above algorithm.

The core of system's medical aid quality evaluation is reference models forming mechanism, that allow to build models of the steps of healthcare process: *registration of white papers, conducting of laboratory tests, conducting of diagnostic tests, conducting of treatment procedures, prescription of medicine, formation documents for insurance company.*

The concept of developed intellectual information system is presented on Fig. 1. Medical standard-based medical insurance forecasting consists of 4 iterations and clinical case-based – consists of 6 iterations.

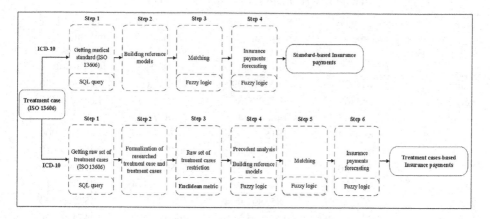

Fig. 1. The concept of decision support system.

The reference model building process can be presented in several steps:

1. Getting a set of treatment cases, which correspond to researched treatment case by ICD-10 code;
2. Formalization of selected treatment cases;
3. Formalization of researches treatment case;
4. Using Euclidian distance for getting distances between treatment cases and treatment case. Gaussian distribution defines set of distances;
5. Making a restriction for the closest treatment cases using three-sigma rule;
6. Getting a restricted set of treatment cases;
7. Getting entities for reference model;
8. Getting probability coefficient of entities.

In the current project, we used archetypes of ISO 13606 [7–10] for storing data.

3   Results

Developed intellectual information system was implemented in the Institute of Microsurgery (Tomsk, Russia). The Institute provides hundreds different surgeries each month. Decision support system was adapted for implementation in the Institute's medical aid process and cooperation with the local information system. The first stage of system implementation was a definition of treatment case base. This stage represented a data acquisition process by the Institute's treatment cases of 2015. The developed algorithm was evaluated using this training set. This evaluation allowed to define the estimation in comparison of real results of medical aid control process and fact sums of insurance payments. After the series of experiment based on the all treatment cases of 2015, were obtained the following results shown in Table 1.

Table 1. The results of system implementation.

Month	Insurance payment	Fact insurance payment	Precedent-based insurance payments forecasting	Standard-based insurance payments forecasting
January	1453078.95	1426719.097	1426719.097	1412451.906
February	1243769.37	1232996.397	1214501.451	1202356.437
March	1416603.47	1400698.491	135877.536	1317917.21
April	1840312.09	1815457.909	1815457.909	1815457.909
Mai	2073797.2	2064890.412	2064890.412	2064890.412
June	1574380.83	1555655.37	1555655.37	1540098.816
July	968507.14	840821.974	815597.3148	815597.3148
August	861201.62	853895.934	853895.934	853895.934
September	1293392.96	1279205.718	1260017.632	1247417.456
October	1214080.05	1204261.377	1168133.536	1156452.2
November	1402607.06	1388928.78	1347260.917	1306843.089
December	1408544.94	1385058.59	1385058.59	1371208.004

By these results, we can conclude that there is a significant divergence between insurance payments computations using treatment cases analysis and medical standards. In the way of using treatment cases, the forecast is more precise. In all treatment, cases received insurance payments values are conformed fully to the real values from learning set of 2015. The graphical results are presented in the Fig. 2.

The forecasting of developed system based on the differences recognition between reference model and a formal model of researched treatment case. The conclusion of

Table 2. Comparative analysis of the results before and after system implementation.

Month	Fine sum before implementation	Fine sum after implementation
January	26359.853	10016.74
February	10772.973	7002.43
March	15904.979	8111.54
April	24854.181	10190.21
Mai	8906.788	1068.81
June	18725.46	0.00
July	2990.136	508.32
August	7305.686	3068.39
September	14187.242	7093.62
October	9818.673	0.00
November	13678.28	6018.44
December	23486.35	6106.45

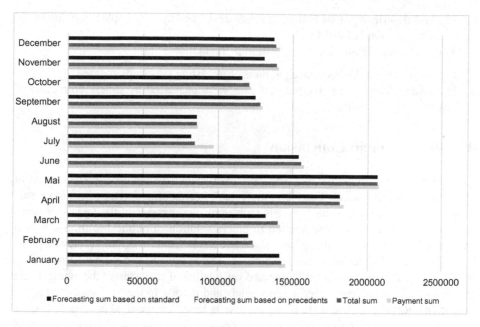

Fig. 2. Graphical results of system implementation.

the end of the first stage of implementation, that the results of inference engine are correspond to the fact. This confirms the accuracy of developed algorithm.

The system implementation in Institute of Microsurgery's treatment process in the beginning of 2016 would allow to significant decrease the total sum of deduction from insurance payments (Table 2).

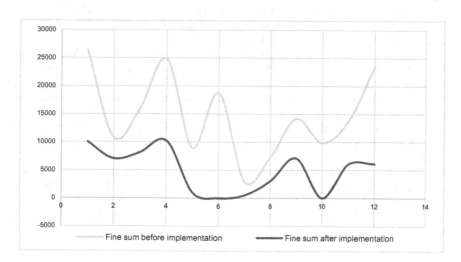

Fig. 3. Graphical results of comparative analysis before and after implementation per month.

Figure 3 describes graphs before and after developed system implementation based on the Institute's data of 2014.

The key results of intellectual system implementation:

- The possibility of the insurance payments forecasting was implemented
- The insurance payments for medical care were increased by timely correction of treatment cases records;

4 Discussion and Conclusion

The results allow to conclude that there is a divergence between quality evaluations of the steps of treatment case. Therefore, the value of sums of insurance payments based on the treatment case reference models represents closer result to the fact. Moreover, presented concept can be also applied to others solution in public health. So, hybrid inference method based on fuzzy logic and CBR can be used for different relevant problems which require decision-making process. The system uses case-based reasoning (CBR) technology and performs automated verification of each step of the medical care process locally based on the reference models and reports to medical specialist about deviations. Reference models building process is based on the dual approach. So, the system contains information not only about medical standards, but also about previous treatment cases and their expertise. The methods presented this research has demonstrated an effectiveness on insurance payments forecasting.

References

1. Taranik, M.A., Kopanitsa, G.D.: Analysis of the process of control quality of medical service in the scope of compulsory health insurance program. J. Control Comput. Sci. Tomsk State Univ. 3(32), 75–85 (2015)
2. Kopanitsa, G., Yampolsky, V.: Approach to extract billing data from medical documentation in Russia – lessons learned. Stud. Health Technol. Inf. 2010, 349–353 (2015)
3. Zadeh, L.A.: Fuzzy sets. Inf. Control 8, 338–353 (1965)
4. Haghighi, P., Burstein, F., Zaslavsky, A., Arbon, P.: Development and evaluation of ontology for intelligent decision support in medical emergency management for mass gatherings. Decis. Support Syst. 54, 1192–1204 (2013)
5. Bequm, S., Barua, S., Ahmed, M.U.: Physiological sensor signals classification for healthcare using sensor data fusion and case-based reasoning. Sensors 14, 11770–11785 (2014)
6. Gonzalez, C., Lopez, D.M., Blobel, B.: Case-based reasoning in intelligent Health Decision Support Systems. Studies in Health Technology and Informatics 189, 44–49 (2013). pHealth 2013
7. Kopanitsa, G., Taranik, M.: Application of ISO 13606 archetypes for an integration of hospital and laboratory information systems. In: Dregvaite, G., Damasevicius, R. (eds.) ICIST 2015. CCIS, vol. 538, pp. 29–36. Springer, Cham (2015). doi:10.1007/978-3-319-24770-0_3
8. Kopanitsa, G., Hildebrand, C., Stausberg, J., Englmeier, K.H.: Visualization of medical data based on EHR standards. Methods Inf. Med. 52(1), 43–50 (2013)

9. Martinez-Costa, C., Menarguez-Tortosa, M., Fernández-Breis, J.T.: An approach for the semantic interoperability of ISO EN 13606 and OpenEHR archetypes. J. Biomed. Inform. **43**, 736–746 (2010)

10. Kopanitsa, G.: Evaluation study for an ISO 13606 archetype based medical data visualization method. J. Med. Syst. **39**(8), 82 (2015)

11. Gu, D., Liang, C., Zhao, H.: A case-based reasoning system based on weighted heterogeneous value distance metric for breast cancer diagnosis. Artif. Intell. Med. **8**, 31–47 (2017)

12. Semenov, I., Kopanitsa, G., Karpov, A., Lakovenko, G., Laskovenko, A.: Implementation of a clinical decision support system for interpretation of laboratory tests for patients (2016)

Information Systems: Special Session on Information and Software Technologies for Intelligent Power Systems

Models of Decision Making
in Planning the Structure of Hybrid
Renewable Energy System

Olha Shulyma(ID), Vira Shendryk(✉)(ID), Yuliia Parfenenko(ID),
and Sergii Shendryk(ID)

Sumy State University, Sumy, Ukraine
{o.shulym, ve-shen}@opm.sumdu.edu.ua,
{yuliya_p, s.shendryk}@cs.sumdu.edu.ua

Abstract. This paper is devoted to the development of scientific and methodological foundations of improvement the information support of decision during planning stage of creation hybrid energy system with renewable energy sources. Here are proposed models of multiple-criteria decision-making for choosing the optimal structure of the grid within three interrelated valuation scenarios by defining a plurality of quality criteria in the form of explicit dependencies from linguistic variables. It was improved the model of structure synthesis of hybrid energy grid by using the methods of combinatorial logic. The model of analysis the technical and economic parameters of the system are proposed accordance to operating logic of the real system. Based on developed models in paper is proposed the information technology of decision support planning hybrid renewable energy system structure.

Keywords: Information technology · Multiple-criteria decision-making of planning hybrid renewable energy system · Decision support system

1 Introduction

Climate change and limited fossil fuels are the greatest global problems facing the world today. Residual houses use about 40% of primary energy consumption. Under these circumstances, energy saving is required. Additionally, the world trends of consistent growth in the cost of energy carriers and severe restrictions in their impact on the environment define significant changes in the requirements for energy systems (ES). The development and the introduction of the energy-saving technologies by increasing the share of renewable energy sources (RES) is a way to meet those needs [1].

Availability of several energy sources makes such system a hybrid renewable energy system (HRES). The process of hybrid system creation is conceived as a set of problems to be solved at each stage, such as planning, designing, installation and operation. Installation and operation are those stages which should be considered during creation and work of the real energy system, so this study is focused on the stages of planning and designing.

© Springer International Publishing AG 2017
R. Damaševičius and V. Mikašytė (Eds.): ICIST 2017, CCIS 756, pp. 213–225, 2017.
DOI: 10.1007/978-3-319-67642-5_18

Despite the significant advantages of such systems, it is very difficult to assess what capacity of RES use in economy. The non-determination of power generation process complicates a decision making process at the stages of planning and designing of a distributed grid; the amount of primary energy depends on the season, day, weather conditions, and RES plants available on the market. In addition, the high cost of the construction of the energy grids with renewable energy sources requires the preliminary detailed analysis of all energy efficiency indexes. This complicates making the right decision regarding the planning system components.

The methodological basis of the planning process of HRES is a system analysis, based on the process of building of generalized model system. In practice, this is connected with the creation of relevant information decision support systems that provide advice on choosing components of HRES.

2   Analysis of the Current State

Tymchuk S. [2], Schur I.Z, Klymko V.I. [3], S. Lazarou, D.S. Oikonomou, L. Ekonomou [4], T.V. Ramachandra [5], I.M. Muslih, Y. Abdellatif [6] studied scientific and methodological bases of energy system modeling. Control technologies of autonomous energy system with renewable energy sources are examined by Holyk E.P. [7], H. Dagdougui, R. Minciardi, A. Ouammi, M. Robba, R. Sacile [8]. Problems of information support in decision-making during designing of grids with RES are discussed by Sabirzyanov T.G., Kubkina M.V., Soldatenko V.P. [9], C. Tiba, A.L.B. Candeias, N. Fraidenraich [10], Choong-Sung Yi, Jin-Hee Lee, Myung-Pil Shim [11].

In spite of extensive use of information technology to solve specific problems, there is not for the moment a unified integrated approach to addressing the problem of improving the quality of decision-making processes when planning the structure of hybrid energy systems with renewable energy sources.

Improvements of information support decision-making processes will allow to increase the effectiveness of the decisions on the planning of grid structure, thereby reducing the cost of building the grid while ensuring a sufficient level of energy efficiency.

3   Aims and Objectives of the Study

This study aims at development of a model that solves a multiple-criteria decision-making problem to choose the best structure of the hybrid renewable energy system.

The achievement of the aim stated in this study will require solving the following interrelated problems:

- To formalize the decision-making problem when planning the structure of a hybrid energy system by developing a set of models;
- To develop a planning model for structure of energy grid with renewable energy sources by using the method of structure synthesis;

- To develop a model that defines technical-and-economical indexes of energy grid;
- To generate a set of quantitative and qualitative criteria to evaluate alternatives of HRES structure
- To develop a model of decision support when planning the structure of hybrid energy grids of renewable energy;
- To develop decision support system models when planning the structure of hybrid energy systems with renewable energy sources.

4   Decision-Making Processes When Planning the Structure of Hybrid Energy Systems

Decision support when planning the structure of hybrid energy systems with renewable energy sources is carried out according to the scheme shown in Fig. 1.

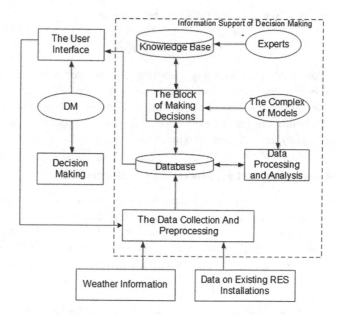

Fig. 1. The scheme of the decision making process

During information gathering and its preprocessing, the database (DB) receives data about the implication of factors influencing on energy grid structure.

Information support for decision making when planning the structure of hybrid energy systems with renewable energy sources is carried out using a set of models: a model of information gathering and processing, a model that defines technical-and-economical indexes of energy grid, a model that generates the set of alternatives of energy grid structure, a model that creates effective decisions when planning the structures of hybrid energy systems with renewable energy, a model that defines estimation criteria.

To make a decision on planning the best structure of grid, expert knowledge stored in the knowledge base is used. A decision maker (DM) analysing all data used in the decision-making process receives a feasibility data of the best alternative of grid structure and ranked list of decisions being the closest to the best one.

A decision-support system (DSS) that performs the information support for decision making when planning the structure of hybrid energy systems with renewable energy sources is proposed, such DSS contains next components:

$$DSS = \langle O, Sw, Z, Ds \rangle \tag{1}$$

where O – the set of users, who make decision; Sw – the set of software; Z – the set of tasks which are performed in DSS; Ds – the set of data on which decisions are made.

5   DSS Tasks

The set of problems Z, which serve DSS can be given as:

$$Z = Z_0 \cup Z_1 \cup Z_2 \cup Z_3 \cup Z_4 \tag{2}$$

where $Z0$ – set of problems concerning gathering and preprocessing of information, $Z1$ – set of problems concerning the alternative generation, $Z2$ – set of problems concerning the definition of technical-and-economical indexes of alternatives, $Z3$ – set of problems to generate criteria for evaluation, $Z4$ – set of problems concerning the estimation of efficiency and decision making.

5.1   Tasks of Gathering and Preprocessing of Information

Set Z_0 is formed by gathering data about plant Res available on the market, weather conditions Wcg, power consumption Ec, distribution grids available in the area which is planned to be connected to the HRES Pl. This results in formation of the set of the solar panels (P) available on the market, wind turbines (W), batteries (A), determination of the external grid capacity Tpl, day with the worst weather conditions in the area (Objs) which forms the basis for decision-making.

$$Z_0 = Step^0 : \{Res, W_{cg}, E_c, Pl\} \rightarrow \{P, W, A, Objs, W_c, Tpl\} \tag{3}$$

$$Z_o = W_c \cup E_c \cup Res \cup Tpl \tag{4}$$

$$Res = P \cup W \cup A \ (6) \tag{5}$$

The data set of weather conditions

$$W_{cg} = \{t, v, c, sd\} \tag{6}$$

where t – ambient temperature in °C, v - wind speed in meters per second, c – cloudiness – is value from the set from 1 to 5, sd - duration of solar day in hour.

The set of data on the solar panel/wind turbines/storage battery

$$P|W|A = \{price, power, manuf\} \tag{7}$$

where price – equipment price in euro, power – power for solar panels and Wind turbines in Wh/capacity in AH, manuf – name of manufacturer.

5.2   Tasks of Generating a Set of System Structure Alternatives

The planning process of HRES structure refers to the problems of the structural synthesis. The identification of the system configuration is considered within the morphological analysis for day with a worse weather conditions in the place (*Objs*).

$$Z_1 = Step^1 : \{Objs, P, W, A\} \rightarrow \{i, I\} \tag{8}$$

Each alternative is characterized by the presence of solar panels P and/or wind turbines W and as well as battery A [12].

$$I = \{i_e\}, \text{ де } i =< pv_e, wt_e, ab_e >, \quad e = \overline{1, n} \tag{9}$$

The problem of sorting of all possible configurations is proposed to solve using combinatorial analysis. Total number of alternative structures of HRES:

$$I' = (P_m^n + W_k^l) * A_o^p \quad \text{при } A_o^p \geq 1, \ n \in \overline{0, m}, \ k \in \overline{0, l}, \ o \in \overline{0, p} \tag{10}$$

where PV_m^n, W_k^l – is a number of all possible combinations of solar panels and wind turbines, AB_o^p is a number of all possible alternatives of batteries, n, l, p is a certain type of solar panel, wind turbine, battery consequently, m, k, o is the total number of types of solar panel, wind turbine, battery.

5.3   Tasks of Forming a Set of Technical-and-Economical Indexes

The set of technical-and-economical indexes $B(i)$ of alternatives is generated with regard to a operating logic of HRES.

$$Z_2 = Step^2 : \{Objs, i, Wc, E_c, Tpl\} \rightarrow \{i, B(i)\} \tag{11}$$

The set Z_2 for each alternative i forms with the reference to gathering data on capacity of the external grid Tpl, weather conditions W_c based on it the day with the whorse condition is determined (*Objs*).

The level of a battery charge depending on the consumption in the economy and the real capacity of the solar panel/wind turbine – the capacity that can be generated in areas where the HRES is planned to be built under the worst weather conditions is obtained. Indexes of technical and economical efficiency and their limit value are calculated for each alternative [13].

Consumption in the household:

$$RH = \sum_{i=1}^{N} RH_i \qquad (12)$$

The value of energy generated by solar panels:

$$0 \leq E_s \leq E_{smax} \qquad (13)$$

The value of energy generated by wind turbines:

$$0 \leq E_w \leq E_{wmax} \qquad (14)$$

The value of the battery capacity:

$$0 \leq E_{bmin} \leq E_b \leq E_{bmax} \qquad (15)$$

The value of the total available generated energy:

$$E_a = E_s + E_b + E_w \qquad (16)$$

The limit value of excess generated energy that may not exceed the grid capacity:

$$0 \leq REPG^* \leq Tpl \qquad (17)$$

The limit value of energy deficiency:

$$DPSP^* \leq 0 \qquad (18)$$

Energy and economic efficiency of the system is calculated on the bases of the following parameters:

1. Deficiency of power supply probability which depends on hourly possible energy scarcity:

$$DPSP = \frac{\sum_{t=1}^{T} (RH(t) - Ea(t))}{\sum_{t=1}^{T} RH(t)} \qquad (19)$$

2. Relative excess power generated which depends on hourly possible excess energy which can be sold according to a "green" tariff to an external grid.

$$REPG = \frac{\sum_{t=1}^{T} (Ea(t) - RH(t))}{\sum_{t=1}^{T} RH(t)} \qquad (20)$$

3. The total cost of building the system COE.

5.4   Tasks of Definition of Value Criterion

The set of definition problems of value criterion includes the problems of determining the set of $K = \{j_m\}, m = \overline{1,m}$ quantitative and qualitative criteria, calculation of membership functions of qualitative criteria given in the form of fuzzy variables, reduction to one space with quality quantitative estimates.

$$Z_3 = Step^3 : \{Objs, i, B(i)\} \rightarrow \{i, K\} \qquad (21)$$

Such quantitative assessment criteria include the following: deficiency of power supply probability (DPSP), relative excess power generated (REPG) and total cost of building the system (COE).

Qualitative criteria are: noise (N), aesthetic integrity (EV), possible repair works (RC), scheduled maintenance (SC) and influence of characteristic features of areas on the energy generation (SA). The list of criterion may be supplemented by experts.

$$K = \{REPG, DPSP, COE, N, EV, RC, SC, SA\} \qquad (22)$$

The fuzzy-set theory and expert evaluation methods are used to calculate the membership functions of qualitative criteria

$$\mu_{l_h}(u_b) = \frac{1}{K} \sum_{k=1,K} b^k_{h,b} \qquad (23)$$

where K – the amount of experts; $b^k_{h,b}$ opinion of k-th expert on the presence of properties fuzzy sets in the element u_b.

In general the model of fuzzy inference for decision on the value of quality criteria can be expressed by:

$$Z = F(Z1, Z2, \ldots, ZN) \qquad (24)$$

where $Z1, Z2, \ldots, ZN$ is linguistic variables that characterize the quality criterion.

Mamdani's method is used for fuzzy inference for decision on the value of quality criteria. The centroid method is used for defuzzification.

The example of the rule of fuzzy inference decision on the identification of noise level (Z) is given in Table 1.

Table 1. An example of fuzzy rule of value output for criterion "Noise"

The preconditions	*ZY is ZY1, BY is BY2*
The rule formulation	*If ZY is ZY1 and BY is BY2 then Z = Z2.*
Interpretation	If "TheDistancetoHousehold" = ZY1 and "ThePowerOfWindturbines" = BY2, then value output for criterion "Noise" = Z2.

Unfussy variable values "TheDistancetoHousehold" (ZY) and "ThePowerOfWind-turbines" (BY) make up the rules as prerequisites predicates.

$$Z = \{Z1, Z2, \ldots Z9\} \tag{25}$$

$$Z = F(ZY, BY) \tag{26}$$

$$ZY = ZY1, ZY2, ZY3 \tag{27}$$

$$BY = BY1, BY2, BY3 \tag{28}$$

The compilation of quantitative criteria estimation to a single space with quality is carried out according to normalization procedure. This procedure involves reducing the criteria to a dimensionless form on the interval [0; 1]. In addition to the current value of the criterion, the maximum and minimum values from all possible values within criterion are taken into account.

$$s_{ij} = \left(\frac{v_i(s) - v_i^-}{v_i^+ - v_i^-} \right)^{\vartheta_i} \tag{29}$$

5.5   Tasks of Estimation of Efficiency and Decision-Making

The set of efficiency and decision-making estimation problems contains problems of alternative utility functions and methods for the final ranking of alternatives used to determine the best one in term to estimation scenarios.

$$Z_4 = Step^4 : \{Objs, i, I, EF^*\} \rightarrow \{i^o, K(i^o)\} \tag{30}$$

The estimation of efficiency consists of two stages:
In the first stage all alternatives are ranked on social and economic scenario:

$$\begin{cases} REPG(s) \geq REPG^* \\ COE(s) \leq COE^* \quad (32) \\ i_o \rightarrow \arg\max(R_i(z)) \end{cases} \tag{31}$$

as well as energy efficiency scenario according to excess power generated:

$$\begin{cases} COE(s) \leq COE^* \\ REPG(s) \geq REPG^* \\ i_o \rightarrow \arg\max(R_i(z)) \end{cases} \tag{32}$$

The estimation of alternatives at the first stage results in generation of Pareto-optimal alternatives set that are combined for estimation in term of energy efficiency scenario according to deficiency of power supply probability:

$$\begin{cases} DPSP(s) \leq DPSP^* \\ i_o \rightarrow \ \arg\max(R_i(z)) \end{cases} \tag{33}$$

Where $R_i(z)$ is the additive function of general utility, COE^* is limit values of the cost of the system, $REPG^*$ is limit values of the energy efficiency of the system, $DPSP^*$ is limit values of the energy deficiency in the system.

In terms of each scenario the alternative efficiency is estimated according to typical procedure:

1. The calculation of total fuzzy utility function alternatives:

$$R_i(z) = \sum_{j=1}^{m} w_j s_{ij}, \ z = (w_1 \ldots w_m; s_{i1} \ldots s_{im}) \tag{34}$$

According to relation 31 the total fuzzy utility function of each alternatives is produced by considering criterion weight within universal space [0, 1]. The weight of criterion is distributed according to three scenarios. The procedure of criterion weightening is performed by experts and is as follows: in the first stage all criterion is divided into low, medium, high priority. Then, criteria are classified as more or less important within each of this group (Table 2).

Table 2. Weight distribution of criteria

Socio-economic scenario					
High priority		Medium priority		Low priority	
Less important	More important	Less important	More important	Less important	More important
SC, RC	COE	EV	N	REPG,N	SA
Energy efficient scenario of first level					
High priority		Medium priority		Low priority	
Less important	More important	Less important	Less important	More important	Less important
SA	REPG	N	EV, DPSP	COE, SC	RC
Energy efficient scenario of second level					
High priority		Medium priority		Low priority	
Less important	More important	Less important	Less important	More important	Less important
REPG	DPSP	SA, SC	RC	N, EV	COE

2. The final ranking of alternatives: for scenarios of stage I - generation of Pareto-optimal solutions, for s of stage II - generation of the matrix of concessions and selection of effective alternative according to max min approach [14]:

$$\mu_m = \min\{\mu_{im}^{-i}(x)\} \tag{35}$$

$$\mu(x) = \max\{\mu_k\} \tag{36}$$

A decision maker receives feasibility data of the best alternative in terms of estimation according to estimation criterion and weight of criterion as well as recommendations for alternative planning of the latter, which is closest to the best structure of the energy grid.

6 Information Technologies for Decision Support When Planning a Structure of Energy Grid

SADT-methodology and IDEF-technology were used as the mathematical tools for modeling. These technologies provide the possibility to display and analyze models of complex systems in a graphic representation of functional, information and logical structures of processes. As a result of the system analysis of information relationships between the planning process components of the grid structure, the functional models for numerical calculation of technical and economic parameters of energy grid, planning of several alternatives of energy grid structure as well as decision generation on planning the structure of hybrid energy systems with renewable energy were developed. The information technology for decision support when planning the structure of the energy grid with RES combining models and algorithmic support the abovementioned process was developed.

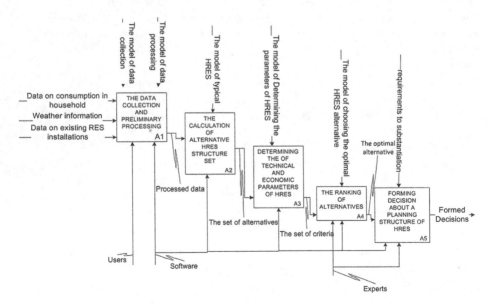

Fig. 2. The functional model of information technology of decision support

The information technology for decision support when planning the structure of the energy grid with RES consists of five interrelated stages. Figure 2 shows the functional model of the proposed information technology.

The stage 1 includes gathering of data, verification of data correctness and data storage. The sets of data consist of data about weather conditions in the area, power consumption in the economy, plant RES available on the market. In the stage 2 data received at the stage 1 are used for calculation of all possible combinations of energy grid according to model (8) reported in the Sect. 2. In the stage 3 energy and economic indexes for each configuration is calculated according to model (11) presented at the Sect. 2. The output data are interpreted into quantitative criteria indicating the boundary conditions. In the stage 4 all alternatives are estimated based on the developed rating model for alternatives according to three optimization scenarios (32, 33, 34). In the stage 5 the decision on choice of the best structure of hybrid energy grid among the alternatives ranked on the basis of the utility function model is generated. Thus the decision maker receives recommendations for the best grid structure.

7 Results and Comparison to the Other Methods Outcomes

According to proposed methodology were generated 28356 all alternatives which can satisfy household consumption. After socio-economic scenario it were chosen 16 alternatives and after energy efficiency scenario according to excess power generated it were chosen 6775 alternatives. After was formed the new set with 9 alternatives as the intersection of results, and was determined the optimal configuration in term of energy efficiency scenario according to deficiency of power supply probability. This approach helped to determine the best alternative within 3 interrelated estimation scenarios. For a temperate climate with a cold and gloomy winter, it was determined that the configuration consisted of 160 solar panels with a power of 160 W and 7 batteries with a capacity of 1000 Ah.

In order to verify the correctness of the calculations, the results were compared with the opinion of the expert group and using software based on the use of ELECTRE III and Promethee methods.

The results show that correctness of proposed methodology is higher on 13,5% in accordance to ELECTRE III method, and higher on 16,8% in accordance to Promethee method.

8 Conclusions

This study resulted in theoretical generalization of existed approaches regarding to information support of planning the grid structure and developing the model set that implement the task of gathering, processing and analyzing the data on the basis of which decisions on planning of building energy efficiency using RES considering operation logic of real grid and factors influencing on generation and consumption of electric energy are taken on.

1. The analysis of models, methods and tools used for information support when planning the structure of hybrid energy system was carried out. The aims and objectives of this study were produced at the basis of the results of this analysis.
2. The model of structure synthesis of hybrid energy grid was improved by using the methods of combinatorial logic analysis.
3. The model of technical and economic parameters of the system which allows to consider the operating logic of the real system was improved.
4. The models of multiobjective problem choosing the best structure of the energy grid within three interrelated estimation scenarios were developed.

References

1. Shendryk, V., Shulyma, O., Parfenenko, Y.: The topicality and the peculiarities of the renewable energy sources integration into the ukrainian power grids and the heating system. In: Promoting Sustainable Practices Through Energy Engineering and Asset Management, pp. 162–192 (2015)
2. Tymchuk, S.O., Shendryk, V.V., Shendryk, S.O., Shulyma, O.V.: Pidtrymka pryynyattya rishen' dlya optymal'noho keruvannya elektropostachannya vid vidnovlyuval'nykh dzherel enerhiyi. Problemy enerhoresursozberezhennya v elektrotekhnichnykh systemakh. Nauka, osvita i praktyka, vol. 1, pp. 208–210 (2016)
3. Shchur, I.Z., Klymko, V.I.: Prohnozuvannya efektyvnosti roboty fotoelektrychnykh paneley u misti L'vovi. Visnyk Natsional'noho universytetu "L'vivs'ka politekhnika". Elektroener-hetychni ta elektromekhanichni systemy, vol. 785, pp. 88–94 (2014)
4. Lazarou, S., Oikonomou, D.S., Ekonomou, L.: A platform for planning and evaluating distributed generation connected to the hellenic electric distribution grid. In: Proceedings of the 11th WSEAS International Conference on Circuits, Systems, Electronics, Control & Signal Processing, pp. 80–86 (2012)
5. Ramachandra, T.V.: RIEP: Regional integrated energy plan. Renew. Sustain. Energy Rev. 13(2), 285–317 (2009)
6. Muslih, I.M., Abdellatif, Y.: Hybrid micro-power energy station; design and optimization by using HOMER modeling software. In: Proceedings of The 2011 International Conference on Modeling, Simulation and Visualization Methods, pp. 183–193 (2011)
7. Golik, E.P.: Avtomaticheskoe upravlenie processom jenergosnabzhenija avtonomnyh potrebitelej na osnove apparata nechetkoj logiki s nejrosetevoj adaptaciej. Jelektronnoe modelirovanie 35(3), 113–123 (2013)
8. Dagdougui, H., Minciardi, R., Ouammi, A., Robba, M., Sacilea, R.: A dynamic optimization model for smart micro-grid: integration of a mix of renewable resources for a green building. In: Proceedings of the 2010 International Congress on Environmental Modelling and Software, pp. 1–8 (2010)
9. Sabirzyanov, T.H., Kubkin, M.V., Soldatenko, V.P.: Metodyka vyboru struktury i skladu system elektropostachannya z vidnovlyuvanymy dzherelamy. Zbirnyk naukovykh prats' KNTU 24(2), 146–151 (2011)
10. Tiba, C., Candeias, A.L.B., Fraidenraich, N., de Barbosa, E.M., de Carvalho Neto, P.B., de Melo Filho, J.B.: A GIS-based decision support tool for renewable energy management and planning in semi-arid rural environments of northeast of Brazil. Renew. Energy 35(12), 2921–2932 (2010)

11. Yi, C.-S., Lee, J.-H., Shim, M.-P.: Site location analysis for small hydropower using geo-spatial information system. Renew. Energy **35**(4), 852–861 (2010)
12. Shulyma, O., Shendryk, V., Baranova, I., Marchenko, A.: The features of the smart microgrid as the object of information modeling. In: Dregvaite, G., Damasevicius, R. (eds.) Information and Software Technologies, ICIST 2014. Communications in Computer and Information Science, vol. 465, pp. 12–23 (2014)
13. Pakštas, A., Shulyma, O., Shendryk, V.: On defining and assessing of the energy balance and operational logic within hybrid renewable energy systems. In: Dregvaite, G., Damasevicius, R. (eds.) ICIST 2016. CCIS, vol. 639, pp. 151–160. Springer, Cham (2016). doi:10.1007/978-3-319-46254-7_12
14. Dubois, D., Fargier, H., Prade, H.: Refinements of the maximin approach to decision-making in a fuzzy environment. Fuzzy Sets Syst. **81**(1), 103–122 (1996)

Software Architecture for an ORC Turbine – Case Study for an Intelligent Technical System in the Era of the Internet of Things

Carsten Wolff[✉], Mathias Knirr, Tobias Pallwitz, Hüseyin Igci, Klaus-Peter Priebe, Peter Schulz, and Jörn Strumberg

Dortmund University of Applied Sciences, Otto-Hahn-Str. 23, 44227 Dortmund, Germany
carsten.wolff@fh-dortmund.de

Abstract. Intelligent Technical Systems are the consequent extension of the concept of Mechatronic Systems into the world of software-intensive, networked systems. The concept enhances the functionality and variability of physical (or electro-mechanical) technical systems by adding embedded electronics and software. This adds degrees of freedom (DoF) and controllability to the technical systems. It enhances the effectivity of integrating such systems into distributed infrastructures (e.g. smart grids) via a public network like the internet. Therefore, it enables them for an effective integration into the internet-of-things (IoT) since such Intelligent Technical Systems can add and draw significant functionality and optimisation potential from networking with other systems. They can become an integral part of a distributed system which is coupled via the IoT. Nevertheless, it is important to leverage between local control and distributed control carefully according to the requirements of the technical application. A smart heating grid is an example of a distributed cyber-physical system (CPS) which can be coupled via IoT. Such systems include components like block heat and power plants which produce electricity (fed into the public smart grid) and heat. Smart heating grid benefit from components which can convert heat into electricity in a flexible and controllable way and which can change fast from heat provision to electricity provision and vice-versa. An Organic Rankine Cycle (ORC) Turbine is such a component since it converts exhaust heat into electricity. This takes heat out of the heating grid and puts electricity into the electricity grid instead. Making such an ORC turbine intelligent means optimizing it for the usage in a smart heating grid. The challenge is to design a control software architecture which allows coupling via IoT on the required interaction level of the distributed system while guaranteeing a safe operation on the local level. The paper presents the software architecture of an ORC turbine based on the architecture of the Operator-Controller-Module (OCM). The OCM provides an architecture pattern which allows a seamless integration into a smart heating grid based on an IoT infrastructure while enabling maximum flexibility and efficiency of the local functionality of the turbine.

Keywords: Intelligent technical systems · Operator-Controller-Module (OCM) · Smart heating grid · Organic Rankine Cycle (ORC) turbine

© Springer International Publishing AG 2017
R. Damaševičius and V. Mikašytė (Eds.): ICIST 2017, CCIS 756, pp. 226–237, 2017.
DOI: 10.1007/978-3-319-67642-5_19

1 Introduction

1.1 Challenges for IoT in Technical Applications

Smart-X applications are an important domain for the market deployment of Internet-of-Things (IoT) technology [30]. For smart heating grids and smart electricity grids a major progress is expected if the coupling is moving from proprietary standards to open protocols as with the IoT. Nevertheless – apart from general challenges in communication via public infrastructure like security, reliability and standards for interfacing [29] – technical applications like smart grids face some specific challenges which need to be addressed carefully [30]:

- "Dealing with critical latencies, e.g. in control loops": Technical systems like the example of the ORC turbine contain control loops which operate the system and its subsystems in certain operation points which are safe, reliable and efficient. The control loop has to react in a defined time to deviations. This requires the fulfilment of certain real-time requirements. Dependent on the re-action time this cannot be fulfilled via the internet. Therefore, the system architecture has to partition the functionality into control loops with different real time requirements.
- "System partitioning (local/cloud based intelligence)": During partitioning of the system the decision needs to be taken which functionality is implemented locally without coupling via IoT and which functionality can be implemented e.g. as a cloud service. Apart from real-time considerations this has to take into account that the technical system should be able to operate safely or at least to fail safely without IoT connection. Functionality which requires coupling via IoT or certain cloud services needs to be separated from local functionality.
- "Real-time models and design methods describing reliable interworking of heterogeneous systems. Identifying and monitoring critical system elements. Detecting critical overall system states in due time.": The ORC turbine of our example will be embedded into such a heterogeneous system and needs to signal critical states. Furthermore, it has to react appropriately to critical states from the overall system.
- "Power grids have to be able to react correctly and quickly to fluctuations" in demand and supply: This ability to react to fluctuations is the main benefit of an intelligent ORC turbine. Only with this flexibility it becomes useful to integrate the turbine into a smart heating grid and therefore connect it to the IoT.

The following sections are dealing with the respective steps to design the software architecture of an ORC turbine according to the requirements of an operation in a smart heating grid which is coupled via IoT. This serves as an example and a blue print for the design of Intelligent Technical Systems [15] for effective and efficient integration into IoT-coupled smart systems. The example case of the ORC turbine with its specific characteristics and requirements is presented in Sect. 1.2. Section 2 summarizes the relevant related work on IoT device architectures (briefly in Sect. 2.1) and the applied Operator-Controller-Module (OCM) architecture [3, 17, 20] (in Sect. 2.2). Section 3 describes the software and system architecture of the ORC turbine in more detail. It contains the main consequences for the integration of such an Intelligent Technical

System into the IoT. Section 4 presents results from the implementation of the ORC turbine and the integration into a district heating system. Section 5 summarizes the work and draws the main conclusions.

1.2   Case Study ORC Turbine

Organic Rankine Cycle (ORC) turbines implement a thermodynamic process which converts low temperature heat (e.g. exhaust heat from a motor) into electricity [7]. With this functionality, it serves as a valuable component in sustainable energy systems and contributes to long term strategies for mitigating global warming [22]. Nevertheless, ORC turbines are not a big market success so far [25] which is caused by several factors. The price is too high compared to the power which is generated and the flexibility in terms of reaction to the fluctuation in heat and electricity demand is too low due to the slow changes of efficient operating points in the thermodynamic processes. Therefore, we developed the ORC system [31] according to the following main requirements:

- Flexibility in electricity production (and heat usage) due to several efficient operating points for different heat sources, temperatures and electricity demands.
- Fast and robust change between the different operating points with guaranteed thermodynamic stability.
- Intelligent control and planning system with the ability to be connected to electricity and heat production control systems (e.g. smart grid) and to the overall energy system control and planning levels.
- Modular system with complete automation of the control and maintenance systems.

The main challenge is the design of an ORC turbine with several efficient operating points and a fast and robust change between the operating points. For using different temperature ranges, respective working fluids have been selected [27]. The result is a flexible, cascaded two-stage ORC turbine [8] which is based on four coupled thermodynamic modules:

- The first module contains a direct evaporator driven by exhaust gas from a waste heat source (e.g. biogas block heat and power plant) with temperature levels up to 600 °C, cooling the exhaust gas down to 75 °C.
- The second module contains the high temperature and high pressure ORC with a sophisticated turbo generator (HT TuGen). This module contains also the condenser of the working fluid, which produces heat at a level between 90 °C to 110 °C carried by a specific working fluid.
- The third module uses solar or waste heat sources in the temperature range between 90 °C and 200 °C. It contains the low temperature und low pressure ORC, also with a sophisticated turbo generator (NT TuGen) using a grouping of nozzles for best efficiency at variable loads. Condensation energy is released on levels between 35 °C and 65 °C.
- The fourth module – if required – contains the liquefier of the working fluid of the low temperature ORC.

The ORC turbine and the thermodynamic system were developed in a research project conducted by the authors [31].

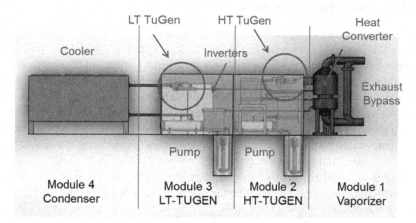

Fig. 1. Organic Rankine Cycle (ORC) turbine [31]

One target application for the ORC turbine is the conversion of conventional District Heating Systems in the Ruhr-Metropolitan Area [18]. These heating grids have been supplied with heat from conventional coal and gas fired power plants or from large steel mills in the past. The conventional power plants go offline step by step. They are replaced by de-central heat sources. The university-industry-cluster ruhrvalley [32] is dealing with the development and set up of a smart heating grid for the Ruhr-Metropolitan Area – the so-called Ruhr Valley. The research on the flexible and smart ORC turbine is part of the efforts in ruhrvalley. It is a demonstrator and nlue print for future smart energy systems within ruhrvalley. The IoT-based system and software architecture will be multiplied into a variety of system components. Smart combined heat and power district heating systems [10] are a major area of research for the sustainable energy system of the future. Heat (and cooling) is a bigger amount of energy than electricity in many countries. Since such systems are by nature very heterogeneous and distributed, a centralized control and steering system is not feasible. Technology based on big data and cloud computing [2] is perceived as a way of managing such systems. The Internet-of-things will play an important role in web-enabled smart grid system [5]. For the overall system architecture of the networked energy grids, the reference model for industry 4.0 (RAMI 4.0) [16] can serve as a architecture model. In ruhrvalley, based on this template, a model-driven architecture for the Internet of Things [26] is developed as a smart heating grid platform. Components like the ORC turbine have to fit into this architecture to play a beneficial role in future smart heating grids. Therefore, the ORC turbine is developed according the reference architecture model for intelligent technical systems in ruhrvalley, the Operator-Controller-Module (OCM) [3, 17, 20].

2   Related Work

2.1   Architectures for Devices in IoT Systems

Within a smart heating grid, the intelligent technical system – the ORC turbine in our case study – is not only connected to the information network formed via the IoT. It is also connected with energy and material (e.g. hot water) flows via the physical (tube) network. Meaning, the smart heating grid is a "real" cyber-physical system (CPS) [1, 19] and not just a set of sensors and actuators of independent sub-systems connected via internet, but without physical connection. For such systems, the CERP-IoT [29] roadmap foresees a growing importance of the device architecture in terms of the trend "towards the autonomous and responsible behaviour of resources". Therefore, it is not sufficient to see the "device" only as an electronic IoT gateway. Devices in smart systems are smart objects or systems themselves. In many cases they are complex mechatronic systems which are equipped with embedded devices which are connected via an IoT gateway to the cloud (Fig. 2).

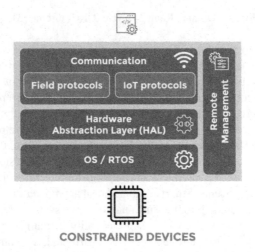

Fig. 2. Constrained Device Architecture according to Eclipse IoT [9]

The Eclipse IoT project [9] is a major endeavour to develop an open source ecosystem for all aspects of the IoT. Within its IoT architecture, the constrained device architecture plays an important role. Such IoT devices are perceived as traditional (microcontroller based) embedded systems. The IoT functionality is delivered by the implemented communication stacks. For the communication, various standards and interfaces emerged in the past years, e.g. for M2M system (ETSI oneM2M Release 2 specifications [12]), the OGC standards, e.g. the OGC SensorThingsAPI [23], and MQTT - Message Queue Telemetry Transport Protocol [21] as the dominating communication protocol for IoT applications. In automation industry, the OPC UA Unified Architecture [24] is an important standard to make programmable logic controllers (PLC) communicate with each other. This technology is typically used to connect systems like the ORC turbine to the internet or other energy systems. Nevertheless, such standards focus on data exchange with guaranteed qualities without looking deeper into the technical system. Wider approaches like the European Technology Platform on Smart Systems Integration (EPoSS) [11] strive for a system integration of the technical sub-systems. Several technical sub-systems cooperate as multi-agent systems [6] in that case. For the ORC-turbine, such standards (e.g. OPC UA and MQTT) are used, but the focus of this paper is more into the software architecture of the ORC itself then on the technologies for connecting it to the IoT.

2.2   The Operator-Controller-Module (OCM)

The architecture of the Operator-Controller-Module (OCM) can be connected to the very basic analysis and structuring provided by Ropohl in his description of a systems theory of technical systems (called "Technology at large") [28]. Ropohl provides a three-layer-model of a general activity system – which can be a technical system, any ecosystem or even a biological system. The basic execution system deals with the "things" or the interaction with the "real world". The information system could be IT or a nervous system in biology. We can easily guess that it would be the layer connecting the things in the Internet-of-Things (IoT). The target setting system is a kind of a "brain". In technical systems, it can be seen as the place where data analytics (in some case with "big data" methods – another buzzword) or artificial intelligence methods find their place. It can be the place where the user or the socio-economic system comes in (Fig. 3).

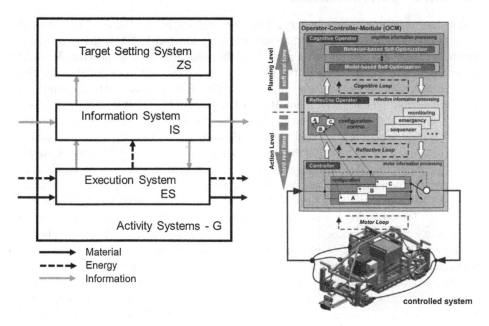

Fig. 3.   Technology stack according to Ropohl [28] and Operator Controller Module [13, 14]

The OCM technology stack [13, 14] is based on such a three layer approach and supports the separation of controllers with hard real time requirements from more complex and strategy oriented planning and controlling tasks. On the lowest level the *motor loop* is controlled by "classical" controllers. To make the approach flexible, these controllers can be configured with different parameters, that may be exchangeable according to the operation mode and the parameter or controller change may be done during operation (re-configuration). The development and the technology stack for this kind of controllers is state-of-the art. The re-configuration is done by the next layer, the *reflective operator*. This is a rule-based system with state machines and service functions, e.g. for emergency notification. The reflective controller is not allowed to interact directly with the technical but only via the controllers of the motor loop. With the reflective operator, the overall system can be operated and it can be connected to other systems in a network or to a smart grid. For intelligent technical systems, a more sophisticated layer for planning, reasoning and learning is added, the *cognitive operator*. This layer can include strategies for self-optimization and machine learning [3]. The user interaction can be added to this layer or to the reflective operator. In general, the implementation of this technology stack and the combination with a networking module turns mechatronics systems into networked mechatronic systems (NMS) [13, 14].

3   Software and System Architecture

3.1   Overall System Architecture

The system and software architecture for the ORC turbine is based on the 3-layer model of the OCM technology stack. The thermodynamic system (see Fig. 1) with its vaporizor, the two turbines (NT and HT), the pumps and tubes and the condenser plus the electrical system with the generators and the electrical converters are considered to be the *controlled system*. The *motor loop* with its controllers is based on a real time control via a real-time programmable logic controller (PLC) and operates the system autonomously around the desired operation points. The *reflective operator* implements the state machines for driving the machine from one operation point to another operation points (and from power on to operation and again back to power off). Furthermore, it implements the coupling and synchronization to the electric grid and the service, monitoring and alarm function via the IoT and up to the planning layer. The *cognitive operator* plans the operating sequence of the ORC turbine system based on the demand for heat and electricity. The controller knows the capabilities of the ORC system and may plan and optimize e.g. daily sequences of operation modes. It can take maintenance intervals into account and it can use self-optimizing and learning strategies. The cognitive operator is connected to smart power grid and smart heating grid interfaces and to the overall optimization instance of the regional energy system. On the different layers of the system, different architectural concepts, description of components and languages are deployed. The implementation is done on a distributed PLC and Industry-PC system and connected via IoT technology to an IoT cloud [26].

3.2   Motor Controller Loop

The controllers of the motor loop are developed in a model-based development approach by setting up a mathematical model of the controlled systems and by developing optimized controllers which are simulated with the model and later with the real system (Hardware in the Loop – HiL). They are basically data driven continuous systems which need to react real-time to any change of the system (Fig. 4).

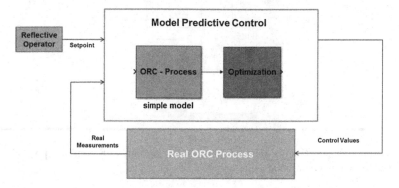

Fig. 4.   Model Predictive Control (MPC) approach for the motor control loop

The Model Predictive Control (MPC) is used for the controllers [31]. In such a system, the (simplified) mathematical model of the thermodynamic and electro-mechanical processes of the ORC turbine (controlled system) are simulated online at any time. With this model, the controller can calculate (predict) what actuator values need to be set to achieve a certain system behaviour based on the current state of the system (which is signalled by the sensors). Furthermore, based on the model the optimum placement of the actuators and sensors can be derived and the dynamics of the controlled system can be simulated. The MPC approach is quite powerful but consumes a lot of processing power. Therefore, it is better suited for slower processes like thermodynamic processes. For the high speed supersonic turbine a faster independent control loop is implemented. The controllers are initiated and started by the state machines of the reflective controller. They read their parameters from a shared memory controlled by the reflective controller. All controllers and the system models are described and validated in Matlab/Simulink and deployed via automatic code generation into C-Functions of the PLC [31].

3.3   Reflective Controller Loop

The main functionality of the reflective controller loop is implemented into several state machines and interrupt service functions. It follows a control driven and an event driven paradigm. The functionality is described in CoDeSys which is a domain specific language (DSL) for state charts and event driven systems [4]. The main state machines for ramping the system up (to power up), ramping it down (to safe off) and operating it with changing operation points are coupled via a central shared memory (called SVI) (Fig. 5).

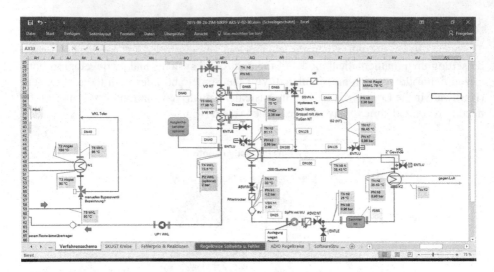

Fig. 5. Thermodynamic Circuit diagram of the ORC turbine with coupling points between reflective controller and motor controller loops

The SVI contain all states of the system and all relevant values for sensors and actuators. Furthermore, it is used to set the operation points for the controllers. The data structure of the SVI is automatically generated from a master system scheme which contains the main thermodynamic circuits and defines the coupling points. The MPC controllers read their parameters from the SVI but can operate the system safely afterwards independently. The SVI implements connectivity via OPC-UA [24], too (Fig. 6).

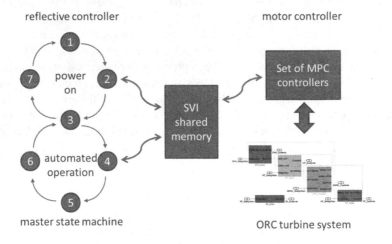

Fig. 6. Coupling of state machines and controllers via SVI shared memory

3.4 Cognitive Controller – Planning Level

The cognitive controller implements the integration of the ORC turbine into a biogas power plant (which supplies the exhaust heat via its block heat and power plant) and into a smart heating grid providing heat to residential areas and industry. The cognitive controller is partly implemented on an industrial PC and partly within an M2M cloud solution. The M2M cloud solution provides online access and monitors all operation data since the ORC system is a research prototype where the data is needed for evaluation and validation. The industrial PC implements the operating strategy of the biogas power plant and the smart heating grid. It provides the ORC system with the required information about how much heat and how much electricity is needed at certain times of the day. The cognitive controller will be extended with simulation and optimization components (a learning system for optimized heat and power production planning) in future.

4   Implementation

The MPC motor controllers and the main parts of the reflective controller are implemented on a Bachmann control system [4] which is tailored to the requirements of renewable energy systems. It includes the required real-time PLC functionality for the MPC and for some additional C++ functionality. It connects to the high speed controllers of the super-sonic turbo generators via CAN-Bus. Bachmann provides the functionality for the SVI shared memory, too. Other features of the reflective operator are implemented within the industrial PC part of the Bachmann system. This allows the connection to OPC UA Unified Architecture [24]. The connection to the cognitive operator is done via the Bachmann WebMI which connects to the SVI, too. All components have been tested on a Bachmann laboratory installation. The ORC system prototype is currently under test at a biogas power plant in Germany (Fig. 7).

Fig. 7. Vaporizer, NT Turbo Generator and PLC cabinet of the ORC prototype

5   Conclusion and Future Work

The ORC system and software architecture will be evaluated and validated during the coming 12 month. Afterwards, the full integration into the ruhvalley smart heating grid platform will be done (see Sect. 1.2). The described system and software architecture allows coupling via IoT into smart systems based on the functionality of the reflective operator and/or the cognitive operator. Therefore, it enables system integration beyond traditional systems which are just extended with an IoT gateway. It will serve as a blue print for the development of other intelligent technical systems as components in smart systems, specifically within the context of ruhrvalley.

References

1. Acatech: AgendaCPS: Integrierte Forschungsagenda Cyber Physical Systems (2012)
2. Agrawal, D., Das, S., El Abbadi, A.: Big data and cloud computing: current state and future opportunities. In: Proceedings of the 14th International Conference on Extending Database Technology, pp. 530–533. ACM (2011)
3. Adelt, P., Donoth, J., Gausemeier, J., Geisler, J., Henkler, S., Kahl, S., Klöpper, B., Krupp, A., Münch, E., Oberthür, S., Paiz, C., Podlogar, H., Porrmann, M., Radkowski, R., Romaus, C., Schmidt, A., Schulz, B., Vocking, H., Wittkowski, U., Witting, K., Znamenshchykov, O.: Selbstoptimierende Systeme des Maschinenbaus – Definitionen, Anwendungen, Konzepte. HNI-Verlagsschriftenreihe, Band 234, Paderborn (2008)
4. Bachmann M1 Automation System (2015). http://www.bachmann.info/branchen/erneuerbare-energien/. Accessed 20 Nov 2015
5. Bui, N., Castellani, A.P., Casari, P., Zorzi, M.: The internet of energy: a web-enabled smart grid system. Network **26**(4), 39–45 (2012). IEEE
6. Bellifemine, F.L., Caire, G., Greenwood, D.: Developing Multi-agent Systems with JADE. Wiley, Hoboken (2007)
7. Chen, H., Goswami, D.Y., Stefanakos, E.K.: A review of thermodynamic cycles and working fluids for the conversion of low-grade heat. Renew. Sustain. Energy Rev. **14**, 3059–3067 (2010)
8. Dubberke, F.H., Priebe, K.-P., Vrabec, J., Roedder, M., Neef, M.: Thermodynamic simulation and experimental validation of a cascaded two-stage organic rankine cycle turbine. In: 3rd International Seminar on ORC Power Systems, Belgium (2015)
9. Eclipse IoT Constrained Devices. https://iot.eclipse.org/devices/. Accessed Mar 2017
10. Elci, M., Oliva, A., Herkel, S., Klein, K., Ripka, A.: Grid-interactivity of a solar combined heat and power district heating system. In: International Conference on Solar Heating and Cooling for Buildings and Industry, SHC2014 (2014)
11. EPoSS: Strategic Research Agenda of The European Technology Platform on Smart Systems Integration, Version 2 (2013). www.smart-systems-integration.org
12. ETSI oneM2M Release 2 specifications. http://www.onem2m.org/technical/published-documents. Accessed Mar 2017
13. Gausemeier, J., Steffen, D., Donoth, J., Kahl, S.: Conceptual design of modularized advanced mechatronic systems. In: 17th International Conference on Engineering Design (ICED 2009), August 24–27, 2009, Stanford, CA, USA (2009)
14. Gausemeier, J., Kahl, S.: Architecture and design methodology of self-optimizing mechatronic systems. In: Mechatronic Systems Simulation Modeling and Control. InTech (2010)

15. Gausemeier, J., Rammig, F.J., Schäfer, W. (eds.): Design Methodology for Intelligent Technical Systems: Develop Intelligent Technical Systems of the Future. LNME. Springer, Heidelberg (2014). doi:10.1007/978-3-642-45435-6
16. Hankel, M., Rexroth, B.: Industrie 4.0: Das Referenzarchitekturmodell Industrie 4.0 (RAMI 4.0), Zentralverband Elektrotechnik- und Elektronikindustrie e.V (2015)
17. Hestermeyer, T., Oberschelp, O., Giese, H.: Structured information processing for selfoptimizing mechatronic systems. In: Proceedings of 1st International Conference on Informatics in Control, Automation and Robotics (ICINCO 2004), Setubal, Portugal (2004)
18. Knutzen, L.K., Stolpe, H., Bracke, R., Beese, E.: Conversion of conventional District Heating Systems in the Ruhr-Metropolitan Area, Western Germany, by stepwise integration of Geothermal Sources. In: Proceedings World Geothermal Congress (2015)
19. Lee, E.A.: Cyber physical systems: design challenges. In: International Symposium on Object/Component/Service-Oriented Real-Time Distributed Computing (2008)
20. Lückel, J., Hestermeyer, T., Liu-Henke, X.: Generalization of the cascade principle in view of a structured form of mechatronic systems. In: 2001 IEEE/ASME International Conference on Advanced Intelligent Mechatronics (AIM 2001), Como, Italy (2001)
21. MQTT - Message Queue Telemetry Transport Protocol. http://www.ibm.com/developerworks/webservices/library/ws-mqtt/index.html. Accessed Mar 2017
22. Nakicenovic, N., Grubler, A., Inaba, A., Messner, S., Nilsson, S., Nishimura, Y., Rogner, H.-H., Schafer, A., Schrattenholzer, L., Stubegger, M., Swisher, J., Victor, D., Wilson, D.: Long term strategies for mitigating global warming. Energy Int. J. **18**(5), 401–609 (1993)
23. OGC, OGC SensorThingsAPI. http://www.opengeospatial.org/standards/sensorthings. Accessed Mar 2017
24. OPC-UA, OPC Unified Architecture (UA) (2008). https://opcfoundation.org/about/opc-technologies/opc-ua/. Accessed Mar 2017
25. Quoilin, S., Van Den Broek, M., Declaye, S., Dewallef, P., Lemort, V.: Techno-economic survey of Organic Rankine Cycle (ORC) systems. Renew. Sustain. Energy **22**, 168–186 (2013)
26. Rademacher, F., Peters, M., Sachweh, S.: Model-driven architecture for the internet of things. In: 41st Euromicro Conference on Software Engineering and Advanced Applications, Madeira, Portugal (2015)
27. Roedder, M., Neef, M., Laux, C., Priebe, K.-P.: Systematic fluid selection for organic rankine cycles (ORC) and performance analysis for a combined high and low temperature cycle. In: Proceedings ASME Turbo Expo 2015: Turbine Technical Conference and Exposition, Montreal, Canada (2015)
28. Ropohl, G.: Allgemeine Technologie, Eine Systemtheorie der Technik, 3. überarbeitete Auflage, Universitätsverlag Karlsruhe (2009)
29. Vermesan, O., Friess, P., Guillemin, P., Gusmeroli, S., et al. (eds.) Internet of Things Strategic Research Roadmap, Cluster of European Research Projects on the Internet of Things, CERP-IoT (2011)
30. Vermesan, O., Friess, P. (eds.): Internet of Things – From Research and Innovation to Market Deployment. River Publishers Series in Communications. River Publishers, Aalborg (2014)
31. Wolff, C., Knirr, M., Schulz, P., Priebe, K.P., Strumberg, J., Vrabec, J.: Flexible and controllable ORC turbine for smart energy systems. In: Proceedings of the IEEE EnergyCon 2016. IEEE Xplore, Leuven (2016)
32. Wolff, C., Telgmann, L.: Systems engineering for metropolitan mobility and energy – RuhrValley. In: Proceedings of the Dortmund International Research Conference 2016 (2016)

Business Intelligence for Information and Software Systems: Special Session on Intelligent Methods for Data Analysis and Computer Aided Software Engineering

Data Mining in Agri Warehouses Using MODWT Wavelet Analysis

Ken Bailey[1]([✉]), Mark Roantree[1], Martin Crane[2],
and Andrew McCarren[1]

[1] INSIGHT: Insight Centre for Data Analytics, School of Computing,
Dublin City University, Glasnevin, Dublin 9, Ireland
{ken.bailey4,mark.roantree,andrew.mccarren}@dcu.ie
[2] School of Computing, Dublin City University, Glasnevin, Dublin 9, Ireland
martin.crane@dcu.ie

Abstract. Agri-data analysis is growing rapidly with many parts of the agri-sector using analytics as part of their decision making process. In Ireland, the agri-food sector contributes significant income to the economy and agri-data analytics will become increasingly important in terms of both protecting and expanding this market. However, without a high degree of accuracy, predictions are unusable. Online data for use in analytics has been shown to have significant advantages, mainly due to frequency of updates and to the low cost of data instances. However, agri decision makers must properly interpret fluctuations in data when, for example, they use data mining to forecast prices for their products in the short and medium term. In this work, we present a data mining approach which includes wavelet analysis to provide more accurate predictions when events which may be classified as outliers are instead patterns representing events that may occur over the duration of the data stream used for predictions. Our evaluation shows an improvement over other uses of wavelet analysis as we attempt to predict prices using agri-data.

1 Introduction

The purpose of this paper is to show how the predictive power of ARIMA models can be improved using Wavelet Analysis. A series is first decomposed by a wavelet transform and ARIMA models are applied to each series produced by the decomposition from the transform and ARIMA predictions for each level produced. The hypothesis being explored here is whether modelling each of the decomposed wavelet levels with an ARIMA prior to reconstructing the series provides a more accurate prediction than using ARIMA prediction models on the original series.

Future prices are regularly used to construct agricultural commodity forecast prices. Both grain elevators and livestock packer buyers forward price off the board, generally using a number of formulae, [1]. These methods are largely used in the United States where well traded future prices exist. Forecasts can be made on commodity future prices, however, long term accuracy and reliability are often found to be weak. Additionally, European markets do not possess high volume trading meat or dairy futures and while prices from the US do correlate with European commodity prices the

© Springer International Publishing AG 2017
R. Damaševičius and V. Mikašytė (Eds.): ICIST 2017, CCIS 756, pp. 241–253, 2017.
DOI: 10.1007/978-3-319-67642-5_20

relationship is not strong enough to be relied upon on a commercial basis. In many cases, this is caused by market access to individual countries and irregularities within individual markets. Typically, production of animals for a particular product is very much dependent on individual regulations within a country. Much of this knowledge can be found in online data sources.

An Autoregressive Integrated Moving Average (ARIMA) model uses regressive components of lags of both the variable in question and the error terms to make predictions of future values in a series. Differencing of the data is also incorporated in these models in order to reduce the effect of non-stationary data. ARIMA models are widely used to model time series data and provide forecasts. In ARIMA methods the parameter settings are extremely difficult to find when dealing with complex combinations of the Moving Average and Auto Regressive components. Implementing wavelet analysis decomposes the complexity of the series and allows the researcher a much higher chance of identifying simpler ARIMA models for each level of the decomposed series.

Paper Structure. The paper is structured as follows: in the remainder of this section, we provide the background which motivates this work and provide a statement of our contribution; in Sect. 2, we provide a discussion on early work in this field to more recent application to financial time series; in Sect. 3, we present our algorithm to create predicted prices and compare a Wavelet/ARIMA model generated with the Maximal Overlap Discrete Wavelet Transform to a typical ARIMA prediction; in Sect. 4 we present the experiments that were conducted to compare the predictive power of the DWT and MODWT methods; and finally in Sect. 5, we conclude the paper.

Contribution. We investigate the technique introduced by [3] which used a high frequency dataset for forecasting electricity day ahead prices using the Discrete Wavelet Transform (DWT). We apply this technique to a lower frequency dataset, weekly pig prices, with a longer prediction window of 8 weeks. We compare the DWT method with our own method which uses the non-decimated Maximal Overlap Discrete Wavelet Transform (MODWT). We apply the two techniques to the two different datasets with a view to identifying a reliable forecasting method for weekly price data. Bootstrapping was used by resampling with replacement samples of equal size from the datasets, to provide a more robust analysis of the efficacy of our algorithms.

In contrast to the related work presented in [3, 14–16], we provide a detailed description of our algorithm to enable it to be used or improved. Our algorithm can be used with any wavelet filter, not just the Haar filter. The Haar filter allows reconstruction of a series by a simple summation of wavelet coefficients. This property does not apply to any other filter although other authors declare that they used this property for the inverse transform with other filters.

2 Related Research

The authors of [5] provide a basic introduction to wavelets with a more applied focus on financial time series. Their view is that the benefit of wavelets is to reveal features in the original time series at different scales which are possibly hidden in the original time series. The decomposed levels form time series which are then more amenable to techniques such as ARIMA.

In [3], the authors proposed a method for forecasting day ahead electricity prices in the Spanish market using a combination of wavelets and ARIMA techniques and compared this approach to an ARIMA forecasting method alone. Their rationale is that using wavelets, the decomposition of historical electricity price series results in a less volatile set of representations of the behaviour of the original time series at several scales. ARIMA models of these constituent series are proposed to be more stable for forecasting techniques. The ARIMA-forecasted constituent series form the input to the wavelet reconstruction process to provide forecast values for the original series. In the paper it is found that these forecast values provide greater accuracy than forecasts from an ARIMA of the original series alone. In our work, we use the MODWT transform to generate the coefficients for the wavelet-ARIMA and ARIMA predictive process which we believe is a more robust method than using DWT.

In [4], a similar approach is used to [3] to forecast day ahead electricity prices. The method is extended to apply appropriate prediction models to each wavelet decomposition level. Thus, GARCH models are applied to the high frequency elements of the wavelet decomposition combined with the ARIMA modelling of the low frequency element. The wavelet reconstruction series, created from subseries are then used for prediction.

In [6], the approach considers the influence of exogenous variables on the decomposed levels of the wavelet transformation. The process includes selecting the most appropriate variable by a feature selection technique based on the data model. The process combines lagged values of the wavelet subseries and time domain features of the subseries to include lags from the original time series and the exogenous variables. Multiple candidate forecast series are created. They are differentiated by validation error and the inverse wavelet transform applied to produce the overall forecast series.

The authors of [7] highlight the limitations of using wavelets for forecasting and instead, make use of a non-decimated form of the discrete wavelet transform. The decimated form DWT halves the number of coefficients produced at each subsequent decomposition. The non-decimated form MODWT results in the same number of coefficients as the original series at each level of decomposition to feed into a predictive model. We use an MODWT transform in our approach to provide a consistent number of coefficients for ARIMA modelling to make the process more robust.

The authors of [16] are most similar to our approach. They use the MODWT and ARIMA predictions from the decomposed series. However, the method of reconstruction of the series after prediction at the decomposition levels does not make use of the inverse wavelet transform for the filter which created the decomposition. Instead they make use of a feature of the most basic filter, Haar, which uniquely, allows reconstruction of a series by simply summing corresponding decomposed coefficients.

We show that this method of reconstruction can be used with a Haar filter but is not appropriate for any other filter.

3 Wavelet Analysis of Time Series

In this section, we present our methodology for incorporating wavelet analysis into predictive algorithms. We begin by covering some background work necessary to understand the ARIMA and MODWT algorithms for prediction of time series data. We then describe our own approach which uses a combination of both of these algorithms in order to improve the quality of predictions. Finally, we provide a more detailed description of our algorithm.

3.1   Background

A time series consists of a set of observations related to some particular measurement at fixed time intervals. A univariate ARIMA model [2] represents a time series in the form of an *algebraic statement* describing how values of the variable are statistically related to past values of the same variable [12]. The ARIMA model requires the specification of 3 parameters termed (p,d,q): p, the number of past observations required in the auto regression; d, the levels of differencing to produce a stationary (constant mean and variance) form of the series; and q, the number of past observations required in the moving average. There should be at least 50 past values to use an ARIMA for prediction [12]. Once the methods for identifying the most appropriate values for (p,d,q) e.g. in [2, 12], the ARIMA model can be used to forecast future values.

Wavelet Analysis is an approach to signal analysis which identifies patterns of frequencies at different time scales occurring in a signal. This approach applies a well-defined mathematical transform to observed values to produce details of frequencies contained therein while retaining the location of the frequencies in the time domain. In an application where the signal can be observed over very short time intervals, such as a sound wave, a very fine resolution form of the wavelet transform, the Continuous Wavelet Transform (CWT) can be applied. Where the observations are more sparse such as in a financial time series, measured hourly, daily or weekly, the Discrete Wavelet Transform (DWT) is more appropriately applied [10].

The DWT uses a filter which is applied to the data. Fundamentally, a filter is a pair of orthogonal vectors which when applied to the time series produces a decomposed representation of the signal in terms of high frequency components and low frequency components. This representation is in the form of a set of coefficients. The low frequency coefficients can be decomposed repeatedly in the same fashion by the filter to the level of resolution required. The most commonly used wavelet filters are the Haar [13] filter and Daubechies filters [11].

Each iteration or level of the DWT on N values produces a set of $N/2$ values, producing a *decimated* transform. Therefore, the limitation on the number of levels L that can be produced is $2^L \leq N$. In addition, coefficients at each level are out of phase with respect to each other in the DWT with the result that decomposed coefficients are different depending on the starting point chosen within the time series.

When dealing with time series analysis, these limitations can be overcome by using the Maximal Overlap Discrete Wavelet Transform (MODWT). This is a non-decimated transform which produces N coefficients at each level of decomposition. The MODWT uses the same parameters as the DWT to specify the filter being used and the number of levels of decomposition required. Having a constant high number of coefficients makes the ARIMA modelling of these series more robust.

3.2 MODWT Assisted ARIMA Model

A dataset whether in the form of a continuous signal such as sound or a set of discrete points in a financial time series contains a number of underlying frequencies. Frequencies can extract crucial information that is hidden in the aggregated data. The development of *wavelets* provides a mechanism to identify the frequencies in a signal at different times. A wavelet transform takes a signal and identifies the high frequencies at shorter intervals while smoothing the remaining low frequencies. This process is repeated to the desired number of levels which are particular to the domain from which the data set is drawn, with each level representing the frequencies at higher scales.

In the discrete wavelet transform (DWT) case, which is appropriate for financial time series, the transform consists of two functions, a father and mother wavelet. The functions are applied to the data at successively smaller scales, typically reducing the detail by 50% each time. At each level of decomposition, the mother wavelet captures the high frequency components in a zero mean series while the father wavelet captures the remaining smoother components. In this paper, we make use of the Haar transform [13], to extract different frequency levels together with their location in time.

The result of a DWT decomposition is 2 vectors representing the wavelet coefficients for the high frequencies and scaling coefficients for the low frequencies of the scale. The coefficients relating to the high frequencies at level 1 are denoted by D_1 and the low frequency coefficients by S_1. The S_1 coefficients are further decomposed into D_2 and S_2 and so on. The resulting set of coefficients for a J-level decomposition is known as a crystal, as in Definition 1.

Definition 1. *Decomposition Crystal*

$$C = \{S_J, D_J, D_{J-1}, D_{J-2}, \ldots, D_1\}$$

The Haar wavelet samples data points 2 at a time and the coefficient is generated from a sample value and its preceding value. In the case of the first value in the time series, the previous value is taken from the end of the series (periodicity) or from a reflection of the series. The number of coefficients affected by this boundary problem increase at each level of decomposition. In our case, the transform used, MODWT, locates the affected boundary coefficients at the beginning of the series and thus, do not affect the coefficients at the end of the series which are primarily required for prediction.

The Maximal Overlap Discrete Wavelet Transform (MODWT) addresses some of the issues with the DWT but is a non-orthogonal redundant transform [8]. The MODWT is a non-decimated transform and so the number of coefficients produced at each level has the same cardinality as the time series.

In our method the price data is divided into a training set and a testing set. The training set is modelled with an ARIMA and predictions produced. The training set is then decomposed using the MODWT. Each of the series of coefficients produced are modelled by an appropriate ARIMA for the series and future values predicted. The inverse MODWT is applied to the sets of predicted values from the coefficients to produce a prediction for the prices. The two sets of predictions from the training set ARIMA and the wavelet coefficients ARIMA are compared against the testing set using a root mean square error (RMSE) test to allow comparison between the results. Our evaluation uses a price dataset consisting of historic weekly pigmeat prices to predict forward prices over an 8 week period.

3.3   Algorithm Description

In Algorithm 1, we present our MODWT Assisted ARIMA (MAM) algorithm for time series prediction, which follows the approach described earlier in this section. It uses the Haar filter to decompose the series into wavelet and scale coefficients.

Alg 1. MODWT Assisted ARIMA (MAM) with the Haar filter

1. Select dataset $X = \{x_1, x_2, .., x_n\}$
2. Select prediction period of width k
3. Divide the data into a training set $T = \{x_1, x_2, ..., x_{n-k}\}$ and a testing set $Q = \{x_{n-k+1}, ... x_n\}$
4. Use wavelet to transform T using a MODWT function outputs crystal $C = \{S_J, D_J, D_{J-1}, D_{J-2}, ... D_1\}$, each element consisting of $n-k$ coefficients
5. Construct ARIMA for each decomposition $C^a = \{S_J^a, D_J^a, D_{J-1}^a, D_{J-2}^a, ... D_1^a\}$
6. Generate k predictions for each decomposition $P_{sJ}, P_{dJ}...P_{d1}$.
7. Reconstruct Wavelet/Arima prediction series W_p, adding the corresponding terms from $P_{sJ}, P_{dJ}...P_{d1}$
8. Construct ARIMA model for T and predict forward a set of k values T_p. Append T_p to the end of T to produce series P of m values.
9. Compare the Root Mean Square Error (RMSE) of the MAM prediction W_p against the testing set Q and the RMSE of the ARIMA prediction set T_p against the testing set Q.

In Steps 1–3 the dataset of cardinality n is selected and referred to as X, the number of elements, k, to be predicted is decided and the dataset is split into a training set labelled T and testing set Q.

In step 4 the MODWT transform using an appropriate filter, in this case Haar, is applied to the training set T to the level of decomposition required J to produce a crystal C consisting of series of coefficients the same length as T.

In step 5 a separate ARIMA model is produced for each series of coefficients in the crystal C. Step 6 uses a *forecast* function in R for ARIMA models to predict the k future values for each series in the crystal C.

Step 7 of Algorithm 1 produces k predictions, W_p, for the training set T. In the case of the Haar filter, this can simply be done by adding the corresponding predicted coefficients from the D_j j = 1..J and corresponding predicted coefficients from S_J. In the case of filters other than Haar the steps in Algorithm 2 replace this step.

Step 8 produces a predicted set of values T_p from an ARIMA model of the training set T.

Step 9 use the Root Mean Square Error (RMSE) to compare the MAM predictions W_p against the testing set Q and the ARIMA predictions T_p against the training set Q.

Alg 2. MODWT Assisted ARIMA (Generic filter)

If a filter other than Haar is used in step 4 in Alg.1, replace step 7 with the following

- Apply the wavelet transform to the original series X to provide a container W, with n coefficients, for the wavelet prediction W_p, with n coefficients
- Append each prediction set to the corresponding decomposition e.g. S_{Jp} = S_J&P_{sJ} to produce a crystal C_p = $\{S_{Jp}, D_{Jp}, ... D_{1p}\}$
- Swap C_p into the container W
- Apply the inverse transform to W, the last k values of the result being W_p

---

Algorithm 2 is a modified version of step 7 in Algorithm 1. This is used in the inverse transform procedure for experiments where a non-Haar filter such as a Daubechies filter [11] is used in step 4 of Algorithm 1.

Algorithm 2 uses the Inverse MODWT Transform to reconstruct the predicted series. The MODWT is applied to the complete series X to create a container W to hold the coefficients for the inverse transform. The coefficients in the container are replaced at each level j with the corresponding ARIMA model from the C^α and predictions. The inverse transform is applied to the amended container W to generate a series where the last k values form the MAM prediction set W_p.

4 Evaluation

In this section, we describe our evaluation process and provide a discussion on the results from each series of experiments.

Data. The DATAS project collects agricultural price data from around the world at the frequencies with which the data is published. For this paper, we downloaded the market price of pig meat in Ireland, Denmark and Germany. This data is available weekly. We used a dataset of 459 values from week 1 2007 to week 42 2015. Primarily all initial investigations were carried out with the Irish dataset. The experiments in [3] try to forecast hourly electricity prices over a period of 1 day for the Spanish Electricity market. The data used in [3] provides a contrast to our dataset in that the data has a high frequency of samples, 24 per day, and the historical data is known for a long period. Our data uses weekly pigmeat prices from markets in Ireland, Germany and Denmark and so has a much lower frequency.

Software. Experiments were developed using RStudio with libraries 'forecast' and 'wtmsa' providing the necessary functionality. The wavModwt function was used with the Haar and Daubechies wavelets with varying filter lengths and levels of decomposition.

Hardware. The machine used was a Dell Optiplex 7020 3.6 GHz, 16 GB RAM, running Microsoft Windows 7 Professional.

4.1   Approach

Four separate experiments were carried out as part of our evaluation.

1. Replicating the Conejo experiments [3] as a starting point for our evaluation.
2. Using our MAM Algorithm with Conejo's high frequency dataset to provide baseline results for comparative purposes.
3. Using Conejo algorithm on our low frequency dataset.
4. Using MAM Algorithm on our low frequency dataset.

Replicating Experiment from [3]. As our approach is similar to [3], we set out to duplicate their original experiment and required similar results to act as a baseline for our own approach. Their method used the DWT with a Daubechies 5 wavelet to 3 levels of decomposition, to predict forward using 24 hourly wholesale electricity prices from a training dataset of 1152 instances of hourly values. As the authors did not provide precise details of their DWT implementation nor the ARIMA parameters, it was not possible to deliver an exact replica of their experiments but we achieved similar results.

The [3] experiments produced predictions for hourly prices each day from 4 test weeks - labelled Winter, Spring, Summer and Fall weeks - with a total of 28 experiments. The predictions from the ARIMA and DWT/ARIMA are measured and compared by a daily error presented in Definiton 2 where p is hourly price.

Definition 2. *Daily Error Definition*

$$\frac{1}{24}\sum_{h=1}^{24} \frac{\left|p_h^{true} - p_h^{est}\right|}{p_{day}^{-true}}$$

where

$$p_{day}^{-true} = \frac{1}{24}\sum_{h=1}^{24} p_h^{true}$$

Using MAM Algorithm with High Frequency Dataset. We applied our MAM approach using the same Spanish electricity data as used in [3]. We implemented the MAM algorithm using both the Haar filter and the Daubechies 5 filter used in [3]. For both experiments, we used the daily error for comparing against our replication of the original approach.

Using [3] algorithm on Low Frequency datasets. For this experiment, we applied the approach in [3] on the pig meat dataset from Ireland. This experiment used 20 subsets of the data in a sliding window, to produce 8 predicted values for each subset in 20 tests.

Using MAM Algorithm on Low Frequency datasets. Our initial experiments aimed at determining an optimum prediction period for Daubechies wavelets of lengths 2 (Haar), 4, 6 and 8. This was repeated for each of 3 to 8 levels of decomposition. The proportion of the data given over to the testing set was varied from 4 to 56 weeks with the remainder used as the training set. The test runs were compared by calculating the Root Mean Square Error (RMSE) of the predicted values against the actual values.

The main focus of our experiments was to look at a prediction period of 8 weeks for pigmeat prices from the Irish, German and Danish markets. This provided a maximum of 451 data points in the training set with 8 points to validate the predictions. Using both the suggestions in [7] and our own empirical evidence, we selected a Haar (Daubechies order 1 with 2 coefficients [9]) wavelet with 3 levels of decomposition and the non-decimated MODWT wavelet transform. We split the training set into 20 sliding subsets of 299 values, sliding 8 values at a time. This provided 291 values in the training set and 8 points to compare against our predictions. We then compared the RMSE of the MAM predictions to the ARIMA predictions for each of the 20 experiments for each of the 3 datasets from Ireland, Germany and Denmark in Experiments *4a*, *4b* and *4c* respectively.

4.2 Experiment Results

The results of our experiments are illustrated in Tables 1, 2, 3 and 4. The number of tests within each experiment are shown. The number of tests which showed a lower daily error or RMSE for each method being compared are given. The column headings have the following meaning:

Table 1. Experiment 1 results

Exp	Tests	Dataset	Size	Period	Transform	Filter	Levels	Results	
								DWT/ARIMA	ARIMA
1a	28	Electricity	1152	24	DWT	D5	3	20	8
1b	28	Electricity	1152	24	DWT	D5	3	22	8

Table 2. Experiment 2 results

Exp	Tests	Dataset	Size	Period	Transform	Filter	Levels	Results	
								MAM	DWT/ARIMA
2a	28	Electricity	1152	24	MODWT	Haar	3	12	16
2b	28	Electricity	1152	24	MODWT	D5	3	13	15

Table 3. Experiment 3 results

Exp	Tests	Dataset	Size	Period	Transform	Filter	Levels	Results	
								MAM	DWT
3	20	Irish Pigmeat	299	8	DWT	Haar	3	14	6

Table 4. Experiment 4 results

Exp	Tests	Dataset	Size	Period	Transform	Filter	Levels	Results	
								MAM	Arima
4a	20	Irish Pigmeat	299	8	MODWT	Haar	3	11	9
4b	20	German Pigmeat	299	8	MODWT	Haar	3	8	12
4c	20	Danish Pigmeat	299	8	MODWT	Haar	3	8	12

- **Exp** identifies the experiment (1–4 described earlier) being undertaken.
- **Tests** is the number of individual tests run for each experiment. – **Dataset** is either *Electricity* for Spanish Electricity Prices or *Pigmeat* for Irish, German or Danish pigmeat prices.
- **Size** is the cardinality of the dataset used.
- **Period** is the cardinality of the prediction set.
- **Transform** is either the Discrete Wavelet Transform (DWT) or Maximal Overlap Discrete Wavelet Transform (MODWT).
- **Filter** is the wavelet used: the Haar filter or D5 to represent the Daubechies 5 filter.
- **Level** is the number of levels of decomposition by the transform.
- **Results** summarises the number of tests for which the specified parameter was more successful. DWT/AR refers to the Wavelet ARIMA method in [3]

For Experiment 1, we sought to replicate the results in [3] to benchmark our tests. The results from [3] show that the Wavelet/ARIMA produced a lower daily error rate than the ARIMA predictions on 20 days of the 28 days predicted (Experiment 1a). When we replicated the Conejo experiment, our results produced a lower daily error rate than ARIMA predictions on 22 days of the 28 days predicted which we felt was a satisfactory reproduction (Experiment 1b).

In the second series of experiments, the MAM approach generated *lower* daily errors in 12 tests compared to lower daily errors in the Conejo experiments in 16 tests (Experiment 2a). However, the MAM process produced lower daily errors in 13 tests compared to lower daily errors in the Conejo in 15 tests (Experiment 2b).

In the third series of experiments, the DWT transform is a decimated transform and so the number of coefficients related to 8 values in a prediction series are too few: at the level 3 decomposition there is only one coefficient. The MAM approach produced lower errors in 14 tests with DWT/Conejo producing lower errors in just 6 tests (Experiment 3), as a result of applying the inverse transform.

In the final series of experiments, the MAM approach produced a lower RMSE in 11 tests and ARIMA in 9 tests on the Irish pigmeat prices data. MAM produced a lower RMSE in 8 tests and ARIMA was lower in 12 tests for the German pigmeat prices data. Using the Danish pigmeat prices data, MAM produced a lower RMSE in 8 tests and ARIMA was lower in 12 tests. These results show some promise in that in 45% of cases, the MAM approach produced better results than the established and widely used ARIMA prediction model.

4.3   Analysis

ARIMA modelling requires significant domain knowledge together with a lot of trial and error runs, to find an appropriate model for a time series. The advantage of the MAM process is that by decomposing a signal, using an MODWT, into statistically better behaved series, ARIMA models can be more readily produced on the decomposed levels. The series produced from recombining the predictions from the decomposed series is as statistically accurate as predictions from an ARIMA method applied to the original series.

In our experiments, we have seen that wavelet analysis with ARIMA in both MAM and the process in [3] can produce different results from different subsets of the same dataset. In [3], the test results are presented for each of 4 weeks - Winter, Spring, Summer and Fall. The results indicate that there is an unknown factor affecting certain weeks. For example, the results using the same Daubechies 5 filter with the DWT and MODWT produce significantly different results in *Winter* and *Fall* as compared with *Spring* and *Summer*. This suggests that further investigation to identify characteristics of this data could potentially further optimise wavelet analysis to time series.

The results of the experiments in 2a and 2b show statistically different results between MAM with the HAAR and Daubechies 5 filters against the results using the DWT method. Paired t-tests were carried out to compare the MAM and DWT methods using the daily error measurement from [3] for each of the 4 weeks Winter, Spring, Summer and Autumn.

The Winter week showed no significance between MAM with Haar and DWT ($p = .419$, $t = 0.214$) but a significant improvement with MAM with Daubechies 5 ($p = .032$, $t = 2.27$).

The Spring week showed the daily error for DWT to be significantly lower than either MAM with Haar ($p = .012$, $t = 3.0$) and MAM with Daubechies 5 ($p = .002$, $t = 4.52$).

The Summer week showed different results for the different MAM filters. The MAM with Haar showed no significant difference to DWT ($p = .418$, $t = 0.216$) whereas DWT had a lower error than MAM with Daubechies 5 ($p = .005$, $t = 3.71$).

The Autumn week showed that both the MAM methods produced lower errors than DWT, Haar ($p = .089$ $t = 1.525$) and Daubechies 5 ($p = .121$, $t = 1.298$).

The results of applying a DWT to the pigmeat prices dataset show a significantly poorer result than using an MODWT. This is likely due to the cardinality of the pig meat dataset being too small to allow the application of the decimated transform necessary to produce predictions from the decomposed series for longer prediction windows than the 8 predictions used. The MODWT approach which produces the same number of coefficients at each level of decomposition is more suited to a smaller, infrequent dataset.

Experiments 3 and 4 (pig pricing data) show that there is statistically no significant difference between applying ARIMA and the MAM process in a long term dataset with low frequency. 20 datasets were extracted for usage as test data. Each method was applied to the test sets and a mean square error was calculated. Paired t-tests were carried out between ARIMA, MAM and DWT methods, with no statistical differences found between the ARIMA and the MAM methods with regard to the mean square error. However, the DWT had significantly greater mean square error over the other 2 methods over all the test runs (p = 0.0159, t = −2.3173 & p = 0.02, t = 2.2)

5 Conclusions

Pricing predictions from agri datasets are very difficult to achieve mainly due to *events* occurring at different timelines that are present within the datasets. This requires more complex algorithms for prediction.

In ARIMA methods, it is extremely difficult to find the correct parameter settings when dealing with complex combinations of Moving Average and Auto Regressive components. Implementing a MODWT decomposes the complexity of the series and allows the researcher a much higher chance of identifying simpler ARIMA models for each level of the decomposed series.

While a number of different wavelet approaches have been tested, our approach is to use both the MODWT and ARIMA methods in combination for better predictions in time series data. As a baseline for our results, we used the approach and similar evaluation as [3] to determine what is currently possible using a wavelet approach to time series data. Our evaluation used 4 sets of experiments to try to determine if our approach was better than [3]. The MODWT in conjunction with the ARIMA method was comparable with the DWT ARIMA method proposed by [3] for the high frequency Spanish electricity price data.

However, our MAM approach showed superior results to [3] when attempting forecasts for low frequency data streams such as the pig price data. For low frequency data, MAM and ARIMA demonstrated equivalent results, but importantly, MAM demonstrates a resilience and robustness that neither of the other 2 methods demonstrated as it achieved equally good results for both low and high frequency data. The choice of wavelet filter is very much dependent on the characteristics of the data. A suitable wavelet and decomposition level might only be identifiable by trial and error. However, in all uses of wavelets and in particular for prediction, the issue of coefficients affected by the boundary problem becomes more intrusive, the wider the wavelet and the deeper the decomposition. This is of particular concern when using the DWT wavelet transform as opposed to MODWT.

Our process, MAM, gives the researcher a level of comfort knowing that it will produce predictions that are robust to the frequency components of the data.

References

1. Kastens, T.L., Jones, R., Schroeder, T.C.: Futures-based price forecast for agricultural producers and buisnesses. J. Agric. Resour. Econ. **23**(1), 294–307 (1998)
2. Box, G.E.P., Jenkins, G.M.: Time Series Analysis, Forecasting and Control, 2nd edn. Holden-Day, San Francisco (1976)
3. Conejo, A.J., et al.: Day-ahead electricity price forecasting using the wavelet transform and ARIMA models. IEEE Trans. Power Syst. **20**(2), 1035–1042 (2005)

4. Zhongfu, T., et al.: Day-ahead electricity price forecasting using wavelet transform combined with ARIMA and GARCH models. Appl. Energy **87**(11), 3606–3610 (2010)
5. Schleicher, C.: An Introduction to Wavelets for Economists. Bank of Canada (2002)
6. Amjady, N., Keynia, F.: Day ahead price forecasting of electricity markets by a mixed data model and hybrid forecast method. Int. J. Electr. Power Energy Syst. **30**(9), 533–546 (2008)
7. Nguyen, H.T., Nabney, I.T.: Short-term electricity demand and gas price forecasts using wavelet transforms and adaptive models. Energy **35**(9), 3674–3685 (2010)
8. Percival, D.B., Walden, A.T.: Wavelet Methods for Time Series Analysis, vol. 4. Cambridge University Press, Cambridge (2006)
9. Yousefi, S., Weinreich, I., Reinarz, D.: Wavelet-based prediction of oil prices. Chaos, Solitons Fractals **25**(2), 265–275 (2005)
10. Crowley, P.M.: A guide to wavelets for economists. J. Econ. Surv. **21**(2), 207–267 (2007)
11. Daubechies, I.: Ten Lectures on Wavelets. Society for Industrial and Applied Mathematics, Philadelphia (1992)
12. Pankratz, A.: Forecasting with Univariate Box-Jenkins Models: Concepts and Cases, vol. 224. Wiley, New York (2009)
13. Haar, A.: Zur theorie der orthogonalen funktionensysteme. Math. Ann. **69**(3), 331–371 (1910)
14. Al Wadi, S., Hamarsheh, A., Alwadi, H.: Maximum overlapping discrete wavelet transform in forecasting banking sector. Appl. Math. Sci. **7**(80), 3995–4002 (2013)
15. Zhu, L., Wang, Y., Fan, Q.: MODWT-ARMA model for time series prediction. Appl. Math. Model. **38**(5), 1859–1865 (2014)
16. Kriechbaumer, T., et al.: An improved waveletARIMA approach for forecasting metal prices. Resour. Policy **39**, 32–41 (2014)

Database Inconsistency Measures and Their Applications

Hendrik Decker[1]([✉]) and Sanjay Misra[2]

[1] PROS, DSIC, Universidad Politecnica de Valencia, Valencia, Spain
hdecker@pms.ifi.lmu.de
[2] Covenant University, Canaanland, Ota, Nigeria

Abstract. We investigate the measuring of inconsistency of formal sentences, a field with increasing popularity in the literature about computer science, mathematics and logic. In particular, we look at database inconsistency measures, as featured in various publications in the literature. We focus on similarities and differences between inconsistency measures for databases and for sets of logic sentences. Also some differences to quality measures are pointed out. Moreover, we pace some characteristic applications of database inconsistency measures, which are related to monitoring, maintaining and improving the quality of stored data across updates.

1 Introduction

An inconsistency measure is a mathematical or procedural description to determine the amount of inconsistency of a given set of formal sentences that may contain or imply conflicts, and hence an infringement of informational quality. Conflicts can be described as formal inconsistencies.

The innovative feature of the concept of inconsistency measures is its constructive, positivistic handling of inconsistency, uninhibited by the no-go connotations of inconsistency and its potentially devastating effects in classical logic theories [51]. That confident posture is not original of inconsistency measuring, but the latter has helped much to pave the way for the acceptance of paraconsistency and inconsistency tolerance in database theory and artificial intelligence [3,14]. It is hoped that it may have a similar effect in the development of (as of yet still depauperate) formal foundations of data quality theory.

The history of inconsistency measuring has its roots in John Grant's seminal article [27]. After years of ignorance, the field started to blossom about a quarter century later, sparked by papers such as [30,31,34,35]. An early survey is provided in [32], which also traces precursor topics and related subjects in the fields of information theory [38,46], knowledge evolution [24,25,41], paraconsistency [10,13,42] probabilistic logic [11] and possibilistic logic [22].

Most conventional measures in the literature that serve for assessing the amount of inconsistency in a logic setting usually are sculpted to be applied to what is frequently called "knowledge bases", but what effectively corresponds,

© Springer International Publishing AG 2017
R. Damaševičius and V. Mikašytė (Eds.): ICIST 2017, CCIS 756, pp. 254–265, 2017.
DOI: 10.1007/978-3-319-67642-5_21

in most cases, either to propositional sets of formulas [4,5,33–35,39,44,47], or first-order theories [27,28,31,40].

As opposed to that, measures for assessing database inconsistency cannot be easily subsumed by any conventional classification of measures for classical logic theories (be they propositional or arbitrary first-order), essentially because, while being closely related, database logic is not classical logic. Moreover, the main application of the database inconsistency measures as defined in [15,17,20] is not to quantify the amount of inconsistency in given databases per se, but to compare the inconsistency of consecutive database states for inconsistency-tolerant integrity maintenance. For that purpose, the values of inconsistency between database states before and after updates do not necessarily have to be computed, to become comparable in terms of their level of inconsistency. Rather, only the difference of inconsistency between such states is of interest for integrity checking and repairing. That feature obviously yields a big Brownie point for our database inconsistency measures, since inconsistency measures tend to be notoriously hard to compute [48]. Conceptually speaking, database inconsistency measures are more general than conventional inconsistency measures, since the range of the mappings that define former is not necessarily numerical, and the ordering of that range is not necessarily total.

After some preliminaries, we first are going to recall some pertinent similarities and differences between classical logic and database logic. Then, we differentiate the notion of inconsistency in databases from inconsistency in classical logic. Then we elaborate on essential distinctions between measures of inconsistency for databases and conventional measures of quality and inconsistency. After that, we recapitulate two applications of database inconsistency measures that have been investigated so far: integrity checking and inconsistency repair checking.

2   Basic Concepts

As in previous papers about database inconsistency measuring [18,21],we use common database research terminology and formalisms. We now shortly recapitulate some key definitions.

Throughout, let D, IC, I, U, μ always stand, respectively, for a database, an integrity theory (i.e., a finite set of first-order sentences called integrity constraints or, simply, constraints), an integrity constraint, an update, and inconsistency measure that determines the amount of integrity violation in pairs (D, IC).

We may use ";" for delimiting clauses in sets, instead of ",", since the latter symbolizes conjunction of literals in database clauses.

In Sects. 3 and 4, we are going to determine some further characteristics of the kind of databases and integrity theories dealt with in the remainder.

3   Classical Logic and Databases

Database logic and classical logic have been closely intertwined since the inception of relational databases [9]. This connection has been boosted and further tightened by the rise of deductive databases [23]. Indeed, each relational and each deductive database essentially consists of logic sentences in a restricted syntactic form. However, their interpretation deviates to some extent from both the proof- and model-theoretic semantics of classical logic.

In brief, the main differences, which are elaborated in more detail in [1,7], can be summarized as follows. The logic sentences used to describe databases are not as general as to allow arbitrary first-order predicate logic syntax. Rather, the stored relational data consist of ground atomic facts only. More generally, deductive databases contain clauses of the form $A \leftarrow B$ where the head A is an atom, the body B is a (possibly empty) conjunction of atoms, and all variables in A and B are taken to be universally quantified.

To infer negative answers from such sets of clauses, the latter need to be supplemented by the assumption that formulas that are not true of the database in terms of classical logic are considered to be false by default. Well-known formalizations of that intuition are the *closed world assumption* [45], the *database completion* [8] and the distinction of a *standard model*, i.e., a particular Herbrand model of the database as its meaning (e.g., the least Herbrand model [49] or the stable [26] or the perfect [43] or the well-founded model [50]). where all atoms that are not in that model are taken to be false. Once such an assumption of default negation is taken, also the atoms in the body of clauses can be generalized to contain not only positive, but also negated atoms, where negation again is interpreted by default. Default negation makes database logic non-monotonic [6]. However, in order to guarantee that the standard model is two-valued, unique and total, some syntatic restrictions usually are imposed on clauses that define predicates recursively in terms of negations of themselves.

To avoid out-of-context answers, database clauses, queries and constraints usually are asked to be domain-independent [37]. Since domain-independence is undecidable, sufficient syntactic restrictions such as range-restrictedness [12] are imposed. Thus, we assume, for simplicity, that all considered databases are range-restricted, have a consistent completion and a unique and total Herbrand model. Also, queries and integrity theories are required to be range-restricted. Moreover, as soon as any concrete integrity checking method is substituted for the unspecified integrity checking methods that are going to appear in later sections, the restrictions of their applicability to certain classes of databases, queries and constraints also have to be imposed.

Queries and integrity constraints (which are processed as queries about the consistency of stored data) may be specified in a more general first-order syntax, but each such query can be mechanically re-written into a normal query of the form $\leftarrow B$, where B is a non-empty conjunction of positive or negated atoms, plus a set of database clauses which are added to the database [12].

As opposed to database logic, classical logic is monotonic, i.e., for each set of sentences S and each sentence s, the logical consequences derivable from S is always a subset of the consequences derivable from $S \cup \{s\}$. As we are going to see, non-monotonicity may invalidate a monotonicity property that is frequently postulated for conventional inconsistency measures, since the addition of new data may render an inconsistent database consistent.

4   Inconsistency

It is well-known that each sentence whatsoever (and hence also the negation of each sentence) is derivable in inconsistent classical logic theories, according to the *ex-falso-quodlibet rule* (*EFQ*). Due to that, inconsistency may amount to a problem of monstrous proportions. Not so, however, in databases. Let us see why.

A set D of database clauses can never be inconsistent, but the union of D with a set IC of integrity constraints can. Yet, inconsistency in databases can be hedged to become a simple syntactic issue, simply by replacing each integrity constraint of the form $\leftarrow B$ in IC by the database clause $incon \leftarrow B$, where $incon$ is a distinguished 0-ary predicate that does not occur in D, thus obtaining a set IC' of database clauses about the predicate $incon$. Then, inconsistency of $D \cup IC$ is equivalent to the answer 'yes' to the query $\leftarrow incon$ against the database $D \cup IC'$.

Moreover, even if an inconsistent (D, IC) is not rewritten to $(D \cup IC, \leftarrow incon,$ the usual inference rules employed in database query answering (no matter if logic-programming-style backward reasoning or fixpoint-generating forward reasoning procedures) are not at all computing arbitrary answers that would be invalidated by EFQ, as observed in [13]. In fact, since the disjunctive thinning inference rule of classical logic is not used in database logic, the EFQ sting is taken out of inconsistency, as observed in [16,36]. In fact, one can argue that database logic is inconsistency-tolerant, as done in [14]. However, care must be taken if, for checking the integrity of databases across updates, some procedures on top of database logic are employed. For instance, some well-respected integrity checking procedures are not inconsistency-tolerant, as shown in [19]. In Subsects. 6.1–6.2, we'll come back on the issue of inconsistency tolerance in more detail, in the context of several examples of inconsistency-tolerant applications based on database inconsistency measures.

5   Inconsistency Measures

In mathematical measure theory [2], a *measure* μ maps elements (typically, sets) of a *measure space* $\mathbb{S}$ (typically, sets of sets) to the set of non-negative real numbers, which sometimes is augmented with an additional greatest element ∞. Intuitively, for $S \in \mathbb{S}$, $\mu(S)$ tells how 'big' S is. Well-known examples of mathematical measures are statistical measures, whose range is the real numbers interval $[0,1]$, for indicating the probability of certain "events", formalized as elements of the measure space [29].

Standard properties of measures μ are that they are *positive definite*, i.e., $\mu(\mathcal{S}) \geq 0$ for each $S \in (S)$ (which holds by definition, given the prescribed range of measures) and $\mu(\emptyset) = 0$, and *additive*, i.e., $\mu(S \cup S') = \mu(S) + \mu(S')$, for disjoint sets $S, S' \in \mathbb{S}$.

Measures for quantifying the inconsistency of sets of logical formulas are axiomatized similarly, in the literature. The positive definiteness of mathematical measures corresponds to the postulate that each consistent set is mapped to 0, and each inconsistent set to a value greater than 0.

Apart from that, there is a large diversity of different properties postulated for inconsistency measures, but there is no widely accepted agreement on their stringency, except additivity, although even that is not unanimously agreed upon [47]. A property which is weaker than additivity is *monotony*, i.e., for S, S' such that $S \subsetneq S'$, $\mu(S) \leq \mu(S')$ is postulated. But even that is not cogent for inconsistency measures, since, e.g., the set $I = \{p, \neg p\}$ can easily be considered more inconsistent than sets such as $S \cup I$, where S is a very large consistent set that is disjoint from I.

In fact, neither additivity nor monotony hold, in general, for database inconsistency measures, due to the non-monotonic logic at work. Moreover, as argued in [17], it is possible to imagine database inconsistency measures such that even the inconsistency value of a database with only negligible inconsistency may be mapped to 0.

In general, a database inconsistency measure μ maps pairs (D, IC) from a measure space of pairs of databases D and integrity theories IC to a *metric space* $(\mathbb{M}, \preccurlyeq, \emptyset, \oplus)$, i.e., a commutative monoid $(\mathbb{M}, \oplus, \emptyset)$ that is partially ordered by $\preccurlyeq$, with neutral element o that also is the infimum of $\preccurlyeq$. The algebraic structure of such measure spaces is further detailed in [17,18]. Intuitively speaking, $\mu(D, IC)$ sizes the amount of inconsistency in (D, IC).

As already indicated in the previous section, database inconsistency measures do not comply with many postulates imposed on conventional inconsistency measures for sets of propositional or first-order predicate logic formulas, mainly because of the non-monotonicity brought about by default negation inference rules in databases.

6   Applications of Inconsistency Measures

Important applications of mathematical measures are of probabilistic or statistical kind. The main application of conventional inconsistency measures is to quantify the amount of inconsistency in sets of logic formulas which formalize a description of some real-world or imagined scenario. As opposed to that, the main application area of database inconsistency measures is the comparison of the amount of inconsistency in databases before and after updates, in order to support decisions of whether to accept, amend or reject the updates.

The most essential difference between conventional inconsistency measures and database inconsistency measures is that the latter do not have to be computed for the two applications discussed in this section. Also for mathematical measures μ, there are applications where μ does not have to be determined numerically. For instance, to compare who is the taller one of two persons, their measured height needs not be known; rather, it suffices to put them side by side. Similarly, for determining if an update U of a database D changes the amount of constraint violation in *IC*, it is easy to see that it suffices to run an inconsistency-tolerant integrity checking method, which tells if U may violate a constraint, or an instance thereof, that has been satisfied before updating D with U. If U violates a hitherto satisfied constraint, it obviously does not decrease the set of extant cases of integrity violation, nor does it leave it invariant.

In the remainder of this section, we look into two applications of database inconsistency measures, viz., inconsistency-tolerant relaxations of integrity checking and inconsistency repair checking. More applications will be addressed in an extended version of this paper (in preparation).

6.1   Measure-Based Integrity Checking

The main difference between conventional and measure-based integrity checking is that the former is inconsistency-intolerant while the latter is inconsistency-tolerant. Conventional integrity checking is based on the premise that total consistency can be achieved and maintained in databases, irrespective of their size and the complexity of their dynamics. Thus, conventional integrity checking requires that, for an update U to be checked for integrity preservation, the database state to be updated be consistent with its integrity constraints, and only updates that preserve consistency are acceptable. As opposed to that, inconsistency-tolerant integrity checking recognizes that total consistency in real-life databases is rarely achievable and thus a matter of wishful thinking, rather than an assumption with which can be reasoned in practice. Thus, inconsistency-tolerant integrity checking does not pursue the illusionary goal to maintain an absolute control in order to completely ban inconsistency from any database. Rather, inconsistency is, for better or worse, not excluded, and the goal is to contain its amount across updates.

The basic idea of measure-based integrity checking is to find out, for a given update request U in a database D, whether the amount of inconsistency, i.e., of integrity violation, in the updated database (D^U, IC) is equal to or less than the amount of inconsistency in (D, IC) or not. If it is equal or less, then the update may be accepted. If it is neither equal nor less, then the amount of inconsistency in (D^U, IC) is either greater than that of (D, IC), or it is incomparable. If inconsistency in (D^U, IC) is greater than in (D, IC), then U usually is to be rejected.

Incomparability of the amount of inconsistency before and after an update may occur only if the metric space to which the database inconsistency measure maps its output is not totally ordered. For example, if U violates a constraint ι that has been satisfied before but also repairs a previous violation of some other constraint I', and if the measure is the set of violated constraints (i.e., the metric space is the powerset of *IC*, partially ordered by $\subseteq$), then, the set of violated constraints in the updated state clearly is neither a subset nor a superset of the set of violated constraints before the update, nor are both sets equal. Hence, they are not comparable. In such cases, the usual policy of integrity checking methods is to either reject the update, or to compute a consistency-preserving repair of I', or to use some preference criteria that decide which of the two violations of

ι and I' is more tolerable, which may include the option to ask the user which of the states before and after the update should be preferred.

In case the amount of inconsistency in (D, IC) and (D^U, IC) is the same, then that does not necessarily mean that the violations in (D, IC) are the same as the one in (D^U, IC), no matter if the metric space is totally ordered or not. For instance, the set of violated constraints is theasure same before and after the update $U = \{delete\,p(a,a),\ insert\,p(b,b)\}$ in $D = \{p(a,a)\}$ and $IC = \{\leftarrow p(x,x)\}$, but the cases of violated instances of $\leftarrow p(x,x)$ obviously are different before and after applying U.

The preceding example also shows that different measures may yield different kinds of inconsistency tolerance. In fact, several different measures can be illustrated. One is the measure ι that maps pairs (D, IC) to $\{I \mid I \in v(D, IC)\}$, where $v(D, IC)$ is the set of constraints in IC that are violated in D. In the example, $vc(D, IC) = \{\leftarrow p(x,x)\}$. Related to ι, the measure $|\iota|$ simply counts the violated constraints in IC, i.e., $|\iota|$ maps (D, IC) to $|\iota(D, IC)|$. Similar to ι, the database inconsistency measure ζ maps pairs (D, IC) to $\{\zeta \mid C \in vc(D, IC)\}$, where $vc(D, IC)$ is the set of violated cases of constraints in IC. Recall from [19]: Cases are instances of a constraint in prenex form where all $\forall$- quantified variables that are not governed by an $\exists$ quantifier are consistently substituted by a ground term. In the example, $vc(D, IC) = \{\leftarrow p(a,a)\}$ and $vc(D^U, IC) = \{\leftarrow p(b,b)\}$. Instead of sets of cases of violated constraints, the database inconsistency measure κ maps pairs (D, IC) to $\{\zeta \mid C \in c(D, IC)\}$, where $c(D, IC)$ is the set of causes of the violation in IC. Causes are instances of if- and only-if halves of the completion of D where all $\forall$-quantified variables that are not governed by an $\exists$ quantifier are consistently substituted by a ground term. In the example, $c(D, IC) = \{p(a,a)\}$ and $c(D^U, IC) = \{p(b,b)\}$. In analogy to ι and to $|\iota|$, there are also cardinality measures $|\zeta|$ and $|\kappa|$, which map to $|\zeta(D, IC)|$ and, resp., $|\zeta(D, IC)|$. In the example, $|\iota(D, IC)| = |\iota(D^U, IC)| = |\zeta(D, IC)| = |\zeta(D^U, IC)| = |\kappa(D, IC)| = |\kappa(D^U, IC)| = 1$.

Of course, mode measures can be imagined, e.g., those which assign a weight of inconsistency to violated constraints or their cases or their causes, for quantifying their severity, and sum up the weights of elements in the results of ι, ζ or κ, respectively. Or measures that compute the ratio of $|\iota|$, $|\zeta|$ or $|\kappa|$ by the cardinality of D. Then, the amount of extant integrity violations or their causes become less important with each increase of the database that does not increase the amount of violations or of their causes. There are also conventional inconsistency measures that can be adapted to become database inconsistency measures, at least for the monotonic case of relational or definite databases and integrity theories that only consist of conjunctive denial constraints. An example is the inconsistency measure in [28,30], which has been molded as a database inconsistency measure in [20].

6.2   Measure-Based Repair Checking

Repair checking is to find out if a given update repairs violations of database integrity. Conventional repair checking evaluates the integrity of each constraint brute-force. Alternatively, the authors of [21] propose to compute repair checking by measure-based integrity checking (cf. Subsect. 6.1), as sketched below.

Let μ be a database inconsistency measure. A μ-based repair of a tuple (D, IC) is defined as an update of D such that $\mu(D^U, IC) \preccurlyeq \mu(D, IC)$ and there is no update U' such that $U' \subsetneq U$ and $\mu(D^{U'}, IC) \preccurlyeq \mu(D^U, IC)$.

According to this definition, to check if a given update U is a μ-based repair of (D, IC), it is necessary to check two things. Firstly, if U is a μ-based inconsistency reduction of (D, IC), i.e., if $\mu(D^U, IC) \preccurlyeq \mu(D, IC)$ holds, and, secondly, ifn μ is minimal in the sense defined above.

Now, let us succinctly recapitulate the main characteristics that differentiate the concept and the implementation of generalized measure-based repair checking from conventional brute force repair checking. The main conceptual difference between brute-force and measure-based repair checking: the latter is inconsistency-tolerant, i.e., accepts reductions of integrity violations that do not totally eliminate inconsistency. Brute-force repair checking disqualifies each update that does not yield total consistency. The main technical difference: measure-based repair checking can be implemented by measure-based simplified integrity checking, brute-force repair checking evaluates all constraints brute-force. The main practical difference: An implementation of measure-based repair checking by simplified integrity checking is more efficient since it exploits the incrementality of updates. In particular, the incrementality of updates makes it possible to refrain from computing the inconsistency measure explicitly. Rather, only the difference of inconsistency between old and new states needs to be looked at for deciding if an update is a repair or not.

In terms of the efficiency-enhancing use of measure-based inconsistency-tolerant integrity checking, perhaps the most surprising thing with measure-based repair checking is that not only the inconsistency reduction check can be done by measure-based integrity checking, but also the minimality check can recur on that same technology, based on the given database inconsistency measure. Below, we re-state the main results in [21], where measure-based integrity checking is used for the inconsistency reduction check and the minimality check of generalized repair checking. As argued in [21], this way of repair checking is significantly cheaper than brute-force repair checking.

Theorem 1. Let ic be a sound μ-based integrity checking method, and rc a function that maps triples (D, IC, U) to yes, no. rc is a complete μ-based repair checking method if rc obeys the following equivalence, where $U'' = U \setminus U'$.

$$rc(D, IC, U) = yes \iff ic(D^U, IC, \overline{U}) = no \text{ , and}$$
$$\text{for each } U' \subsetneq U, \ ic(D^U, IC, \overline{U}'') = no.$$

Theorem 2. Let μ be an inconsistency measure, ic a sound and complete μ-based integrity checking method, and rc a function that maps triples (D, IC, U) to $\{yes, no\}$. rc is a sound and complete μ-based repair checking method if rc obeys the following equivalence, where $U'' = U \setminus U'$.

$$rc(D, IC, U) = yes \iff ic(D^U, IC, \overline{U}) = no,$$
$$ic(D, IC, U) = yes, \text{ and}$$
$$\text{for each } U' \subsetneq U, \ ic(D^U, IC, \overline{U}'') = no.$$

Theorem 3. Let μ be an inconsistency measure with a totally ordered range, ic a sound and complete μ-based integrity checking method, and rc a function that maps triples (D, IC, U) to $\{yes, no\}$. rc is a sound and complete μ-based repair checking method if rc obeys the following equivalence, where $U'' = U \setminus U'$.

$$rc(D, IC, U) = yes \iff ic(D^U, IC, \overline{U}) = no, \text{ and}$$
$$\text{for each } U' \subsetneq U, \ ic(D^U, IC, \overline{U}'') = no.$$

Note that the key differences between the three theorems are determined by the different premises, that either don't postulate or do postulate the completeness of ic, and also don't or do postulate the totality of the order of the metric space. Depending on the guarantee of completeness and totality, or the lack thereof, more or less strong consequences are obtained, as expressed by the respective equivalences.

Further note that the line $ic(D^U, IC, \overline{U}) = no$, which is common to each of the three theorems, precisely corresponds to the inconsistency reduction check of the repair checking method rc, realized by the μ-based integrity checking method ic. The last line, *for each* $U' \subsetneq U$, $ic(D^U, IC, \overline{U}'') = no$, on the right side of the equivalence symbol in each theorem, corresponds to the minimality check. The middle line on the right side of the equivalence symbol in Theorem 2 guarantees the soundness of the inconsistency reduction of rc.

Special mention must also be made of the use of the inverse updates $\overline{U}$ and $\overline{U}''$. The rationale for that is the following. Given an update U of (D, IC), an integrity checking method based on database inconsistency measure μ outputs *yes* only if $\mu(D^U, IC) \preceq \mu(D, IC)$. On the other hand, U properly reduces the amount of integrity violation if and only if $\mu(D^U, IC) \prec \mu(D, IC)$. So, the use of the inverse update simply is to find out if $\mu(D^U, IC) = \mu(D, IC)$ holds or not. If not, then the desired $\prec$ relation holds, i.e., U then is a proper inconsistency reduction.

7   Conclusion

The main contribution of this paper is to point out the originality and significance of database inconsistency measures, by comparing them to conventional mathematical measures and inconsistency measures of sets of logical formulas in the literature. For that purpose, we have first scrutinized the differences of the concepts of classical logic and database logic, and the differences of inconsistency in classical theories and in databases. On that basis, the differences between conventional inconsistency measures and database inconsistency measures could be elaborated more clearly and with more poignancy that it had been done in [15, 18–23, 25]. Yet, we refer to the latter for more technical details on various applications of database inconsistency measures, which we have paced in Sect. 6.

To conclude, we briefly recapitulate the main differences that we have carved out in this paper. As opposed to mathematical measures and logical inconsistency measures, the range of database measures is not necessarily numerical, since their main purpose is not to quantify the amount of inconsistency in a given database (although they can be used for that purpose too), but rather to compare the amounts of inconsistency in two consecutive database states. Such comparisons are key for an inconsistency-tolerant monitoring, maintenance and repairing of database quality, and also for an assessment of the quality of answers given in potentially inconsistent databases.

An equally important difference is that, for comparing the amount of consistency of consecutive database states by measure-based integrity checking methods, it is not necessary to compute the absolute values of inconsistency measures. Rather, it suffices to gain evidence of the relative difference (i.e., decrease or increase or invariance) between such states, for supporting decisions about accepting or dismissing updates. Also for computing answers that have integrity in inconsistent databases, it is not necessary to compute absolute inconsistency measures. Rather, it suffices to check if there is any overlap of causes that explain a given answer with the causes of integrity violation. Computation of the latter tends to be more expensive than computing causes of answers. However, computing causes of integrity violation can be done in quiescent states, after update requests have been processed, and hence does not have to cope with real-time requirements that are more likely to occur at update time, i.e., the time when causes of answers are computed.

References

1. Abiteboul, S., Hull, R., Vianu, V.: Foundations of Databases. Addison-Wesley, Reading (1995)
2. Bauer, H.: Maß- und Integrationstheorie, 2nd edn. De Greuter, Berlin (1992)
3. Bertossi, L., Hunter, A., Schaub, T. (eds.): Inconsistency Tolerance. LNCS, vol. 3300. Springer, Heidelberg (2005)
4. Besnard, P.: Revisiting postulates for inconsistency measures. In: Fermé, E., Leite, J. (eds.) JELIA 2014. LNCS (LNAI), vol. 8761, pp. 383–396. Springer, Cham (2014). doi:10.1007/978-3-319-11558-0_27
5. Besnard, P.: Forgetting-based inconsistency measure. In: Schockaert, S., Senellart, P. (eds.) SUM 2016. LNCS (LNAI), vol. 9858, pp. 331–337. Springer, Cham (2016). doi:10.1007/978-3-319-45856-4_23
6. Brewka, G., Dix, J., Konolige, K.: Nonmonotonic Reasoning: An Overview. CSLI Lecture Notes, vol. 73. CSLI Publications, Stanford (1997)
7. Ceri, S., Gottlob, G., Tanaka, L.: Logic Programming and Databases. Surveys in Computer Science. Springer, Heidelberg (1990)
8. Clark, K.: Negation as failure. In: Gallaire, H., Minker, J. (eds.) Logic and Data Bases, pp. 293–322. Plenum, New York (1978)
9. Codd, E.: A relational model of data for large shared data banks. CACM 13(6), 377–387 (1970)
10. da Costa, N.: On the theory of inconsistent formal systems. Notre Dame J. Form. Log. 15(4), 497–510 (1974)
11. de Bona, G., Finger, M.: Notes on measuring inconsistency in probabilistic logic. University of Sao Paulo (2014)

12. Decker, H.: The range form of databases and queries or: how to avoid floundering. In: Retti, J., Leidlmair, K. (eds.) 5th ÖGAI, pp. 114–123. Springer, Heidelberg (1989)

13. Decker, H.: Historical and computational aspects of paraconsistency in view of the logic foundation of databases. In: Bertossi, L., Katona, G.O.H., Schewe, K.-D., Thalheim, B. (eds.) SiD 2001. LNCS, vol. 2582, pp. 63–81. Springer, Heidelberg (2003). doi:10.1007/3-540-36596-6_4

14. Decker, H.: A case for paraconsistent logic as a foundation of future information systems. In: 17th CAiSE Workshops, vol. 2, pp. 451–461. FEUP Ediçoes (2005)

15. Decker, H.: Quantifying the quality of stored data by measuring their integrity. In: Proceedings of ICADIWT 2009, Workshop SMM, pp. 823–828. IEEE (2009)

16. Decker, H.: How to confine inconsistency or, wittgenstein only scratched the surface. In: 8th ECAP, pp. 70–75. Technical University of Munich (2010)

17. Decker, H.: Measure-based inconsistency-tolerant maintenance of database integrity. In: Schewe, K.-D., Thalheim, B. (eds.) SDKB 2011. LNCS, vol. 7693, pp. 149–173. Springer, Heidelberg (2013). doi:10.1007/978-3-642-36008-4_7

18. Decker, H.: New measures for maintaining the quality of databases. In: Murgante, B., Gervasi, O., Misra, S., Nedjah, N., Rocha, A.M.A.C., Taniar, D., Apduhan, B.O. (eds.) ICCSA 2012. LNCS, vol. 7336, pp. 170–185. Springer, Heidelberg (2012). doi:10.1007/978-3-642-31128-4_13

19. Decker, H., Martinenghi, D.: Inconsistency-tolerant integrity checking. IEEE Trans. Knowl. Data Eng. 23(2), 218–234 (2011)

20. Decker, H., Martinenghi, D.: Modeling, measuring and monitoring the quality of information. In: Heuser, C.A., Pernul, G. (eds.) ER 2009. LNCS, vol. 5833, pp. 212–221. Springer, Heidelberg (2009). doi:10.1007/978-3-642-04947-7_26

21. Decker, H., Misra, S.: Measure-based repair checking by integrity checking. In: Gervasi, O., et al. (eds.) ICCSA 2016. LNCS, vol. 9790, pp. 530–543. Springer, Cham (2016). doi:10.1007/978-3-319-42092-9_40

22. Dubois, D., Prade, H.: Possibilistic logic: a retrospective and prospective view. Fuzzy Sets Syst. 144(1), 3–23 (2004)

23. Gallaire, H., Minker, J., Nicolas, J.-M.: Logic and databases: a deductive approach. ACM Comput. Surv. 16(2), 153–185 (1984)

24. Alchourron, C., Gardenfors, A., Makinson, D.: On the logic of theory change: partialo meet contraction and revision functions. J. Symb. Log. 50(2), 510–521 (1985)

25. Gaye, M., Sall, O., Bousso, M., Lo, M.: Measuring inconsistencies propagation from change operation based on ontology partitioning. In: 11th SITIS, pp. 178–184 (2015)

26. Gelfond, M., Lifschitz, V.: The stable model semantics for logic programming. In: 5th ICLP, pp. 1070–1080. MIT Press (1988)

27. Grant, J.: Classifications for inconsistent theories. Notre Dame J. Form. Log. 19(3), 435–444 (1978)

28. Grant, J., Hunter, A.: Measuring inconsistency in knowledgebases. J. Intell. Inf. Syst. 27(2), 159–184 (2006)

29. Hand, D.: Statistics and the theory of measurement. J. R. Statist. Soc. Ser. A 159(3), 445–492 (1996)

30. Hunter, A.: Measuring inconsistency in knowledge via quasi-classical models. In: 18th AAAI, pp. 68–73 (2002)

31. Hunter, A.: Evaluating significance of inonsistencies. In: 18th IJCAI, pp. 468–478 (2003)

32. Hunter, A., Konieczny, S.: Approaches to measuring inconsistent information. In: Bertossi, L., Hunter, A., Schaub, T. (eds.) Inconsistency Tolerance. LNCS, vol. 3300, pp. 191–236. Springer, Heidelberg (2005). doi:10.1007/978-3-540-30597-2_7

33. Hunter, A., Konieczny, S.: On the measure of conflicts: shapley inconsistency values. AI **174**(14), 1007–1026 (2010)

34. Knight, K.: Measuring inconsistency. J. Philos. Log. **31**, 77–98 (2002)

35. Konieczny, S., Lang, J., Marquis, P.: Quantifying information and contradiction in propositional logic. In: 18th IJCAI, pp. 106–111 (2003)

36. Kowalski, R.: Logic for Problem Solving. North-Holland, New York (1979)

37. Kuhns, J.: Answering Questions by Computer: A Logical Study. Rand Corporation, Santa Monica (1967)

38. Lozinskii, E.: Information and evidence in logic systems. JETAI **6**(2), 163–193 (1994)

39. Lang, J., Marquis, P.: Reasoning under inconsistency: a forgetting-based approach. Artif. Intell. **174**(12–13), 799–823 (2010)

40. Ma, Y., Guilin Qi, G., Hitzler, P.: Computing inconsistency measure based on paraconsistent semantics. J. Log. Comput. **21**(6), 1257–1281 (2011)

41. Popper, K.: Objective Knowledge: an Evolutionary Approach, Revised edn. Oxford University Press, Oxford (1979)

42. Priest, G.: Paraconsistent logic. In: Gabbay, D., Guenthner, F. (eds.) Handbook of Philosophical Logic, vol. 6. Kluwer, Dordrecht (2002)

43. Przymusinski, T.: Perfect model semantics. In: 5th ICLP, pp. 1081–1096. MIT Press (1988)

44. Qi, G., Hitzler, P.: Inconsistency-tolerant Reasoning with Networked Ontologies. Deliverable D1.2.4 of NeOn project. University of Karlsruhe (2008)

45. Reiter, R.: On closed world data bases. In: Gallaire, H., Minker, J. (eds.) Logic and Databases, pp. 55–76. Plenum, New York (1978)

46. Shannon, C.: A mathematical theory of communication. Bell Syst. Tech. J. **27**(3), 379–423 (1948)

47. Thimm, M.: On the compliance of rationality postulates for inconsistency measures: a more or less complete picture. KI **31**(1), 31–39 (2017)

48. Thimm, M., Wallner, J.: Some complexity results on inconsistency measurement. In: 15th KR, pp. 114–123. AAAI (2016)

49. van Emden, M., Kowalski, R.: The semantics of predicate logic as a programming language. J. ACM **23**(4), 733–742 (1976)

50. Van Gelder, A., Ross, K., Schlipf, J.: The well-founded semantics for general logic programs. J. ACM **38**(3), 620–650 (1991)

51. Wikipedia: akri. https://en.wikipedia.org/wiki/Principle_of_explosion

Migration from COBOL to SOA: Measuring the Impact on Web Services Interfaces Complexity

Cristian Mateos[1,4(✉)], Alejandro Zunino[1,4], Sanjay Misra[2],
Diego Anabalon[3,4], and Andres Flores[3,4]

[1] ISISTAN-UNICEN-CONICET Research Institute, Tandil, Argentina
{cristian.mateos,
alejandro.zunino}@isistan.unicen.edu.ar
[2] Covenant University, Ota, Nigeria
ssopam@gmail.com
[3] GIISCO Research Group, National University of Comahue,
Neuquén, Argentina
{diego.anabalon,andres.flores}@fi.uncoma.edu.ar
[4] CONICET, National Scientific and Technical Research Council,
Buenos Aires, Argentina

Abstract. SOA and Web Services allow to easily expose business functions to build larger distributed systems. However, legacy systems – mostly in COBOL – are left aside unless applying a migration approach. Main approaches are: direct and indirect migration. The former implies to wrap COBOL programs with a thin layer of a Web Service oriented language/platform. The latter needs reengineering COBOL functions to a modern language/platform. In a previous work, we presented an intermediate approach based on direct migration where developed Web Services are later refactored to improve their interfaces quality. Refactorings mainly capture good practices inherent to indirect migration. In this paper, we measure the complexity of Web Services' interfaces generated by the three approaches. Both comprehension and interoperability can be affected according to the service interface complexity level. We apply a metric suite (by Baski & Misra) to measure complexity on services interfaces – i.e., WSDL documents. Migrations of two real COBOL systems upon the three approaches were compared on the complexity level of the generated WSDL documents.

Keywords: Legacy system migration · Service-oriented architecture · Web services · Direct migration · Indirect migration · WSDL complexity

1 Introduction

Organizations still relying on out-of-date supporting systems – e.g., in COBOL – are lately in the urgency to migrate towards new technologies such as Web 2.0, Web Services or mobile devices. The need is mainly avoiding high IT operational costs – e.g., mainframes – while increasing visibility to reach new markets [13]. System migration implies moving to new software environments/platforms while preserving

© Springer International Publishing AG 2017
R. Damaševičius and V. Mikašytė (Eds.): ICIST 2017, CCIS 756, pp. 266–279, 2017.
DOI: 10.1007/978-3-319-67642-5_22

legacy data and business functions [1]. Nowadays, a common architectural option is SOA (Service Oriented Architecture) [13], where systems are built from independent building blocks called *services* that can be invoked remotely. Services expose functionality that any system can use within/across the owner organization boundaries. The Web Services technology is the common way to materialize SOA, where services interfaces are described in WSDL (Web Service Description Language). Then, legacy to SOA migration mainly produces a *SOA frontier*, the set of WSDL documents describing the functionality of a service oriented system, as shown in Fig. 1.

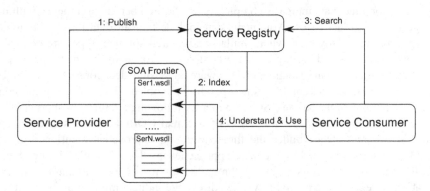

Fig. 1. SOA frontier and SOA roles.

Two main approaches for migration to SOA are: *direct* and *indirect* migration [13, 14]. The former implies to add a new software layer to wrap the legacy functionality that remains implemented with old technologies – being rapid and low cost. The latter requires reengineering concepts and techniques, driven by properties of the service-based system from a (non)functional standpoint – leading to higher time/cost.

In a previous work [14], we presented an intermediate approach based on direct migration in which developed Web Services are later improved on their interfaces quality – attending concerns inherent to an indirect approach. A quick migration is less costly but WSDLs (the SOA frontier) might suffer from anti-patterns – e.g., bad naming conventions and redundant operations [12] – affecting services readability and discoverability. Direct migration to SOA is often performed via a *1-to-1* mapping between legacy modules and Web Services. Hence, identifying and avoiding anti-patterns is disregarded [13]. Indirect migration may address this issue but at a large investment on cost/time. The intermediate migration approach, called COB2SOA is focused on COBOL systems, and identifies refactoring opportunities to be applied on SOA frontiers. Through an automatic analysis of WSDL documents and COBOL files, anti-patterns evidence detection is done. Specific refactorings are then proposed as remedy actions, to increase the quality level of WSDL documents.

All in all, organizations truly need a suitable approach to migrate legacy systems to SOA, and capable to ensure best quality of SOA frontiers. Hence, in this paper we address a specific quality concern related to the complexity of WSDL documents, which may seriously affect comprehension and interoperability. This may impact on new business opportunities and partners relationships, as services must be consumed from heterogeneous systems. Tightly closed functional constraints of data processing implemented in legacy modules are now openly exposed as operational data exchange protocols through WSDL documents. The use of XML (eXtensible Markup Language) documents serve to data message exchange. Certain message data structure definitions into WSDLs and XMLs might affect understandability.

Thereby, we make use of a recent metric suite (proposed by Baski and Misra [2]) to measure complexity of services interfaces – i.e., WSDL documents. Measurable aspects entail the structure of requesting and responding messages of WSDLs operations. A factor that may increase complexity is the number of arguments within a message and their data types. Arguments can include built-in data types or complex data type structures. However, when similarly-structured complex types are defined, a familiarity factor arises that may decrease complexity. As such, this metric suite produces further trade-off information to be aware of design decisions about WSDLs. Concretely, we could prevent from interoperability problems by measuring the complexity that might be injected on a SOA frontier by following a migration approach. We apply the metric suite onto the migration of two real COBOL systems to SOA performed in different stages under the three migration approaches mentioned above. The SOA frontiers produced by the three approaches involved 431 WSDL documents.

Our contribution in this paper is threefold: (a) to review the main migration approaches of legacy systems to SOA – i.e., direct and indirect migration; (b) to present an intermediate migration approach, namely COB2SOA, focused in COBOL systems; and (c) to analyze the migration of two real COBOL systems upon the three migration approaches. The complexity level of the generated WSDLs is compared through the Baski & Misra metric suite, which has been designed for that specific purpose.

2   Preliminary Concepts

As Web Services functionality is exposed through WSDL documents, their proper specification becomes crucial not to affect understanding and exceed development effort and cost to a consumer application. This can be addressed through identifying anti-patterns affecting services interfaces, and measuring their complexity by a set of metrics – e.g. the Baski & Misra metric suite. These two options are presented below.

Anti-Patterns. The catalog of Anti-Patterns in [12] describes bad practices that make WSDL documents less readable. Anti-patterns are concerned with how *port-types*, *operations* and *messages* are structured and specified in WSDLs. Table 1 summarizes the catalog of anti-patterns, classified in three categories: *high-level service interface specification*, *comments and identifiers*, and *service message exchange*. Consumer application developers prefer properly designed WSDL documents [12], so quality should be attended by service providers when building SOA frontiers. In the context of legacy to SOA migration scenarios, applying indirect migration favors achieving good WSDL document quality [13]. However, software engineers usually choose between direct or indirect migration based on classical criteria (e.g., time), disregarding those that may impact on readability and discoverability of SOA frontiers.

Table 1. Catalog of WSDL anti-patterns.

Anti-patterns	Symptoms
High-level service interface specification	
Enclosed data model	Type definitions are placed in the WSDL rather than in separate XSD documents
Redundant port-types	Several port-types offer the same set of operations, on different binding types (e.g., HTTP, HTTPS, or SOAP)
Redundant data models	Many types to represent the same domain objects within a WSDL
Low cohesive port-type	Port-types have operations with weak semantic cohesion
Comments and identifiers	
Inappropriate or lacking comments	(1) a WSDL document has no comments, or (2) comments are non explanatory
Ambiguous names	Ambiguous names are used for denoting the main elements of a WSDL document
Service message exchange	
Whatever types	A data-type might represent any domain object
Undercover fault information	Output messages are used to notify service errors

Baski and Misra Metric Suite. The metric suite ("BM suite") presented in [2] is concerned with the effort required to understand data flowing to/from a service interface, that can be characterized by the structures of messages used for data exchange. The BM suite includes four metrics, whose formulas are shown in Table 2, which can be computed from a service interface in WSDL. Metrics are explained as follows.

Data Weight metric (DW). This metric, with Formula (1), computes the structural complexity of service messages data-types. In (1), $C(m_i)$ broadly counts and weights the various XSD elements (simple/complex data-types) exchanged by the parts of message m_i. Each element or data-type definition in XSD is assigned with a weight value wp_j as a complexity degree. This wp_j is equals to we if the part references an element declaration in XSD, or wt if the part references an XSD element definition. In turn, wt depends on the data-type (simple or complex). See [2] for details about we and wt. Then, DW values are positive integers. The bigger the DW of a WSDL is, the more dense the parts of its messages are. Then, DW values should be kept low.

Distinct Message Ratio metric (DMR). This metric, with Formula (2), considers that a WSDL may have many messages with the same structure. As the number of similarly-structured messages increases, less effort is likely needed to reason about them. Repetitive messages might allow to gain familiarity when inspecting the WSDL. The DMC function counts the number of distinct-structured messages in a WSDL, from the $[C(m_i), \#parts(m_i)]$ pairs, i.e., the complexity value and the total number of parts (input/output operation arguments) that each message m_i contains. Then, the DMR metric is in range $[0, 1]$, where 0 means that all messages are similarly-structured (lowest complexity), and 1 means that all messages are dissimilar (highest complexity). Then, DMR values should be kept low.

Table 2. BM metric suite.

Metrics formulas	
$DW(wsdl) = \sum_{i=1}^{n_m} C(m_i)$ (1) n_m: number of messages (input/output) of a WSDL	$C(m) = \sum_{j=1}^{\#parts(m)} wp_j$ wp_j: weight value of the j-th part of message m n_m: total number of messages in the WSDL
$DMR(wsdl) = \frac{DMC(wsdl)}{n_m}$ (2)	
$ME(wsdl) = \sum_{i=1}^{DMC(wsdl)} P(m_i) * (-log_2 P(m_i))$ (3)	$P(m_i) = \frac{nom_i}{n_m}$ nom_i: number of occurrences of the i-th message n_m: total number of messages in the WSDL
$MRS(wsdl) = \sum_{i=1}^{DMC(wsdl)} \frac{nom_i^2}{n_m}$ (4)	nom_i: number of occurrences of the i-th message, n_m: total number of messages in the WSDL

Message Entropy metric (ME). This metric, with Formula (3), exploits the percentage of similarly-structured messages that occur within a given WSDL. ME also assumes that repetition of the same messages makes a developer more familiar with the WSDL, but ME bases on an alternative differentiation among WSDLs in this respect. The ME metric has values in the range $[0, log_2(n_m)]$. A low ME value means that messages are consistent in structure, i.e., the complexity of a WSDL is lower than others with equal DMR values [2]. Then, ME values should be kept low.

Message Repetition Scale metric (MRS). This metric, with Formula (4), analyzes variety in structures of a WSDL. MRS measures the consistency of messages by considering $[C(m_i), \#parts(m_i)]$ pairs in the given WSDL. MRS values are in the range $[1, n_m]$. A higher MRS means less effort to reason about messages structures due to repetition of similarly-structured messages. Then, MRS values should be kept high.

3 Related Work

Direct migration. In [16] individual functions of legacy code are wrapped with an XML shell to be offered as Web Services. For each relevant function/program, a new subroutine of the parent program is built, to be associated to a WSDL document. A proxy is generated to link the Web Services to the underlying legacy business logic. In [3] interactive legacy functions are wrapped to make it accessible as Web Services. A Finite State Automaton is used to manually describe the interaction model between users and the legacy system. For GUI-centered programs, a wrapper produces the request/response scheme interaction with the SOA system on behalf of users. In [10] are presented three design patterns for wrapping legacy systems as Web Services. The Lowest Common Denominator Interface, Most Popular Interface and the Negotiated

Interface patterns are used to create a common interface to wrap similar software components, to be used modularly within the resulting SOA system.

Indirect migration. In [5], a reengineering methodology towards SOA is presented, based in the 4 + 1 view model [8]. Some software architectures are combined: 3-tier for business logic design, n-tier for service deployment, and SOA for integrating the legacy system with the new environment. In [6] reengineering of legacy code is based on a three-step process: legacy architecture recovery, evolution plan creation, and plan execution. The QAR workflow is used to recover the architecture on three analysis-based steps: documentation, static and dynamic. For the new architecture is used the OGSi standard framework for service lifecycle management and execution. Finally, the set of services is generated. In [17] is presented the SOAMIG COBOL to SOA migration methodology that consists of four iterative phases. COBOL code is translated to Java that is easier to expose as Web Services. Translation is straightforward without any good object-oriented (OO) design criteria. As such, COBOL limitations are transferred to the SOA frontier – e.g. routine names and comments.

Combining direct and indirect migration. In [11] legacy components are identified to be used as services, by the Architecture Reconstruction and MINing (ARMIN) method. Dependencies (functional/data) between legacy components help to identify candidate services. This is used to generate a component view. Some issues found involve implementation and documentation inconsistencies, indicating the need for deeply studying the code prior to migration. In [15] the Service-Oriented and Reuse Technique (SMART) can help to expose legacy functions as Web Services. Wrapping is the initial option, otherwise specific interactions prescribed by SOA are considered to modify legacy modules. The initial step implies architectural design, to then analyze the gap between the target SOA system and the original system. Finally, a migration technique is selected (e.g., quick and dirty or wrapping). Several migration approaches can be combined, but no supported tools are provided.

4   The COB2SOA Migration Approach

COB2SOA relies on refactoring opportunities applied upon the SOA frontier of a legacy system, by detecting evidences of anti-patterns. The hypothesis is that enhancing the SOA frontier of a wrapped legacy system can be done in a cheap and fast way by analyzing legacy source code and WSDL interfaces, and supplying developers with guidelines (*refactoring opportunities*) for manually refining WSDLs based on the evidence of anti-patterns. Main activities of COB2SOA are shown in Fig. 2.

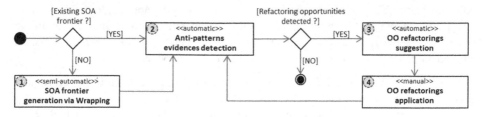

Fig. 2. COB2SOA: main activities.

The input is a legacy system source code (COBOL files) and the set of WSDL documents that result from a direct migration. If the legacy system does not have a SOA frontier yet, a semi-automatic process generates one Web Service per COBOL program. As a pre-processing, COBOL data-types are converted into XSD data-types for WSDLs. Data exchanged by COBOL programs is manually identified to then create a wrapper for it (e.g., using.NET or Java). Then, the WSDLs are automatically generated from the source code of the wrapper. The initial SOA frontier is automatically analyzed to detect evidences of WSDL anti-patterns. Then a list of concrete suggestions is generated to improve the services frontier. After that, developers apply all or some of the suggested refactoring actions. These steps can be done in successive iterations and refinements, where a new, improved SOA frontier can be obtained.

To detect the anti-patterns evidences, some heuristics were defined and implemented, allowing assistance during the system migration. Evidences of anti-patterns can be combined to create *refactoring opportunities*. Six refactoring opportunities have been defined – explained in Sect. 4.1. Most of the heuristics help to analyze WSDLs to detect evidences of anti-patterns that may affect service readability and discoverability (see Sect. 2). Also, two anti-patterns for COBOL source code were added, namely *unused parameters* and *shared dependencies* among two COBOL programs representing service implementations. To detect evidences of these two anti-patterns, COBOL code files are reverse engineered with an analysis of the common area for data-type exchange, called COMMAREA. Once evidences of anti-patterns have been identified, practical guidelines to remove them must be provided. For this, OO refactorings are applied, considering that services are described as OO interfaces exchanging messages, with data-types described using XSD. Then, a sub-set of Fowler et al.'s catalog [7] was selected.

4.1 SOA Refactoring Opportunities

The six refactoring opportunities applicable over a SOA frontier are now briefly explained. They allow to remove the evidences of the ten anti-patterns explained in the previous section. Table 3 shows how refactoring opportunities – referred as *Legacy-System-to-SOA (LSSOA) Refactorings* – are related into one or more logical combinations to *OO refactorings* from the Fowler et al.'s catalog [7]. For space reasons, the reader is referred to [14] for details of refactoring opportunities.

Remove redundant operations. Redundant operations in a SOA frontier is similar to duplicate code in other contexts [12]. This can be detected both in COBOL source code and in WSDLs. Each service exposes an interface that wraps COBOL programs, whose business logic involves an interface including COBOL data-types and dependencies to other programs. The *Extract Method* OO refactoring may be applied, to create a single operation in a WSDL (grouping several redundant operations) to be invoked for all the points where the redundancy was detected. At the class level, the *Extract Class* is applied to generate a new service from the redundant services.

Improve error handling definitions. This is related to improper handling of errors and exceptions in services, which occurs when WSDL operations exclude <fault> elements. Instead, errors are exchanged along with pure data. Thus, the actual result

Table 3. SOA frontier refactorings and Fowler et al.'s refactorings.

LSSOA refactoring	OO refactoring
Remove redundant operations	1: Extract Method ⇒ Extract Class
Improve error handling definitions	1: Replace Error Code With Exception
Improve business object definitions	1: Convert Procedural Design to Object ; Replace Conditional with Polymorphism 2: Inline Class 3: Extract Class ; Extract Subclass ; Extract Superclass ;Collapse Hierarchy 4: Remove Control Flag ; Remove Parameter 5: Replace Type Code with Class ; Replace Type Code with Subclasses
Expose shared programs as services	1: Extract Method ⇒ Extract Class
Improve names and comments	1: Rename Method ⇒ Preserve Whole Object ⇒ Introduce Parameter Object ⇒ Replace Parameter with Explicit Methods
Improve service operations cohesion	1: Inline Class ; Rename Method 2: Move Method ⇒ Move Class

Numbers means the steps to be performed to fulfill the OO refactorings.
"⇒" means that only one OO refactoring should applied.
";" means that all OO refactorings should be applied in that strict order.

(correct or error) from an operation is unknown until invoking the service. The *Replace Error Code With Exception* OO refactoring can be applied here. This refactoring adds the missing <fault> elements to WSDLs and the refinement of data-types mixing output and error data. A textual description (string) or a <complexType> can be used to report details of the error.

Improve business object definitions. This can be detected with the lack of a single XSD file for a set of services within the same frontier. This means, a bad business model definition (or the lack of a unique data-type schema) hinders the general readability of services and their reusability. As shown in Table 3, up to five steps and many OO refactorings should be done here. In fact, several aspects of a service are involved: *Too many output/input parameters, Redundant data-types definitions, Data-types with inconsistent names and types,* and *Unused parameters.* Some of them can be solved with one OO refactoring, while others require more than one in alternate combinations. For example, *Too many output/input parameters,* evidences the use of many variables as parameters of procedural modules, that should be arranged among different business objects. The *Convert Procedural Design to Object* OO refactoring can be applied, to restructure common data-types schema for a set of Web Services.

Expose shared programs as services. Usually some programs/routines contain functionality that represents core business itself. Such routines might have several client routines dependents, representing highly reusable business logic modules. Exposing these routines as services can reduce the chance of redundant operations, increasing the possibility of Web Services composition. The *Extract Method* OO refactoring can be applied, which is similar to having a long method. In SOA, it means generating new service operations that might help service consumers to identify the requested functionality. If a decomposition of a long routine expose several service operations, a new service could be generated, i.e., by applying *Extract Class*.

Improve names and comments. WSDLs must precisely describe how to invoke certain functionality as well as the meaning of that functionality. This implies to improve names of operations, messages, port-types, parts and elements present in a WSDL, by adding documentation according to the meaning of the service. Improving these elements implies dealing with semantics, and hence they cannot be fully automated. This situation implies several alternatives. For example, renaming service operations is equivalent to apply the *Rename Method* OO refactoring.

Improve service operations cohesion. This improvement consists in grouping semantically similar operations and/or Web Services in terms of business functionality. For similarity between two services is assumed a 1-to-1 association between COBOL programs and Web Services, i.e., produced Web Services contain a single operation. Therefore, this also represents the similarity between two COBOL programs. This implies some aspects with different alternatives as solutions. For example, the *Move Method* OO refactoring can be applied, which is used to re-locate methods being odd within a class, and mostly invoked by other classes. In SOA, this would be equivalent to moving operations between services. When a group of similar services (of one operation) is identified, a new service could be built by applying *Move Class*.

5 Experimental Evaluation

This section evaluates the effectiveness of migration approaches to SOA regarding frontier complexity in terms of the BM suite (see Sect. 2). Two case studies, concerning COBOL systems, have been subject of migration to SOA by employing the three approaches: Direct and Indirect migration, and COB2SOA. The first case study is the legacy system of the largest Argentinian government agency [13]. The second case study is a legacy system providing support for mill sales management [14].

5.1 Direct and Indirect Migration

The first system manages information of the entire population in Argentina [13]. It runs on an IBM AS/400 *mainframe*. Some programs are used via an *intranet* and others are grouped in CICS transactions that are consumed by Web applications. *Direct migration* was done by wrapping the CICS-enhanced programs, creating a preliminary Web Services frontier. One 1-operation Web Service for each COBOL program was generated, adding a thin C# .NET service layer. Then, WSDLs were automatically generated from the C# source code. Developers migrated 32 COBOL programs, generating 32 services in about 5 days. *Indirect migration* was done to completely re-implement the 32 COBOL programs in C#. An indirect SOA frontier was built, consisting of 7 services, and 1 XSD file representing a single data model. The generated WSDLs were manually refined until an antipatterns-free SOA frontier was obtained. The whole migration process demanded 13 months: 1 month to manually define WSDLs, 3 months to analyze legacy functions, 1 month to refine WSDLs, 6 months to rewrite the business logic, and 2 months to test the obtained indirect SOA frontier.

The Mill Sales Management system provides support for sale transaction management between clients, suppliers and creditors [14]. The system comprises 211 COBOL programs and an extra COBOL program acting as a program selector (menu). No databases or CICS transactions are involved. Data storage is programmatically handled via ".dat" files. An independent file – the COMMAREA – is used for data definition of each COBOL program. First, *direct migration* was done, generating 211 Web Services by wrapping each COBOL program via a 1-to-1 mapping strategy. WSDL interfaces were also generated by building a thin service layer. The migration to SOA demanded 21 days. Then, *indirect migration* of the original system was also done. Similar to the first case study, the goal was to generate a high quality SOA frontier, i.e., without anti-patterns. After 6 months process, 50 Web Services were built – 2 months to analyze the legacy functions, 1 month to design the WSDLs, and 3 months to refine WSDLs. Since this case study had experimental purposes only, no actual deployment was done. Hence, testing the obtained indirect SOA frontier was left out – which might require more than 2 months compared to case study 1.

5.2   COB2SOA Migration

The direct SOA frontiers of both case studies were taken as input for the COB2SOA approach, to identify refactoring opportunities (see Sect. 4.1). Table 4 summarizes the refactoring opportunities detected. After that, the new SOA frontier – the set of refactored WSDL documents – for both case studies were obtained.

For case study 1, there were refactoring opportunities applicable to all the services/programs and others applicable to a subset of the services/programs. Besides, a suggestion came up that the 32 services should be grouped in just 16 services. One specialist applied the proposed refactorings in 2 days, to create the new SOA frontier of

Table 4. Case studies: detected LSSOA refactorings.

LSSOA refactoring	Case study 1 (32 services)	Case study 2 (211 services)
Remove redundant operations	7 redundant operations detected	35 redundant operations detected
Improve error handling definitions	32 services needed to be improved	0 services needed to be improved
Improve business object definitions	32 services needed to be improved	209 services needed to be improved
Expose shared programs as services	6 COBOL programs to be exposed	0 COBOL programs to be exposed
Improve names and comments	32 services needed to be improved	211 services needed to be improved
Improve service operations cohesion	16 services identified	115 services identified

16 services + 1 XSD file. For case study 2, one refactoring opportunity was applicable to all the services/programs (211) and other was applicable to most of them (209 services). Finally, after the specialist applied the proposed refactorings (in about 1 month), the new SOA frontier was created containing 115 services + 1 XSD file.

5.3   Comparison of Service Interfaces Quality

SOA frontiers obtained by direct migration strongly depend on the original system design. In turn, interfaces obtained by indirect migration might be more independent [13], since the legacy system functionality is re-implemented using modern technologies and new design criteria. The main goal of this work is to assess the trade-off between cost/time and services frontier quality. Thereby, setting forth empirical evidence can reveal how a migration approach influences a SOA frontier quality – mainly focusing on the complexity level according to the BM suite (see Sect. 2). Besides, a quantitative analysis highlights some results from the migration processes, as follows.

Quantitative analysis. Table 4 shows the quantitative results regarding the interfaces generated by the three migration alternatives, for both case studies. The first advantage of indirect migration and COB2SOA compared to direct migration is the unique XSD document generated, to share the definition of common data-types across all WSDLs. In addition, the fewer number of WSDLs means they include more operations, fostering a functional definition of related cohesive operations within a WSDL.

In case study 1, 32 COBOL programs were directly migrated, that resulted in 38 operations (one program was divided into 7 operations). After manually analyzing the business logic was detected that only 2 operations were useful and the remaining ones were marked as duplicate. For case study 2, after directly migrating 211 COBOL programs the result was 252 operations – because operations were classified into three transaction types: add, update, or delete of data. In turn, indirect migration and COB2SOA migration resulted in 202 and 206 operations, respectively. There are fewer operations due to redundant operations that were removed in both cases.

Qualitative analysis. The BM metric suite was applied on both case studies upon the three migration approaches. The aim is to evaluate how a migration approach influences the complexity level of a generated SOA frontier – with a likely impact on comprehension and interoperability. Before analyzing measurement results from both case studies, we recall the expected (good/bad) values on each metric of the BM suite.

Results for case study 1 are shown in Fig. 3. The COB2SOA migration outperforms the direct migration in both DMR and MRS. However, the indirect migration obtained the best values for these two metrics – i.e., the lowest DMR and the highest MRS. This means, refactorings have produced higher use of similarly-structured messages, that improves WSDL comprehension. However, the ME metric, was affected by COB2SOA and indirect migration – the worst value (highest) for indirect migration. This means, a high distribution of similarly-structured messages, instead of being consistent in structure. Finally, the DW metric was also affected by COB2SOA and indirect migration – obtaining higher values than for direct migration. This means, refactorings have produced a larger number of complex data types – probably with a goal to better reflect business domain objects (see Table 4).

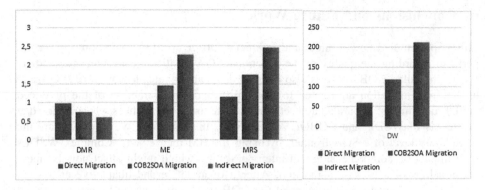

Fig. 3. Case study 1: BM suite metrics upon migration approaches.

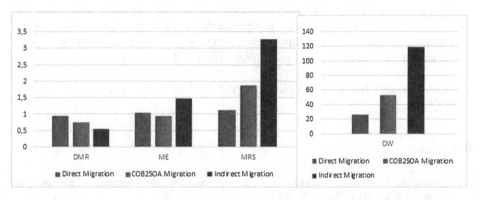

Fig. 4. Case study 2: BM suite metrics upon migration approaches.

Results for case study 2 are shown in Fig. 4. The general trends are quite similar to case study 1 for the DMR, MRS and DW metrics. However, the ME metric was particularly benefited by COB2SOA, obtaining the lowest (better) value. Then, after the refactorings, most WSDLs resulted with few data structures largely repeated (wrt other similar-structures) being as such highly consistent within the given WSDLs.

Discussion. From the quantitative and qualitative analysis above, it can be seen that the COB2SOA migration approach has a midway performance. Regarding the time vs. quality trade-off there is a better performance, considering a quality trend towards the indirect approach, but with a time trend very close to the direct approach and largely far from the indirect migration. As such, the COB2SOA approach comes up as an optimized option for the industry when engaging in a COBOL to SOA migration.

6 Conclusions and Future Work

This paper studied how a direct and indirect COBOL to SOA migration approaches perform regarding the quality of the generated SOA frontier. Besides an intermediate approach, called COB2SOA, is also evaluated. Qualities attended by COB2SOA and the indirect migration are related to readability and discoverability of the produced WSDL documents. In particular, a set of anti-patterns – bad practices – is considered at the levels of WSDL and COBOL source code. In this study, we also evaluate the complexity level of a SOA frontier, by using the BM metric suite. Complex WSDLs may impact on comprehension and interoperability, which might affect new business relationships of a target organization. After a quantitative and qualitative analysis a conclusive evidence arises in favor of the COB2SOA approach, in terms of balanced trade-off between quality and time. As future work, we expect to conduct another study concerning well-known OO metrics from Chidamber and Kemerer [4], from which we have found a correlation with the BM metric suite [9]. By considering the OO back-ends of the SOA frontiers that are generated in the three approaches we might early analyze another refactoring opportunities to then generate improved WSDLs with lowest complexity – i.e., increasing comprehension and interoperability.

Acknowledgments. This work is supported by PIP 2013-2015 GI code 11220120100185CO (CONICET).

References

1. Almonaies, A., Cordy, J., Dean, T.: Legacy system evolution towards service-oriented architecture. In: SOAME, pp. 53–62 (2010)
2. Baski, D., Misra, S.: Metrics suite for maintainability of extensible markup language web services. IET Softw. **5**(3), 320–341 (2011)
3. Canfora, G., Fasolino, A., Frattolillo, G., Tramontana, P.: A wrapping approach for migrating legacy system interactive functionalities to service oriented architectures. J. Syst. Softw. **81**(4), 463–480 (2008)
4. Chidamber, S., Kemerer, C.: A metrics suite for object oriented design. IEEE Trans. Softw. Eng. **20**(6), 476–493 (1994)
5. Chung, S., An, J., Davalos, S.: Service-oriented software reengineering: SoSR. In: Proceedings of the 40th IEEE HICSS, pp. 172c (2007)
6. Cuadrado, F., Garcia, B., Dueñas, J., Parada, H.: A case study on software evolution towards service-oriented architecture. In: Proceedings of the 22nd IEEE AINA, pp. 1399–1404 (2008)
7. Fowler, M., Beck, K., Brant, J., Opdyke, W., Roberts, D.: Refactoring: Improving the Design of Existing Code. Addison-Wesley Professional, Massachusetts (1999)
8. Kruchten, P.: The 4 + 1 view model of architecture. IEEE Softw. **12**(6), 42–50 (1995)
9. Mateos, C., Zunino, A., Misra, S., Anabalon, D., Flores, A.: Keeping web service interface complexity low using an OO metric-based early approach. In: Proceedings of the 42nd CLEI, pp. 1–12 (2016)

10. Millard, D., Howard, Y., Chennupati, S., Davis, H., Jam, E., Gilbert, L., Wills, G.: Design patterns for wrapping similar legacy systems with common service interfaces. In: ECOWS (2006)
11. O'Brien, L., Smith, D., Lewis, G.: Supporting migration to services using software architecture reconstruction. In: Proceedings of the 13th IEEE STEP, pp. 81–91 (2005)
12. Ordiales Coscia, J., Mateos, C., Crasso, M., Zunino, A.: Refactoring code-first web services for early avoiding WSDL anti-patterns: approach and comprehensive assessment. Sci. Comput. Program. **89**(Part C), 374–407 (2014)
13. Rodriguez, J., Crasso, M., Mateos, C., Zunino, A., Campo, M.: Bottom-up and top-down cobol system migration to web services. IEEE Internet Comput. **17**(2), 44–51 (2013)
14. Rodriguez, J., Crasso, M., Mateos, C., Zunino, A., Campo, M., Salvatierra, G.: The SOA frontier: experiences with 3 migration approaches. In: Migrating Legacy Applications: Challenges in Service Oriented Architecture and Cloud Computing Environments, pp. 26–152. IGI Global (2013)
15. Smith, D.: Migration of legacy assets to service-oriented architecture environments. In: Proceedings of the 29th ICSE, pp. 174–175. IEEE (2007)
16. Sneed, H.: Wrapping legacy software for reuse in a SOA. In: Multikonferenz Wirtschaftsinformatik, vol. 2, pp. 345–360. GITO-Verlag, Berlin (2006)
17. Zillmann, C., Winter, A., Herget, A., Teppe, W., Theurer, M., Fuhr, A., Horn, T., Riediger, V., Erdmenger, U., Kaiser, U., Uhlig, D., Zimmermann, Y.: The SOAMIG process model in industrial applications. In: Proceedings of the 15th CSMR, pp. 339–342. IEEE (2011)

Quality Model for Evaluating Platform as a Service in Cloud Computing

Temitope Olokunde, Sanjay Misra[(⊠)], and Adewole Adewumi

Center of ICT/ICE Research, CUCRID, Covenant University, Ota, Nigeria
{temitope.olokunde,sanjay.misra,
wole.adewumi}@covenantuniversity.edu.ng

Abstract. Cloud computing is a style of computing in which dynamically scalable and often virtualized resources are provided as a service over the Internet. Cloud computing can be offered in three ways namely: Software as a Service (SaaS), Platform as a Service (PaaS), and Infrastructure as a Service (IaaS). Researchers have begun to investigate quality in SaaS and have proposed quality models in this regard. There is however a dearth of literature investigating quality in PaaS and IaaS which form the motivation for this work. In this paper, therefore a model is proposed for evaluating quality of PaaS. We first define key features of PaaS. And then, we derive quality attributes from the key features, and define metrics for the quality attributes. To validate our quality model for PaaS, we conduct assessment based on case studies using the Analytic Hierarchy Process. By using the proposed PaaS quality model, developers will be able to select suitable PaaS solutions among alternatives.

Keywords: PaaS · Quality · Analytical hierarchy process

1 Introduction

Cloud computing has become an increasingly adopted computing phenomenon. It is defined as a model for enabling convenient, on-demand network access to a shared pool of configurable computing resources (e.g. networks, servers, storage applications and services) that can be rapidly provisioned and released with minimal management effort or service provider interaction [1]. Cloud computing services can be offered in three ways namely: Software as a Service (SaaS), Platform as a Service (PaaS), and Infrastructure as a Service (IaaS). Figure 1 shows these service offerings in layers.

SaaS is a model in which software is provided by a vendor [2]. The software being provided is hosted at the vendor's data center under agreed terms of use. The key strength of SaaS is that users do not have to develop their own software but rather can patronize SaaS vendors [3]. An example of this is the Gmail service offered by Google [4]. PaaS is a model where the manufacturers supply services to the users such as development environment, server platform and hardware resources [5]. The users can then use such platforms to develop their own applications and make it available to other customers through their server and Internet. PaaS thus provides the middleware platform, applications development environment, database management systems, and application server for the enterprise and the individual [6]. Examples of PaaS include:

© Springer International Publishing AG 2017
R. Damaševičius and V. Mikašytė (Eds.): ICIST 2017, CCIS 756, pp. 280–291, 2017.
DOI: 10.1007/978-3-319-67642-5_23

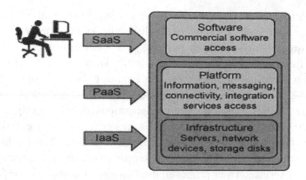

Fig. 1. Cloud computing layered architecture (http://www.ibm.com/developerworks/cloud/library/cl-cloudintro/)

Google App Engine offered by Google, Windows Azure offered by Microsoft. IaaS is a model that provides the consumer with the capability to provision processing, storage, networks, and other fundamental resources. It also allows the consumer to deploy and run arbitrary software, which can include operating systems and application [7].

In recent times, interest has been shown in investigating quality in cloud computing research and this is pioneered by the work of [8] who proposed a quality model for evaluating the quality of SaaS. However, no work was seen in literature proposing a quality model for IaaS and in particular PaaS. This forms the motivation for this present paper. The aim of this study therefore is to propose a model for evaluating quality of PaaS. We first define key features of PaaS. And then, we derive quality attributes from the key features, and define metrics for the quality attributes. To validate our quality model for PaaS, the Analytic Hierarchy Process (AHP) was applied on three known PaaS systems. The AHP is a multi-criteria decision-making approach introduced by [9]. By using the proposed PaaS quality model, PaaS systems can be evaluated by developers. Furthermore, the evaluation results are utilized as an indicator for PaaS quality management. The rest of this study is organized as follows: Sect. 2 examines related work. In Sect. 3 the proposed model is shown along with all the criteria used in its creation. In Sect. 4 the model is evaluated using specific case studies. In Sect. 5 we discuss the results of the evaluation process and conclude the paper in Sect. 6.

2   Related Work

A comprehensive model for evaluating quality of SaaS was proposed by [8]. They achieved this by first defining the key features of SaaS and went on to derive quality attributes for the key features. Metrics were then defined for the quality attributes. They validated their quality model for SaaS by conducting an assessment based on IEEE 106.1. They argued that by using their proposed model, SaaS could be evaluated by service providers. Their evaluation result could also be used as indicator for SaaS quality management. The proposed model however is limited to evaluating quality in SaaS.

Also, a model based on fuzzy logic for assessing SaaS quality was proposed by [10]. They argue that such a model of quality criteria provides a ground for more comprehensive quality model, which may assist a SaaS customer to choose a higher quality service from available services on Cloud. They also argued that the quality model serves as a guideline to SaaS providers enabling them to improve the quality of service provided. Although the study examined quality assessment using an Artificial Intelligence (fuzzy logic) technique, the model proposed does not apply to PaaS.

In addition, researchers in [11] proposed a newer quality model, which addressed the limitation of previously, proposed SaaS quality models. The quality models that existed before their work did not factor in security, quality of service and software quality of the SaaS service. Their proposed quality model is able to clarify SaaS service into four levels, which are: basic level, standard level, optimized level and integrated level. They argued that by using their quality model, a customer could evaluate the provider. The provider on the other hand could use it for quality management. Their quality model however is only suited for SaaS.

All the models reviewed in literature focused on evaluating the quality of SaaS cloud computing delivery model. However, apart from SaaS, there is still the PaaS and IaaS model which both have unique attributes separate from SaaS [12]. As a result, there is need to evaluate quality in these other aspects of cloud computing service delivery models. In this study therefore, we will be confining on PaaS, which is the layer directly below the SaaS layer in the Cloud computing layered architecture (as shown in Fig. 1).

3   The Proposed Model

In order to propose a quality model, there is a need to first identify the factors that affect quality in PaaS. First, developers do not like to be locked in by any technology platform; as such they would go for a platform that allows them a certain level of freedom especially as it relates to programming languages and operating systems. The quality of a PaaS platform therefore is determined by its ability to interact with specified systems (i.e. interoperability) [13]. Also, the degree to which PaaS enables developers to learn its usage affects such developer's perspective about its quality [14]. In addition, the degree to which PaaS can be successfully ported to various operating environment can affect its quality [15]. The model in this section therefore measures the quality of PaaS by examining its quality based on its interoperability, usability and portability. These are collectively referred to as the quality criteria. They are discussed as follows.

3.1   Interoperability

This has been defined by ISO as the attribute of software (PaaS) that bear on its ability to interact with specified systems. A PaaS system would be said to be of more quality if it reduces or eliminates vendor-lock-in [16]. The metrics to measure this in PaaS therefore includes number of operating system supported as well as the number of programming languages supported.

3.2 Usability

This refers to the ease with which a developer is able to master the use of a given platform. Learnability is an important sub-attribute in this regard. It is the degree to which a software product enables users to learn its application [17]. Developers therefore would consider a platform to be of higher quality if such a platform offers documentation and useful learning resources in multiple formats such as wikis, PDF files and video tutorials. Therefore metrics to measure learnability is number of documentation formats available.

3.3 Portability

This refers to the ease with which a system can be transferred from one environment to another. An important sub-attribute in this regard is installability, which refers to the degree of ease with which a software product can be installed and uninstalled in a specified environment. In the context of PaaS, environment can be seen as the operating systems [18]. Metrics to measure installability therefore include installation time on Windows, installation time on Linux and installation time on Mac OS.

The quality model proposed in this section is shown in Fig. 2. The goal of the model is to evaluate PaaS alternatives as depicted at the root of the decision hierarchy. As a result, three quality attributes namely: portability, usability and interoperability (taken from the ISO 25010 product quality model) were considered as evaluation criteria. From Fig. 2, interoperability has two metrics – number of operating systems supported as well as number of programming languages supported. Usability has one sub-criterion called learnability which in turn has a metric – number of documentation formats available. Similarly, portability has one sub-criterion (i.e. installability) as well. Installability being a sub-criteria has three metrics as given in Fig. 2.

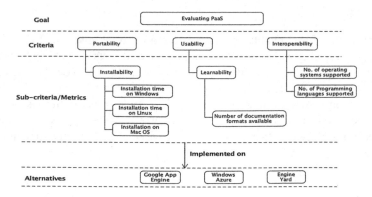

Fig. 2. Proposed model

4   Validation of the Model

There exist quite a number of PaaS offerings today. To evaluate our model, we will be selecting three namely: Google App Engine, Windows Azure and Engine Yard (GWE). These three are well known among developers. We evaluated the model based on data gotten from their respective websites: (cloud.google.com/appengine, azure.microsoft. com, engineyard.com). We applied the Analytic Hierarchy Process technique to the data in order to validate our model. This technique was adopted because it had earlier been used to evaluate quality in the cloud domain [19]. This section discusses the evaluation process.

4.1   Interoperability

This quality criterion that was formerly a sub-attribute of functionality in ISO 9126 was evaluated using two measures. The first measure determines the number of operating systems on which a PaaS solution is able to run [20]. The second determines the number of programming languages supported by the PaaS solution. In order to measure interoperability therefore in GWE the metrics used are given as follows:

Number of operating systems supported: Google App Engine and Windows Azure both support the three major operating system platforms namely: Windows, Mac OSX and Linux/other Unix-based systems. Engine Yard however does not support newer versions of Mac OSX such as 10.9 and 10.10. It only supports the Gentoo Linux distribution[1].

Number of programming languages supported: Windows Azure demonstrated the highest support for six programming languages namely:.NET, Java, Python, Ruby, PHP and Node.js. In addition to the above, we noted that it also provides support for mobile development especially iOS, Android and Windows phone development. Google App Engine and Engine Yard both come in second place as both equally support four programming languages. Google App Engine supports Python, Java, Go and PHP while Engine Yard supports PHP, Ruby, Node.js and Java.

4.2   Usability

The sub-attribute of this quality criterion is learnability as given in ISO 9126. The metric proposed here is the number of documentation formats available which include: wikis, video tutorials and PDF files. For this metric, we observed that all the PaaS platforms considered had just two formats of presenting documentation. The first was as wiki pages on their website and through video. Videos were often used to record tutorials. We discovered that because of these other sources of documentation pro-vided, platform service providers did not see any need to include PDF documentation.

---

[1] https://support.cloud.engineyard.com/categories/20033681-Engine-Yard-Cloud-Documentation.

4.3   Portability

Installability is the sub-criteria given for this quality criterion. We measure installability through the following metrics namely:

Installation time on Windows: Google App Engine and Engine Yard take the lead in this metric being able to install within 5 min on an average Windows machine running Windows 7. It takes about 30 min however to install on Windows Azure due to the installation of dependencies like SQL Server.

Installation time on Linux: Engine Yard requires only 5 min to install on a typical Linux machine; followed closely by Google App Engine which requires 6 min to install. Windows Azure however takes longer requiring about 25 min to install.

Installation on Mac OSX: In this regard, Google App Engine clearly takes the lead requiring only 3 min to install. Engine Yard takes 15 min to install while Windows Azure takes 25 min.

4.4   Validating the Model with AHP

With reference to Fig. 2, the goal of our metric is to evaluate quality in PaaS and the factors being considered are: Usability, Interoperability and Portability. We now determine the relative ranking of the factors to each other. As given in [22] Usability is more important to the developer followed by Interoperability and then Portability. Hence, Table 1 shows the relative ranking of factors.

Table 1. Relative ranking of the proposed model's criteria

	Usability	Interoperability	Portability
Usability	1/1	2/1	3/1
Interoperability	1/2	1/1	2/1
Portability	1/3	1/2	1/1

From Table 1 we observe a 1/1 relationship (for Usability to Usability, Interoperability to Interoperability and Portability to Portability). The value 2/1 between Usability and Interoperability implies that Usability is twice as important as Interoperability. The value 1/3 between Portability and Usability implies that Usability is thrice as important Portability. Normalizing Table 1 data, we obtain the following matrix (rounding to four decimal places):

$$\begin{bmatrix} 1.0000 & 2.0000 & 3.0000 \\ 0.5000 & 1.0000 & 2.0000 \\ 0.3333 & 0.5000 & 1.0000 \end{bmatrix}$$

We square the normalized result to get the following matrix:

$$\begin{bmatrix} 1.0000 & 2.0000 & 3.0000 \\ 0.5000 & 1.0000 & 2.0000 \\ 0.3333 & 0.5000 & 1.0000 \end{bmatrix} * \begin{bmatrix} 1.0000 & 2.0000 & 3.0000 \\ 0.5000 & 1.0000 & 2.0000 \\ 0.3333 & 0.5000 & 1.0000 \end{bmatrix}$$

$$= \begin{bmatrix} 2.9999 & 5.5000 & 10.0000 \\ 1.6666 & 3.0000 & 5.5000 \\ 0.9166 & 1.6666 & 2.9999 \end{bmatrix}$$

Table 2. Process of obtaining the eigenvector for the first iteration

	Sum of rows	Normalization process	Normalized result
2.9999 + 5.5000 + 10.0000	18.4999	18.4999/34.2490	0.5402
1.6666 + 3.0000 + 5.5000	10.1660	10.1660/34.2490	0.2968
0.9166 + 1.6666 + 2.9999	5.5831	5.5831/34.2490	0.1630
Total	34.2490		1.0000

Summing the rows and normalizing the result we obtain the eigenvector for this first iteration given in Table 2 below.

The values in the normalized matrix are added as shown in the table below which results in the sum of rows. We then normalize the result to by dividing each sum by the sum total; this is the normalization process.

The resulting eigenvector is:

$$\begin{bmatrix} 0.5402 \\ 0.2968 \\ 0.1630 \end{bmatrix}$$

In the next iteration, we square the previous matrix obtained to get the following matrix:

$$\begin{bmatrix} 2.9999 & 5.5000 & 10.0000 \\ 1.6666 & 3.0000 & 5.5000 \\ 0.9166 & 1.6666 & 2.9999 \end{bmatrix} * \begin{bmatrix} 2.9999 & 5.5000 & 10.0000 \\ 1.6666 & 3.0000 & 5.5000 \\ 0.9166 & 1.6666 & 2.9999 \end{bmatrix}$$

$$= \begin{bmatrix} 27.3317 & 49.6655 & 90.2480 \\ 15.0407 & 27.3326 & 49.6655 \\ 8.2770 & 15.0407 & 27.3317 \end{bmatrix}$$

Table 3. Process of obtaining the eigenvector for the second iteration

	Sum of rows	Normalization process	Normalized result
27.3317 + 49.6655 + 90.2480	167.2452	167.2452/309.9334	0.5396
15.0407 + 27.3326 + 49.6655	92.0388	92.0388/309.9334	0.2970
8.2770 + 15.0407 + 27.3317	50.6494	50.6494/309.9334	0.1634
Total	309.9334		1.0000

Summing the rows and normalizing the result we again obtain the eigenvector for the second iteration in Table 3.

Subtracting the eigenvector obtained in the second iteration from the first iteration we get the following, which show that should another iteration be performed, the difference in value will be insignificant.

$$\begin{bmatrix} 0.5402 \\ 0.2968 \\ 0.1630 \end{bmatrix} - \begin{bmatrix} 0.5396 \\ 0.2970 \\ 0.1634 \end{bmatrix} = \begin{matrix} 0.0006 \\ -0.0002 \\ -0.0004 \end{matrix}$$

Thus our resultant eigenvector can be taken as

$$\begin{bmatrix} 0.5396 \\ 0.2970 \\ 0.1634 \end{bmatrix}$$

We now proceed to normalize the proposed metrics.

For the metrics under the Interoperability criteria we have the following as results, which we normalize (see Tables 4 and 5) to get eigenvectors:

The resulting eigenvectors for Interoperability is thus given as:

$$\begin{bmatrix} 0.4286 \\ 0.4286 \\ 0.1429 \end{bmatrix} + \begin{bmatrix} 0.2857 \\ 0.4286 \\ 0.2857 \end{bmatrix} = \begin{bmatrix} 0.7143 \\ 0.8572 \\ 0.4286 \end{bmatrix}$$

For the metrics under usability we have the following Table 6:

The resulting eigenvector for Usability is thus given as:

$$\begin{bmatrix} 0.3333 \\ 0.3333 \\ 0.3333 \end{bmatrix}$$

For the metrics under Portability, Table 7 shows the different installation times on Windows. It takes 5 min for Google App Engine to install, 30 min for Windows Azure and 5 min for Engine Yard. The results are normalized in Table 7.

Table 8 shows the time it takes for each PaaS platforms to be installed on Linux. It takes 6 min for Google App Engine to install, 25 min for Windows Azure and 5 min for Engine Yard. The results are normalized as seen in Table 8.

Table 9 shows the time it takes for each PaaS platforms to be installed on Mac OS. It takes 3 min for Google App Engine to install, 25 min for Windows Azure and 15 min for Engine Yard. The results are normalized as seen in Table 9.

The resulting eigenvector for Portability is given as:

$$\begin{bmatrix} 0.1250 \\ 0.7500 \\ 0.1250 \end{bmatrix} + \begin{bmatrix} 0.1667 \\ 0.6944 \\ 0.1389 \end{bmatrix} + \begin{bmatrix} 0.0697 \\ 0.5814 \\ 0.3488 \end{bmatrix} = \begin{bmatrix} 0.3614 \\ 2.0258 \\ 0.6127 \end{bmatrix}$$

Table 4. Interoperability metric 1

Number of operating systems		
Google App Engine	3/7	0.4286
Windows Azure	3/7	0.4286
Engine Yard	1/7	0.1429
		1.0000

Table 5. Interoperability metric 2

Number of programming languages supported			
Google App Engine	4	4/14	0.2857
Windows Azure	6	6/14	0.4286
Engine Yard	4	4/14	0.2857
	14		1.0000

Table 6. Usability metric

Number of documentation formats			
Google App Engine	2	2/6	0.3333
Windows Azure	2	2/6	0.3333
Engine Yard	2	2/6	0.3333
	6		**1.0000**

Table 7. Portability metric 1

Installation time on windows			
Google App Engine	5 min	5/40	0.1250
Windows Azure	30 min	30/40	0.7500
Engine Yard	5 min	5/40	0.1250
	40		1.0000

Table 8. Portability metric 2

Installation time on Linux			
Google App Engine	6 min	6/36	0.1667
Windows Azure	25 min	25/36	0.6944
Engine Yard	5 min	5/36	0.1389
	36		1.0000

Multiplying the eigenvectors of Interoperability metrics, Usability metrics and Portability metrics with that of the proposed model's criteria gives the following whose interpretation is given in Table 10:

Table 9. Portability metric 1

Installation time on Mac OS			
Google App Engine	3 min	3/43	0.0697
Windows Azure	25 min	25/43	0.5814
Engine Yard	15 min	15/43	0.3488
	43		1.0000

Table 10. Result of validating the proposed model using GWE

PaaS systems considered	Normalized result
Google App Engine	1.4435
Windows Azure	0.8925
Engine Yard	0.4304

$$\begin{bmatrix} 0.7143 & 0.3333 & 0.3614 \\ 0.8572 & 0.3333 & 2.0258 \\ 0.4286 & 0.3333 & 0.6127 \end{bmatrix} * \begin{bmatrix} 0.5396 \\ 0.2970 \\ 0.1634 \end{bmatrix} = \begin{bmatrix} 1.4435 \\ 0.8925 \\ 0.4304 \end{bmatrix}$$

5 Discussion

The challenge of measuring quality in any domain can be regarded as a multiple criteria decision problem. AHP is suited for addressing such problems. It is an approach that allows for objective evaluation and decision making in the midst of multiple criteria. In order to apply AHP, it is important to first define the purpose for adopting it. In this study, the reason was to evaluate quality in PaaS. The next thing to do is to define the quality criteria for PaaS, which include: usability, interoperability and portability. Having performed the aforementioned step, alternatives are selected and in this study, the alternatives that were considered included: Google App Engine, Windows Azure and Engine Yard. These are just three of the several PaaS systems that exist.

The preliminary information specified for AHP is then arranged in a hierarchical tree similar to the structure of our model in Fig. 2. The information is then synthesized to determine the relative rankings of the alternatives. AHP allows for comparison of both qualitative and quantitative criteria and can be compared using informed judgments to derive weights and priorities. The metrics of our model however was strictly quantitative. Pairwise comparison was used to determine the relative importance of one criterion over another. In the PaaS domain, usability is crucial. If the platform were not easy to use (e.g. providing relevant documentation to developers) then it would be difficult to adopt. Interoperability is the next important factor in the PaaS domain and then portability. In order to get the ranking of the priorities from the pairwise matrix, eigenvector solution is used as proposed by Saaty in 1990.

The way to go about obtaining the eigenvector solution is to raise the pairwise matrix to powers that are successively squared each time. The row sums are then calculated and normalized as seen in Tables 2 and 3. The process is discontinued when the difference between these sums in two consecutive calculations is small and insignificant (e.g. 0.0006 or -0.0002). Computing the eigenvector determines the relative ranking of the alternatives under each criterion. Since our model provides only quantitative metrics, the value of each metric is obtained for the alternatives and the result is normalized (as seen in Tables 4, 5, 6, 7, 8 and 9) and used with other rankings.

The result of the validation process using Google App Engine, Windows Azure and Engine Yard as case studies (alternatives) shows that AHP ranks Google App Engine higher (1.4435) in terms of the quality criteria defined in the model. Windows Azure is the next highest ranked of the three alternatives with a score of 0.8925. Engine Yard is ranked with a score of 0.4304 as seen in Table 10.

6   Conclusion and Future Work

In this paper, a model has been proposed for evaluating quality in PaaS. Although such a model has been proposed for SaaS, no literature was seen addressing PaaS. A model was composed by first identifying the factors that affect quality in PaaS. Sub-factors were also identified and metrics proposed drawing from the ISO 25010 model. The proposed model was then evaluated by applying it to measure quality in Google App Engine, Windows Azure and Engine Yard. The results show that Google App Engine is the candidate software based on the evaluation of the proposed model using AHP.

As future work, more factors can be incorporated into the proposed model. Also, more PaaS systems can be evaluated with the resulting model to observe the kind of result it produces compared to this. A tool can also be developed or leveraged to ease the computation process.

Acknowledgements. We acknowledge the support and sponsorship provided by Covenant University through the Centre for Research, Innovation and Discovery (CUCRID).

References

1. Mell, P., Grance, T.: The NIST definition of cloud computing. National Institute of Standards and Technology Special Publication (2011). csrc.nist.gov/publication/nistpubs/800-145/SPSD-1485.pdf
2. Subashini, S., Kavitha, V.: A survey on security issues in service delivery models of cloud computing. J. Netw. Comput. Appl. **34**(1), 1–11 (2011)
3. Buyya, R., Yeo, C.S., Venugopal, S., Broberg, J., Brandic, I.: Cloud computing and emerging IT platforms: vision, hype and reality for delivering computing as the 5th utility. Future Gener. Comput. Syst. **2009**, 599–616 (2009)

4. Chang, V., Wills, G., De Roure, D.: A review of cloud business models and sustainability. In: 2010 IEEE 3rd International Conference on Cloud Computing (CLOUD), pp. 43–50. IEEE (2010)
5. Xu, X.: From cloud computing to cloud manufacturing. Rob. Comput.–Integr. Manuf. **28**(1), 75–86 (2012)
6. Chavan, P., Kulkarni, G.: PaaS cloud. Int. J. Comput. Sci. Inf. Secur. (IJCSIS) **1**, 22–26 (2013)
7. Zissis, D., Lekkas, D.: Addressing cloud computing security issues. Future Gener. Comput. Syst. **28**(3), 583–592 (2012)
8. Lee, J.Y., Lee, J.W., Kim, S.D. A quality model for evaluating software-as-a-service in cloud computing. In: 7th ACIS International Conference on Software Engineering Research, Management and Applications, SERA 2009, pp. 261–266. IEEE (2009)
9. Saaty, T.L.: Decision making with the analytic hierarchy process. Int. J. Serv. Sci. **1**(1), 83–98 (2008)
10. Baliyan, N., Kumar, S.: Quality assessment of software as a service on cloud using fuzzy logic. In: IEEE International Conference on Cloud Computing in Emerging Markets (CCEM), pp. 1–6. IEEE (2013)
11. Wen, P.X., Dong, L.: Quality model for evaluating SaaS service. In: Fourth International Conference on Emerging Intelligent Data and Web Technologies (EIDWT), pp. 83–87. IEEE (2013)
12. Zhang, S., Zhang, S., Chen, X., Huo, X.: Cloud computing research and development trends. In: Second International Conference on Future Networks, pp. 93–97. IEEE (2010)
13. Sheth, A., Ranabahu, A.: Semantic modeling for cloud computing. Part 2 Internet Comput. IEEE **14**(4), 81–84 (2010)
14. Garg, S.K., Versteeg, S., Buyya, R.: A framework for ranking of cloud computing services. Future Gener. Comput. Syst. **29**(4), 1012–1023 (2013)
15. Leavitt, N.: Is cloud computing really ready for prime time? Computer **42**(1), 15–20 (2009)
16. Lewis, G.A.: Role of standards in cloud computing interoperability. In: 46th Hawaii International Conference System Sciences (HICSS), pp. 1652–1661. IEEE (2013)
17. Goyal, P.: Enterprise usability of cloud computing environments: issues and challenges. In: Enabling Technologies: Infrastructures for Collaborative Enterprises (WETICE), pp. 54–59 (2010)
18. Takabi, H., Joshi, J.B., Ahn, G.J.: Security and privacy challenges in cloud computing environments. IEEE Secur. Priv. **8**(6), 24–31 (2010)
19. Kolb, S.: Towards application portability in platform as a service. In: IEEE 8th International Symposium Service Oriented System Engineering (SOSE), pp. 218–229. IEEE (2014)
20. Godse, M., Mulik, S.: An approach for selecting software-as-a-service (SaaS) product. In: IEEE International Conference on Cloud Computing, CLOUD 2009, pp. 155–158. IEEE (2009)
21. Zhang, Z., Wu, C., Cheung, D.W.: A survey on cloud interoperability: taxonomies, standards, and practice. ACM SIGMETRICS Performance Eval. Rev. **40**(4), 13–22 (2013)
22. Haigh, M.: Research versus practice in software engineering: comparison of expert opinions to measured user priorities (2009)

Constraint Modularization Within Multi-level Meta-modeling

Zoltán Theisz[1(✉)], Dániel Urbán[2], and Gergely Mezei[2]

[1] evopro Innovation Ltd., Hauszmann Alajos u. 2, Budapest 1116, Hungary
zoltan.theisz@evopro.hu
[2] Department of Automation and Applied Informatics,
Faculty of Electrical Engineering and Informatics, Budapest University of
Technology and Economics, Magyar tudósok krt. 2, Budapest 1117, Hungary
urb.daniel7@gmail.com, gmezei@aut.bme.hu

Abstract. Traditional meta-modeling strictly differentiates between internal and external constraints attached to the meta-models. While for example cardinality and annotations are usually considered existential parts of the meta-modeling techniques, OCL expressions are treated as an independent layer of constraint mechanism. The result is a patchwork because the external constraint notation will not become part of the meta-model, its semantics is only referentially integrated, and thus meta-levels are to be harmonized. In comparison, multi-level meta-modeling may enable a uniform self-contained interpretation of the constraint semantics by encapsulating the constraint modeling constructs into the fabric of the multi-level meta-modeling framework. In this paper, we describe such a modular constraint modeling technique that has been formalized in Dynamic Multi-Layer Algebra (DMLA), an algebraic multi-level meta-modeling method. The paper first describes our constraint modeling approach and then elaborates on the concept of cardinality and its trivial generalization to regular expression patterns. As motivated by one of the interface modeling languages of network management, the approach is also demonstrated on a simple YANG language construct.

Keywords: Multi-level meta-modeling · Modeling constraints · Cardinality

1 Introduction

Model-based network management systems mirror the deployed network infrastructure inside a centralized model store. The modeled network elements are managed through their interfaces, which are precisely defined by simple data types and their compositions. One of the preferred languages for interface definition is called YANG [1]. YANG is an XML schema like textual notation that has been conceived for data modeling for the purposes of network management through configuration. In that sense, YANG plays a similar role to that the EMF community has bestowed on emfatic [2]. Although meta-type definitions work very similarly in both languages, the correspondence stops quickly when it comes to introducing additional type constraints. Simple cardinality constraints are still shared by both formalisms, but there exists, for

© Springer International Publishing AG 2017
R. Damaševičius and V. Mikašytė (Eds.): ICIST 2017, CCIS 756, pp. 292–302, 2017.
DOI: 10.1007/978-3-319-67642-5_24

example, no genuine concept of pattern constraints in MOF [3]. Although annotations are part of Ecore and might be taken advantage of in order to mimic pattern like constraints, the clean EMF Ecore solution would require full-fledged meta-modeling of the particular pattern constraint and a corresponding promotion operation in order to shift the meta-levels.

An essential aspect of any model-based network management solution is that the utilized run-time model store shall be able to validate the compliance of the interface instances to their interface type definition(s) on the various network elements. This requirement can be easily satisfied by our multi-level meta-modeling framework, the so called Dynamic Multi-Layer Algebra (DMLA) [4, 5]. Nevertheless, its first version has limited the allowed sorts of type constraint to the mere checking of cardinality. Therefore, DMLA's constraint handling facilities had to be modularized in order to be able to incorporate more complex modeling constraints in a consistent way by instantiation.

In this paper, the aim is to introduce DMLA's modular constraint modeling and to illustrate it by a simple YANG pattern construct. The paper is structured as follows: Sect. 2 introduces some technical background; it covers both constraint modeling ideas and YANG's pattern constraint. Then, in Sect. 3, we introduce DLMA 2.0 [6], mainly focusing on its revamp by describing the most important core entities. Next, in Sect. 4, we focus on DMLA's constraint entities and their application, as an example, on YANG's pattern construct. Finally, Sect. 5 concludes the paper and mentions our future research goal.

2 Background

2.1 Constraint Modeling

Constraint modeling is an essential part of any kind of meta-modeling. Unfortunately, the actual implementation of constraint conceptualization is highly dependent on the constraint itself. For example, in Ecore, *ETypeElement* provides *lowerbound* and *upperbound* EInt attributes that containment cardinality originates from. However, for all other purposes Ecore relies on *EAnnotation* that is used to encode any kind of information not being part of the meta-metamodel, such as OCL constraints in OCLInECore.

In multi-level meta-modeling constraint handling is more flexible, but it is not straight-forward to incorporate constraint expressions such as OCL directly into the meta-modeling framework [7]. With DMLA, we provide a flexible and universal modeling formalism, which strongly supports customization by its idea of interchangeable bootstraps. Since constraints are modeled like any other elements in DMLA they can be applied to any "slots" of entity representation in the model. Another important feature of the bootstrap is that none of the constraints must be prioritized or handled exceptionally: both type and cardinality constraints are handled by validation formulae.

2.2 YANG

YANG is a complex data modeling language for interface definition. Since traditional network management relied on hierarchical structuring of the configuration interfaces,

YANG also relies on a hierarchical data modeling technique with explicitly placed references. The usual basic data types such as string and various sorts of integer can be combined into modules and containers, and also restricted by, for example, range and pattern constraints. One of the most frequently used string constraints is the so called "pattern's substatement", which applies a regular expression on a string.

```
type string {pattern "[0-9a-fA-F]*";}
```

Similar "additional" constraints are frequently taken advantage of in YANG model files, which further challenges any Ecore-based model representation of network elements because Ecore does not provide a built-in mechanism to incorporate them in its meta-metamodel. An ad-hoc solution could be the introduction of a new type for each constrained type, but that would not solve the problem of validating them. However, that would lead to a proliferation of types and the addition of Java code in annotations.

3 DMLA 2.0

Dynamic Multi-Layer Algebra (DMLA) is a multi-level instantiation technique based on Abstract State Machines (ASM). It consists of three major parts: The first part lays out the modeling structure and also defines the core ASM functions operating over this structure. In essence, it defines an ASM and a set of connected functions that specify the transition logic between the states. The second part is the initial set of modeling elements (e.g. built-in types) that are necessary to facilitate the modeling of any practical application. This second part is also referred to as the bootstrap of the algebra. Finally, the third part defines the rules of correct instantiation in the form of validation formulae, which are activated by generic instantiation mechanics.

DMLA is structurally self-contained, thus it can work with various bootstraps. Moreover, any concrete bootstrap selection seeds the concrete meta-modeling capability of the generic DMLA framework, which we consider as an additional benefit compared to other potency notion [8] based techniques.

3.1 Data Representation

In DMLA, the model is represented as a Labeled Directed Graph. Each model element can have labels, which represent the attributes of the model elements. For simplicity, we use a dual field notation in labeling Name/Value pairs, thus we refer to a label with the name N of the model item X as X_N. In the following, the word *entity* is only used if we refer to an element with a label structure. The following labels are defined:

- X_{ID}: a globally unique ID of the model element
- X_{Meta}: the ID of the meta-model definition
- X_{Value}: the values of the model element
- $X_{Attributes}$: a list of attributes

Definition. The superuniverse $|\mathfrak{A}|$ of a state $\mathfrak{A}$ of the Multi-Layer Algebra consists of the following universes:

- U_{Bool} containing logical values {true/false}
- U_{Number} containing rational numbers {$\mathbb{Q}$} and a special symbol ∞ representing infinity
- U_{String} containing character sequences of finite length
- U_{ID} containing all the possible entity IDs
- U_{Basic} containing elements from {$U_{Bool} \cup U_{Number} \cup U_{String} \cup U_{ID}$}

Additionally, all universes contain a special element, *undef*, which refers to an undefined value. The labels of the entities take their values from the following universes: (i) X_{ID}: U_{ID} (ii) X_{Meta}: U_{ID} (iii) X_{Value}: $U_{Basic}[]$ (iv) X_{Attrib}: $U_{ID}[]$. The label Value is an indexed list of Basic values, and the label Attrib is an indexed list of IDs, which refers to other entities.

A simple example could be:

```
RouterInst_ID = "RouterI", RouterInst_Meta = "RouterM", Router_Value =
undef, Router_Attrib = ["RouterAddr"]
```

This definition encodes entity RouterInst with its ID being RouterI, the ID of its meta-model being RouterM, and a contained attribute with ID RouterAddr. A more compact textual representation of equal semantics:

```
{"RouterI", "RouterM", undef, [ID"RouterAddr"]}
```

3.2   Functions

Functions serve to determine how state transition in ASM takes place. In DMLA, we rely on *shared* and *derived* functions. The current attribute configuration of any model item is represented via *shared* functions. The values of these functions are modified either by the algebra or the environment thereof. *Derived* functions represent calculations which must not change the model; they are only utilized to obtain or restructure existing information within the ASM. The vocabulary $\sum$ of DMLA is assumed to contain the following characteristic functions: (i) Meta(U_{ID}): U_{ID}, (ii) Value(U_{ID}, U_{Number}): U_{Basic}, and (iii) Attrib(U_{ID}, U_{Number}): U_{ID}. The functions are used to access the values stored in the corresponding labels. We suppose that the Value and Attrib functions return undef, whenever index is beyond the available number of stored entities. Note that the functions are not only able to query the requested information, but they can also update it.

Moreover, there are two derived functions: (i) Contains(U_{ID}, U_{ID}): U_{Bool} and (ii) DeriveFrom(U_{ID}, U_{ID}): U_{Bool}. The first function takes an ID of an entity and the ID of an attribute and checks if the entity contains the attribute. The second function checks if the entity identified by the first parameter is an instantiation, also transitively, of the entity specified by the second parameter.

3.3   Bootstrap Mechanism

The ASM functions define the basic structure of the algebra and allow to query and change the model. However, based only on these constructs, it would be hard to use the algebra due to the lack of basic built-in constructs. The bootstrap solves this problem by defining those principal entities that must be available in order to go ahead with further domain specific modeling. In the following, only the core part of the principal entities are introduced, cardinality handling will be dealt with in Sect. 4.

The entity Base is the root meta of every entity. In order to eliminate the problem of self-meta recursion, the meta of the *Base* entity is set to *undef*. Since *Base* acts as the root meta, it must be based on the most flexible structure DMLA can facilitate: it consists of an arbitrary amount of slots of any type. This is formally expressed by adding the *SlotDef* entity as an attribute to *Base*. We have also added an additional slot called *IsPrimitive* in order to draw a clear distinction among the instances of *Base*. *IsPrimitive* attribute marks only basic types (e.g. string), other entities eliminate this slot, when they get instantiated from *Base*. Since Base is the meta of every entity in this bootstrap, and Base only has SlotDef attributes.

```
{"Base", undef, undef,
[
 "SlotDef",
 {"IsPrimitive", "SlotDef", undef, [{"BOOL"}, {0, 1}]}
]}
```

For the rest of the paper, we rely on an intuitive graphical notation of equal semantics to visualize entities:

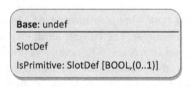

The entity Entity is the root meta of every model element except the slots. Flexibility is a key feature here similarly to *Base*, but we must restrict the type of the contained elements to *Base*. This restriction is applied via an instance of *SlotDef*. *Entity* also clones the *IsPrimitive* flag of *Base* because every basic type must be an instance of *Entity*.

The basic type entities represent built-in primitive types of the bootstrap. Basic types instantiate the Entity, and fill in the IsPrimitive slot with true.

The entity SlotDef defines a slot of the containing entity. In the bootstrap tailored for modularized constraints, *SlotDef* has an arbitrary number of contained constraints, which impose particular conditions on the values of the slot, e.g. their type or cardinality.

SlotDef has two options of being instantiated: either a value is substituted which conforms to the constraints set in the meta of *SlotDef*, or no value is provided, but some of the constraints within the *SlotDef definition is further concretized*. Hence, *SlotDef* is the formal expression of the generic instantiation principle set by DMLA. In effect, *SlotDef* prescribes and then helps validate the correct contained values, thus *SlotDef* is the only element which is allowed to be able to contain a value.

SlotDef makes DMLA 2.0 more powerful than its original version used to be since being a separate entity in the bootstrap, it can represent every further constraint in the model independently of its nature. Furthermore, by now the bootstrap handles all constraint concretizations explicitly as they were normal instantiations instead of delegating them as hidden additions to the validation formulae.

The entity Constraint represents the conditions to be imposed on the values of a SlotDef instance. This entity is defined only as a common meta for every constraint in the bootstrap. *Constraint* only differs from *Entity* by dropping its *IsPrimitive* slot.

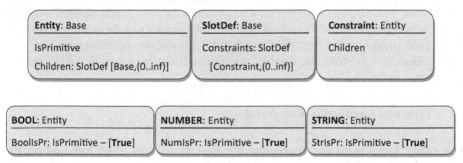

3.4   Dynamic Instantiation

Based on the structure of the algebra and the bootstrap, we can now represent our models as states of DMLA. During the instantiation process, instances are being created by constantly checking that no defined constraints have been violated. Thus, we distinguish between valid and invalid models, where validity checking is based on a set of predefined formulae. We also assume that whenever the state of the algebra changes these formulae are evaluated on the current state of the model.

The instantiation process is fully determined by the validation rules that ensure that if an invalid model is found it is rejected and an alternative instantiation is selected for validation. The procedure consists of instructions that involve a selector and an action, $\{\lambda_{selector}, \lambda_{action}\}$. $\lambda_{selector}$ takes an entity ID and returns a possibly empty list of IDs referring to the selected entities. λ_{action} takes an entity ID and executes an abstract function on it. Hence, the functions $\lambda_{selector}$ and λ_{action} can be defined by their signature, which allows us to treat them as black box implementations.

3.5   Validation Formulae

The validation of the model is based on validating every model entity against its meta. The actual validation is carried out by two sorts of formulae. The first kind of formula (alpha formula) validates a meta entity against one instance entity, checking if the instance violates any constraints. The second kind of formula (beta formulae) validates a meta entity *within its context*, that is, it operates on a list of clone and instance entities. This formula is mostly needed to check the constraints defined by the meta element. The *in context* checks (beta formulae) are evaluated while validating the first kind (alpha formula) of the validation formula, checking the validity of every child of the meta entity against the relevant children of the instance entity.

4   Extending DMLA's Constraint System

The enabler of DMLA's constraint customization is the easily extendable *Constraint* entity, which allows uniform handling of constraints throughout the model. In order to better understand its role, first, the *Type* and the *Cardinality* constraints will be presented. Then, we illustrate the flexible constraint system by a simple YANG pattern constraint.

4.1   Type and Cardinality Constraint

The entity TypeConstraint represents the type constraint to be imposed on the values of a slot. The type constraint checks the meta-hierarchy of the value to be validated: if the value is an ID, the referred element has to be a direct, or indirect instance of the provided type. If the value is a built-in type, the respective basic type has to satisfy the same check. Since *Base* is the topmost meta entity of every other element in the model, setting *Base* as the type of an attribute implies to allow any sort of entities as its value.

The entity Cardinality represents the cardinality constraint one can impose on the values of a slot. Although cardinalities can be of various kinds (e.g. range, min-max, sequence of ranges etc.), the bootstrap default one is defined as min-max semantics for Cardinality. However, the mechanism is flexible as it is based on instantiation.

TypeConstraint: Constraint	**Cardinality**: Constraint
Type: Children [Base,(1..1)]	CardMin: SlotDef [NUMBER,(1..1)]
	CardMax: SlotDef [NUMBER,(1..1)]

In order for Cardinality to possess its wanted semantics some validation formulae must be plugged-in into the generic modular constraint validation mechanism. As discussed in Sect. 3.5, a formula can be either of type alpha or beta. The constraint validator formulae extend these alpha and beta type formulae, providing additional logic for validating their container entities.

The helper formula *PossMin* calculates the possible minimum cardinality of slot instance S based on the number of values and the "structural encoding" of minimum cardinality. The *Cont* is the meta of a possibly present *Cardinality* constraint.

$$\varphi_{PossMin}(S, Cont) : result :$$
$$(\exists c : c = ChildByMeta(S, Cont) \wedge imin = \varphi_{CardMin}(Value(c, 0)) \vee imin = 0)$$
$$\wedge\ result = ValueCount(I) + imin$$

The helper formula *PossMax* works similarly on the possible maximum cardinality of slot instance S based on the number of values and the maximum cardinality. The *Cont* is the meta of a possibly present *Cardinality* constraint.

$$\varphi_{PossMax}(S, Cont) : result :$$
$$(\exists c : c = ChildByMeta(S, Cont) \wedge imax = \varphi_{CardMax}(Value(c, 0)) \vee imax = 0)$$
$$\wedge\ result = ValueCount(I) + imax$$

The alpha type constraint formula of *Cardinality* checks if the *SlotDef* instance (I) violates the cardinality constraint $(Card)$ of its meta (M). Note that *Cont* is the direct container of *Card*, and *Cont* is an attribute of M. The formula checks if all of the constraints were discarded by I, or the *Cardinality* instance was cloned or instantiated. Discarded constraints mean that the slot cannot be instantiated again, but if it is not a final slot, the cardinality constraint must be kept or concretized. Finally, the formula checks if the sum of the maximum cardinality and the number of values contained in I exceeds the meta cardinality maximum.

$$Constr\alpha_{Card}(I, M, Cont, Card) :$$
$$(ChildrenByMeta(I, ID_{Constraints}) = \emptyset \vee \exists c : c = ChildByMeta(I, Cont)) \wedge$$
$$\varphi_{PossMax}(I, Cont) \leq \varphi_{CardMax}(Card))$$

The beta type constraint formula of *Cardinality* checks if the list of relevant *SlotDef* clones and instances (R) violate the cardinality constraint $(Card)$ of their meta (M). The formula sums the possible minimum and maximum cardinality for every entity in list R, then validates them against the cardinality of M.

$$Constr\beta_{Card}(R, M, Cont, Card) :$$
$$min = \sum m | \forall i : r = R[i] \wedge m = \varphi_{PossMin}(r, Cont) \wedge$$
$$max = \sum m | \forall i : r = R[i] \wedge m = \varphi_{PossMax}(r, Cont) \wedge$$
$$min \geq \varphi_{CardMin}(Card) \wedge max \leq \varphi_{CardMax}(Card)$$

4.2   Pattern Constraint

The modular constraint mechanism based on the entity *Constraint* enables the quick introduction of YANG like patterns into the bootstrap. The regular expressions are composed of "min-max cardinalities": the pattern sequence and the quantifier operators. Therefore, it is enough to define the constituent entities, the corresponding validation formulae can be derived almost mechanically thanks to the cardinality analogy thereof. However, the concrete formulae are left out due to the page limits of the paper.

A YANG pattern has four options, which are reflected in DMLA as five *Constraint* instances. The first instance is the common meta for the different pattern operators, it also contains a cardinality slot to simplify the validation of the pattern hierarchy. The second instance is the string pattern element, which contains a simple string to be matched against. The third instance represents the quantifier operators which control the occurrence of the pattern groups, such as ?, + or *. In DMLA, they are formalized by their min-max range, which is exactly the semantics of *Cardinality*! The fourth instance is the | operator, which enables alternatives taken from multiple patterns. The fifth instance is the pattern sequence itself, which allows the concatenation of multiple sub-patterns up to a maximum cardinality of the groups.

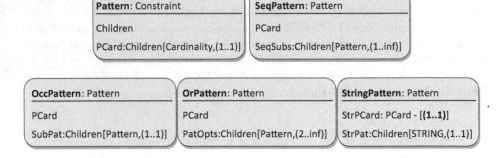

4.3   Using the Pattern Constraint

We will now demonstrate the pattern constraint by a simple example. In this example, we model the service identification string of a modular router (*Router* entity) for selecting one of its components. The components (*RouterModule*) of a *Router* instance can be accessed through a hierarchical service name. We will add a *Pattern* constraint to the name part of *RouterModule* entity in order to enable only valid hierarchical names. A hierarchical name consists of a security category, an optional subsystem name, and a hierarchical ID. The regular expression enforced on the name is as follows:

$$(Secure|Public)(-[A-Z]+)?(-[0-9]+)+$$

This can be easily projected onto DLMA *Pattern* instances. The first section is a simple *OrPattern* with two *StringPatterns*:

SecureOptPat: OrPattern	**SecP**: StringPattern	**PubP**: StringPattern
SOCard: PCard − [(**1..1**)]	StrPCard	StrPCard
SecOpts: PatOpts−[**SecP,PubP**]	SecS:StrPat−[**"Secure"**]	PubS:StrPat−[**"Public"**]

The second group can be interpreted as an *OccPattern* with a [0..1] range having a sequence inside it. The sequence contains a *StringPattern* (-), and an *OccPattern* with [1..inf] range, wrapping an *OrPattern* containing all uppercase letters:

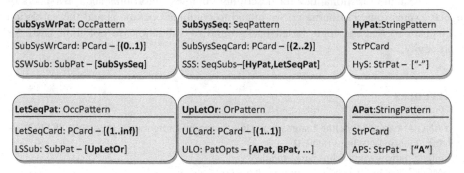

SubSysWrPat: OccPattern	**SubSysSeq**: SeqPattern	**HyPat**:StringPattern
SubSysWrCard: PCard − [(**0..1**)]	SubSysSeqCard: PCard − [(**2..2**)]	StrPCard
SSWSub: SubPat − [**SubSysSeq**]	SSS: SeqSubs−[**HyPat,LetSeqPat**]	HyS: StrPat − ["-"]

LetSeqPat: OccPattern	**UpLetOr**: OrPattern	**APat**:StringPattern
LetSeqCard: PCard − [(**1..inf**)]	ULCard: PCard − [(**1..1**)]	StrPCard
LSSub: SubPat − [**UpLetOr**]	ULO: PatOpts − [**APat, BPat, ...**]	APS: StrPat − [**"A"**]

The third section consists of an *OccPattern* with [1..inf] range, which contains a sequence of *HyPat* and an *OccPattern* with [1..inf] range, wrapping an *OrPattern* containing all digits from 0 to 9:

UIDOccPat: OccPattern	**UIDSeq**: SeqPattern
UIDOccCard: PCard − [(**1..inf**)]	UIDSeqCard: PCard − [(**2..2**)]
UIDOSub: SubPat−[**UIDSeq**]	USS:SeqSubs−[**HyPat,DigSeqPat**]

DigSeqPat: OccPattern	**DigitOr**: OrPattern	**0Pat**:StringPattern
DigSeqCard: PCard − [(**1..inf**)]	DigitOrCard: PCard − [(**1..1**)]	StrPCard
DSSub: SubPat − [**DigitOr**]	DigitO: PatOpts−[**0Pat, 1Pat, ...**]	OPS: StrPat − [**"0"**]

Finally, we need to wrap the sub-patterns in a *SeqPattern*:

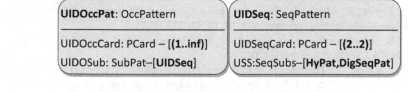

RouterModNameSeq: SeqPattern
RMNSeqCard: PCard - [(**2..3**)]
RMNSS: SeqSubs − [**SecureOptPat, SubSysWrPat, UIDOccPat**]

5   Conclusion and Future Work

DMLA's flexible multi-level modeling formalism proved to be modular enough to incorporate the concept of a generic constraint handling mechanism through a selected set of bootstrap entities. Although cardinality is simple enough to be extended to similar constraints such as patterns, the modification of the validation formulae may be more challenging in general cases. Also, the parsing mechanism is black box implemented now. Nevertheless, DMLA has managed to establish a modular formal handling of constraint within the model, through its instantiation mechanism. Our future research will investigate how to include operations into DMLA so that models could attain executable functionalities for describing complex algorithms such as parsers of regular expressions. Furthermore, we intend to combine operations and the validation mechanism so that the logic based background of validation do not limit DMLA's expressivity.

References

1. YANG – A Data Modeling Language for the Network Configuration Protocol (NETCONF). https://tools.ietf.org/html/rfc6020
2. Emfatic. https://www.eclipse.org/emfatic/
3. OMG's MetaObject Facility. http://www.omg.org/mof/
4. Theisz, Z., Mezei, G.: An Algebraic Instantiation Technique Illustrated by Multilevel Design Patterns. MULTI@MoDELS, Ottawa, Canada (2015)
5. Theisz, Z., Mezei, G.: Multi-level dynamic instantiation for resolving node-edge dichotomy. In: Proceedings of the 4th International Conference on Model-Driven Engineering and Software Development, Rome, Italy (2016)
6. Urbán, D., Theisz, Z., Mezei, G.: Formalism for static aspects of dynamic meta-modeling. Period. Polytech. Electr. Eng. Comput. Sci. **61**(1), 34–47 (2017)
7. Gogolla, M.: Experimenting with Multi-level Models in a Two-Level Modeling Tool. MULTI@MoDELS, Ottawa, Canada (2015)
8. Atkinson, C., Kühne, T.: The essence of multilevel metamodeling. In: Gogolla, M., Kobryn, C. (eds.) UML 2001. LNCS, vol. 2185, pp. 19–33. Springer, Heidelberg (2001). doi:10.1007/3-540-45441-1_3

Statistical Arbitrage Trading Strategy in Commodity Futures Market with the Use of Nanoseconds Historical Data

Mantas Vaitonis[(⊠)] and Saulius Masteika

Vilnius University, Kaunas Faculty, Muitines 8, 44280 Kaunas, Lithuania
{mantas.vaitonis, saulius.masteika}@knf.vu.lt

Abstract. This paper confirms the existence of statistical arbitrage opportunities by employing the nanosecond historical data in high frequency trading (HFT). When considering the possible options, the Daniel Herlemont pairs trading strategy has been selected. In order pairs trading could operate, the pair selection algorithm had to be developed. Herlemont pairs trading strategy has not been tested before by using the nanosecond information and the proposed pair selection algorithm. The main objective of the given research is to test the pairs trading strategy in HFT by calculating the returnability in commodity futures market. The statistical arbitrage strategy attempts to achieve profit by exploiting price differences of the futures contracts. The strategy takes long/short positions when the spread between the prices widens with an expectation that the prices will converge in the future. In the given paper, the nanosecond historical data was provided by the Nanotick Company. The applied strategy has been subsequently tested with MatLab software.

1 Introduction

The global finance market is hard to predict and is characterized by risky trading. Many investors make profit by using the available information and applying different strategies. The common method, employed by investors, is technical analysis, applied by using high frequency trading.

High-frequency trading refers to algorithmic trading that involves the usage of specialized infrastructure and ultra-low latency computing to execute a wide range of strategies on financial markets [29]. While HFT has been present since the digitization of markets, it has only become wide spread over the past decade. Evidence suggests that a very large percentage of the trading activity in many markets is now carried out via HFT algorithms across a variety of assets. Projections indicate that this presence is likely to stay, and even to increase over the next years [30]. HFT has been the recent focus of researchers, particularly, those focusing on the market microstructure, as well as regulators and even the popular media, mainly owing to increasingly frequent incidents of abnormal market behavior supposedly linked to HFT algorithms. [25] HFT accounts for a growing share of total market turnover in a wide-range of financial markets.

© Springer International Publishing AG 2017
R. Damaševičius and V. Mikašytė (Eds.): ICIST 2017, CCIS 756, pp. 303–313, 2017.
DOI: 10.1007/978-3-319-67642-5_25

High frequency trading can be found in almost all stocks, currencies, futures and options markets. [4, 5] Although there are many advantages of HFT, e.g., bringing liquidity to the markets, making market more efficient, etc. [6, 7], there are a few papers that explain the trading strategy behavior with high frequency data. Most papers that covers high frequency data consist milliseconds or microsecond data, and only few use nanoseconds, thus this type of data was selected for this research. The objective of this paper is to test high frequency trading, statistical arbitrage and the pair selection algorithm with 5 different futures contracts. The main results of the research are presented in the paper.

2 What Is High-Frequency Trading?

High frequency traders seek profit from short-term pricing inefficiencies. However, as there are plenty of market players building more sophisticated algorithms, this will only reduce profitability. Meanwhile, high frequency trading refers to effective trading strategies adopted to perform the trade with guaranteed success [5, 6].

HFT also refers to fully automated trading strategies in different securities as equities, derivatives, and currencies. These types of opportunities have life span from nanoseconds to seconds. Thus, capturing a tiny fraction of profit from each trade in huge number makes HFT an efficient way to generate substantial profit [14].

In general, those traders, who employ HFT strategies, seek to earn small amounts of profit per trade. Evidence suggest that some arbitrage strategies can earn profits close to 100% of the time. However, previous reports concluded that these strategies might make money on only 51% of the trades. Nevertheless, as the trades are transacted hundreds or thousands of times per day, the strategies may still be profitable [26].

3 Pairs Trading

Pairs trading is a market neutral statistical arbitrage strategy, based on the convergence of financial instruments prices. First, the pairs of financial instruments, characterized by significant statistical correlation, are selected, then, by adding equivalent long and short positions, zero-investment portfolios can be created. Moreover, if the pairs of financial instruments abnormally deviate for a short period, the excess return can be gained. Thus, this strategy results in abnormal return [3].

It should be noted that pairs trading is a relative-value arbitrage strategy that has been known in the quantitative finance community ever since the mid 1980s [22]. The strategy involves identification of two securities with prices that tend to travel together. Upon divergence, the cheaper security is bought long and the more expensive one is sold short. When the prices converge back to their historical equilibrium, the trade is closed and the profit collected. Thus, the idea is to obtain a quantitative trading strategy by exploiting relative mispricing between two securities [28].

In fact, all financial markets are based on the following general trading rule: buy with low price and sell with high price. Thus, the key aim is to develop the strategies with low risk. It should be noted that pure arbitrage is a category of the strategies with zero risk. As an example, the case could be of buying and selling a financial instrument with a different value in two different exchanges at the same time. The profit results from the difference in prices, breaking the law of one price. Another category is statistical arbitrage, which is not risk free. The strategies of this type are aimed at the expected gain which is greater than the risk. The profit results from the mispricing of the financial instrument. To achieve this, one needs to assess whether the price of a financial instrument is overvalued or undervalued relative to the actual value, however, it is hard to determine. The fundamentals of the financial instrument, the demand of each period and the general economic environment are some of the factors that make the fair value evaluation difficult [24].

3.1   The Object of Research

The nanosecond data was provided Nanotick company. Historical data used comes from CME group which consist of NYMEX, COMEX and CBOT. All data was used to test the statistical arbitrage and pair selection algorithm with five futures contracts. The five futures contracts used in this research were: NG (natural gas), BZ (Brent crude oil), CL (crude oil), HO (NY Harbor ULSD), RB (RBOB Gasoline). The period for trading covered the futures contract historical data form 01-08-2015 to 31-08-2015. The main objective of this research is to check whether HFT can be applied on these futures contracts with nanosecond information and how efficient the selected trading strategy and the pair selection algorithm is. Efficiency of the strategy was measured by its profitability. More precisely, the pairs trading strategy was applied to high frequency data, and its profitability and risk was calculated. The research was based on the strategy, proposed by D. Herlemont [6]. However, this pairs trading strategy was modified to be able to work with high frequency data. At the end of the research, strategy was measured, according to the generated profit.

3.2   Methodology of Pairs Trading Strategy

The underlying idea of the pairs trading is to identify two financial instruments that move together, taking long and short positions simultaneously when they start to act abnormally. It is expected that in the future the prices of two financial instruments will return to the mean.

In order to carry out the research, six main steps of the pairs trading strategy were identified [23, 24]. The proposed methodology for the pairs trading strategy is illustrated in Fig. 1:

The steps for creating the algorithm are the following:

- Identification of window for training and data normalization;
- Data normalization;
- Selection of the correlated pairs;
- Selection of the trading period;
- Definition of the parameters for long/short positions;
- Assessment of the trading strategy [23, 24].

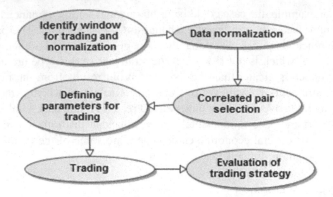

Fig. 1. Pair trading methodology.

First, the window for the training period should be identified. Then, as high frequency data can be sent to the trading strategy, a trader must select the training period. The training period should not be too long, since the algorithm will overtrain. On the other hand, it cannot be too short as the strategy will not be able to notice the abnormal behaviour of the futures contract prices [13, 24].

Next, data normalization follows, which is applied for the trading period too. As this period could be used for both, it is essential to select the right size. Thus, it should be noted that the size of this window is subject to the extent of sensitivity of the strategy: the shorter the period, the more sensitive the trading strategy. In this research, the training window of 5 min and the data normalization window of 10 s was used.

Before starting testing the strategy, data must be normalized. Normalization includes the following stages:

1. Normalization of time stamps;
2. Normalization of the futures contract price.

3.3   High Frequency Data Normalization

The algorithmic trading system requires to normalize HFT data. The main problem, related with HFT data, is caused by discrepancies between the time stamps of correlated contracts. The time stamp problem is shown in Tables 1 and 2 below.

From Tables 1 and 2 it might be observed that time stamps for trades or bid/ask changes during the same trading second differ, for example, in Table 1 there is a time stamp of Quote for NG contract change at 17:00:00.869053009, while the other contract (HO) has Quote changes at nanoseconds 17:00:00.867756129, and no activity at 17:00:00.869053009. This fact requires comparing the time stamp sequences of correlated financial instruments. If the time stamps differ, the contract, which lacks the time stamp, is filled in with missing time stamp and the previous bid/ask or trade prices. As a result, not only the time stamps of correlated contracts are brought together, but also the prices are kept accurate.

Table 1. High frequency data

ReceivingDate	ReceivingTime	Symbol	Asset	EntryType	EntryPrice
20150809	17:00:00.869053009	NGF6	NG	A	3227
20150809	17:00:00.869053009	NGF6	NG	B	3221
20150809	17:00:00.930168164	NGF6	NG	A	3226
20150809	17:00:00.930168164	NGF6	NG	B	3221
20150809	17:00:01.017456320	NGF6	NG	A	3226
20150809	17:00:01.017456320	NGF6	NG	B	3219
20150809	17:00:01.059840559	NGF6	NG	A	3227
20150809	17:00:01.059840559	NGF6	NG	B	3219
20150809	17:00:01.156791713	NGF6	NG	A	3238
20150809	17:00:01.156791713	NGF6	NG	B	3216
20150809	17:00:01.204683812	NGF6	NG	A	3238
20150809	17:00:01.204683812	NGF6	NG	B	3216
20150809	17:00:01.205605232	NGF6	NG	A	3238
20150809	17:00:01.205605232	NGF6	NG	B	3215
20150809	17:00:01.206755867	NGF6	NG	A	3238
20150809	17:00:01.206755867	NGF6	NG	B	3215
20150809	17:00:01.207350519	NGF6	NG	A	3231
20150809	17:00:01.207350519	NGF6	NG	B	3215
20150809	17:00:01.208805474	NGF6	NG	A	3231
20150809	17:00:01.208805474	NGF6	NG	B	3217
20150809	17:00:01.224604710	NGF6	NG	A	3233
20150809	17:00:01.224604710	NGF6	NG	B	3217

Obviously, normalization of high frequency data is significant for recalculating the prices of correlated contracts to the certain unit, thus, removing the noise of price changes and being able to compare the changes in a more qualitative way. The normalization steps were the following: price $P(i, t)$, empirical mean $\mu(i, t)$ and standard deviation $\sigma(i, t)$ were calculated for each contract i. Afterwards, the Eq. (1) was applied. Perlin [4] in his research, related to the pairs trading in Brazilian financial market, also used this method.

$$p(i,t) = \frac{P(i,t) - \mu(i,t)}{\sigma(i,t)} \tag{1}$$

Here, value $p(i, t)$ stands for the normalized price of asset i at time t. Normalized prices were calculated within a particular moving window of the time series, discussed in details in the next section. As Eq. (1) is used, all prices of the correlated contracts are converted into normalized units. The total number of records after normalization was 287872500.

Table 2. High frequency data

RecevingDate	ReceivingTime	Symbol	Asset	EntryType	EntryPrice
20150809	17:00:00.825207610	HOF6	HO	A	16040
20150809	17:00:00.825207610	HOF6	HO	B	15950
20150809	17:00:00.826021615	HOF6	HO	A	16035
20150809	17:00:00.826021615	HOF6	HO	B	15950
20150809	17:00:00.838609766	HOF6	HO	A	16040
20150809	17:00:00.838609766	HOF6	HO	B	15950
20150809	17:00:00.865890817	HOF6	HO	A	16040
20150809	17:00:00.865890817	HOF6	HO	B	15945
20150809	17:00:00.866430043	HOF6	HO	A	16040
20150809	17:00:00.866430043	HOF6	HO	B	15944
20150809	17:00:00.867756129	HOF6	HO	A	16040
20150809	17:00:00.867756129	HOF6	HO	B	15943
20150809	17:00:00.869125205	HOF6	HO	A	16040
20150809	17:00:00.869125205	HOF6	HO	B	15938
20150809	17:00:00.875541527	HOF6	HO	A	16040
20150809	17:00:00.875541527	HOF6	HO	B	15934
20150809	17:00:00.884336757	HOF6	HO	A	16040
20150809	17:00:00.884336757	HOF6	HO	B	15928
20150809	17:00:01.025686712	HOF6	HO	A	16040
20150809	17:00:01.025686712	HOF6	HO	B	15950
20150809	17:00:01.029573686	HOF6	HO	A	16019
20150809	17:00:01.029573686	HOF6	HO	B	15950

3.4 Pair Selection Algorithm

It is important to note that one of two main parts of this trading methodology is a pair selection algorithm, based on cointegration testing. In our previous research, while selecting the trading pairs, the method of minimum squared distance was applied [13, 23, 24]. However, this research employs cointegration method. What is more, in order to work with nanosecond historical data, new pair selection method must be developed.

Cointegration method includes the below steps:

1. Identification of the futures contract pairs that could potentially be cointegrated.
2. Upon identification of the potential pairs, the hypothesis that the futures contract pairs are cointegrated based on information from historical data needs to be verified.
3. Examination of the cointegrated pairs to find out whether they can be trade on [22].

The objective of this phase is to identify the pairs the linear combination of which exhibits a significant predictable component that is uncorrelated with underlying movements in the entire market. Thus, first, it is checked, whether all the series are integrated of the same order. This is done by applying the Augmented Dickey Fuller Test (ADF). Following the ADF test, cointegration tests are performed on all possible combination of pairs. To test for cointegration, the Engle and Grangers 2-step approach and the Johansen test were adopted. All the above procedures were implemented on MATLAB. For the detected cointegrating relations, the second part of the algorithm creates trading signals based on the predefined investment decision rules [5].

4 Proposed Pairs Trading Strategies

The suggested methodology presents six steps of the pair trading strategy. In the diagram below, a more detailed view of each step is given in respect of strategy, proposed D. Herlemont.

Before research, a window for training and trading need to be defined. As it has already been mentioned, the training window of 5 min and the trading and normalization window 10 s were selected. Upon defining all windows, normalization is in order as it was explained in the previous section (Fig. 2).

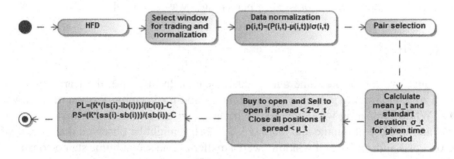

Fig. 2. D. Herlemont pairs trading strategy

According to this strategy, the trading signals are created by calculating the mean μ_t and the standard deviation σ_t of the difference for normalized prices of paired futures contract for a given trading window. Signals are created, if the difference between the futures contract A and B pair prices is $<2\ \sigma_t$:

When $A_t > B_t$, open short position with A_t and long position with B_t;
When $A_t < B_t$, open long position with A_t and short position with B_t [6].

If the difference between prices of A_t and $B_t < \mu_t$ or the period for keeping positions opened is reached, all positions are closed [6]. Importantly, a position is kept opened until threshold is reached or a given time to keep the positions open ends. 10 s was the maximum time for keeping the position opened.

Lastly, it is essential to assess the performance of the algorithm, based on the pairs trading strategy, offered by D. Herlemont, in a high frequency environment. Thus, it was measured by calculating the price differences, while trading the correlated futures contracts for a given period. Upon passing all data through the algorithm, the arrays with the prices of opening and closing positions were employed, in order to find the profit/loss of the certain period. The following equations were used for calculating the profits from long and short positions:

$$PL = \sum_{i=1}^{K} (ls(i) - lb(i)) \tag{2}$$

$$PS = \sum_{i=1}^{K} (ss(i) - sb(i)) \tag{3}$$

Here, the variable PL stands for the profit from a long position, and PS – the profit from a short position, while the variable i represents the trade, where the profit or loss is calculated. In other words, the profit from a long position is equal to the difference between assets i sell – ls and buy – lb values, multiplied by K (number of contracts). Accordingly, the profit from a short position is equal to the difference between assets i sell – ss and buy – sb, multiplied by K (number of contracts). The total profit was found by using the below Eq. (4):

$$TP = PL + PS \tag{4}$$

Then, the total profit, expressed in percentage, was given [4].

5   Results

All criteria were kept the same during this research. In this case, the learning period was 5 min, the trading period – 10 s, and the period for keeping position opened was 10 s. While comparing with other research, based on milliseconds information, where all windows were of minute and more [13, 23, 24], it might be observed that in case of nanosecond information, all windows were smaller as one second time stamp consist of more data in nanoseconds than in milliseconds. The main idea of this research was to test the effectiveness of the pair trading strategy, thus, the commissions were not taken into account (Fig. 3).

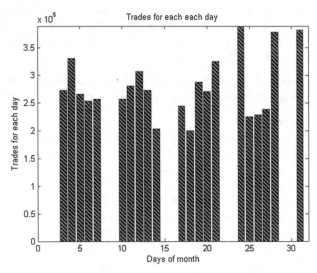

Fig. 3. Trades made each day

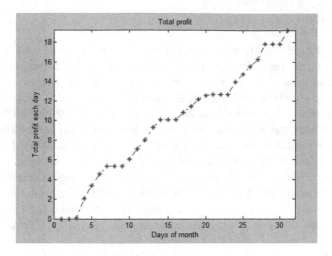

Fig. 4. Total profit

The total number of trades made for the entire period was 5869860. The daily number of trades is shown in the figure above (Fig. 4).

As it has already been stated, the effectiveness of this strategy was measured by the generated profit. Based on the result, the strategy presented by D. Herlemont did perfume with no days of loss. At the end of the research, it generated 19,27% of profit. It should be noted that previous research have tested the considered strategy by using millisecond data [13, 23, 24]. Importantly, it also resulted in profit. However, this paper changed the method of pair selection and increased the frequency of data from milliseconds to nanoseconds. These changes might have affected the better performance of the strategy (Table 3).

Table 3. Trading strategy result

	Pair trading strategy
Profit	19,27%
Number of total trades	5869860

As it has already been mentioned, trading costs were not calculated as this paper focused only on the performance of the strategy. In case of applying this strategy to the real market, the results might differ due to commissions. However, there are many markets, which want to attract high frequency traders, offering very low or even no commissions. The reason of this is the fact that high frequency traders bring liquidity to the market.

6 Conclusion

Five different futures contracts with nanosecond were used for this research. To compare the futures contracts, this historical data had to be normalized. Data normalization is necessary as you must compare each different futures contract price. Importantly, one disadvantage of normalization is the fact that it requires additional resources. The total number of record after normalization was 287872500.

For this research, the strategy proposed by D. Herlemont was used. Before applying on low frequency information and this research, it had to be modified for work with high frequency data. In this research nanosecond information was used.

Pair selection was done by implementing the Augmented Dickey Fuller Test (ADF). If a pair passes the ADF test, cointegration tests are performed on all possible combination of pairs. In order to test for cointegration, the Engle and Grangers 2-step approach and the Johansen test were adopted. All calculations were done using MATLAB.

At the end of the research, the performance of D. Herlemont pair trading strategy was measured by calculating its profitability. Based on the calculations, the profit generated was equal to 19,27% from the primary investments. The total number of trades was 5869860. When trading in real market, one trades with margin, which could be 1:2 or even 1:4, thus, the generated profitability of 19,27% is fairly high.

Before applying the strategy to real market conditions, the performance with different parameters should be tested, the trading infrastructure costs, bidirectional arbitrage should be considered, and the ones that suit the best should be identified. Pair trading, using high frequency data, gives positive results and can be an attractive option for market infrastructure developers and market participants, especially low latency traders.

Acknowledgements. We would also like to show our gratitude to the NANOTICK for providing with high frequency data in nanoseconds of 5 futures commodity contracts.

References

1. Barry, E.J.: Hedge funds and financial market dynamics. Intl. Monetary Fund, p. 83 (1998)
2. Madhavaram, G.R.: Statistical arbitrage using pairs trading with support vector machine learning. Saint Mary's University (2013)
3. Burton, G.M.: The efficient market hypothesis and its critics. J. Econ. Perspect. **17**(1), 59–82 (2003)
4. Perlin, M.S.: Evaluation of Pairs-trading strategy at the Brazilian financial market. J. Deriv. Hedge Funds **15**(2), 122–136 (2009)
5. Caldeira, J.F., Moura, G.V.: Selection of a portfolio of pairs based on cointegration: a statistical arbitrage strategy. Revista Brasileira de Financas **11**(1), 49–80 (2013)
6. Herlemont, D.: Pairs trading, convergence trading, cointegration. Quant. Finan. **12**(9) (2013)
7. Zubulake, P., Lee, S.: The high frequency game changer: how automated trading strategies have revolutionized the markets. Aite Group. Wiley Trading (2011)
8. Cifu, D.A.: FORM S-1, Registration Statement Under The Securities Act Of 1933. Virtu Financial, Inc. (2014)

9. AFM: Authority for the Financial Markets, High frequency trading: The application of advanced trading technology in the European marketplace (2010). http://www.afm.nl/~/media/files/rapport/2010/hft-report-engels.ashx. Accessed 20 Feb 2014
10. Aldridge, I.: High-Frequency Trading: A Practical Guide to Algorithmic Strategies and Trading Systems, 2 edn., p. 306. Wiley (2013)
11. Hagströmer, B., Norden, L.: The diversity of high-frequency traders. J. Financ. Mark. 16(4), 741–770 (2013)
12. Driaunys, K., Masteika, S., Sakalauskas, V., Vaitonis, M.: An algorithm-based statistical arbitrage high frequency trading system to forecast prices of natural gas futures. Transform. Bus. Econ. 13(3), 96–109 (2014)
13. Masteika, S., Vaitonis, M.: Quantitative research in high frequency trading for natural gas futures market. In: Abramowicz, W. (ed.) BIS 2015. LNBIP, vol. 228, pp. 29–35. Springer, Cham (2015). doi:10.1007/978-3-319-26762-3_3
14. Cvitanic, J., Kirilenko, A.: High frequency traders and asset prices (2010). SSRN: http://ssrn.com/abstract=1569067 or http://dx.doi.org/10.2139/ssrn.1569067
15. Carrion, A.: Very fast money: high – frequency trading on the NASDAQ. J. Financ. Mark. 16(4), 680–711 (2013)
16. George, M.J.: High frequency and dynamic pairs trading based on statistical arbitrage using a two-stage correlation and cointegration approach. Int. J. Econ. Financ. 6(3), 96–110 (2014)
17. Antoine, B., Cyrille, G., Carlos, A.R., Christian, W., Steffen, N.: High-frequency trading activity in EU equity markets. In: Economic Report, vol. 1 (2014)
18. Botos, B., Nagy, L., Ormos, M.: Pairs Trading Arbitrage Strategy in the Old and New EU Member States, ICFB (2014)
19. Vaitonis, M.: Porų prekybos strategijų taikymo gamtinių dujų rinkose tyrimas. Informacinės Technologijos 117–120 (2015)
20. Krauss, C.: Statistical arbitrage pairs trading strategies: review and outlook. IWQW Discussion Paper Series, No. 09/2015 (2015)
21. Miller, S.J.: The method of least squares. Mathematics Department Brown University (2006)
22. Vidyamurthy, G.: Pairs Trading – Quantitative Methods and Analysis, p. 210. Wiley, New Jersey (2004)
23. Vaitonis, M., Masteika, S.: Research in high frequency trading and pairs selection algorithm with Baltic region stocks. In: Dregvaite, G., Damasevicius, R. (eds.) ICIST 2016. CCIS, vol. 639, pp. 208–217. Springer, Cham (2016). doi:10.1007/978-3-319-46254-7_17
24. Vaitonis, M.: Pairs trading using HFT in OMX Baltic market. Baltic J. Modern Comput. 5 (1), 37–49 (2017)
25. Bogoev, D., Karam, A.: An empirical detection of high frequency trading strategies. In: 6th International Conference of the Financial Engineering and Banking Society, 10–12 June 2016, Melaga (2016)
26. Miller, R.S., Shorter, G.: High frequency trading: overview of recent developments. Report, Washington, D.C., 4 April 2016
27. Drakos, S.: Statistical arbitrage in S&P500. J. Math. Financ. 6, 166–177 (2016)
28. Ahmet, G.: Statistical arbitrage in the Black-Scholes framework. Quant. Financ. 15(9), 1489–1499 (2015)
29. O'Hara, M.: High frequency market microstructure. J. Financ. Econ. 116(2), 257–270 (2015)
30. Goldstein, M.A., Pavitra, K., Frank, C.G.: Computerized and high-frequency trading. Financ. Rev. 49(2), 177–202 (2014)

Knowledge-Based UML Models Generation from Enterprise Model Technique

Ilona Veitaitė[(⊠)] and Audrius Lopata

Department of Informatics, Kaunas Faculty,
Vilnius University, Kaunas, Lithuania
{Ilona.Veitaite,Audrius.Lopata}@knf.vu.lt

Abstract. The scope of this article is to present knowledge-based Unified Modelling Language (UML) behaviour (dynamic) models generation from Enterprise Model (EM) technique. The main advantage of this method is that problem domain knowledge inducted during user requirements specification and business modelling IS lifecycle phases are validated and verified before formal criteria defined. In this case empirical factors which could adversely influence the whole IS development process are decreased. The beginning of generation process is a selection of concrete UML model and specific element from EM as the main one. In this article main steps of generation from EM are presented. The conclusive result of the generation from EM are UML dynamic models that specifies structure of specific problem domain and can be used by IS developers in further lifecycle phases.

Keywords: UML · Enterprise model · Knowledge-based IS engineering · Transformation algorithms

1   Introduction

There are diverse advanced information system development approaches. Traditional methods and techniques are continually updated, but in spite of this, some fundamental IS development issues are nevertheless essential [4, 5].

One of the most important issues of IS engineering is software validation and verification ahead of user requirements. The essence of this issue contains of: expert is main participant in the problem domain knowledge gaining and analysis process, accordingly user requirement analysis and enterprise modelling process strongly rely on the experience of that expert. That causes insufficient analysis of problem domain and incoherent user requirements [5, 6, 9].

The importance of UML in software development has become more significant since the appearance of model-driven architecture [3]. UML as a modelling language is mostly used in the context of traditional model-driven development, where models are used by IS development process participants as the basis for implementation [8]. This phase is mostly manual and based on empirics. Also it depends on many factors such as analysts' or designers' experience, time constraints and user requirements [10, 11, 16].

The main components of IS life cycle design phase models, such as UML, can be generated in semi-automatic mode from knowledge repository – Enterprise model, that

© Springer International Publishing AG 2017
R. Damaševičius and V. Mikašytė (Eds.): ICIST 2017, CCIS 756, pp. 314–325, 2017.
DOI: 10.1007/978-3-319-67642-5_26

implementation will enhance the productivity of the following participants of IS development process: system analyst, system designer and developer [1, 17, 18].

It is important to notice that some elements in UML models store information about EM element from different point of view. Comparing these points of view first level knowledge validation will be executed. It insures data consistency among particular UML models. In case inconsistent data take place among the models, the issues will be resolved at this initial phase. It means that internal EM validation (prior to EMM rules) will be implemented after basic UML models consistency validation [2, 6, 12].

The introduced improvement will intellectualize knowledge-based models composition process by enriching their consistency and reducing the affection of the empirical information in composition process.

2 Relationship Between Enterprise Model and UML

Enterprise model elements are sturdy related with UML model's elements by its matter and value for IS development process.

2.1 Enterprise Meta-model Concept

Enterprise meta-model (EMM) is formally determined enterprise model composition, which contained of a formalized enterprise model alongside with the general principles of control theory (Fig. 1). Enterprise model is the main source of the requisite knowledge of the specific problem domain for IS engineering and IS reengineering processes [7].

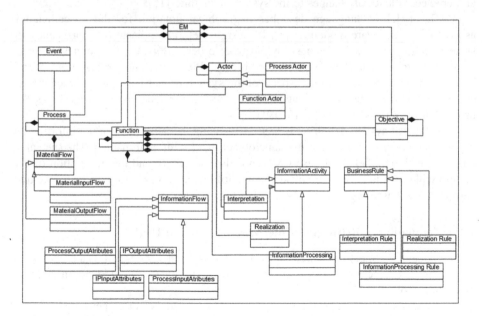

Fig. 1. Class diagram of enterprise meta-model [7]

Enterprise meta-model manages Enterprise model structure. Enterprise model stores knowledge that is obligatory for IS development process solely and will be used during all phases of IS development life cycle [13, 14]. Enterprise model is main source of knowledge, which is obligatory for models in life cycle design phase and source code generation process. In particular research UML dynamic models are included.

2.2   OMG UML Description

The Unified Modelling Language (UML) from Object Management Group (OMG) is general language for software architects, business analysts and developers used to indicate, determine, project and document the present or latest business processes and structure. UML specification clarifies software development process: represents control as to the course of a command's actions, indicates what artefacts should be developed, refers the tasks of the command as whole and individual participants and suggests parameters for evaluating and controlling a project's actions and products [15, 19].

The current version of UML is UML 2.5, released in June 2015. 2.5 tools maintains a whole UML specification. Information flows, models, and templates are no longer auxiliary UML constructs. Simultaneously, use cases, deployments, and the information flows becomes UML supplementary concepts [15].

UML specification describes two basic types of UML models: structure and behaviour (dynamic). Structure models show the static structure of the system and its parts on different fulfilment and abstraction levels and how they are connected to each other. The elements in structure diagrams represent the meaningful concepts of a system. The elements may include abstract, real world and implementation concepts. Behaviour models reveal the dynamic behaviour of the objects in a system, which can be depicted as a set of changes to the system over time [15].

UML modelling language describes a graphical notation for the miscellaneous aspects of the software modelling [1]. IS design methods indicate the consistency of systems engineering activities, i.e. how, in what order and what UML model to use in the design process and how to realize the process? Plenty of them are based on several kinds of models defining various aspects of the system properties. Sense of each model can be described individually, but more relevant is the fact that each model is the projection of the system model [15, 19].

This type of system definition is pretty confusing, because most of the information in the model overlap and define the same object just in different manner. The specialist without much experience can use UML models improperly and the description of the system will potentially be incomplete, incompatible and contradictory. In cases like that current UML based tools cannot help much for the specialist.

2.3   Compatibility Between of Enterprise Model and UML

UML is one of the most widespread software specification standards. It is a universal IS modelling language used to a number of methodologists and applied in popular modelling tools.

In a knowledge-based IS engineering, all project models can be generated interactively by using transformation algorithms, if the requisite knowledge will be collected into knowledge repository into Enterprise model. A minimum analyst and designer participation is demanded for insuring a lacking knowledge enlisting. Knowledge is verified to insure automatically generated design models and software code quality in knowledge collection into knowledge repository phase.

Liaison between UML models and Enterprise model is also implemented via the transformation algorithms. All elements stored in Enterprise model can be generated as UML models elements by using these algorithms. The usage of knowledge-based enterprise model in generation process makes it possible to generate knowledge proven by formal parameters into the UML model (Fig. 2). Usage of Enterprise model in knowledge-based IS development process automatization saves working hours of all participants.

Enterprise model and enterprise meta-model make UML project models generation process more effective and qualified and ensure lower number of mistakes in the final IS development phase.

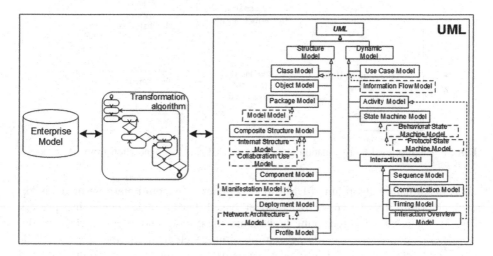

Fig. 2. The transformation algorithm role in UML models generation process [1]

3 Enterprise Model Based Generation Process

Enterprise model as organization's knowledge repository permits to generate UML models after using the transformation algorithms. Such repository can be used not only for knowledge of the organization gathering, but also as a tool that minimizes IS reengineering volume of work if changes take place in an organization. UML models generation from Enterprise model is implementation of knowledge-based design phase in the IS development life cycle.

In knowledge-based IS engineering all project models are implemented from enterprise model. Enterprise model contains significant elements of business modelling techniques and methodologies, which ensures a appropriate UML models generation process.

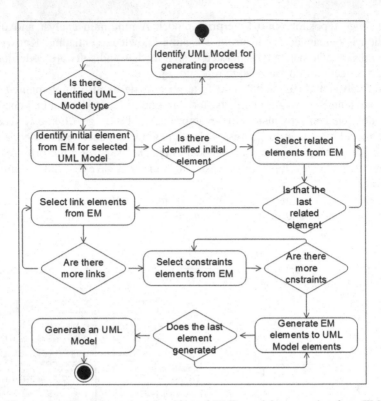

Fig. 3. The top level transformation algorithm of UML models generation from EM process

Transformation algorithm of UML models generation from Enterprise model is top level algorithm for enterprise meta-model based UML model generating process (Fig. 3). Main steps for generating process are identifying and selecting UML model for generating process, identifying starting (initial) element for the selected UML model and selecting all elements related to this UML model, generating enterprise model elements to UML model elements and generating the selected UML model.

Identifying particular UML model and selecting the initial model element is quite significant, because further generating process depends on it. A lot UML model elements repeats in different UML model, but these elements define various aspects of the system. In example Enterprise model element Actor into several different UML models elements (Table 1).

3.1   UML Use Case Model Generation from EM

UML Use Case models are usually referred to as dynamic models used to describe a series of actions that some system or systems should or can implement in contribution with one or more external users of the system. Each use case should grant some observable and valuable result to the actors or other participants of the system. UML Use Case model elements [15, 19].

Table 1. EM Actor elements role variations in UML models [15, 19].

EM element	UML model element	UML model	Description
Actor	Actor	Use Case Model	Represents a role played by some person or system external to the modelled system
	Subject	Use Case Model	Represents behaviour of participant
	Partition	Activity Model	Describes actor or actor group actions that have some common characteristic
	Lifeline	Sequence Model	Represents the lifeline of the actor
	Lifeline	Communication Model	Represents part of sequence model lifeline
	Lifeline	Timing Model	Represents an individual participant in the interaction

Input (objects from Enterprise model) and output (objects generated to UML Use Case model) elements are presented in the table (Table 2).

Table 2. UML Use Case model elements [15, 19].

EM element	UML Use Case model element	Description
Actor	Actor	An actor is behavioural classifier which defines a role played by an external entity
	Subject	A subject is a classifier which represents business, software system, physical system or device under analysis, design, or consideration, having some behaviour, and to which a set of use cases applies
Function, process	Use Case	A use case is a type of behavioural classifier that describes a unit of functionality performed by actors or subjects to which the use case applies in collaboration with one or more actors
Business rule	Extend	Extend is a directed relationship that specifies how and when the behaviour defined in usually supplementary (optional) extending use case can be inserted into the behaviour defined in the extended use case
	Include	Use case include is a directed relationship between two use cases which is used to show that behaviour of the included use case is inserted into the behaviour of the including use case
	Association	Each use case represents a unit of useful functionality that subjects provide to actors. An association between an actor and a use case indicates that the actor and the use case somehow interact or communicate with each other

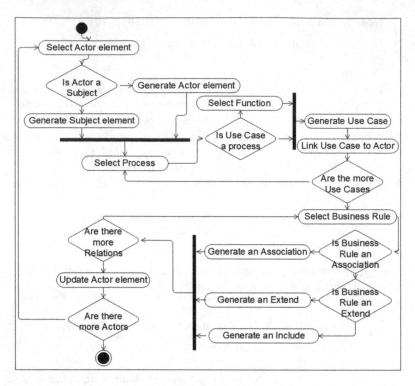

Fig. 4. The transformation algorithm of UML Use Case model generation from EM process

Figure presents transformation algorithm of UML Use Case model generation from EM process (Fig. 4). Initial element in this generation process is Actor, after actor element is generated, Use Case element is selected and then Include, Extend and Association relationships.

3.2   UML Activity Model Generation from EM

Activity model is UML dynamic model which shows flow of control or object flow with emphasis on the sequence and conditions of the flow. The actions which are coordinated by activity models can be initiated because other actions finish executing because objects and data become available, or because some events external to the flow occur [19].

Input (objects from Enterprise model) and output (objects generated to UML Activity model) elements are presented in the table (Table 3).

3.3   UML State Machine Model Generation from EM

UML State machine model is used for modelling discrete behaviour through finite state transitions. In addition to expressing the behaviour of a part of the system, state machines can also be used to express the usage protocol of part of a system. These two

Table 3. UML Activity model elements [15, 19].

EM element	UML Activity model element	Description
Actor	Partition	Describes actor or actor group actions that have some common characteristic
Function, Process	Activity	Represents a parameterized behaviour as coordinated flow of actions
Material flow, informational flow	Object Nodes	Used to define object flows in an activity
Business rules	Control Nodes	Used to coordinate the flows between other nodes. It includes: initial, flow final, activity final, decision, merge, fork, join

types of state machines are referred to as behavioural state machines and protocol state machines [19].

Input (objects from Enterprise model) and output (objects generated to UML State Machine model and UML Protocol State Machine model) elements are presented in the tables (Tables 4 and 5).

Table 4. UML State Machine model elements [15, 19].

EM element	UML State Machine model element	Description
Process, function	Behavioural State Machine	Used to specify discrete behaviour of a part of designed system through finite state transitions
Information flow	Simply State	Defined as state that has not substates
	Composite State	Defined as state that has substates
Business rule	Pseudostate	An abstract node that encompasses different types of transient vertices in the state machine graph

Table 5. UML Protocol State Machine model elements [15, 19].

EM element	UML State Machine model element	Description
Process, function	Protocol State Machine	Used to express a usage protocol or a lifecycle of some classifier
Information flow	Protocol State	Present an external view of the class that is exposed to its clients
Business rule	Protocol Transition	Used for the protocol state machines which specifies a legal transition for an operation

3.4 UML Sequence Model Generation from EM

UML Sequence model is most common kind of interaction models which focuses on the message interchange between objects (lifelines). Sequence model shows how the objects interact with others in a particular scenario of a use case [19].

Input (objects from Enterprise model) and output (objects generated to UML Sequence model) elements are presented in the table (Table 6).

Table 6. UML Sequence model elements [15, 19].

EM element	UML Sequence model element	Description
Actor	Lifeline	Represents an individual participant in the interaction. While parts and structural features may have multiplicity greater than 1, lifelines represent only one interacting entity
Process, function	Message	Defines one specific kind of communication between lifelines of an interaction
Business rules	Execution Specification	Represents a period in the participant's lifetime
	Combined Fragment	Defines a combination (expression) of interaction fragments. A combined fragment is defined by an interaction operator and corresponding interaction operands
	Interaction Use	Allows to use (or call) another interaction
	State Invariant	Represents a runtime constraint on the participants of the interaction.
	Destruction Occurrence	Represents the destruction of the instance described by the lifeline.

3.5 UML Communication Model Generation from EM

UML Communication Model (called collaboration model in UML 1.x) is a type of UML interaction model which shows interactions between objects and/or parts (represented as lifelines) using sequenced messages in a free-form arrangement [19].

Input (objects from Enterprise model) and output (objects generated to UML Sequence model) elements are presented in the table (Table 7).

3.6 UML Timing Model Generation from EM

UML Timing model are interaction models which shows interactions when a primary scope of the model is to reason about time. Timing model focus on terms changing within and among lifelines along a linear time axis. Timing models defines behaviour of both individual classifiers and interactions of classifiers, focusing attention on time of events causing changes in the modelled terms of the lifelines [19].

Input (objects from Enterprise model) and output (objects generated to UML Timing model) elements are presented in the table (Table 8).

Table 7. UML Communication model elements [15, 19].

EM element	UML Communication model element	Description
Process, function	Frame	Represents a unit of behaviour that focuses on the observable exchange of information between connectable elements
Actor	Lifeline	Represents an individual participant in the interaction
Information flow	Message	Indicates direction of the communication

Table 8. UML Timing model elements [15, 19].

EM element	UML Timing model element	Description
Actor	Lifeline	Represents an individual participant in the interaction. While parts and structural features may have multiplicity greater than 1, lifelines represent only one interacting entity
Information flow	State or Condition Timeline	Shows states of the participating classifier or attribute, or some testable conditions
Business rules	Duration constraint	Refers to a duration interval. The duration interval is duration used to determine whether the constraint is satisfied
	Time Constraint	Refers to a time interval. The time interval is time expression used to determine whether the constraint is satisfied
	Destruction Occurrence	Represents the destruction of the instance described by the lifeline

3.7 UML Interaction Overview Model Generation from EM

UML Interaction Overview model identifies interactions through a variant of activity models in a way that sustains overview of the control flow. Interaction Overview model focus on the overview of the flow of control where the nodes are interactions or interaction uses. The lifelines and the messages do not fulfil at this overview level. UML Interaction Overview model coordinates elements from activity and interaction models [19]:

- from the activity model: initial node, flow final node, activity final node, decision node, merge node, fork node, join node;
- from the interaction models: interaction, interaction use, duration constraint, time constraint.

Table 9. UML Interaction Overview model element [15, 19].

EM element	UML Interaction Overview model element	Description
Process, function	Frame	Represents a unit of behaviour that focuses on the observable exchange of information between connectable elements
Business rules	Duration constraint	Refers to a duration interval. The duration interval is duration used to determine whether the constraint is satisfied
	Time Constraint	Refers to a time interval. The time interval is time expression used to determine whether the constraint is satisfied
	Interaction Use	Allows to use (or call) another interaction
	Control Nodes	Used to coordinate the flows between other nodes. It includes: initial, flow final, activity final, decision, merge, fork, join

Input (objects from Enterprise model) and output (objects generated to UML Timing model) elements are presented in the table (Table 9).

4 Conclusions

The detailed UML dynamic models generation algorithms are requisite for knowledge-based generation from Enterprise model technique. According to previous researches there are presented top level and UML Use Case transformation algorithm in the article. All the UML model elements, which can be generated from Enterprise model are presented in tables of this article. The described solution insures data sequence inter specific Use Case, Activity, State Machine, Sequence, Communication, Timing and Interaction Overview models accordingly granting more precise whole IS development process. All the attention must be concentrated to separate elements, which can define system in different ways according to model which they represent.

The future work is to acknowledge the use of described technique with more detailed UML models examples. Moreover, in future works plan is knowledge-based tool's prototype partial implementation.

References

1. Butleris, R., Lopata, A., Ambraziunas, M., Veitaite, I., Masteika, S.: SysML and UML models usage in knowledge based MDA process. Elektronika ir elektrotechnika **21**(2), 50–57 (2015). Print ISSN: 1392-1215, Online ISSN: 2029-5731
2. Eichelberger, H., Eldogan, Y., Schmid, K.: A comprehensive analysis of UML tools, their capabilities and compliance. Softw. Syst. Eng., versio 2.0, August 2011. Universität Hildesheim

3. Dunkel, J., Bruns, R.: Model-driven architecture for mobile applications. In: Abramowicz, W. (ed.) BIS 2007. LNCS, vol. 4439, pp. 464–477. Springer, Heidelberg (2007). doi:10. 1007/978-3-540-72035-5_36

4. IEEE Computer Society. Guide to the Software Engineering Body of Knowledge SWEBOK. Version 3.0 (2014). Paperback ISBN-13:978-0-7695-5166-1

5. Jenney, J.: Modern methods of systems engineering: with an introduction to pattern and model based methods (2010). ISBN-13:978-1463777357

6. Gudas, S.: Informacijos sistemų inzinerijos teorijos pagrindai. Vilniaus universiteto leidykla (2012). ISBN: 978-609-459-075-7

7. Gudas, S., Lopata, A.: Meta-model based development of use case model for business function. Inf. Technol. Control 36(3) (2007). ISSN: 1392-124X 2007

8. Fouad, A., Phalp, K., Kanyaru, J.M., Jeary, S.: Embedding requirements within model-driven architecture. Softw. Q. J. 19(2), 411–430 (2011)

9. Gailly, F., Casteleyn, S., Alkhaldi, N.: On the symbiosis between enterprise modelling and ontology engineering. In: Ng, W., Storey, Veda C., Trujillo, Juan C. (eds.) ER 2013. LNCS, vol. 8217, pp. 487–494. Springer, Heidelberg (2013). doi:10.1007/978-3-642-41924-9_42

10. Kerzazi, N., Lavallée, M., Robillard, P.N.: A knowledge-based perspective for software process modeling. e-Informatica Softw. Eng. J. 7, 25–33 (2013)

11. Lopata, A.: Disertacija. Veiklos modeliu grindziamas kompiuterizuotas funkcinių vartotojo reikalavimų specifikavimo metodas (2004)

12. Lopata, A., Ambraziunas, M., Gudas, S., Butleris, R.: The main principles of knowledge-based information systems engineering. Electron. Electr. Eng. 11(1), 99–102 (2012). ISSN: 2029-5731

13. Lopata, A., Ambraziunas, M., Gudas, S.: Knowledge based MDA requirements specification and validation technique. Transform. Bus. Econ. 11(1), 248–261 (2012)

14. Morkevicius, A., Gudas, S.: Enterprise knowledge based software requirements elicitation. Inf. Technol. Control 40(3), 181–190 (2011). 1392-124X

15. OMG UML. Unified Modelling Language version 2.5. Unified Modelling (2017). http://www.omg.org/spec/UML/2.5

16. Perjons, E.: Model-driven process design. aligning value networks, enterprise goals, services and IT Systems. Department of Computer and Systems Sciences, Stockholm University, Sweden by US-AB, Stockholm (2011). ISBN: 978-91-7447-249-3

17. Soares, M.S., Vrancken, J.: Model-driven user requirements specification using SysML. J. Softw. 3(6), 57–68 (2008). ISSN: 1796-217X

18. Stirna, J., Persson, A., Sandkuhl, K.: Participative enterprise modeling: experiences and recommendations. In: Krogstie, J., Opdahl, A., Sindre, G. (eds.) CAiSE 2007. LNCS, vol. 4495, pp. 546–560. Springer, Heidelberg (2007). doi:10.1007/978-3-540-72988-4_38

19. UML diagrams. The Unified Modeling Language (2017). http://www.uml-diagrams.org/

Design Automation Systems. Prospects of Development

Viktoriia Zakharchenko, Anna Marchenko$^{(\boxtimes)}$, and Viktor Nenia

Sumy State University, Sumy, Ukraine
victoriaIT@ukr.net, anna.marchnko@gmail.com,
victor.nenja@gmail.com

Abstract. The researches of the design automation systems as systems which themselves manage their work have been considered in this paper. It has been established that insignificant attention is paid to this problem. The structure of the design process as the manufacturing process using the example of a typical process has been examined. The design automation system in its state "As is" has been analyzed on the basis of time factor as a stable and objective indicator. The improved organization of the design process in its state "To be" has been proposed by implementing reserves of time. On the basis of the minimum functional requirements to the design system, which itself manages its work, the function diagram of the information design automation system has been offered as a part of the interacting subsystems such as design, controlling, management, planning and data protection.

Keywords: Design system · Manufacturing process · State "As is" · State "To be" · Automation · Information system

1 Introduction

Humanity always will have the need for technical objects. It is due to the fact that they significantly help people at home and at manufacturing. Thus the improvement of design and manufacturing of technical objects not only now but also in future will be urgent and topical tasks.

According to modern views on the nearest future [1], conditioned by wide experience of experts, the equipment will develop in the direction of creation of cyber and technical systems. It will allow technical objects and the complexes "independently" to solve problems which arise due to the environment or their own discrepancy between them and current tasks.

For example, as for safety of nuclear power plants (NPP) International Atomic Energy Agency (IAEA) requires that models and calculations of probabilistic safety assessment accurately maintained throughout the whole life cycle NPP [2]. Besides, it is necessary to have all the information about the NPP and the environment for calculation of possible scenarios of events development during the design accidents [3].

Also it is claimed that "Quality Assurance Programme is a basis for the tasks analysis, development of methods, establishment of standards and defining the necessary skills and equipment". This basis includes quality assurance, standards or other requirements

© Springer International Publishing AG 2017
R. Damaševičius and V. Mikašytė (Eds.): ICIST 2017, CCIS 756, pp. 326–339, 2017.
DOI: 10.1007/978-3-319-67642-5_27

that must be implemented in the form of instructions, calculations, specifications, draw-ings and other documentation" [2].

The last thesis can be implemented due to the presence of the technical object project in it during its functioning. The functioning of the design automation system in a cyber-netic subsystem of a technical object is necessary for the possibility of use of a project and performance of modeling using this project.

The current state of the design automation systems development does not allow to transfer them from the design organization to technical object as they consist of many diverse subsystems (Computer-aided design (CAD), Computer-aided engineering (CAE), Product Data Management (PDM), Product lifecycle management (PLM) etc.) and integrated with each other by the processes of conversion and data reformatting and structure changes [4]. All this determines the topicality of the design automation system development.

2   Related Work

Subject of the design automation is very popular among experts in various fields. It is so because using a computerization of the design works leads to the acceleration of the design [5]. It allows to reduce the price on the design works implementation. In this paper it is also claimed that such process provides the enterprises with significant competitive advantages which are the driving force of development of methods and software applied to the improvement of the design quality.

In the work [6] advantages of the design automation are confirmed. A new view on this process is provided there. Two new components – master model and knowledge base that supports it, are added to architecture of the design system. The model of a design object is built on the basis of the master model. This significantly increases the reliability and quality of design objects for which the knowledge base has been accu-mulated. However, this little promotes creation of essentially new objects and subjects of new constructive schemes. Nevertheless, it is an essential contribution to the views development on the design automation. Additionally, it should be noted two essential moments. The first one is that the design automation development is focused on the construction industry as authors mention. The second one is the lack of the design process management means.

The application of parallel calculations gains an expansion in the design automation field. The work [7] provides convincing arguments in favor of the fact that existing software should be remained unchanged according to economic reasons, and to develop new programs using previously approved templates that cover a lot of problems. A concrete example of achieving 750-fold acceleration of the computation performance on GPUs (Graphics processing unit), which confirms the topicality of this design computerization direction, is shown in [8]. At the same time the existing design systems are used for development of technical means of parallel calculations, exactly the systems of mass and parallel data processing [9]. Such development is very urgent as its devel-opers have encountered the difficulties of the design object modeling.

Electronics developers continue to remain as leaders in the design automation. They have already changed the paradigm of CAD on EDA – Electronic design automation, as a higher level of the design computerization. Among the directions of EDA tools in [10] proposed the following:

1. To divide problems into separate tasks according to the concrete tasks aspects (the users requirements, functional design, the interface etc.).
2. To use component-oriented structures as a basis for the complex systems creation.
3. To highlight the semantic sequences in the problems of each aspect. It allows to use formalism within the sequence. This formalism is determined by semantics.
4. To provide the structure correctness that guarantees a correctly performed function.

The authors of this work support the position that "the term "mechanization" is often used to refer to the simple replacement of human labour by machines during the processing of raw materials into a product; the term "automation" generally implies the integration of machines into the management process of the manufacturing process (exactly the processing of raw materials into a product) and into the human resource management within previous process. The aim of automation is to create a self-managed system [11].

Analyzed the publications provided in this work and many other researched papers separately the authors haven't found the researches according to transformation of the design systems into the self-managed systems meant the design automation systems with its own management. The authors interpret the term automation exactly in this sense. Guided by the presented arguments and considerations the aim of this paper is to examine the performance processes of the design works, to identify the characteristic features of the subprocesses and to offer the functional diagram that corresponds to the concept of the design automation system.

3   Research of the Design in the State "As is"

Design can be considered from the different angles and highlight various aspects. There are different types of the design: integrated, cross-cutting, optimal, competitive etc. We will consider the design as a manufacturing process. Observation of designers' and constructors' work at mechanical engineering enterprises, analysis of organizational documents and normative standards allow to represent some conventional and simple design process as a set of precedents (Fig. 1) – the set of processes and persons who carry out them or interact with them.

If there is a presence of Terms of References (ToR), the Chief Supervisor of the design organization (design office, design group) analyzes it and initiates the beginning of the design process performance by the elected group of workers. He is the person who is interested in the effectiveness of design and approves its results. The Chief Supervisor delegates to the supervisor of lower level – the Supervisor a part of his powers according to the consultation of the designer, the monitoring and controlling of designer's work, the management of the design process. The results of the designer's work are checked for mistakes not only by this Supervisor, but also by other corresponding

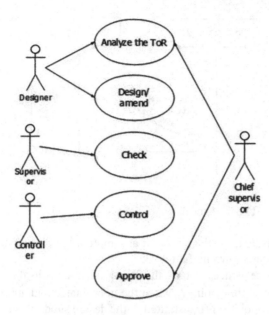

Fig. 1. Use Case Diagram of the design process at the design organization

experts. They check the designer's work according to the observance of standard requirements for the project documentation and of requirements of technological processes of the designed object manufacturing. The designer not only develops the project as the description of the designed object, but also rectifies the mistakes determined during the checking. If there are mistakes, the designer amends the proposed design solution, and, if it is necessary, the designer remakes it from the very beginning.

For the purpose of the objective analysis of the manufacturing design process, it will be considered as the Use Case Diagram within one scenario of design. The time axis of all subjects and objects involved into the process of the researched activity are specified in this type of diagram. At some time point the message is sent from one object to another. During the organization of the design process a typical term "message transmission" from *Performer_1* to *Performer_2* must be understood correctly: in addition to the actual message that means manufacturing operation, the ToR and necessary design documentation for its implementation are also transmitted. The message transmission takes certain time Δt_T. On the basis of this statement the diagram of the message transmission must be considered as follows presented in Fig. 2.

In fact, the considered process begins at the time T_0 and finishes at the time $T_1 = T_0 + \Delta t_T$. Considering that transition of the design system from a state "As is" to a state "To be" will be carried out by a computerization of technological design process on the basis of information networks, the time interval of the message transmission will be much less than the period of the design work performance Δt_J, i.e. $\Delta t_T \ll \Delta t_J$. Based on this ratio we accept that $\Delta t_T = 0$. Further we will represent the "vector" of the message transmission horizontally, i.e. without any delay in the time.

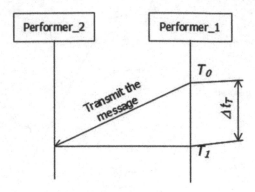

Fig. 2. Time diagram of message transmission

Taking into consideration the specified assumption the current state of the design has the following view shown in the Fig. 3.

The diagram of sequences details the researched scenario during the time. The process begins at some time point T_0 when the coordinated and approved ToR for the design of the technical object is transmitted to the design subdivision. The Chief Supervisor of the subdivision analyzes the ToR in terms of specifics of the design work connected with a concrete technical object, transmits the ToR to Archive, appoints the executive performer – the Supervisor and transmits him the copy of the ToR. The Supervisor analyzes the ToR in terms of the essence and the volume of the design work, appoints a certain performer (the Designer) for the design work performance and transmits him the ToR.

The designer analyzes the ToR and performs the formation of the design solution. Then, perhaps after some time, he properly prepares the design documentation. The formed design solution is checked by the corresponding performer for compliance with the ToR. Then the design documentation is transmitted to the Design Rule Check. After that starts the Technical supervision of the design solution. There are chances of the identification of mistakes, defects or discrepancies to requirements during the checking and control of the design solutions and the design documentation. It is so because during the work performance by a person it is impossible to avoid influence of a subjective factor. The processes of bringing the design solution to the ToR requirements and manufacturing conditions are shown as the iterative cycles of the project return for the amending.

The last development stage is the approval of the project by the Chief Supervisor, its transmission to the Archive and to the Client in accordance with the established procedure at some timepoint T_n.

It is established that each expert, who is involved into the design process, begins his work after some period of time, performs it during some time, and then after some time sends results to the next performer. Delays can be caused by the manufacturing need (the need to complete the performance of previously launched work, the need to perform the work with higher priority, the organizational inconsistency) or by the subjective factors.

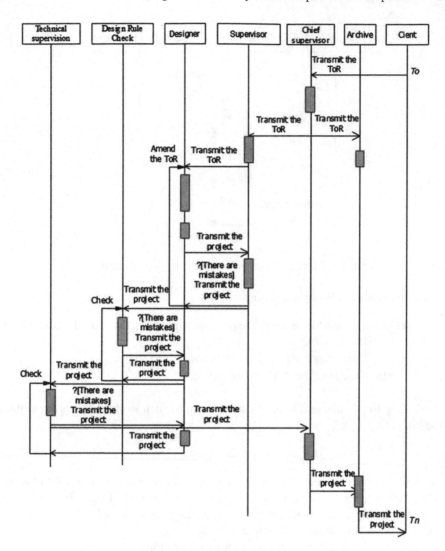

Fig. 3. Diagram of the design processes state "As is"

All types of performed work have certain consequences. Experience shows that not all of them are equal due to various objective and subjective circumstances. Of course there are rather simple works and only the fact of their performance is controlled. Works of design are subject to obligatory check for mistakes.

Let's consider the performance of the first type of works. We select a diagram fragment in the Fig. 3 which shows the process of work performance and this work isn't checked for mistakes. For example, it will be the ToR analysis by an expert who is responsible for its implementation in the project. This process is presented in Fig. 4.

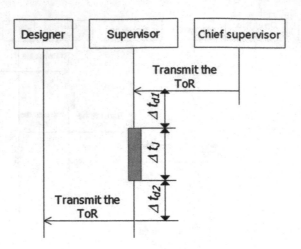

Fig. 4. Diagram of the uncontrollable work performance

We introduce the following notations:

Δt_J – the time of the performance of the process implementation. In this case, it is the ToR analysis (J = Job);

Δt_{d1} – the delay time before the work performance (d = Delay);

Δt_{d2} – the delay time after the work performance.

According to this the total time of performance of such work (ΔT_{J1}) is determined by the Eq. (1):

$$\Delta T_{J1} = \Delta t_{d1} + \Delta t_J + \Delta t_{d2} \tag{1}$$

A detailed scheme of work of the design process implementation, the results of which are checked for mistakes, controlled and approved, is shown in Fig. 5. It is presented using as the example the sequences of both the design process and the check process with the introduced notations of the time intervals.

According to the Fig. 5 we have the following notations:

Δt_{Jt} – the performance time of the design results check (t = Test = Check);

Δt_{dt1} – the delay time before the check performance;

Δt_{dt2} – the delay time after the check performance;

Δt_{Ja} – the performance time of the amending process implementation – correction of shortcomings by results of the project check (a = Amending);

Δt_{da1} – the delay time before the amending performance;

Δt_{da2} – the delay time after the amending performance.

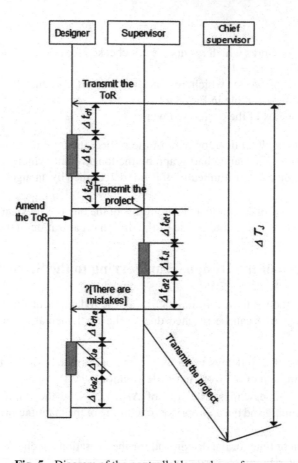

Fig. 5. Diagram of the controllable works performance

The time interval of the work performance that is checked for mistakes or controlled (ΔT_{J2}) is determined by the Eq. (2):

$$\Delta T_{J2} = \Delta t_{d1} + \Delta t_J + \Delta t_{d2} + \sum_{l=1}^{k} (\Delta t_{dt1} + \Delta t_{Jt} + \Delta t_{dt2})_l + \sum_{l=1}^{k-1} (\Delta t_{da1} + \Delta t_{Ja} + \Delta t_{da2})_l \qquad (2)$$

where

k – the number of checks or controls;
l – the current index of the check iteration.

The time interval of the performance of the considered design process (ΔT_J) is determined by the Eq. (3):

$$\Delta T_J = \sum_{i=1}^{n1} \Delta T_{J1i} + \sum_{i=1}^{n2} \Delta T_{J2i} \qquad (3)$$

where

$n1$ – the number of works which results are not checked for mistakes (according to the example in Fig. 3 $n1 = 4$);

$n2$ – the number of works which results are checked for mistakes or controlled (according to the example in Fig. 3 $n2 = 3$);

i – the current index of the performed work.

At the multi procedural development of the project the total time interval is determined on the basis of the Gantt chart graph by the longest path which is called critical. This path is determined algorithmically. It is not determined by an algebraic formula of the fixed form.

The average value of ΔT_J indicator for groups of the one type designed objects is an objective indicator for the characteristic of the design organization in the state "As is".

4   Justification of the Design Transferring to the State "To be"

The reduction of the value of ΔT_J indicator, i.e. the reduction of time for the design process implementation can be reached due to the implementation of the following actions:

1. The exclusion of Δt_{d2} delays by releasing the performer from the function of the results transmission of his work to the destination.
2. The exclusion or essential reduction of Δt_{d1} delays by the improvement of the processes planning and the appropriate scheduling of the manufacturing tasks on the design works.
3. The reduction of time for the design and for the operations of check and control Δt_J by the computerization of these processes. This time is the basic time of the design work performance. Such solution carries out an essential role in the quality improvement of the design documentation and a rather significant role in the quality improvement of the design solutions.

Taking into account the aforesaid recommendations 1–3, the diagram of the processes sequences in the scenario of the design is presented in Fig. 6.

Delays Δt_{d1} and Δt_{d2} have been excluded for the scenario of design represented in Fig. 6. The duration and content of works at the stages of the design work and check of its results don't influence on the improvement essence of the design process. It is inexpedient to change its composition and the sequence confirmed by the practice of the industry to a full-fledged exception of the person from this process. The reduction of the process duration by an exception of the subprocesses and the effect evaluation from this don't cause the complications according to the formula (3).

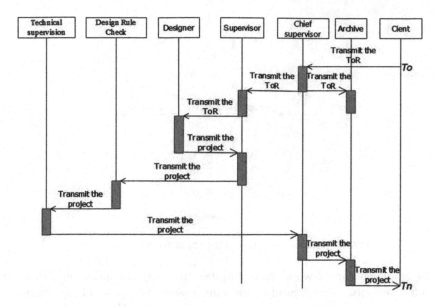

Fig. 6. Diagram of the design processes state "To be"

5 Proposed Composition of the Design Automation Systems

The UML graphical notation that has been used before, supports the development of information systems only according to the "bottom-up" diagram – the rising development [12, 13].

This approach does not allow to carry out the controlling requirements formed for the developed information system. Therefore, for the development of the design automation system we use the IDEF0 approach [14] for the functional modeling of systems.

As a fact we perceive the existed statement that the developed system accepts the ToR as the input and gives a full description of the designed object as a set of the design documentation as the output. Design is performed by experts, and their supervisors perform the functions of management. The specified approach to the organization of the design is reflected by the diagram of the highest hierarchical level. It is presented in Fig. 7.

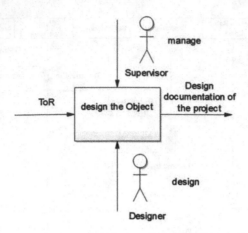

Fig. 7. Functional diagram of the organization of the design

The main way for the work improvement of the design organization is to use the computers and network equipment for the transmission of the part of functions (ideally all functions) performed by a person to the technical means. The complex of technical means that make up the basis of the design automation system must provide the following functions:

1. The computerized support of the organization of the technical objects design and construction.
2. The computerized support of the management of the staff, software and technical means during the design process.
3. The computerized support of the management of designer's actions and software works algorithms during the design procedures performance.

The functional diagram of the design automation system of the design organization as the decomposition of the general diagram is shown in Fig. 8.

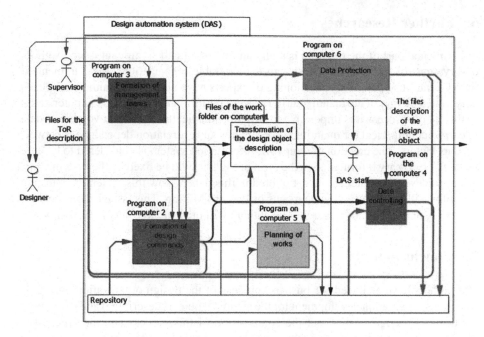

Fig. 8. Functional diagram of the design automation system

The working area is central. It has a previous description of the technical object. There is also the next description which is more detailed. The design process of the corresponding technical object or a separate its part is implemented by the same way.

The designer influences on the selected working area by using the computer software over the network equipment.

The designer has his supervisor. This supervisor influences on the designer's work. Management influence occurs both outside and inside the design system. The supervisor can change the employee's work results in this system.

The control subsystem monitors the state of the design object description. If necessary, it notifies the management subsystem about the making the necessary actions. The management subsystem delegates the responsibility to the supervisor in case of contingencies.

The management subsystem informs the performers about planned tasks for them according to the results of the planning subsystem work. Then it warns them about the deadlines oncoming and finally transfers the task for its performance in time.

The data protection subsystem monitors the commands that submit supervisors and designers, the running programs in the system and the processed information. This subsystem also makes the necessary decisions and executes planned actions according to the adopted strategy and tactics of the information security.

All subsystems use data from a single repository and store data in it. This allows simply to combine the data of a design stage and the data of other stages of the technical object life cycle if necessary.

6   Further Researches

Experimental part of the research is really an important and significant issue. Authors' observations of the design processes in the available organizations, measurements of time for various operations, questioning of experts have allowed the authors to receive only a clear picture of the manufacturing process performance. Without computerization of this whole process it is impossible to save up statistically significant volume of data, to carry out numerical (or quantitative) estimates and correlation dependences between various factors. The creation of a separate information system is considered to be inexpedient. Necessary information in the form of log files will be fixed by the system which has been developed on the concept offered in this paper. Now this system is in testing. Log files will be analyzed by the means of Process Mining. This issue is considered as a separate and important research. The authors will present its results in further works.

7   Conclusions

The authors have analyzed the business process of the design organization during the design documentation development for the technical objects description and their manufacturing. They have found out the composition of this process and the order of its components performance, the interdependences between them and the interaction between experts, as the subprocesses performers. The functional diagram of the design automation system has been proposed according to the reasonable consideration of the design as the manufacturing process.

Additionally have been done the following:

1. The time balance during the design processes implementation in the design organization has been considered. This has allowed specifically and objectively to characterize the activity of the organization according to the design as a research object in its state "As is".
2. The reserves of time reduction for the design documentation development have been established. The use of these reserves allows reasonably to transfer the activity of the design organization into the new state "To be". It is expedient to keep the existing composition of processes of the design procedures performance as the design components of the complex objects until the complete exclusion of the person from the composition of outlines of the design work performance and replacing the person's intellectual abilities by the computer software.
3. The functional diagram of the design automation system has been offered. It provides a partial exclusion of the person from the outlines of the design work performance and from the outlines of the management of the design processes performers. This system also guarantees the declared system functionality.

References

1. Beihoff, B., Oster, C., Friedenthal, S., Paredis, C., Kemp, D., Stoewer, H., Wade, J., et al.: A World in Motion–Systems Engineering Vision 2025. INCOSE-SE Leading Indicators Guide (2014)
2. Doklad mezhdunarodnoj konsul'tativnoj gruppy po jadernoj bezopasnosti: Osnovnye principy bezopasnosti atomnih jelektrostancij 75-INSAG-3 Rev.1 INSAG-12. Mezhdunarodnoe agentstvo po atomnoj jenergii, Vienna (2015)
3. Bukrinskij, A.M.: Upravlenie zaproektnymi avarijami v dejstvujushhih normativnyh dokumentah Rossii. Jadernaja i radiacionnaja bezopasnost' **1**, 16–25 (2010)
4. Chang, K.H.: Design Theory and Methods Using CAD/CAE. The Computer Aided Engineering Design Series. Academic Press, Burlington (2014)
5. Cederfeldt, M., Elgh, F.: Design automation in SMEs–current state, potential, need and requirements. In: DS 35: Proceedings ICED 05, the 15th International Conference on Engineering Design, Melbourne, Australia, August 15–18, 2005 (2005)
6. Sandberg, M., Gerth, R., Lu, W., Jansson, G., Mukkavaara, J., Olofsson, T.: Design automation in construction: an overview. In: CIB W78 Conference (2016)
7. Catanzaro, B., Keutzer, K., Su, B.Y.: Parallelizing CAD: A timely research agenda for EDA. In: Proceedings of the 45th annual Design Automation Conference, pp. 12–17. ACM, June 2008
8. Probst, M., Rothlauf, F., Grahl, J.: An implicitly parallel EDA based on restricted boltzmann machines. In: Proceedings of the 2014 Annual Conference on Genetic and Evolutionary Computation, pp. 1055–1062. ACM, July 2014
9. Brown, A., Lester, D., Plana, L., Furber, S., Wilson, P.: SpiNNaker: the design automation problem. In: Köppen, M., Kasabov, N., Coghill, G. (eds.) ICONIP 2008. LNCS, vol. 5507, pp. 1049–1056. Springer, Heidelberg (2009). doi:10.1007/978-3-642-03040-6_127
10. Sifakis, J.: System design automation: challenges and limitations. Proc. IEEE **103**(11), 2093–2103 (2015)
11. Groover, M.: Automation. Encyclopedia Britannica (2017)
12. Macjashek, L.A.: Analiz trebovanij i proektirovanie sistem. Razrabotka informacionnyh sistem s ispol'zovaniem UML (2002)
13. Maciaszek, L.: Requirements Analysis and System Design: Developing Information Systems with UML. Addison-Wesley, Harlow (2001)
14. Lightsey, B.: Systems engineering fundamentals. Defense acquisition univ ft belvoir va (2001)

Software Engineering: Special Session on Intelligent Systems and Software Engineering Advances

Ensemble of Classifiers Based on Simple Granules of Knowledge

Piotr Artiemjew[(⊠)]

Faculty of Mathematics and Computer Science,
University of Warmia and Mazury in Olsztyn,
Sloneczna 54, 10-710 Olsztyn, Poland
artem@matman.uwm.edu.pl

Abstract. The idea of classification based on simple granules of knowledge (CSG classifier) is inspired by granular structures proposed by Polkowski. The simple granular classifier turned up to be really effective in the context of real data classification. Classifier among others turned out to be resistant for damages and can absorb missing values. In this work we have presented the continuation of series of experimentations with boosting of rough set classifiers. In the previous works we have proven effectiveness of pair and weighted voting classifier in mentioned context. In this work we have checked a few methods for classifier stabilization in the context of CSG classifier - Bootstrap Ensemble (Simple Bagging), Boosting based on Arcing, and Ada-Boost with Monte Carlo split. We have performed experiments on selected data from the UCI Repository. The results show that the committee of simple granular classifiers stabilized the classification process. Simple Bagging turned out to be most effective for CSG classifier.

Keywords: Rough sets · Rough inclusions · Granules of knowledge · Classification of data · Bootstrap ensemble · Ada-Boost · Arcing

1 Introduction

In the previous works we have developed the group of rough set classifiers based on the granular structures developed by Polkowski [15]. Classification turned out to be really effective with significant reduction in the training decision system size. The ensemble scheme of classification, in the context of rough set methods is really effective - see [7–11, 16] thus we decided to check the selected methods on our classifiers. In the previous experimentations we have proven the effectiveness of boosting scheme for our pair and weighted voting classifier.

In this work we have selected for experiments the granular classifier based on simple granules of knowledge [1].

The Boosting consists of sequential production of classifiers, where each classifier is dependent on the previous one and focuses on the previous one's error [12, 18, 21]. Incorrectly classified objects are chosen more often to training sets The Ensemble of Bootstraps [22] forms the group of classifiers, where each classifier is dependent on the previous one, but there is no influence of classification accuracy.

© Springer International Publishing AG 2017
R. Damaševičius and V. Mikašytė (Eds.): ICIST 2017, CCIS 756, pp. 343–350, 2017.
DOI: 10.1007/978-3-319-67642-5_28

We have conducted three types of experiment, where the first one consists of the stabilisation of classification based on the mentioned Committee of Boot- straps [17], the second on Boosting based on Arcing [5, 19], and the third on Ada-Boost with Monte Carlo split [12, 18, 21].

Let us to start with the theoretical basics.

1.1   Theoretical Background

An information system [13] is a pair $I = (U, A)$, where U is a set of objects, entities, and A is a set of attributes; decision system is a triple $DS = (U, A, d)$, where $d \notin A$. The basic form of granulation in decision and information systems consists in partitioning U into classes of the indiscernibility relation $IND(A)$ defined as $IND(A) = \{(u, v) : a(u) = a(v), \forall a \in A\}$. Each class $[u]_A = \{v \in U : IND_A(u, v)\}$ is interpreted as a elementary granule and unions of elementary granules are granules of knowledge. Another approach to granulation, proposed in [15], consists in using rough inclusions, cf. [15]

A rough inclusion [15] is a relation $\mu \subseteq U \times U \times [0, 1]$ which can be regarded as graded similarity relation extending the indiscernibility relation by relaxing restrictions on attribute values. We let $IND(u, v) = \{a \in A : a(u) = a(v)\}$.

In our approach we use rough inclusion proposed by [15], to classify test objects. Test object u is classified by granules, which have been formed from training set as follows,

$$g_{r_{gran}}(u) = \left\{ v \in U : \frac{|IND(u,v)|}{|A|} \geq r_{gran} \right\}, \text{ where } r_{gran} \in [0, 1] \text{ is the granulation radius.}$$

The most numerous decision class transfers decision to our testing object. If tie occurs, it is resolved by a random choice. This type of classification is the simplest among studied by the author cf. [3, 4, 14]. The results of research for optimal parameters for this method is available in [2]. In this work we continue this approach and our main purpose is to find the threshold of the optimal parameter stability for the random damage of the decision system.

In the work [2] we have proposed a method for experimental detecting of the optimal radius value for a given data set, by means of multiple CV-5 and subsequent confirmation by means of Leave One Out method. Once the optimal value is found for the test data, it can be used for classifying incoming objects without any need for full granulation procedure.

The rest of the paper has the following content. In Subsects. 1.1–1.3 we have the theoretical introduction to CSG classifier. In Sect. 2 we have described the Boosting methods used in this work. In Sect. 3 we show the results of the experiments, and we conclude the paper in Sect. 4.

We now describe background information about how the classifiers are considered in terms of rough set theory.

1.2 Classification by Simple Granules of Knowledge Theoretical Background

The Rough inclusion is defined as $\mu_\pi(x, y, r)$, where x, y are individual objects, $r \in [0, 1]$, which satisfies the following requirements, relative to a given part relation π on a set U of individual objects, see [15],

$$1.\, \mu_\pi(x, y, 1) \Leftrightarrow ing_\pi(x, y);$$
$$2.\, \mu_\pi(x, y, 1) \Rightarrow [\mu_\pi(z, x, r) \Rightarrow \mu_\pi(z, y, r)];$$
$$3.\, \mu_\pi(x, y, r) \wedge s < r \Rightarrow \mu_\pi(x, y, s)$$

Those requirements seem to be intuitively clear. 1. demands that the predicate μ_π is an extension to the relation ing_π of the underlying system of Mereology; 2. does express monotonicity of μ_π, and 3. assures the reading. "to degree at least r". We use here only one rough inclusion, albeit a fundamental one, viz., see [15] for its derivation,

$$\mu_L(u, v, r) \Leftrightarrow \frac{|IND(u, v)|}{|A|} \geq r.$$

A granule $g_\mu(u, r)$ about $u \in U$ of the radius r, relative to μ, is defined by letting,

$$g_\mu(u, r) \quad \text{is} \quad \text{ClsF}(u, r),$$

where the property F(u,r) is satisfied with an object v if and only if $\mu(v, u, r)$ holds, and Cls is the class operator, see, e.g., [15]. Practically, in case of μ_L, the granule $g(u, r)$ collects all $v \in U$ such that $|IND(v,u)| \geq r \cdot |A|$.

1.3 Voting by Granules on Decision Values

For granule $g = g_{r_{gran}}(u)$ of test objects u in a training decision system (U_{trn}, A, d), for each test object u, the value of decision assigned to u by the granule g is defined as, $d(u) = d'$ such that, for D as the set of granule's $g_{r_{gran}}(u)$ decision classes,

$$d' = \left\{ d'' \in D : \max \left| \left\{ v \in g_{r_{gran}}(u) : d(v) = d'' \right\} \right| \right\}$$

The ties are resolved in a random way.

1.4 The Procedure of Classification by Means of Standard Granules (CSG Algorithm)

1. The training decision system (U_{trn}, A, d) and the test system (U_{tst}, A, d) has been input, where U_{tst}, U_{trn} is respectively universe of test and training objects, A is a set of attributes and d is a decision reflecting a partition of objects into classes.
2. The granular radius $r_{gran} \in \{\frac{0}{card\{A\}}, \frac{1}{card\{A\}}, \ldots, \frac{card\{A\}}{card\{A\}}\}$ has been chosen.

3. For classified test object $u \in U_{tst}$, the classification granule $g_{r_{gran}}(u)$ has been found in the training set Utrn as follows,

$$g_{r_{gran}}(u) = \{v \in U_{trn} : \frac{|IND(u, v)|}{|A|} \geq r_{gran}\}, \text{ where } r_{gran} \in [0, 1]$$

4. The most numerous decision class of granule $g_{r_{gran}}(u)$ transfers decision to our test object. If tie occurs, it is resolved randomly.

2   Classifiers Stabilisation Methods

In order to perform the experimental part we have selected three methods to check the boosting, stabilisation effect on our classifier. The brief description is as follows.

2.1   Bootstrap Ensembles

It is the random committee of bootstraps [22], a method, in which the original decision system - the basic knowledge - is split into (TRN) training data set, and (TSTvalid) validation test data set. And from the TRN system, for a fixed number of iterations, we form new Training systems (NewTRN) by random choice with returning of card {TRN} objects. In all iterations we classify the TRNvalid system in two ways: the first based on the actual NewTRN system and the second based on the committee of all performed classifications. In the committee majority voting is performed and the ties are resolved randomly.

2.2   Boosting Based on Arcing

The similar method to the frst one, but here the TRN is split into two data sets NewTRN and NewTST - see [5, 19]. The split is based on Bootstraps and the NewTRN system is formed by weights assigned to training objects. The objects are chosen for the NewTRN with a fixed probability determined by weights. The weights are initially equal, but after the first classification of the NewTST system based on NewTRN, the weights are modified in such a way that well-classified objects have lowered weights, and after that the normalization of weights is performed. This method of forming Bootstraps is called Arcing. After the classification, the NewTRN classifies the TSTvalid in a single iteration and as the committee of classifiers. In Arcing the factor for weights modification is equal 1-Accuracy/Accuracy.

2.3   Boosting Based on Ada-Boost with Monte Carlo Split

We use a similar method of classification to the one previously described, but here we use a different method for NewTRN and NewTST forming - see [12, 18, 21]. We split the TRN data set according to the fixed ratio, and choose the objects in the NewTRN based on weights. The good split ratio is about 0.6, because it is close to the approximate size of the distinguishable objects in the bootstraps. The rest of the algorithm works in a similar way to the previous one.

3 Results of Experiments

We have carried out experiments with use of multiple Cross Validation 5 (CV-5) [6] method and we use the exemplary data from UCI Repository [20], the list of data is in the Table 1. Due to short space we have selected only one exemplary result for three methods of boosting. See the results in the Figs. 1, 2 and 3. In case of Fig. 1 we have results for ensemble of bootstraps for Australian credit data set, we have stable

Table 1. The list of examined data sets

Name	Attr. type	Attr.no.	Obj.no.	Class no.
Adult	*Categorical, integer*	15	48842	2
Australian-credit	*Categorical, integer, real*	15	690	2
Diabetes	*Categorical, integer*	9	768	2
German credit	*Categorical, integer*	21	1000	2
Heart disease	*Categorical, real*	14	270	2
Hepatitis	*Categorical, integer, real*	20	155	2
Congressional voting	*Categorical*	17	435	2
Mushroom	*Categorical*	23	8124	2
Nursery	*Categorical*	9	12960	5
Soybean large	*Categorical*	36	307	19

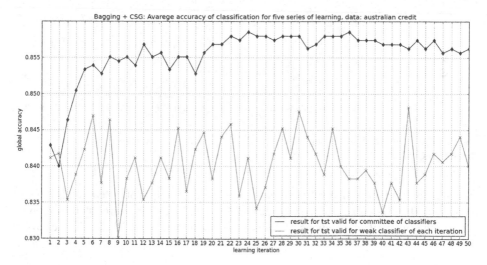

Fig. 1. The result for Bagging based on Arcing with CSG classifier – 50 iterations of learning. Data: Australian Credit

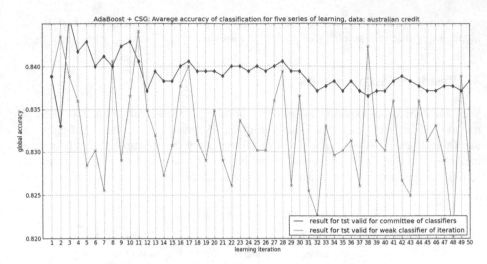

Fig. 2. The result for Ada Boost with CSG classifier – 50 iterations of learning. Data: Australian Credit

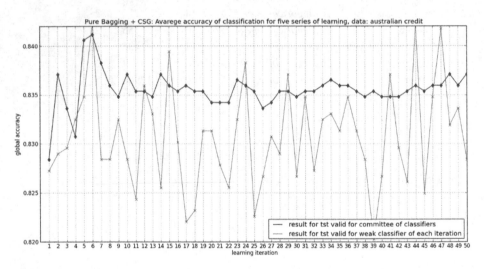

Fig. 3. The result for Simple Bagging with CSG classifier – 50 iterations of learning. Data: Australian Credit

classification starting from the 20th iteration, accuracy error upto 30th iteration is around 0.002 with 0.855 accuracy. In the Figs. 2 and 3 we have similar results, stabilization is in the same interval of iterations, the results is slightly worse with similar accuracy error.

4   Conclusions

In the paper we have investigated the possibility of stabilization of the classifier based on simple granules of knowledge, which is based on the granules formed from rough inclusions proposed by Polkowski [15]. We have performed the series of experiments based on data from University of Irvine repository. The results show the effectiveness of all investigated boosting methods. The simple granular classifier is significantly stabilized and the simple Bagging wins among checked methods. In the future works we have plan to check the effect of boosting for classifiers based on approximated decision systems.

Acknowledgement. The research has been supported by grant 1309-802 from Ministry of Science and Higher Education of the Republic of Poland.

References

1. Artiemjew, P.: Stability of optimal parameters for classifier based on simple granules of knowledge. Tech. Sci. **14**(1), 57–69 (2011). UWM Publisher, Olsztyn
2. Artiemjew, P.: In search of optimal parameters for classifier based on simple granules of knowledge. In: III International Interdisciplinary Technical Conference of Young Scientists (InterTech 2010), vol. 3, pp. 138–142. Poznan University Press (2010)
3. Artiemjew, P.: On strategies of knowledge granulation and applications to decision systems, Ph.D. dissertation, Polish Japanese institute of Information Technology. L. Polkowski, Supervisor, Warsaw (2009)
4. Artiemjew, P.: Natural versus granular computing: classifiers from granular structures. In: Chan, C.-C., Grzymala-Busse, J.W., Ziarko, W.P. (eds.) RSCTC 2008. LNCS, vol. 5306, pp. 150–159. Springer, Heidelberg (2008). doi:10.1007/978-3-540-88425-5_16
5. Breiman, L.: Arcing classifier (with discussion and a rejoinder by the author). Ann. Stat. **26** (3), 801–849 (1998). Accessed 18 Jan 2015. Schapire (1990) proved that boosting is possible. (p. 823)
6. Devroye, L., Gyorfi, L., Lugosi, G.: A Probabilistic Theory of Pattern Recognition. Springer, New York (1996)
7. Hu, X.: Construction of an ensemble of classifiers based on rough sets theory and database operations. In: Proceedings of the IEEE International Conference on Data Mining (ICDM 2001) (2001)
8. Hu, X.: Ensembles of classifiers based on rough sets theory and set-oriented database operations. In: Presented at the 2006 IEEE International Conference on Gran-ular Computing, Atlanta, GA (2006)
9. Lei, S.H.I., Mei, W.E.N.G., Xinming, M.A., Lei, X.I.: Rough set based decision tree ensemble algorithm for text classification. J. Comput. Inf. Syst. **6**(1), 89–95 (2010)
10. Murthy, C.A., Saha, S., Pal, S.K.: Rough set based ensemble classifier. In: Kuznetsov, S.O., Ślęzak, D., Hepting, D.H., Mirkin, B.G. (eds.) RSFDGrC 2011. LNCS, vol. 6743, p. 27. Springer, Heidelberg (2011). doi:10.1007/978-3-642-21881-1_5

11. Nowicki, R.K., Nowak, B.A., Woźniak, M.: Application of rough sets in k nearest neighbours algorithm for classification of incomplete samples. In: Kunifuji, S., Papadopoulos, G.A., Skulimowski, A.M.J., Kacprzyk, J. (eds.) Knowledge, Information and Creativity Support Systems. AISC, vol. 416, pp. 243–257. Springer, Cham (2016). doi:10.1007/978-3-319-27478-2_17

12. Ohno-Machado, L.: Cross-validation and Bootstrap Ensembles, Bag-ging, Boosting, Harvard-MIT Division of Health Sciences and Technology. HST.951J: Medical Decision Support, Fall 2005. http://ocw.mit.edu/courses/health-sciences-and-technology/hst-951j-medical-decision-support-fall-2005/lecture-notes/hst951_6.pdf

13. Pawlak, Z.: Rough sets. Int. J. Comput. Inf. Sci. **11**, 341–356 (1982)

14. Polkowski, L., Artiemjew, P.: On granular rough computing: factoring classifiers through granulated decision systems. In: Kryszkiewicz, M., Peters, J.F., Rybinski, H., Skowron, A. (eds.) RSEISP 2007. LNCS, vol. 4585, pp. 280–289. Springer, Heidelberg (2007). doi:10. 1007/978-3-540-73451-2_30

15. Polkowski, L.: A unified approach to granulation of knowledge and granular computing based on rough mereology. a survey. In: Pedrycz, W., Skowron, A., Kreinovich, V. (eds.) Handbook of Granular Computing, pp. 375–401. Wiley, New York (2008)

16. Saha, S., Murthy, C.A., Pal, S.K.: Rough set based ensemble classifier for web page classification. Fundamenta Informaticae **76**(1–2), 171187 (2007)

17. Steinhaus, H.: Remarques sur le partage pragmatique. Annales de la SocitPolonaise de Mathmatique **19**, 230–231 (1946)

18. Schapire, R.E.: The boosting approach to machine learning: an overview. In: Denison, D.D., Hansen, M.H., Holmes, C.C., Mallick, B., Yu, B. (eds.) Nonlinear Estimation and Classification. LNS, vol. 171, pp. 149–171. Springer, New York (2003)

19. Schapire, R.E.: A Short Introduction to Boosting (1999)

20. UCI Repository. http://www.ics.uci.edu/mlearn/databases

21. Zhou, Z.-H.: Boosting 25 years, CCL 2014 Keynote (2014)

22. Zhou, Z.-H.: Ensemble Methods: Foundations and Algorithms, p. 23. Chapman and Hall/CRC (2012). ISBN: 978-1439830031. The term boosting refers to a family of algorithms that are able to convert weak learners to strong learners

A Method for Solving the Time Fractional Heat Conduction Inverse Problem Based on Ant Colony Optimization and Artificial Bee Colony Algorithms

Rafał Brociek and Damian Słota[⊠]

Institute of Mathematics, Silesian University of Technology,
Kaszubska 23, 44-100 Gliwice, Poland
damian.slota@polsl.pl

Abstract. The paper presents an application of ant colony optimization and artificial bee colony algorithms to solve the inverse heat conduction problem of fractional order. In a given fractional heat conduction model, one of the parameters – thermal conductivity coefficient is missing. With output of the model - temperature measurements, functional defining error of approximate solution is created. In order to reconstruct thermal conductivity coefficient we apply swarm intelligence algorithms to minimize created functional.

Keywords: Fractional heat conduction equation · Artificial bee colony algorithm · Ant colony algorithm · Inverse problem

1 Introduction

Ant colony optimization and artificial bee colony algorithms are swarm intelligence algorithms which can be used to deal with optimization problems. They are inspired by behavior of swarm of ants and bees, which are regarded as intelligent community. Generally, swarm intelligence algorithms have a wide range of applications [1–7].

In this paper, we deal with fractional heat conduction inverse problem. Considered model contains differential equation with fractional derivative. Fractional differential equations can be used to model phenomena of subdiffusion or superdiffusion, for example, the process of heat conduction in porous media [8]. More about fractional calculus and fractional differential equations can be found in [9–11]. Ismailov and Cicek [12] considered an inverse problem of determining a time-dependent source term in a one-dimensional time-fractional diffusion equation from the energy measurement. They proved that the considered inverse problem has a uniqueness solution. Dou and Hon [13] presented a kernel based approximation technique and an efficient and accurate numerical scheme to solve a backward space-time fractional diffusion problem. They used Caputo fractional derivative. The authors in their computation used fast inverse Fourier transform. They also gave a numerical verification of the proposed method. Chen et al. [14] presented an algorithm to solve an inverse problem for identifying the fractional derivative indices in a two-dimensional space-fractional nonlocal model based on a generalization of the two-sided Riemann–Liouville

© Springer International Publishing AG 2017
R. Damaševičius and V. Mikašytė (Eds.): ICIST 2017, CCIS 756, pp. 351–361, 2017.
DOI: 10.1007/978-3-319-67642-5_29

formulation with variable diffusivity coefficients. First, the authors presented an algorithm for solving a direct problem, and discussed the stability and convergence of the presented method. In order to solve an inverse problem a fast bi-conjugate gradient stabilized method was used. They also applied the Levenberg–Marquardt regularization technique combined with the Armijo rule. In the end, a numerical example is presented. Also, the authors of this paper dealt with inverse problem of fractional order [2, 15]. For example, in [2] a heat transfer coefficient in time fractional diffusion equation is reconstructed. To minimize the functional defining the error of approximate solution, the Nelder-Mead algorithm was used. Various applications of bio inspired solutions can be found in the literature. In [20], these approaches were used to simulate dynamic object over time interval. In [21], an imf demixing method was based on some intelligent algorithm. Similarly, other sounds can be processed, i.e. for classification from the voice samples by the use of Gabor filter [22]. It is also presented that these methodologies can benefit from devoted processing based on latest technology for parallel computing [23].

This paper is organized as follows. In Sect. 2 we present a model – time fractional heat conduction equation with Neumann and Robin boundary conditions. We considered fractional derivative defined in the sense of Caputo. The inverse problem consists of determining thermal conductivity coefficient based on temperature measurements. The problem under consideration is reduced to the optimization problem. A short description of finding a solution of direct problem is presented in Sect. 3. More about solution of direct problem can be found in [16]. In order to solve the optimization problem two algorithms were implemented and compared – Artificial Bee Colony algorithm [17] and a parallel version of the Ant Colony Optimization algorithm [18]. Section 4 presents a numerical example with conclusions.

2 Formulation of the Problem

Consider the following time fractional heat conduction equation:

$$c\varrho \frac{\partial^\alpha u(x,t)}{\partial t^\alpha} = \lambda(x)\frac{\partial^2 u(x,t)}{\partial x^2}, \tag{1}$$

where $x \in [0, L_x]$, $t \in [0, T]$ and c, ϱ, λ denote specific heat, density and thermal conductivity coefficient. We also add an initial-boundary conditions, respectively

$$u(x, 0) = f(x), \quad x \in [0, L_x],$$
$$-\lambda(0)\frac{\partial u(0,t)}{\partial x} = q(t), \quad t \in (0, T),$$
$$-\lambda(L_x)\frac{\partial u(L_x,t)}{\partial x} = h(t)(u(L_x, T) - u^\infty), \quad t \in (0, t^*).$$

Function f defines the initial condition, when heat flux q, heat transfer coefficient h and ambient temperature u^∞ specifies boundary conditions of second and third kind. Fractional derivative occurring in the left-hand of Eq. (1) is defined in Caputo sense as follows (for $\alpha \in (0, 1)$):

$$\frac{\partial^\alpha u(x,t)}{\partial t^\alpha} = \frac{1}{\Gamma(1-\alpha)} \int_0^t \frac{\partial u(x,s)}{\partial s}(t-s)^{-\alpha}\,ds, \qquad (2)$$

where Γ is the Gamma function.

In the presented model, we determine the thermal conductivity coefficient λ as quadratic polynomial:

$$\lambda(x) = a_2 x^2 + a_1 x + a_0. \qquad (3)$$

Additional information, which we have to find parameters a_0, a_1, a_2, are temperature measurements in selected points of the considered region. Considered inverse problem consists of restoring the parameters a_i (and therefore thermal conductivity coefficient). Additional information about temperature measurements (values of function u) at selected points inside considered region (x_i, t_k) is called input data and denoted by:

$$u(x_i, t_k) = \widehat{U}_{ik}, \quad i = 1, 2, \ldots, N_1, \quad k = 1, 2, \ldots, N_2,$$

where N_1 is the number of measurement points and N_2 denotes the number of measurements at each point. Solving the direct problem for fixed values of the coefficients a_i, we obtain values approximating function u in selected points (x_i, t_k). These values will be denoted by $U_{ik}(\lambda)$. Therefore, based on this computation and input data, we create functional defining the error of approximate solution:

$$F(\lambda) = \sum_{i=1}^{N_1} \sum_{k=1}^{N_2} \left(U_{ik}(\lambda) - \widehat{U}_{ik} \right)^2. \qquad (4)$$

The inverse problem is transformed into an optimization problem. By minimizing the functional (4), we determine thermal conductivity coefficient in the form (3).

3   Description of Algorithms

In order to solve the inverse problem, first we need to find numerical solution of the direct problem. Using finite difference method, approximation of boundary conditions and Caputo fractional derivative to Eq. (1), we derive numerical scheme of considered equation. More details about numerical solution of the direct problem can be found in [16].

In this section, we focus on the description of Ant Colony Optimization (ACO) and Artificial Bee Colony (ABC) optimization algorithms. Let us start from describing a parallel version of the ACO algorithm. We use the following notations:

F	– minimized function,
nT	– number of threads,
$M = nT \cdot p$	– number of ants $(p \in \mathbb{Z})$,
L	– number of pheromone spots,
I	– number of iterations,
$\xi = 1.0, q = 0.9$	– parameters of the algorithm.

Below, we present a step-form of the parallel version of the ACO algorithm.

ACO algorithm

Initialization of the algorithm

1. Setting parameters of the algorithm L, M, I, nT.
2. Generating L pheromone spots (solutions) at random and creating the initial archive T_0.
3. Computing values of minimized function for every pheromone spot (solution) and ordering elements in T_0, according to their qualities (descending).

Iterative process

4. Assigning the probabilities to the pheromone spots (solutions) according to the formula:

$$p_l = \frac{\omega_l}{\sum_{l=1}^{L} \omega_l} \qquad l = 1, 2, ..., L,$$

where ω_l is the weight associated to the l-th solution and expressed by the formula

$$\omega_l = \frac{1}{qL\sqrt{2\pi}} e^{\frac{-(l-1)^2}{2q^2L^2}}.$$

5. The ant chooses the l-th solution according to probabilities p_l.
6. The ant transforms the j-th ($j=1,2, ... , n$) coordinate of the l-th solution s_j^l by sampling the neighborhood by using the probability density function (Gaussian function):

$$g(x, \mu, \sigma) = \frac{1}{\sigma\sqrt{2\pi}} e^{\frac{-(x-\mu)^2}{2\sigma^2}},$$

where $\mu = s_j^l$, $\sigma = \frac{\xi}{L-1}\sum_{p=1}^{L} |s_j^p - s_j^l|$.
7. Steps 5-6 are repeated for each ant. Hence, we obtain M new solutions (pheromone spots).
8. Dividing the population into nT groups (groups are processed in parallel way).
9. Determinating the value of the minimized function for each new solution in population (parallel calculation).
10. Updating the archive T_i.
11. Repeating steps 4-10 I times.

For fixed values of parameters L, M, I, the number of minimized function F evaluations is equal to $L + M \cdot I$.

The second algorithm, which we used to apply to the considered problem, is the ABC algorithm. We use the following notations:

F — minimized function,
SN — number of food sources = number of employed bees, number of onlookers,

MCN – number of iterations,
n – number of sought parameters.

ABC algorithm

1. Setting parameters of the algorithm SN, MCN, n.
2. Generating randomly initial population P (vectors $x^i = \left(x_1^i, x_2^i, ..., x_n^i\right), i = 1, 2, ..., SN$).
3. Calculating the value of the minimized function for every element in P.
4. Modify the location of all food sources according to the formula:

$$v_j^i = x_j^i + \phi_{ij}\left(x_j^i - x_j^k\right),$$

where $j \in \{1, 2, ..., n\}$, $k, i \in \{1, 2, ..., SN\}$ and $k \neq i$ – random index, $\phi_{ij} \in [-1, 1]$ is a random generated number.
5. Comparing x^i with v^i. If $F(v^i) \leq F(x^i)$, then $x^i = v^i$, otherwise the source x^i remains unchanged.
6. Repeat steps 4 and 5 $SN \cdot n$ times.
7. Assign probabilities to all sources x^i according to the formula:

$$p_i = \frac{fit(x^i)}{\sum_{j=1}^{SN} fit(x^j)}, \qquad i = 1, 2, ..., SN,$$

where

$$fit(x^i) = \begin{cases} \dfrac{1}{1 + F(x^i)}, & if \ F(x^i) \geq 0, \\ 1 + \left|F(x^i)\right|, & if \ F(x^i) < 0. \end{cases}$$

8. Each onlooker selects one source in accordance to the probability p_i (some sources may be repeated) and begins its modification in the same way as it was in steps 4 and 5.
9. Choose the best sources (solutions) from existing sources. If it is the best one, we save it, denoted by x^{best}. Otherwise, skip it and remember the previous best solution.
10. If after steps 4 and 5, a bee could not improve the position of the food source (could not find a better solution), then it is abandoned and replaced by a new source specified by the formula:

$$x_j^i = x_{min}^i + \omega_{ij}\left(x_{max}^i - x_{min}^i\right), \quad i = 1, 2, ..., SN,$$

where $\omega_{ij} \in [0, 1]$ is a pseudo-random number.
11. Repeat steps from 4 to 10 MCN times.

For fixed values of parameters SN, MCN, n, the number of function F evaluations is equal to $SN + (SN^2 \cdot n + SN) \cdot MCN$. More about both described algorithms can be found in [17–19].

4 Numerical Verification

Assume the following data in the considered model: $t \in [0, 500], x \in [0, 0.2], c = 1000, \varrho = 2680, \alpha = 0.5, u^\infty = 300, f(x) = 900, q(t) = 0$ and $h(t) = 1400 \exp \left[\frac{t-45}{455} \ln \left(\frac{7}{4} \right) \right]$. Thermal conductivity coefficient λ is sought in the form:

$$\hat{\lambda}(x) = a_2 x^2 + a_1 x + a_0,$$

while the exact value of λ is $100 + 400 \sin(15t)$. By finding parameters a_0, a_1, a_2 we reconstruct λ. Solving the direct problem for exact λ, we obtain values of temperature (values of function u) at selected points of grid created in finite difference method. Then, from these values, we select only those corresponding to the predetermined grid points (location of the thermocouple). These values simulate temperature measurements. They are input data $\widehat{U}_{ik}$ and were generated in grid 300×5000. In order to avoid inverse crime problem, the grid used in the algorithm to reconstruct λ was of size 100×1000.

Additionally, we assume one measurement point $x_p = 0.5 (N_1 = 1)$, the measurements from this point are taken every 0.5 s and 1 s $(N_2 = 1001, 501)$. In order to investigate the effect of measurement errors on stability of the proposed method and the results of reconstruction, the input data were perturbed by the pseudo-random error of sizes 1 and 2%.

To find the minimum of functional (4), we use and compare two algorithms, namely ABC and ACO. Both algorithms are heuristic, therefore it is required to repeat calculations a certain number of times. In this paper, we assumed that the calculations for each case will be repeated ten times. In these algorithms, we assume the following data:

ABC

$SN = 5, MCN = 4, n = 3,$
$a_0 \in [0, 150], a_1 \in [7500, 8500], a_2 \in [-39000, -37500].$

ACO

$L = 8, M = 12, I = 25, nT = 4,$
$a_0 \in [0, 150], a_1 \in [7500, 8500], a_2 \in [-39000, -37500].$

The data for the algorithms were chosen to compare algorithms, the number of function evaluations in both algorithms is similar. For ABC it is equal to 325, and for ACO it is equal to 308. Additionally, ACO is adopted to parallel computing.

Tables 1 and 2 present results of determining a_0, a_1, a_2 depending on the size of perturbation input data for measurements every 0.5 s and 1 s. The error of reconstruction function λ is defined in the following form:

$$Err = \sqrt{\frac{\int_0^{0.2} \left| \lambda(x) - \hat{\lambda}(x) \right|^2 dx}{\int_0^{0.2} |\lambda(x)|^2 dx}} \cdot 100\%.$$

Both algorithms give similar results, particularly in case of measurements every 0.5 s. Errors of reconstruction function λ are approximately 4.80% (exact input data), 5.30% (1% perturbed input data) and 17% (2% perturbed input data). We must remember that the exact function of the coefficient λ was in the form of a trigonometric function, while the sought function was in the form of a polynomial. The difference in errors of reconstruction function λ can be seen in the case of one-second measurements. However, the values of the minimized function F are almost equal in both algorithms

Table 1. Results of calculation in case of measurements every 0.5 s ($\overline{a}_i$ – restored value of a_i (i = 0, 1, 2), σ^p – ratio of standard deviation to the best solution, F(x) – value of minimized function, Err – error of reconstruction λ)

Noise	$\overline{a}_i$	$|\sigma^p|$	$F(x)$	$Err[\%]$	$\overline{a}_i$	$|\sigma^p|$	$F(x)$	$Err[\%]$
	ACO				ABC			
0%	51,24	0.344	0.721	4.82	51.32	0.303	0.722	4.80
	7992,89	0.022			7993.22	0.013		
	−37500	0.015			−37500	0.008		
1%	48.09	0.292	8329.37	5.23	47.65	0.126	8329.40	5.38
	8013.29	0.020			8007.59	0.009		
	−37521.84	0.014			−37504.55	0.006		
2%	0	-	33414.78	17.00	0.05	-	33414.86	16.98
	8012.98	0.013			8013.55	0.012		
	−37500	0.009			−37500	0.009		

Table 2. Results of calculation in case of measurements every 1 s ($\overline{a}_i$ – restored value of a_i (i = 0, 1, 2), σ^p – ratio of standard deviation to the best solution, F(x) – value of minimized function, Err – error of reconstruction λ)

Noise	$\overline{a}_i$	$|\sigma^p|$	$F(x)$	$Err[\%]$	$\overline{a}_i$	$|\sigma^p|$	$F(x)$	$Err[\%]$
	ACO				ABC			
0%	41.76	0.332	0.629	5.64	51.29	0.187	0.361	4.81
	8117.84	0.016			7993.06	0.010		
	−37908.91	0.011			−37500.13	0.007		
1%	28.86	0.398	4313.00	5.89	42.45	0.300	4313.24	4.53
	8436.37	0.015			8293.22	0.011		
	−39000	0.010			−38532.90	0.008		
2%	51.36	0.274	17042.05	6.08	53.18	0.245	17042.10	5.69
	7921.98	0.020			7918.99	0.017		
	−37506.62	0.013			−37503.30	0.011		

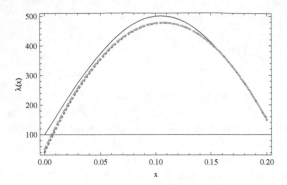

Fig. 1. Plots of exact (solid line) and reconstructed (red line - ACO, green line - ABC) thermal conductivity coefficient λ in case of the 0% input data perturbation. (Color figure online)

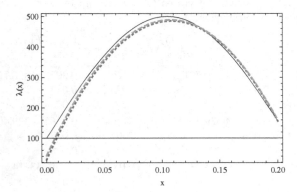

Fig. 2. Plots of exact (solid line) and reconstructed (red line - ACO, green line - ABC) thermal conductivity coefficient λ in case of the 1% input data perturbation. (Color figure online)

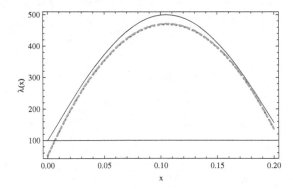

Fig. 3. Plots of exact (solid line) and reconstructed (red line - ACO, green line - ABC) thermal conductivity coefficient λ in case of the 2% input data perturbation. (Color figure online)

(except one case where the ACO algorithm gives a little bit smaller values of the minimized function F).

In the Figs. 1, 2 and 3, we can see plots of reconstructed and exact function λ. As we can see plots of reconstructed λ function fit to the plot of exact λ function, especially in case of 0% and 1% input data. Both algorithms give similar results.

The most important criterion for evaluating the obtained results are errors of temperature reconstruction in the measurement point. Tables 3 and 4 present such errors. In each case, the temperature in measurement point is reconstructed very good. The relative error is small enough and does not exceed 0.09%. Both algorithms give similar results. However, we should note that the ACO algorithm is adapted for multithreads computation, so the calculation time is shorter in case of the ACO algorithm.

Table 3. Errors of temperature reconstruction in measurement point $x_p = 0.5$ in case of measurements every 0.5 s (Δ_{avg} – average absolute error, Δ_{max} – maximal absolute error, δ_{avg} – average relative error, δ_{max} – maximal relative error)

Noise	0%		1%		2%	
	ACO	ABC	ACO	ABC	ACO	ABC
$\Delta_{avg}[K]$	0.0235	0.0234	0.1111	0.1101	0.3978	0.2204
$\Delta_{max}[K]$	0.0626	0.0643	0.1818	0.1773	0.7618	0.4823
$\delta_{avg}[\%]$	0.0026	0.0026	0.0126	0.0125	0.0458	0.0250
$\delta_{max}[\%]$	0.0073	0.0075	0.0206	0.0201	0.0891	0.0539

Table 4. Errors of temperature reconstruction in measurement point $x_p = 0.5$ in case of measurements every 1 s (Δ_{avg} – average absolute error, Δ_{max} – maximal absolute error, δ_{avg} – average relative error, δ_{max} – maximal relative error)

Noise	0%		1%		2%	
	ACO	ABC	ACO	ABC	ACO	ABC
$\Delta_{avg}[K]$	0.0311	0.0232	0.0694	0.0687	0.2228	0.4030
$\Delta_{max}[K]$	0.0792	0.0666	0.1935	0.1835	0.4826	0.7659
$\delta_{avg}[\%]$	0.0035	0.0026	0.0079	0.0079	0.0253	0.0464
$\delta_{max}[\%]$	0.0092	0.0077	0.0226	0.0214	0.0540	0.0896

Acknowledgement. Publication supported within the framework of grants in the area of scientific research and developmental works founded by Rector of the Silesian University of Technology, 09/010/RGJ17/0020.

References

1. Birvinskas, D., Jusas, V., Martisius, I., Damasevicius, R.: Data compression of EEG signals for artificial neural network classification. Inf. Technol. Control **42**, 238–241 (2013)
2. Brociek, R., Słota, D.: Reconstruction of the boundary condition for the heat conduction equation of fractional order. Therm. Sci. **19**, 35–42 (2015)
3. Das, R., Akay, B., Singla, R.K., Singh, K.: Application of artificial bee colony algorithm for inverse modelling of a solar collector. Inverse Probl. Sci. Eng. **25**, 887–908 (2017)
4. Hetmaniok, E., Słota, D., Zielonka, A.: Parallel procedure based on the swarm intelligence for solving the two-dimensional inverse problem of binary alloy solidification. In: Wyrzykowski, R., Deelman, E., Dongarra, J., Karczewski, K., Kitowski, J., Wiatr, K. (eds.) PPAM 2015. LNCS, vol. 9574, pp. 287–297. Springer, Cham (2016). doi:10.1007/978-3-319-32152-3_27
5. Hetmaniok, E.: Inverse problem for the solidification of binary alloy in the casting mould solved by using the bee optimization algorithm. Heat Mass Transf. **52**, 1369–1379 (2016)
6. Jafrasteh, B., Fathianpour, N.: A hybrid simultaneous perturbation artificial bee colony and back-propagation algorithm for training a local linear radial basis neural network on ore grade estimation. Neurocomputing **235**, 217–227 (2017)
7. Woźniak, M., Połap, D., Napoli, C., Tramontana, E.: Graphic object feature extraction system based on cuckoo search algorithm. Expert Syst. Appl. **66**, 20–31 (2016). doi:10.1016/j.eswa.2016.08.068. Elsevier
8. Obrączka A., Kowalski J.: Modeling the distribution of heat in the ceramic materials using fractional differential equations. In: Szczygieł, M. (eds.) Materiały XV Jubileuszowego Sympozjum "Podstawowe Problemy Energoelektroniki, Elektromechaniki i Mechatroniki", PPEEm 2012. Archiwum Konferencji PTETiS, Komitet Organizacyjny Sympozjum PPEE i Seminarium BSE, vol. 32, pp. 133–132 (2012). (in polish)
9. Das, S.: Functional Fractional Calculus for System Identification and Controls. Springer, Berlin (2008)
10. Klafter, J., Lim, S., Metzler, R.: Fractional Dynamics: Resent Advances. World Scientific, New Jersey (2012)
11. Podlubny, I.: Fractional Differential Equations. Academic Press, San Diego (1999)
12. Ismailov, M.I., Cicek, M.: Inverse source problem for a time-fractional diffusion equation with nonlocal boundary conditions. Appl. Math. Model. **40**, 4891–4899 (2016)
13. Dou, F.F., Hon, Y.C.: Fundamental kernel-based method for backward space-time fractional diffusion problem. Comput. Math. Appl. **71**, 356–367 (2016)
14. Chen, S., Liu, F., Jiang, X., Turner, I., Burrage, K.: Fast finite difference approximation for identifying parameters in a two-dimensional space-fractional nonlocal model with variable diffusivity coefficients. SIAM J. Numer. Anal. **56**, 606–624 (2016)
15. Brociek, R., Słota, D.: Application and comparison of intelligent algorithms to solve the fractional heat conduction inverse problem. Inf. Technol. Control **45**, 184–194 (2016)
16. Brociek, R.: Implicit finite difference method for time fractional diffusion equations with mixed boundary conditions. Zesz. Nauk. Politech. Śląskiej Matemat. Stosow. **4**, 73–87 (2014)
17. Karaboga, D., Akay, B.: A comparative study of artificial bee colony algorithm. Appl. Math. Comput. **214**, 108–132 (2009)
18. Socha, K., Dorigo, M.: Ant Colony Optimization in continuous domains. Eur. J. Oper. Res. **185**, 1155–1173 (2008)
19. Karaboga, D.: Basturk B,: A powerful and efficient algorithm for numerical function optimization: artificial bee colony (ABC) algorithm. J. Global Optim. **39**, 459–471 (2007)

20. Woźniak, M., Połap, D.: Hybrid neuro-heuristic methodology for simulation and control of dynamic systems over time interval. Neural Netw. (2017). doi:10.1016/j.neunet.2017.04.013. Elsevier

21. Damaševičius, R., Napoli, C., Sidekerskiene, T., Woźniak, M.: IMF mode demixing in EMD for jitter analysis. J. Comput. Sci. (2017). doi:10.1016/j.jocs.2017.04.008. Elsevier

22. Połap, D., Woźniak, M.: Voice recognition through the use of Gabor transform and heuristic algorithm. Int. J. Electron. Telecommun. **63**(2), 159–164 (2017). doi:10.1515/eletel-2017-0021. De Gruyter Open Ltd

23. Woźniak, M., Połap, D.: On the manipulation of the initial population search space in heuristic algorithms through the use of parallel processing approach. In: Proceedings of the IEEE Symposium Series on Computational Intelligence – SSCI 2016, December 6–9 Athens, Greece (2016). doi:10.1109/SSCI.2016.7850033

Automated Scheduling for Tightly-Coupled Embedded Multi-core Systems Using Hybrid Genetic Algorithms

Pedro Cuadra[✉], Lukas Krawczyk, Robert Höttger, Philipp Heisig,
and Carsten Wolff

Institute for Digital Transformation of Application and Living Domains (IDiAL),
Dortmund University of Applied Sciences and Arts,
Otto-Hahn-Str. 23, 44227 Dortmund, Germany
pedro.cuadrachamorro001@stud.fh-dortmund.de
http://www.idial.institute

Abstract. Deploying software to embedded multi- and many-core hardware has become increasingly complex in the past years. Due to the heterogeneous nature of embedded systems and the complex underlying Network on Chip structures of many-core architectures, aspects such as the runtime of executable software are highly influenced by a variety of factors, e.g. the type, instruction set, and speed of the processor an executable is allocated to as well as its predecessors, their location, ordering and the communication channels in between them. In this work, we propose a semi-automated Hybrid Genetic Algorithm based optimization approach for distributing and re-scheduling executional software to heterogeneous hardware architectures in constrained solution spaces, along with an evaluation of its applicability and efficiency. The evaluation is based on both, publicly available as well as real world examples of automotive engine management systems.

Keywords: Hybrid Genetic Algorithms · Many-core · Automotive

1 Introduction

Nowadays, most of the innovation achieved within the automotive domain is driven by software. For instance, cars in 2014 already featured over 100 million lines of code and had the computing power of 20 PCs [10], which required over 100 Electronic Control Unit (ECU)s. Since then, the complexity increases even further, demanding more and more computation power that can only be addressed by multi- and many-core hardware.

One of the challenges in developing embedded multi- and many-core systems is the deployment process, which combines challenges from different domains.

The research leading to these results has received funding from the Federal Ministry for Education and Research (BMBF) under Grant 01|S14029K in the context of the ITEA3 EU-Project AMALTHEA4public.

© Springer International Publishing AG 2017
R. Damaševičius and V. Mikašytė (Eds.): ICIST 2017, CCIS 756, pp. 362–373, 2017.
DOI: 10.1007/978-3-319-67642-5_30

In terms of multi- and many-core, it is necessary to allocate various elements of the software (executables, data, and communications) to hardware components (processing units, memories, and communication channels), while maintaining constraints such as deadlines or the order of execution.

From an embedded point of view, the allocation target usually contains a heterogeneous architecture that consists of processing units (e.g. cores) with a variety of instruction sets and frequencies, multiple communication paths to and from peripherals, and a mixture of shared and distributed memories. Due to their heterogeneous nature, finding valid allocations can become a challenging task, as e.g. allocating data to a single shared memory may result in unnecessary bottlenecks in the same manner as distributing shared data among distributed memories, which would instead increase the overhead on the communication network. Consequently, the satisfaction of constraints highly depends on the allocation decisions, which are well-known to be NP-complete.

To support this process, proper tooling has to be utilized. Such tooling, with focus on supporting the development of automotive embedded systems, is provided by the open-source Eclipse Project APP4MC [2]. It allows creating customized tool chains by providing interfaces for both open source as well as proprietary tools and supports a semi-automated artifact exchange. We extended the platforms deployment functionality [9] with a customized Hybrid Genetic Algorithm (HGA) [7] for distributing executable software to multi- and many-core hardware platforms while optimizing the overall execution time in due consideration of all communication overheads.

Genetic Algorithms (GAs) are a specific class of evolutionary algorithms and have several disadvantages, such as an extensive search space, slow convergence speed, and they tend to be easily trapped in local optima. To address the later downside, this work implements an Hybrid Genetic Algorithm (HGA) that is constructed by adding Simulated Annealing (SA) to a standard GA. As a result, the HGAs convergence speed is enhanced by decreasing the probability of accepting worse result over time, which allows it to escape local optima [7]. As an evolution over [7], our approach is designed to consider both the load balance across the processors as well as the communication overhead in between them.

This paper is organized as follows. Section 2 discusses related work, followed by a detailed description of our proposed HGA based software distribution algorithm in Sect. 3. It provides details about the problem definition and implementation, such as the chromosome encoding, fitness function, operators and the simulated annealing process. Our experimental evaluation of the approach is presented in Sect. 4. Finally, a conclusion along with a further outlook on future work closes this paper in Sect. 5.

2   Related Work

Over the past years, a large amount of approaches using various techniques, such as GA, Integer Lintear Programing (ILP), or Ant Colony Optimization (ACO) have been developed and published for scheduling and allocating software to multi- any many-core hardware.

The paper [13] introduces a heuristic called Combined dynamic BLevel (CBL) for non-preemptive task scheduling solutions that minimizes the schedule length of a application. While it considers communication overheads as well as heterogeneous architectures, the authors did not mention the applicability of this approach regarding its scalability or runtime for optimizing real-world scenarios.

Another heuristic is presented in [12], which proposes a task scheduling algorithm based on the HEFT approach to maximize the performance on heterogeneous systems. The algorithm considers the effect of heterogeneity and performs especially well on systems with large numbers of communicated messages.

The work in [4] targets the softwares performance and is realized as a two stage based ACO algorithm for scheduling tasks in heterogeneous embedded systems. Due to the nature of ACO, the approach performs well on a large search space of hard NP-complete problems.

The paper [3] proposes an algorithm, which uses SA to minimize the communication costs between `Runnables` in an AUTOSAR framework. The algorithm effectively finds a schedule with minimal communication overhead and also proposes a refinement approach that attempts to merge the tasks, which communicate among each other and are allocated on the same core to reduce the communication cost between the resp. `Runnables`.

3   Hybrid GA

The implementation of our HGA, which has been implemented as a `Jenetics`' [11] evolution stream, is shown in Algorithm 1. It should be noted that the mutation and crossover operations can be undone if the SA criteria are not fulfilled. The implementation of the mentioned genetic alterers internally check the SA criteria and update the individual if passed.

Data: P, G, p_m, p_c
Result: Best fitness chromosome
initialize random population of size P;
set $g = 1$;
while $g \leq G$ **do**
> compute fitness of each individual;
> $O, S = rouletteWheel(generations[g])$;
> **foreach** *individual ind of O* **do**
>> mutate with probability, p_m;
>> crossover with probability, p_c;
>
> **end**
> $g = g + 1$;
> $generations[g] = merge(O, S)$;

end

Algorithm 1. Genetic Algorithm factory [7]

3.1   Problem Definition

Let $R = \{\rho_1, \rho_2, \ldots, \rho_m\}$ denote the computing resources available in the Heterogeneous Computing Environment (HCE), with m being the maximum number of resources. Similarly, let $T = \{\tau_1, \tau_2, \ldots, \tau_n\}$ denote the tasks to be scheduled to run on $\rho_k \in R \mid k = 0 \ldots, k \leq n$, with n being the maximum number of tasks to schedule.

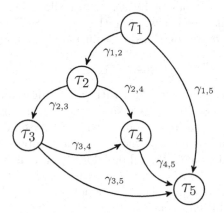

Fig. 1. Exemplary DAG definition consisting of five tasks and their interdependencies

Given a Directed Acyclic Graph (DAG) $G = (V, E)$, with $V = \{v_1, v_2, \ldots, v_n\}$ being the vertex set and E the edge set with edges (v_i, v_j), v_i being the source vertex and v_j the destination vertex. For representing a set of tasks and their dependencies as a DAG let $V = T$ and E denote the set of inter-task dependencies. Since the only type of dependencies considered in our work are inter-task dependencies, we'll refer to them as task dependencies or only dependencies. Figure 1 shows a DAG representation of a task set with task dependencies. The edges of the graph in Fig. 1 are annotated with the communication cost $\gamma_{i,j}$, i.e. the cost of communicating the data that τ_j needs and τ_i generates. Equation 1 shows the definition of the communication cost matrix C.

$$C = [\gamma_{i,j}]_{n \times n} \mid \forall \gamma_{i,j} \neq 0 \tag{1}$$

The dependency matrix is defined using E in Eq. 2. Task's dependencies also denote its precedence constraints, meaning that this task can't start executing until all the tasks on which it depends are finished.

$$D = [\delta_{i,j}]_{n \times n} \mid \delta_{i,j} = \begin{cases} 1 & (i, j) \in E \\ 0 & otherwise \end{cases} \tag{2}$$

Communication costs matrix and dependency matrix can be merged together given the fact that the existence of communication between tasks denote explicit dependencies. It was decided to keep them separate to consider the case where no communication exists between τ_i and τ_j while a precedence constraint exists.

$$\Pi = \{T, R, S, D, \Gamma(C, \Omega), \Omega\} \tag{3}$$

Our work is focused on obtaining an optimal schedule Π as defined in Eq. 3, with S being the Expected Time to Compute (ETC) matrix, Ω the allocation matrix and Γ a transform operation performed on the communication costs matrix to modify its elements taking the given allocation into account. S, Ω, and Γ are further explained below. Note that T, R, S, D and C are constants; and $\Gamma(C, \Omega)$, Ω vary from one schedule solution to another depending on the given allocation Ω.

$$S = [\sigma_{i,j}]_{n \times m} \tag{4}$$

The ETC matrix is defined in Eq. 4 with $\sigma_{i,k}$ being the total execution time of τ_i when executed in ρ_k. Our work assumes pre-calculation of the ETC values for each task in each computing resource, these could be done by profiling the tasks or running a simulation using models of the computing resources.

Let $A = T \times R$ denote the set of all possible allocations of tasks to computing resources. Then $\tau_i \mapsto \rho_k = a_{i,k} \mid a_{i,k} \in A$, denotes the allocation of task τ_i to computing resource ρ_k. Now, let $A_\Pi \subset A$, denotes the set allocations comprising a possible schedule solution defined in Eq. 5

$$A_\Pi = \{\alpha_{0,k_0}, \alpha_{1,k_1}, \ldots, \alpha_{n,k_n}\} \mid k_i \in \{0, 1, \ldots, m\} \tag{5}$$

Using the matrix representation of A_Π, the allocation matrix can be defined as in Eq. 6.

$$\Omega = [\omega_{i,k}]_{n \times m} \mid \omega_{i,k} = \begin{cases} 1 & \tau_i \mapsto \rho_k \in A_\Pi \\ 0 & otherwise \end{cases} \tag{6}$$

The Γ transform operation in Eq. 7 sets the communication costs to zero if two tasks are allocated to the same computing resource.

$$\Gamma(C, \Omega) = [\gamma'_{i,j}]_{n \times n} \mid \gamma'_{i,j} = \begin{cases} 0 & \tau_i \mapsto \rho_k, \tau_j \mapsto \rho_k \in A_\Pi \\ \gamma_{i,j} & otherwise \end{cases} \tag{7}$$

For a schedule Π, its makespan MS can be calculated using Eq. 8. Makespan stands for the total execution time of a given schedule, taking into account communications as shown in Eq. 9 with $FT(\tau_i)$ being the finish time of task i.

$$MS(\Pi) = \max(FT(\tau_1), \ldots, FT(\tau_n)) \tag{8}$$

$$FT(\tau_i) = \max\left(FT(\tau_j) + \sum_{k=1}^{n_r} \sigma_{i,k} \cdot \omega_{i,k} + \gamma'_{i,j} \mid \forall \tau_j \in preds(\tau_i)\right) \tag{9}$$

The load balancing is performed using the standard deviation calculated in Eq. 10 using the makespans per computing resource as defined in Eq. 11.

$$\sigma(\Pi) = \sqrt{\frac{1}{n_r - 1} \sum_{k=1}^{n_r} (MS_k(\Pi) - \overline{MS_k(\Pi)})^2} \tag{10}$$

$$MS_k(\Pi_s) = \max(FT(\tau_i) \mid \forall \tau_i \mid (\tau_i \mapsto \rho_k) \in A_\Pi) \tag{11}$$

Chromosome Encoding. The chromosome encoding is needed to represent a temporal running sequence of the tasks. Therefore, the encoding shown in Fig. 2 is used as in [7]. Each gene comprises of a task and the resource to which it is allocated to. The gene's sequence represents the temporal running sequence of the tasks.

τ_1	τ_2	τ_3	$\cdots$	τ_n
ρ_{τ_1}	ρ_{τ_2}	ρ_{τ_3}	$\cdots$	ρ_{τ_n}

Fig. 2. Chromosome Encoding used for describing the running sequence and resource allocation

The chromosomes are randomly created as stated in Algorithm 2.
Data: One list per topological level with all tasks in the corresponding level
Result: Random chromosome
get maximum topological level l_{max};
set $l = 0$;
while $l = l + 1 \leq l_{max}$ **do**
    get topological level list, T_l;
    while T_l *is not empty* **do**
        shuffle T_l;
        $\tau_i = T_l[0]$;
        select random resource, ρ_k;
        create gene, g, with $\{\tau_i, \rho_k\}$;
        push g to chromosome sequence;
        remove τ_i form T_l;
    end
end

Algorithm 2. Chromosomes factory [7]

The topological level of a task is given by the maximum numbers of vertices of every possible path between all source vertices (vertices without incoming edges) and the task's vertex. By definition, a source vertex has topological level 1, while the maximum topological level is given by maximum number of vertices of all possible paths.

3.2 Optimization Approach

Fitness Function. The fitness function in Eqs. 12–14 combines load balancing and makespan functions from [1], but also factors in the communication overhead in the schedule sequence; replacing the load balancing function with the standard deviation of the makespans of the computing resources as calculated in Eq. 10.

$$f_T(\Pi_s) = \alpha \cdot f_l(\Pi_s) + (1 - \alpha) \cdot f_e(\Pi_s) \tag{12}$$

$$f_l(\Pi_s) = \sigma_{MS_k}(\Pi_s) \tag{13}$$

$$f_e = MS(\Pi_s) \tag{14}$$

Crossover inherits "characteristics" or "genes" by an offspring from its parents by combing the genes from both parent chromosomes to produce one or more offsprings. Our paper uses an improved Single-point crossover which eliminates the possibility of an invalid offspring. The crossover point is selected so that the tasks across the crossover site have the same topological levels. The implementation of our mutation algorithm is shown in Algorithm 3.

> **Data:** C_1, C_2
> **Result:** C_1', C_2'
> select random crossover site, g_c;
> **if** $topoLevel(g_c) == topoLevel(g_{c-1})$ **then**
> > $C_1' = C_1$;
> > $C_2' = C_2$;
> > swap C_1' and C_2' genes sequence from g_c and on;
> > **if** $not\ checkSACriteria(C_1, C_1')$ **then**
> > > $C_1' = C_1$;
> >
> > **end**
> > **if** $not\ checkSACriteria(C_2, C_2')$ **then**
> > > $C_2' = C_2$;
> >
> > **end**
>
> **end**

Algorithm 3. Crossover operation

Mutation. This paper's mutation operator is inherited from the single point mutation in [7]. However, the gene is not randomly mutated and the task at the mutation point is interchanged with another task at the same topological level. This ensures a valid solution after every mutation, though the probability of retaining it is decided by the simulated annealing criteria. Although mutation is vital to a genetic algorithm to maintain genetic diversity across generations, the mutation probability should be kept low. If set too high, the search will turn into a random search. The implementation of our mutation algorithm is shown in Algorithm 4.

Data: C
Result: C'
get topological level task list, T_l, of random level, l;
$T_s = shuffle(T_l)$;
get locus in C of $T_s[0]$, l_0;
get locus in C of $T_s[1]$, l_1;
$C' = C$;
swap C''s genes in l_0 and l_1;
if *not checkSACriteria(C, C')* then
$\quad | \quad C' = C$;
end

Algorithm 4. Mutation operation

Simulated Annealing is inspired by annealing in metallurgy, which is based on the principle that slow cooling of a molten solid results in large crystals with less structural defects. Simulated annealing interprets slow cooling as a slow decrease in the probability of accepting worse solutions as it explores the solution space. A fundamental property of such meta-heuristics is accepting even worse solutions, thus allowing the algorithm to 'go with a leap' through a more extensive search for the global optimum.

In this paper, we combine GA with the principle of another randomized meta-heuristic, i.e. SA, to equip the algorithm with a higher probability of avoiding the local optimum trap. This heuristic ensures that after every genetic alteration, the new solutions are first screened through an acceptance criteria and only inserted into the genetic pool. The worse solutions are also accepted to avoid a local optimum trap and converge faster with better results.

Data: Old chromosome, C_{old}, new chromosomes, C_{new}
Result: SA criteria fulfillment
Set an initial temperature $T_k = T_0$;
Compute fitness value of old and new chromosomes;
if $f(C_{new}) > f(C_{old})$ then
$\quad |$ SA criteria fulfilled;
end
generate a random number r such that $r \in [0], [1]$;
if $\min\{1, \exp[-(f(C_{old}) - f(C_{new}))/T_k]\} > r$ then
$\quad | \quad T_{k+1} = \beta * T_k, k \to k+1$. Where, $\beta \in [0], [1]$;
$\quad |$ SA criteria fulfilled;
else
$\quad |$ SA criteria unfulfilled;
end

Algorithm 5. Simulated annealing acceptance criteria [7]

4   Experimental Evaluation

In order to evaluate the efficiency of our proposed HGA w.r.t its runtime as well as the generated outcome we have implemented and integrated it into the software distribution functionality of the APP4MC Plattform [2] and applied it in on the problem models of three unrelated engine control applications with different sizes and levels of difficulty.

The major characteristics of the models are illustrated in Table 1 along with their level of parallelism and the amount of tasks per topological level in Table 3. The evaluation results for applying our HGA are shown in Table 2. All results are based on the average of 5 subsequent runs of the HGA on a Linux PC with 8 GB of RAM and an i7-3632QM CPU with up to 3.20 GHz. The algorithm is configured to evolve over 10000 Generations, with a mutation probability of 0.01%, crossover probability of 0.50%, and a population size of 15. Moreover, it is set to an initial temperature of 900 and a cooling factor of 0.9.

Table 1. Comparison of evaluated engine control applications

Application	Instructions	Labels	Runnables	Tasks
Democar	4260966	71	43	6
FMTV	5814540	10000	1250	21
Industrial	3600000	46929	1297	77

Our first application is based on an re-engineered engine control ECU from the ETAS DemoCar Project [5] and is publicly available as part of the APP4MC platform. It consists of 6 Tasks, 43 Runnables and 71 Labels with a total of 4260966 instructions. It was initially developed to operate on a single-core ECU and, as shown in Table 3, consists completely of sequential Task.

Our second application is publicly available as part of the Formal Methods for Timing Verification (FMTV) Challenge [6] and describes a modern and accordingly more complex engine management system. It consists of 10000 Labels and 1250 Runnables with 5814540 instructions, which are already partitioned into 21 Tasks. Due to its complexity, it is supposed to be executed on a 200 Mhz quad core ECU. Compared to the Democar Example, this application has much potential for concurrent execution in the first topological level (up to 12 concurrently executable tasks). All other tasks are strictly sequential.

Finally, the industrial application is based on a real-world engine control system and consists of 46929 Labels, 1297 Runnables consisting of 3600000 Instructions distributed to 77 Tasks. It provides the highest potential for concurrent execution, having 50 concurrently executable Tasks of the first topological level, while Tasks in other topological levels have a medium to low level of parallelism.

For the evaluation, we have applied our HGA based approach on all application models using three different hardware platform models [8] consisting of one, three, and six cores. The single core hardware platform consists of an single NXP e200z7 core with 300 MHz and is used to illustrate the sequential execution on a single-core hardware platform with no parallelization and inter-core communication. The triple core hardware platform is based on an NXP MPC5777M consisting of two e200z7 cores operating at 300 Mhz and one e200z4 core operating at 200 MHz. Both cores are connected using a High Bandwidth Crossbar Switch. Finally, the hexa-core example consists of two NXP MPC5777M boards which have been connected to each other using a CAN bus.

Table 2. Outcome of evaluated engine control applications

	Democar	FMTV	Industrial
HGA run-time 1 Core (rt1c)	1.68 s	12.83 s	100.76 s
HGA run-time 3 Cores (rt3c)	1.70 s	13.72 s	103.01 s
HGA run-time 6 Cores (rt6c)	1.64 s	14.78 s	106.76 s
Makespan 1 Core (ms1c)	16.53 ms	19.38 ms	14.91 ms
Makespan 3 Cores (ms3c)	16.53 ms	18.56 ms	13.67 ms
Makespan 6 Cores (ms6c)	16.53 ms	18.50 ms	13.61 ms
Max. computing time 1 Core (ct1c)	16.53 ms	19.38 ms	14.91 ms
Max. computing time 3 Cores (ct3c)	11.20 ms	16.65 ms	8.88 ms
Max. computing time 6 Cores (ct6c)	7.47 ms	9.94 ms	4.83 ms

As shown in Table 2, the run-times $rt1c$, $rt3c$, and $rt6c$ for *deploying* the applications on all three hardware platforms were almost constant and only minimally influenced by the hardware attributes, e.g. number of cores. Because of the nature of the HGA and its chromosome encoding, this behavior is expected. On the other hand, we can see that the run-times are highly dependent on the complexity of the software, more specific on the number of Tasks and inter-Task dependencies. The first makes the chromosomes longer and the second increases the operations needed to get valid chromosomes. Both these factors affect directly the computation needed by our HGA.

The makespan values $ms1c$, $ms3c$, and $ms6c$, i.e. the total execution time of a single schedule, for the DemoCar application remains constant along all hardware platforms. This is caused by the strictly sequential nature of the applications Tasks. Since the Industrial and FMTV examples have a slightly greater level of parallelism, the evaluation of their makespan values $ms1c$, $ms3c$, and $ms6c$ shows a constant reduction with an increasing number of cores by up to 4% (FMTV) resp. 8.6% (Industrial). However, this increase is not proportional to the number of cores, due to the sequential Tasks in later topological levels as shown in Table 3. Consequently, a hardware platform with a fast processor for the sequential parts as well as additional (comparable slower) co-processors for the parallel executable parts of the software would likely represent a better suited hardware target for these applications.

Table 3. Concurrently executable Tasks per topological level

Application	1	2	3	4	5	6	7	8	9	10	11	12	13
Democar	1	1	1	1	1	1	-	-	-	-	-	-	-
FMTV	12	1	1	1	1	1	1	1	1	1	-	-	-
Industrial	50	2	2	1	1	1	1	2	5	6	1	3	2

Finally, the max. computing times $ct1c$, $ct3c$, and $ct6c$ illustrate how long the core with the highest utilization on a hardware platform is performing its computations during a single schedule (makespan). Obviously, this value equals the makespan of a single core platform, and should ideally decrease with a rising amount of cores without increasing the makespan. Although all three applications have a high amount of sequential Tasks, our approach is capable of reducing the load by up to 66% (Industrial application) for the core with the highest utilization. Interestingly, it also reduces the highest load by over 54% on the DemoCar application without noticeably increasing its makespan, despite its strictly sequential nature. This is caused by its low number of data transfers as well as the High-Bandwidth Crossbar Switch of the hardware.

5   Conclusion and Future Outlook

In this work we presented a new HGA based approach for deploying executable software to processing hardware components, i.e. cores. We discussed which steps are required to adapt an existing GA and how to enrich it with SA to enhance one of its disadvantages. Our integration to the open-source APP4MC platform, allowed extensive evaluation on three independent engine control examples on three hardware platforms. Our evaluation shows that the approach is indeed capable of creating results in a reasonable short amount of time (≤ 2 minutes) and provides a minor speedup for tightly-coupled software on multi-core platforms while balancing the load among cores and revealing opportunities for further optimizations, e.g. energy minimization.

In the future, we will extend the approach and integrate further optimization goals, such as increasing reliability, reducing memory accesses or a more detailed energy model for lowering the energy consumption. Especially the later would be highly beneficial due to the heterogeneous nature of embedded systems. Moreover, the approach could be further extended to support multi-criteria optimization, which would allow to fine-tune the deployment as well as supporting design space exploration in early development phases. Other important aspects are the degrees of freedom, i.e. the criteria which are altered by the approach. As mentioned in the introduction, the allocation of data to memories as well as communications to channels can be crucial for the execution time. Consequently, we intent to extend our HGA accordingly.

References

1. Alexandrescu, A., Agavriloaei, I., Craus, M.: A genetic algorithm for mapping tasks in heterogeneous computing systems. In: 15th International Conference on System Theory, Control and Computing, pp. 1–6, October 2011
2. Eclipse: App4mc website (2017). http://www.eclipse.org/app4mc/
3. Faragardi, H.R., Lisper, B., Sandström, K., Nolte, T.: An efficient scheduling of autosar runnables to minimize communication cost in multi-core systems. In: 2014 7th International Symposium on Telecommunications (IST), pp. 41–48, September 2014
4. Ferrandi, F., Lanzi, P.L., Pilato, C., Sciuto, D., Tumeo, A.: Ant colony heuristic for mapping and scheduling tasks and communications on heterogeneous embedded systems. IEEE Trans. Comput. Aided Design Integr. Circuits Syst. **29**(6), 911–924 (2010)
5. Frey, P.: A timing model for real-time control-systems and its application on simulation and monitoring of autosar systems (2011). doi:10.18725/OPARU-1743
6. Hamann, A., Ziegenbein, D., Kramer, S., Lukasiewycz, M.: Demo abstract: demonstration of the FMTV 2016 timing verification challenge. In: 2016 IEEE Real-Time and Embedded Technology and Applications Symposium (RTAS), p. 1, April 2016
7. Jiang, Z., Feng, S.: A fast hybrid genetic algorithm in heterogeneous computing environment. In: 2009 Fifth International Conference on Natural Computation, vol. 4, pp. 71–75, August 2009
8. Krawczyk, L., Kamsties, E.: Hardware models for automated partitioning and mapping in multi-core systems. In: 2013 IEEE 7th International Conference on Intelligent Data Acquisition and Advanced Computing Systems (IDAACS), vol. 02, pp. 721–725, September 2013
9. Krawczyk, L., Wolff, C., Fruhner, D.: Automated distribution of software to multi-core hardware in model based embedded systems development. In: Dregvaite, G., Damasevicius, R. (eds.) ICIST 2015. CCIS, vol. 538, pp. 320–329. Springer, Cham (2015). doi:10.1007/978-3-319-24770-0_28
10. Mohr, D., Kaas, H.W., Gao, P., Cornet, A., Wee, D., Inampudi, S., Krieger, A., Richter, G., Habeck, A., Newman, J.: Connected car, automotive value chain unbound (2014)
11. Wilhelmstötter, F.: Jenetics: Java genetic algorithm library (2017). http://jenetics.io/
12. Xie, G., Li, R., Xiao, X., Chen, Y.: A high-performance dag task scheduling algorithm for heterogeneous networked embedded systems. In: 2014 IEEE 28th International Conference on Advanced Information Networking and Applications, pp. 1011–1016, May 2014
13. Zeng, B., Wei, J., Liu, H.: Research of optimal task scheduling for distributed real-time embedded systems. In: 2008 International Conference on Embedded Software and Systems, pp. 77–84, July 2008

The Bag-of-Words Methods with Pareto-Fronts for Similar Image Retrieval

Marcin Gabryel[✉]

Institute of Computational Intelligence, Częstochowa University of Technology,
Al. Armii Krajowej 36, 42-200 Częstochowa, Poland
marcin.gabryel@iisi.pcz.pl

Abstract. This paper presents an algorithm for similar image retrieval which is based on the Bag-of-Words model. In Computer Vision the classic BoW algorithm is mainly used in image classification. Its operation is based on processing of one image, creating a visual words dictionary, and specifying the class to which a query image belongs. In the presented modification of the BoW algorithm two different image feature have been chosen, namely a visual words' occurrence frequency histogram and a color histogram. As a result, using multi-criteria comparison, which so far has not been used in the BoW algorithms, a set of images similar to a query image is obtained, which is located on the Pareto-optimal non-dominated solutions front.

Keywords: Image features · Bag-of-Words · Multi-objective optimization

1 Introduction

One of the most popular and widely spread algorithms used for indexation and image retrieval is the Bag-of-Words model (BoW, which is also known as the Bag-of-Visual-Words or the Bag-of-Features algorithm) [1]. The classic BoW algorithm is used in natural language processing. A text (such as a sentence or a document) is represented as a bag of words. In image retrieval or image classification this algorithm also works on one characteristic image feature and most often it is a descriptor defining the surrounding of a keypoint obtained by using e.g. the SURF algorithm.

In presented method each image is assigned two histograms of features. One histogram stores information connected with visual words' occurrence frequency, i.e. it stores information on local image features. The other histogram contains information on grayscale intensity occurrence frequency, i.e. it stores global information on a given image. Those histograms are compared by the distance metric between them. Thus, it is possible to obtain two distances between the histograms, i.e. two probability criteria: the distance between the histograms of visual words occurrence and the distance between the histograms of grayscale. By using multiple criteria comparison of the two distances it becomes possible to obtain a set of similar non-dominated images from the so-called Pareto front. In order to search for similar images the first two Pareto fronts are used, and to obtain that a fast sorting algorithm called Fast Non Dominated Sort, which actually constitutes a fragment of the well-known NSGA-II algorithm [2], is used.

© Springer International Publishing AG 2017
R. Damaševičius and V. Mikašytė (Eds.): ICIST 2017, CCIS 756, pp. 374–384, 2017.
DOI: 10.1007/978-3-319-67642-5_31

An example comparison process is shown in Fig. 1. Figure 1a shows a schematic representation of images stored in a database and query image. Each image $\mathbf{I}_i$ has two histograms: $\mathbf{h}_i^p$ – representing visual words occurrence in an image, and $\mathbf{h}_i^c$ – the color histogram. In the search process the distances d_i^p and d_i^c between query image histograms and histograms stored in the database are calculated. Those distances are used in multiple-criteria comparison, where fronts of non-dominated points are created. This is presented in Fig. 1b. Each point in the diagram corresponds to one of the images stored in the database. The points are located on the intersections of the values of the distances d_i^p and d_i^c. It can be seen in the Figure that the sample points 1, 3 and 4 are located on the first non-dominated front. These are non-dominated solutions, i.e. solutions which it is not possible to improve in relation to any of the criteria without simultaneously compromising the others. Having rejected the images from the first front subsequent Pareto fronts can be created. In the presented algorithm the images which are most similar to the query image are the images whose points are located on the first two fronts.

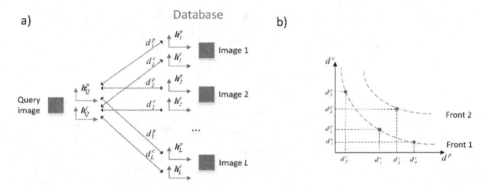

Fig. 1. (a) Schematic representation of the process of retrieving similar images by calculating the metric between the query image histograms and the images stored in the database, (b) two example Pareto fronts obtained as the result of multiple-criteria comparison of 4 different query images with the query image.

In the algorithm being presented in this paper an analytical model is used. This model is supposed to analyze visual words occurrence in images stored in a database [3, 4]. The main idea behind this algorithm is to eliminate those visual words which have spare occurrence in the cluster of all images stored in the whole database. The algorithm starts its task with the count of each visual word occurrence in histograms of a given cluster of images. If the occurrence number is lower than the previously set threshold value, then the visual word is removed from the dictionary for this image cluster. In practice occurrence of such visual word in all histograms in a given image cluster is reset. For the purpose of this paper this algorithm is called the Nonactive Visual Words Tresholding (NVWT).

The algorithm which is proposed in this paper has been divided into three main modules:

1. The initiating module – in this phase histograms describing each image are created and stored in the database. Its operation is similar to the operation of the classical BoW method.
2. The analytical module – an analysis of the visual words dictionary is conducted, which results in changes of the values of histograms' bins.
3. The retrieval and classification module –in this phase the database is searched so as to classify and retrieve images similar to the query image.

The diagram with particular elements of the algorithm along with its division into three main modules as well as the methods which are used and which are discussed in Sect. 3 are all presented in Fig. 2. A more detailed description of particular algorithm components is presented in Sect. 3.

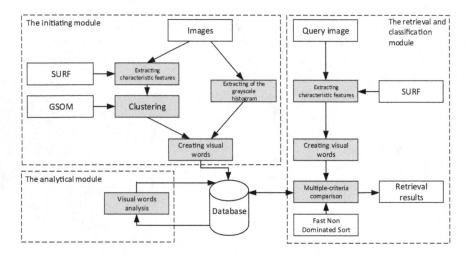

Fig. 2. Diagram of the algorithm with its division into the three main modules.

This article is divided into the following parts. Section 2 presents familiar algorithms such as Speeded Up Robust Features (SURF), the GSOM algorithm, Fast Non-Dominated Sort, and the classical Bag-of-Words method. In the last section the results of the experiments as well as a summary of this work are presented.

2 Algorithms Used in the Proposed Approach

This section contains short descriptions of all the algorithms used in the proposed BoW method including Speeded Up Robust Features, Growing Self-Organizing Map, Fast Non-Dominated Sort, and the classical BoW algorithm).

2.1 Speeded up Robust Features

The Speeded Up Robust Features (SURF) algorithm is a Fast algorithm used for retrieving and describing characteristic points in an image [13]. A characteristic feature of those points is that they are not sensitive to any changes in the scale of an image, image rotation or changes in illumination. When applied this algorithm produces descriptors describing the surroundings of the located key points. In this paper an algorithm generating descriptors in the form of 64 element vectors is used.

2.2 Growing Self-organizing Map

The Growing Self-Organizing Map (GSOM) algorithm is a modification of Self Organizing Map (SOM) which additionally was equipped in the ability of expansion. When in operation the number of neurons adjusts to the number of data. One of the parameters which has to be defined and given as τ_{max} (and called neuron activity threshold) determines how fast a neural network grows, which directly affects the number of neurons. Operation of this algorithm is supposed to generate N_C number of neurons whose weights $\mathbf{w}_j = \left[w_{i1}, w_{i2}, \dots, w_{iK} \right]$ are used as cluster centers, $i = 1, \dots, N_C$, K is data dimensions size in a given problem. A detailed presentation of the operation of the GSOM algorithm can be found in [3].

2.3 Fast Non-dominated Sort

Operation of the BoW algorithm involves comparing image representation histograms, which carry the count of particular clusters of visual words. It is assumed that the images between which there is the minimum distance are similar to each other. At this stage, when comparing two images with each other the minimum distance between their histograms needs to be found. In the presented algorithm it has been suggested to add the second histogram to the image representation. This histogram is the histogram of the grayscale intensity, which stores global information about the image. Correspondingly, in this case the similarity between the images is computed on the basis of the minimum distance between their histograms. Having two independent histograms and comparing the images with each other two similarity criteria are obtained, on the basis of which a set of non-dominated solutions (known as Pareto-optimal solutions) is created. These non-dominated solutions are solutions for which it is not possible to find better solutions in relation to any of the criteria without compromising the other criteria at the same time. Generally, in the case of objective function minimization this problem can be presented by the following formula:

$$x \succ y \Leftrightarrow \exists i f_i(x) \leq f_i(y) \tag{1}$$

where the solution x dominates over y if and only if the value of the function for the objective for x is not greater for y.

In the method which is being proposed the images are retrieved from the first two non-dominated Pareto fronts. In order to find Pareto-optimal solutions the Fast Non-Dominated Sort algorithm presented in [2] has been used. This algorithm boasts fast operation as its computational complexity is $O(MN^2)$ as opposed to the other algorithms searching for non-dominated solutions, whose complexity is $O(MN^3)$.

2.4   The Bag-of-Words Algorithm

The classical Bag-of-Words algorithm is based on a concept of text search methods within collections of documents. Single words are stored in dictionaries with an emphasis on appearing in various documents. The Bag-of-Words version applied in Computer Vision comprised three main steps: (i) feature extraction, (ii) learning visual vocabulary and (iii) image representation. In the first phase characteristic features are detected from an image. Characteristic features are usually descriptions of the surroundings of the points which do not respond to changes in the image scale, illumination and rotation, [1, 5], and they are also color features [6], texture features [7], features of selected image fragments [8, 9], and others. The number of data obtained in such way is extremely high and thus, it is rather difficult to compare it. In order to reduce the number of data clustering algorithms are applied. Those algorithms generate clusters of similar image features. Cluster centers are called visual words and they work in a similar way to the way in which words work in text documents. The last phase of the BoW algorithm is supposed to create a normalized histogram of visual words occurrence frequency in a given image, which in the literature on the subject is referred to as code-book or image representation. Those histograms are vectors which are stored in a database. Such database can then be searched in order to retrieve similar images with regard to minimum distances between histograms or its data is used to learn a classifier. Classification, i.e. determining to which class a particular image belongs, uses all images from a given database along with class labels assigned to them. They form the basis on which a classifier learns (Support Vector Machine SVM is the most frequently used one) by providing positive examples (containing histograms of a particular class) and negative examples (remaining histograms not belonging to a particular class).

3   The Proposed Method

The algorithm presented herein is different from the classical BoW model in terms of innovative elements:

- When creating visual words it is not necessary to give the initial number of clusters of image characteristic features. When using the clustering algorithm which is applied herein will automatically choose the number of clusters.
- Two histograms are used to represent each of the images stored in the database, i.e. the histogram of the frequency of occurrence of characteristic keypoints' clusters and the histogram of grayscale intensity.
- The proposed algorithm is used for both image classification and image retrieval.
- Two criteria are used as a metric to evaluate image similarity: the minimum distance between visual words' occurrence frequency histograms and the minimum distance between the histograms of colors. Having two comparison criteria a multi-criteria comparison is applied, which results in retrieval of a set of similar images from the Pareto front.
- As a result of the conducted phase of the analysis each of the histograms of an image stored in the database is modified. The histograms bins assigned to those visual words

whose number is below a certain threshold are reset. Threshold value is set for each class separately.

As it is said in the introduction (Sect. 1), the presented algorithm consists of three parts:

- the initiating module, which is supposed to prepare the images stored in a database,
- the analytical module, responsible for the visual words' dictionary analysis and histogram modification,
- the retrieval module, whose task is to retrieve and classify similar images.

The initiating module is meant to save images in a data base in the way the Bag-of-Words algorithm does. Local characteristic features are retrieved from an image, and next, they are clustered in order to create a visual words' dictionary. Each image $\mathbf{I}_i$ has the following histograms saved in the database to which it belongs: histogram $\mathbf{h}_i^p$ – mapping characteristic points to group centers and histogram $\mathbf{h}_i^c$ – the color histogram created on the basis of the grayscale intensity. The number of the grayscale intensity levels H_c is one of the algorithm's parameters. There are 256 grayscale intensity levels most often used when creating a histogram. However, it has turned out during the work on this algorithm that using a smaller number of grayscale intensity levels produces better results.

The operation of the initiating algorithm looks as follows:

1. Finding characteristic points $\mathbf{x}_i = [x_{i1}, x_{i2}, \ldots, x_{iK}]$, for each image $\mathbf{I}_i$, $i = 1, \ldots, L$, L – the total number of all characteristic points, K – the dimension of the vector describing characteristic points.
2. Grouping obtained points $\mathbf{x}_i$ with the use of the GSOM algorithm. Obtain group centers $\mathbf{w}_j$ of neurons N_j, $j = 1, \ldots, N_c$, N_c – the number of groups.
3. Creating and storing in a database histograms $\mathbf{h}_i^p = \left[h_{i1}^p, \ldots, h_{iN_c}^p \right]$ for an image $\mathbf{I}_i$, where

$$h_{ik}^p = \sum_{n=1}^{L} \delta_{nk}(i), k = 1, \ldots, N_c \tag{2}$$

Variable $\delta_{nk}(i)$ is an indictor if a group w_k is the closest vector (a winner) for any sample $\mathbf{x}_i$ from an image $\mathbf{I}_i$.

4. Create a color histogram $\mathbf{h}_i^c = [h_{i1}^c, \ldots, h_{iH_c}^p]$ for each image $\mathbf{I}_i$, where H_c is the length of the histogram.

The next module of the proposed algorithm analyzes the words dictionary $\mathbf{w}_j$ creating histograms $\mathbf{h}_i^p$ so as to improve the BoW recognition and classification. The applied NVWT algorithm involves the following steps:

(i) analyzing occurrence of the visual words in images in a given group (all the images or in a given class of images),

(ii) removing from the dictionary those visual words whose occurrence number is below the set threshold, and

(iii) filtering histogram $\mathbf{h}_i^p$ and to reset those histogram elements which contain information on removed visual words.

After this operation the histograms are normalized and the remaining histogram element values which have not been reset increase their values automatically. This is why the histogram has information on the most significant visual words occurring in a given group of images. Detailed information on the algorithm along with the experiment description can be found in of [3].

The last module of the presented algorithm is responsible for retrieving similar images of the query image (marked as I_Q) from the database. The process starts with initiation of the SURF algorithm and retrieval of the image local features from I_Q. Next, similar to formula a histogram of visual words' frequency occurrence $\mathbf{h}_Q^p$ and a color histogram $\mathbf{h}_Q^c$ with the grayscale intensity of H_c are created. The next stage involves calculating distances d_i^p (between histograms $\mathbf{h}_i^p$ and $\mathbf{h}_Q^p$) and d_i^c (between histograms $\mathbf{h}_i^c$ and $\mathbf{h}_Q^c$) using the L1 metric; yet, for the histogram $\mathbf{h}_Q^p$ we also use the NVWT algorithm. The next stage comprises multi-criteria comparison of the obtained values d_i^p and d_i^c, and obtaining the first two non-dominated Pareto-optimal fronts by using the Fast Non Dominated Sort algorithm (see Sect. 2.3). The images which belong to the first two Pareto fronts are treated as images similar to the query image I_Q, and they can be retrieved as the retrieval operation result.

4 Experiments

This section presents the operation of the proposed algorithm which shows how the parameters affect its operation and efficiency of the image retrieval algorithm. The algorithm is in Java and uses JavaCV library [10], which makes the function of the commonly used OpenCV library [11].The experiments utilize 6 image classes selected from the Caltech 101 database [12]. Each of the image classes has been divided into two parts in the proportion of 80/20 with one part used for creating a database with the use of the BoW algorithm, and the other part used for testing of the algorithm operation. A database utilizing 180 images has been created in which 100,000 characteristic points generated by the SURF algorithm have been processed.

The first of the experiments aimed at identifying the optimum grayscale intensity number value of the color histogram $\mathbf{H}_c$. For the purpose of the research grayscale intensity histograms with the power value of number 2 i.e. from 8 to 256 were chosen. At the same time, the experiments were conducted for five sample values τ_{max} (see the operation of the GSOM algorithm in Sect. 2.2). The system being launched comprises only the initiating part and the retrieval and classification part. The NVWT algorithm is not applied. In the Table 1 the recall values on the intersections of rows and columns are expressed as percentage. The recall value expressed as a percentage was used to calculate the classification efficiency according to the following formula:

$$Recall = \frac{TruePositiveCount}{TruePositiveCount + FalseNegativeCount} \cdot 100\% \qquad (3)$$

Table 1. Recall values obtained by presented algorithm in the experiment searching for the optimum length values of the color histogram H_c in relation to the parameter τ_{max}.

		Parameter τ_{max} for the GSOM network				
		125	250	500	750	1000
Color	8	72.20	69.93	69.41	68.29	68.71
histogram	16	72.45	70.63	69.44	69.37	69.02
length H_c	32	72.36	70.80	70.59	69.62	69.69
	64	**73.38**	**71.40**	**70.73**	**69.72**	**69.79**
	128	73.18	71.05	**70.73**	69.62	69.69
	256	72.97	70.77	70.15	69.65	69.37

The rows show the results for various length of the color histogram H_c, while in the columns the values change in relation to the value τ_{max}.

As it can be noticed the most optimum value of H_c is 64. For each value τ_{max} the classification results are the best. Hence, for the other experiments it is assumed that $H_c = 64$. The Fig. 3 present the recall values for various values of the parameter τ_{max} (neuron activity threshold, cf Sect. 2.2) in relation to the parameter H_c.

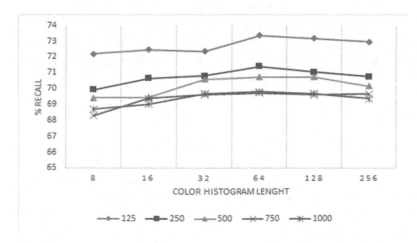

Fig. 3. Diagram show recall classification efficiency [%] for different values of H_c in relation to parameter τ_{max}.

The next experiments aims at presenting retrieval efficiency of the proposed algorithm. The whole complete algorithm with the following parameters $\tau_{max} = 250, H_c = 64$ was operated and the NVWT module had the option of individual selection of the threshold. The results of the experiment are presented in the Fig. 4. They are sample retrieval results of the query image. On the left there are sample query images from the testing image set and on the right there are the responses of the system from the first two Pareto-optimal fronts.

Fig. 4. Sample images from the 6 classes (revolver, car side, leopard, motorbike, wrench, airplane) selected for learning.

5   Conclusions

In this paper a version of the BoW is presented. This version makes it possible to generate a list of images similar to the query image. This is a result of using multi-criteria comparison in which distances from the two histograms containing information about two image features are compared. Additionally, the NVWT analysis histogram has been applied to the histogram containing key point descriptors, which improved image recognition efficiency. In the case of simple calculations the presented.

The algorithm presented in this paper can still be improved by adding new methods from the realm of artificial intelligence in the initial image recognition, for example adding elements of evolutionary algorithms or similar [14, 15, 18] or neuro-fuzzy systems [19]. The presented algorithm can be successfully used in computer systems which do not require additional equipment including databases [16, 17].

References

1. Csurka, G., Dance, C.R., Fan, L., Willamowski, J., Bray, C.: Visual categorization with bags of keypoints. In: Workshop on Statistical Learning in Computer Vision, ECCV, pp. 1–22 (2004)
2. Deb, K., Pratap, A., Agarwal, S., Meyarivan, T.: A fast and elitist multiobjective genetic algorithm: NSGA-II. IEEE Trans. Evol. Comput. **6**(2), 182–197 (2002)
3. Gabryel, M., Grycuk, R., Korytkowski, M., Holotyak, T.: Image indexing and retrieval using GSOM algorithm. In: Rutkowski, L., Korytkowski, M., Scherer, R., Tadeusiewicz, R., Zadeh, Lotfi A., Zurada, Jacek M. (eds.) ICAISC 2015. LNCS, vol. 9119, pp. 706–714. Springer, Cham (2015). doi:10.1007/978-3-319-19324-3_63
4. Gabryel, M., Capizzi, G.: The bag-of-words method with dictionary analysis by evolutionary algorithm. In: Rutkowski, L., Korytkowski, M., Scherer, R., Tadeusiewicz, R., Zadeh, Lotfi A., Zurada, Jacek M. (eds.) ICAISC 2017. LNCS, vol. 10246, pp. 43–51. Springer, Cham (2017). doi:10.1007/978-3-319-59060-8_5
5. Sivic, J., Russell, B., Efros, A., Zisserman, A., Freeman, W.: Discovering objects and their location in images. In: 2005 Tenth IEEE International Conference on Computer Vision, ICCV 2005, Vol. 1, pp. 370–377 (2005). doi:10.1109/ICCV.2005.77
6. Chang, B.-M., Tsai, H.-H., Chou, W.-L.: Using visual features to design a content-based image retrieval method optimized by particle swarm optimization algorithm. Eng. Appl. Artif. Intell. **26**(10), 2372–2382 (2013). doi:10.1016/j.engappai.2013.07.018
7. Nanni, L., Melucci, M.: Combination of projectors, standard texture descriptors and bag of features for classifying images. Neurocomputing **173**, 1062–1614 (2015). doi:10.1016/j.neucom.2015.09.032
8. Lazebnik, S., Schmid, C., Ponce, J.: Beyond bags of features: Spatial pyramid matching for recognizing natural scene categories. In: 2006 IEEE Computer Society Conference on Computer Vision and Pattern Recognition, Vol. 2, pp. 2169–2178 (2006). doi:10.1109/CVPR.2006.68
9. Li, W., Dong, P., Xiao, B., Zhou, L.: Object recognition based on the region of interest and optimal bag of words model. Neurocomputing **172**, 271–280 (2016). doi:10.1016/j.neucom.2015.01.083
10. Audet, S.: JavaCV. http://bytedeco.org/. Accessed 22 May 2017
11. Bradski, G.: The OpenCV Library, Dr. Dobb's Journal of Software Tools
12. Fei-Fei, L., Fergus, R., Perona, P.: Learning generative visual models from few training examples: An incremental bayesian approach tested on 101 object categories. In: 2004 Conference on Computer Vision and Pattern Recognition Workshop, CVPRW 2004, pp. 178–178 (2004). doi:10.1109/CVPR.2004.109
13. Bay, H., Tuytelaars, T., Van Gool, L.: SURF: Speeded up robust features. In: Leonardis, A., Bischof, H., Pinz, A. (eds.) ECCV 2006. LNCS, vol. 3951, pp. 404–417. Springer, Heidelberg (2006). doi:10.1007/11744023_32
14. Woźniak, M.: Novel image correction method based on swarm intelligence approach. In: Dregvaite, G., Damasevicius, R. (eds.) ICIST 2016. CCIS, vol. 639, pp. 404–413. Springer, Cham (2016). doi:10.1007/978-3-319-46254-7_32. ISBN 1865-0929
15. Woźniak, M., Połap, D., Napoli, C., Tramontana, E.: Graphic object feature extraction system based on cuckoo search algorithm. Expert Syst. Appl. **66**, 20–31 (2016). doi:10.1016/j.eswa.2016.08.068. Elsevier

16. Gabryel, M.: The bag-of-features algorithm for practical applications using the MySQL database. In: Rutkowski, L., Korytkowski, M., Scherer, R., Tadeusiewicz, R., Zadeh, Lotfi A., Zurada, Jacek M. (eds.) ICAISC 2016. LNCS, vol. 9693, pp. 635–646. Springer, Cham (2016). doi:10.1007/978-3-319-39384-1_56

17. Gabryel, M.: A bag-of-features algorithm for applications using a NoSQL database. In: Dregvaite, G., Damasevicius, R. (eds.) ICIST 2016. CCIS, vol. 639, pp. 332–343. Springer, Cham (2016). doi:10.1007/978-3-319-46254-7_26

18. Damaševičius, R., Maskeliūnas, R., Venčkauskas, A., Woźniak, M.: Smartphone user identity verification using gait characteristics. Symmetry 8(10), 1001–10020 (2016). doi:10.3390/sym8100100

19. Cpalka, K.: A new method for design and reduction of neuro-fuzzy classification systems. IEEE Trans. Neural Netw. 20(4), 701–714 (2009)

Buffer Overflow Duration in a Model of WSN Node with Power Saving Mechanism Based on SV Policy

Wojciech M. Kempa[✉]

Faculty of Applied Mathematics, Institute of Mathematics,
Silesian University of Technology, 23 Kaszubska Str., 44-100 Gliwice, Poland
wojciech.kempa@polsl.pl

Abstract. A model of a wireless sensor network node with power saving mechanism based on single vacation policy is investigated. The input/output traffic is supposed to be described by an $M^X/G/1/N$-type queueing system with finite buffer capacity and batch packets' arrivals. In the case the queue of packets directed to the node becomes empty the radio transmitter/receiver is switched off for a random and generally distributed period of time (single vacation). During the vacation the transmission of packets via the node is suspended. Using analytical approach, based on the total probability formula, integral equations and linear algebra, the closed-form representation for the cumulative distribution function of the first buffer overflow duration is found. Hence, the corresponding results for next such periods are obtained. Finally, probability distributions of the number of losses in successive buffer overflow periods are derived.

Keywords: Buffer overflow · Packet loss · Power saving · Single vacation policy · Wireless sensor network

1 Introduction

Wireless sensor networks (WSNs) are commonly used nowadays in control of different-type activities and phenomena, e.g. in fire prevention, road traffic and hospital patients' monitoring. A typical wireless sensor node is equipped with an energy source (battery), a radio transmitter/receiver and a microprocessor. Since sensors are often located in places being hardly to reach, where the replacement of the battery (or the whole sensor) is problematic and costly, the power saving monitoring is essential one in WSNs.

One can observe variety of different-type mechanisms proposed in the literature for power saving modelling. An infinite-buffer M/G/1-type system with multiple vacation policy is considered in [17] as a model of WSN's node with energy saving. The M/G/1/N-type queueing model of the base station in Mobile WiMAX network is analyzed in [18] according to modelling system vacations. In [1] a queue with repeated vacations is proposed in modelling the node sleep-mode operation. An infinite-capacity M/G/1-type queueing system with the threshold-type policy is investigated as a model of WSN's node with battery saving mechanism in [9] (compare also [7, 8]). As it can

© Springer International Publishing AG 2017
R. Damaševičius and V. Mikašytė (Eds.): ICIST 2017, CCIS 756, pp. 385–394, 2017.
DOI: 10.1007/978-3-319-67642-5_32

be noted, the analytical results are obtained mainly for performance measures in the steady state of the system. As it seems, however, transient (time-dependent) investigation is often recommended or even necessary, e.g. during the analysis of the model just after a repair, technical break or together with application of the new control algorithm. Besides, in practice, the system behavior can be destabilized, especially in relation to wireless communication, by the phenomena like fade-out or interference.

The phenomenon of packet losses is a typical one in packet-oriented networks with finite buffer capacities. Because during the buffer overflow period all the arriving packets are rejected without processing, the knowledge of the probabilistic behavior of successive buffer overflow periods' durations is essentially important. Besides, the statistical structure of the loss process is important (it makes a difference whether the arriving packets are rejected in long series or not).

Results on probability distributions of buffer overflow durations in the finite- and infinite-buffer M/G/1-type models without "perturbations" in access to the service station can be found e.g. in [2–5]. In [6, 19] the system with general independent input flow and single server vacations is considered and optimized by using genetic algorithms. The closed-form formulae for the distributions of the time to buffer overflow are derived in [10, 15], where the GI/M/1/N-type model and the M/G/1/N-type queue with setup and closedown periods are considered, respectively. In [11–14] the non-stationary analysis of queueing systems with single vacation policy (SVP for short) or some other control mechanisms implemented in the service process can be found.

In the article we consider the M/G/1/N-type finite-capacity queueing model operating under SVP. Using the analytical approach based on the concept of embedded Markov chain, integral equations and linear algebra, we obtain the explicit formula for the tail of cumulative distribution function (CDF for short) of the first buffer overflow duration, conditioned by the initial buffer state. Hence we obtain similar result for next such periods' durations. Besides, we get the formulae for the total numbers of losses during successive buffer overflow periods.

The paper is organized as follows. In the next section we give the mathematical description of the considered queueing model and necessary notations. In Sect. 3 we obtain the formula for the tail of conditional CDF of the first buffer overflow duration. Section 4 is devoted to next buffer overflow periods and to probability distributions of the number of consecutively lost packets. Finally, the last Sect. 5 contains a short conclusion.

2 Description of Queueing System

We deal with the M/G/1/N-type queue in which packets occur according to a Poisson process with intensity λ in batches of random sizes and are being processed individually with a CDF $F(\cdot)$, according to the FIFO service discipline. The size of the arriving group equals k with probability p_k. The capacity of the system equals N packets, i.e. we have $N - 1$ places in the buffer queue and one place "in processing". The system may start the operation with a number n of packets accumulated in the buffer, where $0 \leq n \leq N - 1$. Every time when the server becomes idle, the single server vacation with a general-type CDF $V(\cdot)$ is being initialized. During the vacation

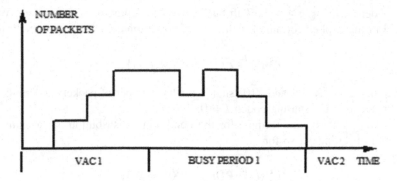

Fig. 1. The scheme of the considered system's evolution

period the processing of packets is suspended. At the completion epoch of the vacation period, if there is at least one packet accumulated in the buffer, the service station restarts processing immediately. In the case of empty buffer, the service station remains active and waits for the first packet occurrence (see Fig. 1). If the arriving packet finds the system being saturated, it is lost without processing (see Fig. 2).

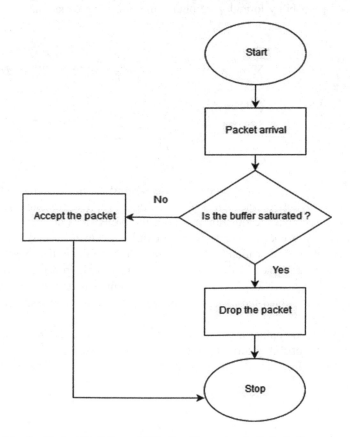

Fig. 2. Typical Tail Drop (TD) algorithm using in finite-buffer queues

Let us denote by $\gamma_k, k \geq 1$, the k th buffer overflow duration of the system. We are interested in the explicit formula for the tail of conditional CDF of γ_k, namely for

$$G_n^{(k)}(t) \stackrel{\text{def}}{=} \mathbf{P}\{\gamma_k > t | X(0 = n)\}, \tag{1}$$

where $t > 0, 0 \leq n \leq N - 1$ and $X(0)$ stands for the number of packets accumulated in the buffer queue at the starting epoch $t = 0$.

Moreover, we derive the formula for the conditional distribution of the number h_k of packets lost during γ_k, so for

$$H_n^{(k)}(l) \stackrel{\text{def}}{=} \mathbf{P}\{h_k = l | X(0 = n)\}, \tag{2}$$

where $l \geq 1$.

3   First Buffer Overflow Duration

Let us start with the first buffer overflow duration, and consider firstly the case of the buffer being empty before the opening of the system. By virtue of the continuous version of total probability formula, we obtain the following equation:

$$
\begin{aligned}
G_0^{(1)}(t) \\
= \int_{u=0}^{\infty} dV(u) &\left[\int_{x=0}^{u} \sum_{k=1}^{N-1} p_k \lambda e^{-\lambda x} \sum_{r=0}^{N-k-1} \sum_{j=0}^{r} p_r^{j*} \frac{[\lambda(u-x)]^j}{j!} e^{-\lambda(u-x)} G_{k+r}^{(1)}(t) dx \right. \\
&+ \int_{x=0}^{u} \sum_{j=1}^{N} p_N^{j*} \frac{\lambda^j}{(j-1)!} x^{j-1} e^{-\lambda x} \overline{F}(t - u + x) dx \\
&\left. + e^{-\lambda u} \left(\sum_{k=1}^{N-1} p_k G_k^{(1)}(t) + \overline{F}(t) \sum_{k=N}^{\infty} p_k \right) \right],
\end{aligned} \tag{3}
$$

where $\overline{F}(x) \stackrel{\text{def}}{=} 1 - F(x)$. Let us comment (3) in few words. If the system is empty at the starting moment, the server vacation begins at this $t = 0$. The first summand on the right side of (3) describes the situation in which the buffer does not become saturated before the completion epoch u of the vacation time, however at least one group of packets occurs during the vacation. In the second summand the buffer overflow period starts at time $x < u$ and hence its duration exceeds t if only the processing time of the first packet will be greater than $t - u + x$. The last summand on the right side of (3) relates to the case in which the first group of packets arrives after completion of the server vacation.

For the system containing n packets at the starting epoch, where $1 \leq n \leq N - 1$, applying the total probability formula with respect to the first departure moment after the opening (renewal or Markovian moment), we obtain the following equations:

$$G_n^{(1)}(t) = \int\limits_0^\infty \sum_{k=0}^{N-n-1} \sum_{j=0}^{k} p_k^{j*} \frac{(\lambda y)^j}{j!} e^{-\lambda y} G_{n+k-1}^{(1)}(t) dF(y)$$

$$+ \int\limits_{y=0}^\infty dF(y) \int\limits_{x=0}^y \sum_{j=1}^{N-n} p_{N-n}^{j*} \frac{\lambda^j}{(j-1)!} x^{j-1} e^{-\lambda x} I\{y-x>t\} dx, \tag{4}$$

where $I\{A\}$ stands for the indicator of the random event A. The first summand on the right side of (4) relates to the case in which the buffer does not become saturated before the first departure occurring at time $y > 0$. In the second summand the first buffer overflow period starts at time $0 < x < y$.

Introduce the following functionals:

$$a_k \stackrel{\text{def}}{=} \int\limits_0^\infty \sum_{j=0}^{k} p_k^{j*} \frac{(\lambda t)^j}{j!} e^{-\lambda t} dF(t), \tag{5}$$

$$b_k(t) \stackrel{\text{def}}{=} \int\limits_{y=0}^\infty dF(y) \int\limits_{x=0}^y \sum_{j=1}^{k} p_k^{j*} \frac{\lambda^j}{(j-1)!} x^{j-1} e^{-\lambda x} I\{y-x>t\} dx, \tag{6}$$

$$c_k \stackrel{\text{def}}{=} \int\limits_0^\infty \sum_{j=0}^{k} p_k^{j*} \frac{(\lambda t)^{j+1}}{(j+1)!} e^{-\lambda t} dV(t), \tag{7}$$

$$d(t) \stackrel{\text{def}}{=} \int\limits_{u=0}^\infty dV(u) \int\limits_{x=0}^u \sum_{j=1}^{N} p_N^{j*} \frac{\lambda^j}{(j-1)!} x^{j-1} e^{-\lambda x} \overline{F}(t-u+x) dx. \tag{8}$$

Now we can convert the system (3) and (4) into the following one:

$$G_0^{(1)}(t) = \sum_{k=1}^{N-1} p_k \sum_{r=0}^{N-k-1} c_k G_{k+r}^{(1)}(t) + v(\lambda) \left(\sum_{k=1}^{N-1} p_k G_k^{(1)}(t) + \overline{F}(t) \sum_{k=N}^\infty p_k \right) + d(t), \tag{9}$$

$$G_n^{(1)}(t) = \sum_{k=0}^{N-n-1} a_k G_{n+k-1}^{(1)}(t) + b_{N-n}(t), \tag{10}$$

where $1 \le n \le N-1$ and $v(\lambda) \stackrel{\text{def}}{=} \int_0^\infty e^{-\lambda t} dV(t)$.

Moreover, if we use in (9) and (10) the following substitution:

$$T_n(t) \stackrel{\text{def}}{=} G_{N-n}^{(1)}(t), 1 \le n \le N, \tag{11}$$

then we obtain for $1 \le n \le N-1$

$$\sum_{k=-1}^{n-1} a_{k+1} T_{n-k}(t) - T_n(t) = \phi_n(t), \tag{12}$$

where

$$\phi_n(t) \stackrel{\text{def}}{=} T_1(t) a_n - b_n(t), \tag{13}$$

and, moreover,

$$T_N(t) = \sum_{k=1}^{N-1} p_k \sum_{r=1}^{N-k} c_{N-k-r} T_r(t) + v(\lambda) \left(\sum_{k=1}^{N-1} p_k T_{N-k}(t) + \overline{F}(t) \sum_{k=N}^{\infty} p_k \right) + d(t). \tag{14}$$

In [16] it is shown that each solution of the infinite-sized (written for $n \geq 1$) system of equations of type (12) can be written in the form

$$T_n(t) = M(t) R_n + \sum_{k=1}^{n} R_{n-k} \phi_k(t), \tag{15}$$

where successive terms of the sequence $(R_n)_{n=0}^{\infty}$ can be found from the representations

$$\sum_{k=0}^{\infty} z^k R_k = \frac{z}{A(z) - z}, \quad |z| < 1, \tag{16}$$

where

$$A(z) \stackrel{\text{def}}{=} \sum_{k=0}^{\infty} a_k z^k. \tag{17}$$

In consequence, to find the representations for successive functions $T_n(t)$, we need the formulae for $T_1(t)$ (see (13)) and for $M(t)$. Because the number of equations in (12) is finite, we can use the Eq. (14) as a specific-type boundary condition.

Substituting $n = 1$ into (15), we get

$$T_1(t) = M(t) R_1. \tag{18}$$

Implementing (15) in (14) and referring to (18), we obtain

$$M(t)R_N + \sum_{k=1}^{N}(M(t)R_1 a_k - b_k(t))R_{N-k}$$

$$= \sum_{k=1}^{N-1} c_k \left[M(t)R_{N-k} + \sum_{i=1}^{N-k} (M(t)R_1 a_i - b_i(t))R_{N-k-i} \right] \qquad (19)$$

$$+ v(\lambda) \left[M(t)R_{N-1} + \sum_{k=1}^{N-1}(M(t)R_1 a_k - b_k(t))R_{N-1-k} \right]$$

$$+ d(t).$$

If we denote

$$B_1(t) \overset{\text{def}}{=} \sum_{k=1}^{N} b_k(t)R_{N-k}$$

$$- \sum_{k=1}^{N-1} c_k \sum_{i=1}^{N-k} b_i(t)R_{N-k-i} - v(\lambda) \sum_{k=1}^{N-1} b_k(t)R_{N-1-k} + d(t) \qquad (20)$$

and

$$B_2(t) \overset{\text{def}}{=} \left[R_N + R_1 \sum_{k=1}^{N} a_k R_{N-k} \right.$$

$$- \sum_{k=1}^{N-1} c_k \left(R_{N-k} + R_1 \sum_{i=1}^{N-k} a_i R_{N-k-i} \right) \qquad (21)$$

$$\left. - v(\lambda) \left(R_{N-1} + R_1 \sum_{k=1}^{N-1} a_k R_{N-1-k} \right) \right]^{-1},$$

we can eliminate $M(t)$ from (19) as

$$M(t) = \prod_{i=1}^{2} B_i(t). \qquad (22)$$

Now, the formulae (11), (13), (15), (18) and (22) lead to the following main result:

Theorem 1. *In the $M^X/G/1/N$-type queueing model operating under the SVP the tail $G_n^{(1)}(t)$ of CDF of the first buffer overflow duration, conditioned by the number n of packets accumulated in the buffer before the opening can be found as follows:*

$$G_n^{(1)}(t) = \left(R_{N-n} + R_1 \sum_{k=1}^{N-n} a_k R_{N-n-k} \right) \prod_{i=1}^{2} B_i(t) - \sum_{k=1}^{N-n} b_k R_{N-n-k}, \qquad (23)$$

where $0 \le n \le N-1$ and the representations for $a_k, b_k(t), R_k, B_1(t)$ and $B_2(t)$ are given in (5), (6), (16), (20) and (21), respectively.

4 Next Buffer Overflow Periods

As it can be easily noticed, after finishing each buffer overflow period, due to the fact that the service process is organized "individually", the number of packets present in the system always equals $N - 1$. In consequence, distribution functions of next buffer overflow periods' durations γ_k, where $k \geq 2$, are independent on the number of packets accumulated in the buffer at the opening. Moreover, these distributions coincide with the distribution of the first buffer overflow period γ_1 conditioned by $X(0) = N - 1$. Concluding, from Theorem 1 we get

Corollary 1. *The CDF of the k th buffer overflow duration for $k \geq 2$ in the $M^X/G/1/N$-type model with SVP can be found from the formula*

$$G^{(k)}(t) = \mathbf{P}\{\gamma_k > t\} = G_{N-1}^{(1)}(t) = R_1 \prod_{i=1}^{2} B_i(t), \qquad (24)$$

where $0 \leq n \leq N - 1$.

The following theorem is a consequence of the fact that the arrival process in the considered queueing system is described by a compound Poisson process with rate λ:

Theorem 2. *Probability mass function $H_n^{(k)}(l)$ of the number h_k of consecutively lost packets during the k th buffer overflow period in the $M^X/G/1/N$-type queueing model with SVP can be found from the following formulae:*

$$H_n^{(1)}(l) = \int_0^\infty \sum_{j=0}^{l} p_l^{j*} \frac{(\lambda t)^j}{j!} e^{-\lambda t} dG_n^{(1)}(t) \qquad (25)$$

and

$$\begin{aligned} H_n^{(k)}(l) = H^{(k)}(l) &= \int_0^\infty \sum_{j=0}^{l} p_l^{j*} \frac{(\lambda t)^j}{j!} e^{-\lambda t} dG^{(k)}(t) \\ &= \int_0^\infty \sum_{j=0}^{l} p_l^{j*} \frac{(\lambda t)^j}{j!} e^{-\lambda t} dG_{N-1}^{(1)}(t), \end{aligned} \qquad (26)$$

where $0 \leq n \leq N - 1$ and $k \geq 2$.

5 Conclusion

In the article the explicit formulae for the tails of CDFs of successive buffer overflow durations in the $M^X/G/1/N$-type finite-buffer queueing model with SVP are found. Moreover, probability mass functions of the number of losses in successive buffer overflow periods are derived. The investigated system can be used in modelling of energy saving mechanism in nodes of WSN. The analytical methods is based on the concept of embedded Markov chain, integral equations and linear algebraic approach.

References

1. Alouf, S., Altman, E., Azad, A.: M/G/1 queue with repeated inhomogeneous vacations applied to IEEE 802.16e power saving. In: Proceedings of ACM SIGMETRICS 2008, Performance Evaluation Review, vol. 36, pp. 451–452 (2008)
2. de Boer, P.T., Nicola, V.F., van Ommeren, J.C.W.: The remaining service time upon reaching a high level in M/G/1 queues. Queueing Syst. **39**, 55–78 (2001)
3. Chae, K.C., Kim, K., Kim, N.K.: Remarks on the remaining service time upon reaching a target level in the M/G/1 queue. Oper. Res. Lett. **35**, 308–310 (2007)
4. Chydziński, A.: On the remaining service time upon reaching a target level in M/G/1 queues. Queueing Syst. **47**, 71–80 (2004)
5. Fakinos, D.: The expected remaining service time in a single server queue. Oper. Res. **30**, 1014–1018 (1982)
6. Gabryel, M., Nowicki, Robert K., Woźniak, M., Kempa, W.M.: Genetic cost optimization of the $GI/M/1/N$ finite-buffer queue with a single vacation policy. In: Rutkowski, L., Korytkowski, M., Scherer, R., Tadeusiewicz, R., Zadeh, L.A., Zurada, J.M. (eds.) ICAISC 2013. LNCS, vol. 7895, pp. 12–23. Springer, Heidelberg (2013). doi:10.1007/978-3-642-38610-7_2
7. Jiang, F.-C., Huang, D.-C., Wang, K.-H.: Design approaches for optimizing power consumption of sensor node with N-policy M/G/1. In: Proceedings of QTNA 2009, Singapore, 29–31 July 2009 (2009)
8. Jiang, F.-C., Huang, D.-C., Yang, C.-T., Wang, K.-H.: Mitigation techniques for the energy hole problem in sensor networks using N-policy M/G/1 queueing models. In: Proceedings of the IET International Conference: Frontier Computing: Theory, Technologies and Applications 2010, Taichung, 4–6 August 2010 (2010)
9. Jiang, F.-C., Huang, D.-C., Yang, C.-T., Leu, F.-Y.: Lifetime elongation for wireless sensor network using queue-based approaches. J. Supercomput. **59**, 1312–1335 (2012)
10. Kempa, W.M.: On the distribution of the time to buffer overflow in a queueing system with a general-type input stream. In: 35th International Conference on Telecommunication and Signal Processing (TSP 2012), Prague, Czech Republic, 3–4 July 2012, Piscataway, pp. 207–211 (2012)
11. Kempa, W.M.: On transient queue-size distribution in the batch-arrivals system with a single vacation policy. Kybernetika **50**, 126–141 (2014)
12. Kempa, W.M.: On queueing delay in WSN with energy saving mechanism based on queued wake up. In: Mustra, M., et al. (eds.) Proceedings of 21st International Conference on Systems, Signals and Image Processing (IWSSIP 2014), Dubrovnik, Croatia, 12–15 May 2014, Zagreb, pp. 187–190 (2014)
13. Kempa, W.M.: Time-dependent analysis of transmission process in a wireless sensor network with energy saving mechanism based on threshold waking up. In: IEEE 16th International Workshop on Signal Processing Advances in Wireless Communications (SPAWC 2015), Stockholm, Sweden, June 28–July 1, 2015, Piscataway, pp. 26–30 (2015)
14. Kempa, W.M.: Transient workload distribution in the M/G/1 finite-buffer queue with single and multiple vacations. Ann. Oper. Res. **239**, 381–400 (2016)
15. Kempa, W.M., Paprocka, I.: Time to buffer overflow in a finite-capacity queueing model with setup and closedown times. In: Świątek, J., Wilimowska, Z., Borzemski, L., Grzech, A. (eds.) Information Systems Architecture and Technology: Proceedings of 37th International Conference on Information Systems Architecture and Technology – ISAT 2016 – Part III. AISC, vol. 523, pp. 215–224. Springer, Cham (2017). doi:10.1007/978-3-319-46589-0_17

16. Korolyuk, V.S.: Boundary-value problems for compound Poisson processes. Naukova Dumka, Kiev (1975)
17. Mancuso, V., Alouf, S.: Analysis of power saving with continuous connectivity. Comput. Netw. **56**, 2481–2493 (2012)
18. Seo, J., Lee, S., Park, N., Lee, H., Cho, C.: Performance analysis of sleep mode operation in IEEE 802.16e. In: Proceedings of IEEE VTC 2004-Fall, Los Angeles, vol. 2, pp. 1169–1173 (2004)
19. Woźniak, M., Kempa, W.M., Gabryel, M., Nowicki, R.: A finite-buffer queue with a single vacation policy: an analytical study with evolutionary positioning. Int. J. Appl. Math. Comput. Sci. **24**, 887–900 (2014)

Departure Counting Process in a Wireless Network Node with Sleep Mode Modelled via Repeated Vacations

Wojciech M. Kempa[(⊠)] and Rafał Marjasz

Faculty of Applied Mathematics, Institute of Mathematics,
Silesian University of Technology, 23 Kaszubska Str, 44-100 Gliwice, Poland
{wojciech.kempa, rafal.marjasz}@polsl.pl

Abstract. A finite-capacity queueing model with Poisson packet arrivals and generally-distributed processing times is investigated. The system operates under the multiple vacation policy, i.e. every time when the server becomes idle a number of independent vacation times is initialized until at least one packet is accumulated in the buffer. Using the analytical approach based on the concept of embedded Markov chain and total probability law, the explicit representation for the mixed double transform of the probability distribution of the number of packets completely processed until the given time t is found. Hence the mean number of departures in a fixed-length time period can be obtained easily. The considered queueing system can be efficiently used in modelling the nodes in wireless telecommunication networks, where the multiple vacation policy is a kind of energy saving mechanism. An illustrating numerical example is attached.

Keywords: Departure process · Finite buffer · Markov chain · Multiple vacation policy · Wireless communication

1 Introduction

Queueing systems with finite buffer capacities have wide network applications, in particular in modelling network nodes' operation. Due to the fact that the energy saving problem is one of the most essential in wireless communication, systems with different-type limitations in the access to the service station are of particular importance. Evidently, each busy period of the queueing system may correspond to the active mode and, similarly, each idle time may correspond to the sleep mode in the operation of wireless network node (e.g. in sensor network). Different mechanisms are proposed in the literature for supporting power saving modelling. One of them is the so called multiple vacation policy (MVP in short). The idea of MVP is in that the node (more precisely, the radio transmitter/receiver of the node), every time when the queue of packets directed to the node empties, initializes a number of repeated independent vacation periods, until at the end of one of them at least one packet accumulated in the buffer is detected. An infinite-buffer M/G/1-type queue with repeated (multiple) server vacations is proposed e.g. in [19] as a model of Type I power-saving mode in IEEE 802.16e standard, and some performance measures are derived there (compare also [4, 20]).

© Springer International Publishing AG 2017
R. Damaševičius and V. Mikašytė (Eds.): ICIST 2017, CCIS 756, pp. 395–407, 2017.
DOI: 10.1007/978-3-319-67642-5_33

As one can observe, analytical results obtained for different-type queueing models with different service limitations relate mainly to the stable queues, i.e. to the stochastic characteristics in the case of $t \to \infty$. However, quite often time-dependent analysis of the system behavior seems to be more desired, in particular due to the high variability network traffic, e.g. in TCP/IP connections. Moreover, in rare traffic (like in some wireless sensor networks) the system stabilizes longer, so the investigation of its performance shortly after the opening or the application of a new control mechanism requires transient analysis (at fixed time t).

In the paper we deal with the transient departure process in the M/G/1-type queueing model of the wireless network node with the mechanism of energy saving based on MVP. The departure process at any fixed time epoch t takes a random value equal to the number of packets completely processed by the node until t and is one of the most important stochastic characteristics of each queueing model. Indeed, in network applications, the departure process from one node corresponds to the arrival process to the next node. Applying the analytical approach based on the idea of embedded Markov chain and total probability law, the explicit representation for the mixed double transform of the probability distribution of the number of packets completely processed until the given time t is found. Hence the mean number of departures in a fixed-length time period can be obtained easily.

The bibliography on transient departure process analysis is rather modest. In [8] a stationary-case joint density function of k successive departure intervals is obtained in the M/G/1/N system. Some results related to the service process in the M^X/G/1/N model are derived in [5]. In [9] a technique based on the of resolvent sequences of the process being the difference of a compound Poisson process and a compound general-type renewal process is proposed in the case of finite systems. Transient results for the departure process in the case of the system with batch arrivals and infinite queue can be found in [10], and in [11, 12], where additionally multiple and single vacation policies are analyzed. Analytical results for the transient departure counting process in some other queueing models with different-type limitations in the access to server can be found in [13–17].

The remaining part of the article is organized as follows. In the next section we give the detailed description of the considered queueing system. In Sect. 3 we build a system of equations for conditional departure process. The main result, namely the solution of the corresponding system written for double transforms, is stated in Sect. 4. In Sect. 5 we discuss the mean number of departures as a consequence of the result from previous section. Finally, the last section contains examples of numerical results.

2   Queueing System

We deal with an M/G/1/N-type queueing system in which packets arrive according to a Poisson process with rate λ and are being processed individually under the FIFO service discipline. The processing time is assumed to be generally-distributed with cumulative distribution function (CDF in short) $F(\cdot)$ and Laplace-Stieltjes transform

(LST in short) $f(\cdot)$. The number of packets that are allowed to be present in the system simultaneously is bounded by a non-random value N, so there are $N - 1$ places in the buffer queue and one place in the processing station (service unit). Whenever the system becomes empty an MVP is initialized, during which successive vacations are being started, one by one, until at least one job accumulated in the buffer is detected at the completion epoch of one of them. We assume that all the vacations are independent and identically distributed random variables with a common general-type CDF $G(\cdot)$ with LST $g(\cdot)$.

Let us denote by $h(t)$ the (random) number of packets completely processed up to the fixed time t (departure process). We are interested in the explicit compact-form representation for the double transform of the probability distribution of $h(t)$, i.e. for the functional

$$\tilde{h}_n(s,z) \stackrel{\text{def}}{=} \sum_{m=0}^{\infty} z^m \int_0^{\infty} e^{-st} \mathbf{P}\{h(t) = m | X(0) = n\} dt, \tag{1}$$

where $|z| \langle 1, \Re(s) \rangle 0, 0 \leq n \leq N$ and $X(0)$ denotes the number of packets present in the buffer at the starting epoch.

In [18] the following linear system with infinite number of equations is considered:

$$\sum_{i=-1}^{n} a_{i+1} y_{n-i} - y_n = \varphi_n, \quad n \geq 0, \tag{2}$$

where $(y_n)_{n=0}^{\infty}$ is the sequence of unknowns, and $(a_n)_{n=0}^{\infty}$ and $(\varphi_n)_{n=0}^{\infty}$ are, respectively, the sequences of coefficients and free terms, where $a_0 \neq 0$. As it was proved in [18], each solution of (2) can be written in the following form:

$$y_n = C R_{n+1} + \sum_{i=0}^{n} R_{n-i} \varphi_i, \quad n \geq 0, \tag{3}$$

where C is a constant and the sequence $(R_n)_{n=0}^{\infty}$ is defined by means of coefficients of the system, namely the following relationship holds:

$$\sum_{k=0}^{\infty} z^k R_k = \frac{z}{A(z) - z}, \quad |z| < 1, \tag{4}$$

where

$$A(z) \stackrel{\text{def}}{=} \sum_{k=0}^{\infty} a_k z^k. \tag{5}$$

In the next sections, applying the paradigm of embedded Markov chain and total probability law, and using Volterra-type integral equations and the formula (3), we obtain the formulae for the mixed double transform $\tilde{h}_n(s, z)$, namely the probability generating function (PGF in short) of the Laplace transform (LT in short) of $h(t)$, conditioned by the initial level of buffer saturation.

3 Integral Equations for Conditional Departure Process

In this section, by using the idea of embedded Markov chain, we build a system of integral equations for conditional departure process. Next we convert it to a corresponding system written for double mixed transforms and rewrite it in a specific form similar to (2).

Assume firstly that the system is empty at the starting time, so the first MVP begins at $t = 0$. Utilizing the notation introduced in Sect. 2, the formula of total probability leads to the following equation:

$$
H_0(t, m)
$$
$$
= \sum_{i=0}^{\infty} \int_{u=0}^{t} dG^{i*}(u) \int_{y=u}^{t} \lambda e^{-\lambda y} dy \left\{ \int_{v=y-u}^{t-u} \left[\sum_{k=0}^{N-2} \frac{[\lambda(u+v-y)]^k}{k!} e^{-\lambda(u+v-y)} H_{k+1}(t-u-v, m) \right. \right.
$$
$$
\left. + H_N(t-u-v, m) \sum_{k=N-1}^{\infty} \frac{[\lambda(u+v-y)]^k}{k!} e^{-\lambda(u+v-y)} \right] dG(v) + \delta_{m,0} \bar{G}(t-u) \right\}
$$
$$
+ \delta_{m,0} e^{-\lambda t},
$$

$$(6)$$

where $H_n(t, m) \overset{\text{def}}{=} \mathbf{P}\{h(t) = m | X(0) = n\}$, $G^{i*}(\cdot)$, is the $i-$ fold Stieltjes convolution of CDF $G(\cdot)$, $\delta_{i,j}$ stands for the Kronecker delta function and $\bar{L}(x) \overset{\text{def}}{=} 1 - L(x)$ for any CDF $L(\cdot)$.

Consider now the case of the system being non-empty at the starting time $t = 0$. Due to the fact that successive departure epochs are Markov moments in the evolution of the M/ · /· FIFO queue, applying the total probability law with respect to the first departure epoch after $t = 0$, we get

$$
H_n(t, m) = I\{m \geq 1\} \int_0^t \left[\sum_{k=0}^{N-n-1} \frac{(\lambda y)^k}{k!} e^{-\lambda y} H_{n+k-1}(t-y, m-1) \right.
$$
$$
\left. + H_{N-1}(t-y, m-1) \sum_{k=N-n}^{\infty} \frac{(\lambda y)^k}{k!} e^{-\lambda y} \right] dF(y) + \delta_{m,0} \bar{F}(t),
$$

$$(7)$$

where $1 \leq n \leq N$ and $I\{A\}$ denotes the indicator of random event A.

It is easy to verify that the following identity holds (compare the first summand on the right side of (6)):

$$\frac{\lambda^{k+1}}{k!} \int_{t=0}^{\infty} e^{-st} dt \int_{u=0}^{t} e^{-\lambda u} dG^{i*}(u) \int_{y=u}^{t} dy \int_{v=y-u}^{t-u} e^{-\lambda v}(u+v-y)^k H_{k+1}(t-u-v,m) dG(v)$$

$$= \frac{\lambda^{k+1}}{k!} \int_{u=0}^{\infty} e^{-(\lambda+s)u} dG^{i*}(u) \int_{y=u}^{\infty} dy \int_{v=y-u}^{\infty} (u+v-y)^k$$

$$e^{-(\lambda+s)v} dG(v) \int_{t=u+v}^{\infty} e^{-s(t-u-v)} H_{k+1}(t-u-v,m) dt$$

$$= \frac{\lambda^{k+1}}{k!} \tilde{h}_{k+1}(s,m) \int_{u=0}^{\infty} e^{-(\lambda+s)u} dG^{i*}(u) \int_{v=0}^{\infty} e^{-(\lambda+s)v} dG(v) \int_{y=u}^{u+v} (u+v-y)^k dy$$

$$= \frac{\lambda^{k+1}}{k!} \tilde{h}_{k+1}(s,m) g^i(\lambda+s) \int_{0}^{\infty} e^{-(\lambda+s)v} v^{k+1} dG(v),$$

$$\tag{8}$$

where

$$\tilde{h}_j(s,m) \overset{\text{def}}{=} \int_{0}^{\infty} e^{-st} H_j(t,m) dt, \quad \Re(s) > 0. \tag{9}$$

Similarly, we have

$$\int_{t=0}^{\infty} e^{-st} dt \int_{u=0}^{t} \bar{G}(t-u) dG^{i*}(u) \int_{y=u}^{t} \lambda e^{-\lambda y} dy$$

$$= \int_{u=0}^{\infty} e^{-(\lambda+s)u} dG^{i*}(u) \int_{t=u}^{\infty} \left[e^{-s(t-u)} - e^{-(\lambda+s)(t-u)} \right] \bar{G}(t-u) dt \tag{10}$$

$$= g^i(\lambda+s) \left[\frac{1-g(s)}{s} - \frac{1-g(\lambda+s)}{\lambda+s} \right].$$

Now, putting

$$a_j(s) \overset{\text{def}}{=} \int_{0}^{\infty} e^{-(\lambda+s)x} \frac{(\lambda x)^j}{j!} dF(x), \tag{11}$$

$$b_j(s) \overset{\text{def}}{=} \frac{1}{1-g(\lambda+s)} \int_{0}^{\infty} e^{-(\lambda+s)x} \frac{(\lambda x)^j}{j!} dG(x) \tag{12}$$

and

$$d(s,m) \overset{\text{def}}{=} \frac{\delta_{m,0}}{1-g(\lambda+s)} \left[\frac{1-g(s)}{s} - \frac{1-g(\lambda+s)}{\lambda+s} \right], \tag{13}$$

we can obtain from (6) and (7) the following corresponding system for LTs:

$$\tilde{h}_0(s,m) = \sum_{k=1}^{N-1} b_k(s)\tilde{h}_k(s,m) + \tilde{h}_N(s,m)\sum_{k=N}^{\infty} b_k(s) + d(s,m) + \frac{\delta_{m,0}}{\lambda+s} \quad (14)$$

and

$$\tilde{h}_n(s,m) = I\{m \geq 1\}\left[\sum_{k=0}^{N-n-1} a_k(s)\tilde{h}_{n+k-1}(s,m-1) + \tilde{h}_{N-1}(s,m-1)\sum_{k=N-n}^{\infty} a_k(s)\right] + \delta_{m,0}\frac{1-f(s)}{s},$$
$$(15)$$

where $1 \leq n \leq N$.

In order to avoid inconveniences caused by indicators $I\{\cdot\}$, introduce the following PGF (compare (1)):

$$\tilde{h}_n(s,z) \overset{\text{def}}{=} \sum_{m=0}^{\infty} z^m \tilde{h}_n(s,m), \quad 0 \leq n \leq N, |z| < 1. \quad (16)$$

Defining also

$$\tilde{a}_j(s,z) \overset{\text{def}}{=} z a_j(s), \quad (17)$$

$$\gamma(s,z) \overset{\text{def}}{=} \sum_{m=0}^{\infty} z^m\left(d(s,m) + \frac{\delta_{m,0}}{\lambda+s}\right) = \frac{1-g(s)}{s[1-g(\lambda+s)]}, \quad (18)$$

the Eqs. (14) and (15) lead to

$$\tilde{h}_0(s,z) = \sum_{k=1}^{N-1} b_k(s)\tilde{h}_k(s,z) + \tilde{h}_N(s,z)\sum_{k=N}^{\infty} b_k(s) + \gamma(s,z), \quad (19)$$

$$\tilde{h}_n(s,z) = \sum_{k=0}^{N-n-1} \tilde{a}_k(s,z)\tilde{h}_{n+k-1}(s,z) + \tilde{h}_{N-1}(s,z)\sum_{k=N-n}^{\infty} \tilde{a}_k(s,z) + \frac{1-f(s)}{s}, \quad (20)$$

where $1 \leq n \leq N$.

Let us apply to the system (19) and (20) the following transformation:

$$\tilde{u}_n(s,z) \overset{\text{def}}{=} \tilde{h}_{N-n}(s,z), 0 \leq n \leq N. \quad (21)$$

We obtain now for $0 \leq n \leq N - 1$

$$\sum_{k=-1}^{n} \tilde{a}_{k+1}(s,z)\tilde{u}_{n-k}(s,z) - \tilde{u}_n(s,z) = \psi_n(s,z) \quad (22)$$

and

$$\tilde{u}_N(s,z) = \sum_{k=1}^{N-1} b_k(s)\tilde{u}_{N-k}(s,z) + \tilde{u}_0(s,z) \sum_{k=N}^{\infty} b_k(s) + \gamma(s,z), \tag{23}$$

where

$$\psi_n(s,z) \stackrel{def}{=} \tilde{a}_{n+1}(s,z)\tilde{u}_0(s,z) - \tilde{u}_1(s,z) \sum_{k=n+1}^{\infty} \tilde{a}_k(s,z) - \frac{1-f(s)}{s}. \tag{24}$$

4 Exact Solution for Departure Process

Due to the specific form of (22) (compare to (2)), the solution can be written as (see (3))

$$\tilde{u}_n(s,z) = C(s,z)R_{n+1}(s,z) + \sum_{k=0}^{n} R_{n-k}(s,z)\psi_k(s,z), \quad n \geq 0, \tag{25}$$

where (see (4) and (5))

$$\sum_{k=0}^{\infty} \theta^k R_k(s,z) = \frac{\theta}{A(\theta,s,z) - \theta}, \quad |\theta| < 1, \tag{26}$$

and

$$A(\theta,s,z) \stackrel{def}{=} \sum_{k=0}^{\infty} \tilde{a}_k(s,z)\theta^k. \tag{27}$$

Obviously, we must find the representation for $C(s,z)$. Substitution of $n=0$ to (25) leads to the equation

$$C(s,z) = \tilde{u}_0(s,z)\tilde{a}_0(s,z), \tag{28}$$

since from (26) and (27) follows that $R_1(s,z) = \frac{1}{\tilde{a}_0(s,z)}$. Taking $n=0$ in (22), we obtain

$$\tilde{a}_0(s,z)\tilde{u}_1(s,z) + \tilde{a}_1(s,z)\tilde{u}_0(s,z) - \tilde{u}_0(s,z) = \psi_0(s,z). \tag{29}$$

Because of $\sum_{j=0}^{\infty} \tilde{a}_j(s,z) = zf(s)$, we get from (24)

$$\psi_0(s,z) = \tilde{a}_1(s,z)\tilde{u}_0(s,z) - \tilde{u}_1(s,z)[zf(s) - \tilde{a}_0(s,z)] - \frac{1-f(s)}{s}, \tag{30}$$

and hence, applying (29), we eliminate $\tilde{u}_1(s,z)$ in the form

$$\tilde{u}_1(s,z) = [zf(s)]^{-1}\left[\tilde{u}_0(s,z) - \frac{1-f(s)}{s}\right].$$ (31)

Having in mind (24), (28) and (31), we obtain from (25)

$$\begin{aligned}
\tilde{u}_n(s,z) &= \tilde{a}_0(s,z)R_{n+1}(s,z)\tilde{u}_0(s,z)\\
&\quad + \sum_{k=0}^{n} R_{n-k}(s,z)\Big[\tilde{a}_{k+1}(s,z)\tilde{u}_0(s,z)\\
&\qquad -\tilde{u}_1(s,z)\sum_{i=k+1}^{\infty}\tilde{a}_i(s,z) - \frac{1-f(s)}{s}\Big]\\
&= \tilde{a}_0(s,z)R_{n+1}(s,z)\tilde{u}_0(s,z)\\
&\quad + \sum_{k=0}^{n} R_{n-k}(s,z)\Big[\tilde{a}_{k+1}(s,z)\tilde{u}_0(s,z) - (zf(s))^{-1}\\
&\qquad \left(\tilde{u}_0(s,z) - \frac{1-f(s)}{s}\right)\sum_{i=k+1}^{\infty}\tilde{a}_i(s,z) - \frac{1-f(s)}{s}\Big]
\end{aligned}$$ (32)

that gives

$$\tilde{u}_n(s,z) = A_n(s,z)\tilde{u}_0(s,z) + B_n(s,z),$$ (33)

where

$$\begin{aligned}
A_n(s,z) &\stackrel{\text{def}}{=} R_{n+1}(s,z)\tilde{a}_0(s,z)\\
&\quad + \sum_{k=0}^{n} R_{n-k}(s,z)\left[\tilde{a}_{k+1}(s,z) - (zf(s))^{-1}\sum_{i=k+1}^{\infty}\tilde{a}_i(s,z)\right]
\end{aligned}$$ (34)

and

$$B_n(s,z) \stackrel{\text{def}}{=} \frac{1-f(s)}{zsf(s)}\sum_{k=0}^{n} R_{n-k}(s,z)\left(\sum_{i=k+1}^{\infty}\tilde{a}_i(s,z) - zf(s)\right).$$ (35)

Substituting the representation (33) into (23), we obtain

$$\begin{aligned}
A_N(s,z)&\tilde{u}_0(s,z) + B_N(s,z)\\
&= \sum_{k=1}^{N-1} b_k(s)[A_{N-k}(s,z)\tilde{u}_0(s,z) + B_{N-k}(s,z)]\\
&\quad + \tilde{u}_0(s,z)\sum_{k=N}^{\infty} b_k(s) + \gamma(s,z)
\end{aligned}$$ (36)

and hence we eliminate $\tilde{u}_0(s, z)$ as follows:

$$\tilde{u}_0(s, z) = \frac{\sum_{k=1}^{N-1} b_k(s) B_{N-k}(s, z) - B_N(s, z) + \gamma(s, z)}{A_N(s, z) - \sum_{k=1}^{N-1} b_k(s) A_{N-k}(s, z) - \sum_{k=N}^{\infty} b_k(s)}. \tag{37}$$

Now, taking into consideration the formulae (21), (33) and (37), we can state the following main result:

Theorem 1. *The PGF of LT (mixed double transform) of the conditional probability distribution of the number of departures up to fixed time t (departure process at time t) $\tilde{h}_n(s, z)$ can be found using the following formulae:*

$$\tilde{h}_n(s, z) = A_{N-n}(s, z)\tilde{h}_{N-n}(s, z) + B_{N-n}(s, z), 0 \le n \le N - 1, \tag{38}$$

and

$$\tilde{h}_N(s, z) = \frac{\sum_{k=1}^{N-1} b_k(s) B_{N-k}(s, z) - B_N(s, z) + \gamma(s, z)}{A_N(s, z) - \sum_{k=1}^{N-1} b_k(s) A_{N-k}(s, z) - \sum_{k=N}^{\infty} b_k(s)}, \tag{39}$$

where the formulae for $b_k(s), \gamma(s, z), A_k(s, z)$ and $B_k(s, z)$ are given in (12), (18), (34) and (35), respectively.

5   Mean Number of Departures

As a conclusion from Theorem 1, we can find the representation for the mean number of successful departures up to fixed time epoch t, conditioned by the number of packets being accumulated in the buffer initially. Indeed, denoting

$$\mathbf{E}_n[h(t)] \overset{\text{def}}{=} \sum_{m=0}^{\infty} m \mathbf{P}\{h(t) = m | X(0) = n\}, \tag{40}$$

we get

$$\mathbf{E}_n[h(t)] = \mathrm{LT}^{-1} \left[\int_0^{\infty} e^{-st} \sum_{m=0}^{\infty} m \mathbf{P}\{h(t) = m | X(0) = n\} dt \right]$$
$$= \mathrm{LT}^{-1} \left[\frac{\partial}{\partial z} \tilde{h}_n(s, z) \right]_{z=1}, \tag{41}$$

where the notation LT^{-1} stands for the inverse LT operator.

6 Numerical Examples

In this section we illustrate theoretical results by numerical examples, for which we discuss the dependence of the successful departures counted to fixed time epoch t on server vacation duration, intensity of arrivals and processing speed. Assume that packets of average sizes 500 B arrive at the wireless sensor network node according to Poisson process with rate λ and are being individually processed accordingly to FIFO service discipline, with exponentially distributed service time with mean μ^{-1}. For numerical calculations we also assume that an MVP consists of independent exponentially distributed server vacations, each one with mean $\frac{1}{\lambda_v}$. Firstly we use the formulae (38) and (39) from Theorem 1 to obtain explicit representations the mixed double transform of the conditional probability distribution of the number of departures up to fixed time t. Secondly we calculate the mean number of successful departures using the formula (41), where the LT^{-1} operator is calculated using the procedures of numerical Laplace transform inversion, based on algorithms of Abate-Choudhury-Whitt (presented in [1]) and the Gaver-Stehfest algorithm proposed in [2, 3], which is a combination of two approaches given in [7, 21]. The results are illustrated in successive figures.

Firstly, we visualize the dependence of the mean number of successful departures up to fixed time epoch t on the single server vacation duration, by subsequent changes of single vacation period parameter taking values $\lambda_v = 10^3, 5 * 10^3, 15 * 10^3$ and $40 * 10^3$. The remaining system parameters are $\lambda = 15 * 10^3$ packets/s (corresponding to intensity 60 Mb/s), $n = 0, N = 10$ and $\mu = 25 * 10^3$ packets/s (corresponding to 100 Mb/s). The results are given in Fig. 1.

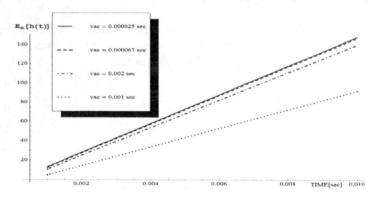

Fig. 1. $E_n[h(t)]$ in dependence on single vacation duration for $n = 0$

Next, let us investigate the dependence of the mean number of successful departures up to fixed time epoch t on the intensity of packet arrivals for $\lambda = 10^4, 2 * 10^4$ and $3 * 10^4$ packets/s (corresponding to intensities 40 Mb/s, 80 Mb/s and 120 Mb/s, respectively), where the initial buffer state $n = 1$, $n = 1$, the maximum system capacity $N = 10$, the processing rate $\mu = 25 * 10^3$ (corresponding to intensity 100 Mb/s), and the parameter of exponentially distributed server vacation $\lambda_v = 6 * 10^4$. The results are given in Fig. 2.

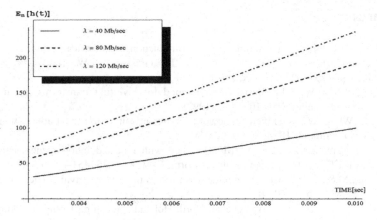

Fig. 2. $\mathbf{E}_n[h(t)]$ in dependence on the arrival intensity λ

Finally, we visualize the impact of the service speed on the mean number of successful departures up to fixed time epoch t for three different exponential processing rates $\mu = 15 * 10^3, 20 * 10^3$ and $25 * 10^3$ packets/s (corresponding to 60 Mb/s, 80 Mb/s and 100 Mb/s, respectively), where the arrival rate $\lambda = 2 * 10^4$ packets/s (corresponds to intensity of 80 Mb/s), the initial buffer state $n = 3$, the maximum system capacity equals $N = 10$, and $\lambda_v = 6 * 10^4$. The results are presented in Fig. 3.

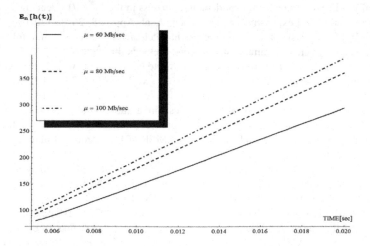

Fig. 3. $\mathbf{E}_n[h(t)]$ in dependence on the processing rate μ

Acknowledgements. The infrastructure was supported by "PL-LAB2020" project, contract POIG.02.03.01-00-104/13-00.

References

1. Abate, J., Choudhury, G.L., Whitt, W.: An introduction to numerical transform inversion and its application to probability models. In: Grassmann, W. (ed.) Computational Probability, pp. 257–323. Kluwer, Boston (2000)
2. Abate, J., Whitt, W.: The fourier-series method for inverting transforms of probability distributions. Queueing Syst. **10**, 5–88 (1992)
3. Abate, J., Whitt, W.: A unified framework for numerically inverting Laplace transforms. INFORMS J. Comput. **18**, 408–421 (2006)
4. Alouf, S., Altman, E., Azad, A.: M/G/1 queue with repeated inhomogeneous vacations applied to IEEE 802.16e power saving. Perform. Eval. Rev. **36**, 451–452 (2008)
5. Bratiichuk, M.S., Chydziński, A.: On the loss process in a batch arrival queue. Appl. Math. Model. **33**, 3565–3577 (2009)
6. Cohen, J.W.: The Single Server Queue. North-Holland Publishing Company, Amsterdam (1982)
7. Gaver, D.P.: Observing stochastic processes, and approximate transform inversion. Oper. Res. **14**, 444–459 (1966)
8. Ishikawa, A.: On the joint distribution of the departure intervals in an M/G/1/N queue. J. Oper. Res. Soc. Jpn. **34**, 422–435 (1991)
9. Kadankov, V., Kadankova, T.: Busy period, virtual waiting time and number of the customers in $G^d/M^k/1/B$ system. Queueing Syst. **65**, 175–209 (2010)
10. Kempa, W.M.: The departure process for queueing systems with batch arrival of customers. Stoch. Models **24**, 246–263 (2008)
11. Kempa, W.M.: On one approach to study of departure process in batch arrival queues with multiple vacations. In: Applied Stochastic Models and Data Analysis, ASMDA-2009, Vilnius, Lithuania, pp. 203–207 (2009)
12. Kempa, W.M.: Some new results for departure process in the $M^X/G/1$ queueing system with a single vacation and exhaustive service. Stoch. Anal. Appl. **28**, 26–43 (2010)
13. Kempa, W.M.: Analysis of departure process in batch arrival queue with multiple vacations and exhaustive service. Commun. Stat.-Theory Methods **40**, 2856–2865 (2011)
14. Kempa, Wojciech M.: Departure process in finite-buffer queue with batch arrivals. In: Al-Begain, K., Balsamo, S., Fiems, D., Marin, A. (eds.) ASMTA 2011. LNCS, vol. 6751, pp. 1–13. Springer, Heidelberg (2011). doi:10.1007/978-3-642-21713-5_1
15. Kempa, W.M.: On transient departure process in a finite-buffer queueing model with probabilistic packet dropping. In: AIP Conference Proceedings of the Applications of Mathematics in Engineering and Economics, AMEE 2014, Sozopol, Bulgaria, vol. 1631, pp. 42–49 (2014)
16. Kempa, Wojciech M.: Output process in batch-arrival queue with N-policy and multiple vacations. In: Dudin, A., De Turck, K. (eds.) ASMTA 2013. LNCS, vol. 7984, pp. 247–261. Springer, Heidelberg (2013). doi:10.1007/978-3-642-39408-9_18
17. Kempa, W.M.: Transient analysis of the output process in the GI/M/1-type queue with finite buffer. In: AIP Conference Proceedings of the Application of Mathematics in Technical and Natural Sciences, AMiTaNS 2012, St. Constantine and Helena, Bulgaria, vol. 1487, pp. 193–200 (2012)
18. Korolyuk, V.S.: Boundary-Value Problems for Compound Poisson Processes. Naukova Dumka, Kiev (1975)

19. Mancuso, V., Alouf, S.: Analysis of power saving with continuous connectivity. J. Comput. Netw. **10**, 2481–2493 (2012)
20. Seo, J., Lee, S., Park, N., Lee, H., Cho, C.: Performance analysis of sleep mode operation in IEEE 802.16e. In: Proceedings of VTC2004-Fall (Los Angeles), vol. 2, pp. 1169–1173 (2004)
21. Stehfest, H.: Algorithm 368: Numerical inversion of laplace transforms. Commun. ACM **13**, 47–49 (1970)

Parallelization of Fast Sort Algorithm

Zbigniew Marszałek[(⊠)]

Institute of Mathematics, Silesian University of Technology,
ul. Kaszubska 23, 44-100 Gliwice, Poland
Zbigniew.Marszalek@polsl.pl

Abstract. Sorting algorithms are widely used in databases and various information systems to organize and search for information. In this paper, author describes version of parallization of fast sort algorithm for large data sets. Examination of the paralization of fast sort algorithm performance was subject to performance tests, that showed validity.

Keywords: Parallel algorithm · Data sorting · Data mining · Analysis of computer algorithms

1 Introduction

Advances in technology allowed the construction of computers with high computing power and store huge data sets [6, 7, 14, 20]. This implies a need to create dedicated software to enable efficient processing of such huge datasets and ability to search the requested information under managed queues [11, 13, 19, 26, 28, 30, 34]. Similarly modern devices enable implementing of intelligent software created to assist people [9, 10] by processing information encoded in vision [12, 14] and sound [22], what brings crucial help for data mining [1, 5, 21, 24]. As always in such a case, the special role play sorting algorithms and parallelization of computational processes which can improve efficiency. Widely appropriate sorting algorithm in NoSQL databases is a merge sort. Very powerful sorting algorithms are also described in [3, 4, 16] where research showed that devoted versions of sorting methods improve systems work since faster data management helps on reduction of power consumption [2, 8, 25]. However, sorting algorithms in its present versions do not have the capacity to perform well on multiple processors. Therefore this paper presents a modification of the algorithm that allows parallelization of sorting process and reducing the time complexity to $\vartheta(n)$ using $n/3$ processors. Constant presented in the algorithm remains unchanged from the original version [16] and the algorithm can be used in the same version on any computer with a limited number of processors.

1.1 Related Works

There is a large discrepancy between theory and practice of parallelization algorithms. In the 1960s and at the end of last century were carried out research on the achievement of the best possible asymptotic complexity of sorting algorithms, e.g. Richard Cole in 1988, in [4] described merge sort algorithm of complexity $O(\log_2 n)$ using n processors.

© Springer International Publishing AG 2017
R. Damaševičius and V. Mikašytė (Eds.): ICIST 2017, CCIS 756, pp. 408–421, 2017.
DOI: 10.1007/978-3-319-67642-5_34

This algorithm was disproportionately high fixed. Proposed in [3, 15, 23, 32] or [33] ways of sorting are hard to apply to parallel systems. Recent research results on improved quicksort [29] and merge sort [17, 27] sowed it is possible to make an attempt to bridge the gap between theory and practice, what resulted in new method [16]. Although there various approaches to parallel [18] and dynamic [31] versions of sorting, multiway methods seems to be still far from practical application in NoSQL databases. Therefore in this article will be discussed a derivative from our recent research. The most commonly used model for analysis of parallel algorithms is machine PRAM. In practice, we distinguish between three variants of this model. The first model EREW PRAM gives you the ability to read and write memory by only one processor. The second model CREW gives the right memory read by any processor and the right to write at the same time by only one processor. The third model of the CRCW PRAM enables simultaneous access of all processors to computer memory. In this work will be used first model EREW PRAM. Tasks will be distributed so that the processor does not operate on the same memory space.

1.2 Parallel Sort Algorithms and Big Data Sets

Traditional way of storing and accessing data in a database employs a row format. However, analytics run best on a columnar format. A set of algorithms is automatically run on the data being stored in the memory columnar. In memory column we can store units, as shown in Fig. 1. In memory columnar data is fragmented into smaller units, so that parallelization is possible when running a query on overall data. Processing large data sets requires efficient and stable algorithms. Parallelization of fast sort algorithm allows to sort in parallel while maintaining low computational complexity. To compare speed of the algorithm by using different numbers of processors has been used in tests time measured by the CPU (Central Processing Unit) and clock cycles (clock rate). This allows objective assessment of operation of parallel calculation process.

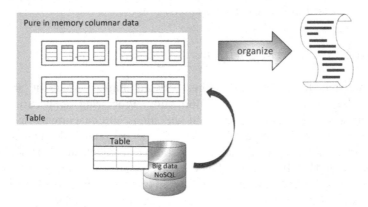

Fig. 1. In memory columnar data is fragmented into smaller units to enable parallelization.

1.3   Statistical Research on Algorithm Performance

Let $a_1, a_2, \ldots, a_n$ denote disordered number of distributed results of observations of some features of A, and let $\bar{a}$ be arithmetic mean of these results

$$\bar{a} = \frac{a_1 + a_2 + \cdots + a_n}{n} \tag{1}$$

Standard deviation of sample describes amount of information we have. In study for large data sets we used formula

$$\sigma = \sqrt{\frac{(a_1 - \bar{a})^2 + (a_2 - \bar{a})^2 + .. + (a_n - \bar{a})^2}{n - 1}} \tag{2}$$

where n is the number of elements in sample, $a_1, a_1, \ldots, a_n$ are values of the random variable in the sample, $\bar{a}$ is the arithmetic mean of the sample. In order to find the most efficient algorithm is carried out analysis of average time for sufficiently large set of data. The analysis for sorting time was carried out in 100 benchmark tests for each of the fixed dimension of the task on the input.

Algorithm's stability is best described on basis of coefficient of variation. Coefficient of variation is a measure that allows determining value of diversity in examined population. It is determined by the formula

$$V = \frac{\sigma}{\bar{a}} \tag{3}$$

where we use arithmetic mean (1) and standard deviation (2). The coefficient of variation reflects the stability of the method in a statistical sense. Benchmark tests of the newly proposed method for sorting sets were taken for 100, 1000, 10000, 100000, 1000000, 10000000 and 100000000 elements on the input. The results are presented in graphs and discussed in the following sections.

2   Parallel Fast Sort Algorithm

Big data and real time analytics requires forward thinking solutions and enough computer power to obtain necessary information. Processing applications of huge information requires algorithms to perform operations in a concurrent way, so that it was possible to access them in real time. They play an important role in parallel sorting algorithms such as parallel merge sort. Let's think of parallelism of the sorting algorithm presented in [16]. In order to allow the performance of the fast sorting algorithm FSA we should resign from the recording merged first two strings to a buffer. This can be done by declaring an array of dimension tasks and save merged string into an array, so that index merged within temporary table was the same as the index of the first merged strings. Figure 2 shows how to merge the input of numbers in the first step. This way of writing merged sequences allows division merge between processors, because none of them will use the same memory resources.

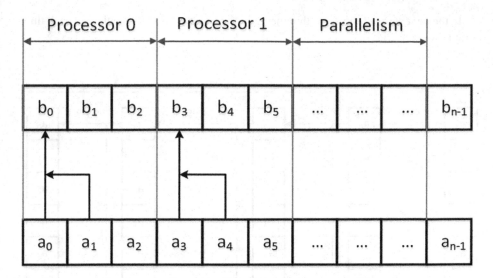

Fig. 2. Parallel merge of the first two numeric strings in the first step of FSA.

The algorithm then merges the string stored in temporary array to third string located in the input array. The result of merge is stored in input array. Way to parallelize the process of merging n/3 strings is shown in Fig. 3.

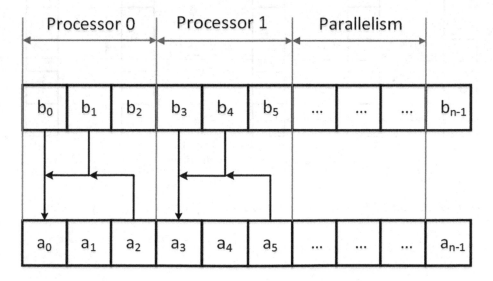

Fig. 3. Parallel merge of temporary array to the third string located in the input array.

In the next steps of the algorithm merge in the same way, strings enlarged each time three times, see Fig. 4.

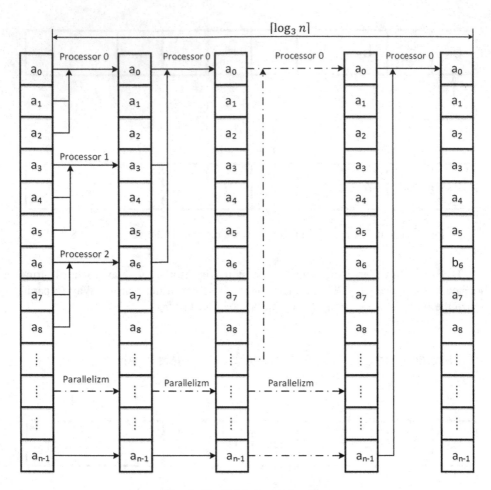

Fig. 4. Parallel fast sort algorithm.

Theorem 1. Parallel Fast Sort Algorithm using $n/3$ processors has time complexity

$$T_{max} = \frac{5}{2}n - 2\log_3 n - \frac{5}{2} \tag{4}$$

Proof. We are limiting deliberations to $n = 3^k$, where $k = 1, 2, \ldots$.

Let us first notice that tree sequences $x_1 \leq \cdots \leq x_t$, $y_1 \leq \cdots \leq y_t$ and $z_1 \leq \cdots \leq z_t$ of t elements, we can merge into one sequence $a_1 \leq \cdots \leq a_{3t}$, using twice merging two sequences, making no more $5t - 2$ comparison elements of sequences X, Y and Z.

In the first step $t = 1$ and $n/3$ processors perform in a concurrent merge three one element strings by doing no more than $5 \cdot 1 - 2 = 3$ comparisons for each processor. In fact, the time to complete the entire operation is such as the duration of one processor. In each time step t, $n/3^t$ processors performs the integration of three strings 3^{t-1} elements by doing no more than

$$5 \cdot 3^{t-1} - 2 \tag{5}$$

comparisons. All operations performed in a simultaneous we can save in the form of

$$\sum_{t=1}^{k} \left(5 \cdot 3^{t-1} - 2\right) = 5 \cdot \sum_{t=1}^{k} 3^{t-1} - 2 \cdot \sum_{t=1}^{k} 1$$
$$= 5\left(1 + 3 + \cdots + 3^{k-1}\right) - 2k = 5 \cdot \left(\frac{3^k - 1}{2}\right) - 2\log_3 n \tag{6}$$
$$= \frac{5}{2}n - 2\log_3 n - \frac{5}{2}$$

which was to prove.

Presented method was implemented in C# Visual Studio Ultimate 2013. The algorithm uses a parallel loop, which takes as arguments the start index, number of iterations, and action (Action object<int>). Loop Paraller. For reduces created program code, because there is no need to create separate tasks, run them and wait for them to finish. The algorithm presented in Fig. 5 uses maximum number of processors available on the system.

2.1   The Study of the Proposed Parallel Method of Sorting

Performance analysis of presented method is based on benchmark tests for the algorithm implemented in C# in Visual Studio 2013 Ultimate on MS Windows Server 2012. The study was conducted on 100 input samples randomly generated for each dimension of the task. Tests were carried out on quad core amd opteron processor 8356 8p. The purpose of the analysis and comparison is to check how parallel calculation process speeds up sorting large data sets. For the benchmark were applied input samples of 100, 1000, 10000, 100000, 1000000, 10000000 and 100000000 elements. Each sorting operation by examined methods was measured in time [ms] and CPU (Central Processing Unit) usage represented in tics of CPU clock.

These results are averaged for 100 sorting samples. Benchmark comparison for PFSA are describe in Tables 1 and 2, Figs. 6 and 7.

Comparison of coefficient of variation for PFSA methods for large data sets is presented in Tables 3 and 4.

Analyzing Tables 3 and 4 we see that algorithm for any number of CPUs used in statistic has the same stability for large data sets. Some variations in stability of the algorithm for small inputs are due to the fact that the system exceed sorting algorithm.

```
Start
Load table a
Load dimension of table a into n
Create an array of b of dimension n
Set options for parallelism to use all
processors of the system
Remember 1 in tt
While tt is less than n then do
Begin
     Remember 2*tt in zz0
     Remember 3*tt in zz1
     Remember (n - tt - 1) / zz1 in it
     Parallel for each processor at index j greater
     or equal 0 and less than it + 1 do
     Begin parallel for
         Remember j * zz1 in i
         Remember i + tt in tz1
         Remember i in tra
         Remember i in tr0
         Remember tz1 in tr1
         Remember i + zz0 in tr2
         If tr2 greater than n then do
         Begin
             Remember n in tr2
         End
         While tr0 less than tr1
         and tz1 less than tr2 then do
         Begin
             If a[tr0] less or equal a[tz1] then do
             Begin
                 Remember a[tr0] in b[tra]
                 Add to index tr0 one
             End
             Else
             Begin
                 Remember a[tz1] in b[tra]
                 Add to index tz1 one
             End
             Add to index tra one
         End
         While tr0 less than tr1 then do
         Begin
             Remember a[tr0] in b[tra]
             Add to index tr0 one
             Add to index tra one
         End
```

Fig. 5. Parallel fast sort algorithm

```
                    Remember i in txa
                    Remember i in tr0
                    Remember i + zz1 in tr3
                    If tr3 greater than n then do
                    Begin
                          Remember n in tr3
                    End
                    While txa less than tra
                    and tr2 less than tr3 then do
                    Begin
                          If b[txa] less or equal a[tr2] then do
                          Begin
                                Remember b[txa] in a[tr0]
                                Add to index txa one
                          End
                          Else
                          Begin
                                Remember a[tr2] in a[tr0]
                                Add to index tr2 one
                          End
                          Add to index tr0 one
                    End
                    While txa less than tra then do
                    Begin
                          Remember b[txa] in a[tr0]
                          Add to index txa one
                          Add to index tr0 one
                    End

              End of the parallel for
              Multiply variable tt by three
        End
        Stop
```

Fig. 5. (*continued*)

2.2   Analysis and Comparison of Sorting Time

Analysis and comparison will describe efficiency for sorting large data sets. Let us compare the algorithm assuming that duration of the method using one processor and let as examine if the duration of action is shorter for the method using multiple processors. The results are shown in the graphs Figs. 8 and 9.

The study shows that FSA operates in shorter time measuring tasks from 10 000 to 1 000 000. With the increase in the number of sorted elements of the effectiveness of the methods of parallelism becomes visible, what improves sorting for large data sets.

Table 1. The results of sorting parallel fast sort algorithms in [ms].

Method – average time sorting for 100 samples in [ms]				
Elements	1–processor	2–processors	4–processors	8–processors
100	1	1	1	1
1 000	2	2	2	2
10 000	7	6	6	6
100 000	55	41	32	24
1 000 000	661	420	315	217
10 000 000	7537	4461	3323	2230
100 000 000	84896	49478	35825	23967

Table 2. The results of sorting parallel fast sort algorithms in [ti].

Method – average time sorting for 100 samples in [ti]				
Elements	1–processor	2–processors	4–processors	8–processors
100	1759	1675	1606	1605
1 000	3211	3048	3059	3043
10 000	11021	10005	9628	9318
100 000	85543	67273	49045	36679
1 000 000	1029981	658732	476982	325985
10 000 000	11746618	6953534	5080104	3317956
100 000 000	132323223	77118348	55837661	36356198

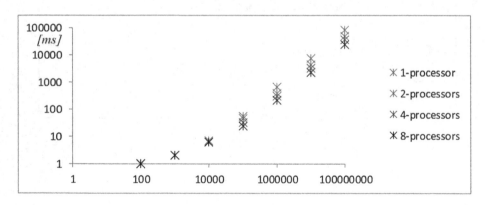

Fig. 6. Comparison of benchmark time [ms]

3 Final Remarks

The article presented Parallel Fast Sort Algorithm for rapid sorting of large data sets. The tests demonstrate stability of the method and confirm theoretical time complexity. Parallel Fast Sort Algorithm can find practical application in NoSQL databases,

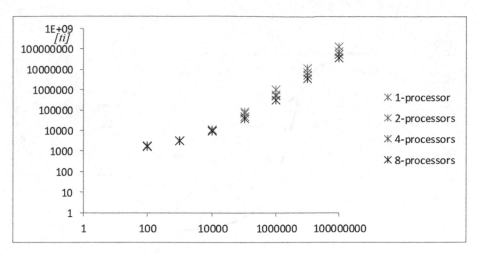

Fig. 7. Comparison of benchmark time [ti]

Table 3. Coefficient of variation for FSA [ms].

Coefficient of variation [ms]				
Elements	1–processor	2–processors	4–processors	8–processors
100	0,3779644	0,4367821	0,4183471	0,4629100
1 000	0,3273268	0,4225771	0,4225771	0,2817180
10 000	0,3818017	0,3392334	0,2886751	0,3622089
100 000	0,1893255	0,2993231	0,1619496	0,1079664
1 000 000	0,1844882	0,1837794	0,1753136	0,1427409
10 000 000	0,1967079	0,2122525	0,1769588	0,1449125
100 000 000	0,2010331	0,2039987	0,1939415	0,1393479

Table 4. Coefficient of variation for FSA [ti].

Coefficient of variation [ti]				
Elements	1–processor	2–processors	4–processors	8–processors
100	0,3572552	0,3434650	0,4285883	0,3373299
1 000	0,2613546	0,2181388	0,1969925	0,2113027
10 000	0,2590488	0,3066372	0,1775589	0,3563180
100 000	0,1895242	0,2956528	0,1650359	0,1024241
1 000 000	0,1845861	0,1843094	0,1751595	0,1426187
10 000 000	0,1967101	0,2122440	0,1769479	0,1449022
100 000 000	0,2010302	0,2040005	0,1939433	0,1393424

however newly proposed method gives better effects in case of limited amount of processors in the system.

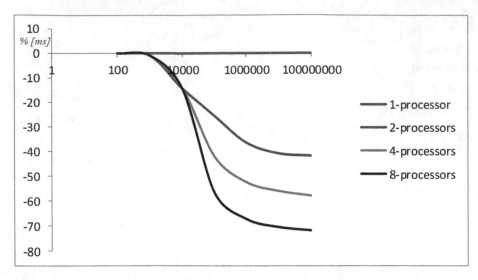

Fig. 8. Comparison of the method using multiple processors in terms of operational time [ms].

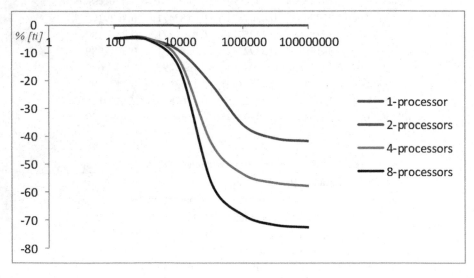

Fig. 9. Comparison of the method using multiple processors in terms of operational time [ti].

References

1. Artiemjew, P., Nowak, B.A., Polkowski, L.T.: A new classifier based on the dual indiscernibility matrix. In: Dregvaite, G., Damasevicius, R. (eds.) ICIST 2016. CCIS, vol. 639, pp. 380–391. Springer, Cham (2016). doi:10.1007/978-3-319-46254-7_30
2. Bonanno, F., Capizzi, G., Napoli, C.: Some remarks on the application of RNN and PRNN for the charge-discharge simulation of advanced lithium-ions battery energy storage. In: Power Electronics, Electrical Drives, Automation and Motion, SPEEDAM 2012, pp. 941–945. IEEE (2012). doi:10.1109/SPEEDAM.2012.6264500
3. Carlsson, S., Levcopoulos, C., Petersson, O.: Sublinear merging and natural merge sort. In: Asano, T., Ibaraki, T., Imai, H., Nishizeki, T. (eds.) SIGAL 1990. LNCS, vol. 450, pp. 251–260. Springer, Heidelberg (1990). doi:10.1007/3-540-52921-7_74
4. Cole, R.: Parallel merge sort. SIAM J. Comput. 17(4), 770–785 (1988). doi:10.1137/0217049
5. Czerwinski, D.: Digital filter implementation in hadoop data mining system. In: Gaj, P., Kwiecień, A., Stera, P. (eds.) CN 2015. CCIS, vol. 522, pp. 410–420. Springer, Cham (2015). doi:10.1007/978-3-319-19419-6_39
6. Czerwinski, D., Przylucki, S., Matejczuk, P.: Resource management in grid systems. In: Kwiecień, A., Gaj, P., Stera, P. (eds.) CN 2012. CCIS, vol. 291, pp. 101–110. Springer, Heidelberg (2012). doi:10.1007/978-3-642-31217-5_11
7. Czerwinski, D.: Numerical performance in the grid network relies on a grid appliance. In: Kwiecień, A., Gaj, P., Stera, P. (eds.) CN 2011. CCIS, vol. 160, pp. 214–223. Springer, Heidelberg (2011). doi:10.1007/978-3-642-21771-5_23
8. Damaševičius, R., Toldinas, J., Grigaravicius, G.: Modelling battery behaviour using chipset energy benchmarking. Elektronika Ir Elektrotechnika 19(6), 117–120 (2013). doi:10.5755/j01.eee.19.6.4577
9. Damaševičius, R., Vasiljevas, M., Salkevicius, J., Woźniak, M.: Human activity recognition in AAL environments using random projections. In: Computational and Mathematical Methods in Medicine, vol. 2016, pp. 4073584:1–4073584:17. Hindawi Publishing Corporation (2016). doi:10.1155/2016/4073584
10. Damaševičius, R., Maskeliunas, R., Venckauskas, A., Woźniak, M.: Smartphone user identity verification using gait characteristics. Symmetry 8(10), 100:1–100:20 (2016). doi:10.3390/sym8100100. MDPI
11. Gabryel, M.: The bag-of-features algorithm for practical applications using the MySQL database. In: Rutkowski, L., Korytkowski, M., Scherer, R., Tadeusiewicz, R., Zadeh, L.A., Zurada, J.M. (eds.) ICAISC 2016. LNCS, vol. 9693, pp. 635–646. Springer, Cham (2016). doi:10.1007/978-3-319-39384-1_56
12. Gabryel, M., Grycuk, R., Korytkowski, M., Holotyak, T.: Image indexing and retrieval using GSOM algorithm. In: Rutkowski, L., Korytkowski, M., Scherer, R., Tadeusiewicz, R., Zadeh, L.A., Zurada, J.M. (eds.) ICAISC 2015. LNCS, vol. 9119, pp. 706–714. Springer, Cham (2015). doi:10.1007/978-3-319-19324-3_63
13. Gabryel, M., Woźniak, M., Damaševičius, R.: An application of differential evolution to positioning queueing systems. In: Rutkowski, L., Korytkowski, M., Scherer, R., Tadeusiewicz, R., Zadeh, L.A., Zurada, J.M. (eds.) ICAISC 2015. LNCS, vol. 9120, pp. 379–390. Springer, Cham (2015). doi:10.1007/978-3-319-19369-4_34

14. Grycuk, R., Gabryel, M., Scherer, R., Voloshynovskiy, S.: Multi-layer architecture for storing visual data based on WCF and microsoft SQL server database. In: Rutkowski, L., Korytkowski, M., Scherer, R., Tadeusiewicz, R., Zadeh, L.A., Zurada, J.M. (eds.) ICAISC 2015. LNCS, vol. 9119, pp. 715–726. Springer, Cham (2015). doi:10.1007/978-3-319-19324-3_64

15. Gubias, L.J.: Sorting unsorted and partially sorted lists using the natural merge sort. Softw. Pract. Exp. **11**(12), 1339–1340 (2006). doi:10.1002/spe.4380111211

16. Marszałek, Z.: Novel recursive fast sort algorithm. In: Dregvaite, G., Damasevicius, R. (eds.) ICIST 2016. CCIS, vol. 639, pp. 344–355. Springer, Cham (2016). doi:10.1007/978-3-319-46254-7_27

17. Marszałek, Z., Woźniak, M., Borowik, G., Wazirali, R., Napoli, C., Pappalardo, G., Tramontana, E.: Benchmark tests on improved merge for big data processing. In: Asia-Pacific Conference on Computer Aided System Engineering APCASE 2015, pp. 96–101. IEEE, 14–16 July, Quito, Ecuador (2015). doi:10.1109/APCASE.2015.24

18. Axtmann, M., Bigmann, T., Schulz, C., Sanders, P.: Practical massively parallel sorting. arXiv:1410.6754v2 [cs.DS]. 25 Feb 2015

19. Kempa, W.M.: A comprehensive study on the queue-size distribution in a finite-buffer system with a general independent input flow. Perform. Eval. **108**, 1–15 (2017)

20. Kempa, W.M.: Transient workload distribution in the M/G/1 finite-buffer queue with single and multiple vacations. Ann. Oper. Res. **239**(2), 381–400 (2016)

21. Nowak, B.A., Nowicki, R.K., Woźniak, M., Napoli, C.: Multi-class nearest neighbour classifier for incomplete data handling. In: Rutkowski, L., Korytkowski, M., Scherer, R., Tadeusiewicz, R., Zadeh, L.A., Zurada, J.M. (eds.) ICAISC 2015. LNCS, vol. 9119, pp. 469–480. Springer, Cham (2015). doi:10.1007/978-3-319-19324-3_42

22. Damaševičius, R., Napoli, C., Sidekerskiene, T., Woźniak, M.: IMF mode demixing in EMD for jitter analysis. J. Comput. Sci. (2017). doi:10.1016/j.jocs.2017.04.008,Elsevier

23. Rauh, A., Arce, G.: A fast weighted median algorithm based on quick select. In: Proceedings of the IEEE International Conference on Image Processing, pp. 105–108 (2010)

24. Szypulski, J., Artiemjew, P.: The rough granular approach to classifier synthesis by means of SVM. In: Yao, Y., Hu, Q., Yu, H., Grzymala-Busse, J.W. (eds.) RSFDGrC 2015. LNCS, vol. 9437, pp. 256–263. Springer, Cham (2015). doi:10.1007/978-3-319-25783-9_23

25. Woźniak, M., Połap, D., Napoli, C., Tramontana, E.: Application of bio-inspired methods in distributed gaming systems. Inf. Tech Control **46**(1), 150–164 (2017)

26. Woźniak, M., Gabryel, M., Nowicki, R.K., Nowak, B.A.: An application of firefly algorithm to position traffic in NoSQL database systems. In: Kunifuji, S., Papadopoulos, G.A., Skulimowski, A.M.J., Kacprzyk, J. (eds.) Knowledge, Information and Creativity Support Systems. AISC, vol. 416, pp. 259–272. Springer, Cham (2016). doi:10.1007/978-3-319-27478-2_18

27. Woźniak, M., Marszałek, Z., Gabryel, M., Nowicki, Robert K.: Preprocessing large data sets by the use of quick sort algorithm. In: Skulimowski, A.M.J., Kacprzyk, J. (eds.) Knowledge, Information and Creativity Support Systems: Recent Trends, Advances and Solutions. AISC, vol. 364, pp. 111–121. Springer, Cham (2016). doi:10.1007/978-3-319-19090-7_9

28. Woźniak, M., Kempa, W., Gabryel, M., Nowicki, R.: A finite-buffer queue with single vacation policy - analytical study with evolutionary positioning. Int. J. Appl. Math. Comput. Sci. **24**(4), 887–900 (2014). doi:10.2478/amcs-2014-0065

29. Woźniak, M., Marszałek, Z., Gabryel, M., Nowicki, Robert K.: Modified merge sort algorithm for large scale data sets. In: Rutkowski, L., Korytkowski, M., Scherer, R., Tadeusiewicz, R., Zadeh, L.A., Zurada, J.M. (eds.) ICAISC 2013. LNCS, vol. 7895, pp. 612–622. Springer, Heidelberg (2013). doi:10.1007/978-3-642-38610-7_56

30. Woźniak, M.: On applying cuckoo search algorithm to positioning GI/M/1/N finite-buffer queue with a single vacation policy. In: Proceedings of the 12th Mexican International Conference on Artificial Intelligence – MICAI 2013, 24–30 November, Mexico City, Mexico, pp. 59–64. IEEE (2013). doi:10.1109/MICAI.2013.12

31. Zhang, W., Larson, P.A.: Dynamic memory adjustment for external mergesort. In: Proceedings of Very Large Data Bases Conference, pp. 376–385 (1997)

32. Zhang, W., Larson P.A.: Buffering and read-ahead strategies for external mergesort. In: Proceedings of Very Large Data Bases Conference, pp. 523–533 (1998)

33. Zheng, L., Larson, P.A.: Speeding up external mergesort. IEEE Trans. Knowl. Data Eng. **8** (2), 322–332 (1996). doi:10.1109/69.494169

34. Tikhonenko, O.M., Kempa, W.M.: Performance evaluation of an M/G/n-type queue with bounded capacity and packet dropping. Appl. Math. Comput. Sci. **26**(4), 841–854 (2016)

Extraction and Analysis of Voice Samples
Based on Short Audio Files

Dawid Połap and Marcin Woźniak[✉]

Institute of Mathematics, Silesian University of Technology,
Kaszubska 23, 44-100 Gliwice, Poland
{dawid.polap,marcin.wozniak}@polsl.pl

Abstract. Some voice defects may be removed from a recording in such a way that the remainder of the sample contains only the relevant data. However processing of input sounds to achieve this goal requires methodology that will be able to distinguish between clear sound and noise. In this paper, we propose data extraction technique and defect analysis. Developed methodology may allow for possible use in various life support systems, where sounds are processed to verify identity, control, communicate, etc. Proposed method has been tested and compared to other indirect methods.

Keywords: Short-Time Fourier Transform · Key-Point analysis · Heuristic algorithm · Spectrograms · Voice defects · Short audio files

1 Introduction

Sound is one of the features which we use to communicate. Over the years we have developed various methods of processing sounds to be forwarded between users in communication technology. Starting from the invention of the telephone it was possible to communicate over the remote distance using voice. With the development in technology voice became passed on the radio. Recent years showed a boost of computer technology, it become possible to process sounds in a digital way. Various devices use sounds to control but also now it is possible to use voice for registering and access management. To use a digital form of the sound we need to compute methodologies to process, manage and store information encoded in a digital form.

Storing of the information mainly involves data base systems. There are mainly two kinds of data bases: with some implemented methodologies that use a specific languages like various sql [10] and without it, so called nosql approaches [9] in which we need to implement management algorithms i.e. to sort the data [7, 11]. The efficiency of data base lays upon infrastructure and implemented approaches. Among these we have data mining techniques that assist in information retrieval with devoted information classifiers [15] and approaches for incomplete data using boosted techniques [16] or fuzzy-neural systems [17]. For all these implementations we need programming languages. There are many technologies which use programming to customize connections and transfer [4, 20] but also give annotations to make human oriented source code [5, 6].

© Springer International Publishing AG 2017
R. Damaševičius and V. Mikašytė (Eds.): ICIST 2017, CCIS 756, pp. 422–431, 2017.
DOI: 10.1007/978-3-319-67642-5_35

1.1 Related Works

There are various possibilities to use sounds as a source of information about humans. In medicine we can use sounds from ECG examination to help doctors evaluate heart actions [12] or use other analytical approaches to evaluate human activity [1]. Similarly we can use information from environment sounds to compose images of objects, i.e. for bathymetric purposes [18]. Human voice can be used to verification processes in various control systems. However voice is a type of sound, which is connected to language and therefore may undergo dialects. Therefore before we start to develop a system for voice processing we must think about possible language compositions and topic classifications [8] which both may depend on the age group, country, etc. Therefore we need to work on intelligent methodologies that make it possible to extract from voice samples the information which is crucial in ongoing situations. Computational intelligence give possibilities to improve gaming systems [14], routing problems [13], and some technical simulations [19]. Intelligent algorithms are developed to simplify operations in decision making processes. Mainly we try to change computationally complex methods to some intelligent ones which extract the information we need in a smart and therefore simple and faster way.

In this paper we propose to use a key-points extraction from voice by the use of methods developed for image processing. This idea is based on assumption that each of sounds can be represented in a spectrogram. Therefore this graphical form of voice presentation become a prefect input for key-points search methods. We propose to use algorithms like SIFT and SURF for extraction of most important features from spectrograms, and therefore make corrections to original vice samples by removing unnecessary sounds from the background.

2 Data Extraction from Short Audio Files

The proposed solution uses image analysis, so each sound sample will be converted to a spectral image. In the next step, well-known key-point detection algorithms are used to create areas that define a person's sample. So prepared samples are used to detect and diagnose defects on a given sound input.

2.1 Spectrograms

Graph of an amplitude signal spectrum is called spectrogram. The graph is spread over two axes represented by time and frequency. Each point on the graph determines the intensity, which value is determined by the colour change. Technically, the spectrogram is defined by Short-Time Fourier Transform (STFT) for discrete signal $x[n]$, what is represented by

$$STFT\{x[n]\}(m, \omega) \equiv X(m, \omega) = \sum_{n=-\infty}^{\infty} x[n]w(n - m) \exp(-j\omega n), \qquad (1)$$

where w is the Hann window in the following form

$$w(n) = 0.5\left(1 - \cos\left(\frac{2\pi n}{N-1}\right)\right). \tag{2}$$

Such defined transform is used to determine the spectrogram by

$$spectrogram\{x(t)\}(\theta, \omega) = |X(\theta, \omega)|^2. \tag{3}$$

2.2 Key-Points Algorithms

The key-points of the image are points or sometimes even fragments that define certain unique features for the image. Detection of these points will depend on the definition of the uniqueness that may be a certain colour or area within a certain neighbourhood, or even the edges of objects.

2.2.1 SIFT

In 1999, David Lowe presented Scale-Invariant Feature Transform [2] to detect and describe important areas on 2D images. The first stage of the algorithm is to create the Difference of Gaussian (DoG) Pyramid. $D(x, \sigma)$ is understood as a difference of two filtrated images and described by

$$D(x, \sigma) = L(x, k\sigma) - L(x, \sigma), \tag{4}$$

where x is a given point and $L(\cdot)$ is calculated as

$$L(x, \sigma) = g(x, \sigma)I(x) \tag{5}$$

where $g(x)$ is Gaussian kernel in two dimension represented by

$$g(x, \sigma) = \frac{1}{2\pi\sigma^2} \exp\left(-\frac{1}{2}\frac{x^T x}{\sigma^2}\right). \tag{6}$$

So, the input image is filtered with a Gaussian filter at different scales (divided by the constant coefficient k). Then the differential images are calculated and local extremes are found by comparison with neighboring values. If the value is greater or lower than the neighborhood, it is suspected to be a key-point. Then points are located by interpolating the extremes

$$D(x) = D + \frac{\partial D^T}{\partial x}x + \frac{1}{2}x^T\frac{\partial^2 D}{\partial x^2}x. \tag{7}$$

In addition, the points along the edge are removed by the following condition

$$\frac{Tr(H)^2}{Det(H)} < \frac{(r+1)^2}{r}, \tag{8}$$

where H means Hessian matrix for image I defined as

$$H(x, \omega) = \begin{bmatrix} L_{xx}(x, \omega) & L_{xy}(x, \omega) \\ L_{xy}(x, \omega) & L_{yy}(x, \omega) \end{bmatrix}, \tag{9}$$

where $L_{xx}(x, \omega)$, $L_{yy}(x, \omega)$ and $L_{xy}(x, \omega)$ are the convolution of I with the second derivative represented as

$$L_{xx}(x, \omega) = I(x)\frac{\partial^2}{\partial x^2}g(\omega), \tag{10}$$

$$L_{yy}(x, \omega) = I(x)\frac{\partial^2}{\partial y^2}g(\omega), \tag{11}$$

$$L_{xy}(x, \omega) = I(x)\frac{\partial^2}{\partial xy}g(\omega), \tag{12}$$

wherein $g(\omega)$ is the Gaussian kernel defined in Eq. (6) with declared parameter value of σ. The complete algorithm assumes calculating the orientation of key-point and generation of descriptors.

2.2.2   SURF

Speeded Up Robust Features (SURF) [3] is a detector partly inspired by SIFT. It was proposed in 2006 as a faster version of SIFT algorithm. The detector uses an approximate value of Hessian blob detector, again the descriptor is based on the response of Haar's wavelet for a given point.

The SURF algorithm approximates kernels calculated using Eqs. (9)–(12) through rectangular boxes. As $I(x)$, we understand an integral image where x is a point which stores the neighbourhood information calculated as

$$I(x) = \sum_{l=0}^{i \leq x} \sum_{j=0}^{j \leq y} I(x, y). \tag{13}$$

The most important feature of SURF is non-maximal-suppression of determinant of Eq. (9). The determinant of the hessian matrix can be represented as

$$det\left(H_{approximate}\right) = D_{xx}D_{xy} - \left(wD_{xy}\right)^2. \tag{14}$$

Approximate and discrete kernels refer respectively as D_{xx} for $L_{xx}(x, \omega)$, and w is the weight. In the next step, the extremes are found and can be understand as key-points. The full algorithm assumes that after detection, the process of description based on Haar's wavelet will have a place.

2.3   Data Extraction Using Spectrograms and Key-Points

For verification purposes, the best sample is that one which contains only specific data such as name and surname. There are situations when the sample may contain other information such as coughing or other defect that may indicate the onset of influenza or cold. This are just a few examples of the use of defects, but good separation of specific information is a very desirable tool for different decision support systems.

Proposed method is based on extraction of original data consisting for instance name and surname and image analysis of deleted part of the sample. At the beginning, the pattern for specific person is created. In this process, a several dozen well-recorded samples are used to generate a pattern identifying this person. For each sample, spectrogram is made. For each spectrogram, key-point detection algorithm is used to find a certain points of that sample.

An array of the same size as the sample is created and it is fulfill with 0. For all the position of key-points and their neighborhood (in the form of a circle, where the key-point is the center and a radius r), the corresponding cell in the array is incremented by 1. New bitmap with the same size as an array is created and it will be called general pattern for all these samples. If the value in the array is higher or equal to ϕ, black pixel is set. Otherwise, white pixel is set. In this way, one pattern is formed, which contains the most common areas for all given samples.

2.4   Voice Defects Analysis

In the case of identity verification systems, recorded sample must be reduced to the minimum. So, we create a spectrogram and locate key-points. Each of these points is transferred to a new bitmap and surrounded by a circle fulfil with black colour. In this way we get the processed sample ready for the analysis. The analysis will consist extraction of the information contained in the general pattern (formed according to Sect. 2.3). If the similarity will be higher that 90%, than this area has the same information and it may be extracted for the purpose of verification. The remaining rest may contain other information or even some voice defect that may be useful for other purposes.

While extraction of specific data according to the general pattern may seem simple, analysis of specific voice defects is a more arduous task. In the case of cough, keypoints on the spectrogram should create some regular asymmetrical areas. The situation is when it might be a siren signal or a sound of signalling light – the area should represents regular and symmetrical areas. Classification may work by checking the regularity of the space between black areas. Visualization of selected noise or defects is shown in Fig. 1.

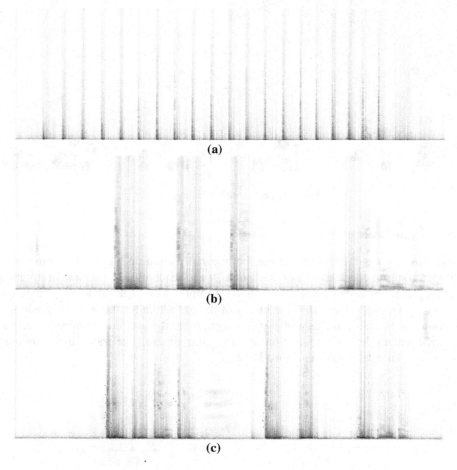

Fig. 1. Spectrogram for selected disturbances – (a) signaling light, (b)–(c) cough.

3   Experiments

A database of *200* voice samples was created with the first and last name ("*Luke Skywalker*"). Then *100* samples were prepared with cough (before the name) and *100* samples with traffic lights sounds. All samples were used to verify the performance of the proposed extraction and signal analysis method (Fig. 2).

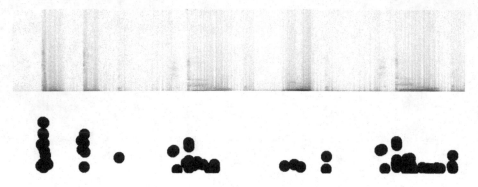

Fig. 2. Spectrogram and the pattern.

3.1 Data Extraction

Data extraction is made by matching the original pattern on the newly downloaded sample. If we cover at least *80%* of black areas, we have identified important information in this place. The tests were done for all *400* samples. For sound samples without any defects no error occurred. The correctness of the extraction for the remaining samples is shown in Fig. 3. In the case of cough, irregular areas were often confused with the original pattern, but in the situation when regular signals (like traffic lights sounds) occurred, extracted data were almost ideal.

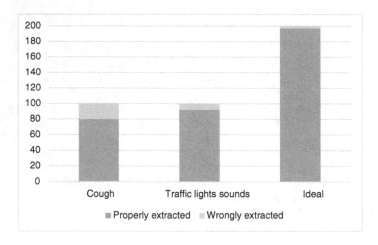

Fig. 3. Extraction results.

3.2 Selected Defects Detection

After data extraction, the remaining areas were checked for the regularity of black space intervals. The result of such a simple classification is shown in Fig. 4.

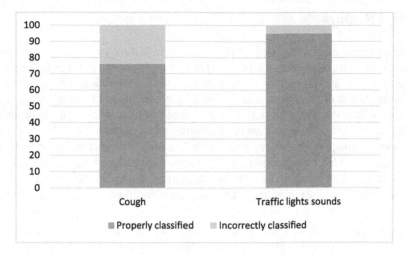

Fig. 4. Defects classification results.

3.3 Conclusions

The proposed solution has two main applications. The first is the extraction of a specific information, which is a big asset for various neural network classifiers where the smallest input vector at the entrance can efficiently reduce training time. The second use is the analysis of additional signals before or after the extracted data on the sample. Such an analysis may indicate problems with voice or isolate important information about the situation around the microphone. The obtained results show, first of all, the effectiveness of data extraction, but not only. The selected two noise problems were rated at *83%*. Such a result could have been caused by too little samples with noise or the wrong selection of parameters during its creation (Fig. 5).

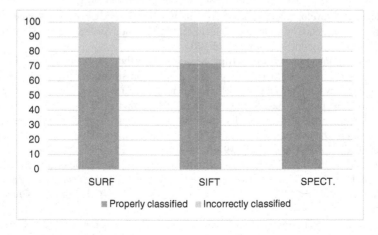

Fig. 5. Comparison of the results for implemented methods.

4   Final Remarks

Nowadays, voice analysis is used in numerous decision support systems or identity verification systems more often than ever. This is one of the main motives for improving and creating more accurate analysis of sound samples. In the article we have discussed an implementation of the novel idea to use efficient methods of image processing to search for the important information in voice samples. The novelty of this approach lies in the fact that after simple operation of computing a spectrogram for each voice sample we retrieve an image of the voice, which now becomes a prefect input for using key-points search to extract most important information. The results have shown that this type of approach can reach about *80%* of correct processing, and show high potential for implementations in security at the level of user identity verification using voice.

Acknowledgments. Authors acknowledge contribution to this project to the Diamond Grant 2016 No. 0080/DIA/2016/45 funded by the Polish Ministry of Science and Higher Education.

References

1. Aggarwal, J., Ryoo, M.: Human activity analysis: a review. ACM Comput. Surv. **43**, 1–43 (2011)
2. Lowe, D.G.: Object recognition from local scale-invariant features. In: The Proceedings of the Seventh IEEE International Conference on Computer vision (1999)
3. Bay, H., Tuytelaars, T., Van Gool, L.: SURF: speeded up robust features. In: Leonardis, A., Bischof, H., Pinz, A. (eds.) ECCV 2006. LNCS, vol. 3951, pp. 404–417. Springer, Heidelberg (2006). doi:10.1007/11744023_32
4. Nosáľ, M., Porubän, J., Sulír, M.: Customizing host IDE for non-programming users of pure embedded DSLs: a case study. Comput. Lang. Syst. Struct. **49**, 101–118 (2017). doi:10.1016/j.cl.2017.04.003
5. Nosál, M., Sulír, M., Juhár, J.: Language composition using source code annotations. Comput. Sci. Inf. Syst. **13**(3), 707–729 (2016). doi:10.2298/CSIS160114024N
6. Chodarev, S.: Development of human-friendly notation for XML-based languages. In: 2016 Federated Conference on Computer Science and Information Systems (FedCSIS), pp. 1565–1571. IEEE (2016). doi:10.15439/2016F530
7. Marszałek, Z.: Performance test on triple heap sort algorithm. Tech. Sci. **20**(1), 49–61 (2017)
8. Kapočiūtė-Dzikienė, J., Krilavičius, T.: Topic classification problem solving for morphologically complex languages. In: Dregvaite, G., Damasevicius, R. (eds.) ICIST 2016. CCIS, vol. 639, pp. 511–524. Springer, Cham (2016). doi:10.1007/978-3-319-46254-7_41
9. Gabryel, M.: A bag-of-features algorithm for applications using a NoSQL database. In: Dregvaite, G., Damasevicius, R. (eds.) ICIST 2016. CCIS, vol. 639, pp. 332–343. Springer, Cham (2016). doi:10.1007/978-3-319-46254-7_26
10. Gabryel, M.: The bag-of-features algorithm for practical applications using the MySQL database. In: Rutkowski, L., Korytkowski, M., Scherer, R., Tadeusiewicz, R., Zadeh, L.A., Zurada, J.M. (eds.) ICAISC 2016. LNCS, vol. 9693, pp. 635–646. Springer, Cham (2016). doi:10.1007/978-3-319-39384-1_56
11. Marszałek, Z.: Novel recursive fast sort algorithm. In: Dregvaite, G., Damasevicius, R. (eds.) ICIST 2016. CCIS, vol. 639, pp. 344–355. Springer, Cham (2016). doi:10.1007/978-3-319-46254-7_27

12. Birvinskas, D., Jusas, V., Martisius, I., Damasevicius, R.: Fast DCT algorithms for EEG data compression in embedded systems. Comput. Sci. Inf. Syst. **12**(1), 49–62 (2015). doi:10.2298/CSIS140101083B

13. Mandziuk, J., Zychowski, A.: A memetic approach to vehicle routing problem with dynamic requests. Appl. Soft Comput. **48**, 522–534 (2016). doi:10.1016/j.asoc.2016.06.032

14. Swiechowski, M., Mandziuk, J.: Fast interpreter for logical reasoning in general game playing. J. Log. Comput. **26**(5), 1697–1727 (2016). doi:10.1093/logcom/exu058

15. Artiemjew, P., Nowak, B.A., Polkowski, L.T.: A new classifier based on the dual indiscernibility matrix. In: Dregvaite, G., Damasevicius, R. (eds.) ICIST 2016. CCIS, vol. 639, pp. 380–391. Springer, Cham (2016). doi:10.1007/978-3-319-46254-7_30

16. Artiemjew, P.: The boosting and bootstrap ensemble for classifiers based on weak rough inclusions. In: Yao, Y., Hu, Q., Yu, H., Grzymala-Busse, J.W. (eds.) RSFDGrC 2015. LNCS, vol. 9437, pp. 267–277. Springer, Cham (2015). doi:10.1007/978-3-319-25783-9_24

17. Nowicki, R.K., Scherer, R., Rutkowski, L.: Novel rough neural network for classification with missing data. In: 21st International Conference on Methods and Models in Automation and Robotics MMAR 2016, Miedzyzdroje, Poland, 29 August–1 September 2016, pp. 820–825 (2016) doi:10.1109/MMAR.2016.7575243

18. Wlodarczyk-Sielicka, M.: importance of neighborhood parameters during clustering of bathymetric data using neural network. In: Dregvaite, G., Damasevicius, R. (eds.) ICIST 2016. CCIS, vol. 639, pp. 441–452. Springer, Cham (2016). doi:10.1007/978-3-319-46254-7_35

19. Brociek, R., Slota, D.: Application and comparison of intelligent algorithms to solve the fractional heat conduction inverse problem. Inf. Tech. Control **45**(2), 184–194 (2016). doi:10.5755/j01.itc.45.2.13716

20. Jaworski, M., Duda, P., Rutkowski, L., Najgebauer, P., Pawlak, M.: Heuristic regression function estimation methods for data streams with concept drift. In: Rutkowski, L., Korytkowski, M., Scherer, R., Tadeusiewicz, R., Zadeh, L.A., Zurada, J.M. (eds.) ICAISC 2017. LNCS, vol. 10246, pp. 726–737. Springer, Cham (2017). doi:10.1007/978-3-319-59060-8_65

Detection of Important Features
from Images Using Heuristic Approach

Dawid Połap and Marcin Woźniak[⊠]

Institute of Mathematics, Silesian University of Technology,
Kaszubska 23, 44-100 Gliwice, Poland
{dawid.polap,marcin.wozniak}@polsl.pl

Abstract. Digital systems offer high quality images, for which information is encoded with precision. Pixels represent the features of objects, therefore we can use this information to detect purposes. In this article we present our research on methodology based on a heuristic approach. A model of bio inspired algorithm was used to search between the pixels and evaluate which of them are representing important components of the objects. Therefore this methodology serves as detection model to find the features of interest. Presented research results show that the developed approach show high potential and proposed methodology makes the search efficient.

Keywords: Feature detection · Image processing · Heuristic method

1 Introduction

In multimedia systems digital images are widely used. This type of imaging brings many advances to the processing and information retrieval. A construction of the image is composed of pixels, located in a structure where each represents some special features of the depicted objects. Since this construction has a form of a matrix we can easily process information encoded in it using computational methods. Most often we process images to find some important features useful in decision making systems, which have various applications in medical systems, tracking, routing, recognition, etc.

Medical applications focus on proposed computing functions for input image, where encoded information is processed to find differences in color, saturation, and other basic features. Results of this calculations help in evaluation of the context. Recent research have shown that it is possible to use ECOC matrix for classification of glaucoma symptoms [1]. Prostate cancer can be detected by time-intensity curves from DCEMRI image series [2]. Similarly we can evaluate brain and some of it's pathologies by the use of EEG signals [3].

Tracking and detection from images also involves processing of pixels for verification. In these processes objects are detected by the selection of some special attributes like shape and size. It is possible to use quality degradation for visual tracking, some interesting performance evaluations of these type algorithms was presented in [4].

© Springer International Publishing AG 2017
R. Damaševičius and V. Mikašytė (Eds.): ICIST 2017, CCIS 756, pp. 432–441, 2017.
DOI: 10.1007/978-3-319-67642-5_36

We can also develop intelligent methods to that can predictively target occurrence of objects by the use of fuzzy logic controllers [5].

Routing problems also involves some image processing techniques. Complexity of the system depends on the environment for which routing system is being modeled. For water transportation mainly bathymetric data is of an importance, since these information help to compose an image of bottom of the sea, rivers, and lakes. We can find complex approaches using bio-inspired system to navigate on the water [33, 36]. While for vehicle transportation some intelligent models play crucial role to support routing on the communication map [38].

Recognition mainly involves processing of special features that are unique for people like biometrics, or in case of object classification features that can define some particular objects. We can recognize people faces by collaborative techniques based on local convolution of features from face images [6]. In other cases, sometimes we can use trajectories to boost recognition of actions [7].

All image processing techniques involve input data processing, therefore data storage and management play a very important role in efficiency. The aspects that make the data proper for processing are various and complex, an importance of visual object extraction from multimedia was discussed in [8]. While Bag-of-Features Algorithm, which involves selection of most important aspects from data stored in MySQL Database was proposed [9]. Some techniques use devoted models, where planar representations of colors are used for information retrieval [10], while the other focus on context based processing by intelligent approaches based on bioinspired methods [11]. Other data mining approaches base on fast sorting [37] and information retrieval [35]. While programming developments for complex systems use devoted solutions for host interfaces [17] and personalized language annotations [34].

1.1 Related Works

For the purpose of extraction of the objects, we mainly compute algorithms that focus on selection of the key-points. Key-points are mainly selected using methodologies that process the image to localize some differences in the shape, these are evaluated by the developed methods to extract only the most important pixels responsible for composition of the shapes. Some approaches use probabilistic theories, which show efficiency for 3-D objects recognition [12], while other ideas are based on large scale comparisons [13]. Development in efficiency of key-points extraction comes parallel to the development in technology, since for more complex images in higher resolutions it is necessary to process more information encoded in the input images. Extraction of key features from images can be done using global model of detection where we search for differences comparing global features in images [14]. Computing power made it possible to analyze several aspects and gave a boost to the new intelligent technologies with various new applications [15]. We can detect defects in fruits peel by selection of most important areas of images, where these defects are visible as done for apple sorting systems [16]. Techniques based on artificial intelligence give many important advances to the multimedia systems. Using techniques based on bio-inspired methods we can gain on intelligent detection what benefits in precision and computing complexity. That kind of systems are useful in extraction of features important to evaluate duplicates in forgery detection systems, but also in video frames capturing which help in real-time intelligent and adaptive processing of information for surveillance systems [18]. These methods have been used in multimedia systems for multilevel thresholding [19]; grey images watermarking [20]; video tracking [21]; and several other aspects [22]. Bio inspired methods can work alone or in cooperation with other methods. These have been proved in gaming aspects with adapting strategies of multi agent systems [23], neuro-heuristic forex trading simulations [24], and adaptive intelligent strategies for visual information retrieval [25] where some additional boosted fuzzy classifiers can efficiently increase precision of extraction [26].

In this article we present research on modeling intelligent methodology to process input images for extraction of important features from input images. Proposed approach is based on bio-inspired method, that simulates strategy from nature to search the image for most important pixels representing information that can be used for extraction of the objects. The novelty of this approach is in intelligent processing of the image pixels. We propose a model to move from pixel to pixel in search of features. Motion model is using fitness functions that help to detect pixels of interest. Presented research results show that developed solution works with good efficiency and helps on extraction of shapes from input images.

2   Proposed Image Processing Technique

Bio-inspired methods allow intelligent processing of images. We can use developed model, in which we simulate free and efficient search, to find pixels that can extract important features of the objects in the image. Proposed technique is based on mathematical model of life behaviours that were observed in life spices. An extensive studies of convergence of these approaches with some models developed to simulate various life phenomena in engineering purposes can be found in [27, 28].

2.1   Proposed Version of Dragonfly Algorithm

An example of bio-inspired algorithm, that we used for feature extraction from images, is a dragonfly algorithm introduced in [29]. There, the author has shown a model of a static and a dynamic movement of dragonflies. In our approach we have modified this idea to fit image processing.

We assume that the life environment of a dragonfly is a two dimensional image, so each dragonfly in the population will be represented by a pixel $X_i = (x_i; y_i)$. Each individual has a velocity V which is a random value at the beginning. Moreover, each dragonfly can see only in a certain area defined as a circle with radius r_0. All individuals in the initial population are selected at random and to describe their movement for the proposed model some factors must be introduced. As A_i, we understand an alignment factor, C_i is consistency value, F_i is a rate of attractiveness into some direction of flight and E_i represents enemies dispersion in this environment. These factors are defined as

$$
\begin{cases}
S_i = -\sum_{j=1}^{N} X_i - X_j \\
A_i = \frac{1}{N}\sum_{j=1}^{N} V_j \\
C_i = \frac{1}{N}\sum_{j=1}^{N} X_j - X_i \\
F_i = X^+ - X_i \\
E_i = X^- + X_i
\end{cases}
\tag{1}
$$

where X_j is a neighbor, X^+ means food source and X^- represents the enemy. All these definitions of the dragonflies movement are defined as

$$
X_i^{t+1} = X_i^t + \Delta X_i^{t+1}
\tag{2}
$$

where $t\psi$ is the number of iteration ΔX_i^{t+1} is the correlation of all factors calculated as

$$
\Delta X_i^{t+1} = sS_i + aA_i + cC_i + fF_i + eE_i + \Delta X_i^t
\tag{3}
$$

where $\{s, a, c, f, e\} \in [0, 1]$ are the weights. To make some simplification, in the first iteration, all individuals has $\Delta X_i^{t=0} = 0.5$. The original idea makes some randomness of the movement by

$$
X_i^{t+1} = X_i^t + L(d)X_t
\tag{4}
$$

where $L(d)$ is a Lévy's flight defined as

$$
L(d) = 0.01\frac{r_1\gamma}{|r_2|^2}
\tag{5}
$$

with $r_1, r_2 \in [0, 1]$ ψ are selected at random, β ψ is a constant, and γ is calculated as

$$
\gamma = \left(\frac{\Gamma(1+\beta)\sin\frac{\pi\beta}{2}}{\Gamma\left(\frac{1+\beta}{2}\right)\beta2^{\frac{1+\beta}{2}}}\right)^{\frac{1}{\beta}}
\tag{6}
$$

where $\Gamma(x) = (x-1)!$. At the end of each iteration, all individuals are evaluated in terms of fitness function $f(X_i)$, and the best of them is chosen as X^+, and the worst as X^-.

2.2 Modifiable Fitness Function

Fitness function for bio-inspired approaches is a very important part of the model. In all developed techniques, this part of the model helps to solve the task with appropriate precision. There are various approaches to model it, i.e. we can use it for cooperative multiagent systems [30], classification of medical problems [31], and compose a special family of fitness function that fit the purpose of processing [32].

In our research we have modeled fitness function to work as detection tool for selection of pixels related to object shapes. In each iteration, each individual in a given population is evaluated for adaptation to the environment (in our case two dimensional image). Unfortunately, in the case of an image, the important search areas may differ in many places, but all of them could be important for shape detection because of different properties. For this purpose, we proposed a set of tree functions. In our approach individuals can be considered using one of the three fitness functions describing each of the properties of the HSL model.

Suppose that $x \psi$ is a pixel, and functions $R(\cdot), G(\cdot), B(\cdot)$ denote the color value at a given point. Moreover, $\delta(x) = max(R(x); G(x); B(x))$ and $\mu(x) = min(R(x); G(x); B(x))$. So defined relations allow to determine the fitness function in the following way

$$
f_1^{hue}(x) = \begin{cases} 60^{\circ} \left[\frac{G(x)-B(x)}{\delta(x)-\mu(x)} \, mod \, 6 \right] if \ \delta(x) = R(x) \\[2mm] 60^{\circ} \left[\frac{B(x)-R(x)}{\delta(x)-\mu(x)} \, mod \, 6 \right] if \ \delta(x) = G(x) \\[2mm] 60^{\circ} \left[\frac{R(x)-G(x)}{\delta(x)-\mu(x)} \, mod \, 6 \right] if \ \delta(x) = B(x) \end{cases} \tag{7}
$$

$$
f_2^{saturation}(x) = \frac{\delta(x) - \mu(x)}{1 - |\delta(x) + \mu(x) - 1|} \tag{8}
$$

$$
f_3^{lightness}(x) = \frac{\delta(x) + \mu(x)}{2} \tag{9}
$$

Of course, such decision model will be beneficial only if the individual move will be done with a respect to only one of them. Therefore we have implemented a very simple mechanism to select the function. After the first iteration, each individual will be verified for the best fit for each of these functions. The best result will determine the fitness condition. Algorithm presents implemented ad-hoc filtering.

Algorithm   Dragonfly Algorithm.

Define the parameters N – size of population, t - the maximum number of iteration and rest like r_0, s, c, f, e, w Load an image and define fitness conditions Create an initial population at random **for** *each individual* **do**

    if $f^{brightness}(X_i) > 0.7$ **then**

        Assign the given function $f^{brightness}(\cdot)$ to the individual

    else if $f^{hue}(X_i) > 0.7$ **then**

        Assign the given function $f^{hue}(\cdot)$ to the individual

    else if $f^{saturation}(X_i) > 0.7$ **then**

        Assign the given function $f^{saturation}(\cdot)$ to the individual

end

T=0 **while** $T < t$ **do**

    Evaluate dragonflies according to selected fitness condition Find best and worst in whole population X^+, X^- Update the coefficient $\{s, c, f, e\}$ Update the parameters using (1) **if** *a neighbor of X_i in the field of view r_0 exists* **then**

        Calculate new postion of X_i by (2)

    else

        Move dragondly using (4)

    end

    if $T == t - 1$ **then**

        Evaluate all individuals according to selected fitness condition

    end

    T++

end

Return all dragonflies

---

3   Experiments

In the research we have tested proposed model on sample images presenting various objects. Results of proposed bio-inspired extraction model are presented in Fig. 1.

In the figures we can see that the use of various components of the fitness function result in various selected key-points. The difference lies mainly in the fact that each of the components is focused on other aspects of the input image. Therefore each of them concentrate on some specific aspects, which are most fitted to the component equation. Red selections represent hue component, blue represent brightness component and green represent saturation component. However if we use all of them extracted in one image as important key-points for we can see that composed in this way information contains knowledge about various aspects of the objects. Therefore this results can serve as a very good source for decision support systems.

Fig. 1. In the image we can see extracted key-points for all three components of proposed fitness function, where red represents hue, green represents saturation and blue represents brightness. For the research we have used data from https://homepages.cae.wisc.edu/~ece533/ images/. (Color figure online)

3.1 Conclusion

Research results have shown that our method by the use of fitness condition with conjunction with various number of particles in population and iterations in the algorithm can fit to the purpose of search. After comparing our results we can see that the number of particles may influence quality of extraction giving more details of extracted objects. While the number of iterations in the algorithm does not influence this so much, however to extract the object with necessary precision we need at least 40 iterations. If we increase this number, our model gains on details in extracted objects, but if the number of iterations is bigger than 60 this do not boost extraction. Therefore we can conclude that above 50–60 iterations the changes are so small that it is not necessary to compute the image longer. Developed solution helps on fast and efficient extraction of objects from images. The solution is giving enough precision to help in automatic detection support. Although since this is an early stage of the research, we are working on changes to the model to increase precision i.e. by introduction of some improvements to the motion model. We also think about introducing some preprocessing methodology that will be selecting only some areas in the images in which it will be easier to find important features. This can be done i.e. by implementation of neural network processing tool.

4 Final Remarks

We have developed methodology to process images for detection of important features. Proposed method is based on bio-inspired algorithm, in which we simulate some life phenomena to detect pixels representing features of interest. This detection is done using proposed fitness function, which represents selection of changes in brightness, hue and saturation. Each pixel in the image is evaluated in the following iterations using this function. Those that fit this criterion are extracted in the image as potentially representing important object features. The novelty of the proposed method is that we have implemented bio-inspired algorithm to search over input image for the features that may be important for detection. In this way we have developed methodology that is using behaviour of life organisms to search where proposed fitness function simulates adaptation to natural conditions. The results of the research show that proposed method works properly showing pixels of importance. In future work, we plan to improve model of search and add additional components to the fitness function.

Acknowledgments. Authors acknowledge contribution to this project to the Diamond Grant 2016 No. 0080/DIA/2016/45 funded by the Polish Ministry of Science and Higher Education.

References

1. Bai, X., Niwas, S.I., Lin, W., Ju, B., Kwoh, C.K., Wang, L., Sng, C.C., Aquino, M.C., Chew, P.T.K.: Learning ECOC code matrix for multiclass classification with application to glaucoma diagnosis. J. Med. Syst. **40**(4), 781–7810 (2016)
2. Fabijanska, A.: A novel approach for quantification of time-intensity curves in a DCE-MRI image series with an application to prostate cancer. Comput. Biol. Med. **73**, 119–130 (2016)
3. Hou, X., Liu, Y., Lim, W.L., Lan, Z., Sourina, O., Mueller-Wittig, W., Wang, L.: CogniMeter: EEG-based brain states monitoring. In: Gavrilova, Marina L., Tan, C.J. Kenneth, Sourin, A. (eds.) Transactions on Computational Science XXVIII. LNCS, vol. 9590, pp. 108–126. Springer, Heidelberg (2016). doi:10.1007/978-3-662-53090-0_6
4. Fang, Y., Yuan, Y., Li, L., Wu, J., Lin, W., Li, Z.: Performance evaluation of visual tracking algorithms on video sequences with quality degradation. IEEE Access **5**, 2430–2441 (2017). doi:10.1109/ACCESS.2017.2666218
5. Harik, E.H.C., Guerin, F., Guinand, F., Brethé, J., Pelvillain, H., Parédé, J.: Fuzzy logic controller for predictive vision-based target tracking with an unmanned aerial vehicle. Adv. Robot. **31**(7), 368–381 (2017). doi:10.1080/01691864.2016.1271500
6. Yang, M., Wang, X., Zeng, G., Shen, L.: Joint and collaborative representation with local adaptive convolution feature for face recognition with single sample per person. Pattern Recogn. **66**, 117–128 (2017). doi:10.1016/j.patcog.2016.12.028

7. Qiao, R., Liu, L., Shen, C., van den Hengel, A.: Learning discriminative trajectorylet detector sets for accurate skeleton-based action recognition. Pattern Recogn. **66**, 202–212 (2017). doi:10.1016/j.patcog.2017.01.015

8. Burdescu, D.D., Stanescu, L., Brezovan, M., Slabu, F., Ebânca, D.: Multimedia data for efficient detection of visual objects. In: Proceedings of the 11th International Conference on Ubiquitous Information Management and Communication, IMCOM 2017, Beppu, Japan, 5–7 January 2017

9. Gabryel, M.: The bag-of-features algorithm for practical applications using the MySQL database. In: Rutkowski, L., Korytkowski, M., Scherer, R., Tadeusiewicz, R., Zadeh, Lotfi A., Zurada, Jacek M. (eds.) ICAISC 2016. LNCS, vol. 9693, pp. 635–646. Springer, Cham (2016). doi:10.1007/978-3-319-39384-1_56

10. Kazimierski, W., Wlodarczyk-Sielicka, M.: Technology of spatial data geometrical simplification in maritime mobile information system for coastal waters. Pol. Marit. Res. **23**(3), 3–12 (2016). Gdansk University of Technology

11. Grycuk, R., Gabryel, M., Nowicki, R., Scherer, R.: Content-based image retrieval optimization by differential evolution. In: IEEE Congress on Evolutionary Computation, CEC 2016, Vancouver, BC, Canada, 24–29 July 2016, pp. 86–93 2016. doi:10.1109/CEC.2016.7743782

12. Pope, R., Lowe, D.: Probabilistic models of appearance for 3-D object recognition. Int. J. Comput. Vis. **40**(2), 149–167 (1998)

13. Nelson, R., Selinger, A.: Large-scale tests of a keyed, appearance based 3-D object recognition system. Vis. Res. **38**(15), 2469–2488 (1998)

14. Se, S., Lowe, D., Little, J.: Global localization using distinctive visual features. In: Proceedings of the ICIROS 2002 , pp. 226–231 (2002)

15. Parker, J.: Algorithms for Image Processing and Computer Vision. Wiley, New York (2010)

16. Wen, Z., Tao, Y.: Dual-camera NIR/MIR imaging for stem-end/CALYX identification in apple defect sorting. Trans. ASAE **43**(2), 449–452 (2000)

17. Nosál, M., Porubän, J., Sulír, M.: Customizing host IDE for non-programming users of pure embedded DSLs: A case study. Comput. Lang. Syst. Struct. **49**, 101–118 (2017). doi:10.1016/j.cl.2017.04.003

18. Wozniak, M., Polap, D., Capizzi, G., Sciuto, G.L.: Toward adaptive heuristic video frames capturing and correction in real-time. In: Proceedings of the 2016 Federated Conference on Computer Science and Information Systems, FedCSIS 2016, Gdansk, Poland, 11–14 September 2016, pp. 849–852 (2016), doi:10.15439/2016F143

19. Panda, R., Agrawal, S., Bhuyan, S.: Edge magnitude based multilevel thresholding using cuckoo search technique. Expert Syst. Appl. **40**(18), 7617–7628 (2013)

20. Mishra, A., Agarwal, C., Sharma, A., Bedi, P.: Optimized grayscale image watermarking using DWT–SVD and firefly algorithm. Expert Syst. Appl. **41**(17), 7858–7867 (2014)

21. Walia, G.S., Kapoor, R.: Intelligent video target tracking using an evolutionary particle filter based upon improved cuckoo search. Expert Syst. Appl. **41**(14), 6315–6326 (2014)

22. Baonabeau, E., Dorigo, M., Theraulaz, G.: Swarm Intelligence: From Natural to Artificial Systems. Oxford University Press, Oxford (1999)

23. Swiechowski, M., Mandziuk, J.: Fast interpreter for logical reasoning in general game playing. J. Log. Comput. **26**(5), 1697–1727 (2016). doi:10.1093/logcom/exu058

24. Mandziuk, J., Rajkiewicz, P.: Neuro-evolutionary system for FOREX trading. In: IEEE Congress on Evolutionary Computation, CEC 2016, Vancouver, BC, Canada, 24–29 July 2016, pp. 4654–4661 (2016). doi:10.1109/CEC.2016.7744384

25. Grycuk, R., Gabryel, M., Scherer, R., Voloshynovskiy, S.: Multi-layer architecture for storing visual data based on WCF and microsoft SQL server database. In: Rutkowski, L., Korytkowski, M., Scherer, R., Tadeusiewicz, R., Zadeh, Lotfi A., Zurada, Jacek M. (eds.) ICAISC 2015. LNCS, vol. 9119, pp. 715–726. Springer, Cham (2015). doi:10.1007/978-3-319-19324-3_64

26. Korytkowski, M., Rutkowski, L., Scherer, R.: Fast image classification by boosting fuzzy classifiers. Inf. Sci. **327**, 175–182 (2016). doi:10.1016/j.ins.2015.08.030

27. Koziel, S., Yang, X.: Computational Optimization, Methods and Algorithms. Springer, Berlin (2011)

28. Yang, X.: Engineering Optimisation: An Introduction with Metaheuristic Applications. Wiley, Hoboken (2010)

29. Mirjalili, S.: Dragonfly algorithm: a new meta-heuristic optimization technique for solving single-objective, discrete, and multi-objective problems. Neural Comput. Appl. **27**(4), 1053–1073 (2016). doi:10.1007/s00521-015-1920-1

30. Colby, M.K., Tumer, K.: Fitness function shaping in multiagent cooperative coevolutionary algorithms. Auton. Agents Multi-Agent Syst. **31**(2), 179–206 (2017). doi:10.1007/s10458-015-9318-0

31. Cheruku, R., Edla, D.R., Kuppili, V.: Sm-ruleminer: Spider monkey based rule miner using novel fitness function for diabetes classification. Comput. Biol. Med. **81**, 79–92 (2017). doi:10.1016/j.compbiomed.2016.12.009

32. Lissovoi, A., Witt, C.: MMAS versus population-based EA on a family of dynamic fitness functions. Algorithmica **75**(3), 554–576 (2016). doi:10.1007/s00453-015-9975-z

33. Wlodarczyk-Sielicka, M.: Importance of neighborhood parameters during clustering of bathymetric data using neural network. In: Dregvaite, G., Damasevicius, R. (eds.) ICIST 2016. CCIS, vol. 639, pp. 441–452. Springer, Cham (2016). doi:10.1007/978-3-319-46254-7_35

34. Nosál, M., Sulír, M., Juhár, J.: Language composition using source code annotations. Comput. Sci. Inf. Syst. **13**(3), 707–729 (2016). doi:10.2298/CSIS160114024N

35. Artiemjew, P., Nowak, Bartosz A., Polkowski, Lech T.: A new classifier based on the dual indiscernibility matrix. In: Dregvaite, G., Damasevicius, R. (eds.) ICIST 2016. CCIS, vol. 639, pp. 380–391. Springer, Cham (2016). doi:10.1007/978-3-319-46254-7_30

36. Wlodarczyk-Sielicka, M., Stateczny, A.: Clustering bathymetric data for electronic navigational charts. J. Navig. **69**(05), 1143–1153 (2016)

37. Marszałek, Z.: Novel recursive fast sort algorithm. In: Dregvaite, G., Damasevicius, R. (eds.) ICIST 2016. CCIS, vol. 639, pp. 344–355. Springer, Cham (2016). doi:10.1007/978-3-319-46254-7_27

38. Mandziuk, J., Zychowski, A.: A memetic approach to vehicle routing problem with dynamic requests. Appl. Soft Comput. **48**, 522–534 (2016). doi:10.1016/j.asoc.2016.06.032

A Comparison of the Deep Learning Methods for Solving Seafloor Image Classification Task

Tadas Rimavicius[(⊠)] and Adas Gelzinis

Department of Electric Power Systems, Kaunas University of Technology,
Studentu 50, 51368 Kaunas, Lithuania
tadas.rimavicius@ktu.edu, adas.gelzinis@ktu.lt

Abstract. An accurate interpretation of seabed images is relevant for evaluating and monitoring ecosystem states, assessing environmental impact, mapping seabed sediment, tracking life forms, and carrying out many other tasks. The main scope of this study is to establish an automated, accurate and efficient classification system of seabed images using state-of-the-art techniques. A convolutional neural network and other deep learning algorithms have been used to solve the seafloor images classification problem. To test the proposed techniques, images of five benthic classes were used, and the classes include "Red algae", "Sponge", "Sand", "Lithothamnium" and "Kelp". The task has been solved with the overall accuracy of 92.78% using a dataset consisting of 18356 image regions and the 10-fold cross-validation to assess the performance. The advantages of the convolutional neural network are presented and compared with the results obtained using two other deep learning techniques following different dataset formation approaches. The comparison of the classification results has shown that deep learning methods are suitable for seabed images classification, where the best precision has been shown by the convolutional neural network.

Keywords: Seabed image recognition · Deep learning · Deep features · Deep neural network · Deep belief network · Convolutional neural network

1 Introduction

Image processing techniques in combination with artificial intelligence methods are widely used in various over ground and underwater objects recognition tasks. Fish detection and recognition or corals classification problems are the most popular tasks related to underwater fauna and flora recognition. The importance of seafloor images recognition is based on various ecological tasks; however, the difficulties related to environment features such as variations in colours during the depth changes and turbidity or movement of underwater fauna make this task not trivial. Moreover, while a task for an expert is to manually detect, recognize, and evaluate the seabed coating, the limited human and time resources make this problem even more complicated. A huge amount of data should be pre-processed, which requires a lot of time; therefore, only less than 2% of the gathered images are manually annotated [3].

© Springer International Publishing AG 2017
R. Damaševičius and V. Mikašytė (Eds.): ICIST 2017, CCIS 756, pp. 442–453, 2017.
DOI: 10.1007/978-3-319-67642-5_37

Usually the flora variety recognition is implemented using videos-based technologies in cooperation with machine learning techniques, which seems to be promising for large datasets processing. However, the recognition accuracy of video images achieved in multi-class classification tasks is still rather low when using conventional machine learning methods, though deep learning techniques are increasingly used to solve multi-class classification problems [5, 22, 24]. Over the last years, increased computational resources and large image datasets, such as ImageNet [6], have caused highly developed usage of the convolutional neural network (CNN). Consequently, state-of-the-art results have been produced in classification, recognition and detection tasks [7, 15, 19]. The deep learning techniques have also been applied in the underwater images recognition tasks, where a vast variety of methods differing in image augmentation techniques, the size of training images, the depth of neural network or final classifier has been applied [12–14, 16]. The achieved segmentation accuracy also greatly depends on a dataset (image resolution, quality and the number of samples) and the depth of the CNN. Deep neural networks with convolutional layers from three layers [2, 17, 18, 20] to five layers [10] have been used to extract the features. Finally, the classification is done by adopting various approaches such as multilayer perceptron [13], random forest (RF) [2], support vector machines (SVM) [2, 20], nearest neighbour classifier (k-NN) [20] or the softmax [11, 17] function. Recent studies have shown that going deep is becoming the norm. However, no guidelines on the effective designing of a very deep convolutional neural network exist.

This article implements a technique for seabed coating classification into five benthic classes. The technique used is capable of achieving a relatively high classification accuracy. The state-of-the-art technique, which solves the image classification problem in recent study, is the convolutional neural network. We compare the results of the proposed method with the results obtained classifying the same images by using different approaches which cover various dataset formation methods and different deep learning techniques.

2 Data Organization and Feature Extraction

2.1 Data Collection and Preparation for Computer Vision Algorithms

The video transects used in this study were collected in the Norwegian seafloor in September 2010 and September 2011. A HDTV video camera and a xenon light source (400 W in total) were installed on a remotely operated vehicle (ROV), which was used to collect video transects. The data have been collected at depths varying between 20 and 40 m, while the duration of one video is approximately 10 min and includes 200 m transects [21]. The frame width and height are 960 and 540 pixels respectively.

The images have been selected from the whole span of sequences to have a larger data variety. A human expert has segmented and labelled seabed images manually to have the labelled data for the evaluation of the classification results. In total, 4589 regions differing in shape, colour and texture have been analysed and prepared for using in computer vision algorithms. A representative seafloor image is illustrated on the left-hand side of Fig. 1.

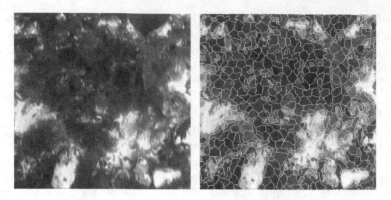

Fig. 1. A fragment of a seabed image (left), the SLIC segmented part of the same image (right).

2.2 SLIC Algorithm in Data Pre-processing

Lighting condition (varying brightness, hue, dimness) and turbidity limit accuracy and robustness when classifying the underwater images. The quality of seafloor images used in this study highly depends on the sea depth where the data have been taken. When necessary, additional lighting has been used to light up the seafloor. All the images were segmented into small nearly uniform regions using the simple linear iterative clustering (SLIC) algorithm, which achieves good segmentation quality at low computational cost [1]. The SLIC is an adaptation of the k-means clustering for perceptually meaningful group of pixels generation. The main distinction between the k-means and the SLIC is that the search space in SLIC is proportional to the super-pixel size, which helps to reduce the number of distance calculations. An image fragment segmented using the SLIC algorithm is shown on the right-hand side of Fig. 1. In the present study, the regions generated by the SLIC algorithm has been used to create algorithms for the recognition of the benthic classes covering the seafloor (patches extraction, training the classifiers and assessing performance of the algorithms).

2.3 Forming Data Sets

The datasets in the study were formed using three methods. Firstly, the patches (50 × 50) were extracted for every region. The patch size was chosen so that every region fits within the patch. The first dataset DS1 was composed of information, where a classified region was centred in the patch after cropping it from the seabed images. The small part of this dataset is shown in Fig. 2. The experiments have shown that the convolutional neural network requires substantial number of training data to reach eligible results. The first dataset was augmented from 4589 samples to 18356 samples rotating all the patches every 90°. The whole dataset was split into 10 equal parts to assess model performance using 10-fold cross-validation. The data in each part is proportional to the distribution in each sediment class.

All training/testing data samples have been composed of five classes. However, the domination of the "Red algae" class is observed (62.91% of all samples). The

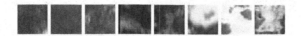

Fig. 2. Image patches of regions of interests.

additional partly data augmentation technique has been adopted to alleviate this problem. The second dataset DS2 has been composed of the dataset DS1 samples and the additional samples created flipping dataset DS1 image patches of the "Lithothamnium", "Kelp", "Sand" and "Sponge" classes by the first dimension. This allows to reduce the dominance of the "Red algae" specie by 17% to 45.91%. This way augmented dataset is composed of 25160 image patches. The third dataset DS3 has been formed from carefully hand-crafted features. Colour (18 features), texture (87) and shape (6) information (in total 111 features) extracted from the regions of interest have been used to train deep learning algorithms. A detailed list of hand crafted features is presented in Table 1. Finally, the fourth dataset DS4 has been constructed from the extracted image patches by converting them from RBG image patches to grey-scale image patches and reshaping data arrays of 50×50 to data arrays of 1×2500.

3 Deep Learning Models for Seafloor Image Classification

In this study, deep learning techniques have been used to classify seafloor images. To approach the seabed image recognition task, three different classifiers have been selected. The classifiers are as follows: deep neural network (DNN), deep belief network (DBN) and convolutional neural network. The DNN and the DBN have been used to classify carefully handcrafted features and reshaped images patches, while the CNN have been used to classify two dataset of image patches. The results of the classification are presented using region-wise and pixel-wise evaluation techniques.

3.1 Deep Neural Network and Deep Belief Network

A neural network is a computing system formed of simple, highly interconnected elements which process information by their dynamic state response to external inputs [4]. The main idea of the neural network is to extract a linear combination of the input as derived features and model the target as a nonlinear function of these features. The importance of the respective inputs to the output can be expressed using real numbers, stated as weights. The weighted sum of neuron's inputs determines the neuron output. In binary classification, the task is expressed as follows:

$$output = \begin{cases} 1 & if \ \sum_{j=1}^{m} w_j x_j + b > 0 \\ 0 & otherwise \end{cases} \qquad (1)$$

where x is a real valued input vector, w is real valued weights, m is the number of inputs to the neuron and b is the bias. The bias could be interpreted as a decision

Table 1. List of features included in dataset DS3.

#	Feature set	Size	#	Feature set	Size
	Colour (*L*, *a*, *b* channels)	18	21	Inverse difference normalized	
1	Mean		22	Inverse difference moment normalized	
2	Standard deviation			**Texture, *GLRLM***	11
3	Minimum		1	Short run emphasis	
4	Maximum		2	Long run emphasis	
5	Skewness		3	Gray-level non-uniformity	
6	Kurtosis		4	Run length non-uniformity	
	Texture, *GLCM*	22	5	Run percentage	
1	Angular second moment		6	Low gray-level run emphasis	
2	Contrast		7	High gray-level run emphasis	
3	Correlation		8	Short run low gray-level emphasis	
4	Sum of squares: variance		9	Short run high gray-level emphasis	
5	Inverse difference moment		10	Long run low gray-level emphasis	
6	Sum average		11	Long run high gray-level emphasis	
7	Sum variance			**Texture, *Gabor filter*** (9 frequencies)	54
8	Sum entropy		1	Mean	
9	Difference variance		2	Standard deviation	
10	Difference entropy		3	Minimum	
11	Information measures of correlation 1		4	Maximum	
12	Information measures of correlation 2		5	Skewness	
13	Maximal correlation coefficient		6	Kurtosis	
14	Entropy			**Geometric**	6
15	Dissimilarity		1	Area	
16	Homogeneity		2	Major axis length	
17	Autocorrelation		3	Minor axis length	
18	Cluster Shade		4	Orientation	
19	Cluster Prominence		5	Equivalent diameter	
20	Maximum probability		6	Perimeter	
Total 111					

boundary. The network is called *deep* neural network if it is composed of more than one hidden layer.

The deep belief network is a stack of layers where a small network, formed of restricted Boltzmann machines (RBM), is placed in each layer. A RBM is formed of hidden and visible units, which may have a symmetric connection between different units but no connection between the same units [8]. A RBM follows the paradigm of an encoder which transforms the input into a feature vector from which the decoder reconstructs the original input. Training of the deep belief network consists of training each of the restricted Boltzmann machines that compose the net. Firstly, the lower-level layers are trained and progressively moving forward in hierarchy while all the layers are being trained. Three groups of parameters are updated in the DBN, and the groups include visible units bias, hidden unit bias, and weights between units. The structures of the DNN and the DBN were selected experimentally.

3.2   Convolutional Neural Network

A convolutional neural network is a state-of-the-art deep learning technique. This network stands out from all the other neural networks by the ability to create feature maps from input data and successfully classify them. The first layer receives the input data, while the last one returns the probability of the object to belong to a certain class. All the other layers located between the input and output layers are called *hidden*. The construction of such network could be separated into two main parts. Firstly, the features are extracted using convolutional layers. The deeper the network, the more complex features it could learn, and the more computational resources is required. The primary convolutional layers learn low level features, such as pixel intensities. The middle layers learn more complex features, such as edges. Finally, in the last convolutional layers the most sophisticated features such as objects are learnt [23]. The second part of the CNN is dedicated to classification task solving; this part could be a fully connected neural network or another classifier (e.g. SVM, RF, k-NN). A convolutional layer used together with a non-linear layer and/or with a max pooling layer forms a stage. A deep CNN could consist of several stages.

Mathematically convolution is an operation which describes how to combine two functions or pieces of information. The first function is the input data (image) or the output from previous layers, and the second function is a set of learnable filters (kernels). These filters are used to extract hierarchical contextual features of the input data. Between the convolutional layers, often the pooling layers are used to reduce the number of parameters and computation in the network. The pooling layer reduces the spatial size of the representation and resizes input spatially using a max operation. The element-wise nonlinearity activation layers are immediately applied after applying the convolution layers. Rectified Linear Units (ReLU) is a layer of neurons that applies the non-saturating activation function $f(x) = max(0; x)$. This function increases non-linear properties of the overall network without affecting the receptive fields of the convolutional layer. After applying all the convolutional and max pooling layers, which represent high-level features of the input image, the high-level reasoning in the neural network is done via fully connected layers. The aim of the fully connected layer is to use the features extracted for classifying the input image into various classes based on the training dataset. The output of the last fully connected layer is recalculated to probabilities of the predicted class using the SoftMax function.

3.3   CNN Structure for Seafloor Images Classification

The structure of CNN used in the study is composed of two main parts. Firstly, five convolutional layers are used as feature descriptors. The second classification part is formed of two fully connected layers followed by soft-max function. The first and the second feature extraction stages are formed of a convolutional layer followed by a sub-sampling layer where we use the max-pooling function. The first stage input is a region of interest patches, while the second stage input is the result of max-pooling layer from the first convolutional stage. Next, two of three feature extraction stages are composed of convolution layers followed by a rectified linear unit's layers. The fifth feature extraction stage is composed of a convolution layer, a nonlinear layer and a sub-sampling layer. The feature extraction part is finished after these five convolution stages. The output of feature extractor is transferred to classifier which consist of two fully connected layers, where ReLU and dropout layers are embedded in between. Finally, in the last layer, the probability of region belong to class is presented by the softmax function. The architecture of the CNN in this research has been implemented using the Caffe framework [9]. The structure and parameters of the network have been selected based on related studies [11, 16] and experimental investigations, where the accuracy were assessed using several sets of parameters and the depth of network from two to six convolution layers. All the details of the network architecture are presented in Table 2.

Table 2. Detailed network architecture for sea-floor images classification.

#	Layer	Input w × h	Kernel w × h × n	Stride w × h	Padding w × h	Output w × h
1	Conv1	50 × 50	5 × 5 × 64	1 × 1	2 × 2	46 × 46
2	Pool1	46 × 46	2 × 2	2 × 2		23 × 23
3	Conv2	23 × 23	5 × 5 × 128	1 × 1	2 × 2	23 × 23
4	Pool2	23 × 23	2 × 2	2 × 2		12 × 12
5	Conv3	12 × 12	3 × 3 × 256	1 × 1	2 × 2	14 × 14
6	ReLU3					14 × 14
7	Conv4	14 × 14	3 × 3 × 256	1 × 1	2 × 2	16 × 16
8	ReLU4					16 × 16
9	Conv5	16 × 16	3 × 3 × 512	1 × 1	2 × 2	18 × 18
10	ReLU5					18 × 18
11	Pool5	18 × 18	2 × 2	2 × 2		9 × 9
12	FC6	9 × 9	512			41472
13	ReLU6					
14	Dropout6					
15	FC7		5			

The values of the parameters determining the behaviour of the CNN were chosen experimentally. The training bath size of 2048 image patches was chosen experimentally, too. A larger bath size requires more computational resources; however, a smaller bath size requires more training iterations to train the network. The testing batch size of 2048 image patches was chosen to evaluate all the testing samples in one test iteration. Periodically, after every 20 train iterations, when all training samples are fed into the network, test iteration is performed.

4 Experimental Analysis of Seafloor Image Classification

Three measures accuracy, precision and recall were used to evaluate the performance of implemented models. The accuracy is given by:

$$Accuracy = \frac{\sum TP + \sum TN}{\sum (TP + FP + TN + FN)} \tag{2}$$

where TP is a true positive classification result, when region is classified as class i, while the region belongs to class i. TN is a true negative classification result, when the region is not classified as class i, while the region does not belong to class i. FP is a false positive classification result, when region is classified as class i, while the region does not belong to class i and FN is a false negative classification result, when the region is not classified as class i, while the region belongs to class i. The precision shows how many classified elements are relevant and are given by:

$$Precision = \frac{\sum TP}{\sum (TP + FP)} \tag{3}$$

The recall show how many relevant elements is classified and is given by:

$$Recall = \frac{\sum TP}{\sum (TP + FN)} \tag{4}$$

Firstly, the CNN was applied to classify the DS1 dataset, where the cropped patches of the classified region were provided. After making 8000 iterations, the network reached the overall accuracy of 88.74%. The CNN has shown the best classification results when classifying the dominating "Red algae" class, with a precision score of 93.77%. The second largest class "Sand" was classified with the second-best results and reached 83.23%. The third best results were achieved in "Kelp" recognition, where the precision score reached 82.74%. The species of "Lithothamnium" and "Sponge" were more difficult to classify correctly. The classification precision is 74.13% and 79.27% respectively. The recall values do not show the real situation of how many relevant elements were classified to a specific class. Due to the unbalanced data to the distribution on each sediment class, the worst recall measure was observed in the small classes "Sponge" and "Lithothamnium", 53.17% and 76.27% respectively. The results

Table 3. Precision of all used algorithms for specific seabed species.

#	Approach	Red algae	Lithoth	Kelp	Sand	Sponge
1	CNN-DS1	93.77%	74.13%	82.74%	83.23%	79.27%
2	CNN-DS2	81.89%	76.64%	71.89%	66.59%	58.03%
3	DNN-DS3	86.77%	76.31%	90.04%	78.49%	85.36%
4	DNN-DS4	85.42%	37.94%	51.25%	54.19%	37.04%
5	DBN-DS3	89.86%	75.34%	61.92%	72.18%	69.51%
6	DBN-DS4	81.89%	42.99%	46.26%	48.36%	33.33%

Table 4. Recall values of all used algorithms for specific seabed species.

#	Approach	Red algae	Lithoth	Kelp	Sand	Sponge
1	CNN-DS1	93.13%	76.27%	88.49%	86.08%	53.17%
2	CNN-DS2	88.15%	52.84%	60.66%	73.66%	65.28%
3	DNN-DS3	92.75%	59.73%	79.56%	80.05%	67.31%
4	DNN-DS4	76.97%	41.94%	59.26%	73.12%	45.45%
5	DBN-DS3	89.36%	58.79%	79.82%	80.82%	79.17%
6	DBN-DS4	78.18%	37.34%	46.26%	64.82%	37.50%

Table 5. Classification results using various approaches.

#	Approach	Overall accuracy	
		Region	Pixel
1	CNN-DS1	**88.74%**	**92.78%**
2	CNN-DS2	77.52%	79.66%
3	DNN-DS3	84.29%	88.30%
4	DNN-DS4	71.40%	73.12%
5	DBN-DS3	82.98%	87.21%
6	DBN-DS4	68.36%	70.35%

of the classification precision, recall and overall accuracy are presented in Tables 3, 4 and 5 respectively.

The dataset DS2 composed of the dataset DS1 and the partly augmented data were classified using the convolutional neural network. The results of dataset DS2 classification were surprisingly unsatisfying. The partly data augmentation technique have not helped to reduce the dominance of the "Red algae" class, and the results were even worse. The precision has decreased for four out of five classified classes. More specifically, a 11.88% decrease was observed for the "Red algae", 10.85% for "Kelp", 16.64% for "Sand" and 21.24% for "Sponge". However, the recognition rate of "Lithothamnium" has increased by 2.51% and has reached 76.64%.

The deep learning techniques such as the deep neural network and the deep belief network have been used to classify the dataset DS3, and the results have suggested the overall accuracy of 84.29% and 82.98% respectively. The DNN achieved slightly better precision when classifying the "Lithothamnium", whose precision score is 76.31% (DBN

75.3%) and the "Sand", whose precision score 78.49% (DBN 72.18%). Moreover, the DNN has reached considerably better results than the DBN when classifying the "Kelp", whose precision score is 90.04% (DBN 61.92%) and the "Sponge", whose precision rate is 85.36% (DBN 69.51%). However, the DBN has obtained better precision when classifying the "Red algae" class, the precision of which is 89.86% (DNN 86.77%). Both the DNN and the DBN have shown similar recall values for "Lithothamnium", "Kelp" and "Sponge", where values differ about 1%. Importantly, when using the DBN, the recall value of 89.36% has classified more regions from the other species as the dominating "Red algae" class, whereas the recall value for "Red algae" is 92.75% when applying the DNN. By contrast, better precision has been reached by the DNN when classifying the "Sponge" class. Such results have been achieved because the regions of the other classes were classified as "Sponge". This could be observed in the recall values, which are 79.17% for the DBN and 67.31% for the DNN.

Finally, the deep learning algorithms were trained to classify the dataset DS4. The achieved overall accuracies were quite low. The results have revealed that the accuracy for the DNN is 71.40%, whereas the DBN has the accuracy of 68.36%. The classification precisions of four small species have significantly dropped from more than 20% for the "Sand" specie to 40% for the "Kelp" specie. Only the "Red algae" class was classified with higher than 80% precision. The recall values have also reduced. This could account for the highly increased number of features, which could not properly represent the data. The reshaped data lose the spatial information and the ability to be correctly classified. As shown in the classification results, the carefully hand-crafted features better represent the seafloor species than the reshaped image patches.

The classification results show that different techniques used in this study have achieved their best classification precision in different seafloor classes. The three algorithms CNN-DS1, DNN-DS3 and DBN-DS3 show very high results, when classifying dominating "Red algae" class. The highest precision of 93.77% has been reached by CNN-DS1. Only the two techniques CNN-DS2 and DBN-DS4 classified the "Red algae" with lower than 85% precision; both algorithms have reached 81.89%. The "Lithothamnium" specie was difficult to classify for all the techniques, especially for the classifiers which have classified the dataset DS4. The deep neural network and the deep belief network-based algorithms show precision which varies from 37.94% to 42.99%, respectively. However, all the other methods have reached better results, where the precision varies from 74.13% to 76.64%. CNN-DS2 is the most precise classifier for the "Lithothamnium" classification. However, the highest classification results have led to assigning the other classes to the "Lithothamnium" class. The "Kelp" specie has been classified with the highest 90.04% precision by DNN-DS3. All the other methods have shown the results ranging from 46.26% when using DBN-DS4 to 82.74% when using CNN-DS1. As presented in Table 3, the "Sand" class is classified with the highest accuracy by CNN-DS1 and DNN-DS3 classifiers, where the precisions have been reached 83.23% and 79.27% respectively. The smallest "Sponge" class was difficult to recognize for all the algorithms; however, DNN-DS3 has reached the highest precision of 85.36%. When classifying the dataset DS4, the DNN and the DBN have assigned more other classes to the "Sand" class and have shown the lowest recall values varying from 45.45% to 37.50% respectively.

The average classification accuracy is relatively high due to the dominance on the "Red Algae" class in the datasets. As presented in Tables 3 and 4, the smallest species are the most difficult to recognize. Table 5 provides the summary of the classification results using various approaches. In addition to the region classification accuracy, we also provide the accuracy of the pixel-wise classification. The study has revealed that the recognition rates are higher for larger regions than for smaller ones. However, the best seafloor classification result has been reached by the convolution deep neural network CNN-DS1 with the overall accuracy of 88.78%. When the accuracy reached is calculated to the pixel-wise accuracy, it reaches 92.78%.

5 Conclusions

In the present study, we present an approach to solve the multi-class recognition task in benthic imagery recognition by using various deep learning approaches. The presented comparison of the results of six different approaches has proved the importance of the dataset construction to the recognition results. The experimental investigations using the convolutional neural network performed on a dataset containing 18356 image patches substantiated the validity of the approach. The CNN shows better classification results than the DNN and the DBN in three out of five classes. The convolutional neural network reaches better classification results when classifying the "Red algae" (93.77%), the "Lithothamnium" (76.64%) and the "Sand" (86.23%), while the deep neural network approach shows better classification accuracy for the "Kelp" (90.04%) and "Sponge" (85.36%) classes. In general, the CNN-DS1 algorithm reaches the best recognition accuracy of 88.74% for region classification and 92.78% for pixel classification.

Acknowledgement. The authors sincerely thank Sergej Olenin and his team for allowing them to use their video sequences and manual data labelling.

References

1. Achanta, R., Shaji, A., Smith, K., Lucchi, A., Fua, P., Susstrunk, S.: Slic superpixels compared to state-of-the-art superpixel methods. IEEE Trans. Pattern Anal. Mach. Intell. **34** (11), 2274–2282 (2012)
2. Al-Barazanchi, H.A., Verma, A., Wang, S.: Performance evaluation of hybrid CNN for sipper plankton image calssification. In: 2015 Third International Conference on Image Information Processing (ICIIP), pp. 551–556, December 2015
3. Beijbom, O., Edmunds, P.J., Kline, D.I., Mitchell, B.G., Kriegman, D.: Automated annotation of coral reef survey images. In: 2012 IEEE Conference on Computer Vision and Pattern Recognition (CVPR), pp. 1170–1177, June 2012
4. Caudill, M.: Neural networks primer, part I. AI Expert **2**(12), 46–52 (1987)
5. Ciresan, D.C., Meier, U., Gambardella, L.M., Schmidhuber, J.: Convolutional neural network committees for handwritten character classification. In: 2011 International Conference on Document Analysis and Recognition, pp. 1135–1139, September 2011
6. Deng, J., Dong, W., Socher, R., Li, L.J., Li, K., Fei-Fei, L.: Imagenet: a largescale hierarchical image database. In: 2009 IEEE Conference on Computer Vision and Pattern Recognition, pp. 248–255, June 2009

7. Girshick, R., Donahue, J., Darrell, T., Malik, J.: Rich feature hierarchies for accurate object detection and semantic segmentation. In: 2014 IEEE Conference on Computer Vision and Pattern Recognition, pp. 580–587, June 2014
8. Huang, H.B., Huang, X.R., Li, R.X., Lim, T.C., Ding, W.P.: Sound quality prediction of vehicle interior noise using deep belief networks. Appl. Acoust. **113**, 149–161 (2016)
9. Jia, Y., Shelhamer, E., Donahue, J., Karayev, S., Long, J., Girshick, R., Guadarrama, S., Darrell, T.: Caffe: convolutional architecture for fast feature embedding. arXiv preprint arXiv:1408.5093 (2014)
10. Li, X., Shang, M., Hao, J., Yang, Z.: Accelerating fish detection and recognition by sharing CNNs with objectness learning. In: OCEANS 2016 – Shanghai, pp. 1–5, April 2016
11. Li, X., Shang, M., Qin, H., Chen, L.: Fast accurate fish detection and recognition of underwater images with fast r-CNN. In: OCEANS 2015 - MTS/IEEE Washington, pp. 1–5, October 2015
12. Li, Y., Lu, H., Li, J., Li, X., Li, Y., Serikawa, S.: Underwater image de-scattering and classification by deep neural network. Comput. Electr. Eng. **54**, 68–77 (2016)
13. Mahmood, A., Bennamoun, M., An, S., Sohel, F., Boussaid, F., Hovey, R., Kendrick, G., Fisher, R.B.: Automatic annotation of coral reefs using deep learning. In: OCEANS 2016 MTS/IEEE Monterey, pp. 1–5, September 2016
14. Mahmood, A., Bennamoun, M., An, S., Sohel, F., Boussaid, F., Hovey, R., Kendrick, G., Fisher, R.B.: Coral classification with hybrid feature representations. In: 2016 IEEE International Conference on Image Processing (ICIP), pp. 519–523, September 2016
15. Oquab, M., Bottou, L., Laptev, I., Sivic, J.: Learning and transferring mid-level image representations using convolutional neural networks. In: 2014 IEEE Conference on Computer Vision and Pattern Recognition, pp. 1717–1724, June 2014
16. Osterloff, J., Nilssen, I., Jrnegren, J., Buhl-Mortensen, P., Nattkemper, T.W.: Polyp activity estimation and monitoring for cold water corals with a deep learning approach. In: 2016 ICPR 2nd Workshop on Computer Vision for Analysis of Underwater Imagery (CVAUI), pp. 1–6, December 2016
17. Qin, C., Song, S., Huang, G., Zhu, L.: Unsupervised neighborhood component analysis for clustering. Neurocomputing **168**, 609–617 (2015)
18. Qin, H., Li, X., Liang, J., Peng, Y., Zhang, C.: Deepfish: accurate underwater live fish recognition with a deep architecture. Neurocomputing **187**, 49–58 (2016). Recent Developments on Deep Big Vision
19. Razavian, A.S., Azizpour, H., Sullivan, J., Carlsson, S.: CNN features off-the-shelf: an astounding baseline for recognition. In: 2014 IEEE Conference on Computer Vision and Pattern Recognition Workshops, pp. 512–519, June 2014
20. Salman, A., Jalal, A., Shafait, F., Mian, A., Shortis, M., Seager, J., Harvey, E.: Fish species classification in unconstrained underwater environments based on deep learning. Limnol. Oceanogr. Methods **14**(9), 570–585 (2016)
21. Saskov, A., Dahlgren, T.G., Rzhanov, Y., Schläppy, M.L.: Comparison of manual and semi-automatic underwater imagery analyses for monitoring of benthic hard-bottom organisms at offshore renewable energy installations. Hydrobiologia **756**(1), 139–153 (2014)
22. Stallkamp, J., Schlipsing, M., Salmen, J., Igel, C.: The german traffic sign recognition benchmark: a multi-class classification competition. In: The 2011 International Joint Conference on Neural Networks, pp. 1453–1460, July 2011
23. Yu, W., Yang, K., Yao, H., Sun, X., Xu, P.: Exploiting the complementary strengths of multi-layer (CNN) features for image retrieval. Neurocomputing **237**, 235–241 (2017)
24. Zhu, J., Liao, S., Yi, D., Lei, Z., Li, S.Z.: Multi-label CNN based pedestrian attribute learning for soft biometrics. In: 2015 International Conference on Biometrics (ICB), pp. 535–540, May 2015

Information Technology Applications: Special Session on Smart e-Learning Technologies and Applications

Virtual Reality in Education: New Ways to Learn

Tomas Blazauskas[1]([✉]), Rytis Maskeliunas[1], Reda Bartkute[1], Vitalija Kersiene[1],
Indre Jurkeviciute[1], and Mindaugas Dubosas[2]

[1] Kaunas University of Technology, Studentu str. 50, 51392 Kaunas, Lithuania
`{tomas.blazauskas,rytis.maskeliunas,reda.bartkute,`
`vitalija.kersiene}@ktu.lt, indre.jurkeviciute@gmail.com`
[2] Kaunas University of Technology, A. Mickeviciaus str. 37, 44244 Kaunas, Lithuania
`mindaugas.dubosas@ktu.lt`

Abstract. the paper presents new ways of education using virtual reality, new challenges for educators and new models to use it in the practice. Authors worked on the virtual reality to be used for learning a history subject. Empirical research on the learning process effectiveness will be presented and a model for use of virtual reality will be suggested. The overview of the existing practices and researches and conclusions on the topic will be provided.

Keywords: Virtual reality · Augmented reality · Education · Technologies

1 Introduction

Together with the rapid development of information technologies, two types of reality are identified: Augmented Reality (AR) and Virtual Reality (VR). They are concepts that have gained and are forecasted to continue gaining the virtual communication momentum in recent years [1]. These concepts are now being introduced into gamification, game enhanced learning, and pure education [2]: virtual reality, introducing the virtual world for learning and augmented reality, augmenting live data with web-enhanced technologies [3]. How or if it will fit into the classroom will depend on whether developers correctly assess the potential and address the challenges of the technology to be used. Unlike virtual reality, augmented reality does not replace the real world around you entirely, but augments and enriches it instead of adding layers of information on top of the things that are around us [4]. Moving towards increased and improved distance education, through the real-world, AR and VR interfaces are underway and increasing rapidly, while a practical development is already proving itself [5], especially by introducing education enhanced application models [6].

From a technology perspective, current efforts for educational use are aimed at producing and using devices less expensive, less complex, more easily and cheaply sustainable, and as transparent as possible to the users [7]. It also has two special features: representational fidelity and immediacy of control [8, 9]. Despite the cost challenges, educational benefits of implementing virtual reality remain compelling [10]. Results of [11] suggest games, simulations, and virtual worlds are effective in improving learning results. VR features alone might not achieve the desired learning experience. An

© Springer International Publishing AG 2017
R. Damaševičius and V. Mikašytė (Eds.): ICIST 2017, CCIS 756, pp. 457–465, 2017.
DOI: 10.1007/978-3-319-67642-5_38

appropriate set of learning tasks and activities that are considered to be useful and easy to use by learners that are afforded by the VR technology is crucial in enhancing the learning outcomes [12] from realistically reproduced disaster [13] or accident situations [14] to language learning [15] or medical training [16–18]. Many authors [19, 20] agree that computer simulations have been shown to be effective instruments for teaching students about difficult concepts, particularly in the STEM disciplines. Studies suggest that the use of virtual worlds could help foster social interaction among participants through the use of avatars [21]. A significant interaction effect can be distinguished between the learning mode and spatial ability with regard to the performance achievement [22].

Augmented Reality can dramatically shift the location and timing of education and training [23]. However, authors reviewing effectiveness [24], agree that the educational community remains unclear regarding the educational usefulness of AR and regarding contexts in which this technology is more effective than other educational mediums [25]. In order to achieve realistic solutions, multi-disciplinary research is needed and educators themselves must work with researchers to develop augmented reality interfaces [26]. One example is for anatomic education where a user is learning to understand the spatial relations between his body and the virtual interaction plan [27].

This paper focuses on analyzing learning objects (LO) designed by virtual reality tools and LO effectiveness on study process and gained knowledge in a subject of history learning. The aim of the paper is to present the model for design, virtual reality game for students on the "History" topic and to provide the research data based on student's questionnaire.

2   Research Methodology

The paper presents the overview of the literature related to the virtual reality based on learning objects. In our case, learning object (LO) is any electronic resource developed by virtual reality design tools and environments. In addition, the reflection method based on gamification is used for students' engagement and evaluation. The developed learning object based on virtual reality was presented for 2 groups of learners, which one was a control group piloting the training module. During the piloting, the questionnaire was developed and requested to fill the control group and the empirical research results are presented in the paper's exploitation part.

3   Related Works

The analyzed papers show that some authors provide that immersive experiences in a VR environment can be pleasurable as well as disturbing or frightening so acute is the experience [30]. The slow adoption in education of games and VR environments for learning may remain as is for reasons that have little to do with their effectiveness [31]. Virtual reality and games have the potential of embodying abstract concepts in concrete experiences. Perpetual motion machines can be built to demonstrate the force of gravity without the drag of air or any other friction. Complex interacting systems can be seen from the simplest perspective and complex abstractions, such as the meaning of words and the links between concepts shown tangibly in a complex three-dimensional space [29]. The enthusiastic adoption of a public of new technologies has evolved a resounding need for informal education institutions to design increasingly sophisticated exhibits that incorporate immersive VR, augmented reality, game based technologies, visualizations, and other emerging media [29].

Some authors present that virtual reality has great potential for education across a wide spectrum of fields. One such field is surgical education. Currently, aspiring surgeons learn surgical skills in the operating room, and while this provides the most realistic environment, there is much left to be desired from a pedagogical perspective [32]. 3D possibilities are presented at Construct3D where developed an augmented reality mathematics and geometry learning tool that allows students to draw and visualize virtual three-dimensional objects in real three-dimensional space. Student participants in a pilot study were able to learn how to use the VR tool quickly and thought that it created a good environment for experimentation, which suggests that tools like Construct3D can be effective supplements to a traditional classroom curriculum [33].

The authors of the paper could not find the learning modules based on virtual reality game for history learning. Below we present the model for History learning based on the virtual reality game.

4   Virtual Reality Game

To increase the motivation to engage in the learning process while using AR elements, the game for the History subject was designed. The game was created as a virtual tour and it is dedicated to play in the browser. The main purpose of the game is to collect all the lost artefacts and answer all the provided questions while visiting historical places in Sanciai area virtually. Below the model of the game [28] is presented (Fig. 1).

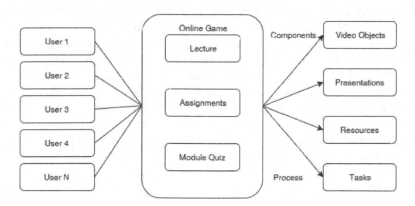

Fig. 1. The model for learning history by virtual reality game.

The structure of the game includes two different areas: the Game scenarios and additional components. The game scenarios include the situations and lines of the game where the tasks are placed and designed. The components describe the additional recourses used for the provision of additional information for a user.

Learners were invited to learn online by joining the game, presenting the history of the city region. There are 23 historical artefacts and 8 questions to test the knowledge in the game. Each of the artefacts or questions is evaluated at points: a correct answer of the question – 20 points; an incorrect answer – 0 points; a picked artefact – 10 points. The game also contains guidance for users on how to find different places related to some historical dates or events and where the questions and artefacts might be hidding. Each of the found/collected artefacts is saved in the player's notebook which can be opened and checked anytime. Learners can go forward just if they find necessary to collect information and to answer the presented questions. However, it is not necessary to answer the questions correctly to go further. The original place view will give a chance to learners to check their knowledge about the geographical skills (Fig. 2). The games ends when all artefacts are collected and all questions are answered.

Fig. 2. The interface of the game.

On the technical point of view, the described game was created using Krpano viewer which is usually used for virtual tours. The completely augmented reality was created using the plugin, which was created for the research porposed. Its aim is to add new augmented elements (artefacts, tests, books and etc.), scenarios and navigation in the virtual tour environment. To reach a better game-database communication, a plugin for users' registration was created which aims to ensure the proper communication between the game and Google Firebase database. The plugin collects data about the registration to the game, the collected points and the final result of the game.

To check the effectiveness of the game the final test was provided to both of the groups. The test included 8 questions about the history of Sanciai and its famous places. Below you will find more exploitation results.

5   Exploitation Results

The experiment was delivered in one of the gymnasiums in Kaunas city. The game was tested with 10th grade students age of 16-17. The sample of the experiment was selected using the random selection. The selected students were distributed into two groups: a control and a pilot group. In the respect of objectivity both groups involved similar number of members. Also, the equal gender distribution was followed in each of the groups. The control group involved 18 and the piloting group involved 19 10th grade students. To test the game, students were using the desktops at school and their personal computers. The members of one group (pilot group) have played a game while another had a regular lesson about Sanciai area.

The results of the research revealed that the piloting group has passed the test with higher scores than the control group (Fig. 3). The dispersion of this question is 1.54. The Confidence interval - 0.95. As it can be seen in Fig. 3, the piloting group was evaluated higher in general questions comparing the average score of each of the questions. The Fig. 3 presents the number of correct answers of each of the group members.

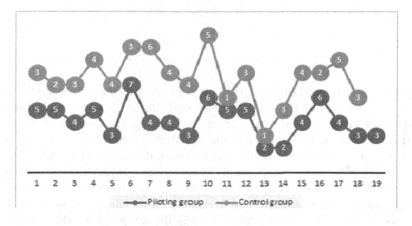

Fig. 3. The results of the final test by users.

To evaluate the overall game, users were asked to decide what impact was made by different aspects of the game. Three most important game aspects were excluded: Engagement, Story and Effectiveness. The Confidence interval of this question is 0.95. The game is engaging, but it lacks some engagement. To evaluate the engagement of the game, respondents were asked if they would play the game at home. 58.82% of users said that game was really engaging and they would like to play it at home. However, 41.28% of users were negative about the game and said that they would not spend their spare time playing this game. Analyzing the impact of the story to the overall evaluation of the game, respondents were asked if the story told in the game was interesting and informative to them (Fig. 4). 82.31% of respondents said that, the story told in the game was interesting and 17.69% of respondents mentioned that it could be more engaging. To find out if the game was effective, the respondents were asked to answer if they understood the history of Sanciai better while playing the game and if they would like to visit the places in the reality. The results showed that 76.55% of respondents evaluated that they learnt history better and would definitely visit the places as in the game in the reality. 23.55% of respondents said that the game did not make any impact and they are not interested in visiting those places. The results show that the overall evaluation of the game is positive, but the game lacks some more engagement elements.

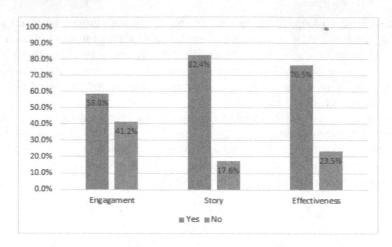

Fig. 4. The evaluation of various aspects of the game.

The members of the piloting group were asked to provide suggestions for the further development of the game. The suggestions are presented in Table 1. As the results of a survey has shown, the game still lacks some functionality. The respondents have noted that the game has no introduction which could include the introduction of the game, its controllers and its aims. Also, according to the users, the control of the game could be easier as it still needs some improvements in navigation (the identified problem is that movements from one place to another are too wide in the game). Another suggestion is to improve the graphic of the game. However, since the user did not mention any details what could be improved, it is difficult to identify the real problem. More and various places could be added to the game as well. Since the game was tested in its early phase, the variety of places were not suggested. More places will be suggested in the next phases of the game.

Table 1. The users' suggestions for improvements of the game

Category	Sub-category	Suggestion
Structure of the game	Introductory information	*"I would add an intro where a user would be introduced with an aim and control of this game."*
Control of the game	Control	*"I would change the control."*
	Navigation	*"The steps could be smaller."*
Graphic	Graphics	*"The graphics could be better."*
Places	More places	*"I would add more places."*

The results of the research revealed the effectiveness of the game. Most of the respondents (82.31%) from the pilot group have evaluated it very positively. However, it is notable that game still lacks more elements for engagement of various people and still struggles with some technical aspects, which will be solved in the next phases of a development. To sum up, the game was a useful tool for students to understand and learn the history better.

6   Conclusions

Virtual Reality opens new ways for learning in the field of education. The Virtual Reality helps students to understand and learn the information better as it is more engaging way of learning. It helps students to learn by stimulating various information perception points while making the learning environment close to the reality. However, as long as it is a new method of information delivery to students, it lacks of the deeper researches and tools for the subject delivery.

The new virtual reality game using VR model was created and tested with students. The effectiveness of the game for learning history was proven by the experiment delivered in the gymnasium in Kaunas. The results of the experiment proved that better learning outcomes were presented by the group learnt using virtual reality games. 76.5% of respondents that were participating in the experiment claimed that they understood history better and it was easier to memorize dates and facts. Also, they mentioned that they would like to visit the places as in the game in the reality. Also, 82.31% of respondents said that, the story told in the game was interesting. the overall evaluation of the game is very positive, but the game lacks some more engagement elements.

References

1. Biocca, F., Levy, M.R.: Communication in the Age of Virtual Reality. L. Erlbaum Associates Inc., Hillsdale (1995). ISBN 0-8058-1550-3
2. Shavinina, L.V.: The Routledge International Handbook of Innovation Education. Routledge, Abingdon (2013). ISBN 978-0-415-68221-3
3. Bower, M., Howe, C., McCredie, N., Robinson, A., Grover, D.: Augmented Reality in education - cases, places and potentials. Educ. Media Int. **51**(1), 1–15 (2014). doi: 10.1080/09523987.2014.889400
4. Kurilovas, E.: Evaluation of quality and personalisation of VR/AR/MR learning systems. Behav. Inf. Technol. **35**(11), 998–1007 (2016)
5. Yuen, S.C.Y., Yaoyuneyong, G., Johnson, E.: Augmented reality: An overview and five directions for AR in education. J. Educ. Technol. Dev. Exch. **4**(1), 119–140 (2011)
6. Fowler, C.: Virtual reality and learning: Where is the pedagogy? Br. J. Edu. Technol. **46**(2), 412–422 (2015)
7. Carrozzino, M., Bergamasco, M.: Beyond virtual museums: Experiencing immersive virtual reality in real museums. J. Cult. Herit. **11**(4), 452–458 (2010)
8. Velev, D., Zlateva, P.: Virtual reality challenges in education and training. Int. J. Learn. Teaching 3(1) (2017)
9. Zhang, X., Jiang, S., de Pablos, P.O., Lytras, M.D., Sun, Y.: How virtual reality affects perceived learning effectiveness: a task–technology fit perspective. Behav. Inf. Technol. **36**(5), 548–556 (2017). ISSN: 1362-3001

10. Abulrub, A.H.G., Attridge, A.N., Williams, M.A.: Virtual reality in engineering education: The future of creative learning. In: IEEE Global Engineering Education Conference (EDUCON) – Learning Environments and Ecosystems in Engineering Education, pp. 751–757 (2011)

11. Merchant, Z., Goetz, E.T., Cifuentes, L., Keeney-Kennicutt, W., Davis, T.J.: Effectiveness of virtual reality-based instruction on students' learning outcomes in K-12 and higher education: A meta-analysis. Comput. Educ. **70**, 29–40 (2014)

12. Lee, E.A.-L., Wong, K.W., Fung, C.C.: How does desktop virtual reality enhance learning outcomes? A structural equation modeling approach. Comput. Educ. **44**(4), 1424–1442 (2010)

13. Farra, S., Miller, E., Timm, N., Schafer, J.: Improved training for disasters using 3-D virtual reality simulation. West. J. Nurs. Res. **35**(5), 655–671 (2013)

14. Lorenz, D., Armbruster, W., Hoffmann, H., Pattar, A., Schmidt, D., Volk, T., Kubulus, D.: A new age of mass casualty education? The InSitu project: realistic training in virtual reality environments. Anaesthesis **65**(9), 703–709 (2016)

15. Choi, D.H., Dailey-Hebert, A., Estes, J.S.: Emerging Tools and Applications of Virtual Reality in Education. IGI Global, Hershey, 360pp. (2016)

16. Olasky, J., Sankaranarayanan, G., Seymour, N.E., Magee, J.H., Enquobahrie, A., Lin, M.C., Aggarwal, R., Brunt, L.M., Schwaitzberg, S.D., Cao, C.G.L., De, S., Jones, D.B.: Identifying opportunities for virtual reality simulation in surgical education: A review of the proceedings from the innovation, design, and emerging alliances in surgery (IDEAS) conference: VR surgery. Surg. Innov. **22**(5), 514–521 (2015)

17. Palter, V.N., Grantcharov, T.P.: Individualized deliberate practice on virtual reality sinylator improves technical performance of surgical novices in the operating room: a randomized controlled trial. Ann. Surg. **259**(3), 443–448 (2014)

18. Jacobsen, M.E., Andersen, M.J., Hansen, C., Konge, L.: Testing basic competency in knee arthroscopy using a virtual reality simulator: exploring validity and reliability. J. Bone Joint Surg. **97**(9), 775–781 (2015)

19. Parmar, D., Babu, S.V., Lin, L., Jörg, S., D'Souza, N., Leonard, A.E., Daily, S.B.: Can embodied interaction and virtual peer customization in a virtual programming environment enhance computational thinking?. In: Research on Equity and Sustained Participation in Engineering, Computing, and Technology (RESPECT), pp. 1–2 (2016)

20. Lindgren, R., Tscholl, M., Wang, Sh, Johnson, E.: Enhancing learning and engagement through embodied interaction within a mixed reality simulation. Comput. Educ. **95**, 174–187 (2016)

21. Hew, K.F., Cheung, W.S.: Use of three-dimensional (3-D) immersive virtual worlds in K-12 and higher education settings: A review of the research. Br. J. Edu. Technol. **41**(1), 33–35 (2010)

22. Lee, E.A.-L., Wong, K.W.: Learning with desktop virtual reality: Low spatial ability learners are more positively affected. Comput. Educ. **79**, 49–58 (2014)

23. Lee, K.: Augmented Reality in Education and Training. Tech Trends **56**(2), 13–21 (2012)

24. Bacca, J., Baldiris, S., Fabregat, R., Graf, S., Kinshuk, : Augmented reality trends in education: a systematic review of research and applications. Educ. Technol. Soc. **17**(4), 133–149 (2014)

25. Radu, I.: Augmented reality in education: a meta-review and cross-media analysis. Pers. Ubiquit. Comput. **18**(6), 1533–1543 (2014)

26. Kesim, M., Ozarslan, Y.: Augmented reality in education: current technologies and the potential for education. Procedia Soc. Behav. Sci. **47**, 297–302 (2012)

27. Blum, T., Kleeberger, V., Bichlmeier, C., Navab, N.: Miracle: An augmented reality magic mirror system for anatomy education. In: Virtual Reality Short Papers and Posters (VRW) (2012). ISSN: 2375–5334
28. Nagata, J.J., Giner, J.R.G.-B., Martinez-Abad, F.: Virtual heritage of the territory: design and implementation of educational resources in augmented reality and mobile pedestrian navigation. IEEE Revita Iberoamericana de Tecnologias del Aprendizaje 11(1), 41–46 (2016)
29. Psotka, J.: Educational games and virtual reality as disruptive technologies. Educ. Technol. Soc. 16(2), 69–80 (2013)
30. Strulle, A., Psotka, J.: Educational games and virtual reality. In: Leadership in Science and Technology, pp. 24–832 (2012)
31. Meltzoff, A., Kuhl, P.K., Movellan, J., Sejnowski, T.J.: Foundations for a new science of learning. Science 325, 284–288 (2009)
32. Cheng, A., Yang, L., Andersen, E.: Teaching language and culture with a virtual reality game. In: CHI 2017 (2017). http://dx.doi.org/10.1145/3025453.3025857
33. Kaufmann, H., Schmalstieg, D., Wagner, M.: Construct3D: a virtual reality application for mathematics and geometry education. Educ. Inf. Technol. 5(4), 263–276 (2000)

Informatics Based Tasks Development in the Bebras Contest Management System

Valentina Dagienė, Gabrielė Stupurienė, and Lina Vinikienė[✉]

Institute of Mathematics and Informatics, Vilnius University,
Akademijos Street 4, 08663 Vilnius, Lithuania
{valentina.dagiene,gabriele.stupuriene,
lina.vinikiene}@mii.vu.lt

Abstract. The paper deals with the contest management system (CMS) of the International *Bebras challenge* on Informatics and Computational Thinking. The challenge is established in 2004 in Lithuania with the aim to engage children in learning Informatics (Computer Science or Computing). Started as a single annual contest on Informatics in a few countries, the *Bebras challenge* has upraised to over 50 countries and successfully developed a worldwide network of Informatics educators. The challenge is one of informatics activities provided for students during informatics lessons. The paper overviews various contest-based learning environments used to engage student's in learning informatics, discusses the main features of activities development and illustrates how *Bebras* CMS is used for purposes of challenge management in Lithuania. This is demonstrated through the description of a system architecture, functionality and tasks development.

Keywords: Bebras challenge · Computer science education · Contest management system · CMS · Informatics education · Informatics activities

1 Introduction

Trying to involve students in learning and keep their attention focused on the basic ideas of informatics – this is real challenge for educators. Informatics education is not mandatory in many countries, sometimes it is integrated with other subjects or involved in some learning activities. Informatics curriculum is implemented according to country's policy, educational trends, skills of the ICT teachers, and marketing. Due to that, educators need to be more flexible in teaching basics and additionally encourage students to participate in various activities during the lessons or during their free time.

Teachers have been proposing a number of suggestions for teaching informatics: attractive activities, contests, camps, programming lessons combined with robotics, special courses, etc. In Lithuania, students are encouraged to learn informatics through annual national or international contests such as programming contests (*International Olympiad in Informatics*[1], *Baltic Olympiad in Informatics*[2]), informatics and computational thinking

---

[1] http://www.ioinformatics.org/.
[2] http://www.boi2017.org/.

© Springer International Publishing AG 2017
R. Damaševičius and V. Mikašytė (Eds.): ICIST 2017, CCIS 756, pp. 466–477, 2017.
DOI: 10.1007/978-3-319-67642-5_39

challenge (*Bebras*[3]), Dr. J.P. Kazickas Information Technologies contest and forums for schoolchildren[4], contests of "*Informikas*"[5], "*Computer Christmas Tale*[6]", etc.

Hakulinen (2011) discussed that informatics contests are not compulsory in education, but they could be integrated in the tradition of education. There exist several remarkable aspects of student participation in the contests: students' engaging, the need of competitive skills in life, encouragement of students to teamwork, feedback on the problem, cognitive skills teaching [1].

Moreover, students are invited to try contests in online platforms, for example *Sphere Online Judge*[7], *ProjectEuler*[8], *CodeChef*[9], *UVA Online Judge*[10], *Kattis*[11]. Additional activities as *Coder Dojo*[12], *Code.org*[13], *Khan Academy*[14], *M-Lab*[15] are proposed as well. Of all listed activities stand out the *Bebras challenge*.

The *Bebras challenge* started in Lithuanian in 2004 and currently spread to more than 50 countries. Over 2 million students participated in the challenge during 2016. The aim of the *Bebras challenge* is to engage students in informatics, deepen their understanding in computer technologies, promote learning by solving short informatics concept-based tasks [2]. Therefore, the tasks are crucial point of the challenge: they should involve at least one informatics concept, tied in an interesting story, they should be attractive, short and interactive [3]. In general, the challenge is divided into six categories according to the age of students: Pre-Primary (grade 1–2), Little Beavers (grades 3–4), Benjamin (grades 5–6), Cadet (grades 7–8), Junior (grades 9–10), Senior (grades 11–12).

A contest management system (CMS) is essential environment in running the challenge effectively and efficiently. It should support simple tools, which enable tasks development, users' management, grading, announcement area, records of solutions, reports, and data storage. For running the *Bebras challenge*, more than 19 different contest management systems have been maintained in participating countries.

In this paper, we analyse the system that supports Lithuanian *Bebras challenge* on informatics and computational thinking. The paper is organized as follows. Section 2 provides features of the informatics activities, problems and learning environment. Section 3 presents a more detailed description of the Lithuanian *Bebras* contest management system. A special attention is paid to systematize development of *Bebras* tasks within the contest management system. Moreover, we end with Conclusion.

---

[3] http://bebras.org/.
[4] https://forumas.ktu.lt/index.php.
[5] http://konkursai.if.ktu.lt/index.php/informikas.
[6] http://www.itmc.lt/kompiuterine-kaledu-pasaka/.
[7] http://www.spoj.com/.
[8] https://projecteuler.net/.
[9] https://www.codechef.com/.
[10] https://uva.onlinejudge.org/.
[11] https://open.kattis.com/.
[12] https://coderdojo.com/.
[13] https://code.org/.
[14] https://www.khanacademy.org/.
[15] https://www.facebook.com/meskenulaboratorija/.

2   Features of a Contest-Based Learning Environment

This section presents related works on informatics activities, problems in order to improve student's computational and algorithmic thinking and engage them to learn informatics.

Teachers should integrate computational activities in teaching and introducing basics of various subjects including informatics (or computer science). According to Hakulinen [1], at the moment there exist many contests in the field of informatics, but their objectives are generally different: test student's knowledge, enable learning, find talent, promote informatics, etc. The aim of his research was to discuss about tasks created for contest development and the educational aspect of it. He emphasizes that "types of tasks vary from tasks solved with pen and paper to complex problems dealing with large datasets and sophisticated algorithms" (p. 12). He mentioned contests as *International Olympiad in Informatics* (IOI), *ACM International Collegiate Programming Contest*[16], *TopCoder, Google Code Jam*[17], *ICFP*[18], *Imagine cup*[19], *CodeCup*[20], *the Bebras* and distinguished following tasks types:

1. **Tasks with programming.** Student are solving problems by writing a program code. The student should then receive feedback and they are expected to write error free code aided by the feedback.
2. **Tasks without programming**. Pen-and-paper problems, problems, which require algorithmic thinking without programming (example, puzzle), attractive activities as *Computer Science Unplugged*[21]are involved. *Computer Science Unplugged* activities could be combined with challenge tasks.
3. **Code understanding**. Student has to find an error on the given code or improve the code.
4. **Subtasks.** There is an emphasis in receiving the score. Student gets points according to what he/she is able to solve.

Hakulinen (2011) also claims that games and puzzles are used in order to motivate students. Games are a type of problems that pay student's attention not by memorizing algorithms but by boosting skills in problem solving and attracting student's interest in algorithms.

Bell et al. [4] describe several educational programs that engage students to explore, and practice computer science concepts. Several activities on Informatics are analysed for example *Bebras* (challenge), *CS Unplugged* (playing without using a computer), *CS4FN*[22] (magazine), *CS Inside*[23] (gaming). These activities enable a deeper understanding of computer science concepts and usefulness. In addition, authors emphasize

---

[16] https://icpc.baylor.edu/.
[17] https://code.google.com/codejam/.
[18] http://www.icfpconference.org/contest.html.
[19] https://imagine.microsoft.com/.
[20] http://www.codecup.nl/intro.php.
[21] http://csunplugged.org/books/.
[22] http://www.cs4fn.org/.
[23] https://csinside.net/.

motivators as contest prizes, the challenge of solving a problem, curiosity, humour, physical exercises, etc. The contents of learning should be chosen carefully (engaging stories, magic, relevant to student's life) in order to create a culture that attracts students.

Wu et al. (2012) described *Online Judge* system as system used to train programming skills. This system is divided into following modules: client, service, database, and judge. Functional requirements of the system include problem, curriculum, contest, user management system, comment communication system, knowledge decision system and platform monitoring system. Knowledge management system, interactive system, evaluation statistical system are the main parts of system's functions. Authors also provide a detailed overview of functionality. The system is composed of *Apache, PHP*, and *MySQL* framework and realized by *C* programming language. After login students choose a course and ACM problem to practice. The problem interface consists of the problem description, input and output requirement, input sample, output sample. Problem is submitted online [5].

Forišek [6] separates the following group of worldwide competition according to the common characteristics (focus on the design of algorithms):

- the *ACM International Collegiate Programming Contest* (ICPC),
- the *International Olympiad in Informatics* (IOI) along with the corresponding national Olympiads for secondary school students,
- company-branded contests such as the *Google Code Jam* and the *Facebook Hacker Cup*[24],
- large portals that host regular contests, such as *CodeForces*[25], *CodeChef* and the *TopCoder*[26].

Students face with difficulties in programming languages, and are not inspired only by programming (write just a program code). Combefis et al. (2013) present *ILPADS* interactive website. The website focus on interactive learning activities based on the development of programming and algorithms design skills. The website is based on three stages: programming, organizing the steps, playing. These stages drive students from the algorithm understanding to the algorithm writing in the programming language. Authors analyse animation as one of the aspects that helps students to understand algorithms. Firstly, students play with the animation, get feedback through it, and follow given instructions. In this way problem is growing and becoming clearer in their mind. Using the first stage animation students have to design a flowchart. Students built the algorithm using blocks. The positive results of using a flowchart could be seen directly. Finally, students have to write algorithms using a programming language. Interactivity on the *ILPADS* website is created by using *HTML5* and *JavaScript* [7].

In the self-paced learning platform used to teach programming research Hiron and Février [8] claim that making learning more interesting for students is not the same as replace learning with games, or put it inside game. Therefore, they separate the ideas to improve learning and engage student's motivation: problem's presentation in the context

---

of a story, making each problem part of a big adventure, recognizing short term and long-term accomplishments, practical problem. Stories should be short due to student's interest in the reading of tasks and his/her time taken to solve the tasks. By solving task student should have the willingness to learn more. They provide several examples of keeping student motivation in learning such as displaying check mark in the front of each problem (students enjoy having a full column of marks) or practical problem after introducing the concept's sequence of instructions. The authors identify features of the learning platform, which is used to teach programming. There are mentioned tools that enable editing, saving, compiling, running programs, group management tools, early feedback. In a web-environment student could directly edit, compile, and run their program.

Ihantola et al. [9] present a detailed and well-done literature review of programming assessment tools. They give deeper understanding about the requirement for the system and its support necessity. The variety of assessment tools depends on their availability, future maintenance and support. The learning management system could be chosen as a tool for assessment. Features as limiting the number of submissions, the amount of feedback, making each task slightly different, programming contest, opportunity for teacher to view student submissions, feedback, statistics and reports are discussed in the article [9].

Sokolova and Totkov [10] offer the classification of the test questions implemented in the *PeU 2.0* e-learning environment. The automatic assessment features such as resource saving, reliability, objective assessment, testing criteria for each students, time, tasks principles and rules, task structure are denoted. The test questions classification is suggested according to Bloom's taxonomy, cognitive objectives, form used to fill, submit, save content in the database, visualization (using text field, labels, multiple-choice questions elements, etc.). This assessment system is based on the client-server technology and realized using a program language *PHP, Apache* web-server and *MySQL* database management system.

Later Koong and Wu [11] present *Interactive Test Item System* (ITIS) used as an interactive multimedia item authoring system, which engage teachers to create an interactive item easily. ITIS is realized using "*Java* and software component technology, while *Java Web Start* technology has made authoring and testing through the web possible" (p. 135). The system consists of tree module: interactive item template, item editor (multimedia authoring tool), and examiner. The overview of these modules is provided in the article in details. Appling ITIS authors studied students learning performances on Social Studies and investigate differences between interactive and paper-and-pencil tests, students' performance by using different testing approaches.

Finally, we should focus on our attractive activities in Informatics, the *Bebras chal-lenge*. In Lithuania the *Bebras contest* is organized in two rounds: a school-wide contest in November together with many other countries over the world, and a nation-wide competition for selected high school students in January next year. During the school-wide round students perform tasks using computers supervised by teachers in schools. Second round of the challenge is performed by universities or colleges in regions. Over 33 thousand participants performed tasks in the first round in 2016 in Lithuania and 385 of them were invited to the second round in January 2017. Detailed discussion on *Bebras* tasks are provided in paper [12]. We are going to overview the development of *Bebras* tasks in the contest management system.

3   Bebras CMS Design

This section presents *Bebras* contest management system's description, functionality, tasks development in detail. Lithuanian *Bebras* contest management system was realized by programmer Rimantas Žakauskas in 2010 and named as *Bebras challenge field* (in Lithuanian - Bebro varžybų laukas, lt.bebras.lt). It was created as a tool to manage an information about participants (students) as well as teachers (coordinators), gather data of solutions of tasks, organise challenge and provide a detailed statistics and reports. The system was tested by exploitation (more than 30 000 student's entered the system during last year) and efficiency-designed for managing challenge. More than 5 500 new accounts were created for primary and secondary school students last year. The number of new user accounts is growing by similar additional accounts each year.

3.1   System Description

The Lithuanian *Bebras* CMS works as a web application and consists of a set of subsystems, which has a well-design interface:

- System administration (security, back up, resource monitoring, etc.),
- User management (registration system, authentication, user profile management),
- Challenge management (creation, administration and monitoring of the challenge),
- School administration (official list of all schools in Lithuania). A school list is updated in accordance with cooperation with the Centre of Information technologies in Education every year.
- Tasks management (create, import tasks),
- Results and communication management (participants and teachers can discuss about particular tasks, preview statistical data).

The Lithuanian *Bebras* CMS is a framework composed of *MySQL* relational database management system (DBMS), *Apache HTTP* server and *PHP* programming language and *Linux* OS. CMS use Model-View-Controller structural pattern. CMS is built to be compatible with all operating system and the latest versions of browsers, except not recommended using of *Internet Explorer* or *Edge* browsers.

3.2   Functional Requirements

Four basic types of roles: system administrator; teacher; student, unregistered user are implemented within the challenge management system (CMS). Each user has his own privileges and responsibilities. Use case diagram of the *Bebras* CMS is shown in Fig. 1.

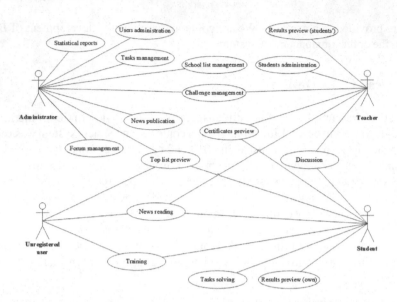

Fig. 1. Use case diagram of the Lithuanian *Bebras* CMS

The *Bebras* CMS design is modular according to the functionality. Modules are shown in Fig. 2. The most important modules for tasks development are challenge management, task management, and discussions.

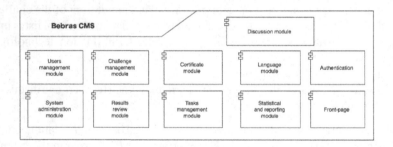

Fig. 2. The modular structure of the Lithuanian *Bebras* CMS

Tasks management module has been designed to create, edit, copy, upload, delete, preview, export task, filter task by tags, create tags for the tasks, search tasks by name or ID.

    Challenge management module involve this actions: create and edit the task, set the challenge date and time, preview tasks in the task set, test tasks, and manage permission to solve the task, participation in the challenge, and answer survey about particular tasks.

    Using discussion module users can follow discussion (read, comment, delete, edit). All user can follow discussion about the tasks solved during the challenge.

    The rest of modules are designed for users' management and data management; they are based on traditional functionally.

The special feature of the CMS is the management of two challenge rounds. The differences between the first and the second round is a permission to solve tasks managed by system administrator. Tasks of first and second round are separated, therefore a system administrator can easily follow the history of the task management (when and which tasks were used in the challenge). The *Bebras* CMS is used as a database for questions (called by a task pool). Over than 1900 tasks are already collected in the system together with solutions, explanations and users' comments.

3.3   Tasks Development in the Contest Management System

A national challenge organizer chooses a list of the tasks from tasks repository using source control software *SVN*. These tasks are prepared by the *Bebras* community countries experts in English during the international task workshop. After selected tasks are translated to the Lithuanian language, organizers develop them using the *Bebras* contest management system. *Bebras* CMS supports multiple-choice questions with opportunity to select one correct answer from four. By default, choices are displayed in random order during the challenge. For multiple-choice tasks, administrator fills these fields: task ID, title, task description and possible answers, answer comment if it is needed, choose task difficulty, age group, language.

To promote students' motivation in the challenge each year organizers provide several interactive tasks. These tasks are developed using *Bebras Lodge*[27] tool and imported to *Bebras* CMS. *Bebras Lodge* consists of two main parts:

- Componental – *JavaScript* library for creating and manipulating components inside a task;
- Lodge UI – interface built on top of Componental to make task development seamless.

Componental library depends on two other libraries: *jQuery* - for easier cross-browser functionality and *RaphaëlJS* – for SVG graphics. In the *Bebras Lodge* users can easily generate interactive tasks if they have a little bit of programming knowledge. A typical task consists of *JavaScript* code, images, cascading style sheets, correct answers, meta information. When user login to *Bebras Lodge*, he can start creating a new task, work on existing task or use the task template. Some basic metadata such as task ID, name, authors, language is added, others components should be added. Components are added by dragging and dropping components onto the tasks canvas in the visual interface or defining them with *JavaScript*.

All components have various parameters. If parameters of components are not enough for users, they can develop new components by writing *JavaScript* code. To make it easier for the users, a list of task templates is developed and added to the system. Users can use these templates to create a simple new interactive task. Interactive tasks are exported in *JSON* format. Exported *JSON* file contain all information needed to render the task, additional resources that might need to be downloaded are images listed

---

[27] http://bebras.licejus.lt/.

in the exported file, *JavaScript* framework for rendering the tasks, and *RaphaëlJS* library.

The interactive tasks' tool is used not only for task preparation for the challenge, but also for programming practice or interactive task development in different online learning environments which don't support interactivity as simulation, animation, etc. Teachers could develop interactive tasks using a tool available at http://spren-dimas.ugdome.lt/ (however, it is only in Lithuanian). The export to a SCORM is supported, so teachers can easily create interactive tasks and import them to a particular system, which supports SCROM standard.

Bebras tasks helps students to understand fundamental concepts of informatics, informatics processes [13], and connect informatics concepts to everyday life. The challenge encourages students to participate in the activity that not require programming skills or experience in technologies. Teachers could easily demonstrate programming practice in the visual way using interactive tasks tool. Tasks' content is based on informatics concepts teaching.

Development of *Bebras* tasks is a process, which involves various activities and needs different resources.

Figure 3 depicts activity diagram and following steps that describes the tasks preparation and usage in the challenge:

1. National challenge organizers (authors) prepare a set of task proposals. They provide 8–10 the best tasks to the task Repository (SVN) at least one month before *Bebras* International Task Workshop. During the workshop experts from the *Bebras* community countries review, improve and prepare final versions of the tasks. Tasks are updated in the task repository.
2. National challenge organizers select tasks from the task pool (download the final version from task repository).
3. Selected tasks are translated into the national language and edited by a linguist.
4. Static tasks (multiple-choice) are developed by using *Bebras* CMS; dynamic tasks (interactive, animated questions, etc.) are developed by using *Bebras Lodge* tool and exported to the *Bebras CMS*.
5. Then all tasks are prepared in the *Bebras* CMS and system administrator creates a set of tasks according the participants age groups (manage approved tasks).
6. During the challenge the teachers give permission for students to solve the task set; a participating student can solve the tasks and submit the answers; and the administrator will manage the whole challenge (users' roles were described in the Sect. 3.2).
7. After the challenge solved task are open for comments and discussions.
8. Later, all tasks are archived in the *Bebras* CMS. All of them can be reused.

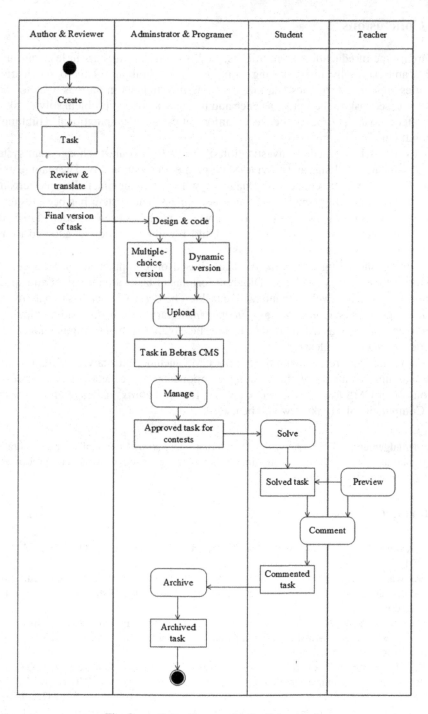

Fig. 3. Activity diagram for the *Bebras* task

4   Conclusions

Different type of educational activities is used to motivate students in learning informatics and especially in supporting Computational Thinking. Game-based learning activities support informatics learning by attracting students in various ages to solve concept-based tasks in computer science and improve students' problem solving skills. The international *Bebras* challenge on informatics and Computational Thinking is among them.

This research is based on investigation of the *Bebras* contest management system that supports the challenge and provides state-of-the-art functionality. The main features of the *Bebras* CMS are created to manage the whole challenge including participants' administration, development of tasks and assessment. The system has been tested by running contests for many years (totally renewed version has been introduced in 2010). Some components of the CMS are revised and rewritten, as well as adopted to new versions of browsers and mobile devices.

Creating interesting and attractive tasks based on computer science concepts is keystone of the *Bebras* challenge. Different formats of tasks are important and special attention is given in developing interactive tasks. The *Bebras Lodge* has two main parts for developing tasks: Componental – *JavaScript* library for creating and manipulating components inside a task, and Lodge UI – interface built on top of Componental to make task development seamless.

The future work related with the *Bebras* CMS includes an analysis of the functionality and improvements of the existing components. More detailed comparison of various other CMS used in different countries for the *Bebras* challenge on informatics and Computational Thinking would be useful.

Acknowledgements. We acknowledge the international *Bebras* Community for collaboration. Truly grateful to Jari Koivisto, our long-time colleague at informatics education, for proofreading the paper and making suggestions.

References

1. Hakulinen, L.: Survey on informatics competitions: developing tasks. Olymp. Inf. **5**, 12–25 (2011)
2. Benaya, T., Zur, E., Dagienė, V., Stupurienė, G.: Computer science high school curriculum in israel and lithuania - comparison and teachers' views. Baltic J. Mod. Comput. **5**(2), 164–182 (2017)
3. Dagiene, V., Stupuriene, G.: Bebras - a sustainable community building model for the concept based learning of informatics and computational thinking. Inf. Educ. **15**(1), 25–44 (2016). doi:10.15388/infedu.2016.02
4. Bell, T., Curzon, P., Cutts, Q., Dagiene, V., Haberman, B.: Overcoming obstacles to CS education by using non-programming outreach programmes. In: Kalaš, I., Mittermeir, R.T. (eds.) ISSEP 2011. LNCS, vol. 7013, pp. 71–81. Springer, Heidelberg (2011). doi:10.1007/978-3-642-24722-4_7
5. Wu, J., Chen, S., Yang, R.: Development and application of online judge system. In: 2012 International Symposium on Information Technologies in Medicine and Education (ITME), vol. 2, pp. 83–86. IEEE (2012). doi:10.1109/ITiME.2012.6291253

6. Forišek, M.: Pushing the boundary of programming contest. Olymp. Inf. **7**, 23–35 (2013)
7. Combefis, S., Schrieck, V., Nootens, A.: Growing algorithmic thinking trough interactive problems to encourage learning programming. Olymp. Inf. **7**, 3–13 (2013)
8. Hiron, M., Février, L.: A self-paced learning platform to teach programming and algorithms. Olymp. Inf. **6**, 69–85 (2012)
9. Ihantola, P., Karavirta, V., Seppala, O.: Review of recent systems for automatic assessment of programming assignments. In: Proceedings of the 10th Koli Calling International Conference on Computing Education Research, pp. 86–93. ACM, New York (2010). doi: 10.1145/1930464.1930480
10. Sokolova, M., Totkov, G.: Accumulative question types in e-learning environment. In: Proceedings of the 2007 International Conference on Computer Systems and Technologies, no. 90. ACM, New York (2007). doi:10.1145/1330598.1330693
11. Koong, C., Wu, C.: An interactive item sharing website for creating and conducting on-line testing. Comput. Educ. **55**(1), 131–144 (2010). doi:10.1016/j.compedu.2009.12.010
12. Dagiene, V., Sentence, S., Stupuriene, G.: Developing a two-dimensional categorization system for educational tasks in informatics. Informatica **28**(1), 23–24 (2017)
13. Stupurienė, G., Vinikienė, L., Dagienė, V.: Students' success in the bebras challenge in lithuania: focus on a long-term participation. In: Brodnik, A., Tort, F. (eds.) ISSEP 2016. LNCS, vol. 9973, pp. 78–89. Springer, Cham (2016). doi:10.1007/978-3-319-46747-4_7

Online Fault Detection Methodology
of Question Moodle Database
Using Scan Statistics Method

Aleksejs Jurenoks[✉], Svetlana Jurenoka, and Leonids Novickis

Riga Technical University, Riga, Latvia
aleksejs.jurenoks@rtu.lv,
{svetlana.jurenoka,lnovickis}@gmail.com

Abstract. This paper describes the methodology for creating the intelligent, user adapted testing system that has been developed using LMS Moodle. The integration of the intelligent processes into the existing training systems will prevent the drawbacks of the existing knowledge assessment systems and will make it possible to assess the learners' ability automatically disable problematics or incorrect questions from database question set.

The methodology to provide fast online fault detection in Moodle question database using scan statistics method is described. Scan statistics have long been used to detect statistically significant bursts of events. This research of student faults in time enables to detect the most problematics topics of educational process, check the efficiency of the decisions taken to select the education strategy.

Keywords: E-learning · Moodle · Scan statistics

1 Introduction

Scan statistics are a powerful method for detecting unusually high rates of events, also called anomalies [2]. Scanning for bursts of events has many applications in diverse fields such as telecommunications, astronomy, quality control, reliability and e-learning [5]. In this paper described method use scan statistics to monitor the occurrence of events in time, a such as status messages, alarms, and faults. As result system can automatically identify unusual bursts in events during educational process.

Nowadays one of the most used ways how to check the learners' knowledge in the e-learning educational system is a test. Test in a broader sense is a standardized assessment of knowledge and comprehension using different types of tasks. In a narrower sense, it is an assessment of knowledge and comprehension through tasks with multiple choice questions. Tests can be used for the initial assessment, the formative assessment as well as the summative assessment. However, tests may be used during the learning process and for self-assessment in an equally successful way.

The tests used for evaluation are based around everything that has been learnt during the learning process. In order to create the task system, it is recommended to progress from simpler to more complex tasks, thus checking the students' knowledge and understanding of using the appropriate knowledge in a standardized situation as well as in a new situation that has not been dealt with prior.

R. Damaševičius and V. Mikašytė (Eds.): ICIST 2017, CCIS 756, pp. 478–486, 2017.
DOI: 10.1007/978-3-319-67642-5_40

Tests are often used for formative assessment purposes. By contrast, summative assessment involves a complex test consisting of test questions and tasks which examine the use of knowledge and creative skills. The summative assessment can also take a combination such as this: test + research.

Nowadays there are many views related to the testing systems. The importance of acquisition of the final result is considered to be the main disadvantage in the classic test system where the learner chooses the correct answer from the suggested set of answers [6]; this does not motivate a person to define the answer themselves or to create a logical chain of problem solutions. This is the reason why testing does not always allow determining the actual level of the learner's knowledge. Other authors have proven [4] that when carrying out the assessment of the learner's knowledge by using open questions and tests, the results obtained by using tests are 48% better than using the open question form.

The integration of the intellectual processes into the existing training systems (utilisation of the artificial intelligence methods) will prevent the drawbacks of the existing knowledge assessment systems and will make it possible to assess the learners' ability to make logical decisions, to clarify the answers using examples and to evaluate the method of achieving the result.

The article describes the methodology for creating the intelligent, user adapted questionnaire; this methodology using scan statistics method can identify faults in educational process as result this will help to choose the educational scenario that help the learner reach the result that is most appropriate to their competence level.

2   Related Works

Thanks to the rapid development of the modern technology, nowadays a new generation of learners has emerged – they use only electronic resources in order to acquire new knowledge [1]. Despite the fact that today's systems can provide full educational process by using the method of presenting information mentioned prior, the way of presenting information is not always acceptable to all groups of learners. Nowadays the online educational systems can be divided into three relative groups [3]: Learning managements system, Synchronous collaboration, and all other computer tools including asynchronous collaboration. Whilst working with training systems, the user must choose the category of the training system for themselves and they must also adapt to the training course methodology. The research nowadays has shown that when using a static training system, the user cannot choose the training style that fits their personal needs which has resulted in: 39% of the time it being a reason to stop learning or 40% of the time it being a reason to simply skip incomprehensible or difficult topics and master them through other systems or courses [1].

In their work [4] it has been proven that using adaptive learning systems lets a person choose the learning content and the way of presenting information; it also increases the quality of the course by 28% by reducing the rate of terminating a course by 60%.

The tools of today only partially solve traditional problems which are related to the intelligent training systems. It is scientifically proven [7] that the main obstacle in implementing the intelligent training systems is related to the integration of the decision-making algorithm in the environment of a training system and its connection with the user model. Nowadays the intelligent training systems mainly have the adaptive rather than the intelligent functions.

3 Application of Scan Statistics Method

Let us introduce N events, distributed at time interval (0, T). In this paper Sw is defined as maximal number of events at a time interval with length w (the window of fixed length w of time). The maximum set Sw is called the scan statistics where one scan process is done in one period of time (0, T) with a window of size w and observes a large number of points. Wk is the shortest period of time containing a fixed number of k events. The distributions of the statistics Sw and Wk are related. If the shortest window that contains k points is longer than w, then there is no window of length w that contains k or more points:

$$P(W_k > w) = P(S_w < k). \tag{1}$$

Let us introduce the distribution of educational system faults using data received from automatic course management system that was implemented in Riga State gymnasium Nr. 3 (http://moodle.r3g.lv) from 01.09.2016 till 31.12.2016. In reviewing the data note that there is a 1 period (from 12.12.16 through 16.12.16) when 80 faults were registered (see Fig. 1). It is justified by the fact, that in this period of time almost in all subject's student knowledge validation process is done.

In Fig. 1 we can see concentration of 8 * 10 points at the time interval from 12.12.16 till 16.12.16. There is a question whether it is possible to explain such concentration proceeding from a null hypothesis [8]. If it is impossible to explain the given concentration of points (faults) by means of a null hypothesis it is necessary to recognize that the given concentration of points (faults) has a special character. It means that process of occurrence of failures in the given situations is influenced by additional factors.

The given conclusion is an objective signal for decision-making in the sphere of data flow management in e-learning system. We might explain this as follows: each of the 190 cases could either fall in the period from 01.09.2016 to 31.12.2016 or not, independently of the other cases. The probability b (k, N, w) found by computing the binomial probability for N = 190, p = 1/16:

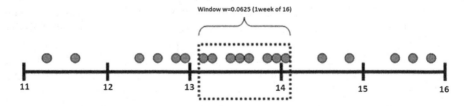

Fig. 1. Scanning the unit time interval with the window of length w = 0.0.625. Black points represent times of occurrence of N = 190 events, $S_{0.0625} = 80$. The centers of the occurred "points" C_i have coordinates $t_1, t_2, ..., t_N$

$$b(k, N, w) = \binom{N}{k} w^k (1 - w)^{N-k} =$$

$$b(k, 190, 0.2) = \binom{19}{k} 0.2^k (1 - 0.2)^{19-k} \tag{2}$$

It is easy to understand that there is an limitation number of sliding windows during the time interval. To solve this problem in a constructive way we must define some limitation set of sliding windows (Fig. 2).

Let us introduce $P(k, 190, 0.0625)$ the distribution of the maximum number of cases in one period of time. The null hypothesis model for 190 cases C_i ($i = 1, 2,...,$ 190) were distributed independently by the binomial distribution function and completely at random over the 4 month period. If the cluster is $k = 80$, the total number of cases over the whole 4 month period is $N = 190$ and the window size w is 1 week out of 16, or $w = 0.0625$. The result provided by the probability $P(80, 190, 0.0625)$ can be calculated using formula 3:

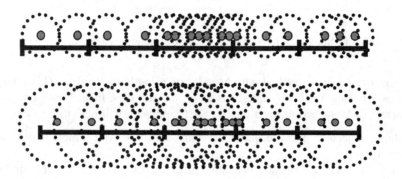

Fig. 2. Illustration of the scanning window of two fixed lengths $w = 0.0,312$ and $w = 0.0625$. The centers of scanning windows are points with time coordinates $t_1, t_2, ..., t_N$

$$P(k, N, w) \approx (N - k + 1)b(k - 1, N, w)$$
$$- (N - k - 1)b(k, N, w) + 2G_b(k + 1, N, w) \tag{3}$$

where

$$b(k, N, w) = \binom{N}{k} w^k (1 - w)^{N-k}$$

$$G_b(k, N, w) = \sum_{i=k}^{N} b(i, N, w)$$

Analyzing the statistics of system faults, it is possible to get an exact analytical solution for the distribution of "incorrect/problematics" questions in database. In this case there exists only one possibility and it is to use intelligent module to make modelling in real time. In the paper we have considered to use the Monte-Carlo method of scan statistics for calculation of p-value and testing null hypothesis H_0 (no clusters). The authors the approach by Wallenstein and Naus [9] in assuming the null hypothesis model which can be used for investigations of similar problems.

To isolate situations causing problems it is necessary to analyze the level of unsolved tasks in e-learning system using method of scan statistics. The paper illustrates the scanning process with a circle window with fixed radius. The illustration of the Monte-Carlo algorithm for cluster detection is presented in Fig. 3.

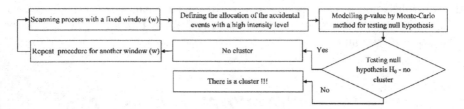

Fig. 3. Illustration of the Monte-Carlo algorithm for cluster detection

Using scan statistics method with Moodle question bank database [11] intelligent module will be able to classify questions using priority tags. In such way unsolved or fault tasks will be tagged to lover metric. Such approach will help to:

- to detect objects in Moodle questioner bank database with utmost fault/unsolved intensity;
- to check significance of fault detection (user process interruption or cancelation) with highest frequency;
- to analyze the dynamics of changes of clusters detected taking into consideration the time factor.

4   The Use of Question Metrics in the Process of Designing a Test

Using scan statistics method any question in database will have dynamic priority value unique for particular user group. (user groups and database structure are defined on Moodle database level). Suppose that a set of questions which can be used to achieve the result D has been assigned a matter of metrics $l(S(s))$, a value which is located in the indexed set and can be used in comparison. In the models suggested by other author [10], the metrics are built using recursive approach from top to bottom, defining the conditions for establishing the selection of best question.

For the question selection algorithm to be effective it is necessary to meet three conditions: determining the importance of the question, preservation of priorities, and the determination of the importance of a question.

Determining the importance of the question. The selectable question v is useful for the test u, if the condition is fulfilled (formula 4):

$$\begin{pmatrix} S(v_1) \\ S(v_2) \\ \dots \\ S(v_n) \end{pmatrix}_T \xrightarrow{t,select} \begin{pmatrix} S(v_{i_1}) \\ S(v_{i_2}) \\ \dots \\ S(v_{i_n}) \end{pmatrix}_T , \tag{4}$$

where $S(v_{i_j}) > S(v_{i_{j+1}})$, j = 1,2, ..., n − 1.

Its condition plays an important role. All metrics, whose rates are low, will be selected from the metrics list S(u) (the questions were not covered before or the learner has made several errors while filling in questions of a similar category). Accordingly, there will be no possibility to choose the test questions which the student can easily answer or has already answered successfully before.

Preserving the priorities. The metric preserves its priority if the $l(S(v)) \le l(S(uv))$ follows with $l(S(u) \le l(S(v)S(u))$ for all $\forall v \in V$ and $\forall u \in N(v)$. This means that before adding a new question u to the list S(v), it is evaluated as to whether it will be better than anyone else from the list S(v).

Defining the importance of a question. It determines the behaviour of the metrics through the full test question reconfiguration. Let us assume that $R(v) = (v_1, v_2, \dots, v_n)$ is the set of questions for the u test. Let us introduce an additional list $R^*(v)$ with questions that are sorted in the ascending order of the metrics - $l(S(v_n)) \le l(S(v_{n+1}))$. The arranged list of metrics will allow choosing the number of the most important questions for the v test (formula 5):

$$l\left[S_{R*(v)}(v) \right] \le \left[S_{R*(v)(v)} \right]. \tag{5}$$

5   The Algorithm of the Intellectual Question Selection

The Dijkstra's procedure is considered to be the basis of the classic information search algorithm in the graph. When implementing the procedure each question in the database is accompanied by two variables – prior(v) indicating the frequency of using the question v and pred(v) which indicates the location of the question v in the test. The starting value of the variable $prior(v) \rightarrow \infty$ has been defined. This means that the question has not been viewed yet. The starting value of the variable $pred(v) = 0$ – this means that the questions do not have a determined location in the test or that the location does not matter.

It is defined that the usage ratio of a question is a positive number. In this case, it is proposed to use the Dijkstra's algorithm provided that - $l(u, v) \ge 0$. As a result, the path of the graph must be built through questions with a minimum utilization coefficient.

```
Dijkstra's Procedure
(set of questions, test set, and achievable result)
for all u∈ V {
        prior(u):=∞;
        pred(u)=0;}
prior(d)=0;
H=CreateQueue(V);
while H is not empty {
u=Fist_Out(H);
for all(v,u) ∈ E {
if (prior(v)=prior(u)+l(v,u))
   { prior(v)=prior(u)+l(v,u);
       pred(v)=u;
       Rearrange_Queue(H,v);}
}
}
```

A significant difference in the procedures is the use of line H where all the elements are sorted using prior(v) values. The procedure *CreateQueue()* creates the line of question priorities H by replacing the question of the start of the line with the lowest usage coefficient *prior(v)* = 0. The procedure *Rearrange_Queue(H,v)* provides the reconfiguration of the line in case of priorities or usage of the questions.

Every time when performing a *while* cycle two conditions are met:

1. There is a $d > 0$ value where all the questions viewed - *prior(v)* $\leq d$ and all the remaining questions of the line - *prior(v)* $\geq d$.
2. The value *prior(v)* for each question v in the line is equal to ∞ or the minimum coefficient which points to the need of including the question; moreover, the frequently used in questions or the questions which do not meet the aim are removed from the line.

When the algorithm is in action, the starting value of the metrics of each question may vary multiple times depending on the results received during the tests. Every time the change in metrics is conducted by using the formula 6:

$$Update\_M(v,u) : prior(v) - min\{prior(v), prior(u)\_l(v,u)\} \tag{6}$$

During the procedure, certain characteristics are conducted:

- the use of the procedure does not increase prior(v) values;
- the most effective result corresponds to a minimal prior(v) value, therefore the regular *Update_M* procedure will not affect the results negatively.

The proposed algorithm creates a test looking at all the questions from the group S (v) if the question usage coefficient is available to the $l(S(v))$ metrics. Where it is not possible to identify the value of the question usage, the algorithm for creating intellectual questions is no longer able to work.

6 Conclusion

The article describes the methodology for creating the intellectual, user adapted questions. The opportunity of using scan statistics methodology for identifying of problematics questions or tasks in Moodle system is presented in this paper. The stochastic modelling of p-value by the method of Monte-Carlo for identifying the faults and Dijkstra algorithm for question selection is described in this paper.

The application of scan statistics enabled:

- to make analysis of question databank of Moodle system;
- to detect objects in Moodle questioner bank database with utmost fault/unsolved intensity;
- to check significance of fault detection (user process interruption or cancelation) with highest frequency;
- to analyze the dynamics of changes of clusters detected taking into consideration the time factor.

In result, general methodology of intelligent questioner module for e-learning intelligent system was described in this paper. The objective is to make a system work like a real teacher which can model the description of pedagogic resources and guide the learner in his educational process according to his assets and to the pedagogic objective that is defined by the teacher.

References

1. Abraham, G., Balasubramanian, V., Saravanaguru, RA.K.: Adaptive e-Learning environment using learning style recognition. Int. J. Eval. Res. Educ. **2**, 23–31 (2013)
2. Berman, M., Eagleson, G.K.: A useful upper bound for the tail probabilities of the scan statistics. J. Am. Stat. Assoc. **80**(392), 886–889 (1985). doi:10.2307/2288548
3. Delgado, M., Gibaja, E., Pegalajar, M.C., Pérez, O.: Predicting students' marks from moodle logs using neural network models. In: Current Developments in Technology-Assisted Education, Badajoz, pp. 586–590 (2006)
4. El Bachari, E., Abelwahed, E., El Adnani, M.: An adaptive learning model using learner's preference. In: International Conference on Models of Information and Communication Systems, ENSIAS, Rabat, Morocco (2010)
5. Glaz, J., Naus, J., Wallenstein, S.: Scan Statistics. Springer Series in Statistics. Springer, New York (2001). pp. 367–360
6. Niemiec, C., Ryan, R.M.: Autonomy, competence, and relatedness in the classroom. Applying self-determination theory to educational practice. Theory Res. Educ. **7**(2), 133–144 (2009)
7. Surjono, H.D.: The design of adaptive e-Learning system based on student's learning styles. Int. J. Comput. Sci. Inf. Technol. (IJCSIT) **2**(5), 2350–2353 (2011)

8. Ward, M.P., Carpenter, T.E.: Methods for determining temporal clusters in surveillance and survey programs. In: Salman, M.D. (ed.) Animal Disease Surveillance and Survey Systems. Methods and Applications, pp. 87–99. Iowa State Press, Ames Iowa (2003)

9. Wallenstein, S., Naus, J.: Statistics for temporal surveillance of bioterrorism. In: Syndrome Surveillance: Reports from a National Conference, Morbidity and Mortality Weekly Report 2004, vol. 53, pp. 74–78 (2003)

10. Гекк, М.В., Истомин, Т.Е., Файзулхаков, Я.Р., Чечендаев, А.В.: Адаптивный алгоритм быстрой доставки сообщений по выделенным направлениям, Вестник молодых ученых "Ломоносов". Выпуск III. С. 55–60 (2006)

11. Moodle question database structure. https://docs.moodle.org/dev/Question_database_structure. Accessed 6 Mar 2017

On Personalised Learning Units Evaluation Methodology

Julija Kurilova[✉], Saulius Minkevicius, and Eugenijus Kurilovas

Institute of Mathematics and Informatics, Vilnius University, Vilniuss, Lithuania
julija.kurilova@vu.mii.lt,
{saulius.minkevicius,jevgenij.kurilov}@mii.vu.lt

Abstract. The aim of the paper is to present a methodology (i.e. model and method) to evaluate suitability, acceptance and use of personalised learning units/ scenarios. Learning units/scenarios are referred here as methodological sequences of learning components (learning objects, learning activities, and learning environment). High-quality learning units should consist of the learning components optimised to particular students according to their personal needs, e.g. learning styles. In the paper, optimised learning scenarios mean learning scenarios composed of the components having the highest probabilistic suitability indexes to particular students according to Felder-Silverman learning styles model. Personalised learning units evaluation methodology presented in the paper is based on (1) well-known principles of Multiple Criteria Decision Analysis for identifying evaluation criteria; (2) Educational Technology Acceptance & Satisfaction Model (ETAS-M) based on well-known Unified Theory on Acceptance and Use of Technology (UTAUT) model, and (3) probabilistic suitability indexes to identify learning components' suitability to particular students' needs according to their learning styles. The methodology to evaluate personalised learning units presented in the paper is absolutely new in scientific literature. This methodology is applicable in real life situations where teachers have to help students to create and apply learning units that are most suitable for their needs and thus to improve education quality and efficiency.

Keywords: Earning styles · Learning units · Probabilistic suitability indexes · Evaluation · UTAUT model

1 Introduction

The main aim of the paper is to present a methodology to evaluate suitability, acceptance and use of personalised learning units/scenarios.

Methodology is refereed here as a model and method to evaluate learning units (or Units of Learning, UoLs). UoLs are referred here as methodological sequences of learning components (learning objects (LOs), learning activities (LAs), and learning environments (LEs) that are often referred to as virtual learning environments). High-quality UoLs should consist of the learning components optimised to particular students according to their personal needs, e.g. learning styles.

© Springer International Publishing AG 2017
R. Damaševičius and V. Mikašytė (Eds.): ICIST 2017, CCIS 756, pp. 487–498, 2017.
DOI: 10.1007/978-3-319-67642-5_41

In the paper, personalised UoLs are referred to as UoLs composed of the learning components having the highest probabilistic suitability indexes [21] to particular students according to Felder-Silverman Learning Styles Model [6].

Probabilistic suitability index is the main value used to establish the preference list of learning components according to their suitability level to students' learning styles. It is based on probabilistic model of students' learning styles and ratings (values) of learning components' suitability to particular students according to their learning styles [21].

Finally, the methodology analysed in the paper is based on acceptance and use evaluation criteria proposed by Educational Technology Acceptance & Satisfaction Model (ETAS-M) which in its turn is based on well-known Unified Theory on Acceptance and Use of Technology (UTAUT) model.

The rest of the paper is organised as follows: related research is presented in the following Section, proposed methodology to evaluate personalised learning units is presented in Sect. 3, and Sect. 4 concludes the paper.

2   Related Research

2.1   Personalisation of Learning Units

Learning personalisation became very popular research object in scientific literature during the last years [1, 5, 10, 17, 22, 23, 28]. Research topic on creating full learning units [13] and smaller learning components (LOs [11, 14], LAs [9] and LEs [16, 20]) that should be optimal (i.e. the most suitable) to particular students based on expert evaluation methods and techniques has also become highly demanded, and there are some relevant methods and techniques proposed in the area [12, 15, 19].

According to [12], suitability of learning unit/scenario to particular learner should be evaluated according to the following framework:

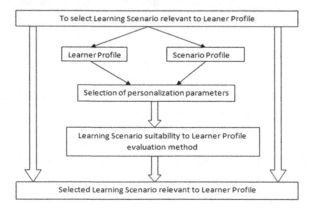

Fig. 1. Framework for evaluating suitability of UoL to learner (according to [12])

According to [18], future education means personalisation plus intelligence. Learning personalisation means creating and implementing personalised UoLs based on recommender system suitable for particular learners according to their personal needs. Educational intelligence means application of intelligent (smart) technologies and methods enabling personalised learning to improve learning quality and efficiency.

In personalised learning, first of all, integrated learner profiles (models) should be implemented. It should be based on e.g. Felder and Silverman Learning Styles Model (FSLSM) [6]. Dedicated psychological questionnaires like Soloman and Felder Index of Learning Styles questionnaire [27] should be applied here. After that, we should integrate the rest features in the learner profile (knowledge, interests, goals, cognitive traits, learning behavioural type etc.).

FSLSM [6] classifies students according to where they fit on a number of scales pertaining to the ways they receive and process information:

(a) By information type: (1) Sensory (SEN) – concrete, practical, oriented towards facts and procedures vs (2) Intuitive (INT) – conceptual, innovative, oriented towards facts and meaning;

(b) By sensory channel: (3) Visual (VIS) – prefer visual representations of presented material e.g. pictures, diagrams, flow charts vs (4) Verbal (VER) – prefer written and spoken explanations;

(c) By information processing: (5) Active (ACT) – learn by trying things out, working with others vs (6) Reflective (REF) – learn by thinking things through, working alone; and

(d) By understanding: (7) Sequential (SEQ) – linear, orderly, learn in small incremental steps vs (8) Global (GLO) – holistic, systems thinkers, learn in large leaps.

According to [21], after filling in Soloman and Felder's Index of Learning Styles questionnaire [27], one could obtain e.g. the following learning style initially stored in his/her student profile/model (Table 1):

Table 1. Example of learning style stored in the student profile (according to [21])

Learning styles							
By information type		By sensory channel		By information processing		By understanding	
SEN	INT	VIS	VER	ACT	REF	SEQ	GLO
0.64	0.36	0.82	0.18	0.73	0.27	0.45	0.55

After that, methodology on creating optimal UoLs for particular learners based on expert evaluation and intelligent technologies should be applied as follows:

According to [18], in personalised learning, first of all, integrated learner profiles should be implemented, and ontologies-based recommender systems should be created to suggest learning components (LOs, LAs and LEs) suitable to particular learners according to their FSLSM-based profiles. Thus, the whole personalised UoLs could be created for particular learners for each topic according to study programmes at Universities or curriculum at schools.

According to [18], a number of intelligent technologies should be applied to implement this approach, e.g. ontologies, recommender systems, intelligent software agents, multiple criteria decision making models, methods and tools to evaluate quality and suitability of the learning components etc.

Ontologies and recommender systems should be based on established interlinks between students' profiles and learning components. While establishing those interlinks, high-quality learning styles models and vocabularies of learning components should be used, on the one hand, and experienced experts should participate in this work generating collective intelligence, on the other.

Since the aim of the paper is to present UoLs suitability, acceptance and use evaluation methodology, first of all, one should identify a system of decision (evaluation) criteria (i.e. model).

According to [13], decision criteria are rules, measures and standards that guide decision-making. Quality criterion is a tool allowing comparison of alternatives according to a particular point of view. When building a criterion, the analyst should keep in mind that it is necessary that all the actors of the decision process adhere to the comparisons that will be deduced from that model. Criteria (relatively precise, but usually conflicting) are measures, rules and standards that guide decision-making, which also incorporates a model of preferences between the elements of a set of real or fictitious actions.

In identifying criteria for the decision analysis, the following considerations (i.e. principles) are relevant to all the multiple criteria decision analysis (MCDA) approaches [13]:

(1) Value relevance; (2) Understandability; (3) Measurability; (4) Non-redundancy; (5) Judgmental independence; (6) Balancing completeness and conciseness; (7) Operationality; and (8) Simplicity vs complexity.

Learning scenario/unit quality evaluation model based on these MCDA criteria identification principles is presented in Fig. 2.

According to [13], UoL is technology consisting of LOs, LAs and LEs. Therefore, UoL quality criteria should consist of the quality criteria identified for all its components:

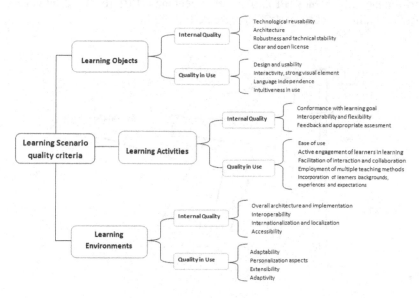

Fig. 2. Learning unit's quality model (according to [13])

2.2 Application of UTAUT Model in Education

The components'-based UoL evaluation model presented in Fig. 1 has its shortages, e.g. there are different criteria to evaluate different learning units' components. This approach is quite time-consuming and requires different and high level expertise from evaluators. According to Sect. 2.1, personalised UoLs are as high-quality as they fit students' personal needs based on FSLSM. Therefore, we could apply the same criteria-based evaluation of all components by the users.

This kind of evaluation is based on Unified Theory on Acceptance and Use of Technology (UTAUT) model. In the paper, UTAUT is examined while being applied in education in terms of acceptance and use of information and communication technologies for personalised learning purposes.

In this section, the original UTAUT model proposed by Venkatesh et al. [31] is analysed supplemented by 10 carefully selected studies on UTAUT application in education.

According to [31], information technology acceptance research has yielded many competing models, each with different sets of acceptance determinants. The eight models reviewed in [31] are the theory of reasoned action, the technology acceptance model, the motivational model, the theory of planned behaviour, a model combining the technology acceptance model and the theory of planned behaviour, the model of PC utilisation, the innovation diffusion theory, and the social cognitive theory. In [31], seven constructs appeared to be significant direct determinants of intention or usage in one or more of the individual models. Of these, the authors theorise that four constructs will play a significant role as direct determinants of user acceptance and usage behaviour: (a) performance expectancy (PE), (b) effort expectancy (EE), (c) social influence (SI), and (d) facilitating conditions (FC) as presented in Fig. 3:

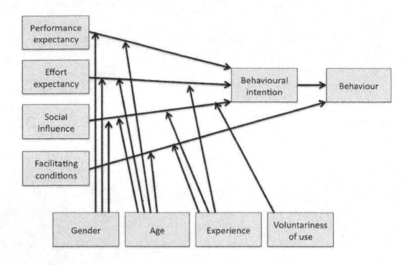

Fig. 3. UTAUT model (according to [31])

Study [7] aimed to investigate students' acceptance and use of Moodle employing the model of UTAUT and further understand the four constructs of the model. Data collected revealed that PE, EE, and SI were the major three keys of the UTAUT model to assess the acceptance of Moodle. Behavioural intention acted as a mediator to urge students to involve in the use of Moodle.

According to [30], acceptance of e-learning by employees is critical to the successful implementation of e-learning in the workplace. To explain why employees might accept the e-learning technology, motivational factors must be considered. According to [30], the effects of intrinsic motivators mediated the effect of extrinsic motivators.

According to [29], the UTAUT proposes that PE, EE, and SI predict behavioural intention towards the acceptance of information technology. The theory further proposes that FC and behavioural intention predicts use behaviour in the acceptance of information technology. Ever since its inception, the theory has been assessed using different applications. In [29], based on 37 selected empirical studies, a meta-analysis was conducted in order to harmonise the empirical evidence. The outcome of the study suggests that only the relationship between PE and behavioural intention is strong, while the relationships between EE, SI and behavioural intention are weak. Similarly, the relationship between FC, behavioural intention and use behaviour is also weak. Furthermore, the significance of the relationship between FC and use behaviour does not pass the fail-safe test while the significance of the relationship between behavioural intention and use behaviour does not pass the fail-safe test satisfactorily.

The main focus of paper [2] is to contrast and combine results from 20 different studies using the UTAUT and its extensions, in the hope of identifying patterns among studied results, sources of discrepancy among those results, or other existing relationships that may come to light in the context of these studies.

The review [3] evidently shows that variables that need to be applied to determine users' acceptance or adoption of technology vary. The effect of exogenous variables EE, PE, SI on endogenous variable 'behavioural intention' is not consistent across countries, within country, and unit of studies. According to the results of [3], EE (0.4, p < .05) significantly predicted Behavioural Intention to use technology, SI and PE were statistically insignificant, as was Behavioural Intention on Use Behaviour. However, FC (β = .26, p < .01) significantly influenced Use Behaviour.

According to [8], technology acceptance studies are a common medium of determining approval and predicting future use of technologies in the field of Information Systems. Numerous technology acceptance studies have been done in the area of education however there still remain hindrances in the use of computers in education. The aim of the study [8] is to analyse published research materials in the area of technology acceptance in education and identify the current research patterns. Upon identifying these patterns, a future research path is presented. For this purpose, initially the popular technology acceptance theories are studied so as to build a firm base for examining the technology acceptance works in education domain. The technology acceptance research works were thoroughly scrutinised to identify important aspects like acceptance theory used, constructs used, causal relationships and user types. Based on all these aspects a future research pathway is suggested. In [8], the acceptance of the two technology enabled phases of education i.e. e-learning and e-assessment was discussed. In the starting, e-learning along with its different types, advantages and disadvantages was explained. The difference between e-assessment and e-learning was explained because they are often thought as the same. Then the different types of e-assessments were discussed so as to show their variety. Next, it was found that the majority of the acceptance studies in education area have been on e-learning barring a few on e-assessment.

According to [26], among the fourteen theories reviewed in the paper, UTAUT seems to be an improved theory that could provide a useful tool to assess the likelihood of success for technology acceptance studies.

According to [4], in understanding how active and blended learning approaches with learning technologies engagement in undergraduate education, current research models tend to undermine the effect of learners' variations, particularly regarding their styles and approaches to learning, on intention and use of learning technologies.

Study [24] seeks to explore the factors that influence students' usage behaviour of e-learning systems. Based on the strong theoretical foundation of the UTAUT and using structural equation modelling, this research paper examines the impact of PE, EE, hedonic motivation, habit, SI, and trust on student's behavioural intention, which is later examined along with FCs on student's usage behaviour of e-learning systems. The results revealed direct positive effect of PE, hedonic motivation, habit, and trust on student's behavioural intention to use e-learning explaining around 71% of overall behavioural intention. Meanwhile, behavioural intention and FC accounted for 40% with strong positive effects on student's usage behaviour of e-learning systems. However, both EE and SI influence did not impact student's behavioural intention.

This review shows that UTAUT was never applied earlier to evaluate technology like learning unit/scenario.

The only study [25] was found in scientific literature which proposed UTAUT-based model that could be applied to evaluate personalised UoLs.

Paper [25] examines various extensions of UTAUT and related frameworks from a theoretical and empirical point of view. The theoretical contribution of the paper consists of substantial extensions/improvements of the UTAUT which are embedded within the theoretical paradigm of social constructivism. It is argued that the usability aspects of e-learning systems cannot be treated independently from their impact on learning behaviour and the pedagogical setting in which they are implemented.

Based on new empirical data from an experimental, undergraduate statistics course the authors provide strong support for a newly proposed Educational Technology Acceptance & Satisfaction Model (ETAS-M) (Fig. 4):

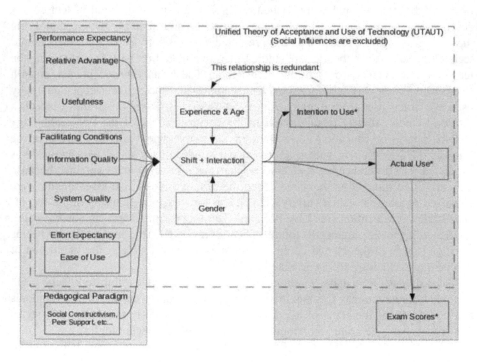

Fig. 4. ETAS-M (according to [25])

In this paper, a novel ETAS-M based methodology is proposed to evaluate personalised learning units.

3   Personalised Learning Units Evaluation Methodology

Based on related research analysis, we propose UoL evaluation model based on MCDA criteria identification principles (Fig. 2), Educational Technology Acceptance & Satisfaction Model (ETAS-M) (Fig. 4), and probabilistic suitability indexes (SI) to identify learning components' suitability to particular students' needs according to their learning styles [21].

Proposed model is components' based, on the one hand, and ETAS-M-based, on the other. Evaluation criteria are performance expectancy (PE), effort expectancy (EE), facilitating conditions (FC), and influence of pedagogical paradigm (IPP) instead of social influence (SI) in UTAUT.

It's more convenient in comparison with purely components-based model presented in Fig. 2 because it is based only on acceptance and use evaluation made by the users, and fully reflects their needs and points of view.

Additionally, this kind of model does not require specific high-level technological expertise from experts-evaluators to evaluate UoL alternatives by learning components' internal quality criteria.

Proposed personalised UoL evaluation model is presented in Fig. 5.

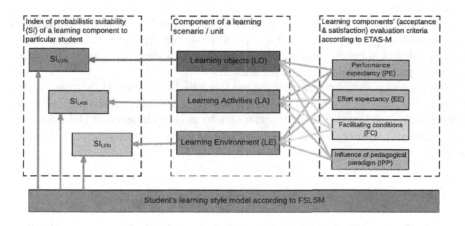

Fig. 5. Proposed personalised UoL evaluation model

After creating personalised UoL evaluation model, we should apply some evaluation method in order to evaluate particular UoL.

Proposed UoL evaluation method is based on Fig. 5. It could be expressed by formula (1):

$$f(x) = \left(\frac{\sum_{i=1}^{n} SI_i}{n} \right) \left(\sum_{j=1}^{m} \alpha_j f_j(x) \right) \tag{1}$$

where i is learning component (LO, LA or LE), $n = 3$, SI_i is probabilistic suitability index of corresponding learning component i to particular student, a_j is a weight of criterion j, and $f_j(x)$ is a value of criterion j, $m = 4$ (PE, FE, FC and IPP). In this paper, the weights of criteria are referred as equal.

Thus, in order to identify numerical value of UoL evaluation function, one should (1) multiply the values of all ETAS-M-based evaluation criteria by their weights for all learning components, (2) add these numbers together and identify the sum, (3) multiply all these sums by average probabilistic suitability indexes of corresponding learning components, and (4) identify the total sum. The higher the numerical value of $f(x)$ the better is the UoL for particular learner.

Practical value of the proposed methodology to evaluate suitability, acceptance and use of UoLs to particular students is as follows:

At any University or school, teachers have to create some kind of UoLs (modules, lessons etc.) for their students composed by learning content (LOs), learning activities, and learning environment. First of all, recommender system should recommend the most suitable learning components to particular students according to appropriate probabilistic suitability indexes applying UoLs personalisation methodology [18] described in Sect. 2.1. Additionally, there are a number of tools created to automatically compose UoLs from the most suitable learning components that teachers could use in their pedagogical practice.

The main problem here is how to create the most suitable UoLs for particular students that should have the highest level of acceptability and use by these students. In Fig. 5 and Formula (1), we present the model and method to evaluate suitability, acceptance and use of particular UoLs to particular students.

Thus, teachers should create personalised UoLs that should be (1) the most suitable for particular students in terms of the highest values of average probabilistic suitability indexes, and (2) the most acceptable and usable by students in terms of UoLs performance expectancy, effort expectancy, facilitating conditions, and influence of pedagogical paradigm used by teachers.

4   Conclusion

In the paper, the authors propose personalised learning units/scenarios suitability, acceptance and use evaluation model based on MCDA criteria identification principles, learning components'-based evaluation model, and Educational Technology Acceptance & Satisfaction Model (ETAS-M) based on UTAUT model. Every UoL's component (LO, LA and LE) should be evaluated according to ETAS-M. Personalisation of UoL components according to FSLSM should be guaranteed by identifying corresponding average probabilistic suitability indexes.

The proposed model is components' based, on the one hand, and ETAS-M-based, on the other. It's more convenient in comparison with purely components-based model presented in Fig. 2 because it is based only on suitability, acceptance and use evaluation made by the users, and fully reflects their needs and points of view. Additionally, this kind of model does not require specific high-level technological expertise from experts-evaluators. On the other hand, proposed model is better than pure ETAS-M/UTAUT-based model because it's more flexible since it takes into consideration all different components of UoL separately as well as corresponding average probabilistic suitability indexes.

Finally, in the paper, personalised UoLs evaluation method was proposed by formula (1).

Proposed methodology is feasible to be applied in real-life pedagogical situations in educational institutions. In order to create and evaluate personalised UoLs, educational institutions should establish FSLSM-based students' profiles, use high quality vocabularies of learning components, and have enough expertise to identify corresponding suitability indexes.

References

1. Arimoto, M.M., Barroca, L., Barbosa, E.F.: AM-OER: an agile method for the development of open educational resources. Inf. Educ. **15**(2), 205–233 (2016)
2. Attuquayefio, S., Addo, H.: Review of studies with UTAUT as conceptual framework. Eur. Sci. J. **10**(8), 249–258 (2014)
3. Attuquayefio, S., Addo, H.: Using the UTAUT model to analyze students' ICT adoption. Int. J. Educ. Dev. Using Inf. Commun. Technol. **10**(3), 75–86 (2014)
4. Chan, K., Cheung, G., Wan, K., Brown, I., Luk, G.: Synthesizing technology adoption and learners' approaches towards active learning in higher education. Electron. J. e-Learn. **13**(6), 431–440 (2015)
5. Dorca, F.A., Araujo, R.D., de Carvalho, V.C., Resende, D.T., Cattelan, R.G.: An automatic and dynamic approach for personalized recommendation of learning objects considering students learning styles: an experimental analysis. Inf. Educ. **15**(1), 45–62 (2016)
6. Felder, R.M., Silverman, L.K.: Learning and teaching styles in engineering education. Eng. Educ. **78**(7), 674–681 (1988)
7. Hsu, H.H.: The acceptance of moodle: an empirical study based on UTAU. Creative Educ. **3**(Supplement), 44–46 (2012)
8. Imtiaz, A., Maarop, N.: A review of technology acceptance studies in the field of education. J. Teknol. Sci. Eng. **69**(2), 27–32 (2014)
9. Jasute, E., Kubilinskiene, S., Juskeviciene, A., Kurilovas, E.: Personalised learning methods and activities for computer engineering education. Int. J. Eng. Educ. **32**(3), 1078–1086 (2016)
10. Juskeviciene, A., Jasute, E., Kurilovas, E., Mamcenko, J.: Application of 1:1 mobile learning scenarios in computer engineering education. Int. J. Eng. Educ. **32**(3), 1087–1096 (2016)
11. Kurilovas, E.: Interoperability, standards and metadata for e-Learning. In: Papadopoulos, G.A., Badica, C. (eds.) Intelligent Distributed Computing III, Studies in Computational Intelligence (SCI), vol. 237, pp. 121–130. Springer, Heidelberg (2009). doi:10.1007/978-3-642-03214-1_12
12. Kurilovas, E., Zilinskiene, I., Ignatova, N.: Evaluation of quality of learning scenarios and their suitability to particular learners' profiles. In: Proceedings of the 10th European Conference on e-Learning (ECEL 2011), Brighton, UK, 10–11 November 2011, pp. 380–389 (2011)
13. Kurilovas, E., Zilinskiene, I.: Evaluation of quality of personalised learning scenarios: an improved MCEQLS AHP method. Int. J. Eng. Educ. **28**(6), 1309–1315 (2012)

14. Kurilovas, E., Serikoviene, S.: New MCEQLS TFN method for evaluating quality and reusability of learning objects. Technol. Econ. Dev. Econ. **19**(4), 706–723 (2013)
15. Kurilovas, E., Serikoviene, S., Vuorikari, R.: Expert centred vs learner centred approach for evaluating quality and reusability of learning objects. Comput. Hum. Behav. **30**, 526–534 (2014)
16. Kurilovas, E., Juskeviciene, A., Kubilinskiene, S., Serikoviene, S.: Several semantic web approaches to improving the adaptation quality of virtual learning environments. J. Univers. Comput. Sci. **20**(10), 1418–1432 (2014)
17. Kurilovas, E., Juskeviciene, A.: Creation of web 2.0 tools ontology to improve learning. Comput. Hum. Behav. **51**, 1380–1386 (2015)
18. Kurilovas, E.: Evaluation of quality and personalisation of VR/AR/MR learning systems. Behav. Inf. Technol. **35**(11), 998–1007 (2016)
19. Kurilovas, E., Vinogradova, I., Kubilinskiene, S.: New MCEQLS fuzzy AHP methodology for evaluating learning repositories: a tool for technological development of economy. Technol. Econ. Dev. Econ. **22**(1), 142–155 (2016)
20. Kurilovas, E., Dagiene, V.: Computational thinking skills and adaptation quality of virtual learning environments for learning informatics. Int. J. Eng. Educ. **32**(4), 1596–1603 (2016)
21. Kurilovas, E., Kurilova, J., Andruskevic, T.: On suitability index to create optimal personalised learning packages. In: Dregvaite, G., Damasevicius, R. (eds.) ICIST 2016. CCIS, vol. 639, pp. 479–490. Springer, Cham (2016). doi:10.1007/978-3-319-46254-7_38
22. Lytras, M.D., Kurilovas, E.: Special issue on information and communication technologies for human capital development. Comput. Hum. Behav. **30**, 361 (2014)
23. Lytras, M.D., Zhuhadar, L., Zhang, J.X., Kurilovas, E.: Advances of scientific research on technology enhanced learning in social networks and mobile contexts: towards high effective educational platforms for next generation education. J. Univers. Comput. Sci. **20**(10), 1402–1406 (2014)
24. Masa'deh, R., Ali Tarhini, A., Mohammed, A.B., Maqableh, M.: Modeling factors affecting student's usage behaviour of e-learning systems in lebanon. Int. J. Bus. Manage. **11**(2), 299–312 (2016)
25. Poelmans, S., Wessa, P., Milis, K., van Stee, E.: Modeling educational technology acceptance and satisfaction. IN: Proceedings of EDULEARN09 Conference, 6–8 July 2009, Barcelona, pp. 5882–5889 (2009)
26. Samaradiwakara, G.D.M.N., Gunawardena, G.G.: Comparison of existing technology acceptance theories and models to suggest a well improved theory/model. Int. Tech. Sci. J. **1**(1), 21–36 (2014)
27. Soloman, B.A., Felder, R.M.: Index of learning styles questionnaire. http://www.engr.ncsu.edu/learningstyles/ilsweb.html
28. Spodniakova Pfefferova, M.: Computer simulations and their influence on students' understanding of oscillatory motion. Inf. Educ. **14**(2), 279–289 (2015)
29. Taiwo, A.A., Downe, A.G.: The theory of user acceptance and use of technology (UTAUT): a meta-analytic review of empirical findings. J. Theor. Appl. Inf. Technol. **49**(1), 48–58 (2013)
30. Yoo, S.J., Han, S.H., Huang, W.: The roles of intrinsic motivators and extrinsic motivators in promoting e-learning in the workplace: a case from South Korea. Comput. Hum. Behav. **28**, 942–950 (2012)
31. Venkatesh, V., Morris, M.G., Davis, G.B., Davis, F.D.: User acceptance of information technology: toward a unified view. MIS Q. **27**(3), 425–478 (2003)

The Study of Gender Equality in Information Sciences Research Institutions in Lithuania

Virginija Limanauskiene[✉], Danguole Rutkauskiene,
Vitalija Kersiene, Eduardas Bareisa, Robertas Damasevicius,
Rytis Maskeliunas, and Aleksandras Targamadze

Kaunas University of Technology, Studentu 50, 51368 Kaunas, Lithuania
virginija.limanauskiene@ktu.lt

Abstract. The aim of this paper is to define the problem and to present the gender equality gaps existing in Information Sciences and Technology (IST) research institutions in Lithuania and to deeply analyze the problem in case study.

The paper presents some research results of the ongoing H2020-EU.5.b. project EQUAL-IST Gender Equality Plans for Information Sciences and Technology Research Institutions (2016–2019).

We analyzed the works of different authors and selected the factors that limit successful scientific carrier in the IST research: gender stereotypes in labor market, unconscious bias among managers, work- life balance, women's confidence and aspirations. In paper we provide evidence of findings by statistical data of Lithuania.

Among all the countries, Lithuania has a gear average of young people looking for a career in computing or engineering, but women are paid less salary; IST economics sector and research of Lithuania needs talented qualified women and men.

We analyze students' gender equality context in Informatics Faculty KTU: amounts of students, degrees of graduates, correlation with study programs. Also we provide results of analysis of staff structure, gender distribution, wages.

Keywords: Women in science · Gender equality · Information sciences

1 Introduction

Equality between women and men is a priority of the EU strategy "Europe 2020". The Recommendations on Equal Opportunities for Women and Men in Institutions of Science and Studies determines the guidelines for actions, measures and monitoring also indicates the need to increase the number of women in research institutions and their number taking the leading vacancies. Today gender equality policy in Lithuanian education system is implemented in accordance with the National Program on Equal Opportunities for Women and Men for 2010–2014, in which one of the tasks is "to ensure the monitoring of application of the principle of equal opportunities for women and men in educational and research institutions" (Planipolis 2014).

This research developed within the framework of Equal IST project presents different activities: literature analysis, statistical data, gender studies, national policy documents,

© Springer International Publishing AG 2017
R. Damaševičius and V. Mikašytė (Eds.): ICIST 2017, CCIS 756, pp. 499–511, 2017.
DOI: 10.1007/978-3-319-67642-5_42

organizational studies and descriptions of best practices implemented in IST (Information Sciences and Technology) research institutions in Lithuania (LT) in recent years.

The aim of this paper is to define the problem and to present the gender equality gaps existing in IST research and economic sector in Lithuania and to deeply analyze the problem in case study. The paper is organized as follows. We analyze the related works in Sect. 2. We describe some gender issues in IST educational sector and research institutions in Lithuania in Sect. 3. We present the case study in Sect. 4.

2   Related Works

2.1   Indicators of the Gap

Through the Global Gender Gap Report, the World Economic Forum quantifies the magnitude of gender disparities and tracks their progress over time, with a specific focus on the relative gaps between women and men across four key areas: health, education, economy and politics. The 2016 Report covers 144 countries. The highest possible score is 1 (equality) and the lowest possible score is 0 (inequality). The methodology of the Index has remained stable since its original conception in 2006, providing a basis for robust cross-country and time-series analysis. Rank of Lithuania was 25, score 0,744 in 2016 year (see Fig. 1). The chart in Fig. 1 compares the country's score for each of the four sub- indexes of the Global Gender Gap Report with the average score weighted by population across all 144 countries.

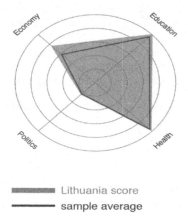

Lithuania score
sample average

Fig. 1. Key indicators and score of Global Gender Gap index: Lithuania 2016.

Country profile in Fig. 1 gives a picture of the relative *strengths* (education- score 1 and health- score 0,979) and *weaknesses* (politics- score 0,239 and economics- score 0,757) of Lithuania performance compared with that of other nations and relative to its own past performance (Global Gender Gap Index 2016). An analysis of gender gaps in the domain of money shows that women are, with few exceptions, disadvantaged compared with men (see Table 1) (EIGE 2017). Due to the presence of various currencies across Member States of Europe income and earnings are assessed in purchasing power standards (PPS), defined as an 'artificial currency' allowing to 'buy the same amount of goods and services in each country' (EIGE 2017).

Table 1. Indicators of Lithuania compared with EU, Gender Equality Index 2012 (EIGE 2015)

Domain	Indicators	Unit	LT		EU-28	
			Women	Men	Women	Men
Money	Mean monthly earnings, 2010 year	PPS	885	1036	2018	2528
Knowledge	Graduates of tertiary education (15–74 population)	%	32	21,8	24,1	22,8
Time	Workers caring for and educating their children or grandchildren, every day for one hour or more (15 + workers)	%	40,6	20,3	44,6	27,4
	Workers doing cooking and housework, every day for one hour or more (15 +)	%	83,3	21	77,1	24

2.2 Barriers to Hiring and Promoting Women in the IST Research Sector

We analyzed the works of different authors and selected the factors that limit women successful scientific carrier in the research andIST sector of economics. Here we provide evidence of findings by statistical data.

First. Gender stereotypes in the labor market. Education, health care, humanities and arts are the areas where women dominate – their employment amounts to 80–90%. Women have been occupying the positions of general education school teachers up to 77,8%. Women make 69,7% of staff in colleges and VET schools, meanwhile, at universities men comprise over 50% of staff (Statistics Lithuania 2015). Noticeably, 55% of researchers in higher education sector are women (see Table 2).

Table 2. R&D staff in Higher Education sector (Statistics Lithuania 2015)

Higher education sector	Year	R&D personnel persons	Males	Females	Percentage of females
Total by category of R&D personnel	2009	13309	5768	7541	56,7
	2011	16492	6961	9531	57,8
	2013	16527	7036	9491	57,4
	2015	14860	6257	8603	57,9
Researchers	2009	10633	4970	5663	53,3
	2011	13664	6130	7534	55,1
	2013	13936	6304	7632	54,8
	2015	12600	5609	6991	55,5

On the other hand, technologies, physical sciences and computer sciences & information technologies are the areas where dominate men in Lithuania. Men who are employed in higher education and government sectors have an academic degree or academic titles in the technology 69,8% and physical sciences 66% (see Fig. 2).

Researchers with a scientific degree by field of science, 2014[1]

	Moterys Women		Vyrai Men		Procentais Per cent		
	iš viso total	%	iš viso total	%	moterys women	vyrai men	
Iš viso	**3905**	**100**	**3976**	**100**	**49,5**	**50,5**	**Total**
Humanitariniai mokslai	753	19,3	522	13,1	59,1	40,9	Humanities
Socialiniai mokslai	1186	30,4	759	19,1	61,0	39,0	Social sciences
Technologijos mokslai	403	10,3	932	23,4	30,2	69,8	Technical sciences
Fiziniai mokslai	433	11,1	855	21,5	33,6	66,4	Physical sciences
Žemės ūkio mokslai	194	4,9	156	4,0	55,4	44,6	Agricultural sciences
Biomedicinos mokslai	936	24,0	752	18,9	55,5	44,5	Biomedical sciences
medicinos mokslai	623	66,6	505	67,2	55,2	44,8	medical sciences
kiti biomedicinos (gamtos) mokslai	313	33,4	247	32,8	55,9	44,1	other biomedical (natural) sciences

Fig. 2. Researchers with a scientific degree by the field of science (Statistics Lithuania 2015).

Second. Unconscious bias among the managers. Žalėnienė et al. lists the social stereotypes which lead to a 'glass ceiling' phenomenon resulting in prejudices and organizational barriers to career-oriented women. Gender stereotypes in Lithuania assign the role of women as a support staff (Žalėnienė et al. 2016).

The survey carried out in universities of the Republic of Lithuania in 2013 and 2015 has demonstrated the existence of asymmetric gender distribution and vertical segregation within Lithuanian higher education system. Women prevail in the lowest administrative positions (70%) in the administration of universities. Top management positions of faculty heads and directors of institutes are dominated by men (71% of deans, 59% of department heads, 56% of faculty councils' members, and 59% of institute directors). There is also vertical segregation by gender in academic staff: women make up the majority of junior researchers (54%) and researchers (56%), while men dominate as senior researchers (53%) and chief researchers (71%); men dominate in professor positions (69%), whereas women prevail in positions of assistants (63%) and lecturers (57%).

Third. Work- life balance. According to various studies it takes longer for females to get their scientific degree. Žalėnienė et al. lists the social obstacles for women to pursue careers in research and occupy managing positions in the administration of universities equally to men: difficulties to reconcile family and career, breaks in research work due to maternity leave (Žalėnienė et al. 2016). The European Institute for Gender Equality (EIGE 2015) provides statistics (see fragment in Table 1) and promote an idea that a more equal distribution of unpaid care work can be the result of men being more involved in the childcare activities and thus increasing their share of care work, or the result of an increase in social infrastructures reducing the time women devote to unpaid care work.

Fourth. Women's confidence, aspirations. According Stanišauskienė findings assessment of women's learning motivation demonstrates a stronger focus on personal and spiritual values, whereas men are more motivated by pragmatic values. Women appreciate spiritual development, they want to know more, to perceive better what is happening globally; they aim for social dimension – being useful to others, meeting new people, getting to know the surrounding environment and themselves; they aim for happiness – women seek to become happier and escape everyday routine. After the analysis of men's motives for learning, the following priorities have been observed: the opportunity to get a new job, the opportunity to be promoted, satisfy employer expectations, obtain a diploma (Stanišauskienė 2005).

The following observations (European Commission 2015) about the factors influencing the negative choice of girls gifted for sciences are: unattractive and inadequate image of scientists; social environment does not motivate girls to choose sciences as profession; teaching of computer sciences is not oriented to women: the textbooks are engaging for boys, given examples reflect masculine hobbies; girls neither see their place in computer science nor foster further career perspectives in science; parents' attitudes and support are invaluable while choosing a scientist's profession; university education does not take into account the peculiarities of the way women think.

2.3 Key Drivers Influencing Young Women Interest in Science and Engineering

Microsoft at 2017 conducted a quantitative survey of 11,500 girls across 12 countries and identified the following drivers, listed in order of importance, and offered some practical steps to sustaining young women's interest in STEM (science, technology, engineering, and mathematics) (Microsoft 2017).:

1. **Female role models.** Having visible female role models sparks girls' interest in STEM careers and helps them to picture themselves pursuing these fields.
2. **Practical experience and hands-on exercises.** The more practical experiences a girl receives during her education– the higher her interest in STEM. Yet 39% say they're not getting enough of either of these. Creativity in the classroom is also a key: girls who like STEM enthuse about being able to choose their own projects.
3. **Teacher mentors.** When educators talk to girls about STEM subjects and actively encourage them, girls become more attracted to these disciplines. Over half (56%) of those we spoke to said they'd like to receive more encouragement from teachers.
4. **Real-life applications.** Girls become more interested in STEM once they're able to conceive what they can do with these subjects, how they can be applied to real-life situations and how relevant they might be relevant to their future.
5. **Confidence in equality.** Young women are more likely to pursue STEM careers when they are confident that men and women will be treated equally working in these disciplines.

3   Some Gender Issues in IST Educational Sector and Research Institutions in Lithuania

According to statistics of educational attainment in 2014–2015 academic years, women comprise 58.8% of students in all types of universities in Lithuania. More women than men completed the tertiary education, received Master degree and doctoral degree (see Fig. 3).

	Baigė ir įgijo kvalifikaciją, kvalifikacinį ar mokslo laipsnį – *Number of graduates with a*							
	Bakalauro *Bachelor's degree*		Magistro *Master's degree*		Profesinę kvalifikaciją *Professional qualification*		Daktaro mokslo ar meno licenciato *Doctoral degree*	
	moterys *women*	vyrai *men*	moterys *women*	vyrai *men*	moterys *women*	vyrai *men*	moterys *women*	vyrai *men*
2005	12030	6282	4900	2587	1409	606	158	117
2010	13466	7596	6770	3075	777	270	216	158
2013	11638	6928	5712	2878	642	171	249	174
2014	8754	5154	5520	2717	410	153	221	151
	Procentais ***Per cent***							
2005	65,7	34,3	65,4	34,6	69,9	30,1	57,5	42,5
2010	63,9	36,1	68,8	31,2	74,2	25,8	57,8	42,2
2013	62,7	37,3	66,5	33,5	79,0	21,0	58,9	41,1
2014	62,9	37,1	67,0	33,0	72,8	27,2	59,4	40,3

Fig. 3. Female and male university graduates by degree (Statistics Lithuania 2015).

Gender proportion in natural sciences and IS sector is opposite. Analysis of the statistical data in the STEM (science, technology, engineering, mathematics) area reveals following results: less and less women choose natural, technological and applied sciences every year (see Fig. 4). Percentage of researchers with a scientific degree in technical science is the following: women 30,2% in physical science: women 33,6% (see Fig. 2).

ICT economics sector and research of Lithuania needs talented qualified women.

The numbers provided by OECD shows expectations to have a career in computing or engineering. Among all the countries, Lithuania has a gear average of young people looking for a career in computing or engineering. A high number of young people educated on the tertiary level, i.e. researchers, is also expected in the future (OECD 2015).

Undertaken steps to fight gender inequality are insufficient to counter historically embedded barriers to gender equality in research. Already at the undergraduate level, female students are an exception in the fields of engineering (Šidlauskiene 2012), technology and physics. In general, participation of women in mathematical and

Number of tertiary level graduates (ISCED 6–8) in natural sciences, technology and applied sciences

Skaičius, tenkantis 1 tūkst. 20–29 metų amžiaus gyventojų
Per 1000 population aged 20–29

	2005	2010	2013	2014	
Iš viso	19,8	21,9	21,4	18,1	*Total*
Moterys	14,1	12,7	11,7	10,6	*Women*
Vyrai	25,4	30,9	30,7	25,2	*Men*

Fig. 4. Number of graduates at tertiary level in STEM (science, technology, engineering, and mathematics) (Statistics Lithuania 2015).

technological fields is low (although the share (33%) is above the EU average (less than 30% for countries with available data) (MOSTA 2015).

Moreover, the share of women is insufficient in better paid research leadership positions both in senior academic positions and managerial positions.

Women are paid less salary. According to the annual income statistics of the persons working in information and communications sector (covering more widely than the higher education and government sectors) in Lithuania in 2014, the average gross monthly earnings of women made up only 72% of those of men: women earned 923,4 Eur while men - 1287,9 Eur; employed persons in this area: women 39,1% and men 60.9% (Statistics Lithuania 2015).

4   Gender Issues at the Faculty of Informatics: A Case Study

The Faculty of Informatics KTU (Kaunas University of Technology) carries out research in Informatics and Information Technologies area, plays a central role in information society of Lithuania.

Students of Informatics Faculty KTU. Study programs offered are listed in Table 3. Statistics of 2013-2016 years show that much larger number of men than women have graduated from the Faculty of Informatics (see Table 4) (KTU 2016).

Table 3. The studies programs in Informatics Faculty KTU, 2017.

Bachelor study (6)	Master study (5)	Doctoral study (2)
Health informatics Informatics Informatics engineering Information systems Multimedia technologies Software systems	Informatics Information and IT security Information systems Engineering IT of distance education Software engineering	Informatics Informatics engineering

Table 4. Female and male graduates from the Faculty of Informatics at KTU by degree

	Bachelor's degree		Master's degree		PhD degree	
Year	men	women	men	women	men	women
2013	188	17	73	10	8	1
2014	201	17	74	16	4	1
2015	178	15	61	15	3	3
2016	174	20	69	21	2	0

Percentage of female and male graduates of the IF (Faculty of Informatics) at KTU is depicted in a chart in Fig. 5. It can be noted that the percentage of women among the Master's degree graduates is higher than the Bachelor's and it is growing over years. Šidlauskiene et al. found, that Multimedia Technologies study program has much more female graduates from Bachelor degree in comparison to other programs (Šidlauskiene et al. 2014), the similar situation is in KTU (see Fig. 6). A very high percentage of women (54,1%) graduated from a Master degree program IT of Distance Education. Interestingly, 20% of Master's graduates from Information technologies, Information Systems Engineering and Informatics study programs are women (see Fig. 7).

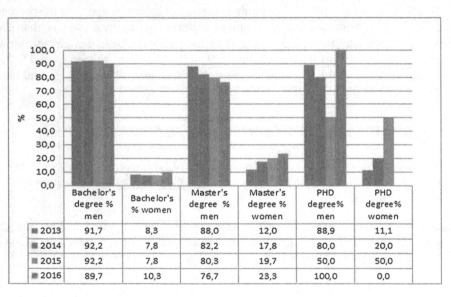

Fig. 5. Percentage of female and male graduates from the Faculty of Informatics at KTU by degree (Updated on: 2016-07-11. KTU 2016).

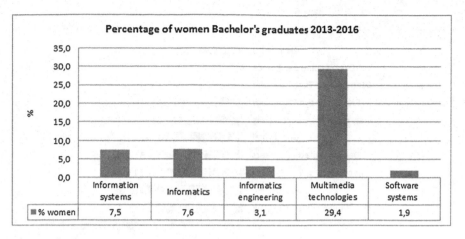

Fig. 6. Percentage of female Bachelor graduates by study programmes from the Faculty of Informatics at KTU (Updated on: 2016-07-11. KTU 2016)

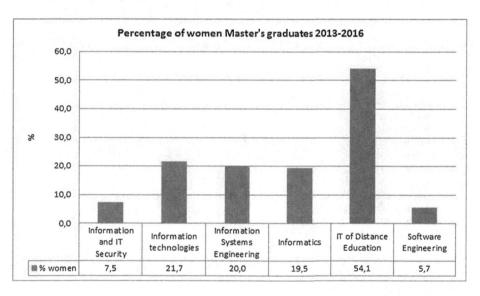

Fig. 7. Percentage of female Master graduates by studies programmes from the Faculty of Informatics at KTU (Updated on: 2016-07-11. KTU 2016).

Staff of the Informatics Faculty KTU. It consists of:

- *Academic staff* of the university (professors, associate professors, lecturers, assistants and contracted teachers) and researchers carrying out projects and other research related activities (analysts, experts, technicians, engineers, programmers);
- *Management staff* members of university administration (dean, heads of departments and other units, coordinators, managers, administrators, academic assistants).

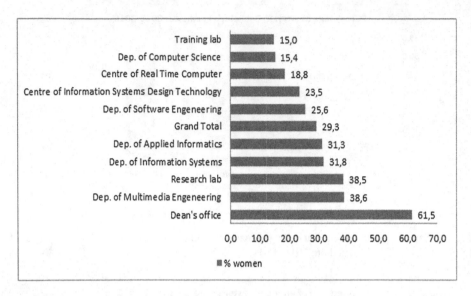

Fig. 8. Percentage of women in the Faculty of Informatics at KTU by subunit (Updated on: 2016-07-11, KTU 2016)

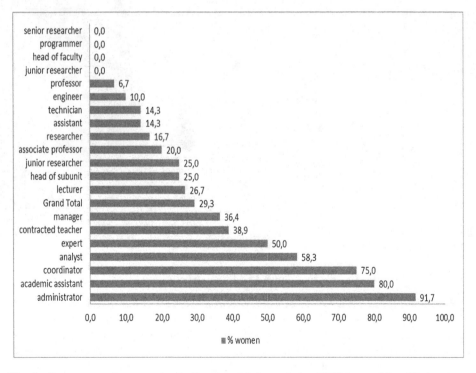

Fig. 9. Percentage of women in the Faculty of Informatics at KTU by position (Updated on: 2016-07-11, KTU 2016).

Women comprise 29,3% of staff in the Faculty of Informatics at KTU. Analysis of the Faculty staff structure has shown that women prevail in the dean's office (61,5%) (see Fig. 8) but in the lowest administrative (91,5%) and coordinating (75%) positions (see Fig. 9). Top management positions of the faculty and departments' heads, directors of research centers are dominated by men (100% of deans/vice deans, 75% of department heads, 100% of center directors).

There is also vertical segregation by gender in research staff: women occupy more than a half of lowest positions as analysts (58,3%) and experts (50%), while men dominate in the highest positions as senior researchers (100%), researchers (83,3%), and junior researchers (75%), also in "technological" positions as engineers (90%), programmers (100%) and technicians (100%).

Notable, women in IF KTU academic positions earn bigger than men salary (see Table 5).

Table 5. Average gross hourly earnings of academic positions in KTU at 2015 year(€) (KTU 2016)

Academic positions	Female		Male	
	IF	KTU	IF	KTU
Full professor	9,55	8,58	8,44	7,70
Associate professor	5,35	5,39	4,96	4,97
Researcher, Temporary researcher	1,89	3,50	2,87	4,07
Research grants, Other academic staff	4,45	3,99	4,08	3,85

Research of gender distribution with regard to academic titles has revealed that men dominate in all positions in IF KTU: professors (93.3%), associate professors (80%), lecturers (73,3%), assistants (85,7%) and contracted teachers (61,1%) (see Fig. 9). Similar proportion we found in statistics of project EQUAL-IST partners (see Fig. 10)

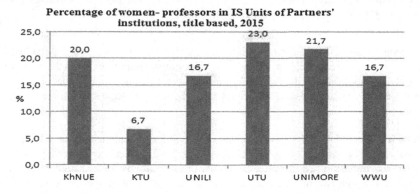

Fig. 10. Women professors' proportions in staff of partners' institutions.

The data of the following EQUAL-IST project partners are used in Fig. 10: KhNUE (Faculty of Economic Informatics Kharkiv National University of Economics, Ukraine), KTU (Informatics Faculty, Kaunas University of Technology, Lithuania), UNILI

(Institute of Information Systems University of Liechtenstein), UTU (Institute of Information Systems Science University of Turku, Finland), UNIMORE (Department of Engineering Università di Modena e Reggio Emilia, Italy), UMinho (Information Systems Department University of Minho, Portugal, WWU (Department of Information Systems University of Muenster, Germany).

5   Conclusions and Future Work

Gender equality has many dimensions; however, they can be categorized into categories: health, educational, economic, political, historical, organization and others. In this work we analyzed social, economic and educational gender inequalities in IST education and research sector in Lithuania. The following key gender equality problems remain significant in IST research sector Lithuania:

1. Women are not proportionally represented in top management positions, academic and research positions.
2. Women are not proportionally represented in STEM and IST fields of science;
3. Women are considerably under-represented in senior academic positions.
4. Lack of qualified talents incoming in IST research sector (Notable: Women made less than 10% of Bachelor's degree, less than 20% of Master's degree and doctoral graduates from the Faculty of Informatics at KTU).
5. Women in interdisciplinary information science study programs have a higher success rate than women in traditional IST study programs.
6. Average gross monthly earnings of women make up only 70% of those of men in Information and communications economic sector Lithuania.

Thanks to the National Program on Equal Opportunities for Women and Men, changes are already noticeable; therefore the likelihood predicting the improvement of current gender inequality rises. For example, women in academic positions earn in average more than men in Informatics Faculty KTU.

Acknowledgements. This research is funded by the European Commission Program H2020-EU.5.b. - Promote gender equality in particular by supporting structural change in the organization of research institutions and in the content and design of research activities, project *EQUAL-IST* Gender Equality Plans for Information Sciences and Technology Research Institutions (2016–2019).

Future work. Methodology for designing and developing concrete customized GEP (Gender Equality Plan) for Informatics Faculty KTU will be created. The measures improving the critical aspects of the university gender equality policies will put into action: career access and development, research governance, working conditions/recruitment, consideration of the gender dimension in research programs and in public research funding.

References

EIGE: Economic benefits of gender equality in the European Union (2017)

European Commission: The EU Mutual Learning Programme in Gender Equality: Gender segregation in the labour market and education Denmark, 29–30 (2015)

Global Gender Gap Index 2016. http://reports.weforum.org/global-gender-gap-report-2016/the-global-gender-gap-report-2016. Accessed 17 May 2017

KTU: Kaunas University of Technology students and employee database (2016)

Microsoft: Why Europe's girls aren't studying STEM (2017)

MOSTA: Research and Higher Education Monitoring and Analysis Centre, Bendrojo priėmimo į Lietuvos aukštąsias mokyklas 2015 m. apžvalga (the Overview of the Admission to Higher Education Schools in 2015) (2015). http://www.mosta.lt/lt/leidiniai

OECD: The ABC of Gender Equality in Education: Aptitude, Behavior, Confidence, PISA, OECD Publishing (2015). http://dx.doi.org/10.1787/9789264229945-en. Accessed 17 May 2017

Planipolis: Education for All 2015: overview of national education, Lithuania, 129p. (2014)

Stanišauskienė, I.V., Urbonienė, A: Moterų ir vyrų įgalinimas mokymuisi:motyvai ir barjerai. Viešoji politika lyčių lygybės aspektu, (Empowering women and men for learning: motivations and barriers. Public Gender equality policy) Vilnius: MRU, pp. 109–122 (2005)

Statistics Lithuania: Women and Men in Lithuania 2014, Vilnius, pp. 35–37 (2015). ISSN: 2029-588X

Šidlauskienė, V.: Influence of the perception of science on engineering & technologies study choices in Lithuania. In: Proceedings of the GIEE HELENA Conference, Paris 23–24 June 2011, pp. 83–103. Sense Publishers (2012)

Šidlauskienė, V., et al.: How Do Universities and Research Institutions in the European Union Foster Gender Equality? Lyčių studijos ir tyrimai, Šiaulių Universitetas, pp. 23–39 (2014)

Žalėnienė, I., Krinickienė, E., Tvaronavičienė, A., Lobačevskytė, A.: Gender equality and its implementation in Universities of Lithuania. Econ. Sociol. 9(1), 237–251 (2016)

Information Technology Applications: Special Session on Language Technologies

Towards Creation of a Lithuanian Lemmatizer for Open Online Collaborative Machine Translation

Jurgita Kapočiūtė-Dzikienė[1(✉)], Vincent Berment[2],
and Erika Rimkutė[1]

[1] Vytautas Magnus University, K. Donelaičio 58, 44248 Kaunas, Lithuania
{jurgita.kapociute-dzikiene,erika.rimkute}@vdu.lt
[2] Institut National des Langues et des Civilisations Orientales,
65 Rue des Grands Moulins, 75013 Paris, France
vincent.berment@imag.fr

Abstract. This paper describes the baseline dictionary-based Lithuanian lemmatizer designed for an open online collaborative Machine Translation system. We evaluated our tool on the gold standard corpus composed of four different domains (official documents, fiction texts, scientific texts, and periodicals) containing ~ 1 million running words in total and obtained an encouraging accuracy equal to $\sim 85.7\%$. Afterwards, we have made an error analysis, which will be used for the further improvements of our lemmatizer.

Keywords: Lithuanian language · Lemmatization · Machine translation · Open-source

1 Introduction and Related Work

Since the Lithuanian language is spoken by only 3.2 million people around the world, it does not attract a lot of investment in its machine translation (MT) research. Despite that, the Lithuanian language is one of the 103 languages supported by Google and one of the 50 supported by Microsoft Translator. Moreover, MT tools for Lithuanian-English (in both directions) and Lithuanian-Russian (in both directions) created by Tilde[1] and English-to-Lithuanian by PROMT[2] are also available online. Unfortunately, all mentioned MT systems are not open-source for further development research practices. Except for a few attempts focusing on Lithuanian as the source or target language (in, e.g., [15]), this Computational Linguistics field is rather poorly researched. The research is also complicated due to the limited resources (e.g., parallel corpora, parsers, etc.) and the complexity of the language itself (rich vocabulary, morphology, word derivation system, relatively free word-order in a sentence).

All previously mentioned Lithuanian language characteristics cannot be ignored especially bearing in mind the fact that without taking into account morphology MT research works fine only on languages with limited (e.g., English) or almost non-existent

---

[1] Available on https://translate.tilde.com.
[2] Available on http://vertimas.vdu.lt.

© Springer International Publishing AG 2017
R. Damaševičius and V. Mikašytė (Eds.): ICIST 2017, CCIS 756, pp. 515–527, 2017.
DOI: 10.1007/978-3-319-67642-5_43

morphology (e.g., Chinese). The published research works provide experimental evidence that the morphological analysis can boost MT performance (e.g., translating Czech-to-English [7] or Malay-English [13]). Many-to-one mapping (when having a morphologically rich source language, but not a rich target language) can be done in a straightforward way by reducing data sparseness of the source language with the lemmatization of an input text. Despite a few recent attempts (e.g., English-to-Czech MT [4], English-to-Russian/Hebrew/Swahili MT [14], English-to-Russian MT [16]) the translation into a morphologically rich language (one-to-many mapping) is still a challenging task due to a high degree of inflection of the target language. Thus, the analysis may cause ambiguity problems because a system must generate a number of word forms, which cannot be directly apparent in the input text.

All MT approaches (based on the statistical packages, rule-based systems, or combining the best characteristics of both methods [5]) are preferable only if they achieve a high accuracy. However, the creation of an accurate automatic MT system requires much more than a corpus of parallel texts: i.e., accurate lemmatizers, morphological analyzers, and parsers are almost inevitable. The Lithuanian language is not resource-scarce regarding all available morphological analyzers-lemmatizers. *Lemuoklis*[3] [17] can solve disambiguation problems in the sentences and is very accurate on the normative texts (reaching up to 94% of accuracy [6]). For the second popular Lithuanian analyzer-lemmatizer[4] the experimental evaluation results have not been reported yet. Unfortunately both lemmatizers are available only as "black boxes" or through Web services: i.e., this fact greatly complicates possibilities of their integration into any MT system.

The development of an accurate MT system consists of several stages. However, in this paper we are focusing on the creation of the open-source Lithuanian lemmatizer only, which afterwards as a separate module will be incorporated into the Ariane's framework [2], which is available to anyone willing to develop "expert" MT systems. Thus, following the Ariane requirements, our lemmatizer is written in the ATEF language provided for this purpose.

In essence, the lemmatization is a shallow morphological analysis, which transforms a word into its base dictionary look-up form (lemma). The most popular dictionary-based lemmatizers (outperforming algorithmic ones) are composed either manually by incorporating handcrafted rules (stems + manually created set of endings) (e.g., for Lithuanian [17], Czech [1]); or with the various automatic training techniques (e.g., by learning rules handling morphological changes in suffixes for Danish, Dutch, English, German, Greek, Icelandic, Norwegian, Polish, Slovene and Swedish [10]); or by combining advantages of both data-driven machine learning and the linguistic techniques to increase the overall performance (e.g., [9]). Nevertheless, comparative experiments (done on the morphologically rich Czech) prove that there is no significant difference in accuracy either the lemmatizer is created manually or automatically [11]. However, the automatic creation of a lemmatizer requires comprehensive manually

---

[3] Available at: http://tekstynas.vdu.lt/page.xhtml;jsessionid=13737278C03300B67C9E5CF2C2AB2734?id=morphological-annotator.

[4] Available at http://www.semantika.lt/TextAnnotation/Annotation/Annotate.

lemmatized (gold-standard) corpus, where words could be found in their lemma and the other inflected forms. Since huge amounts of manually lemmatized corpora even do not exist for the Lithuanian language, we have only one choice – i.e., to create our Lithuanian lemmatizer manually.

2 Production of an Analyzer Written in ATEF

2.1 The Ariane Framework and Its ATEF Language

Ariane is a research product of GETA (see Fig. 1; taken from [3]), the French laboratory dedicated to MT created by Professor Vauquois in 1960 and headed by himself until 1985. This research on Ariane was spread mainly from the early period of the laboratory to the 1990s. Ariane is a system that has referred up the arrival of statistical techniques in the early 2000s and that remains a very powerful solution to setup new MT systems. Its basic principle is to generate a MT system by compilation of linguistic descriptions such as dictionaries or grammars.

The principles of Ariane emerged gradually and the initial version of its first linguistic programming language ATEF was available in 1973. Inside Ariane, ATEF is the language dedicated to writing morphological analyzers. Three other languages complement ATEF: SYGMOR, which at the other end of the chain, specializes in writing morphological generations, ROBRA, which is a tree transducer realizing on trees the equivalent transformations one can do on strings with regular expressions, and EXPANS, allowing in particular the production of lexical transfers. The unique internal data structure is a "decorated" tree, which is able to bear simultaneously representations at syntagmatic, syntactic and logico-semantic levels. Most of the "historical" systems developed with Ariane are transfer-based systems but it is also possible to rely on a

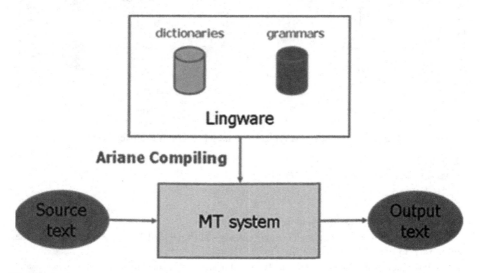

Fig. 1. In Ariane, the MT systems are written in high level linguistic programming languages

double transfer (for example, from Lithuanian to English and then from English to any other language) or through a pivot representation such as UNL[5]. Ariane has been described in many publications (see e.g. John Hutchins' presentations[6]).

In 2010 a new version of Ariane called *Héloïse* or also *Ariane-H* was made available for online collaborative development, especially for under-resourced languages [2, 3]. The first stable version was presented in 2012 [2]. Since then, a number of open-source MT projects were undertaken for under-resourced languages as Khmer, Lao, Burmese, Quechua, etc. Ariane is also used for the languages which are generally not considered as under-resourced, e.g., German for which Guilbaud builds an open-source high quality morphological analyzer that, in 2013, already contained 11,147 verbs, 85,038 nouns and 5,368 adjectives [8].

A minimal transfer-based system developed in Ariane (see Fig. 2; taken from [3]) includes: (1) a monolingual analysis (morphological analysis + structural analysis), (2) a bilingual transfer (lexical transfer + structural transfer), (3) a monolingual generation (structural generation + morphological generation)[7].

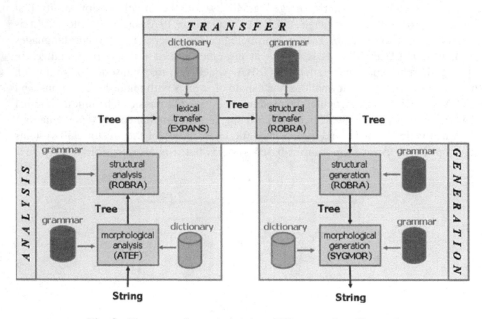

Fig. 2. The steps of a typical Ariane MT system (transfer case)

---

[5] Available at http://www.undlfoundation.org/undlfoundation.

[6] Available at http://www.hutchinsweb.me.uk/Routledge-2014.pdf and http://www.hutchinsweb.me.uk/IntroMT-13.pdf.

[7] Note that the monolingual nature of the analyses and of the generations makes them directly reusable for building new language pairs.

ATEF operates on "words"[8], i.e. character strings between spaces or punctuation marks. Basically, a morphological analysis grammar written in ATEF splits the words into all its possible divisions. See the following example of *būdavai* (you were many times) in the Lithuanian language:

būdavai → nothing found
būdava-i → nothing found
būdav-ai → nothing found
būda-vai → nothing found
būd-avai → *būd* found in a dictionary of radicals but no suffix *avai* matching
bū-davai → *bū* found in a dictionary of radicals but no suffix *davai* matching
b-ūdavai → *b* found in a dictionary of radicals and two matching suffix *ūdavai*

When finding a left part in one of the dictionaries of radicals, like in the case of *b*:
b==VER00101(FSVP, būti)
the entry informs on (1) the potential lemma *būti* (to be), (2) the morphological paradigm of the potential lemma (*VER00101*), (3) its associated morphological information: *verb, positive, non-reflexive (FSVP)*.

The grammar rule triggered by the morphological paradigm *VER00101* will then recursively call other rules by looking for the remaining part *ūdavai* in the dictionaries of suffixes. The algorithm will try to analyse *ūdavai* with the constraint that this string is following a radical whose paradigm is *VER00101*. A usual way of doing that is to store the concatenation of the paradigms with the suffixes in the dictionary of suffixes thus giving entries such as *VER00101ūdavai*. The actual entry is: *VER00101-ūdavai==FTMDES(FVInPiS2)*.

This new entry provides (1) a trigger for the grammar rule (*FTMDES*) and (2) the complementary morphological information coming from the ending: *indicative, past iterative, singular, 2nd person (FVInPiS2)*. Note that the endings dictionaries do not include lemmas. The grammar rule associated to *FTMDES* checks that the word division is completed and returns a success.

2.2 Production of the Analyzer

The lexical and morphological data used as a starting point was made of words taken from the Corpus of the Contemporary Lithuanian Language (created at Vytautas Magnus University [12]) covering different domains: fiction texts, newspaper texts, legislative texts, parliamentary transcripts, etc., and containing ~1 million running words. Found words were grouped into 17 parts-of-speech: nouns (16,321 distinct lemmas); adjectives (4,937); adverbs (2,017); numerals (78); several verb forms differing in their inflection as verbs (11,831), participles (11,831), half participles (11,751), adverbial participles (lith. padalyviai) (11,831), adverbial participles1 (lith. būdiniai) (11,751); pronouns (43); particles (117); interjections (59);

---

[8] ATEF also allows the analysis of multiword expressions. This will not be described here. It can also be used in conjunction with other steps (as in Guilbaud's German analyzer) to produce disambiguated analyses.

onomatopoeias (40); conjunctions (62); prepositions (73); abbreviations (109); and acronyms (156).

A typical entry was given in the following format (see example of *abatė* (abbot in feminine)):

[aba/tė](feminine)→/tė;tės;tei;tę;te;tėje,tėj,ėn;te:tės;čių;tėms;tes;tėmis;tėse,ėsna;tė;/

where (left-hand part):

aba – is a stable part of word.
tė – is not a stable part, that may change depending on the case and number.
abatė denotes the word in the main form/lemma.
(feminine) – the noun is feminine.

and (right-hand part), before the colon are all 7 cases in singular:

tė – nominative
tės – genitive
tei – dative
tę – accusative
te – instrumental
tėje, tėj, ėn – all possible forms in locative separated with the comma (including abbreviated and illative forms still used in the fiction and dialects)
te – vocative

and after the colon are all 7 cases in plural:

tės – nominative
čių – genitive
tėms – dative
tes – accusative
tėmis – instrumental
tėse, ėsna – all possible forms in locative separated with the comma (including abbreviated and illative forms still used in the fiction and dialects)
tės – vocative

More generally, the words were described as:

- [stable part/unstable part]
- () – description of the word: positive/negative
- → – list of possible forms instead of unstable part
- / – separates degrees of comparison
- [] – separates non-pronominal/pronominal forms
- # – separates genders: masculine/feminine/neuter
- : – separates numbers: singular/plural
- ; – separates cases: nominative, genitive, dative, accusative, instrumental, locative, vocative
- , – separates different possible forms of the same case
- – word in such form does not exist

Table 1. Extract from the dictionary table

Id	Lemma	Morphological information[a]	Paradigm
1	abatinis	FSAdjP	ADJ001
2	abdominalinis	FSAdjP	ADJ001
3	abejingas	FSAdjP	ADJ002
4	abejotinas	FSAdjP	ADJ002
5	abiotinis	FSAdjP	ADJ001
6	abipusis	FSAdjP	ADJ001
7	abonentinis	FSAdjP	ADJ001
8	abraomiškas	FSAdjP	ADJ002
9	abrazinis	FSAdjP	ADJ001
10	absoliutus	FSAdjP	ADJ004
...	...	...	...

[a]Syntactic format (FS) for adjectives (Adj), positive word (P).

Table 2. Extract from the paradigm table

Id	Ending	Morphological information[a]	Paradigm	Nb Char[b]
1	is	FAD1MSNN	ADJ001	2
2	io	FAD1MSNG	ADJ001	2
3	iam	FAD1MSND	ADJ001	2
4	į	FAD1MSNA	ADJ001	2
5	iu	FAD1MSNI	ADJ001	2
6	iame	FAD1MSNL	ADJ001	2
8	i	FAD1MSNV	ADJ001	2
9	iai	FAD1MPNN	ADJ001	2
10	ių	FAD1MPNG	ADJ001	2
...	...	...	...	...

[a]Syntactic format (F) for adjectives (AD), 1st degree of comparison (1), masculine (M), singular (S)/plural (P), non-pronominal (N)/pronominal (P), nominative (N)/genitive (G)/dative (D)/accusative (A)/nstrumental (I)/locative (L)/vocative (V).
[b]The *Nb Char* column contains the number of characters that have to be removed from the end of the lemma to build the radical that will be put in the ATEF dictionaries.

Given data has been compiled automatically and a long both manual and automated work was necessary to achieve a clean basis. However, their coverage and organization was quite good so, in the end, we got a satisfying lexical database that could be used for making the analyzer. Basically, this database was obtained by transforming:

- the left-hand part of the original data into a dictionary table (see Table 1) with lemmas and associated morphological information,
- the right-hand part into a paradigm table (see Table 2) with the endings and also their associated morphological information.

From this database, ATEF files were generated automatically with an existing open-source tool DB2ATEF (DataBase to ATEF). Currently this database and the analyzer is publicly available online[9], thus anyone can modify it to get the new version of the lemmatizer.

3   Evaluation and Discussion

3.1   Gold-Standard Corpus

We evaluated our lemmatizer on the lemmatized and morphologically annotated gold-standard corpus of ∼ 1.08 million running words. This manually annotated corpus was created at Vytautas Magnus University and covers 4 domains, in particular, official documents, fiction texts, scientific texts, and periodicals with ∼ 0.32 million, ∼ 0.20 million, ∼ 0.25 million, and ∼ 0.31 running words in each, respectively (statistics about this corpus is in Table 3).

To ensure reliable testing conditions none of the texts in the gold-standard corpus were used for the creation of our lemmatizer.

3.2   Results

We experimentally tested our lemmatizer on the gold-standard corpus (described in the previous section) and evaluated the *accuracy* (*correct lemmas/all lemmatized words*) based on the different parts-of-speech (see Fig. 3) and domains (see Fig. 4).

So far our system does not incorporate the model solving ambiguity problems. Thus, if the lemmatizer provides a number of lemma-solutions based on the different morphological categories (noun, adjective, etc.) and other fine-grained morphological information (case, gender, etc.), the final solution depends on the majority vote or on the random lemma selection.

Nevertheless, it was also important to determine how much the disambiguation problem solving could improve the lemmatization results. Thus, we evaluated our system selecting the correct lemma-solution (if such solution was among the solutions determined by our lemmatizer), or selecting the random lemma-solution (otherwise).

3.3   Discussion

Our baseline lemmatizer for the Lithuanian language, even without the disambiguation problem solving, achieved an *accuracy* equal to ∼ 85.7%. If compared with the refined *Lemuoklis* [6, 17] (solving disambiguation problems and achieving ∼ 94% of accuracy

---

[9] The database and the analyzer (LithuanianMorphoAnalyser.zip) can be downloaded from lingwarium.org/heloise/index.php?Ref=&ws=AnaLTN&lgPair=LTN-ENG.

Table 3. Morphological categories and their frequencies in the gold-standard corpus

Part-of-Speech		Frequency
Noun		382,175
Proper noun		33,956
Adjective		80,937
Adverb		62,263
Numeral		8,215
Verb forms	Inflective form	113,709
	Infinitive	38,434
	Participle	62,751
	Half participle	4,141
	Adverbial participle	7,339
	Adverbial participle1	49
Pronoun		92,801
Particle		21,976
Interjection		1,963
Onomatopoeia		81
Conjunction		83,143
Preposition		51,254
Abbreviation		12,274
Acronym		2,053
Roman number		833
Other (digits, etc.)		18,106
All:		1,078,453

on the normative Lithuanian texts), our results are rather encouraging. And that is not all, because the implemented disambiguation problem solving module could increase the obtained result by $\sim 5.5\%$, thus reaching up $\sim 91.2\%$ of *accuracy*.

As it can be seen in Fig. 3, the main shortcoming of our lemmatizer is proper nouns, which we have not included into our system yet. But $\sim 43.4\%$ of accuracy was reached accidentally due to the lemmatizer specifics or the coincidence with the generic words. Thus, if the lemmatizer does not recognize the word, it lemmatizes it by presenting the original word form (but some proper nouns in the gold-standard corpus are already in their singular nominal case!). Besides, we do not solve disambiguation problems, therefore some part of the proper nouns can be confused with the generic words having the same inflection paradigms, e.g., *Jonas* (name and generic word ion), *Lietuvis* (surname and nationality Lithuanian). The lemmatization of abbreviations, pronouns, and participles seems also problematic. The comprehensive error analysis revealed the problems (absent abbreviations and pronouns; errors in the handcrafted paradigms for particles) that we plan to eliminate by complementing/correcting our lemmatizer in the nearest future.

The big gap between the results obtained, with and without disambiguation solving the problem, signals which parts-of-speech are especially sensitive to this problem. Since the disambiguation problem solving module is also in our nearest future plans, it

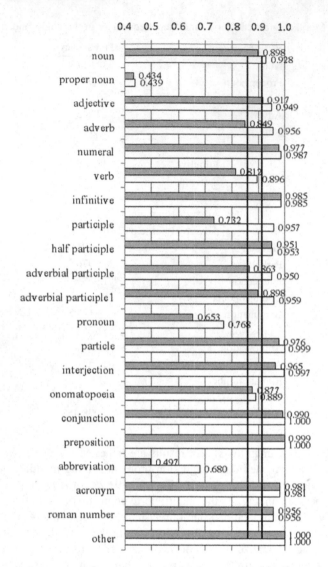

Fig. 3. Accuracies per parts-of-speech: grey/white bars and left/right vertical black lines represent accuracies for the part-of-speech and overall accuracies without and with disambiguation problem solving, respectively.

was important to find out that we will have to take special attention to adverbs, verbs, particles, adverbial particles, pronouns, and abbreviations.

As it can be seen in Fig. 4 the best results were achieved on the fiction texts, the worst – on the periodicals. The detailed content and analysis confirmed that the language in fiction texts is settled and contains less neologisms or specific terminology compared to scientific texts or periodicals. The accuracy, obtained on the official documents and scientific texts, is the second best achieved. Despite when creating our

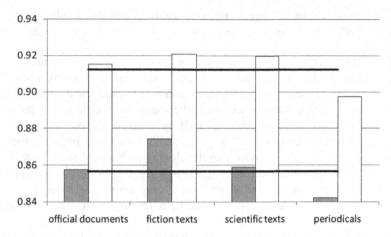

Fig. 4. Accuracies per domains: grey/white columns and upper/lower horizontal black lines represent accuracies for the part-of-speech and overall accuracies without and with disambiguation problem solving, respectively

lemmatizer we considered texts from these domains as well, but the terminology differed significantly. For example, the parliamentary transcript text (where language is more similar to spoken) is absolutely different from the law text (where the language is very formal); the terminology in the scientific paper about medical achievements is absolutely different compared with the paper about the computer science. Some new terms (translated from the English language or left as Anglicisms) in the Lithuanian scientific texts are not settled, but the vocabulary of such words is rather limited, therefore it only slightly affects the overall results. Most of the errors were made on the periodicals. Abbreviations, pronouns, and proper nouns were the worst lemmatized categories in all four domains, but in the periodicals proper nouns were twice often as in the other: i.e., 2.3%, 2.9%, 2.0% and 5.4% of proper nouns in official documents, fiction, scientific texts and periodicals.

We anticipate that the reported error list will help to improve our lemmatizer. However, these improvements may not be very obvious on texts with some other specific terminology. Moreover, due to the language evolvement (neologisms, new terminology), the filling and the maintenance of the lemmatizer have to be performed continuously. We anticipate that the open-source possibility would attract more researches to contribute to this work.

4   Conclusions and Future Work

When we started this work, our concern was "despite the complexity of the Lithuanian language, and especially of its morphology, can we hope setting up a collaborative project around machine translation for Lithuanian, and in particular shall we be able to deal with the difficulty of the morphology?". Thanks to the simple way the lexicographers can handle the lexical data (see Table 1) and to the automaticity of the analyzer generation, the answer to this question is certainly positive for the morphological level.

As for the quality, we initially targeted neither a large coverage nor any other particular objectives but the simplicity of the process, so the quality ($\sim 85.7\%$ of *accuracy*) we achieved certainly satisfied us. From the morphological point of view, we now need to complete the database and also investigate compositional and derivational morphologies currently not addressed, as well as multiword expressions (the ATEF programming language encompasses this). In parallel with this improvement of the morphological analyzer, we will now start developing a structural analyzer and branch it to a transfer between Lithuanian and English (see Fig. 2). We would like to point out that the same database can be used to generate a morphological generation (due to an existing DB2SYGMOR program) so it should help developing the English-Lithuanian direction.

We can now start working on the next step of our MT prototype, the structural analysis. The necessary time will depend on many factors including the availability of bilingual data between Lithuanian and English. Due to the availability of an Ariane open-source generation into Russian language (from GETA lab, BSD license), we can also consider building a Lithuanian-Russian MT system in parallel. As the analysis steps developed for Lithuanian do not depend on the target language (the existing generation into Russian is also monolingual), the only extra work would be the transfer phase. In the longer term, we can also consider connecting automatic speech recognition and text-to-speech to our systems in order to obtain a speech-to-speech MT system, and also to use a UNL pivot in addition to the transfer paradigm to connect our analyzer and our generation of Lithuanian to existing en-converters and de-converters (Russian, Spanish, Hindi, French, etc.).

Acknowledgments. We would like to express our gratitude to Albert Sy Den for his patient contribution to the transfer of lexical data into database form.

References

1. Bejček, E., Hajičová, E., Hajič, J., Jínová, P., Kettnerová, V., Kolářová, V., Mikulová, M., Mírovský, J., Nedoluzhko, A., Panevová, J., Poláková, L., Ševčíková, M., Štěpánek, J., Zikánová, Š.: Prague Dependency Treebank 3.0 (2013)
2. Berment, V., Boitet, C.: Heloise – a reengineering of Ariane-G5 SLLPs for application to p-languages. In: Proceedings of the 24th International Conference on Computational Linguistics (COLING 2012): Posters, pp. 113–124 (2012)
3. Berment, V.: Some thoughts on how to address commercially unprofitable languages and language pairs. In: the 5th Workshop on South and Southeast Asian NLP (WSSANLP) (2014). Keynote speech http://www.sanlp.org/wssanlp2014/KeyNoteSpeech.pdf
4. Bojar, O.: English-to-Czech factored machine translation. In: Proceedings of the Second Workshop on Statistical Machine Translation (StatMT 2007), pp. 232–239 (2007)
5. Costa-jussá, M.R., Fonollosa, J.A.R.: Latest trends in hybrid machine translation and its applications. Comput. Speech Lang. **32**(1), 3–10 (2015)

6. Daudaravičius, V., Rimkutė, E., Utka, A.: Morphological annotation of the Lithuanian corpus. In: Proceedings of the Workshop on Balto-Slavonic Natural Language Processing, Information Extraction and Enabling Technologies of ACL 2007, pp. 94–99 (2007)
7. Goldwater, S., McClosky, D.: Improving statistical MT through morphological analysis. In: Proceedings of the Conference on Human Language Technology and Empirical Methods in Natural Language Processing (HLT 2005), pp. 676–683 (2005)
8. Guilbaud, J.-P., Boitet, C., Berment, V.: Un analyseur morphologique étendu de l'allemand traitant les formes verbales `a particule séparée. [An extended morphological analyzer of German handling verbal forms with separated separable particles] (in French). In: Traitement Automatique des Langues Naturelles – Rencontres des Étudiants Chercheurs en Informatique pour le Traitement Automatique des Langues (TALN-RÉCITAL), pp. 755–763 (2013)
9. Ingason, A.K., Helgadóttir, S., Loftsson, H., Rögnvaldsson, E.: A mixed method lemmatization algorithm using a hierarchy of linguistic identities (HOLI). In: Nordström, B., Ranta, A. (eds.) GoTAL 2008. LNCS, vol. 5221, pp. 205–216. Springer, Heidelberg (2008). doi:10.1007/978-3-540-85287-2_20
10. Jongejan, B., Dalianis, H.: Automatic training of lemmatization rules that handle morphological changes in pre-, in- and suffixes alike. In: Proceedings of the Joint Conference of the 47th Annual Meeting of the ACL and the 4th International Joint Conference on Natural Language Processing of the AFNLP, pp. 145–153 (2009.)
11. Kanis, J., Skorkovská, L.: Comparison of different lemmatization approaches through the means of information retrieval performance. In: Sojka, P., Horák, A., Kopeček, I., Pala, K. (eds.) TSD 2010. LNCS, vol. 6231, pp. 93–100. Springer, Heidelberg (2010). doi:10.1007/978-3-642-15760-8_13
12. Marcinkevičienė, R.: Tekstynų lingvistika: teorija ir praktika [Corpus Linguistics: Theory and Practice] (in Lithuanian). Darbai ir dienos 24, 7–64 (2000)
13. Nakov, P., Ng, H.T.: Translating from morphologically complex languages: a paraphrase-based approach. In: Proceedings of the 49th Annual Meeting of the Association for Computational Linguistics: Human Language Technologies (HLT 2011), pp. 1298–1307 (2011)
14. Schlinger, E., Chahuneau, V., Dyer, C.: morphogen: Translation into morphologically rich languages with synthetic phrases. Prague Bull. Math. Linguist. 100, 51–62 (2013)
15. Skadiņš, R., Goba, K., Šics, V.: Improving SMT for Baltic languages with factored models. In: Proceedings of the 4th International Conference Human Language Technologies – The Baltic Perspective, pp. 125–132 (2010)
16. Tran, K.M, Bisazza, A., Monz, C.: Word translation prediction for morphologically rich languages with bilingual neural networks. In: Proceedings of the Conference on Empirical Methods in Natural Language Processing (EMNLP), pp. 1676–1688 (2014)
17. Zinkevičius, V.: Lemuoklis – morfologinei analizei [Morphological Analysis with Lemuoklis] (in Lithuanian). Darbai ir dienos 24, 246–273 (2000)

Using Sentiment Analysis on Local Up-to-the-Minute News: An Integrated Approach

Joschka Kersting[✉] and Michaela Geierhos

Heinz Nixdorf Institute, University of Paderborn, Paderborn, Germany
{jkers,geierhos}@hni.upb.de

Abstract. In this paper, we present a search solution that makes local news information easily accessible. In the era of fake news, we provide an approach for accessing news information through opinion mining. This enables users to view news on the same topics from different web sources. By applying sentiment analysis on social media posts, users can better understand how issues are captured and see people's reactions. Therefore, we provide a local search service that first localizes news articles, then visualizes their occurrence according to the frequency of mentioned topics on a heatmap and even shows the sentiment score for each text.

Keywords: News aggregation · Local news search · Sentiment analysis · Named entity recognition

1 Introduction

The World Wide Web provides vast kinds of information to its users. Having that in mind, one can find desired information on different pages when actively accessing them. Though, there is a lack of unified information services. Different web sources have to be considered in order to seek information (e.g. Tweets, police news, local newspapers, etc.). Because of missing links between the information bits on various sites, each single page has to be accessed separately by online searchers. Furthermore, there exists no connection to the corresponding location, where an event actually happened. It is an open question to which places news' topics are referenced. Besides, despite the availability of local news, (inter-)national news services are more perceived and visible. For this reason, we want to make local news from different web sources available and locatable on one single search platform.

After having described our initial idea, we want to enhance the search results by sentiment analysis. Therefore, we investigate sentiments towards products, services, events, topics and so on [9, 10] in news texts. Since there exist many different wordings for sentiment analysis, e.g. opinion mining, we will stick to the forenamed [18]. In the era of "fake news" [11], we study how different sources report on (the same) issues. For this purpose, we apply sentiment analysis on news texts in order to show how positively or negatively reports tell about the same issues [7, 12, 13].

To put it short, we sum up our research goals briefly: Due to the vast amount of heterogeneous information, the source has to be known or easy to find. Local information

© Springer International Publishing AG 2017
R. Damaševičius and V. Mikašytė (Eds.): ICIST 2017, CCIS 756, pp. 528–538, 2017.
DOI: 10.1007/978-3-319-67642-5_44

is often widely distributed and can be found on Twitter[1], local newspaper pages, or in police news, etc. [14]. For this reason, we want to aggregate these different information sources via one single service to provide a better overview. Furthermore, on the local level, it can be interesting to know what – but also where – something happened. It is therefore our goal to assign geographic information to news topics (if not provided). Nowadays, it is not sufficient to get to know only the facts (e.g., from newspapers). Even what people think about these issues (e.g., on Twitter) can cause quite a stir. When comparing different news information dealing with the same topic by sentiment score, we enable online searchers to perform some kind of "manual fake news analysis". For our first prototype, we choose the city of Paderborn, Germany as test case because many millennials live there who might use such a search platform [16]. Our goal is to provide a holistic service which creates an overview of what happened, how is it discussed, and when and where did it happen.

The structure of the paper is as follows: In Sect. 2, we provide an overview of the technical background. Then, we present our solution for bundling and location mapping of regional news information (cf. Sect. 3). Here, we describe how we collect and analyze textual information before making the enhanced data accessible. In Sect. 4, we discuss our approach. Finally, we draw a conclusion in Sect. 5.

2 Technical Background

In this section, we firstly list possible competitors before we describe technical challenges that need to be addressed. Then, we move into the technologies that are required for our solution.

There is to the best of our knowledge no online available service that provides exactly what we aim to do: location mapping combined with sentiment analysis on local news. Regarding the city of Paderborn, there is another service called "Stadtplan Paderborn[2]", which literally means "City Map Paderborn." This project uses a map of Paderborn to locate recycling places, or authorities. Different filters can be used to access information about things like train stations, building lots, educational institutions etc. Especially, city-related services are integrated, e.g. parking lots. Up to now, any location mapping or sentiment analysis for news has not been considered [17]. Other competitors might be Google[3], which could itself gather information and show it on the Google Map[4]. For example, Web.de[5], which is a news portal [2], does that already.

Such providers have sufficient know-how and resources. Nevertheless, no direct competitor exists at the moment, which offers the same online service as we plan to develop.

For our solution, we need a full-automatic system that includes a crawler for collecting and storing online data while being able to not get stuck [3]. For topic detection

---

[1] http://www.twitter.com, accessed 2017-04-11.
[2] http://www.googis.de/paderborn/?es=C47S434, accessed 2017-04-11.
[3] http://www.google.de, accessed 2017-03-07.
[4] http://www.google.de/maps, accessed 2017-03-07.
[5] http://www.web.de, accessed 2017-04-10.

and localization purposes, we need to apply named entity recognition (NER). Herewith it is our aim to identify and categorize named entities (e.g. persons, organizations, places, etc.) in the news texts, as it is the purpose of NER [19]. Here, it is important to mention wrong recognitions due to the ambiguity of words. For example, "Washington" can be a name, city or state. Another challenge is domain-dependent sentiment analysis on news reports. Since the opinion holder may vary, it is difficult to assign the sentiment in the right way (i.e. citations state third-party sentiment). However, an opinion, citation or even interpretation of a citation need to be handled adequately [13].

Lastly, a user-friendly web interface is needed that provides online searchers with the gathered information [2]. Therefore, we followed the recommendations made by the international standard ISO 9241-110 [6, 15]. This norm covers the ergonomics of human system interaction. In particular, all texts, labels and notifications should be easy-to-understand and self-descriptive. Furthermore, the usage of applications should be controllable. Therefore, they should help the users to avoid mistakes and be fault tolerant. Moreover, all processes should be designed in such way to support an easy execution of tasks.

After having very briefly shown the scientific and technical background, we now describe the basic requirements of our software architecture.

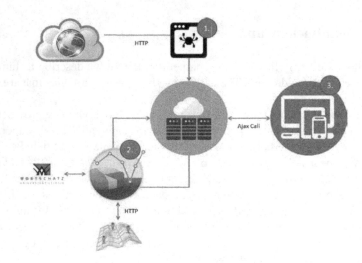

Fig. 1. Overview on our software concept

3   Prototype for Automatic Information Aggregation

In this section, we present our approach. We therefore explain the information gathering and analysis as well as the visualization step.

Figure 1 gives an overview on our basic concept. To provide an up-to-date, easy accessible and integrated technological solution, we aim at using the following architecture. In general, three main steps can be identified: (3.1) Firstly, there is the acquisition of new data. (3.2) Secondly, there is the analysis of the acquired data. (3.3) Thirdly, the visualization of the results is conducted. We separated these steps to run different parts of our application independently and in parallel in order to make it available at any time. In order to achieve this, we have chosen to use a web application because no local installation is necessary and it is freely available and accessible on all operating systems [8]. In the following subsections, we describe the three parts of our prototype.

3.1 Data Acquisition

The first step aims at collecting new data sets from predefined information sources and store them in a database. Although every web source is accessible, we limit our search space to web pages belonging to the administrative district of Paderborn, Germany. Thus, local news reports are adequate. Among others, we have chosen several newspapers, news of the local university, police news and social network posts from Twitter. In general, each news object is structured as follows: Title, publication date and content. It may also contain additional information for distinguishing data records according the *ID* (assigned by the provider) or individual link. Figure 2 shows an excerpt of the entity-relationship diagram for the entity *"news"*. While *globalID* uniquely labels a data record, *ID* marks the data source. This enables filtering by source. The flag "analyzed" says whether a data record has been yet analyzed.

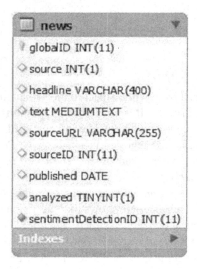

Fig. 2. Data structure of the entity "news"

Crawling once a day is important to keep our database up-to-date. To include more recent information, the crawling interval can be shortened.

For focused crawling, storing and analyzing data, we developed the entity-relationship diagram shown in Fig. 3. As it can be seen, the news entity (cf. Figure 2) is included here. There are several location entities in our database represented by *"ortsentitaet"*. We link news objects to locations using the connecting table *"news_ort_relation"*.

Moreover, the result of the sentiment analysis per news object will be stored in "*sentimentdetection*".

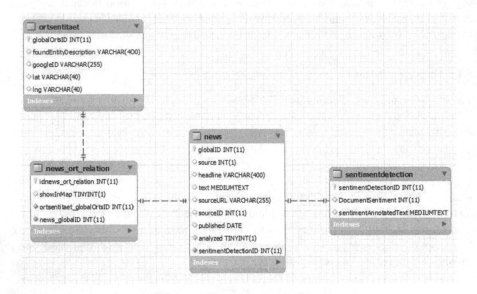

Fig. 3. Entity-relationship diagram

3.2 Data Analysis

After data gathering, we analyze it with respect to the named locations in the given area and the provided sentiment scores. It is challenging to identify places and assign them to the right geographical location on a map. Having analyzed several news articles, we identified three different location categories: urban district ("*Paderborn*"), organization/ facility ("*University of Paderborn*") and street ("*Berliner Ring*"). To illustrate this, we provide an example: "*Paderborn. The University of Paderborn has developed a new method for road safety. This new method will be tested on the following streets: Fürstenallee, Berliner Ring etc.*" This example shows that the action does not take place at the University of Paderborn, but at two named streets. Therefore, a location mapping should be made at least for one of those two streets. For the implementation of our prototype, we defined eight rules that decide how the location can be determined. We assume that the smaller location entities can be identified more accurately. Therefore, we prioritize streets over organizations and these over urban districts.

1. **Information about the urban district[6], street name and organization is available.** The location mapping should be as accurate as possible. When all three location categories are given, the following assumptions are made: Because an urban district is more precise than the whole city (here: Paderborn, Germany), we prioritize the urban district that is not (only) called "Paderborn" but also e.g. "Haxtergrund" in

---

[6] Singular and plural are included.

our case. However, we assume organization names to be more inaccurate concerning their address than street names. If more than one street name is provided, the first one will be selected. In brief, in the first case, we combine the urban district with the street name in order to determine the correct geographic coordinates.

2. **Information about the urban district and street name is available but the organization is not given.** In this case, we proceed analogously to rule no. 1.

3. **Information about the urban district and street name is not available but the organization is given.** If only urban district and organization names are mentioned in the news texts, the urban district will be preferred. If more than one organization is given, the first one will be – analogously to the treatment of multiple street names – chosen.

4. **Information about the urban district is available but the street name and the organization is not given.** If only an urban district is recognized, this will be the only option to choose. The localization is oriented towards the city center.

5. **Information about the urban district is not available but the street name and organization are given.** In this case, we prioritize the street name when both street and organization are provided. We search the first street that is found in the text in given city. This is necessary because the same street names may occur in several cities.

6. **Information about the urban district and the street name is not available but the organization is given.** If only the organization name is provided, we use this information in combination with the predefined city name (here: "Paderborn").

7. **Information about the urban district is not available but the street name is given and the organization is missing.** As it was stated before, we use only the given information and add "Paderborn" as supplementary condition.

8. **Information about the urban district, the street name and even the organization is not available.** The last case inherits the problem that no location information is provided at all. As a general mapping into the city center would not be useful, we do not store any location in the database. However, we add a label that states that the location information is missing. That way, we can filter those news articles without location information by using the web interface.

After having identified the location, we perform sentiment analysis on the news texts. We apply a sentence-based – not aspect-based – sentiment analysis because this method is appropriate for news texts which usually contain only one topic. We regard the acquired news content as a single document. The sentiment score of a document is calculated as the mean of all sentence values. We used SentiWS[7] [4], a sentiment lexicon for the German language, for the rule-based sentiment analysis per sentence and GATE[8], a "General Architecture for Text Engineering" [1] for the NER. Since the AlchemyAPI[9] by IBM showed weak results for the sentiment analysis task on our data, we decided to choose a lexicon-based approach, which performed better. In the SentiWS lexicon, a sentiment value is assigned to each term (i.e. word). A sentiment value of 0

---

[7] http://wortschatz.uni-leipzig.de/de/download, accessed 2017-04-11.

[8] http://gate.ac.uk/, accessed 2017-04-11.

[9] http://www.ibm.com/watson/alchemy-api.html, accessed 2017-05-17.

is neutral. A value higher than 0 represents a positive sentiment, a lower value a negative sentiment.

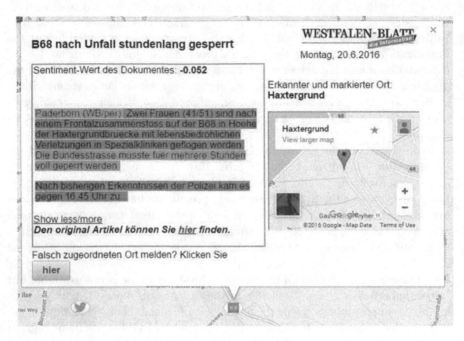

Fig. 4. Sentiment analysis on a sample news article and localization

3.3 Data Visualization

Now, we present the visualization part of our solution shown in Fig. 5. We therefore integrated a map from Google. News articles can be opened when clicking on them. On the top left side, the view can be changed between a standard map and satellite pictures. Underneath this, the date and news sources can be selected. Additionally, the application can determine the user's location. The heatmap [5] represents how much is going on at a specific place and illustrates how often a location is mentioned in the news.

On the top right side, all news information is given that is not mapped to any location. As it can be seen, the "WESTFALEN-BLATT" newspaper and the police ("POLIZEI") provide articles, while there are currently no articles by the University of Paderborn ("UNIVERSITÄTPADERBORN"). When scrolling down, more sources and articles can be found. Further functionality is in included in our solution by zooming and Google Street View[10] is available as well.

---

[10] http://www.google.de/intl/de/streetview/, accessed 2017-04-11.

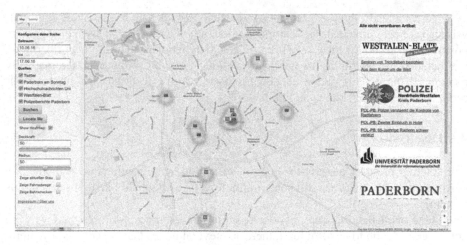

Fig. 5. Visualization frame of our solution

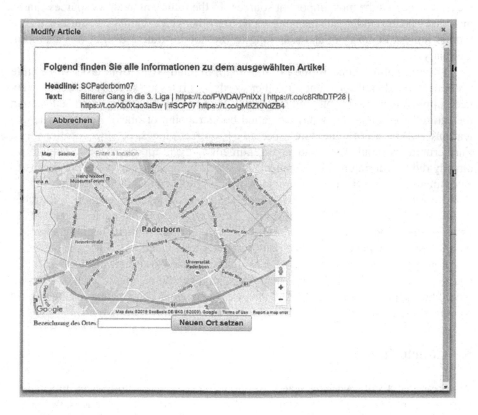

Fig. 6. Location tagging for a sample news article (if the place wasn't identified)

Figure 4 already showed a sample news article. All relevant results of the data analysis step are here provided: the sentiment value, highlighting for each sentence (green: positive, red: negative), the date of the article, and the recognized location. Furthermore, we included the possibility to assign a location to articles without an automatically recognized place. This option encourages users to give feedback and improve our service. This feature is shown in Fig. 6.

4 Discussion

Our solution provides an easy-to-access way to find local information. Although we reached our goals, there are still some limitations that we would like to discuss in this section.

On the one hand, there are, of course, more news sources available than we were able to consider up to now. At least, there are several issues that are covered by supra-local news organizations. These could be accessed and mapped, too. On the other hand, we have accessed the most important sources. In the future, more news sources can be included when extending the mapping service to other cities. Until now, our first prototype is limited in crawling and searching to the administrative district of Paderborn, Germany.

Other limitations concern the location mapping and NER. Both tasks work quite accurately, but do fail sometimes. In other words, our rules are so far sufficient but may need improvement in the long run. Therefore, some alternative rules could be tested in the future based on observations (so-called bootstrapping of rules). Besides, machine learning will be a hot topic, too, especially for street names, or other locations, etc. Furthermore, we could test some more sentiment analysis approaches, even though we already did this during the development. As stated before, we compared our results to a commercial sentiment analysis provider, which produced insufficient results.

Minor limitations can be the following: The usage of machine learning techniques could improve the results of the NER task. Yet it works well, but names and places in news articles appear at least several times throughout time, so that a learning approach would be more reliable (due to the considered textual evidences). Since the design of our prototype is functional and simple, it could be modified to attract more users in future and to work on mobile platforms. Therefore, a study could be conducted which design would best apply to user's needs. Anyhow, we reached our before-mentioned goals but we aim at improving our solution to tackle the already-known limitations.

5 Conclusion

We presented a fully-working search solution that aggregates up-to-date information from different web sources. We map this information to different locations, perform a sentiment analysis and provide a heatmap. These features can be gathered via a user-friendly graphical user interface that is created according to internationally accepted design standards.

Our solution enables people to access local news information and compare how different organizations and users (of Twitter, for example) cover topics in their area. We assume that people are more interested in their local area rather than international topics. Therefore, our prototype allows people to critically read and compare news from different sources. In future, our system will consider more sources and other design patterns. Our prototype is the first local news search service that is able to combine news information with sentiment score and geographical locations.

References

1. Cunningham, H., Wilks, Y., Gaizauskas, R.J.: GATE: a general architecture for text engineering. In: Proceedings of the 16th Conference on Computational Linguistics, vol. 2, pp. 1057–1060. ACL (1996)
2. Djamasbi, S., Siegel, M., Tullis, T.: Generation Y, web design, and eye tracking. Int. J. Hum Comput Stud. **68**(5), 307–323 (2010)
3. Geierhos, M., Bäumer, F.S.: Crawler (fokussiert/nicht fokussiert) (2016). http://www.enzy klopaedie-der-wirtschaftsinformatik.de/lexikon/technologien-methoden/KI-und-Softcomputing/crawler-fokussiert-nicht-fokussiert. Accessed 8 May 2017
4. Goldhahn, D., Eckart, T., Quasthoff, U.: Building large monolingual dictionaries at the Leipzig Corpora collection: from 100 to 200 languages. In: Proceedings of the 8th International Conference on Language Resources and Evaluation, pp. 759–765. ELRA (2012)
5. Google Inc. Heatmap Layer (2017). https://developers.google.com/maps/documentation/javascript/heatmaplayer?hl=de
6. Hörold, S., Kühn, R., Mayas, C., Schlegel, T.: Interaktionspräferenzen für Personas im öffentlichen Personenverkehr. In: Mensch & Computer, pp. 367–370. GI (2011)
7. Kouloumpis, E., Wilson, T., Moore, J.D.: Twitter sentiment analysis: the good the bad and the OMG! In: Proceedings of the 5th International Conference on Weblogs and Social Media, vol. 11, pp. 538–541. AAAI (2011)
8. Leff, A., Rayfield, J.T.: Web-application development using the model/view/controller design pattern. In: Proceedings of the 5th Enterprise Distributed Object Computing Conference, pp. 118–127. IEEE (2001)
9. Liu, B.: Sentiment Analysis and Opinion Mining. Synth. Lect. Hum. Lang. Technol. **5**(1), 1–167 (2012)
10. Medhat, W., Hassan, A., Korashy, H.: Sentiment analysis algorithms and applications: a survey. Ain Shams Eng. J. **5**(4), 1093–1113 (2014)
11. Mie, A.: Uncovering the Truth in the Era of Fake News (2017). http://www.japantimes.co.jp/news/2017/03/31/national/uncovering-truth-era-fake-news/#.WRBCk1L5yJQ. Accessed 8 May 2017
12. Pak, A., Paroubek, P.: Twitter as a corpus for sentiment analysis and opinion mining. In: Proceedings of the 7th International Conference on Language Resources and Evaluation, vol. 10. ELRA (2010)
13. Pang, B., Lee, L., et al.: Opinion mining and sentiment analysis. Found. Trends Inf. Retr. **2**(1–2), 1–135 (2008)
14. Sankaranarayanan, J., Samet, H., Teitler, B.E., Lieberman, M.D., Sperling, J.: Twitterstand: news in tweets. In: Proceedings of the 17th International Conference on Advances in Geographic Information Systems, pp. 42–51. ACM (2009)

15. Schneider, W.: ergo-online - Übersicht über die Grundsätze der Dialoggestaltung nach DIN EN ISO 9241-110 (2010). http://www.ergo-online.de/site.aspx?url=html/software/grund lagen_der_software_ergon/grundsaetze_der_dialoggestalt.htm. Accessed 15 May 2017
16. Stadt Paderborn: Statistisches Jahrbuch der Stadt Paderborn 2014. Technical report, Paderborn – Stadt Paderborn (2014)
17. Stadt Paderborn: TOPO graphics – GOOGIS (2017). http://www.googis.de/paderborn/? es=C47S434. Accessed 15 May 2017
18. Taboada, M., Brooke, J., Tofiloski, M., Voll, K., Stede, M.: Lexicon-based methods for sentiment analysis. Comput. Linguist. **37**(2), 267–307 (2011)
19. Zhou, G., Su, J.: Named entity recognition using an HMM-based chunk tagger. In: Proceedings of the 40th Annual Meeting on Association for Computational Linguistics, pp. 473–480. ACL (2002)

Automatic Spoken Language Identification by Digital Signal Processing Methods. Tatar and Russian Languages

Rustam Latypov$^{(\boxtimes)}$, Ruslan Nigmatullin, and Evgeni Stolov

Kazan Federal University, Kazan 420008, Russia
roustam.latypov@kpfu.ru

Abstract. The paper studies the problem of language identification for audio files. For solving the problem, we use methods of digital signal processing only (without analysis of phonemes distinctive for language). A special attention is drawn to the form of signal in an area close to the position of a stop consonant. The evaluation is performed on a set of two languages; this includes speech records taken from TV programs. It is provided that solely one of the two languages (either Tatar or Russian) is used in each of files. Experimental evidence demonstrates the feasibility of the proposed techniques.

Keywords: Language identification · Tatar and Russian languages · Form of signal

1 Introduction

Automatic spoken language identification (LID) is a process by which the language spoken in a digitized speech sample is recognized by a computer [1]. Applications of LID systems include front-end ones for speech recognition, automated dialogue systems, call routing, call centers, household devices, wiretapping, and information distillation. Research in automatic LID systems possesses a history going back to the early 1970s: Doddington and Leonard [2] have studied frequency of occurrences of certain reference sound units in different languages. Discriminations between languages can be determined by employing paralinguistic information in a speech signal including distinctions in the phonology, morphology, syntax, and prosody [3]. In recent years, great improvements were achieved in different LID fields of research. The most popular modeling techniques used in acoustic systems are in application of some spectral features such as mel frequency cepstral coefficients (MFCC) [5]. In contrast, phoneme n-gram statistics are modeled in order to recognize languages in phonotactic approaches [6, 7]. Note also a widespread use of deep neural networks [8] as well as linear prediction technique [9]. However, such LID systems require greater computing resources to run. The latter narrows the scope of their applications (for example, in online systems or systems without Internet connection). In our work, we search the new speech parameters in LID to reduce computational complexity of LID algorithms. The speech file is treated as a digital signal and recognizing the language of a file is based on digital signal processing methods. The Tatar and Russian are used in the capacity of

R. Damaševičius and V. Mikašytė (Eds.): ICIST 2017, CCIS 756, pp. 539–549, 2017.
DOI: 10.1007/978-3-319-67642-5_45

examples. Throughout the paper, we use the following hypothesis expressed by many linguists: the main features in the considered languages are located in the form of signals related to stop consonants and the environment of that area (see, for example, [4]). The paper has the following structure. In the second section we propose a method for finding onset time as well as automatic voicing localisation by using nonorthogonal wavelet transform and k-means. In the third section the shape of a wave is investigated as a feature for languages identification. Experimental results are presented in the forth section. All the depicted distributions are normalized in the following sense. If $\langle h_0, \ldots, h_{N-1} \rangle$ is a sequence of quantities created by a function *histogram*, then the sequence $\langle h_0, \ldots, h_{N-1} \rangle / \sum_i h_i$ is presented in a figure.

2 Measure of Onset Time

It was mentioned above that the distance between the start of a stop consonant and the beginning of the voicing in a syllable (so-called onset time) is a distinctive feature of both languages under consideration. Localization of a position where the voicing starts is a very subjective process if it is performed by a human being. We present an objective method for calculation of onset time, if the region containing the consonant has been determined. A regular picture of the environment of the stop consonant is presented in Fig. 1.

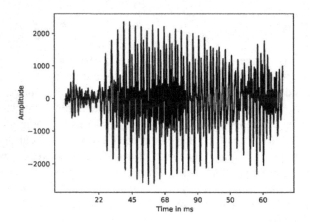

Fig. 1. Example of a syllable that begins with a stop consonant.

Since every wave in the figure looks like a sine wave, we use this function for localizing the positions where the consonant begins. To this end, we implemented the non-orthogonal wavelet technique [10]. Create array Sn_{ln} that will be a mother function in our case:

$$Sn_{ln}(i) = A_{ln} \cdot \sin\left(\frac{2\pi i}{ln}\right), \quad i = 0, \ldots, ln - 1. \tag{1}$$

Here A_{ln} is a constant such that $\sum_i Sn_{ln}^2(i) = 1$. Define function $Corr_{ln}(k)$ as follows:

$$Corr_{ln}(k) = \sum_{k=0}^{ln-1} Data(k+i) \cdot Sn_{ln}(i), \tag{2}$$

and let Set_{ln} be a set of all indexes k for which (2) has a sense. The following algorithm finds position Pos of the beginning of stop consonant, that is inside $Data$, and returns us the value Ln which is the optimal length of the wavelet.

Algorithm 1. Localization of the beginning of stop consonant

```
 1:  Max, Pos, Ln ← 0
 2:  for  ln ← ,3, Freq/1000  do
 3:      max, pos ← 0
 4:      for all  k ∈ Set_ln   do
 5:          Val ← Corr_ln (k)
 6:          if  max < Val  then
 7:              max ← Val
 8:              pos ← k
 9:          end if
10:      end for
11:      if  Max < max  then
12:          Max ← max
13:          Pos ← pos
14:          Ln ← ln
15:      end if
16:  end for
17:  return  Ln, Pos
```

Here $Data$ is a part of an audio file under consideration, $Freq$ is sample frequency. For any Ln we calculate normalized values of the sine function and compare this vector with all frames of $Data$, having length Ln, by means of (2). Since the sum of all values of sine function for the chosen set of arguments is zero, one concludes that the result is independent of the mean value of the signal in interval; hence one might compare the shapes of wavelet and fragment of $Data$. An example of the work of the algorithm is presented in Fig. 2. The vertical line depicts the beginning of the consonant found by the procedure. The described procedure gives us also the other parameter of the blast, namely the parameter Ln. It describes the shape of the blast It will be shown further that the distribution of those values is an important feature of a speaker.

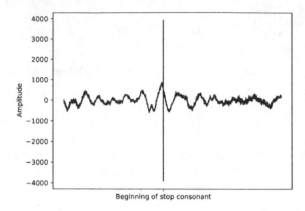

Fig. 2. Localization of the beginning of stop consonant.

2.1   Automatic Localization of Voicing

Let us suppose that the beginning of a consonant is established, and the next step is to determine the position where the voicing starts. Since we want to do it automatically, a formal procedure should be implemented. We denote an interval of audio file by a voicing interval if its spectrum can be successfully divided into three formants. Let $\langle f_0, f_1, \ldots, f_N \rangle$ be the first $N + 1$ Fourier coefficients of an interval of length $2N$. Since we use absolute values of the coefficients, all other coefficients can be omitted. One can implement the standard k-means procedure to the set $\langle d_0, d_1, \ldots, d_N \rangle$, where $d_i = |f_i|$, for dividing the set into three parts, and thus establish c_0, c_1, c_2 as centroids of the clustering. Let d_{ik}, $i = 0, 1, 2$ be all items belonging to the cluster with the centroid c_i. Define

$$Q = \frac{\sum_k (c_0 - d_{0k})^2 + \sum_k (c_1 - d_{1k})^2 + \sum_k (c_2 - d_{2k})^2}{\sum_k (d_k)^2} \qquad (3)$$

as a quality of the clustering. It is easy to see that Q is invariant to scaling of the input data. The lesser is Q the better is the quality of the performed division into three parts of the set. By moving the interval of length $2N$ along an audio file starting from the position of the found consonant, one computes the quality of clustering for each interval. As a result, one obtains the diagram represented in Fig. 3. Without an additional analysis, the graphics is not good enough for evaluation of the onset time. Let us implement the gaussian filter to the curve [12]. After filtering, one gets the picture represented in Fig. 4. Now, the curve has an expected form, since the quality of the division becomes better if the window comes closer to the beginning of the voicing. We suggest to define the beginning of the voicing by the method used for detecting border of object in image processing [12]. Let us implement to the smoothed curve the FIR filter with the coefficients [1, −1.]. This filter approximates the first derivative of function. After applying such a filter to a curve, one searches for the points where the resulting curve reaches its negative minimum. We suggest to declare such point as the

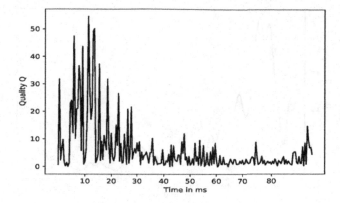

Fig. 3. Graphics of the quality of the division according to (3).

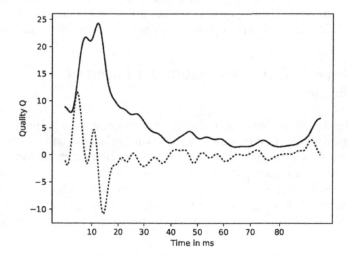

Fig. 4. The result of filtering of the curve in Fig. 3 by the gaussian filter with $\sigma = 4$ and the first derivative (dotted).

beginning of the voicing. In Fig. 4, the result of smooth curve filtering is presented by the dotted line. The minimum of this curve localizes the position where the voicing starts.

We should make a remark related to the graphics in Fig. 4. While moving the window along the file, we set the interval between two adjacent windows being equal to 1.5 ms. If the interval is of order 0.5 ms, then the smooth curve has a form that slightly differs from the curve presented in Fig. 4 (it is a bimodal curve like the one shown in Fig. 5). The reason of the event is in existence of a small interval, that looks like as a stable wave, between the beginning of stop consonant and the voicing (see

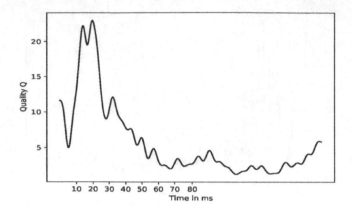

Fig. 5. A bimodal smooth curve. The interval between the two adjacent windows equals 0.3 ms.

Fig. 1). If a part of that interval is inside of the window used for calculating Fourier coefficients, then the k-means procedure creates a good partitioning of the set of the coefficients. That leads to lesser values of Q if compared to the one at the initial points.

3 The Shape of Wave as a Feature for Languages Identification

The technique described above supposes presence of a human being performing some manipulations with file. In this section, we continue the investigation of local parameters of speech files as possible features of a language (for automatic identification of the language used for records in a file). The form of a single wave can be used in the capacity of such feature. The parameter Ln considered above can be thought of as a property of the wave. In [11], some other parameters were suggested for using for that goal. First of all, let us recall the parameters utilized in [11], and then extend the research.

3.1 Distribution of Ln Parameters in an Audio File

Now, describe the procedure intended for investigation of distribution of Ln parameter defined above. The main problem is to distinguish positions of stop consonants and other sine-like regions in a file. What is more, the pure noise regions in file also should be excluded. The respective algorithm is as follows:

1. Normalize loaded *Data* through dividing by standard deviation;
2. Divide the file into fragments of length 1 ms;
3. Calculate Ln for each fragment;
4. Create histogram of the found values of Ln by using proper bin intervals.

Two typical histograms of the distribution of Ln are represented in Fig. 6. In accordance with expectations, one sees a significant distinction between distributions of

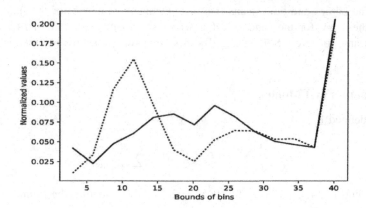

Fig. 6. Normalized distribution of *Ln* parameter for Russian (solid line) and Tatar (dotted line) speakers.

short values of *Ln*. There is a peak for the Tatar speaker, whereas for the Russian speaker one observes a smooth curve. Another interesting feature following from observation is that there is no difference within distribution of long values of *Ln* that are related to the forms of voiced parts of the signal. It is another hint to the fact that all the features intended for distinguishing two languages by means of digital signal processing are concentrated in environment of consonants.

3.2 Fragment of Wave Under Consideration

Let us look at Fig. 7. Here we see a part of a speech file and its fragment situated between two vertical lines. Our goal is to suggest a small number of parameters that describe the depicted fragment. The fragment in Fig. 7 can be thought of as a graphic of a function $f(x)$ with the interval $[A, B]$ of integer numbers (as its domain of definition). All the parameters used for description of the shape of a fragment will be defined in terms of such functions. We want these parameters to be independent of a

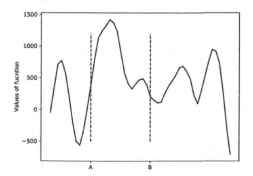

Fig. 7. A fragment of a speech file.

scaling. The latter condition means that any parameter obtained for the function $f(x)$ must be the same for the function $g(x)$ with its domain of definition $tA, tB, g(x) = tf(x/t)$ for any positive t. Some examples of similar functions are presented in the next item.

3.3   Quantiles and Moments

Let F be defined by (4)

$$F(t) = \frac{1}{M}\sum_{x<t} f(x), \quad M = \sum_{x\in[A,B]} f(x). \tag{4}$$

According to (4) $F(A) = 0, F(B+1) = 1$, and we can find the points where the conditions

$$F(q_1) = 0.25, \; F(q_2) = 0.75, \; F(\mu) = 0.5 \tag{5}$$

hold. These points are quantiles and median. They are used in statistics to characterize the form of a distribution [13]. Because of the discrete domain of definition of $f(x)$, these equalities are satisfied only to within a certain given accuracy. It is easy to see that

$$p_1 = \frac{q_1 - A}{B - A}, p_2 = \frac{q_2 - A}{B - A}, p_3 = \frac{\mu - A}{B - A}, m_0 = \frac{M}{(B-A)^2}, m_1 = \sum \frac{xf(x)}{(B-A)^3} \tag{6}$$

are invariant with respect to scaling of the fragment; so they can be used for description of the shape of the fragment. In what follows, the condition $f(A) = f(B) = 0$ will be always fulfilled, so m_0 in (6) is the ratio of the area of domain under the curve $f(x)$ to the area of a square with side being equal to $B - A$. The parameters m_0 and m_1 are the moments of the function f.

3.4   Calculation of Parameters and Their Distributions

There are evident algorithms for calculation of all the parameters in (6), so the main problem consists in obtaining a rule for selection fragments within a file. First of all, signals of a possible noise (which might occupy intervals between syllables) must be omitted, since the parameters calculated on the base of those fragments must have no influence upon the final decision about what language is used. To this end, we calculate standard deviation σ of data in the file and remove all the samples with magnitudes lesser than

$$Threshold = Coe \cdot \sigma. \tag{7}$$

In our experiment we set $Coe = 0.2$. As a result, the saved samples have positive magnitudes, and the file will be split into connected fragments, which are the objects of the investigation. Any fragment has an interval $[A, B]$ of indexes as a domain of definition of the corresponding function f, but we let $f(x) = Dat[x] - Coe \cdot \sigma$, where

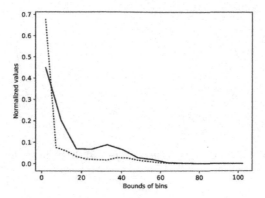

Fig. 8. Normalized distribution of values $B - A$ for Russian (solid line) and Tatar (dotted line) speakers.

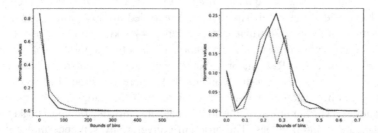

Fig. 9. Normalized distribution of parameters (a) m_0 and (b) p_1 in (6) for Russian (solid line) and Tatar (dotted line) speakers.

$Dat[x]$ is the original value of the sample in the position x. Since A and B are integer x-coordinates of the points, where the line $y = Coe \cdot \sigma$ crosses Dat curve, therefore the conditions $f(A) = f(B) = 0$ are fulfilled only to within a certain given accuracy. It was shown above that just a restricted part of distribution of the parameter Ln is used for identification of language. Now, we have to determine the most informative part of distribution of the values $B - A$. An example of distributions is represented in Fig. 8. There is an evident correlation between the graphics presented in Figs. 8 and 6 showing that only short fragments must be used for language identification. It must be mentioned that the bounds of bins presented in Fig. 8 depend on the value of Coe in (7) although that dependence is rather weak in interval $[0.1, 0.4]$. The bounds in Fig. 6 are independent of that parameter. Only fragments of length lesser than 60 are used in the analysis below. It follows from Figs. 9 and 10 that the parameter m_0 brings us few information and it can be excluded from consideration; as for the parameter p_1, the most interesting region is $[0.15, 0.4]$, for p_2 these will be $[0, 0.1]$ and $[0.3, 0.6]$, and for p_3 we have $[0, 0.1]$ and $[0.45, 0.8]$.

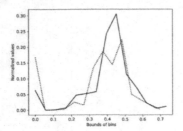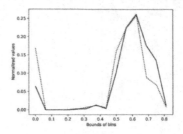

Fig. 10. Normalized distribution of parameters (a) p_2 and (b) p_3 in (6) for Russian (solid line) and Tatar (dotted line) speakers.

4 Experiments

All methods described above were tested on a small corpus created by the authors. The files were recorded on a dictaphone from a TV set during the news broadcast by Tatarstan New Age TV channel. The files were recorded in mp3 format, and then those were converted into the wav format with frequency 44.1 kHz and a bit depth of 16 bit per sample. The corpus consists of short records of about 10 s duration pronounced by native speakers of either Russian or Tatar. We utilized logistic regression from the package scikit-learn for solving the problem [14]. There are about 120 records in our corpus. The training data contains 64 files where both the languages are presented in equal quantities. The amounts of the male speakers and the female speakers in the training data are random values. The program converts any sentence into a vector of length 16. The components of the vectors are parts of the normalized distributions of the parameters $Ln, B - A, p_1, p_2, p_3$ described above. Depending on the choice of the training data, the number of incorrect classifications is in interval [15, 23] percents. The reason of the weak quality of identification lies in small size of the corpus and presence of records of speakers from various regions. A very interesting phenomenon was revealed. Among the files in the corpus, there are records of Tatar native speakers from Tatarstan speaking Russian. Most of them were correctly classified by the program. On the other hand, the corpus contains records of Tatar native speakers, which are living in a Russian region and speaking Tatar. The program failed to identify the language in those records.

5 Conclusion

In this article, methods for automatic separation of two languages are proposed based on local feature of audio signal. Although the verification of the developed algorithms was made by using examples of Tatar and Russian speech files, the methods seem to be also suitable for pairs of other two languages. This is the subject of further researches.

References

1. Li, H., Ma, B., Lee, K.A.: Spoken language recognition: from fundamentals to practice. Proc. IEEE **101**, 1136–1159 (2013)
2. Leonard, R., Doddington, G.: Automatic language identification. Technical report RADC-TR-74-200, Air Force Rome Air Development Center (1974)
3. Schuller, B., Batliner, A.: Computational Paralinguistics: Emotion, Affect and Personality in Speech and Language Processing. Wiley, Hoboken (2013)
4. Diehl, R.L., Lotto, A.J., Holt, L.L.: Speech perception. Annu. Rev. Psychol. **55**, 149–179 (2004)
5. Karafiat, M., Burget, L., Matejka, P., Glembek, O., Cernocky, J.: iVector-based discriminative adaptation for automatic speech recognition. In: Proceedings of the IEEE Workshop on Automatic Speech Recognition and Understanding (ASRU), pp. 152–157 (2011)
6. Zissman, M.A.: Language identification using phoneme recognition and phonotactic language modeling. In: Proceedings of the 1995 International Conference on Acoustics, Speech, and Signal Processing, vol. 5, pp. 3503–3506 (1995)
7. Mathew, N.V., Bai, V.R.: Analyzing the effectiveness of N-gram technique based Feature Set in a Naive Bayesian Spam Filter. In: Proceedings of the 2016 International Conference on Emerging Technological Trends (ICETT), pp. 1–5 (2016)
8. Lopez-Moreno, I., Gonzalez-Dominguez, J., Plchot, O., Martinez, D., Gonzalez-Rodriguez, J., Moreno, P.: Automatic language identification using deep neural networks. In: Proceedings of the 2014 IEEE International Conference on Acoustics, Speech and Signal Processing (ICASSP), pp. 5337–5341 (2014)
9. Nandi, D., Pati, D., Rao, K.S.: Language identification using Hilbert envelope and phase information of linear prediction residual. In: Proceedings of the 2013 International Conference Oriental COCOSDA Held Jointly with 2013 Conference on Asian Spoken Language Research and Evaluation (O-COCOSDA/CASLRE), pp. 1–6 (2013)
10. Mallat, S.: A Wavelet Tour of Signal Processing. Elsevier, Amsterdam (2009)
11. Latypov, R.K., Nigmatullin, R.R., Stolov, E.L.: Classification of speech files by waveforms. Lobachevskii J. Math. **36**, 488–494 (2015)
12. Jain, A.K.: Fundamentals of Digital Image Processing. Prentice-Hall, Upper Saddle River (1989)
13. Cramer, H.: Mathematical Methods of Statistics. Princeton University Press, Princeton (1999)
14. scikit-learn. http://scikit-learn.org

Using Morphological and Semantic Features for the Quality Assessment of Russian Wikipedia

Włodzimierz Lewoniewski[1(✉)], Nina Khairova[2], Krzysztof Węcel[1],
Nataliia Stratiienko[2], and Witold Abramowicz[1]

[1] Poznań University of Economics and Business, Poznań, Poland
{wlodzimierz.lewoniewski,krzysztof.wecel,
witold.abramowicz}@ue.poznan.pl
[2] National Technical University "Kharkiv Polytechnic Institute",
Kharkiv, Ukraine
{khairova,strana}@kpi.kharkov.ua

Abstract. Nowadays, the assessment of the quality and credibility of Wikipedia articles becomes increasingly important. We propose to use morphological and semantic features to estimate the quality of Wikipedia articles in Russian language. We distinguished over 150 linguistic features and divided them into four groups. In these groups, we considered the features of encyclopedic style, readability and subjectivism of the article's text. Based on Random Forest as a classification algorithm, we show the most importance linguistic features that affect the quality of Russian Wikipedia articles. We compare the classification results of our four linguistic features groups separately. We have achieved the F-measure of 89,75%.

Keywords: Quality assessment of texts · Morphological and semantics features · Russian Wikipedia articles · Random forests classification · Encyclopedic · Readability · Subjectivism

1 Introduction

Nowadays, Wikipedia is the biggest public universal encyclopedia with a free content, which includes over 44 million articles. Most articles in the Wikipedia are comparable in quality to those in the Encyclopedia Britannica [1]. Usually, in order for a Wikipedia article to reach the good quality it must be revised by Wikipedia community many times. This is the main reason for the growing interest and popularity of research on assessment of Wikipedia articles quality.

In 2006, during the Opening plenary at Wikimania, Jimmy Wales suggested concentrating on quality of the articles instead of their number [9]. The best articles of Wikipedia must follow the specific style guidelines. Such guidelines can be quantified in many ways. One of the approaches is to use morphological, syntactic and semantic features of words, which allow evaluating the quality of the Wikipedia articles. Obviously, these features strongly depend on a specific language.

© Springer International Publishing AG 2017
R. Damaševičius and V. Mikašytė (Eds.): ICIST 2017, CCIS 756, pp. 550–560, 2017.
DOI: 10.1007/978-3-319-67642-5_46

As of April 2017, the Russian-language edition of Wikipedia had more than 1,3 million articles[1] and more than 1 billion page views per month[2]. The Russian Wikipedia subdomain (ru.wikipedia.org) receives approximately 8% of Wikipedia's cumulative traffic, and takes second place after English subdomain (59%, en.wikipedia.org).[3]

There are a lot of articles that study the correlation between English linguistic characteristics and estimating the quality of articles in English Wikipedia. However, studies examining the use of Russian linguistic characteristics to evaluate the quality of texts are very few.

In this paper we focus on using morphological and semantics features of the Russian language to estimate the quality of Russian Wikipedia articles. We suggest applying the Random Forests algorithm of that is based on these features in order to automatically identify quality classes of Wikipedia articles.

2   Related Work

All experts admit that there are some difficulties in determining the quality of the Wikipedia articles. Furthermore Wikipedia isn't a static resource; their amount keeps growing every day. Also that fact that the articles cover different topics complicates the task [11]. It means it requires that experts from different disciplines judge the quality, but such experts are not always available.

Measuring an article's quality in Wikipedia is not an easy task for human users, complexity of which repeatedly increases in case of the task of automatic evaluation of the article quality. Now there exist enough studies concerning the problems related to automatic estimating the quality of Wikipedia articles. We can divide all research literature into three groups. The first group of researches is based on characteristics related to contributors' reputations and edit network, article status, external factual support and other features [4, 5, 17]. However, often such methods require complex calculations and they do not analyze on the content of the article itself.

The second group of the studies focuses on the calculation of volume of different articles components. These studies showed that a better quality article usually are longer, have more images and sections, use bigger number of references [8, 14, 15]. These quantitative features are used in online service WikiRank[4] for the automatic relative assessment of the articles in various language versions of Wikipedia. In some Wikipedia articles we can find special quality flaw templates, which can also help in articles assessment [3].

The third group of the studies concerning the task of automatic estimating the quality based on linguistic characteristics of text in Wikipedia articles [2, 6]. Other studies used linguistic features to examine how density of factual information impact

---

[1] https://meta.wikimedia.org/wiki/List_of_Wikipedias.

[2] https://analytics.wikimedia.org.

[3] http://www.alexa.com/siteinfo/wikipedia.org.

[4] http://wikirank.net.

on quality of Wikipedia articles [13, 18]. Such approaches that direct to exploring the linguistic characteristics of articles might be useful for improvement of the articles quality. For example, it concerns such characteristics as the writing style of an article, the number of verbs, facts, the number of diverse nouns and similar features. However, linguistic characteristics of the text depend on the article's language. Nowadays, Wikipedia contains articles in approximately 300 languages. One of the main language versions of the online encyclopedia is Russian. There a lot of articles on using linguistic characteristics to estimate the quality of Wikipedia articles in English or Spanish but very few use peculiar properties of Russian linguistic characteristics [10].

This is the first study that use more than 150 features related to Russian language to predict articles quality in Wikipedia. In order to tokenize texts of Russian Wikipedia articles and extract various linguistic features we use own approach. This approach use different open morphological libraries and dictionaries available on the Web. We also add additional rules to this algorithm at the stage of preparation of the text, as well as during the extraction of some features.

3 Description of the Experiment

The best Wikipedia articles must be well-written, comprehensive, well-researched, neutral and must follow the specific style guidelines.[5] The main idea of the approach is that the linguistic features of words or sentences of the articles allow evaluating the style of writing, the brevity, correctness, readable and some others of the Wikipedia articles characteristics. In some cases, semantic and syntactic features of the words allow even to evaluate subjectivity of the article authors.

3.1 Linguistic Features

We distinguish several groups of linguistics features that can affect the quality of Russian Wikipedia articles. The first group includes **morphological features** such as parts of speech, specific morphological characteristics of a particular part of speech. For instance, we determine the number of verbs and then we determine the number of verb categories - tense, person, etc. Herewith, we use more than 50 similar characteristics. In order to analyze the morphological features, we apply the pymorphy2[6], the library for morphological analysis of the Russian language that is based on the OpenCorpora dictionary[7] which is also used to denote grammatical tags (some of them are presented in Table 1).

The second group of the applicable linguistic features includes some **semantic features**, integral morphological features of the words and even the parameters of word formation. We suppose that the features from the second group can explicitly express the existence of some subjective assessment or opinion of the Wikipedia article authors.

---

[5] https://en.wikipedia.org/wiki/Wikipedia:Featured_article_criteria.

[6] http://pymorphy2.readthedocs.io.

[7] http://opencorpora.org.

Table 1. Description of some grammatical tags used in the study. Source: http://opencorpora. org/dict.php?act=gram

NOUN	Noun	NUMR	Numeral
ADJF	Adjective (full)	ADVB	Adverb
ADJS	Adjective (short)	NPRO	Pronoun
COMP	Comparative	PRED	Predicative
VERB	Verb (personal form)	PREP	Preposition
INFN	Verb (the infinitive)	CONJ	Conjunction
PRTF	Participle (full)	PRCL	Particle
PRTS	Participle (short)	INTJ	Interjection
GRND	Gerund	...	

Therefore, the presence of these characteristics in the text can affect the quality of the article.

Typically the value judgments are represented by the various linguistic means and characteristics in the text. For example, such morphological features as personal and possessive pronouns of the first and second person can contribute evaluative-expressive shades to a statement. Herewith, one of the main grammatical means of adding of the author's subjectivity and expressiveness in Russian is affectionate diminutive suffixes.

Moreover, each natural language has a specific vocabulary that expresses emotions, mentality and adds a tinge of author's opinion in the statement. We have created two special vocabularies that express such shade in Russian. The first vocabulary includes more than 300 words and the combination of words (avt_ocenka). The second one includes only verbs that have the certain semantic component of subjectivity (men-verb). It includes 120 speech verbs (such as tell, recall, dictate and others), 154 feelings verbs and 103 emotions verbs (such as wish, rejoice, worry and others) [13]. Additionally, in this group of the features, we use the glossary of introductory turnovers from the Russian National Corpus.[8]

Table 2 shows our full list of the word features that can express some elements of subjective assessment of the Wikipedia article authors.

The third group of the applicable linguistic features allows making exploratory conclusions about the **readability of the texts**. We have included in this group both characteristics that are commonly used to assess the complexity of texts as well as new characteristics based on dictionaries of the Russian National Corpus, the Russian Internet corps I-RU [12] and the Open Corpora. Traditionally the estimation of readability is based on features such as the statistical average word length (in characters and in syllables), the sentence length, the maximum number of words in a sentence, the number of unique words (uslov) and some others [11].

In addition to the listed characteristics, we also highlight the following statistical indicators: the number of words having 3 syllables and more (slog3), the number of words having 4 syllables and more (slog4), the number of words having 5 syllables and more (slog5), the number of unique words of specific parts of speech (uverb, unoun, uadj).

---

[8] http://www.ruscorpora.ru/en/.

Table 2. Linguistic features of the words that can express some elements of subjective assessment of the Wikipedia article authors

lichprit	– personal and possessive pronouns of the first and second person
formal_priz	– dative case with a preposition
ocen	– affectionate diminutive suffixes
avt_ocenka	– the special vocabulary
ruscorp_parenth	– the glossary of introductory turnovers from Russian National Corpus
sl_by	– the use of the subjunctive
menverb	– the special vocabulary of the verbs that have the certain semantic component of subjectivity
VERB_wmv	– the verb that does not have the semantic component of subjectivity

Table 3. Features that take into account different lists of the most frequent words in the Russian language.

frec100 (...500, ...1000, ... 5000)	– the 100 (500, 1 000, 5 000) first most common words in the Russian Internet corps I-RU
slovoformy100 (...500, ...1000, ...5000, ...10000)	– the 100 (500, 1 000, 5 000, 10 000) first most common words in the Russian National Corpus
2grammy100 (...500, 1000, ... 5000, ...10000)	– the 100 (500, 1 000, 5 000, 10 000) first most common bigrams in the Russian National Corpus
3grammy100	– the 100 first most common 3-grams in the Russian National Corpus
4grammy100	– the 100 first most common 4-grams in the Russian National Corpus
5grammy100	– the 100 first most common 5-grams in the Russian National Corpus
oc100un (oc500un, oc1000un, oc5000un, oc10000un	– the 100 (500, 1 000, 5 000, 10 000) first most common unigrams in Open Corpora.
oc100bi (oc500bi, oc1000bi, oc5000bi, oc1000bi)	– the 100 (500, 1 000, 5 000, 10 000) first most common bigrams in Open Corpora.
oc100tri	– the 100 first most common 3-grams in Open Corpora

Furthermore, we assume that the frequency of word usage in texts correlates with their comprehensibility and readability. Therefore, we can include the lists of the most frequent words in the Russian language in the third group of the linguistic features that affect the readability of the texts. Table 3 shows these features that take into account different lists of the most frequent words in the Russian language.

The total number of the third group of the applicable linguistic categories reaches 40.

The fourth group of the applicable linguistic features characterizes an **encyclopedic style** of an article. An encyclopedia-style article should display a comprehensive view of the subject matter in a simple and understandable manner. In the general case, such style means the condensed presentation of material, which identifies the subject sufficiently, completely, naturally and authentically.

We argue that such style can be represented explicitly by the various linguistic means and characteristics in the text. We have included in this group such proper names as the first name of the person (*name*), the last name of the person (*surn*), the middle name of the person (*patr*), a name (*orgn*), and a trademark (*Trad*) of the organisation and toponyms (*Geox*). We also believe that the list of the most popular words of Russian Wikipedia can represent the encyclopedic style of the article (*250wiki*)

Additionally, we have included amounts of simple and complex facts of the article to the fourth group of the applicable linguistic features. According to the logical-linguistic model of fact extraction from English [7] or Russian Texts [13], the simple fact (*fact*) in a Russian sentence is the smallest grammatical clause that includes a verb and a noun; the complex fact (*FactPlus1, FactPlus2*) in Russian texts is a grammatical sentence that includes a verb and a few nouns. Among these nouns, one has to play the semantic role of the Subject (*FactPlus1*) and the other has to be the Object (*FactPlus2*)[9].

3.2   Source Data

Our dataset includes all articles from Russian Wikipedia that have manual evaluation of their quality, i.e. about 130,000 (April 2017). According to the previous studies [14, 15], we distinguish two quality classes of the Russian Wikipedia articles. We called the first class GoodEnough: it includes articles that are evaluated by the Wikipedia community as Featured and Good. The second class is called NeedsWork; it includes I, II, III and IV level (stub) articles. One of the peculiarities of Russian Wikipedia is the availability of such an assessment of the quality of the article as Solid. According to the binary classification, this grade can be classified either as GoodEnough or NeedsWork. In order to show peculiarity of the group of articles that are evaluated as Solid, we consider three versions of the classification. They are *FG-standard*, *FGS-standard* and *FG-S standard*.

Table 4 shows the distributions of the analyzed articles according to the grade of assessment quality.

Table 4. The distributions of the analyzed articles according to the grade of assessment quality.

Quality grade	Number of articles	FG standard	FGS standard	FG-S standard
Featured	997	GoodEnough	GoodEnough	GoodEnough
Good	2738			
Solid	3927	NeedsWork		Disabled
I level	2516		NeedsWork	NeedsWork
II level	9978			
III level	48183			
IV level (stub)	61711			

---

[9] Detailed definitions of the simple and complex facts are given in [13].

4 Implementation Aspects and Experimental Results

Analysis has shown that usually, articles with high-quality grades have the higher value of a particular feature. On Fig. 1 is shown the distribution of some features among different quality grades in Russian Wikipedia. The used Random Forests classifier determines the probability that an article belongs to one of the two classes. The classifier allows us to use the specific analytical methods to explore hidden patterns, rules and dependencies between different linguistic features. At the same time, the Random Forests classifier allows calculating the predictive power of the different features and every group of the applicable linguistic features.

As already mentioned before, better articles usually have more text (including characters, words, sentences). So we can expect that the value of a majority of the considered linguistic characteristics is more in articles with better quality. Therefore, we decided to normalize all features by word count, sentences count and character count (without spaces) separately. On Fig. 2 it is shown distribution of some features normalized by words.

Typically, the encyclopedic style of a Wikipedia article requires that the article includes a brief definition or description of the assigned subject, which is called "The lead section" followed by a broad examination of the topic, which is called "The 1st section" followed by a number of sub-sections. We have evaluated the precision, recall and F-Measure for three way of the normalization and for three analysed areas: the lead section, the 1st section, the whole article's text.

Table 5 shows that the evaluation of the linguistic parameters of the whole article is more significant than the evaluation of the linguistic parameters of the lead section and the 1st section only. According to the table, there is not much difference in F-measure

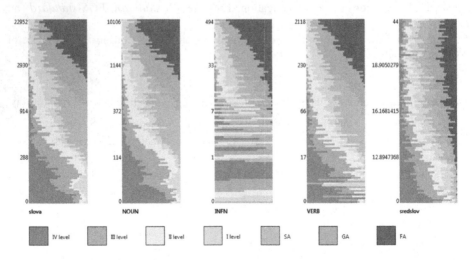

Fig. 1. Value distribution of 5 articles features (from left to right: number of words, nouns, infinitives, verbs, avg. number of words in a sentence) among different quality grades in Russian Wikipedia. Source: own calculation.

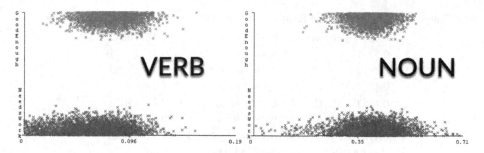

Fig. 2. Distribution of normalized features (by the number of words) in quality classes. Source: own calculations in Weka.

between the various way of the normalization. We decided to normalize our features by the number of words based on the research of corpus linguistics [16].

The Random Forest classifier can show the importance of features in the model. It provides two straightforward methods for feature selection: mean decrease impurity and mean decrease accuracy. Table 6 shows 30 most importance features, which are based on average impurity decrease. Table 7 shows 30 most important features based on number of nodes using that attribute. Every feature is normalized by the number of words of the corpus class. Additionally, as was mentioned before, the linguistic parameters correspond to the whole article.

We found that except for the morphological categories the main features affecting the quality of Russian Wikipedia articles are such semantic characters as the simple fact or the complex fact [13], and such characters of the subjective assessment as a verb that have the certain semantic component of subjectivity. Moreover, one of the main feature

Table 5. Classication results using various types of the normalisation and three versions of the classification standards.

Normalize by	FGS standard		
	Characters	Words	Sentence
Lead section	75,24%	75,04%	75,59%
1st section	75,82%	75,38%	75,89%
Article text	81,47%	81,05%	80,76%
Normalize by	FG standard		
	Characters	Words	Sentence
Lead section	81,68%	81,49%	81,44%
1st section	78,78%	78,74%	78,90%
Article text	89,54%	89,75%	89,50%
Normalize by	FG-S standard		
	Characters	Words	Sentence
Lead section	81,98%	82,01%	82,03%
1st section	79,93%	79,85%	80,40%
Article text	88,81%	89,14%	88,85%

Table 6. 30 most important linguistic features based on average impurity decrease

0,52	VERB_wmv	0,44	PRTF	0,41	GRND
0,5	Fact	0,44	INFN	0,41	ADVB
0,49	FactPlus1	0,44	menverb	0,41	CONJ
0,48	FactPlus2	0,43	PREP	0,4	inan
0,47	FactPlus2_wmv	0,43	COMP	0,4	PRCL
0,47	Fact_wmv	0,43	PRTS	0,4	anim
0,47	FactPlus1_wmv	0,43	sred_dlin_slov	0,39	GNdr
0,46	ADJF	0,42	NUMR	0,39	voct
0,46	NOUN	0,42	ADJS	0,39	INTJ
0,46	VERB	0,42	PRED	0,39	NPRO

Table 7. 30 most important linguistic features based on number of nodes using that features

856	sred_dlin_slov	650	ADJS	588	sing
744	FactPlus1	645	INFN	587	PRTF
738	menverb	635	FactPlus1_wmv	577	anim
733	FactPlus2	621	nomn	576	PREP
723	VERB_wmv	618	NPRO	574	gent
690	makslov	617	FactPlus2_wmv	559	GRND
680	ADJF	608	PRTS	558	VERB
654	sredslov	607	Fact_wmv	551	inan
652	Fact	606	ADVB	538	Sgtm
651	NOUN	590	NUMR	537	PRCL

Table 8. Classication results using the encyclopedic, morphological, readability, subjectivism features groups separately.

Features group	FGS standard			FG standard		
	Precision	Recall	F-Measure	Precision	Recall	F-Measure
Encyclopedic	76,7%	76,5%	76,6%	82,4%	82,4%	82,4%
Morphological	80,7%	80,6%	80,7%	87,9%	87,6%	87,7%
Readability	79,8%	79,7%	79,7%	88,4%	88,0%	88,1%
Subjectivism	76,5%	76,4%	76,4%	85,3%	84,8%	85,0%
All groups	**81,2%**	**81,0%**	**81,1%**	**89,9%**	**89,7%**	**89,8%**

to classify the Russian Wikipedia article are correlated features of the number of the verbs that do not have the semantic component of subjectivity and the number of the facts that do not have the semantic component of subjectivity.

We also analyzed the classification efficiency using separate parameters for each of our four linguistic features groups. The results reported in Table 8 were obtained using the random forest classifier with features of the encyclopedic, morphological, readability, subjectivism groups separately.

Additionally, we analyzed classification results using two versions of the classification standards. They are FGS standard and FG standard.

There are significant differences of results between the FGS version of classification and FG classification. The precision, recall and F-measure are significantly higher when Solid articles are referred to the class NeedsWork articles.

5 Conclusions and Future Works

In this work, we proposed to exploit linguistic features of an article for assessing Wikipedia content quality. We distinguished and categorized over 150 linguistic features of Russian Wikipedia articles. We divided all the linguistic characteristics into four groups: morphological features, semantic features that can explicitly express the existence of some subjective assessment or opinion of the authors, the features that are exploratory conclusions about the readability of the text and the features that characterize the encyclopedic style of the article.

We found that the most important groups of linguistic characteristics that affect the quality of Russian Wikipedia articles are the parts of speech and semantic features of the simple fact and the complex fact. Moreover, such correlated features as the number of the verbs and the number of the facts that do not have the semantic component of subjectivity possess the great predictive power of classification of the quality of the articles. Our experiments on a subset of the Russian Wikipedia revealed that frequency dictionaries are poorly effective in the problem of classifying the quality of articles.

Our experiments showed that the evaluation of the linguistic features of the whole article is more significant than the evaluation of them for some sections of the text. We also investigated the use of three versions of the articles classification standards depending on the position of Solid Articles. Using FG schema allowed achieving the F-measure of the classification results of 89,75%.

While the initial results are very promising, more in-depth investigations of these linguistic features are needed. We guess that the most effective way is to apply our linguistic features with others parameters that affect the Wikipedia articles quality.

In future work, we plan to conduct similar experiments for other languages to analyze how linguistic features of different languages affects the quality of Wikipedia articles. Additionally, we are going to expand the list of semantic variables and also consider the quality of the articles in a more complex categorization.

References

1. Michael, B.: Wikipedia Or Encyclopædia Britannica: Which Has More Bias? Forbes (2015). http://www.forbes.com/sites/hbsworkingknowledge/2015/01/20/wikipedia-or-encyclopaedia -britannica-which-has-more-bias. Accessed 15 June 2017
2. Xu, Y., Luo, T.: Measuring article quality in Wikipedia: Lexical clue model. In Web Society (SWS). In: 2011 3rd Symposium on IEEE, pp. 141–146 (2011)
3. Anderka, M.: Analyzing and predicting quality flaws in user-generated content: the case of wikipedia. Ph.D., Bauhaus-Universitaet Weimar Germany (2013)

4. Kittur, A., Kraut, R.E.: Harnessing the wisdom of crowds in wikipedia: quality through coordination. In: Proceedings of the 2008 ACM conference on Computer Supported Cooperative Work, pp. 37–46. ACM (2008)
5. Velázquez, C.G., Cagnina, L.C., Errecalde, M.L.: On the feasibility of external factual support as Wikipedia's quality metric. Procesamiento del Lenguaje Natural **58**, 93–100 (2017)
6. Lipka, N., Stein, B.: Identifying featured articles in wikipedia: writing style matters. In: Proceedings of the 19th International Conference on World Wide Web, pp. 1147–1148 (2010)
7. Khairova, N., Petrasova, S., Gautam, A.: The logical-linguistic model of fact extraction from english texts. In: International Conference on Information and Software Technologies, CCIS 2016, Communications in Computer and Information Science, pp. 625–635 (2016)
8. Warncke-Wang, M., Cosley, D., Riedl, J.: Tell me more: an actionable quality model for Wikipedia. In: Proceedings of the 9th International Symposium on Open Collaboration (2013)
9. Giles, G.: Internet encyclopaedias go head to head. Nature **438**, 900–901 (2005)
10. Panicheva, P., Ledovaya, Y., Bogolyubova, O.: Lexical, morphological and semantic correlates of the dark triad personality traits in russian facebook texts. In: Artificial Intelligence and Natural Language Conference (AINL), pp. 1–8. IEEE (2016)
11. Lenzner, T.: Are readability formulas valid tools for assessing survey question difficulty? Sociol. Methods Res. **43**(4), 677–698 (2014)
12. Sharoff, S., Umanskaya, E., Wilson, J.: A frequency dictionary of Russian: core vocabulary for learners, Routledge (2014)
13. Khairova, N., Lewoniewski, W., Wecel, K.: Estimating the quality of articles in russian Wikipedia using the logical-linguistic model of fact extraction. In: International Conference on Business Information Systems, pp. 28–42 (2017)
14. Węcel, K., Lewoniewski, W.: Modelling the quality of attributes in wikipedia infoboxes. In: Abramowicz, W. (ed.) BIS 2015. LNBIP, vol. 228, pp. 308–320. Springer, Cham (2015). doi:10.1007/978-3-319-26762-3_27
15. Lewoniewski, W., Węcel, K., Abramowicz, W.: Quality and importance of wikipedia articles in different languages. In: Dregvaite, G., Damasevicius, R. (eds.) ICIST 2016. CCIS, vol. 639, pp. 613–624. Springer, Cham (2016). doi:10.1007/978-3-319-46254-7_50
16. Rebuschat, P.E., Detmar, M., McEnery, T.: Language learning research at the intersection of experimental, computational and corpus-based approaches, Language Learning (2017)
17. Wu, G., Harrigan, M., Cunningham, P.: Characterizing wikipedia pages using edit network motif profiles. In: Proceedings of the 3rd International Workshop on Search and Mining User-Generated Contents, pp. 45–52. ACM (2011)
18. Lex, E., Voelske, M., Errecalde, M., Ferretti, E., Cagnina, L., Horn, C., Granitzer, M.: Measuring the quality of web content using factual information, In: Proceedings of the 2nd Joint WICOW/AIRWeb Workshop on Web Quality, pp. 7–10. ACM (2012)

Analysis of References Across Wikipedia Languages

Włodzimierz Lewoniewski[✉], Krzysztof Węcel,
and Witold Abramowicz

Poznań University of Economics and Business, Poznań, Poland
{wlodzimierz.lewoniewski,krzysztof.wecel,witold.
abramowicz}@ue.poznan.pl

Abstract. Reliable information sources are important to assess content quality in Wikipedia. Using references readers can verify facts or find more details about described topic. Each Wikipedia article can have over 290 language versions. As articles can be edited independently in any language, even by anonymous users, the information about the same topic may be inconsistent. This also applies to sources that can be found in various language versions of particular article, so the same statement can have different sources. In some cases, Wikipedia users, which speak two or more languages, can transfer information with references between language versions. This paper presents an analysis of using common references in over 10 million articles in several Wikipedia language editions: English, German, French, Russian, Polish, Ukrainian, Belarussian. Also, the study shows the use of similar sources and their number in language sensitive topics.

Keywords: Wikipedia · Reference · Source · Citation

1 Introduction

Wikipedia is a popular large collection of human knowledge. In April, 2017 this free online encyclopedia was the fifth most visited website in the world.[1] Nowadays there are over 44 million articles in almost 300 language versions of Wikipedia. The biggest language version is English, which has more than 5 million articles.

Wikipedia offers an innovative way to read and edit the information online for people around the world. Even anonymous users without confirming their skills and experience can collaborate in articles creation in this community knowledge base.

Despite the fact that Wikipedia is often criticized for poor quality of information, for the last 10 years its articles have been cited in over 80 thousands scientific publications.[2] This is almost 10 times more than number articles citing Encyclopaedia Britannica in scientific publications in the same period.

---

[1] http://www.alexa.com/siteinfo/wikipedia.org.
[2] Information about the number of scientific publications is taken from https://www.scopus.com where search query was *REF(wikipedia.org/wiki)* in works published in 2008–2017.

© Springer International Publishing AG 2017
R. Damaševičius and V. Mikašytė (Eds.): ICIST 2017, CCIS 756, pp. 561–573, 2017.
DOI: 10.1007/978-3-319-67642-5_47

One of the most important quality measures for Wikipedia is verifiability. Different language versions of the same topic in Wikipedia can be created and edited independently. Therefore, there are often differences in quality between various language version of the same article. Wikipedia users who speak several languages, try to translate some content between more and less developed language versions. Often along with the content, users also transfer information about references. Referencing verifiable resources enhances the quality of Wikipedia articles [10].

In this paper we analyze number of references included in Wikipedia articles in various languages, the most popular information sources, number of common references in different pairs of Wikipedia language editions. In order to compare the same references with different description we used the unification method based on special identifiers. In this study we analyze all articles with references from some of the most the developed Wikipedia editions and some less developed ones: English (EN), German (DE), French (FR), Russian (RU), Polish (PL), Ukrainian (UK), and Belarussian (BE).

2   Sources in Wikipedia

Wikipedia articles with high quality must be well-researched and have representative survey of the relevant literature.[3] When adding or editing article content, authors must also add reliable and published sources. As a result, people using the encyclopedia can check where the information comes from and verify the facts described in it.

A large number of Wikipedia articles are unassessed or have low quality grade [1]. Differences between language versions about same topic cause an additional difficulty in assessing the quality of articles.

There is a series of studies that use references for assessing quality of Wikipedia articles. One group of scientific works examined how references affected the articles quality. Experiments showed that number of references and derivatives (e.g. references and articles length ratio) were one of the most important predictors in article quality models [2, 3]. Online service WikiRank[4] together with other features uses the number of references to assess and compare the quality of Wikipedia articles in different languages.

Second group of studies focused on quality of references in Wikipedia. One of the first studies in this direction suggested that Wikipedia articles tend to cite articles in high impact journals such as New England Journal of Medicine, Nature, Science [8]. At the same time number of peer reviewed academic papers in the health sciences which are citing Wikipedia is increasing [4]. References can cover a wide range of subjects, but particularly focused on articles from ecology, evolution and other topics that can enrich the encyclopedia with scholarly sources [6]. More than half of the references used in the history articles of the encyclopedia are internet sources, such as news, media, government websites [7]. If users add references connected with academic publications, then they prefer to use book as a source rather than articles [5]. So,

---

[3] https://en.wikipedia.org/wiki/Wikipedia:Featured_article_criteria.

[4] http://wikirank.net.

Wikipedia is especially valuable due to the potential direct linkages to other primary sources through special identifier such as DOIs or PubMed IDs [9]. Additionally, academic status of work is the most important predictor of its appearance in Wikipedia references [12].

Wikipedia has also developed a set of templates for flagging articles that have not enough references or there are no references at all.[5] That template is the most frequent in English Wikipedia from the over 300 specific quality flaw templates [11]. So, we can conclude that Wikipedia community pays special attention to availability of references in articles.

3 Extraction of References

Using Wikipedia dumps from May, 2017, we have extracted all references from over 10 million articles in 7 language editions (BE, DE, EN, FR, PL, RU, UK).

In wiki-code references are usually placed between special tags $< ref > ...</ref >$.[6] In general, we can divide this references into two groups: with special template and without it. In the case of references without special template they usually have URL of source and some optional description (e.g. title).

References with special templates can have different data describing the source. Here in separate fields we can add information about author(s), title, URL, format, access date, publisher and others. Additionally, these templates can contain special identifiers such as DOI, JSTOR, PMC, PMID, arXiv, ISBN, ISSN, and OCLC. The set of possible parameters depends on the type of templates, which can describe web source, book, journal, news, conference, act and others. It is important to note that each

Table 1. Articles and references count in different language versions of Wikipedia in May 2017.

Lang.	Number of articles	Articles with ref.	Number of references	Unique ref.	Ref. with template	Unique ref. domains
BE	143,023	31,522	111,961	82,295	54,456	22,042
DE	2,057,871	874,370	3,777,825	2,988,443	1,275,773	500,560
EN	5,396,615	3,540,201	25,534,467	18,470,122	19,942,239	1,588,692
FR	1,866,412	818,909	4,510,703	3,364,408	2,789,431	389,588
PL	1,219,709	611,247	2,468,167	1,548,696	2,045,508	184,909
RU	1,391,120	714,599	3,852,470	2,873,069	2,184,470	356,896
UK	693,969	260,913	1,010,965	635,149	567,615	114,109
Total	**12,768,719**	**6,851,761**	**41,266,558**	**29,962,182**	**28,859,492**	**3,156,796**

Source: Own calculation based on Wikipedia dumps.

---

[5] https://en.wikipedia.org/wiki/Template:Unreferenced.

[6] Also can be $< ref\ name="..." > ...</ref >$ or $< ref\ name="..."/>$.

language version of Wikipedia can use own group of templates with own names and set of parameters that describe information sources.

In order to extract information about sources we created own parser, which takes into the account different names of references templates and parameters in each Wikipedia language edition. We investigated about 12,7 million articles (which are not redirects to other articles) and found over 42 million references from over 3 million website domains in 7 language versions. More detailed statistics are placed in Table 1.

Zipfian distribution of domains frequency of sources in each language is shown in Fig. 1.

It is important to note that for references with the same special identifiers we can determine equivalency even though they have different parameters in description (e.g. titles in another languages). We can also unify their URL. For example if reference

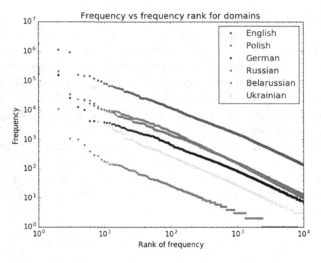

Fig. 1. Zipflaw frequency vs. frequency rank for domains in each language version of Wikipedia

Table 2. Identifiers that used for URL unification of references.

Identifier	Description	New URL
arXiv	arXiv repository identifier	http://arxiv.org/abs/...
DOI	Digital object identifier	http://doi.org/...
ISBN	International Standard Book Number	http://books.google.com/books?vid=ISBN...
ISSN	International Standard Serial Number	https://worldcat.org/ISSN/...
JSTOR	Journal Storage number	https://jstor.org/stable/...
PMC	PubMed Central	https://ncbi.nlm.nih.gov/pmc/articles/PMC...
PMID	PubMed	https://ncbi.nlm.nih.gov/pubmed/...
OCLC	WorldCat's Online Computer Library Center	https://worldcat.org/oclc/...

Table 3. Number of references with particular identifier in Wikipedia articles

Lang.	arXiv	DOI	ISBN	ISSN	JSTOR	PMC	PMID	OCLC
BE	90	1,185	13,656	78	28	53	198	19
DE	2,416	31,014	171,073	12,696	1,591	1,022	3,481	2,671
EN	4,226	1,014,602	1,670,495	79,442	35,709	16,384	52,387	54,995
FR	842	50,381	332,593	25,297	2,045	782	7,406	7,598
PL	577	41,796	245,833	23,319	781	338	11,157	1,131
RU	1,577	33,956	232,427	3,045	785	1,236	5,164	977
UK	301	2,562	37,628	618	96	160	313	400
Total	**10,029**	**1,175,496**	**27,03,705**	**144,495**	**41,035**	**19,975**	**80,106**	**67,791**

Source: own calculations.

have ISBN number "978-3-319-46254-7", we give it URL "https://books.google.com/books?vid=ISBN9783319462547". More detailed information about identifiers which we used to unifying the references is shown in Table 2.

Table 3 present number of unique references with particular identifier in each language version of Wikipedia.

Unification of URLs based on identifiers was used for counting the number of unique references and will be used for comparison of similarity of references in different language versions of Wikipedia articles.

4 Similarity of Sources

In order to examine similarity of sources across different Wikipedia language versions we create three datasets with articles covering different topics (Wiki, Wiki7, Wiki5) and three datasets with language sensitive topics (LST). All data extracted from Wikipedia dumps from May 2017.

4.1 Wiki

We first chose all the articles (about 6.9 million) with references in 7 considered languages. After extraction we had almost 30 million references. Table 4 presents results in a number of common sources on each language intersection.

Table 4. Number of common references used in Wikipedia language versions in Wiki dataset.

Lang.	BE	DE	EN	FR	PL	RU	UK
BE	**82,295**	3,522	19,116	6,127	5,043	47,931	13,100
DE	–	**2,988,443**	345,202	81,572	41,558	69,634	21,097
EN	–	–	**18,470,130**	584,037	244,120	635,546	160,408
FR	–	–	–	**3,364,409**	61,104	118,700	32,470
PL	–	–	–	–	**1,548,696**	71,221	26,022
RU	–	–	–	–	–	**2,873,070**	185,473
UK	–	–	–	–	–	–	**635,149**

Source: own calculations.

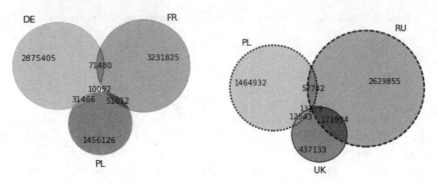

Fig. 2. Unique references overlap between selected language version of Wikipedia. Source: Own calculations.

Table 5. Top 10 most popular reference domains in various Wikipedia language versions in Wiki dataset (Top 100 popular references domains with the number of references in each language version of Wikipedia can be found on page: http://en.lewoniewski.info/2017/top-100-domains-in-wikipedia-references/)

BE	DE	EN	FR
books.google.com	books.google.com	books.google.com	books.google.com
pravo.by	books.google.de	doi.org	doi.org
football.by	spiegel.de	nytimes.com	books.google.fr
doi.org	doi.org	news.bbc.co.uk	worldcat.org
cuetracker.net	welt.de	bbc.co.uk	lemonde.fr
naviny.org	zeit.de	theguardian.com	legifrance.gouv.fr
by.tribuna.com	faz.net	worldcat.org	lefigaro.fr
worldsnooker.com	worldcat.org	news.google.com	insee.fr
web.archive.org	youtube.com	youtube.com	gallica.bnf.fr
gks.ru	sueddeutsche.de	census.gov	interieur.gouv.fr

PL	RU	UK
books.google.com	books.google.com	insee.fr
web.archive.org	doi.org	books.google.com
doi.org	insee.fr	kia.hu
sports-reference.com	billboard.com	w1.c1.rada.gov.ua
archive.is	textual.ru	demo.istat.it
worldcat.org	int.soccerway.com	nsi.bg
stat.gov.pl	lenta.ru	cvk.gov.ua
discogs.com	web.archive.org	pravda.com.ua
allmusic.com	youtube.com	youtube.com
getamap.ordnancesurvey.co.uk	kommersant.ru	web.archive.org

Source: own calculations.

The largest number of references in the English Wikipedia can be explained by the largest number of articles in it. In the next datasets we take equal number of articles in each language. We show unique references overlaps between selected language versions in Fig. 1.

It is noticeable that there are more common sources among Slavic language versions (PL, RU, UK) (Table 5).

Comparing Figs. 2 and 3, we can find that references domains are more international - there are relatively more common across language versions of Wikipedia (Table 6).

Table 6. Number of common references' domains used in Wikipedia language versions in Wiki dataset.

Lang.	BE	DE	EN	FR	PL	RU	UK
BE	**22,042**	10,563	15,393	10,475	9,783	19,030	12,485
DE	–	**500,560**	219,536	104,212	62,595	90,361	41,407
EN	–	–	**1,588,692**	201,601	101,495	183,234	69,437
FR	–	–	–	**389,588**	56,693	86,071	39,426
PL	–	–	–	–	**184,909**	60,130	32,382
RU	–	–	–	–	–	**356,896**	73,254
UK	–	–	–	–	–	–	**114,109**

Source: own calculations.

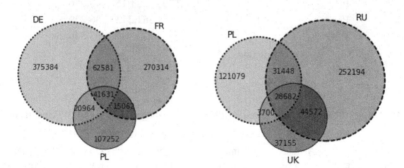

Fig. 3. References' domains overlap between selected language version of Wikipedia. Source: Own calculations.

4.2   Wiki5

In this dataset there are 273,878 articles, that are written in five language versions: DE, EN, FR, PL, RU. Number of articles and extracted references are shown in Table 7.

Table 7. Articles and references count in different language versions of Wikipedia in Wiki5 dataset.

Lang.	Number of articles	Articles with ref.	Number of references	Ref. with template	Unique ref.	Unique ref. domains
DE	273,878	149,664	917,936	326,514	792,077	155,869
EN	273,878	205,503	3,897,533	3,232,357	3,261,656	383,766
FR	273,878	147,655	1,276,342	821,887	1,056,169	148,614
PL	273,878	129,118	745,196	615,556	561,213	83,519
RU	273,878	154,936	1,154,815	712,284	963,545	151,549
Total	**1,369,390**	**786,876**	**7,991,822**	**5,708,598**	**6,634,660**	**923,317**

Source: own calculations.

4.3   Wiki7

In this dataset there are 46,957 articles, that are written in all seven analyzed languages: BE, DE, EN, FR, PL, RU, UK. Number of articles and extracted references are shown on Table 8 (Table 9).

Table 8. Number of common references used in Wikipedia language versions in Wiki5 dataset.

Lang.	DE	EN	FR	PL	RU
DE	**792,077**	90,863	26,797	19,345	31,043
EN	–	**3,261,658**	170,200	104,595	236,229
FR	–	–	**1,056,170**	29,015	49,156
PL	–	–	–	**561,213**	36,239
RU	–	–	–	–	**963,546**

Source: own calculations.

Table 9. Articles and references count in different language versions of Wikipedia in Wiki7 dataset.

Lang.	Number of articles	Articles with ref.	Number of references	Ref. with template	Unique ref.	Unique ref. domains
BE	46,957	10,538	51,387	28,016	43,778	13,497
DE	46,957	27,278	239,520	86,902	217,236	54,640
EN	46,957	37,884	1,089,035	918,726	955,305	152,324
FR	46,957	33,589	415,599	272,618	354,607	61,427
PL	46,957	24,493	203,567	169,139	159,002	31,853
RU	46,957	27,959	353,592	202,034	308,499	65,567
UK	46,957	20,431	111,213	60,023	91,191	26,268
Total	**328,699**	**182,172**	**2,463,913**	**1,737,458**	**2,129,618**	**405,576**

Source: own calculations.

4.4   LST

Additionally to the above analyses, we decided to carry out additional analysis concerning "nationality" of sources. We chose three sub datasets, which described cities in particular country: Poland, Germany, and France. So, these datasets are Language Sensitive. We further chose cities, which were described at least in five languages: DE, EN, FR, PL, RU. As a result we obtained a dataset with articles about 10516 German cities, 10092 French cities, and 904 Polish cities (Table 10).

Table 10. Number of common references used in Wikipedia language versions in Wiki7 dataset.

Lang.	BE	DE	EN	FR	PL	RU	UK
BE	**43,778**	1,378	9,733	2,757	2,637	27,378	6,794
DE	–	**217,236**	17,768	5,467	3,572	5,377	2,585
EN	–	–	**955,305**	44,528	26,139	47,782	21,066
FR	–	–	–	**354,607**	7,262	11,134	4,532
PL	–	–	–	–	**159,002**	8,320	3,711
RU	–	–	–	–	–	**308,500**	28,619
UK	–	–	–	–	–	–	**91,191**

Source: own calculations.

German cities (LST DE)

Similarly to the previous datasets, Table 11 presents number of articles with references and number of references in each language. It is noticeable that German Wikipedia have the highest number of articles with references and the highest total number of references. So, information about German cities is the most verifiable in German Wikipedia.

Table 11. Articles and references count in different language versions of Wikipedia in LST DE dataset.

Lang.	Number of articles	Articles with ref.	Number of references	Ref. with template	Unique ref.	Unique ref. domains
DE	10,516	9,532	64,305	18,893	49,436	16,541
EN	10,516	2,540	11,744	3,168	7,936	3,359
FR	10,516	1,129	2,752	484	1,719	956
PL	10,516	2,805	5,087	1,204	1,572	1,155
RU	10,516	8,820	9,875	292	961	607
Total	**52,580**	**24,826**	**93,763**	**24,041**	**61,624**	**22,618**

Source: own calculations.

From Table 12 we can argue that more common sources have German end English Wikipedia when describing German cities.

Table 12. Number of common references used in Wikipedia language versions in LST DE dataset.

Lang.	DE	EN	FR	PL	RU
DE	**49,436**	1,045	234	80	90
EN	–	**7,936**	77	49	75
FR	–	–	**1,719**	16	24
PL	–	–	–	**1,572**	25
RU	–	–	–	–	**961**

Source: own calculations.

Table 13. Articles and references count in different language versions of Wikipedia in LST FR dataset.

Lang.	Number of articles	Articles with ref.	Number of references	Ref. with template	Unique ref.	Unique ref. domains
DE	10,092	2,568	8,167	3,460	6,959	1,902
EN	10,092	1,738	11,896	5,830	9,652	3,342
FR	10,092	8,763	101,325	52,003	70,817	15,700
PL	10,092	643	1,144	954	497	179
RU	10,092	8,157	38,007	34,844	21,930	1,103
Total	**50,460**	**21,869**	**160,539**	**97,091**	**109,855**	**22,226**

Source: own calculations.

Table 14. Number of common references used in Wikipedia language versions in LST FR dataset.

Lang.	DE	EN	FR	PL	RU
DE	**6,959**	128	368	14	408
EN	–	**9,652**	2,076	10	87
FR	–	–	**70,817**	27	683
PL	–	–	–	**497**	6
RU	–	–	–	–	**21,930**

Source: own calculations.

French cities (LST FR)

Based on Tables 1, 13 and 14 we can make a similar conclusion, that French cities have the most verifiable description in French Wikipedia, and more common references have this language version with English Wikipedia.

Polish cities (LST PL)

Finally, in the case of Polish cities, Table 15 demonstrates similar tendency – Polish Wikipedia have the highest number of references, and therefore is the most prominent for this dataset. However, Table 16 shows that pair EN&PL does not have the biggest number of common references (99) – a little more have EN&FR language version (101).

We can see that in each language sensitive datasets the total number of references is always the biggest in own language. If we look to the biggest number of common sources between two languages, always English version is the first. This could mean that most users that translate content from one language to another often choose English version as a source or a destination.

Table 15. Articles and references count in different language versions of Wikipedia in LST PL dataset.

Lang.	Number of articles	Articles with ref.	Number of references	Ref. with template	Unique ref.	Unique ref. domains
DE	904	608	2,439	387	2,116	932
EN	904	476	2,747	1,930	2,382	1,320
FR	904	253	541	179	472	350
PL	904	904	14,804	9,471	11,098	4,451
RU	904	158	394	151	339	235
Total	**4,520**	**2,399**	**20,925**	**12,118**	**16,407**	**7,288**

Source: own calculations.

Table 16. Number of common references used in Wikipedia language versions in LST PL dataset.

Lang.	DE	EN	FR	PL	RU
DE	**2,116**	81	13	58	9
EN	–	**2,382**	101	99	53
FR	–	–	**472**	37	10
PL	–	–	–	**11,098**	40
RU	–	–	–	–	**339**

Source: own calculations.

5   Conclusions and Future Work

Wikipedia community puts great emphasis on verifiability of information contained in the articles. Using special identifiers we can unify the same references that are present in various Wikipedia editions.

This study shows that different language versions of Wikipedia use common sources in different manner depends on a topic. The biggest number of common references have English and German versions – 345,202. However, we need to take into account total number of articles in these languages – they are the biggest

Wikipedia editions. If we consider only articles that are represented in at least 5 considered languages, than the biggest number of common references have Russian and English Wikipedia editions.

For language sensitive topics we always get the same results – the most verifiable information is available in the respective language. In this case, often this topics have more common references with the biggest language version of Wikipedia – English.

Our future work will be devoted to more in-depth researches about similarity of references. We plan to use some external open citation databases (e.g. WorldCat[7], Google Schoolar[8], Microsoft Academic[9]) to find different data about same sources (URLs, titles, identifiers, etc.). This databases can be also helpful to find information about importance of particular source (e.g. citation index, impact factor). We plan include this analysis to assess the quality of articles and parameters in special templates – infoboxes. This can help to improve the articles quality in less developed language versions of Wikipedia and also enrich other popular open knowledge databases such as DBpedia[10], Wikidata[11], YAGO, Freebase and others.

References

1. Węcel, K., Lewoniewski, W.: Modelling the quality of attributes in wikipedia infoboxes. In: Abramowicz, W. (ed.) BIS 2015. LNBIP, vol. 228, pp. 308–320. Springer, Cham (2015). doi:10.1007/978-3-319-26762-3_27
2. Warncke-Wang, M., Cosley, D., Riedl, J.: Tell me more: an actionable quality model for wikipedia. In: Proceedings of the 9th International Symposium on Open Collaboration (2013)
3. Lewoniewski, W., Węcel, K., Abramowicz, W.: Quality and importance of wikipedia articles in different languages. In: Dregvaite, G., Damasevicius, R. (eds.) ICIST 2016. CCIS, vol. 639, pp. 613–624. Springer, Cham (2016). doi:10.1007/978-3-319-46254-7_50
4. Bould, M.D., Hladkowicz, E.S., Pigford, A.A.E., Ufholz, L.A., Postonogova, T., Shin, E., Boet, S.: References that anyone can edit: review of Wikipedia citations in peer reviewed health science literature. BMJ, vol. 348 (2014)
5. Kousha, K., Thelwall, M.: Are Wikipedia citations important evidence of the impact of scholarly articles and books? J. Assoc. Inf. Sci. Technol. 68(3), 762–779 (2017)
6. Lin, J., Fenner, M.: An analysis of Wikipedia references across PLOS publications. In: Expanding Impacts and Metrics, An ACM Web Science Conference 2014 Workshop, pp. 23–26 (2014)
7. Luyt, B., Tan, D.: Improving Wikipedia's credibility: References and citations in a sample of history articles. J. Am. Soc. Inform. Sci. Technol. 61(4), 715–722 (2010)
8. Nielsen, F.Å.: Scientific citations in wikipedia. First Monday 12(8) (2007)
9. Page, R.D.: Wikipedia as an encyclopaedia of life. Org. Divers. Evol. 10(4), 343–349 (2010)

---

[7] http://www.worldcat.org.

[8] https://scholar.google.com.

[9] https://academic.microsoft.com/.

[10] http://www.dbpedia.org.

[11] https://www.wikidata.org.

10. Mesgari, M., Okoli, C., Mehdi, M., Nielsen, F.Å., Lanamäki, A.: "The sum of all human knowledge": A systematic review of scholarly research on the content of Wikipedia. J. Assoc. Inf. Sci. Technol. **66**(2), 219–245 (2015)
11. Anderka, M.: Analyzing and Predicting Quality Flaws in User-generated Content: The Case of Wikipedia, Doctoral dissertation, Bauhaus-Universität Weimar Germany (2013)
12. Teplitskiy, M., Lu, G., Duede, E.: Amplifying the impact of open access: Wikipedia and the diffusion of science. J. Assoc. Inf. Sci. Technol. **68**(9), 2116–2127 (2016)

Persian Pronoun Resolution Using Data Driven Approaches

Aria Nourbakhsh and Mohammad Bahrani[✉]

Languages and Linguistics Center, Sharif University of Technology, Tehran, Iran
aria.nourbakhsh@mehr.sharif.ir, bahrani@sharif.edu

Abstract. Pronoun resolution is one of the challenges of natural language processing (NLP). The proposed solutions range from heuristic rule-based to machine learning data driven approaches. In this article, we follow a previous machine learning approach on Persian pronoun anaphora resolution. The primary goal of this paper is to improve the results, mainly by extracting more balanced data through using heuristic rules in instance sampling, and utilizing more relevant features in classification. Using PCAC2008 dataset, we consider noun phrase structure as a way to extract more suitable training data. Incorporated features include syntactic and semantic information. Finally, we train and test different classifiers in order to find and compare the results. The best result is achieved by using the C4.5 decision tree classifier. The results show a significant improvement over the previous work by achieving 75% F-measure compared to 45%. An analysis of extracted features and their contribution are also discussed.

Keywords: Pronoun resolution · Coreference resolution · Machine learning algorithms · Persian pronouns

1 Introduction

Every natural language discourse contains mentions about entities, which are referred to in different ways. Some of the referring expressions are definite and indefinite noun phrases, demonstratives, and pronouns [1]. These entities sometimes point to the same entity in the real world. The task of coreference resolution is to extract those entities which have the same reference. In the same way, pronouns are words that substitute for nouns, and in pronoun resolution, we seek to find the reference of pronouns. As a result, pronoun resolution can be thought as a sub-task of coreference resolution. Perhaps, the main difference, aside from the focus on pronouns in pronoun resolution, is that there is usually a second phase to extract coreference chains or clusters in a given document or dataset.

Pronoun resolution has many applications in some of the main area of NLP, including Machine Translation, Text Summarization and Question Answering. Proposed solutions for pronoun resolution range from purely heuristic (e.g. [2]) to statistical methods, by using supervised classification [3] or unsupervised methods (e.g. [4]). In this paper, we tried to continue a previous study on Persian pronoun resolution [5] mainly by improving instance sampling and incorporating different features.

© Springer International Publishing AG 2017
R. Damaševičius and V. Mikašytė (Eds.): ICIST 2017, CCIS 756, pp. 574–585, 2017.
DOI: 10.1007/978-3-319-67642-5_48

This paper is organized as follows: in Sect. 2, we will discuss some related works. In Sect. 3, we will describe characteristics of pronouns in Persian and the dataset we used. In Sect. 4, we will elaborate on how we sampled our instances. Section 5 is about extracted feature vectors. In Sect. 6, we will discuss the results and some methods of reduction of negative instances and finally, in Sect. 7, we will reach our conclusions and state some guidelines for future studies.

2 Related Work

Attempts to solve the task of pronoun resolution dates back to 70's and early days of Natural Language Processing. Most of the earlier works were rule-based approaches using syntactic and semantic information. Since 90s, machine learning approaches have become a trend; many of them were using supervised learning methods. In re-cent years, unsupervised learning also has gotten more attentions. As we can see, there is a big and diverse history of works in this area. In reviewing, we mention some of the works that are more related to what we do in this article. This includes those which are exclusively done for the resolution of pronouns in Persian.

2.1 Supervised Coreference Resolution

Aone and Bennet proposed one of the first classification methods for coreference resolution [6]. They labeled pairs of nouns as coreferent and non-coreferent NPs. These labeled instances were represented by their respective feature vectors. Those features counted to 66 including word level, syntactic role, semantic class and positional information. Soon et al., extended Aone and Bennet" work by changing instance sampling method, namely by extracting negative instances which were between an NP and its antecedent [7]. They also created a subsystem for extracting nested noun phrases. In their work, they used nearest first method that chooses coreferent NPs which are nearest to a positive labeled NP. Ng and Cardie followed Soon et al. steps and improved their work, mainly in three ways [8]. First, they changed instance sampling by choosing the most confident reference for an NP. Second, they used different features and finally, they changed nearest first to best first method in which coreferent NPs were chosen not by being the nearest one labeled as positive in clas-sification, but by choosing the most probable coreferent. The above works are cate-gorized in mention-pair model, because the training and testing data are created by pairing an NP (i.e. pronouns in our work) with another NP as candidate and the feature vector is extracted for these pairs. Similar approaches are common in other languages. For example [9] in Portuguese and [10] in Basque and in some works on Persian which we will discuss in the next subsection.

As mention-pair model works only on pairs of an NP and a candidate, classifier does not consider the relation of these two with other pairs of instances. For solving this problem, two other methods are proposed. One is by Denis and Baldrige in which they used supervised ranking approach [11]. In this approach all candidates for a pronoun are evaluated at the same time. Another method proposed by Yang et al. named twin candidate model in which every training instance is based on features of a pronoun and two candidates at the same time [12].

2.2 Pronoun and Coreference Resolution in Persian

Persian pronouns have some characteristics that make their resolution difficult. Among them are the lack of gender and confusion for number. Persian has no attribute for gender distinction, and for number, some pronouns are used for both singular or plural antecedent in real-world usages of them, regardless of their categorization in traditional grammar books [13].

A few published works can be found on pronoun and coreference resolution of Persian. One is a rule-based method proposed by Fallahi and Shamsfard in which they extracted some heuristic rules for pronoun resolution, including objective and subjective forms of a pronoun which are morphemes concatenated to a noun (clitics) [14]. The reported results were 90% precision and 95% recall. One could find that the proposed rules work for some simple sentences and it does not work on more complicated sentences, structures and noun phrases.

Moosavi and Ghassem-sani made the first attempt for resolution of pronouns in Persian by ways of machine learning approaches [5]. They used mention-pair model in training and testing their model. Feature selection was based on [11], without using extensive syntactic and semantic information. Their returned results are relatively low. One can find some reasons for this unpromising outcome. First of all, they didn't take the structure of noun phrases of Persian into account and, moreover, they used every noun and noun phrases in a given sentence as a candidate. Secondly, they did not use syntactic and semantic information. The best result they achieved was 45% by using C4.5 decision tree. They also used ranking approach by using maximum entropy ranker. Although its result was better than normal maximum entropy classifier, it was still below the result of C4.5 decision tree.

The most recent work, which was proposed by Nazaridoust et al., was concerned with coreference resolution in Persian [15]. They developed a coreference annotated corpus called Lutos. They also used mention-pair model and used features that were easily obtainable from the POS-tagged corpus. Similarly, they did not take syntactic and semantic information into account. Their best result was by Neural Network, and its F-measure was 39.4%.

3   Data Set

In this task, we used a corpus specifically annotated for pronoun resolution called PCAC2008 dataset [5]. This corpus consists of 31 documents from Persian Text Corpus (Peykare) [16] which are POS-tagged on the level of words. The perplexity of the Persian Text Corpus is 198 [24]. In average each documents contains about 6600 words. The entire corpus has about 206000 words and its documents belong to different topics including economics, politics, psychology, art, story, etc. In this corpus, 2006 pronouns are marked with their nearest antecedents. This data set does not include pronouns that are in form of clitics. Annotated pronouns include personal pronouns, reflexive pronouns, reciprocal pronouns and demonstrative pronouns. It should be noted that some of the annotated linguistic entities were not pronouns, and in fact, they were demonstrative adjectives. So, we rightfully ignored them in our instance sampling that we are going to explain extensively in the next section.

4 Instance Sampling

In this article, we used mention-pair model as our model for classification. We paired pronouns with their candidates in range of three sentences with regard to punctuations or 9 sentences with regard to verbs, taking verb as sentence boundary. In this way, we also included some candidates before the antecedent. Intuitively, it seems to model the relation of pronoun and candidates better, instead of just choosing noun phrases that are between a pronoun and its antecedent. For improving the results, we needed more efficient and balanced dataset. To achieve this aim, we used some heuristics in extracting nested NPs. In this section, we review some of the heuristics that we used.

4.1 Nested Noun Phrases

Noun phrases may have dependents. These dependents are pre and post modifiers which include determiners, adjectives, other noun phrases, prepositional phrases (PP), relative clauses and etc. [17]. Among these dependents only heads of other noun phrases, nouns inside PPs and relative clauses can be different entities that may stand as a candidate. By this explanation, four different NPs can be extracted from the noun phrase that follows:

بچه‌های خوب کلاس زبان مدرسه خاتم

Bachehaye xube kelase zabane madreseye xatam.
Good students of language class of Khatam school
The nested NPs are namely:

بچه‌های خوب کلاس زبان مدرسه خاتم

Bachehaye xube kelase zabane madaresye xatam
Good students of language class of Khatam school

کلاس زبان مدرسه خاتم

kelase zabane madreseye xatam
Language class of Khatam school

مدرسه خاتم

Madreseye xatam.
Khatam school

Compound prepositions that include a noun in them, should not be considered as a candidate for a pronoun. This is a problem with this corpus that arises from its POS-tagging.

We used Hazm dependency parser [18] for processing and extracting noun phrases. It should be noted that due to limitation and experimental nature of this article, we used extensive manual annotation in noun phrase extraction.

4.2 Some Heuristics in Instance Sampling

We use some heuristic rules that can be applied to instance sampling. These heuristics can be thought of as when an NP never stands as an antecedent for a pronoun or when some NPs together can be taken as a single candidate. These rules will be explained here:

Coordinated nouns, whether they are joined with "and", "or" or ",", are treated as one candidate.

شیرین و فرهاد آمدند
Shirin va Farhad amadand.
Shirin and Farhad came.

In the above example, the coordinated nouns *Shirin and Farhad* are treated as a single candidate.

If two coordinated nouns have a noun or nouns as their child(ren) in their syntactic representation tree, that noun or nouns should be extracted individually as candidate.

پدر و مادر دانش‌آموزان آمدند.
pedar va madare daneshamouzan amadand.
Father and mother of the students came.

In the above example, the coordinated NP, *father and mother*, and their child, *students* can be assumed as candidates for a given pronoun.

But it should be noted that if every one of those noun phrases have their own genitive dependent, those genitive dependents are not extracted as a candidate.

پدر شیرین و مادر فرهاد به مدرسه آمدند.
Pedare shirin va madare farhad be madrese amadand.
Shirin's father and Farhad's mother came to school.

In the above example, although *Shirin* and *Farhad* are genitive dependent for their respective nouns, the whole noun phrase *Shirin's father and Farhad's mother* is extracted as a single candidate.

Noun phrases that are joined to a pronoun and are in genitive relation (those nouns which govern the pronoun in a representation tree) are never going to be candidates for that pronoun.

به خانه او رفتیم.
Be xaneye ou raftim.
We went to his/her house.

In the above example, *house* cannot stand as a candidate for the pronoun that it governs.

Appositives, even if they include multiple nouns, are treated as a single candidate.

Using these heuristics, we manage to reduce extracted instances enormously. As a comparison to [5], from an example sentence that they managed to extract 13 instances, we extracted only 4 instances.

It should be noted that we ignore cataphoric relations as well as second person pronouns. For a pronoun that its antecedent is a reflexive pronoun, both the reflexive pronoun and reflexive pronoun's antecedent are added as positive instances of the pronoun.

Incorporating these strategies, from 2006 annotated pronoun/antecedent we obtained 1944 positive instances, which were 26.58% of the whole extracted data, com-pared to 2.8% positive instances in the previous study.

5 Feature Set

In machine learning tasks, extracting related and useful features is a very important step. We take features used by [5] which most of them were identical to [11] with minor differences, and add some new ones or alter some of the others. These features can be categorized into 4 categories: morphological features, syntactic features, semantic features and statistical features. Features like syntactic and semantic role and semantic class are among the most important features that we extract. These features describe the pronoun, candidate and the relation between the two. Here is a list of the features used in this work and their respective values. The values may be true or false, multiple values or numerical values.

p_resip: Reciprocal pronoun: T-F

p_pers: Personal pronoun: T-F

p_firsec: First person pronoun: T-F

p_third: Third person pronoun: T-F

p_refl: Reflexive pronoun: T-F

p_num: The pronoun number: sing-pl-com

p_peyro: The pronoun is in a dependent sentence and its candidate is in the main sentence: T-F

p_func: The grammatical function of the pronoun: Multiple values (e.g. Subject, Object, …)

p_hfunc: The grammatical function of the highest node of the noun phrase that governs the pronoun: Multiple values (e.g. Subject, Object, …)

c_func: The grammatical function of the candidate: Multiple values (e.g. Subject, Object, …)

c_hfunc: The grammatical function of the highest node of the noun phrase that governs the candidate: Multiple values (e.g. Subject, Object, …)

c_num: The number of the candidate: sing - pl - coor

c_hcoor: The head of the pronoun is in a coordinate structure with the highest node of the NP candidate: T-F

c_sem: The semantic class of the candidate: Multiple values (e.g. location, orga-nization, time, animate, …)

c_prop: The candidate is a proper noun: T-F

c_quant: The candidate has a quantifier: T-F

c_conj: The pronoun is in a relative clause that describes the candidate: T-F

c_quote: The candidate is the narrator of a quoted sentence: T-F

c_gr: The candidate is a plural name (e.g. team, army, ...): T-F

c_hum: The candidate is human: T-F

c_dem: The candidate has demonstrative: T-F

c_sfunc: The semantic role of the candidate: Multiple values (e.g. agent, theme,...)

c_rec: The candidate is the nearest noun phrase to the pronoun: F-T

c_distc: The candidate-pronoun distance with number of candidate(s) between the two: Nominal value

c_distv: The candidate-pronoun distance with number of verb(s) between the two: Nominal value

c_dists: The candidate-pronoun distance with number of punctuations (dot) between the two: Nominal value

c_hcount: The frequency of the candidate" head in the entire document: Numerical value

c_hlcount: The frequency of the root of candidate's head in the entire document: Numerical value

c_rhcount: The frequency of the candidate" head from the beginning up to the candidate in the document: Numerical value

c_rhlcount: The frequency of the root of candidate's head in the document from the beginning up to the candidate in the document: Numerical value

In morphological perspective, some pronouns that can have both of singular and plural antecedents are distinguished with *com* value for the feature *p_num*. The value of the feature *c_num* for candidates that are coordinated with conjunctions is *coor*. If the antecedent of a given pronoun is a pronoun that points to a human antecedent, then the feature *c_hum* will be true.

6 Evaluation and Results

Like many other NLP tasks, we need a criterion to show the results. We use Precision, Recall and F-measure for positive instances. We use Weka [19] to train and test our classifiers. All evaluations are done with 10-fold cross validation.

Seven different classifiers used for binary classification, four of which were identical to the classifiers used in [5] for the sake of comparison, namely C4.5 decision tree, Maximum entropy, Perceptron, and SVM. Also, the results of three other learning algorithms including Random Forest, k-NN and SMO are reported here. Reports of using Random Forest can be found in [10] with high F-measure of 0.68 just below Perceptron as the best result. A variation of k-NN (TiMBL) is also used in [20] outperforming Maximum Entropy and SVM in some cases. Also, SMO algorithm has good results in our experiments and we decided to include it for comparison.

Although the results are not directly comparable with [5], as different strategies we take into account for this task and remove high distance relations from the data, it is still viable to compare the results with [5].

It can be seen from Table 1 that C4.5 has the highest F-measure of 75.2%. This is mainly a result of the nature of extracted features, as most of them have discrete values. Furthermore, significant gain in recall for all the classifiers is obvious in comparison with Table 2, resulting in higher F-measures for all of them. This is due to having a more balanced dataset. Maximum Entropy which had the lowest F-measure in [5], now with 64.6% has gotten higher result than SVM.

Table 1. Results of different classifiers for positive instances

Classifier	Precision	Recall	F-measure
Decision tree C4.5	78.8	72.8	75.2
Maximum entropy	71	59.3	64.6
Perceptron	78	60.1	67.9
SVM	77.1	33.7	46.9
Random forest	80.5	59.8	68.6
k-NN	71.5	67.7	69.5
SMO	74.2	58.4	65.4

Table 2. results from Moosavi and Ghassem-Sani [5]

Classifier	Precision	Recall	F-measure
Decision tree C4.5	75.99	31.7	44.73
Maximum entropy	19.92	4.017	6.68
Perceptron	49.64	27.47	35.36
SVM	79.12	17	27.98

6.1   Using Semantic Information in Pre-Processing

Pre-processing data in order to have a more balanced dataset is common for this task whether it is a heuristic rule-based [21] or machine learning based anaphora resolution [22]. In this section we remove some of the pronoun/candidate pairs with two semantic rules:

1- Candidates which are labeled as False for *c_hum* feature are deleted for personal pronouns.
2- Human Antecedents are removed for demonstrative pronoun « آن» ("An", that)

After pre-processing with these filters, the ratio of positive to whole instances changed to 36% from 26%. Obtained results from this new dataset are demonstrated in Table 3.

We can see that except for C4.5, all the other classifiers gain a minor improvement compared to Table 1. One reason can be that semantic category already had a significant contribution in selecting the right antecedent, and the second reason is that in some documents of the corpus, personification was used in stories, and it led to removal of some of the positive data. These problems show the importance of having a training and testing data that belongs to specific genera.

Table 3. results after execution of pre-processing filters

Classifier	Precision	Recall	F measure
Decision tree C4.5	78.1	69	73.3
Maximum entropy	70.9	61.2	65.7
Perceptron	72.1	64	67.8
SVM	79	37.7	51.1
Random forest	78.8	64.9	71.2
k-NN	72.1	70.2	70.6
SMO	72.2	60.7	66

Removing negative data up to a certain point randomly, is another common practice in anaphora resolution [22]. After removing negative data from the last stage, we removed further negative instances to reach 1:1 ratio between negative and positive instances. The results are as in table below (Table 4):

Table 4. Results after achieving 1:1 ratio between positive and negative instances

Classifier	Precision	Recall	F measure
Decision tree C4.5	80.4	77.3	78.7
Maximum entropy	75.5	74.9	75.2
Perceptron	76.3	77.8	77
SVM	79.2	46.6	58.7
Random forest	78.9	79.4	79.1
k-NN	77.6	77.6	77.6
SMO	75.5	74.6	75.3

Improved results are expected when we compare to Table 1. However, it should be considered that the results are achieved at a cost for negative instances. For example, the F-measure of negative data for C4.5 decision tree has declined from 91.3 to 79.4. It is also the case for the other classifiers. It means that if we remove more negative data, their results will decline too, which is not a desirable outcome.

6.2 Feature Contribution

One way to assess the contribution of every single feature is by running classification with a single feature once at a time, as it is done in [7]. We do the same by running the classification with the decision tree algorithm as it obtained the highest results among the other algorithms.

Among these features, Feature c_quote has gotten a very high precision and a very low recall. This is because most of the first-person personal pronouns are distinguished by this feature, and it may lead to overfitting. c_spro also has gotten a very high precision. The explanation can be that it is very probable that two same pronouns, which are near each other, are coreferent.

c_hum and *c_sem* have high scores and somehow congruent for both precision and recall. It can be inferred that they are important factors in pronoun resolution in Persian. Even in [23] it can be seen that the *proper noun* feature had a high contribution. It can be reasoned that a proper noun has some kind of semantic meaning in which it refers to a human being most of the time. As a result, semantic features are very important in resolution of pronouns in Persian. Other features that are not in Table 5, have gotten zero scores for precision and recall.

Table 5. Results from running classification by one feature

Feature	Precision	Recall	F measure
c_quote	73.4	2.4	4.7
c_sem	51.4	70.1	59.3
c_prop	52.6	23.1	32.1
c_spro	87.7	17.7	29.5
c_hcoor	29.4	0.03	0.05
c_conj	59	5.5	10
c_hum	54.4	61.5	57.7
c_sfunc	60	31.6	41.4
c_hcount	65.7	30.5	41.7
c_hlcount	66.4	27.3	38.7
c_rhcount	56	20.1	29.5
c_rhlcount	58.9	13.1	21.5

7 Conclusion and Future Works

This study is meant to improve another research in pronoun resolution in Persian. It can be concluded from this study that the method of sampling can be very crucial for reaching more balanced data set. The importance of semantic information in resolution of pronouns in Persian is another factor that can be concluded from this research.

We reported the results of 7 different machine learning classifiers. Decision tree learning classifier seems suitable for this task as it obtains the highest result in the current study and Moosavi and Ghassem-Sani's work [5].

There remains some area to improve pronoun resolution in Persian. Resolution of zero pronouns is one of them. Persian is a pro-drop language, and it can lead to high distance relation between pronoun and its antecedent. The consequence is the introduction of so much noise to the data set. We ignored these high distance relations.

Another important step is the development of automatic tools for NP extraction, robust NER and syntactic and semantic role labeling. In this task we did most of the annotation for these features manually which is time consuming and is not a proper approach for automatic pronoun resolution systems.

Finally, looking at the data, we may find that different genera require different training data, particularly if we want to use semantic class of a noun for pre-processing the data.

References

1. Jurafsky, D., Martin, J.H.: Speech and Language Processing: An Introduction to Natural Language Processing, Computational Linguistics and Speech Recognition. Prentice-Hall, New Jersey (2000)
2. Hobbs, J.R.: Resolving pronoun references. Lingua **44**(4), 311–338 (1978)
3. Ng, V.: Supervised noun phrase coreference research: The first fifteen years. In: Proceedings of the 48th Annual Meeting of the Association for Computational Linguistics, pp. 1396–1411 (2010)
4. Charniak, E., Elsner, M.: EM works for pronoun anaphora resolution. In: Proceedings of the 12th Conference of the European Chapter of the Association for Computational Linguistics, pp. 148–156 (2009)
5. Moosavi, N.S., Ghassem-Sani, G.: A ranking approach to Persian pronoun resolution. In: Advances in Computational Linguistics. Research in Computing Science 41, 169–180 (2009)
6. Aone, C., Bennett, S.W.: Applying machine learning to anaphora resolution. In: Wermter, S., Riloff, E., Scheler, G. (eds.) IJCAI 1995. LNCS, vol. 1040, pp. 302–314. Springer, Heidelberg (1996). doi:10.1007/3-540-60925-3_55
7. Soon, W.M., Ng, H.T., Lim, D.C.Y.: A machine learning approach to coreference resolution of noun phrases. Comput. Linguis. **27**(4), 521–544 (2001)
8. Ng, V., Cardie, C.: Improving machine learning approaches to coreference resolution. In: Proceedings of the 40th Annual Meeting on Association for Computational Linguistics, pp. 104–111 (2002)
9. Cuevas, R.R.M., Paraboni, I.: A machine learning approach to portuguese pronoun resolution. In: Geffner, H., Prada, R., Machado Alexandre, I., David, N. (eds.) IBERAMIA 2008. LNCS, vol. 5290, pp. 262–271. Springer, Heidelberg (2008). doi:10.1007/978-3-540-88309-8_27
10. Arregi, O., Ceberio, K., Díaz de Illarraza, A., Goenaga, I., Sierra, B., Zelaia, A.: A first machine learning approach to pronominal anaphora resolution in basque. In: Kuri-Morales, A., Simari, Guillermo R. (eds.) IBERAMIA 2010. LNCS, vol. 6433, pp. 234–243. Springer, Heidelberg (2010). doi:10.1007/978-3-642-16952-6_24
11. Denis, P., Baldridge, J.: A ranking approach to pronoun resolution. In: IJCAI, pp. 1588–1593 (2007)
12. Yang, X., Su, J., Tan, C.L.: A twin-candidate model for learning-based anaphora resolution. Comput. Linguist. **34**(3), 327–356 (2008)
13. Anvari, H., Givi, H.A.: Persian Grammar Book. Fatemi Cultural Institute, Tehran, Iran (2006). (in Persian)
14. Fallahi, F., Shamsfard, M.: Recognizing anaphora reference in Persian sentences. Int. J. Comput. Sci. Issues **8**, 324–329 (2011)
15. Nazaridoust, M., Bidgoli, B.M., Nazaridoust, S.: Co-reference resolution in Farsi corpora. In: Jamshidi, M., Kreinovich, V., Kacprzyk, J. (eds.) Advance Trends in Soft Computing, pp. 155–162. Springer, Cham (2014)
16. Bijankhan, M., Seikhzadeghan, J., Bahrani, M., Ghayoomi, M.: Lessons from creation of a Persian written corpus: Peykare. Lang. Resour. Eval. J. **45**(2), 143–164 (2011)
17. Samaei, S.M.: Noun phrase processing. Inf. Sci. **18**, 34–41 (2002). (In Persian)
18. www.sobhe.ir/hazm/. Retrieved December 2015
19. Hall, M., Frank, E., Holmes, G., Pfahringer, B., Reutemann, P., Witten, I.H.: The WEKA data mining software: an update. ACM SIGKDD Explor. Newsl. **11**(1), 10–18 (2009)

20. Nøklestad, A.: A Machine Learning Approach to Anaphora Resolution Including Named Entity Recognition, PP Attachment Disambiguation, and Animacy Detection, Ph.D. thesis, Faculty of Humanities, University of Oslo (2009)
21. Lappin, S., Leass, H.J.: An algorithm for pronominal anaphora resolution. Comput. Linguist. **20**(4), 535–561 (1994)
22. Wunsch, H., Kübler, S., Cantrell, R.: Instance sampling methods for pronoun resolution. In: RANLP 2009, pp. 478–483 (2009)
23. Moosavi, N.S.: Using Machine Learning Approaches for Persian Pronoun Resolution, Ms.C. thesis, Faculty of Computer Engineering. Sharif University of Technology, Tehran, Iran (2009). (In Persian)
24. Bahrani, M., Sameti, H.: Building statistical language models for Persian continuous speech recognition systems using the Peykare corpus. Int. J. Comput. Process. Lang. **23**(1), 1–20 (2011)

Information Technology Applications:
Special Session on Internet-of-Things in
Mobility Applications

Channel Dependability of the ATM Communication Network Based on the Multilevel Distributed Cloud Technology

Igor Kabashkin[(✉)]

Transport and Telecommunication Institute, Riga, Latvia
kiv@tsi.lv

Abstract. Air Traffic Management (ATM) systems represent essential infrastructure that is critical for flight safety. Voice communication system (VCS) on the base of embedded cloud technology is a vital part of modern air traffic control operations. In the paper the dependability of VCS based on the multilevel distributed cloud technology is discussed. Mathematical model of the channel reliability for this system is developed. Different strategies for operation of VCS hardware within the embedded clouds and boundary value of reliability parameters for automatics are analysed.

Keywords: Reliability · Dependability · Air Traffic Management · Cloud technology · Communication network

1 Introduction

Air Traffic Management (ATM) systems represent essential infrastructure that is critical for flight safety. Communication between air traffic controllers and pilots remains a vital part of air traffic control operations, and communication problems can result in hazardous situations.

Voice ATM communications include all voice applications used for the purposes of Air Traffic Management (air-ground communications, co-ordination and transfer, emergency, search and rescue, flow management, capacity planning). ATM voice communications covers intra- and inter- centre communications and also ensures the connectivity between the centres and the ground based radio stations on the ground leg of the air-ground communications between controllers and pilots [1].

The telecom industry has undergone drastic changes over the last few decades, from a service only able to deliver voice capabilities, to a service where voice is one of a large number of features delivered across a network. These changes have accumulated to the point where another major change is imminent, a change to an all-Internet Protocol (IP) infrastructure. This change is already happening, but with Time Division Multiplexing (TDM) technology still being used for the majority of voice communications today, it may be further away than first anticipated.

R. Damaševičius and V. Mikašytė (Eds.): ICIST 2017, CCIS 756, pp. 589–600, 2017.
DOI: 10.1007/978-3-319-67642-5_49

Traditionally, voice communication system (VCS) solutions were based on a centralized architecture centered around a TDM-based voice switch constituting a single physical entity located in a specific place. In contrast to this, the modern VCS solutions follow a modern distributed cloud-based approach typical for IP-based solutions [1]. Voice switching functionality is a built-in capability of each deployed communication component (telephony and radio gateways, VCS gateways, radio servers and others).

The ATM voice communication system on the base of cloud technology includes set of human-machine voice interface (VoI) for air traffic controllers and set of VCS monoblocks (VCSM) with main and redundant radio stations and health and usage monitoring systems for utilize data collection and analysis techniques to help ensure availability of all VCS components (Fig. 1).

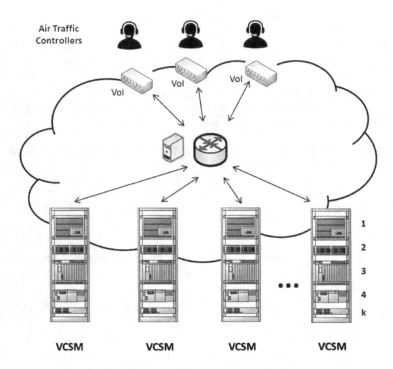

Fig. 1. Cloud-based ATM voice communication system

In practice, the VCS equipment has a modular architecture. Each VCSM includes $i = 1, \ldots k$ independent modules (Fig. 1). In this case the modern VCS components can be distributed like building blocks within the frames of embedded sub clouds of IP infrastructure to achieve more flexibility and to provide additional resilience against failures (Fig. 2). The resulting system is a scalable, fault-tolerant solution for VCS modules switching based on state-of-the-art IP network technology.

In the paper dependability of such ATM voice communication system based on the multilevel distributed embedded cloud technology is discussed.

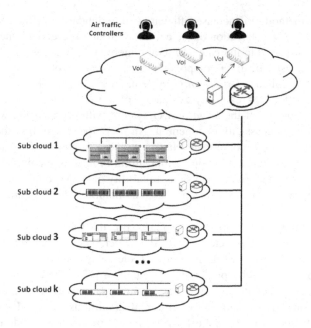

Fig. 2. ATM voice communication system with embedded sub clouds and CS architecture

The rest of this paper is organized as follows. In Sect. 2 some important works in the study area are reviewed. In Sect. 3 the main definitions and assumptions are presented and a model of ATM communication network reliability on the base of VCS multilevel distributed embedded cloud technology is proposed. In Sect. 4 the conclusions are presented.

2 Related Works

The increasing number of flights is a big challenge and it is expected that the current ATM system reaches its capacity limits within the next years in Europe and the US, the world's regions with the highest aircraft densities. Therefore, two major projects have been initiated with the final goal to modernize ATM: SESAR (Single European Sky ATM Research) in Europe [2] and NextGen (Next Generation National Airspace System) in the US. Both projects are globally harmonized under the framework of the International Civil Aviation Organization [3].

In this context, the future radio system infrastructure will consist of a mix of access technologies, each with its own communication elements at the aircraft side (airborne embedded cloud) and its own ground infrastructure (ground embedded clouds) integrated in common frame of internet of things (IoT).

Voice ATM communications include all voice applications used for the purposes of Air Traffic Management. The reliability of traditional VCS with duplicated channels is well studied in the literature [4, 5].

One of the methods to increase efficiency of redundancy in the structures with identical elements is the allocation of the common group of reserve elements. The term *k-out-of-n* system is used to indicate an *n*-component system that works (or is "good") if and only if at least *k* of the *n* components work (or are good).

This system is called a *k-out-of-n:G* system. The works [6–8] provide improved versions of the method for reliability evaluation of the *k-out-of-n:G* system. The work [9] provides an analysis of the *k-out-of-n:G* system with components whose lifetime distributions are not necessarily exponential. An *n*-component system that fails if and only if at least *k* of the *n* components fail is called a *k-out-of-n:F* system [10]. The *k-out-of-n* system structure finds wide applications in telecommunication systems [4, 11]. This model can be used for analysis of reliability of ATM communication network with *k* controllers and *n* radio stations provided availability of communication channels (CC).

In real conditions it is important to know not the reliability of communication network at whole but each selected CC for controller. The channel reliability problem in standby system consisting of independent elements with some units used as a universal component standby pool is investigated in [12]. The reliability of selected communication channel with common set of standby radio stations in the network with periodical sessions of communications for real conditions of ATM communication network is discussed in [13]. In the [14] the model of repairable redundant communication network of ATM system with set of common elements with one single algorithm of radio stations management is developed.

The embedded cloud is about connecting the edge devices to the IT infrastructure and developing a new genre of applications that can make macro-level decisions about the real-world environment and offer value added services [15].

In the book [16] the failure mode effects analysis for canonical configuration of redundant services by pool of mono cloud date centers is described. The model for definition of availability of services protected via client-initiated recovery based on the Markov client-initiated recovery model is proposed.

In the paper [17] the reliability of ATM voice communication system on the base of mono cloud technology includes set of VCS monoblocks with the main and redundant radio stations and health and usage monitoring systems for utilize data collection and analysis techniques to help ensure availability of all VCS components is analysed.

In this paper dependability of such ATM voice communication system based on the multilevel distributed embedded cloud technology is discussed.

3   Model Formulation and Solution

The following symbols have been used to develop equations for the models:

λ – Failure Rate of radio station with VCSM
μ – Repair Rate of radio station with VCSM
q_s – The probability of a switch failure
m – Number of CC in VCS and number of main radio stations with VCSM
n – Number of redundant radio stations with VCSM
$N = m + n$ – Total number of radio stations with VCSM

l	– Number of repair bodies
γ	$= \lambda/\mu, \; \omega = \gamma/l$
k	– Number of modules in VCSM and number of distributed embedded sub clouds
$x_i, i = \overline{1,k}$	– Number of identical modules in each i embedded sub cloud
A	– Channel availability of VCS
$U = 1 - A$	– Channel unavailability of VCS
Q	– Unavailability of single radio station with VCSM
q	– The probability of one module failure in single radio station with VCSM

We will make the assumption that the reliability characteristics of all VCSM modules are identical: $\lambda_i = \lambda_0$ and $\mu_i = \mu_0$ for $i = \overline{1,k}$. There are two types of switching for modules within the distributed embedded sub clouds: architecture with one common switch (CS) for all modules of one sub cloud (Fig. 2) and architecture with individual switches (IS) for each module of one sub cloud (Fig. 3).

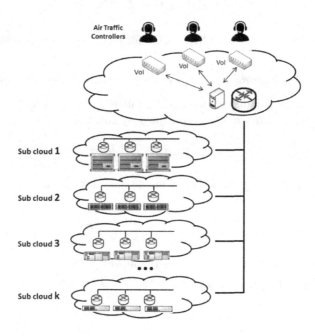

Fig. 3. ATM voice communication system with embedded sub clouds and IS architecture

Let us determine the reliability of the VCS for the case when number of modules in all embedded sub clouds is identical and equal to the total number of radio stations with VCSM: $x_1 = x_2 = \ldots = x_k = m + n$.

In the [13] it is shown that for the system with cloud-based voice communication system and with mono block architecture of radio stations (Fig. 1) for highly reliable systems (for which the condition $N\omega \ll 1$ is realized) the channel unavailability of VCS is defined by the formula

$$U = \begin{cases} \frac{N!l!}{m!l!}\omega^{n+1}, 1 \leq l \leq n \\ \binom{m}{N}\frac{1}{n+1}\gamma^{n+1}, n < l \leq N \end{cases}$$

It is known [12] that for highly reliable systems it is possible to make the assumption

$$Q \approx \gamma \tag{1}$$

In this case the efficiency of redundancy in comparison with non-redundant system can be evaluated with factor of channel reliability improvement V:

$$V = \frac{U}{Q} = \begin{cases} \frac{N!l^{l-1}}{m!l!}\omega^{n}, 1 \leq l \leq n \\ \binom{m}{N}\frac{1}{n+1}\gamma^{n}, n < l \leq N \end{cases} \tag{2}$$

Let us define the channel reliability of VCS for the two options of switch placement in the sub clouds.

1. *Architecture with individual switches for each module of one sub cloud (Fig. 3)*

In this case the probability of one module failure q in single VCSM radio station with unavailability Q and k modules is defined by equation

$$q = 1 - (1 - Q)^{1/k}$$

Taking into account the reliability of the switch, this probability of one module failure is defined by equation

$$q = 1 - (1 - q_s)(1 - Q)^{1/k}$$

In accordance with the assumption that the reliability characteristics of all VCSM modules are identical: $\lambda_i = \lambda_0$ and $\mu_i = \mu_0$ for $i = \overline{1,k}$ we get

$$\lambda_0 = \lambda/k, \ \mu_0 = \mu, \ \gamma_0 = \lambda_0/\mu_0 = \gamma/k \tag{3}$$

The channel reliability improvement V_0 at the level of one sub cloud in accordance with (2) and (3) will be

$$V_0 = V/k^n \tag{4}$$

The probability of one sub cloud failure can be defined with next equation

$$q_0 = V_0 q = V_0 \left[1 - (1 - q_s)(1 - Q)^{1/k} \right]$$

The probability of cloud failure for the first option of sub cloud architecture will be determined by the reliability of all sub clouds:

$$R_1 = 1 - \left\{ 1 - V_0 \left[1 - (1 - q_s)(1 - Q)^{1/k} \right] \right\}^k$$

Expanding the right-hand side of the obtained expression in powers of k and $1/k$ and neglecting terms of higher orders of smallness, we transform the resulting expression to the following form

$$R_1 = kV_0 \left(q_s + \frac{Q}{k} \right) \tag{5}$$

In accordance with (1) and (4) expression (5) can be transformed into the next equation

$$R_1 = FQ^n(kq_s + Q)/k^n \tag{6}$$

where

$$F = \begin{cases} \frac{N! l^{l-n-1}}{m! l!}, & 1 \leq l \leq n \\ \binom{m}{N} \frac{1}{n+1}, & n < l \leq N \end{cases}$$

2. Architecture with common switch for all modules of one sub cloud (Fig. 2)

In this case the probability of one module failure q in single VCSM radio station with unavailability Q and k modules is defined by equation

$$q = V_0 \left[1 - (1 - Q)^{1/k} \right]$$

The probability of cloud failure for the second option of sub cloud architecture will be determined by the reliability of all sub clouds:

$$R_2 = 1 - \left[(1 - q_s) \left\{ 1 - V_0 \left[1 - (1 - Q)^{1/k} \right] \right\} \right]^k$$

Expanding the right-hand side of the obtained expression in powers of k and $1/k$ and neglecting terms of higher orders of smallness, we transform the resulting expression to the following form

$$R_2 = k(q_s + V_0 Q/k) \tag{7}$$

In accordance with (1) and (4) expression for R_2 can be transformed into the next equation

$$R_2 = kq_s + FQ^{n+1}/k^n$$

Let us compare the Eqs. (6) and (7)

$$R_1 - R_2 = kq_s(V_0 - 1) \tag{8}$$

The analysis of expression (8) shows that inequality $R_1 > R_2$ is valid if $V_0 > 1$, but inequality $R_1 < R_2$ is valid if $V_0 < 1$.

As numerical example, at the Fig. 4 the graph for factor of channel reliability improvement $W = U/R_1$ shown as function of the number of levels k in set of sub clouds for different relations q_s/Q. Dependencies are built for typical values of VCSM reliability with $1/\lambda = 10000$ h, $1/\mu = 10$ h and $l = 1$ number of repair bodies.

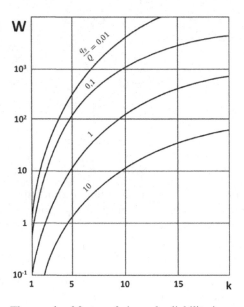

Fig. 4. The graph of factor of channel reliability improvement

Analysis of the presented dependencies shows that with an increase in the number of redundancy levels (the number of sub clouds), a monotonic increase in channel reliability is observed.

The hardware of real VCS usually consists of modules with different reliability and cost parameters. In this case, we can formulate the task of minimizing a set of elements in each sub cloud as an optimal redundancy problem.

Total availability $A(\Omega)$ of VCS with cloud architecture $\Omega \in \{x_i\}, i = \overline{1, k}$ with x_i modules in the i sub cloud is defined as

$$A(\Omega) = \prod_{i=1}^{k} A(x_i)$$

where $A(x_i)$ – channel availability of VCS with set of x_i modules at each of i sub cloud. The cost of hardware with architecture Ω can be expressed as

$$C(\Omega) = \sum_{1=i}^{k} x_i c_i$$

where c_i – cost of one module in i sub cloud.

In this case, the optimal architecture of VCS that provides a specified level of channel availability A_0 can be constructed as

$$\Omega_{opt} = \Omega \in \{x_i\}, i = \overline{1, k} : C(\Omega) = \min |A(\Omega) \geq A_0$$

This problem can be solved by classical methods of optimal reservation [12].

As numerical example let us define the architecture for VCS with mono cloud-based ATM voice communication system (Fig. 1) and with 4 embedded sub clouds ($i = 4$) and optimal modular architecture (Fig. 2) under the assumption of an ideal switch and for reliability and cost parameters of modules shown in the Table 1 (the parameters of VCSM reliability are the same as in previous numerical example).

Table 1. Reliability and cost parameters of VCSM modules.

Modules		Failure rate of module (% of total VCSM failure rate)	Cost of module (the proportion of total VCSM cost)
	1	34	30
	2	20	10
	3	29	30
	4	17	20

The results of calculation of optimal number of modules in each sub cloud for VCS with different number of communication channels m are shown in Table 2 for specified level of channel availability $A_0 = 0,9^40$.

Table 2. Optimal architecture of modular VCS.

m	1	2	3	4	5	6	7	10	15	20
x_1	2	2	2	2	2	2	2	2	2	2
x_2	1	1	1	2	2	2	2	2	2	2
x_3	1	2	2	2	2	2	2	2	2	2
x_4	1	1	1	1	1	2	2	2	2	2

The Fig. 5a illustrates the influence of channel number k on total cost $C(\Omega)$ of VCS with architecture Ω for mono cloud-based ATM voice communication system (curve 1) and with embedded sub clouds for optimal modular architecture (curve 2). The Fig. 5b shows the economic effect $\Delta C(\Omega)$ of proposed separate use of modules within sub clouds for the same channel availability of the system.

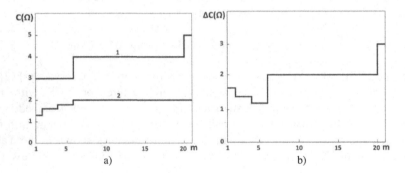

a)   b)

Fig. 5. Economical effectiveness of VCS with embedded sub clouds

4   Conclusions

A key requirement in advanced ATM systems is the migration of all ATM systems and services to a fully IP-based network-oriented VCS. The result is more efficient sharing of information, services and resources. The proposed in the paper solution on the base of multilevel distributed cloud technology ensures smooth integration of the VCS in any IP-based overall ATC architecture and provides additional resilience against failures.

In the paper the reliability of ground communication domain of future multichannel communication ATM system integrated in common frame of internet of things is analyzed.

For ground infrastructure the effective dynamic procedure of monitoring and control of common sets of redundancy radio stations at the level of architectural submodules within the technology of multilevel ground embedded clouds is proposed.

The boundary value of reliability parameters for automatics of VCS embedded cloud for architecture with individual and common switches for modules of one sub cloud is analysed. The value of $V_0 = 1$ is a boundary value of decision making for chose better option for switch placement in the sub cloud. For $V_0 > 1$ the architecture with individual switches for each module of one sub cloud will be better than architecture with one common switch for all modules of one sub cloud. For $V_0 < 1$ the situation will be reversed. Increase in the number of redundancy levels (the number of sub clouds) leads to monotonic increase of VCS channel reliability. This dependence is manifested more strongly for more reliable switching devices.

Acknowledgment. This work was supported by Latvian state research programme project "The Next Generation of Information and Communication Technologies (Nex IT)" (2014–2017).

References

1. Kilpert, J.: Air traffic control: new VoIP-based voice communications system takes off. Secure Communications. Air Traffic Control. Rohde&Schwarz, News 203/11, pp. 60–62
2. The Roadmap for delivering high performing aviation for Europe. European ATM master plan (2015)
3. ICAO: Aeronautical Telecommunication Network (ATN). Manual for the ATN using IPS standards and protocols (Doc 9896). Edition 2.0 (2011)
4. Ayers, M.: Telecommunications System Reliability Engineering, Theory, and Practice. Wiley-IEEE Press, Hoboken (2012)
5. Modarres, M., Kaminskiy, M., Krivtsov, V.: Reliability Engineering and Risk Analysis: A Practical Guide (Quality and Reliability), 2nd edn. CRC Press, Boca Raton (2009)
6. Barlow, R., Heidtmann, K.: On the reliability computation of a k-out-of-n system. Microelectro. Reliab. **33**(2), 267–269 (1993). Elsevier
7. Misra, K.: Handbook of Performability Engineering. Springer, New York (2008)
8. McGrady, P.: The availability of a k-out-of-n: G network. IEEE Trans. Reliab. **34**(5), 451–452 (1985)
9. Liu, H.: Reliability of a load-sharing k-out-of-n: G system: non-iid components with arbitrary distributions. IEEE Trans. Reliab. **47**(3), 279–284 (1998)
10. Rushdi, A.: A switching-algebraic analysis of consecutive-k-out-of-n: F systems. Microelectron. Reliab. **27**(1), 171–174 (1987). Elsevier
11. Chatwattanasiri, N., Coit, D., Wattanapongsakorn, N., Sooktip, T.: Dynamic k-out-of-n system reliability for redundant local area networks. In: 2012 9th International Conference on Electrical Engineering/Electronics, Computer, Telecommunications and Information Technology (ECTI-CON), pp. 1–4, 16–18 May 2012
12. Kozlov, B., Ushakov, I.: Reliability Handbook. International Series in Decision Processes. Holt, Rinehart & Winston of Canada Ltd, New York (1970)
13. Kabashkin, I.: Effectiveness of redundancy in communication network of air traffic management system. In: Zamojski, W., Mazurkiewicz, J., Sugier, J., Walkowiak, T., Kacprzyk, J. (eds.) Dependability Engineering and Complex Systems. AISC, vol. 470, pp. 257–265. Springer, Cham (2016). doi:10.1007/978-3-319-39639-2_22
14. Kabashkin, I.: Resilient communication network of air traffic management system. In: Proceedings of the IEEE International Conference Advances in Wireless and Optical Communications (RTUWO), 3–4 November 2016, Riga, Latvia, pp. 173–177 (2016)
15. Laukkarinen, T., Suhonen, J., Hännikäinen, M.: An embedded cloud design for Internet-of-Things. Int. J. Distrib. Sens. Netw., **2013**, 1–13, Article ID 790130 (2013). Hindawi Publishing Corporation

16. Bauer, E., Adams, R.: Reliability and Availability of Cloud Computing. Wiley-IEEE Press, Hoboken (2012)
17. Kabashkin, I.: Analysing of the voice communication channels for ground segment of air traffic management system based on embedded cloud technology. In: Dregvaite, G., Damasevicius, R. (eds.) ICIST 2016. CCIS, vol. 639, pp. 639–649. Springer, Cham (2016). doi:10.1007/978-3-319-46254-7_52

Security Analysis of VoIP Networks
Through Penetration Testing

Paschal A. Ochang[1] and Philip Irving[2(✉)]

[1] Department of Computer Science,
Federal University Lafia, Lafia, Nasarawa State, Nigeria
`pascosoft@gmail.com`
[2] Department of Computing, Engineering and Technology,
University of Sunderland, Sunderland, UK
`phil.irving@sunderland.ac.uk`

Abstract. The Voice over Internet Protocol (VoIP) is gradually becoming the de facto standard in communications technology and it is now viewed as a cheap alternative to Public Switched Telephone Networks (PSTN) due to its low cost and flexibility. However the flexibility and ability of VoIP to provide a converged data and voice network comes with security vulnerabilities and threats some of which are as a result of the existing IP architecture. However, the use of penetration tests can provide a framework for analysing and identifying vulnerabilities and flaws in a VoIP network which in turn can assist in enhancing security. This research presents how a comprehensive VoIP network security level can be attained by carrying out penetration tests through Ethical Hacking. In this research the VoIP Security Alliance (VoIPSA) taxonomy was used to classify VoIP threats which lead to the design of a penetration test which was carried out against a VoIP network in other to identify vulnerabilities and exploits relating to the VoIPSA threat classification. This resulted in the development of a VoIP penetration testing methodology suitable for VoIP Networks. The developed penetration testing methodology successfully identified vulnerabilities in the VoIP deployment which assisted in providing security recommendations.

Keywords: VoIP · Penetration testing · Ethical Hacking · Security analysis · SIP

1 Introduction

Voice over Internet Protocol (VoIP) has proven to be a successful communications technology that has been widely adopted and deployed by major companies due to its ability to allow voice and multimedia to travel through an existing packet based network along with traditional data (Coulibaly and Liu 2010). VoIP provides numerous advantages and has been used implemented by organisations mainly due to two reasons, the first being due to the fact that it reduces cost because it can be implemented on an existing IP-based network as compared to a Public Switched Telephone Network (PSTN) therefore eliminating service provider fees, while the second reason is due to the fact that it is flexible therefore allowing the easy implementation of new features according to

© Springer International Publishing AG 2017
R. Damaševičius and V. Mikašytė (Eds.): ICIST 2017, CCIS 756, pp. 601–610, 2017.
DOI: 10.1007/978-3-319-67642-5_50

organisational needs such as video conferencing and voicemail (Hanifan and Bandung 2013).

However the convergence of voice and data provides security concerns mostly as a result of the VoIP architecture and the underlying IP architecture (Butcher et al. 2007). The vulnerabilities existing in VoIP architectures brings up the need to implement standard penetration testing procedures and methodologies in other to identify exploitable vulnerabilities which will in turn assist in providing security enhancements.

The rest of this paper is organised as follows. Section 2 gives an overview on VoIP architectures and its protocols while Sect. 3 analyses VoIP threat taxonomy as defined by the VoIPSA. Section 4 provides a brief overview on penetration testing and the possible methodologies that can be adopted, furthermore it goes on to design a penetration test and a VoIP network lab setup. Section 5 implements the deigned penetration test while Sect. 6 provides security recommendations for mitigating the successful test exploits. Finally Sect. 6 summarises and concludes the paper.

2 VoIP Architecture

A simple VoIP architecture makes use of endpoints which can be soft phones or hard phones, control and gateway nodes, and the underlying IP network (Moon et al. 2012) as shown in Fig. 1 below. However, an IP PBX (Private Branch Exchange) can be used to perform the functions of the control and gateway nodes.

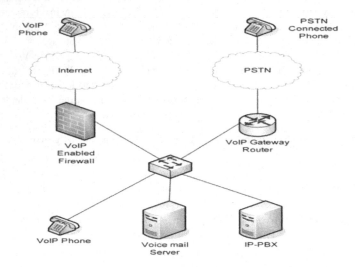

Fig. 1. A simple VoIP architecture

VoIP makes use of media and signalling protocols in other to successfully transport media, set up and carry out a communication sessions. The media protocols include Real-Time Transport Protocol (RTP) which is mainly used to transport the real time media streams while the signalling protocols are used to set up and tear down media sessions (Keromytis 2012). A popular signalling protocol is the Session Initiation

Protocol (SIP) which was developed by the IETF and has today become the de facto standard for creating, modifying and terminating multimedia sessions (Werapun et al. 2009). SIP uses a number of parameters and methods in other to set up call sessions which include INVITE which is use to invite a User Agent (UA) or endpoint to a call, REGISTER which is used to register with a SIP server, BYE which is used to tear down sessions, RINGING which notifies an endpoint of an incoming session and OK which is used to notify an endpoint that a call has been accepted (Keromytis 2012).

3   VoIP Threats

In other to understand and categorise the security threats faced by VoIP deployments a taxonomical approach provided by the Voice over IP Security Alliance (VoIPSA) will be used. The VoIPSA is a non profit vendor neutral organisation consisting of individuals, organisations and vendors with the sole aim of protecting VoIP products and deployments (Coulibaly and Liu 2010). The key factors of the VoIPSA threat taxonomy are:

- **Social Threats** which are threats targeted directly against human users as a result of misconfigurations and bugs in the VoIP protocol interactions. Such threats lead to spamming and phishing.
- **Eavesdropping, interception and modification threats** which covers situations where an adversary can unlawfully listen voice sessions and possible modify the contents of the sessions while avoiding detection. Example of such attacks include interception of RTP traffic.
- **Denial of Service** has the potential of preventing users from having access to the VoIP services. These attacks sometimes exploit flaws in the signalling protocols such as SIP. For example an attacker can send malformed SIP BYE messages to an endpoint preventing the endpoint from receiving calls (Moon et al. 2012) or an INVITE flood can be sent to a SIP server preventing it from attending to legitimate client requests.
- **Service abuse threats** involve situations where improper usage of VoIP services is carried out by users leading to over expenditure by the VoIP service provider (Zhang and Huang 2011). Example of these include billing avoidance and toll fraud.
- **Physical Access threats** comprises of unauthorised access to the physical VoIP equipment or to the physical layer of the network with reference to Layer 1 of the ISO model.
- **Service Interruption** threats which are as a result of non-intentional problems and can lead to the inaccessibility of VoIP services. Example of these include loss of power due to natural disasters and degradation in perceived call quality due to over subscription.

In other to simulate these threats and carry out a penetration test, the work that follows focuses more on the first 4 threats due to the fact that the last two are outside the scope of threats that can be tested in a network laboratory environment.

4 Penetration Testing Methodology and Design

Penetration testing is considered as the bedrock for carrying out security assessments of network models in an ethical manner. Penetration testing goes a long way in revealing to network administrators the consequences of an attacker breaking into a VoIP network and sheds light on any unidentified vulnerabilities (EC-Council 2011). In other to carry out a successful penetration test a methodology has to be adopted from the vast options available. Example of penetration testing methodologies include the Licensed Penetration Tester (LPT) developed by the EC-Council, Information Systems Security Assessment Framework (ISSAF) developed by the Open Information Systems Security Group (OISSG) and the Open Source Security Testing Methodology Manual (OSSTMM) developed by Pete Herzog. However, a penetration test consists of mainly the pre-attack phase which involves planning mainly by carrying out active and passive reconnaissance in other to gather information about the targets, the attack phase which involves exploitation of the vulnerabilities identified during reconnaissance and attacking the targets while the post attack phase presents the results of the test (Bechtsoudis and Sklavos 2012).

For the purpose of this test the ISSAF methodology was adopted in other to develop a VoIP based penetration testing methodology and Fig. 2 below shows the ISSAF methodology.

Fig. 2. ISSAF penetration testing methodology

In other to simulate a VoIP network a virtual lab was created. Using the lab as a real case study a penetration test was carried out against the VoIP network in other to demonstrate the threats and attacks that could exist on a VoIP network due to vulnerabilities in the VoIP architecture. The lab set up is presented in the next section.

4.1   VoIP Penetration Test Set up

As shown in Fig. 3 the lab set up makes use of a Cisco 2800 series router as the gateway while a Cisco 2600 series layer 2 switch was used to connect the hosts. Backtrack 5 R3 was used as the attacking system due to the fact that it has a suite of tools suitable for the test.

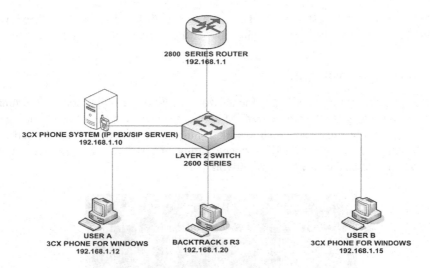

Fig. 3. VoIP penetration testing topology and configuration setup

A 3CX Phone System version 12 was used as the IP PBX while 3CX soft phones for windows were configured as USER A and B respectively. The Table 1 below shows the configuration for the soft phones/SIP User Agents which were also provisioned on the 3CX IP PBX.

Table 1. SIP User Agents configuration

SIP User Agent	Telephone extension number	User ID	Password
USER A	1001	1001	project
USER B	2002	2002	123456

4.2   Test Scenario and Objectives

The test was carried out using an internal testing strategy with the aim of compromising the 3CX IP PBX and the User Agents. The main goal of the test is to compromise the

VoIP network internally by carrying out the VoIP threats specified by the VoIPSA therefore the following steps and threats were drafted out.

- Information gathering
- Extension enumeration
- Spoofing caller ID
- Capturing and cracking SIP authentication
- Denial of Service on the IP PBX
- Capturing voice traffic and eavesdropping

5   Test Implementation

In other to carry out the test implementation we assume that we have access to the Layer 2 Switch, therefore we begin by carrying out getting information about the network.

5.1   Information Gathering

In other to gather information about the network a network mapping tool called nmap was used to identify the IP addresses of the live hosts in the network as shown in Fig. 4. The yellow box in Fig. 4 above shows the router in the network, while the red box identifies the 3CX IP PBX with SIP service running on port 5060 which is open and the green box identifies the clients in the network.

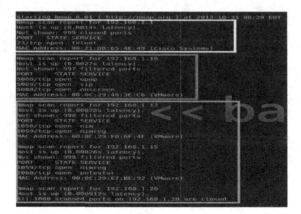

Fig. 4. Network mapping (Color figure online)

Having mapped the network, a SIP scanner tool called svmap was used to scan for SIP devices in the network.

Figure 5 above shows that the SIP devices configured in the lab setup were identified. We went further to carry out fingerprinting of the SIP devices and Fig. 6 below shows that the User Agents were identified, however the 3CX IP PBX rejected the malformed the SIP INVITE message and couldn't be fingerprinted.

```
root@bt:/pentest/voip/sipvicious# ./svmap.py -p1000-6000 192.168.1.1-254

^CWARNING:root:caught your control^c - quiting
| SIP Device          | User Agent | Fingerprint |
-----------------------------------------------------
| 192.168.1.12:1058 | unknown    | disabled    |
| 192.168.1.10:5080 | unknown    | disabled    |
| 192.168.1.15:1059 | unknown    | disabled    |
root@bt:/pentest/voip/sipvicious#
```

Fig. 5. Identifying SIP devices

```
root@bt:/pentest/voip/sipvicious# ./svmap.py -p1058 192.168.1.12 -m INVITE
| SIP Device          | User Agent          | Fingerprint |
-----------------------------------------------------------
| 192.168.1.12:1058 | 3CXPhone 6.0.26523.0 | disabled    |

root@bt:/pentest/voip/sipvicious# ./svmap.py -p1059 192.168.1.15 -m INVITE
| SIP Device          | User Agent          | Fingerprint |
-----------------------------------------------------------
| 192.168.1.15:1059 | 3CXPhone 6.0.26523.0 | disabled    |
```

Fig. 6. Fingerprinting of the SIP User Agents

5.2   Extensions Enumeration

Knowing the live SIP User Agents and their operating ports we proceeded to enumerate the extensions which were configured on the 3CX IP PBX using a tool called svwar. However the scanner was successfully blocked by the 3CX IP PBX as shown in the 3CX server activity log in Fig. 7 below. Other SIP scanners were also used and were blocked as well.

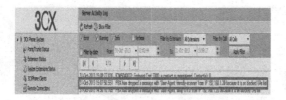

Fig. 7. SIP scanners blocked by the 3CX IP PBX

5.3   Spoofing Caller ID

Having obtained inform information about the ports in which the SIP soft phones operate, we attempted to send specially crafted SIP INVITE messages to USER B pretending to be USER A and pretending to be the bank of USER B by using the IP address and port obtained during information gathering.

Figure 8 above shows USER A receiving a call from the spoofed caller IDs.

```
root@bt:/pentest/voip/sipvicious# ./svmap.py -p1059 192.168.1.15 -m INVITE --fromname="USER A"

root@bt:/pentest/voip/sipvicious# ./svmap.py -p1059 192.168.1.15 -m INVITE --fromname="YOUR BANK"
```

Fig. 8.   USER B receiving spoofed calls

5.4   Capturing and Cracking SIP Authentication

Having successfully carried out a spoofing caller ID attack we attempted to capture SIP authentication messages between the 3CX IP PBX and the SIP clients as shown in Fig. 9 below. The authentication messages were captured and stored in a text file.

```
root@bt:/pentest/passwords/sipcrack# ./sipdump -i eth0 capture.txt
SIPdump 0.3  ( MaJoMu | www.codito.de )
-----------------------------------------
* Using dev 'eth0' for sniffing
* Starting to sniff with packet filter 'tcp or udp or vlan'

* Dumped login from 192.168.1.10 -> 192.168.1.12 (User: '1001')
* Dumped login from 192.168.1.10 -> 192.168.1.12 (User: '1001')
* Dumped login from 192.168.1.10 -> 192.168.1.12 (User: '1001')
* Dumped login from 192.168.1.10 -> 192.168.1.12 (User: '1001')
* Dumped login from 192.168.1.10 -> 192.168.1.15 (User: '2002')
* Dumped login from 192.168.1.10 -> 192.168.1.15 (User: '2002')
* Dumped login from 192.168.1.10 -> 192.168.1.15 (User: '2002')
* Dumped login from 192.168.1.10 -> 192.168.1.15 (User: '2002')
```

Fig. 9.   Capturing SIP authentication

After successfully capturing the SIP authentication messages a brute force attack was launched against the captured MD5 hashes in an attempt to crack the MD5 hashes and reveal the password of the SIP clients in plain text. Figure 10 below shows that the password of extension 1001 which was configured during the planning stage was successfully cracked and revealed to be 'project'.

Fig. 10. Cracking of password for extension 1001

5.5 Denial of Service on the 3CX IP PBX

In other to disrupt VoIP services an attempt to flood the 3CX IP PBX with specially crafted SIP INVITE messages was carried out. This was done by sending an INVITE flood of one million INVITE messages to the IP address of the 3CX server which is 192.168.1.10 and port 5060 which were identified to be running SIP during information gathering by nmap.

Figure 11 above shows that the 3CX IP PBX responded by blacklisting the IP address of the attacking machine which is 192.168.1.20 due to too many unauthenticated requests, therefore the attack was not successful.

Secure Sip (TLS)	Anti-Hacking	IP Blacklist	Allowed Country Codes		
Add Edit Delete					
IP Address	Subnet Mask	Action	Expiration Date	IP address range	Description
192.168.1.20	255.255.255.255	Deny	31-Oct-2013 17:49:04	192.168.1.20	PBX: blocked for too many unauthenticated requests

Fig. 11. Blacklisted IP of attacking machine by the 3CX IP PBX

6   Conclusion and Future Work

VoIP has become a popular candidate in voice and multimedia communications solutions and is widely adopted. This paper analyses security threats directed towards VoIP and the paper has gone further to show that a penetration test can be used to analyse the security of a VoIP network in other to identify and mitigate vulnerabilities and threats. It is also important to know that due to the rapid implementation of VoIP, multiple architectures of deployments have also been realised such as VoIP deployment using Wireless networks. Therefore future research and penetration tests need to be carried out on Voice over Wireless LAN (VoWLAN) and Mobile VoIP (MVoIP) applications in other to enhance security.

References

3CX: 3CX Phone System for Windows Manual Version 12 (2013). http://www.3cx.com/support/3cx-manuals-and-documentation/

Bechtsoudis, A., Sklavos, N.: Aiming at higher network security through extensive penetration tests. Lat. Am. Trans. IIEEE (Rev. IEEE Am. Lat.) **10**(3), 1752–1756 (2012)

Butcher, D., Li, X., Guo, J.: Security challenge and defense in VoIP infrastructures. IEEE Trans. Syst. Man Cybern. Part C (Appl. Rev.) **37**(6), 1152–1162 (2007)

Coulibaly, E., Liu, L.: Security of VoIP networks. In: 2nd International Conference on Computer Engineering and Technology (ICCET) 2010, pp. 104–108 (2010). http://ieeexplore.ieee.org/xpls/abs_all.jsp?arnumber=5485790

EC-Council: Penetration Testing: Procedures and Methodologies. Cengage Learning, Clifton Park, New York (2011)

Hanifan, Y., Bandung, Y.: Designing VoIP security system for organizational network. In: International Conference on ICT for Smart Society, pp. 1–5 (2013). http://ieeexplore.ieee.org/lpdocs/epic03/wrapper.htm?arnumber=6588074

Herzog, P.: OSSTMM 3 – The Open Source Security Testing Methodology Manual (2010). http://www.isecom.org/research/osstmm.html

Keromytis, A.: A comprehensive survey of voice over IP security research. IEEE Commun. Surv. Tutor. **14**(2), 514–537 (2012)

Moon, K., Moon, M.M., Meshram, B.B.: Securing VoIP networks via signaling protocol layer. In: 2012 International Conference on Radar, Communication and Computing (ICRCC), pp. 6–10 (2012)

Open Information Systems Security Group: Information Systems Security Assessment Framework (ISSAF) draft 0.2 (2006). http://www.oissg.org/issaf

Perez-Botero, D., Donoso, Y.: VoIP eavesdropping: a comprehensive evaluation of cryptographic countermeasures. In: 2011 Second International Conference on Networking and Distributed Computing, pp. 192–196 (2011)

VoIP Security Alliance: VoIP Security and Privacy Threat Taxonomy, version 1 (2005). http://www.voipsa.org/Activities/taxonomy.php

Werapun, W., El Kalam, A.: Solution analysis for SIP security threats. In: International Conference on Multimedia Computing and Systems, ICMCS 2009 (2009). http://ieeexplore.ieee.org/xpls/abs_all.jsp?arnumber=5256707

Zhang, Y., Huang, H.: VoIP voice network technology security strategies. In: 2011 2nd International Conference on Artificial Intelligence, Management Science and Electronic Commerce (AIMSEC), pp. 3591–3594 (2011)

Problem of Bathymetric Big Data Interpolation for Inland Mobile Navigation System

Marta Włodarczyk-Sielicka[1(✉)] and Natalia Wawrzyniak[2]

[1] Institute of Geoinformatics, Maritime University of Szczecin, Szczecin, Poland
m.wlodarczyk@am.szczecin.pl
[2] Marine Technology Ltd., Szczecin, Poland
n.wawrzyniak@marinetechnology.pl

Abstract. Depth information is crucial in most navigational analysis and decision support implemented in existing inland navigation systems. Bathymetric data sets needs to be preprocessed and converted into Digital Terrain Model by interpolation methods to provide different vector layer for Electronic Navigational Chart. Data for inland waters needs to be precise and valid due to quickly alternating inland environment and much shallower areas than on marine waters. At the same time visual effect of created layers needs to be readable and easily interpreted by a navigator. In this paper authors analyze different interpolation method for DTM building from the perspective of accepted criteria. Created depth contours are the base of navigational analysis provided by mobile inland navigation system MOBINAV. The experiments used real inland data from bathymetric surveys conducted on waters of Szczecin area.

Keywords: Bathymetric data · Interpolation method · Maritime information systems · Mobile systems

1 Introduction

For many years, existing on-water navigation systems support marine and inland shipping and are essential for ensuring all traffic participants safety. Besides providing spatial and navigational information of navigable area, some of these systems allow users for advance analysis that can help efficiently plan and safely conduct a voyage. There are both professional, standardized systems for commercial units like ECDIS (Electronic Chart Display Information Systems) and simple mobile applications for recreational users as well [1–3], which usually contains only an orthophotomap with smartphones localization feature in order to shows ships geographical location. MOBINAV system, which currently is being evolved by Marine Technology Ltd., is a compromise between professional solutions, their computational achievements and strict visualization standards with mobile technology and decision support. As a result the final product incorporates basic objects of ECDIS systems with achievements of mobile cartography and user-centred pattern.

An absolute basis for all these systems is spatial information in a form of vector or raster map. The most important of all spatial information in such systems is depth

© Springer International Publishing AG 2017
R. Damaševičius and V. Mikašytė (Eds.): ICIST 2017, CCIS 756, pp. 611–621, 2017.
DOI: 10.1007/978-3-319-67642-5_51

information represented as vector layers for various types of analysis purposes. Most of navigational alarms and warnings are generated using this information in combination with GPS position, current water-level information and ships draught. So the base of correct analysis and navigational decision making is precise and valid depth information. However the data not only have to be possibly detailed but the visual effect of presented spatial information must be readable, as not all the analysis that system offers are automatic. Vast of navigational decision are made by a navigator himself using only visual assessment of systems spatial data with reading measurements on board.

Raw bathymetric data are extremely large data sets and they need spatial management and processing methods to be transformed into form that can be used by computer and especially mobile systems in a way to preserve its initial precision. Additionally it is doubly difficult to assure its pleasant visual effect at the same time. That is why the problem of choosing right interpolation methods for constructing a Digital Terrain Model (DTM) of underwater inland areas is not trivial.

In this article authors analyze different methods of bathymetric DTM interpolation to create depth contours in inland mobile navigation system. Taking into consideration the complex character of raw bathymetric data authors focus on finding a solution that generalize data, but preserve shallowest information for the purpose of safety of navigation.

The paper is ordered as follows: Sect. 2 includes specification of a problems related to processing of spatial data comprehending depth information in mobile navigation systems; Sect. 3 describes methodology of conducted analysis to choose the best method for DTM interpolation; Sect. 4 contains experiments results and the publication ends with inference.

2 Background

2.1 Mobinav

MOBINAV system is a semi-professional solution dedicated for inland recreational vessels which is being expanded actually by Marine Technology. MOBINAV takes advantage of spatial datasets combined with information provided by other navigational devices available on board, e.g. unit's positioning is the most important and can be obtained by a GPS (Global Positioning System) receiver of any kind. There is also possibility of using other mobile device raw or derived sensors (magnetometer, barometer, ambient light) or attaching external ships sensors such as echosounder, AIS transponder, compass etc. via blue tooth. Any supplementary, non-spatial information, that assistance navigation can be obtained from available online services, e.g., Web Map Services, River Information System, or to be filled in manually.

MOBINAV system uses different spatial datasets transformed and integrated on server side of the system, according to a created Mobinav Data Exchange Format (MODEF) model. The purposeful vector datasets for each specified geographical area are then supplied to final users through XML/GML and converted into a map in the mobile application. Some raster datasets as an orthophotomap of chosen regions of particular interest (e.g., periodically complicated navigational areas, port, turning area) are also allowed [6]. Server side also makes possible to share information they found interesting users e.g., custom Point of Interest (POI), emergency information like Man Over Board (MOB) alarm.

MOBINAV system is a kind of Geographic Information System solution, which means it is based on geometric vector data objects grouped in feature classes with a defined set of attributes. Neither objects geometry nor attributes that are grouped in core layers can be modified. However, for spatial analyses purposes new dynamic layers may be created and even shared among different users [5]. Moreover, all dynamic, ships traffic information with appearing alerts and warnings that are created as an outcome of conducted analyses is represented as additional layers [4]. Main analysis that uses depth information is proximity analysis for automatic alerting when ship is heading towards shallow areas. System choses safety isobaths based on vessels draught, water-level and the sets of maps depth area vector layer and indicates it on a map with red color (Fig. 1). As background process systems constantly checks if ships position and heading is not too close to indicated contour. If so, system generates a warning and in closer proximity - a danger alert.

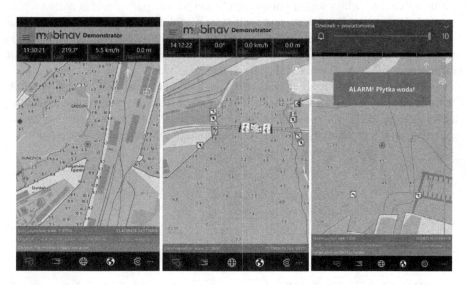

Fig. 1. Screenshots from MOBINAV installed on NOKIA1520 (a) 2D view with active safe depth contour, (b) 2+D view with active safe depth contour, (c) generated alarm for approaching shallow water area (Color figure online)

2.2 Bathymetric Data in Inland Mobile Navigation System

Bathymetry is the study and mapping of seabed topography and it involves obtaining measurements of the depth of water area. Bathymetric maps are mostly created to assistance safety of surface navigation and demonstrate seafloor as selected depths (soundings) and contour lines (called depth contours or isobaths). Charts also provide other navigational information. During the work on building of the mobile navigation system for inland waters it was decided to compile an own spatial data model MODEF (Mobinav Data Exchange Format). Under the development of the model, 28 classes of geometric objects were defined, together with attributes describing them. The individual feature classes in the proposed model correspond to the information layers in the cartographic product, which is used to visualization data on the screen of the mobile device. In the system there are two layers related with depth: soundings and depth areas. The first layer has point geometry and depth attribute at a given location. The second one has polygon geometry and two attributes: minimum and maximum depth.

Depth areas or related with them depth contours can be obtained from a Digital Terrain Model DTM (e.g., a systematic grid of spots connected into a surface) [7–9]. To obtain such model real bathymetric survey of mapped area need to be conducted. From the cloud of point measurements one can build a DTM using either one of triangulation method that preserves measured values in model vertices or proceed gridding algorithm that creates DTM in square GRID net with altered measurements in nodes but regularly structured, which facilitates later processing. On the other hand benefit of using a TIN over a GRID is that the points of a TIN are spread variably depending on an algorithm that determines which points are chosen for the purpose of accurate representation of the terrain. But from visual point of view gridding algorithms allow to create models, which enhance proper users reception, which in this case is important, as navigational decision are mostly taken based on visual assessment of the situation, both in surroundings of the vessel and in the system display as well.

There are few gridding algorithms that can be considered in using for building bathymetric DTM for inland water areas. Commonly used is invert distance weighting interpolation methods which are mostly global methods and which is very simple to implement but it's complexity is O(N). The equation of the method is shown below:

$$z = \frac{\sum_{i=1}^{N} \dfrac{z_i}{(d_i + \sigma)^p}}{\sum_{i=1}^{N} \dfrac{1}{(d_i + \sigma)^p}} \tag{1}$$

where:

z_i – next value in measurement point,
d_i – distance between a node and next measurement point,
p – weighting power,
σ – smoothing factor,

Modified Sheppard's algorithm is also an inverse weighting algorithm but working locally (doesn't take into account measurements that are beyond set radius).

The other commonly used method is Kriging (Gausian process regression) which isn't a deterministic interpolation method as these mentioned above but gives the best linear unblast prediction of the intermediate values. To interpolate values z:

$$z = \sum_{i=1}^{n} w_i z_i \tag{2}$$

One needs to find coefficients w_i from

$$\begin{bmatrix} \gamma_{11} & \gamma_{12} & \gamma_{13} & \cdots & \gamma_{1N} & 1 \\ \gamma_{21} & \gamma_{22} & \gamma_{23} & \cdots & \gamma_{2N} & 1 \\ \cdots & \cdots & \cdots & \cdots & \cdots & \cdots \\ \gamma_{N1} & \gamma_{N2} & \gamma_{N3} & \cdots & \gamma_{NN} & 1 \\ 1 & 1 & 1 & \cdots & 1 & 0 \end{bmatrix} \begin{bmatrix} w_1 \\ w_2 \\ \cdots \\ w_N \\ \lambda \end{bmatrix} = \begin{bmatrix} \gamma_{1,P} \\ \gamma_{2,P} \\ \cdots \\ \gamma_{N,P} \\ 1 \end{bmatrix} \tag{3}$$

where

$\gamma(h_{ij})$ – semivariance as a function of the distance between successive samples i and j,
$\gamma(h_{ip})$ – semivariance as a function of the distance between the next point and the interpolated point,
n – number of interpolated points

Kriging is most appropriate when one knows there is a spatially correlated distance or directional bias in the data [10]. It is often used in soil science and geology.

3   The Experiment

All test methods were implemented using Surface software, developed by Golden Software. Additionally, for visualization purposes ArcGIS software was used. To gather bathymetric datasets the vessel Hydrograf XXI, with interferometric GeoSwath Plus 250 kHz echosounder and extra equipment such as satellite compass, GPS/RTK receiver and motion sensor installed, was used.

3.1   Test Area

Test datasets were collected within Port of Szczecin, on the Babina Canal which is presented in Fig. 2.

Raw bathymetric data are very-high density and consist of XYZ points (latitude, longitude and depth). During the hydrographic exploration a very large amount of data was collected. The raw test dataset included 5864171 points of XYZ elements. Each sample has three attributes: latitude, longitude, and a predetermined true depth at a given position. Very large raw dataset is the primary operational rectriction when using a regular computer. In order to solve this problem, the authors decided to use smaller subsets – data after reduction. For the purposes of this article, a reduced dataset was created using a new author's method – for a scale of 1: 500. Part of this method is presented in [11].

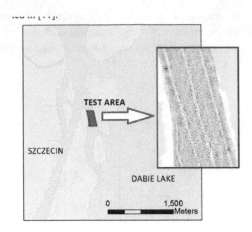

Fig. 2. Test area

Dataset after reduction included 25843 XYZ points and it is shown in Fig. 2. The minimum value of depth is 0.3 m, the maximum value of depth is 8.96 m and the mean value of depth is 6.08 m.

3.2 Research Methodology

For publication purposes, the authors have chosen four different gridding interpolation methods: triangulation with linear interpolation, kriging, modified Shepard's method and inverse distance to a power. The first step involved the development of grid for test dataset using selected method. It was implemented using Surface software with the following parameters:

- Triangulation with Linear Interpolation: anisotropy ratio equal 1, anisotropy angle equal 0;
- Kriging: polynomial drift order equal 0, semi-variogram model: linear component type, anisotropy angle equal 0; anisotropy ratio equal 1, variogram slope equal 1, search parameters: search ellipse radius 1 equal 220, search ellipse radius 2 equal 220, search ellipse angle equal 0, number of search sectors equal 4, maximum data per sector equal 16, maximum empty sectors equal 3, minimum data equal 8, maximum data equal 64;
- Modified Shepard's Method: smoothing factor equal 0, quadratic neighbors equal 13, weighting neighbors equal 19, search ellipse radius 1 equal 44, search ellipse radius 2 equal 44, search ellipse angle equal 0;
- Inverse Distance to a Power: weighting power equal 2, smoothing factor equal 0, anisotropy ratio equal 1, anisotropy angle equal 0, search parameters: search ellipse radius 1 equal 220, search ellipse radius 2 equal 220, search ellipse angle equal 0, number of search sectors equal 4, maximum data per sector equal 16, maximum empty sectors equal 3, minimum data equal 8, maximum data equal 64;

The next step was creation of contour lines for each grid where the default settings were applied - intervals have been set at 0.5 m. The received surfaces and isobaths have been visualized. For all sets of depth contours the following statistics were calculated: total number of isobaths, minimum depth, maximum depth, mean depth and standard deviation. After that the volume to zero level was computed. In the next step, the errors between XYZ point (test data) and model surface were calculated – differences between the height at the XYZ sample and the height calculated in the grid file. The differences are negative and positive, so it is necessary to calculate the absolute value in order to correctly calculate the error. In the last step, using statistical functions, the mean, maximum and minimum error values were calculated.

4   Results

After implementation of the assumed parameters for each method, the authors obtained four surfaces, which are presented in Fig. 3.

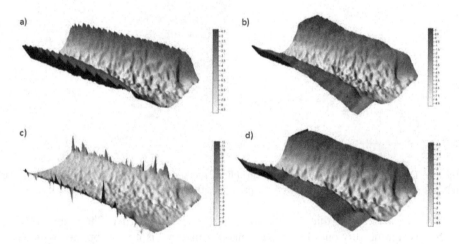

Fig. 3. Surfaces obtained using gridding methods: (a) Triangulation with Linear Interpolation, (b) Kriging, (c) Modified Shepard's Method, (d) Inverse Distance to a Power. (Color figure online)

As we can see in the Fig. 3, each surface has a different depth range. The shallower areas are shown in a darker shade of blue - as is the case in the navigation map. The surface that is most different from the rest is the surface obtained with modified Shepard's gridding method. For each surface volume to zero level was computed. The smallest volume received for triangulation with linear interpolation method – 381429.55 m3. For modified Shepard's method volume equal 382457.91 m3 and for kriging volume equal 391701.77 m3 were received. The biggest volume received for inverse distance to a power method – 416392.95 m3.

In the next step for each of the four surfaces contour lines with 0.5 m intervals were generated. They were visualized using ArcGIS software – comparison is presented in Fig. 4.

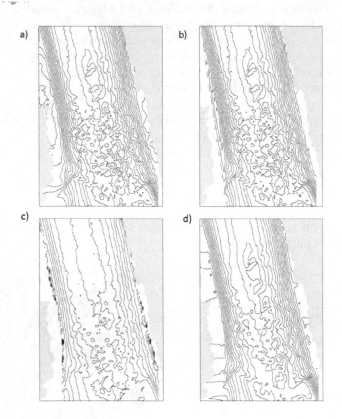

Fig. 4. Depth contour obtained using gridding methods: (a) Triangulation with Linear Interpolation, (b) Kriging, (c) Modified Shepard's Method, (d) Inverse Distance to a Power.

You can also notice that the isobaths obtained with modified Shepard's gridding method is significantly out of place. The most similar are isobaths obtained with triangulation with linear interpolation and kriging methods. It is important that only isobaths obtained with triangulation with linear interpolation do not go beyond the coverage area of the source data. Table 1 contains statistics for all sets of depth contours.

Table 1. Statistics for all sets of depth contours.

Gridding methods	Total number	Min depth [m]	Max depth [m]	Mean depth [m]	σ
Triangulation (L.I.)	155	0.50	8.50	4.92	2.83
Kriging	121	0.00	8.50	5.60	2.60
Modified Shepard's	326	−12.00	8.00	1.11	4.38
Inv. Dist. to Power	90	0.50	8.50	4.76	2.73

All methods except Modified Shepard's method provided depth contours in realistic range, in which real values were measured. However errors in Modified Shepard's methods occur only on edges of created model and can be easily eliminated. Additionally, depth contours for all research method were presented in one map. This can help in visual assessment of received results. Example of this map is shown in Fig. 5 at a 1:250 scale.

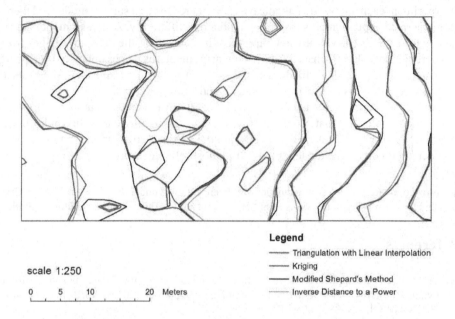

scale 1:250

0   5   10   20   Meters

Legend

——— Triangulation with Linear Interpolation
——— Kriging
——— Modified Shepard's Method
——— Inverse Distance to a Power

Fig. 5. Depth contours obtained using gridding methods at a 1:250 scale

Figure 5 represents the differences between contour lines in the chart, generated at a 1:250 scale. Observed differences refer to few meters (below 3 m) in both directions, which doesn't have crucial influence on navigational analyses – e.g. warning and alarms are generated in distance at least of 100, 200 m from obstacles or shallow waters, to give a navigator time to react.

Table 2 includes the errors between the height at the test XYZ sample and the height calculated in the grid file.

Table 2. The errors between test data and model surfaces.

Gridding methods	Mean error [m]	Max error [m]
Triangulation (L.I.)	0.08	1.05
Kriging	0.08	2.04
Modified Shepard's	0.08	1.94
Inv. Dist. to Power	0.09	2.15

All tested methods method provided minimum error equal to zero. The mean errors are similar: between 0.08 m and 0.09 m. The authors received the smallest error for triangulation method.

5   Conclusions

In experiment each analyzed method gave different results as a surface model and therefore generated depth contours from each model run differently. Although model generated by triangulation is visually not impressive it seems it has the most advantages from all tested methods. First is that it keeps real measurements, as it does not include gridding algorithm. Generated isobaths does not exceed surveyed area and their shape itself closely resembles this of visually more advanced - kriging model.

For the correctness of analysis that ensure safety of navigation the most important is to preserve the information of shallowest areas. Triangulation method with linear interpolation provides unchanged values in model vertices, so assuming the survey was conducted properly – the model provides the most reliable information.

Acknowledgment. This research outcome has been achieved under the grant No 13/MN/IG/16 financed from a subsidy of the Ministry of Science and Higher Education for statutory activities.

References

1. Woźniak, M., Połap, D.: Hybrid neuro-heuristic methodology for simulation and control of dynamic systems over time interval. Neural Netw. **93**, 45–56 (2017). doi:10.1016/j.neunet. 2017.04.013. ISSN: 0893-6080, Elsevier
2. Woźniak, M.: Novel image correction method based on swarm intelligence approach. In: Dregvaite, G., Damasevicius, R. (eds.) ICIST 2016. CCIS, vol. 639, pp. 404–413. Springer, Cham (2016). doi:10.1007/978-3-319-46254-7_32. ISSN: 1865-0929
3. Woźniak, M., Połap, D., Napoli, C., Tramontana, E.: Graphic object feature extraction system based on cuckoo search algorithm. Expert Syst. Appl. **66**, 20–31 (2016). doi:10.1016/j.eswa. 2016.08.068. Elsevier
4. Wawrzyniak, N., Stateczny, A.: MSIS image postioning in port areas with the aid of comparative navigation methods. Polish Marit. Res. **243**(1), 32–41 (2017). ISSN 1233-2585, Gdansk University of Technology
5. Kazimierski, W., Wlodarczyk-Sielicka, M.: Technology of spatial data geometrical simplification in maritime mobile information system for coastal waters. Polish Marit. Res. **23**(3), 3–12 (2016). ISSN: 1233-2585, Gdansk University of Technology
6. Wawrzyniak, N., Hyla, T.: Application of geofencing technology for the purpose of spatial analyses in inland mobile navigation, geodetic congress (Geomatics), Baltic., Gdansk. IEEE (2016). doi:10.1109/BGC.Geomatics.2016.15
7. Wlodarczyk-Sielicka, M., Stateczny, A.: Comparison of selected reduction methods of bathymetric data obtained by multibeam echosounder. In: 2016 Baltic Geodetic Congress (BGC Geomatics). doi:10.1109/BGC.Geomatics.2016.22
8. Shimada, K., Aoki, S., Ohshima, K.I.: Creation of a gridded dataset for the southern ocean with a topographic constraint scheme. J. Atmos. Oceanic Technol. **34**(3), 511–532 (2017). doi:10.1175/JTECH-D-16-0075.1

9. Amante, C.J., Eakins, B.W.: Accuracy of interpolated bathymetry in digital elevation models. J. Coastal Res. **76**(Special Issue), 123–133 (2016). doi:10.2112/SI76-011. ISSN: 0749-0208
10. Li, J., Heap, A.D.: A Review of Spatial Interpolation Methods for Environmental Scientists. Geoscience Australia, Canberra (2008)
11. Wlodarczyk-Sielicka, M.: Importance of neighborhood parameters during clustering of bathymetric data using neural network. In: Dregvaite, G., Damasevicius, R. (eds.) ICIST 2016. CCIS, vol. 639, pp. 441–452. Springer, Cham (2016). doi:10.1007/978-3-319-46254-7_35

Author Index

Printed in the United States
By Bookmasters